The Red Book

on

Real Estate Contracts in Georgia

By: Seth G. Weissman
Ned Blumenthal

Published by the

Georgia Association of REALTORS®

ISSN   1554-3420
ISBN   09765841-0-7

DISCLAIMER

This book is designed to provide accurate and authoritative information with regard to real estate sales contracts in Georgia. Since each transaction is unique and the facts and circumstances will vary from one transaction to another, no representations are made, however, regarding the appropriateness of the sample Special Stipulations and other information contained herein to specific real estate sales transactions. This book is sold with the understanding that neither the authors, publishers, Georgia Association of REALTORS® nor Weissman, Nowack, Curry & Wilco, P.C. are engaged in rendering specific legal or other professional advice. If specific legal advice or other expert assistance is required, the services of a competent professional should be sought.

DEDICATION

This book is dedicated to all past and present members and contributors of the GAR Forms Committee whose hard work, dedication, intellectual curiosity, and true REALTOR® spirit have helped make the GAR Forms so highly regarded. Special thanks and recognition is given to Greg Dunn, David London, Art Robinson, Bert Harrington, Spencer Smith, Melba Franklin, Pat Johnson, Mallory Jones, Brenda Blanton, Frank Mears, Bill Boatman, Larry Hathcock, Tom Wise, Nancy Gay Rowland, Chuck Jonaitis, Jim Smith, Tom Cowan, Linda Mitchell, Nancy Johnson, Sean Brooks, Ceci Osburn, Frank Reinecke, Len Powell, Carol Hayes, Janeece Swainey, Mark Crouch, Stephanie Nielsen and Kathy Murphy. Also special thanks to GAR Staff Liaison to the Forms Committee, Chris Etter, whose attention to detail, good nature and willingness to go the extra mile have been invaluable to the GAR Forms Committee.

ABOUT THE AUTHORS

Seth G. Weissman is an attorney with the real estate and litigation firm of Weissman, Nowack, Curry & Wilco, P.C. He received his undergraduate degree summa cum laude from the University of Pennsylvania in 1975, a Master's degree in land use planning from the University of North Carolina at Chapel Hill in 1978, and a Juris Doctor degree from Duke University in 1979.

Mr. Weissman is general counsel to the Georgia Association of REALTORS® and is actively involved in representing Boards of REALTORS®, real estate brokerage firms, developers and builders throughout Georgia. He is the Editor of the *Georgia Real Estate Law Letter*, a former Chair of the Real Property Law Section of the State Bar of Georgia, and a member of the American College of Real Estate Lawyers. Mr. Weissman is an author and lecturer on a wide variety of real estate and real estate brokerage subjects.

Ned Blumenthal is an attorney with the real estate and litigation firm of Weissman, Nowack, Curry & Wilco, P.C. He received his undergraduate degree from Emory University in 1987, and his Juris Doctor degree from Emory University School of Law in 1990.

Mr. Blumenthal is actively involved in representing and defending REALTORS® and real estate brokerage firms in civil actions and administrative proceedings throughout Georgia. Mr. Blumenthal is a former REALTOR® and lectures frequently on many real estate brokerage topics including risk reduction and claims avoidance.

FOREWORD

When Seth called to ask me if I would write the FOREWORD for this book, I was extremely honored and a bit apprehensive. After much thought, I am pleased to share my feelings about my good friend Seth Weissman and *The Red Book on Real Estate Contracts in Georgia.*

I first met Seth in 1988 when I was hired as a managing broker for a large brokerage firm in Atlanta that had retained a very young Seth Weissman as legal counsel. Over the next seven years, I had the need for legal advice on matters ranging from agency issues to contract matters to employer-employee relationships to anti-trust law. I was always astounded by his remarkable depth of knowledge and his carefully thought-out answers. I quickly learned that he was an extraordinary person who devoted his every waking hour to protecting his clients and offering suggestions for improvements to the real estate profession.

Coincidentally, in 1994 Seth was retained as legal counsel for the Georgia Association of REALTORS® and less than a year later I was offered the position of Executive Vice President for GAR. It has been my privilege to continue to work with Seth on many of the same issues while wearing an entirely different hat. In addition to authoring the Legal Ease articles in the Georgia REALTOR® Magazine, teaching classes all over the state and writing amicus briefs for cases that have industry-changing potential, Seth attends virtually every meeting of the Forms Committee where he offers suggestions for improvements, listens to and participates in debates with some of the smartest brokers, agents and instructors in the business and is frequently asked to rewrite entire paragraphs on the spot.

This book, a new edition of which comes out every four years, is not a book that practitioners will pick up and "read" from cover to cover. However, it is the most valuable resource available regarding the GAR Forms and real estate contracts in Georgia. Owning it is a "must" for every broker and a "should" for every real estate agent in the state. I strongly recommend that you read the Table of Contents in order to familiarize yourself with the depth of information available whenever needed. Additionally, I recommend that you review the table of approximately 200 special stipulations listed in the back of the book.

I will not tell you that you will "enjoy" this book, but I do want you to know that it has been written without regard for return on investment but rather providing the necessary information that will protect the members of the Georgia Association of REALTORS® and keep them out of trouble.

Bob Hamilton
Chief Executive Officer
Georgia Association of REALTORS®

TABLE OF CONTENTS

CHAPTER 4   CLOSING AND POSSESSION

CHAPTER 5   PROPERTY DISCLOSURE STATEMENT

CHAPTER 6   TITLE

CHAPTER 13   REAL ESTATE COMMISSIONS

CHAPTER 14   CONDOMINIUMS, HOMEOWNER ASSOCIATIONS AND OTHER FORMS OF PROPERTY OWNERSHIP

INTRODUCTION

Purpose of the Book

Our goal in writing the Red Book is to provide real estate professionals, including real estate brokers, agents, lawyers, builders and mortgage lenders with an up-to-date reference book on real estate sales contracts in Georgia. The Red Book discusses both the legal and practical issues that arise in real estate sales contracts in Georgia. It also contains a comprehensive analysis of the Brokerage Relationships in Real Estate Transactions Act (also known as "BRRETA"), including the 2000 legislative revisions.[1] We also included numerous sample special stipulations so that real estate professionals can different options for modifying real estate purchase and sale contracts.

A. How to Use This Book

The Red Book also serves as a reference companion when working with the GAR standard real estate forms published by the Georgia Association of REALTORS® (2005 printing). These forms are the most widely used real estate forms in the State of Georgia and are therefore a logical starting point in discussing real estate contracts. The GAR Purchase and Sale Agreements are referred to as "the GAR Contract(s)".

Although the primary focus of the book is the GAR Purchase and Sale Agreements, issues raised in other standard forms contracts are also discussed. There are also separate chapters on the New Construction Purchase and Sale Agreement, the Lot/Land Purchase and Sale Agreement, the Lease/Purchase Agreement and the Condominium Resale Purchase and Sale Agreement, covering only the items in those contracts that are different from the GAR Purchase and Sale Agreement.

Key court decisions with case citations are discussed as they relate to each section of the contract. Multiple case citations to confirm the same point, however, have been avoided. While some of the discussions in the book may by their nature by technical, the book has been written in plain English wherever possible. In an effort to simplify the text, the authors have not used "he or she" but instead have alternated the pronouns, when appropriate, in successive chapters. The Red Book contains a master index all of the sample special stipulations and a subject index at the end for easy reference.

B. Non-Lawyers Writing Contracts

A Georgia statute gives real estate brokers and licensees the authority to complete real estate sales contracts prepared by an attorney and exhibits and

---

1   O.C.G.A. §10-6A-1 et seq.

addenda thereto without having to be licensed as an attorney.[2] The GAR forms have been prepared by an attorney. However, in working with other contracts, real estate licensees should make some effort to determine if an attorney prepared the contract.

Interestingly, when the Georgia legislature granted real estate agents and brokers the limited right to fill out pre-printed real estate sales contracts prepared by an attorney, it effectively legislated an exception to the practice of law in Georgia. The Supreme Court of Georgia has stated very clearly that this is a power reserved exclusively to the Court.[3] The Court has stated, "no statute is controlling as to the civil regulation of the practice of law in this state. Only this Court has the inherent power to govern the practice of law in Georgia. It is the creation and regulation of the State Bar of Georgia, through the decisions and orders of this Court, that now constitute 'the exclusive means of governing the practice of law in Georgia'." Therefore, the legal underpinning for real estate agents and brokers filling out pre-printed real estate sales contracts should not necessarily be taken for granted. However, since the Supreme Court of Georgia has not issued any opinion limiting the right of agents and brokers to fill out pre-printed real estate sales contracts prepared by an attorney, and the statute has been on the books for some 18 years, it can be presumed that the Court through its silence has acquiesced to this change.

Whether this limited grant of authority includes the right to draft special stipulations is unclear. As a practical matter, most real estate agents and brokers regularly draft or assist in drafting stipulations on behalf of their clients and customers. In support of this practice, it can be argued that helping buyers and sellers draft special stipulations is part and parcel to filling out a form contract prepared by an attorney. The argument against real estate agents and brokers drafting special stipulations is that this activity possibly exceeds the limited grant of authority to real estate agents and brokers to perform ministerial functions relative to real estate sales contracts.

By providing in this book numerous sample special stipulations written by attorneys, we have tried to make it easier for real estate brokers and licensees to have access to special stipulations which can serve as a guide or model for special stipulations written by attorneys to avoid the danger of being deemed to be practicing law without a license.

---

2   O.C.G.A. § 43-40-25.1

3   Eckles v. Atlanta Technology Group, Inc. 267 Ga. 801, 485 S.E.2d 22 (1997)

CHAPTER 1
REAL PROPERTY

1

OVERVIEW

A real estate sales contract must include a clear description of the property being conveyed. The most precise description of a property is based on a survey prepared by a licensed Georgia surveyor, which describes the property through metes and bounds attached to the contract. This chapter will discuss the different ways property can be described in a contract and explain why some property descriptions have been upheld by Georgia courts while others have been struck down.

This chapter also includes a discussion of how to determine whether personal property is considered a fixture that must remain with the property and when to use a bill of sale and a financing statement.

§1.1   Real Property

§1.1.1   Description must clearly identify property

When preparing a contract for the sale of real property, it is necessary to include an accurate and definite description of the property to be sold. Many real estate sales contracts provide for an actual legal description to be attached to the contract as an exhibit. The GAR Contracts follow a different approach. Specifically, the property is generally described by reference to the land lot, district, county, address, subdivision, and recorded plat information (if applicable) of the property. The full legal description of the property is then defined as the description of the property as recorded in the country land records. This description is then incorporated into the contract by reference.

There are limitations to describing the property in reference to how it is already described in the land records. Specifically, since most buyers do not search the title to the property they are buying until after the property is put under contract, the actual legal description of the property is unknown to most buyers at the time of contract. To some degree, the buyer is buying "a pig in a poke". This means, for example, that if the property is smaller in size than what the buyer thought or has different boundaries, the buyer may not have a remedy unless the buyer is protected elsewhere in the contract.

One way for the buyer to be protected against the property being smaller than what the buyer thought is for the seller to warrant the property as being at least a minimum specified size and to give the buyer the right to terminate the contract if prior to closing the buyer has a survey done which reveals that the property is smaller than warranted. In this way, if the buyer discovers prior to closing that the property is smaller than the buyer had thought, the buyer can terminate the contract. The GAR Contract also gives the buyer the right to request that the seller attach a survey to the contract. If this is done, the buyer can then obtain a new survey prior to closing and terminate the contract if the new survey is materially different from the old survey.[4]

A property description must describe the amount and location of the property intended to be sold by the seller with sufficient certainty so that it can be reasonably identified.[5] However, even without a precise description, the property description will be valid as long as the contract contains a "key" which will "lead unerringly to the land in question."[6] A "key" allows the reader to consider something outside the terms of the contract to identify the property with certainty. If the description of property is sufficient to furnish a key, parol evidence (evidence outside the terms of the contract) that does not add to, enlarge, or in any way change the description is admissible to identify property intended to be conveyed.[7] So, for example, in one case, a reference to property in Chatham County, Georgia, known as 124, 126, 128, 130 East Waldburg Street being approximately 60 x 55 feet in size was sufficient to constitute a key by which the property could be identified.[8] This "key" allowed the parties to look outside of the terms of the contract (the addresses which were in place at that time in Chatham County, Georgia) to specifically identify the property referenced.

The "key" must help to identify the property with certainty. If the "key" does not do this, the property description will not be valid. For example, in one case, the contract identified the property as "the premises situated at Howard [Road] and more particularly described as all that tract or parcel of land which comprises the 81.14+/-acres lying and being in Land Lots 1153-1154 of the Third District and First Section of Forsyth County, Georgia."[9] At the time of this case, the only tax parcel in Land Lots 1153-1154 was parcel no. 011-009. Moreover, there had been a recent tax appraisal for that parcel which listed the seller as the owner. The tax appraisal also mentioned a warranty deed, which described the property by metes and bounds, and the warranty deed referenced a survey showing the property's precise location. Unfortunately, while the tax appraisal and the contract referred to a parcel of 81.14 acres located in land lots 1153 and 1154, the warranty deed and survey described the property as 93.45 acres of land situated in land lots 1153, 1154, and 1223. Since the deed and survey were inconsistent, the court decided that the contract did not contain a key that led "unerringly to the land in question."

Information not included in the contract cannot be used to aid in locating property described in vague and uncertain terms in the contract itself.[10] If the property description in the contract fails to sufficiently locate and identify a certain tract of land,

---

4   See discussion on surveys at §1.1.8.
5   Wallace v. Adamson, 129 Ga. App. 792, 201 S.E.2d 479 (1973), citing Gainesville Midland Railroad v. Tyner, 204 Ga. 535, 50 S.E.2d 108 (1948).
6   Blumberg v. Nathan, 190 Ga. 64, 66, 8 S.E.2d 374, 375 (1940).
7   Gainesville Midland Railroad v. Tyner, et al., 204 Ga. 535, 50 S.E.2d 108 (1948).
8   Blumberg v. Nathan, 190 Ga. 64, 8 S.E.2d 374 (1940).
9   Makowski v. Waldrop, 262 Ga. App. 130, 584 S.E.2d 714 (2003).
10   Smith v. Wilkinson, 208 Ga. 489, 67 S.E.2d 698 (1951).

evidence outside of the contract, such as discussions of the parties regarding the location of the property or what is included on the property, cannot be used to correct or clarify an otherwise invalid description. In such a case, the property description fails and the contract is void.[11]

While a metes and bounds description based on a professional survey of the property is the best type of description and controls over all other descriptions, many contracts contain far less detailed property descriptions. Discussed below are several general types of property descriptions which are used either alone or in combination in real estate sales contracts, such as street addresses, tax plats, recorded and unrecorded plats, and surveys.

§1.1.2   Identifying air space

Most property is legally described by setting out the property's boundary lines. The property owner also owns the ground beneath and the air space above[12], subject to the rights of flight.[13] However, it is possible to sell the air rights separately from the land and to create a legal description for such air rights parcels. Such legal descriptions must not only describe the boundary lines but also the upper and lower elevation lines enclosing the air rights parcel. An exception is in the case of condominiums, where Georgia law provides that a description of a condominium unit is sufficient if it contains the unit number, condominium name, county, and the deed book and page number of the recorded declaration of condominium.[14]

§1.1.3   Identifying water

When a property's boundary lies within or is adjacent to a body of water, such as a stream, ocean or lake, the following rules apply when determining the exact boundary of the property unless the deed provides otherwise.

§1.1.3.1   Streams

When the boundary line of a property is to the edge of a stream that is non-navigable, the exact boundary of the property is deemed to be where the streambed begins. The owner of the adjacent land owns the bed of the stream. A stream is defined as navigable when it is capable of transporting boats loaded with goods in the regular course of trade, either for the whole or a part of the year. However, merely because timer can be rafted or wood transported in small boats on a stream does not make it navigable.

---

11   Blumberg v. Nathan, 190 Ga. 64, 8 S.E.2d 374 (1940).
12   O.C.G.A. §44-1-2 provides that the property right of the owner of real estate extends downward indefinitely and upward indefinitely.
13   O.C.G.A. §6-2-5.
14   See §1.1.16.

If the stream is a dividing line between two parcels of land, each owner's boundary extends to the center of the main current of the stream. If the current changes gradually over time, the boundary lines of the properties adjacent to the stream changes along with the gradual changes to the current of the stream. However, if the stream suddenly changes its course or direction (for example, as a result of a major storm), the original boundary line, if identifiable, remains the boundary. Sediment on either side accrues to the owner of that side.[15]

In one case, a dispute arose between two adjoining landowners on where the property boundary should be. The property boundary was described in the deed as "commencing on the west bank of the Chattahoochee River at a corner . . . at or near a ford of said river, thence in an eastern direction across the river, thence in a northern direction up said river to a white oak near the bank of said river . . ."[16] The issue was whether the property boundary included the river bed. The court stated that when a deed establishes a non-navigable stream as a boundary line, the owners on either side are entitled to the land running to the center of the main current. It also stated that where the line is described as running to the stream, language which describes it as thereafter running "with," "along," "by," "on," "up," or "down" the stream will be construed to carry the title to the center unless contrary intention appears from the description.

If the property boundary is to the edge of a stream that is navigable, the boundary line of the property extends to the low-water mark.[17] The state will own the streambed from the low-water mark except where there is a state grant that includes the riverbed.

§1.1.3.2   Tidewaters

Tidewaters refer to waters which fall and rise according to the tide, such as in bays and rivers. It does not apply to the open sea. Where property boundary is adjacent to or is covered by non-navigable tidewaters, the boundary of the property ends where the tidewater bed begins.[18] The owner of the adjacent land will own the beds of all non-navigable tidewaters. Where the property is adjacent to or is covered by navigable tidewaters, the boundary of the property extends to the low-water mark.[19]

A navigable tidewater is defined as any tidewater or any other bed of water where the tide regularly ebbs and flows which is used for navigation or is capable of transporting boats loaded with goods in the regular course of trade at mean low tide.

---

15   O.C.G.A. §44-8-2.
16   Westmoreland v. Beutell, 153 Ga.App. 558, 266 S.E.2d 260 (1980).
17   O.C.G.A. §44-8-5.
18   O.C.G.A. §44-8-6.
19   O.C.G.A. §44-8-7.

The rafting of timber or passage of small boats on the waters, whether for the transportation of persons or freight do not make the tidewaters navigable.

If the dividing line between two parcels of land lies within the non-navigable waters, each owner's boundary extends to the main thread or channel of the water. If the main thread or channel of the water changes gradually, the boundary line follows the changing thread or channel. If for any reason the water takes a new channel, the original line, if identifiable, remains the boundary. Sediment on either side accrues to the owner of that side.

§1.1.3.3   Beaches and open seas

Generally, the boundary of private lots adjoining the seashore extends to the high water mark of the tide. The build-up of sediment on the shore accrues to the owner of the lot. The property between the high-water mark and low-water mark belongs to the government.

§1.1.3.4   Lakes

When the boundary line of a property lies next to a lake, the property boundary is deemed to extend to the low-water mark existing at the date of the execution of the deed.[20] However, this is a general rule and will not be applied if the deed provides otherwise. An example is a case where the deed conveyed the land, which was covered by a pond, but stated that the pond was to be maintained at no more than a certain maximum height. The court held that the property boundary to be the line of water in the pond at such height.[21]

If lots are sold in reference to a recorded subdivision plat, which identifies a lake as a recreational area, an easement across the whole lake will arise for the benefit of all of the lot owners in the subdivision.[22]

In the case of a privately owned lake, the owner of the lake has the exclusive right to the use of the waters above his boundary line and may exclude other lakebed owners and fence off his portion.[23] In one case, almost all the land in and around an 880-acre lake was owned by a fishing club, which tried to prevent a lot owner from fishing in the waters. The boundary of the lot owned by the lot owner extended to one-fourth acre below the high water mark of the lake. The lot owner argued that as owner of property adjoining a lake, he has rights over the entire surface waters as long as he does not interfere with the rights of other owners. However, the law in Georgia is that the owner of a bed of a non-navigable lake has the exclusive right to the surface waters above the bed. Therefore, a person who places a boat within that area without

---

20   Boardman v. Scott, 30 S.E. 982 (Ga. 1897).
21   Prescott v. Herring, 212 Ga. 571, 94 S.E.2d 417 (1956).
22   See § 1.1.7.2
23   Lanier v. Ocean Pond Fishing Club, Inc. 253 Ga. 549, 322 S.E.2d 494 (1984).

permission would be trespassing. For this reason, the court found that the lot owner, by fishing in waters beyond the boundary of his lot, was trespassing.

§1.1.4   Use of metes and bounds legal description

A metes and bounds legal description, also known as courses and distances, is a means of describing the boundary lines of land, as measured by distances and angles from designated landmarks and in relation to adjoining properties.[24] This is done by a surveyor creating a survey of the property using both compass directions and distances of the boundaries. The description begins at a definite point and follows the exterior boundary lines of the property until it returns to the point of beginning. These compass directions and distances are reduced to written "calls", which when taken together form the metes and bounds legal description.[25] The legal description created by listing the directions and distances can be attached to the contract and deed in order to fully describe the location and size of the property. A metes and bounds description taken from an accurate survey is, most often, the most complete and definitive means of describing property.

The exception is where the metes and bounds description is different from the boundaries set out by landmarks that have been in place for more than 30 years. In one case, the property boundary was marked by a fence, which crossed an adjoining property for a certain distance.[26] The fence had been in place for more than 40 years and an affidavit stating that the fence line was the boundary was filed and recorded with the deed in a previous sale of the property. Therefore, the court held that it was the fence line, and not the courses and distances in the deed, that defined the true property boundary.

§1.1.5   Use of street address to identify the property

If the street address provides sufficient information to locate the property, it will generally be found to be adequate. However, a street address without any reference to the city, county, or state in which the property is located is generally considered to be too indefinite.

§1.1.5.1   *Examples of street addresses held to be inadequate*

The following are examples of property descriptions containing street addresses, which were held to be inadequate:

---

24   Black's Law Dictionary (8th ed. 2004).

25   Such "calls" often read as follows: Beginning at an iron pin found on the northeasterly right-of-way of Vernon Springs Trail (50 foot right-of-way) 353.40 feet southerly from its intersection with the southerly right-of-way of Mount Vernon Highway (the POINT OF BEGINNING) and run north 75 degrees 14 minutes 30 seconds east 87.88 feet to an iron pin found . . ..

26   <u>Duncan v. Harcourt</u>, 267 Ga.App. 224, 599 S.E.2d 196 (2004).

(1)   "4582 Club Drive" (no indication of the city, county, state, or country in which the property was located).[27]

(2)   "Home on Pine Mountain Road" (no further identification included).[28]

(3)   "All that tract of land shown by the attached sketch showing boundaries and including eight-room brick house, fronting a distance on Victory Drive of 210 feet, and a depth as shown on the attached plat" (attached plat did not disclose location of property or dimensions).[29]

(4)   "All that tract of land being 9 to 10+/- acres near Pendergrass in Jackson County, Georgia near U.S. Highway 129 on the south and Interstate I-85 on the west and being marked parcel 1 (60,000 s.f. Hotel Site) as per Exhibit 'A' attached and made a part of this contract on the attached survey, more particularly described in Exhibit 'B' …"[30]. Exhibit A was a portion of the master plan but did not contain a metes and bounds description. Exhibit B was not attached. The Court held that the property description was insufficient.

§1.1.5.2   *Examples of street addresses held to be adequate*

The following are examples of property descriptions containing street addresses, which were held to be adequate:

(1)   "Houses and lots on South Stevens Street in Thomasville, Thomas County, Georgia, fronting on the northeast side of said street and being designated by…[ten stated numbers]." [31]

(2)   "All that tract of land and improvements thereon known as 344 Wilkerson Drive, S.E., Atlanta, Georgia" (a complete legal description is to be attached hereto and become a part of this contract).[32] In this case, the court concluded that the fact that the description failed to state whether the property was located in Fulton or DeKalb County was not a fatal omission that deprived the seller of an opportunity to prove the allegations of the amended complaint by extrinsic evidence. The better practice, however, is to always include a detailed address, including the city and county.

---

27   Murphy v. Morse, 96 Ga. App. 513, 100 S.E.2d 623 (1957).
28   Bell v. Babb, 139 Ga. App. 695, 229 S.E.2d 511 (1976); overruled on other
          grounds Brack v. Brownlee, 246 Ga. 818, 273 S.E.2d 390 (1980).
29   Bryan v. Rusk, 89 Ga. App. 125, 78 S.E.2d 853 (1953).
30   White v. Plumbing Distributors, Inc., 262 Ga.App. 228, 585 S.E.2d 135 (2003).
31   Silverman v. Alday, 200 Ga. 711, 38 S.E.2d 419, 420 (1946).
32   Essuon v. Raynor, 231 Ga. 297, 201 S.E.2d 416 (1973).

(3) "All that tract of land in Atlanta, Fulton County, Georgia, being improved property located at 126 Ashby Street, S.W., according to the present system of numbering houses in the City of Atlanta; being a 2-story, 14-room frame dwelling".[33]

(4) Property described as "3200 Clairmont Road" which was the address of the entire condominium complex was sufficient to furnish a key by which property could be identified as the individual unit at 3229 Clairmont Road.[34] Based on courts' analyses in more recent cases, it is unclear whether this property description would be deemed to be sufficient today. The Georgia Association of REALTORS® has a form exhibit to be used for a condominium property description.[35]

(5) Property was described as "All that tract of land Wellington Square at Indian Trail-Lilburn and Dickens Road as more particularly described in Exhibit 'A'" (which was not attached). [36] The Court decided that the contract contained several keys. It identified the name of the property, "Wellington Square." It also contained a warranty by the seller in respect of the value and use of the property as a shopping center. Lastly, the contract required the seller to pay Georgia property transfer tax. These "keys" allowed the Court to consider external evidence to identify the property. The Court was exceptionally generous here and its decision does not mean that property descriptions are no longer important. An important fact was that the purchasers had admitted that they contracted to purchase the property in one of their court documents, where they had described the property as "that certain shopping center known as 'Wellington Square' located at the intersection of Indian Trail and Dickens Road, Lilburn, Georgia."

§1.1.5.3   *When street address is not sufficient to describe property*

A street address is not a good way to describe property when: (a) it is unclear how much of the property at the address is being conveyed, or (b) the street address does not include all of the property intended to be transferred. An example is a case where a buyer contracted to purchase property described as "2003 Pinetree Trail, Gainesville, Georgia."[37] The buyers contended that the property also included one-half of the adjoining lot. When the transaction closed, the buyers received a deed describing only one lot in the subdivision. The buyers discovered that they did not own all the property they thought they owned when the seller began constructing a house on the adjoining lot. The buyers sued to have the deed from the sellers reformed to include the disputed property.

The court concluded that the contract of sale merged[38] into the warranty deed from the sellers to the buyers and that there was no evidence that anyone made any

---

33   Greenspan v. Caison, 101 Ga. App. 632, 114 S.E.2d 803 (1960).
34   Romanik v. Buitrago, 153 Ga. App. 886, 267 S.E.2d 301 (1980).
35   GAR Form F127, Condominium Legal Description Exhibit.
36   Nhan et al. v. Wellington Square, LLC, 263 Ga.App. 717, 589 S.E.2d 295 (2003).
37   Fields v. Davies, 235 Ga. 87, 218 S.E.2d 828 (1975).
38   The doctrine of merger generally provides that a real estate sales contract merges

misrepresentations to the buyer, practiced any fraud, or that there was any mutual mistake either in appropriation, delivery, or acceptance by the buyers of the deed sought to be reformed.[39] As such, the court denied the request to reform the deed. When the actual property being sold is more or less than what might be revealed by a street address, it is best to use a metes and bounds property description or survey of the exact property to be transferred.

This case may have had a different outcome if there had been mutual mistake (i.e. a mistake on the part of both the buyer and the seller), in which case it may be possible to reform the warranty deed. In another case, a contract for the sale of property described one lot.[40] At the closing of that contract, two adjoining lots with different street addresses were conveyed to the buyer. There was contradictory evidence as to whether it was the intent of the parties to convey one or two lots. The court concluded that the contract for sale did not merge into the deed where there was evidence of a mutual mistake. The court therefore allowed evidence outside of the contract to be considered in determining whether a mutual mistake had occurred.

§1.1.5.4   When only the "premises" are being conveyed

In using street addresses, the parties must be clear in the contract about whether they intend to convey only the dwelling or the dwelling and the land surrounding the dwelling. In one case, the court concluded that a property description contained in an option and lease which stated "certain premises in state and county aforesaid known as 1310 Butler Avenue and located on Section 3 of Beach Lot 83, Savannah Beach, Chatham County, Georgia" included the entire lot and the building located on the lot and not merely the building alone.[41]

However, the term "premises" has varying meanings. When used in a lease of property without qualifying words, it has been held to mean land and buildings, land and tenements, land and appurtenances, etc.[42] In a case interpreting a will, the Georgia Supreme Court considered whether the phrase "house and land" included an adjacent lot.[43] In that case, item four of the will identified: (a) the "house and lot" at 65 Temple Avenue, the City of Newnan; (b) the "house and land" at 70 Clark Street, Newnan, Georgia; and (c) the "house and lot" at 69 Temple Avenue. The court distinguished between the phrases "house and lot" and "house and land" and concluded that the reference to land meant that the adjacent vacant property, another lot, would be

---

into or is swallowed up into the deed at closing and does not survive afterward except to the extent that the parties have provided in the contract for specific obligations or rights to survive the closing. Anziano v. Appalachee Enterprises, Inc., 208 Ga. App. 760, 432 S.E.2d 117 (1993).

39   Fields v. Davies, 235 Ga. 87, 218 S.E.2d 828 (1975).
40   Rasmussen v. Martin, 236 Ga. 267, 223 S.E.2d 663 (1976).
41   Deich v. Reeves, 203 Ga. 596, 48 S.E.2d 373 (1948).
42   Deich v. Reeves, 203 Ga. 596, 48 S.E.2d 373 (1948).
43   Mathews v. Loftin, 224 Ga. 98, 160 S.E.2d 399 (1968).

included within the property transferred through the will. Given the various interpretations of the term "premises" it is important to specifically describe exactly what property is being conveyed. The following special stipulation may be used in cases of doubt.

Special Stipulation #1-1: Additions to property description

As used herein the term "Property" means that property defined in paragraph 1 hereof, which is further defined as including

_____.

Special Stipulation #1-2: Subtraction from property description

As used herein the term "Property" means that property defined in paragraph 1 hereof, but from which the following is specifically excluded:

_____.

§1.1.6   Use of tax plats to identify property

A tax plat may be used to supplement the property description contained in the contract. A tax plat shows the general configuration of the property; however, it is not clear that a tax plat alone is adequate to locate the property. Generally, an additional description, such as a reference to a prior deed describing the property by metes and bounds, an adequate street address, or some other means of specifically locating the property will be necessary to constitute a complete property description.[44]

§1.1.7   Use of other plats to identify property

Reference in a contract to the deed book and page number of a recorded plat describing the property is sufficient as a legal description of property.[45] In fact, where a description of the property in a sales contract refers to a plat for a more complete description, the plat ordinarily will be considered part of the property description in the contract.[46] The GAR Contracts specifically references and incorporates the plat by identifying the Plat Book and Page numbers.[47]

---

[44]   Sackett v. Wilson, 258 Ga. 612, 373 S.E.2d 10 (1988); Johnson v. Sackett, 256 Ga. 552, 350 S.E.2d 419 (1986) (tax plat attached to a contract supplemented the writing to make a legal description valid).

[45]   Crooke v. Property Management Services, Inc., 215 Ga. 410, 110 S.E.2d 677 (1959).

[46]   Kilby v. Sawtell, 203 Ga. 256, 46 S.E.2d 117 (1948).

[47]   GAR Form F20, paragraph 1.

§1.1.7.1   Use of recorded plats to identify property

Reference to a recorded plat in a property description can constitute a key by which property may be identified. In one case, a property description stated, in part, that:

> "The full legal description of said property Lot 3 and part of Lot 2 . . . is the same as it is recorded with the Clerk of the Superior Court of the County in which the property is located and is made a part of this agreement by reference . . . Plat Book 33, Page 59, Fulton County, Office of Clerk of Superior Court . . ." [48]

The court held that since the description provided a key (deeds and a recorded plat), which was incorporated by reference, the description was valid.

§1.1.7.2   Use of unrecorded plats to identify property

Even if a plat is not recorded, it may be used as a key by which property may be identified. In one case, the court held that an unrecorded plat was incorporated into a contract's property description when the property was described as " . . . tract #3 located in Land Lots 422 & 453 of the 12th Land District of Brooks County, Georgia as by plat made by DeVane Associates, dated 6th December 1968." [49] The court noted that the plat showed the acreage of the tract and all of its boundaries--by compass calls and distances, land lot lines, roads, a water course, and boundaries of adjoining tracts and of lands of other named owners--and the plat stated that "acreage, bearings and distances are derived from deeds, aerial photographs and plats of record." The contract to purchase was a sufficient key by which the property description could be determined by review of extrinsic evidence, such as the deeds, aerial photographs, and plats of record from which the plat was drawn.

§1.1.7.3   Identifying Common Areas on subdivision plat

If lots are sold in reference to a recorded subdivision plat, which identifies an area for the common use and enjoyment of all the property owners in the subdivision, an easement to use those common areas will arise for the benefit of all of the lot owners. For example, when a lake is shown on a subdivision plat and lots are sold according to the plat, the lot owners will acquire an irrevocable easement to use the lake if the lake is not designated as a common area. [50]

---

48   Suttle v. Northside Realty Associates, Inc., 171 Ga. App. 928, 321 S.E.2d 424 (1984).
49   Furney v. Dukes, 226 Ga. 804, 177 S.E.2d 680 (1970).
50   Patterson v. Powell, 257 Ga. App. 336, 571 S.E.2d 400 (2002); Dillard v. Bishop Eddie Long Ministries, Inc. 258 Ga. App. 507, 574 S.E.2d 544 (2002).

One case involved a beach subdivision fronting the Atlantic Ocean. All the land area was subdivided into lots and sold except for a few common areas, such as the beach area, a street and an open area between the beach and the street.[51] There were no reservations made for these common areas on the subdivision plat. The court held that where there was a sale of one or more lots referred to in recorded plat, each purchaser in the subdivision was conveyed an easement to use such common areas as a beach and as means of access to the ocean. The court also held that an easement acquired in such manner is considered an express grant and is an irrevocable property right.

However, a subdivision lot owner may not have a right to use the common areas if his warranty deed did not refer to the subdivision plat that sets out the common areas. In one case, the subdivision was developed as a "fly in" residential community where many residents owned airplanes and have hangers on their lots.[52] Many residents used the gravel roadway for vehicular traffic and taxiing airplanes to and from the airport. When the developers fenced the roadway off, a few of the owners sued the developer, claiming that they had an easement over the roadway. The court held that the owner whose deed referred to the subdivision plat had the easement rights over the roadway, and denied easement rights to owners whose deeds did not refer to the subdivision plat.

§1.1.7.4   Use of plats to clarify metes and bounds description

A reference in a contract to a plat can be used to clarify a detailed metes and bounds description if there is an error in one or more of the calls of the metes and bounds description. A contract which contains such an error will be considered to have an accurate and valid property description if it refers to a plat of survey recorded in the county land records, which contains a definite, certain, and adequate property description.[53]

§1.1.7.5   Insufficient plat does not cure defective property description

If a reference to a plat is itself insufficient (fails to provide a key, fails to show courses and distances, or has no fixed starting point), the person contending that the property description is adequate may not be able to demonstrate that the plat fulfilled the necessary requirements.[54] A map or plat attached and made a part of the contract will generally be considered indefinite and uncertain if it does not show the location of any other properties of the adjoining land owners, the distances or designation of any of the "points" on the plat to which it refers, contains no scale, and shows no directions. Such a plat does not materially aid in the description and will generally be considered

---

51   Smith v. Bruce 241 Ga. 133, 244 S.E.2d 559 (1978).
52   Durham et al. v. Mathis et al. 258 Ga.App. 749, 575 S.E.2d 6 (2002).
53   Barto v. Hicks, 124 Ga. App. 472, 184 S.E.2d 188 (1971).
54   Herrington v. Rose, 225 Ga. 452, 169 S.E.2d 312 (1969).

to be indefinite and uncertain and will not be considered in determining whether the property description in the contract is sufficient.[55]

§1.1.7.6   *Reference to lots on plat may be insufficient description*

Reference to lots on a plat may not be an adequate description if the lots are not sufficiently identified. In one case, a contract referred to 36 lots of a group of 51 shown on a plat.[56] However, there was nothing to identify which specific 36 lots were the subject of the contract. The court held that the property description was inadequate.

§1.1.8   When surveys can be used to supplement description of property

Surveys are often attached to contracts to supplement the property description set out in the contract. If the survey contains sufficient information, such as a metes and bounds description of the property that specifically identifies the property, it can serve as the property description on the condition that it is referenced and attached to the contract as an exhibit.

Surveys can also be used to ensure that the buyer has a clear idea of the property. A buyer and a seller can agree to have a survey done to determine the acreage of the property before the closing and also provided that the purchase price will depend on the acreage set out in the survey.[57] The buyer can also include a special stipulation that allows the buyer to terminate the purchase and sales agreement if a survey obtained after the binding agreement date and prior to closing reveals that the property is smaller than a particular size. An example of such a special stipulation is:

Special Stipulation #1-3: Buyer's right to terminate if survey shows a smaller property

Prior to closing, Buyer may terminate this Agreement upon notice to Seller if Buyer has a survey of the Property prepared by a licensed Georgia surveyor which reveals that the Property is less than _____ acres in size.

A survey cannot supply a property description when it is not attached to the contract. If the parties leave the property description blank in a contract but reference an intent to attach a survey at a later date to provide the description of the property, the contract will be void even if the survey is attached later and provides a clear and

---

55   Smith v. Georgia Indus. Realty Co., 215 Ga. 431, 111 S.E.2d 37 (1959).
56   Delfosse v. Coleman, 211 Ga. 888, 89 S.E.2d 518 (1955).
57   GAR Survey Resolution Exhibit Form F136.

precise description of the property (unless the parties subsequently affirm the contract and survey in writing)[58].

In one case, the seller and buyer agreed that the buyer would pay for a survey and incorporate the description of the property into the sales contract when the survey became available.[59] The seller was unable to meet his obligations under the contract and argued that the contract was void because it did not contain a legal description of the property to be sold. The buyer argued that the seller implicitly, if not expressly, contractually authorized the buyer to enter the legal description of the property after the contract was executed. The court concluded that the arguments made by the buyer might apply to a contract for services or personalty, but did not apply to a contract for the sale of real estate. The court stated: "[a] provision for subsequent survey will not cure a contract which at the time of execution contains no description of the land to be sold at all."

In another case, the buyer entered into a contract to purchase a "house and 10 acres of a 40-acre tract more or less that is now the property of H. C. Tysinger, Jr., on Martain Mill Road, Coweta County, GA. The exact boundaries (sic) to be determined by a survey."[60] The court held that while the larger 40-acre tract may have been identifiable, the ten acres the description refers to were not identifiable and could not be more specifically identified by a survey prepared and attached after the execution of the contract.

Another example is a case where the parties agreed that the metes and bounds of the property, as well as the acreage, were to be determined by a survey to be conducted after the contract was executed.[61] The purchase contract itself did not contain a sufficient legal description of the property because it did not: 1) contain a metes and bounds description; 2) make any reference to the acreage of the tract; or 3) incorporate a plat of survey. It did identify the property as 4190 Cedar Ridge Trail located in Land Lot 192 of District 15 of DeKalb County and the preprinted language in the contract stated that the full legal description "is the same as is recorded by Clerk of the Superior Court of the county in which the property is located and is made a part of this agreement by reference." However, the warranty deed recorded in DeKalb County, which contained a metes and bounds description, referred the tract as located in Land Lots 191 and 192, whereas the sales contract states that the tract is located in Land Lot 192.

The court found that the property description was inadequate and the parties cannot rely on a post-contract survey to provide the legal description. The court

---

58   See Section 1.1.11.

59   McCumbers v. Trans-Columbia, Inc., 172 Ga. App. 275, 322 S.E.2d 516 (1984).

60   McMichael Realty and Ins. Agency, Inc. v. Tysinger, 155 Ga. App. 131, 270 S.E.2d 88 (1980).

61   Gateway Family Worship Centers, Inc. v. H.O.P.E. Foundation Ministries, Inc., 244 Ga.App. 286, 535 S.E.2d 286 (2000).

stated that because "the key relied upon must be sufficient to provide identification by reference to extrinsic evidence which exists at the time that the contract is entered into by the parties."

In one recent case, the parties contracted to purchase property where the contract read: "This agreement is being made [and] finalized on Thursday, December 21, 2000. I agree to trade 5 acres of land behind Doris Masters and Fred Masters for 5 acres of land he owns beside my house at the property line. I also agree to purchase 5 acres of additional property from Fred Masters at the agreed upon purchase price of $5,500 an acre for a total of $27,500."[62]

While the legal description in the contract was obviously vague, the parties apparently understood what properties were being conveyed and were able to have surveys and deeds prepared. However, before all the deeds were signed, the parties got into a dispute and an action was brought to enforce the contract. The Georgia Court of Appeals held that the contract was not enforceable because it did not contain either a legal description of the property or a "key" which would lead to a more precise description of the property. The Court explained that although a contract that contains a valid legal description may rely on a subsequent survey to determine the exact acreage, a survey prepared after the contract is executed could not be used to provide the description itself.

§1.1.8.1   Use of surveys in GAR Contract to identify property

The GAR Contract for residential property provides that if a survey of the property is attached to the contract, it shall be a part of the contract.[63] The GAR Contract further provides that the buyer has the right to terminate the contract upon written notice to the seller if a new survey performed by a licensed surveyor is materially different from the attached survey. It is incumbent upon a buyer of property to ensure that the property described in the contract and the deed is the property that he actually intends to purchase. It is useful to include a survey in the contract for this purpose to avoid mistakes as to the location of property.

In one case, the buyer was showed property in a subdivision.[64] He walked the property he wanted to purchase which was identified as Lot 4 on the subdivision plat which the listing agent gave him. However, the plat was outdated and the recorded revised plat identified the property he walked as Lot 1 instead of Lot 4. The buyer subsequently purchased Lot 4, which was not the lot he had inspected with the listing agent. Soon thereafter, he began construction of a house on the lot he thought he owned. After he completed about 75% of the construction of the house, he received notice from the actual owner of the lot asserting ownership over the lot and stated that

---

62   Redwine v. Masters, 268 Ga.App. 490, 602 S.E.2d 143 (2004).
63   GAR Form F20, paragraph 6C.
64   Dundee Land Co. v. Simmons, 204 Ga. 248, 49 S.E.2d 488 (1948); Reidling v. Holcomb, 25 Ga. App. 229, 483 S.E.2d 624 (1997).

as actual owner, he was taking possession of the house and lot and that he would complete the construction of the house.

The buyer sued the listing agent and the actual owner of the lot. The court held that the buyer was not entitled to damages from the listing agent who had given him the incorrect plat and that the actual owner was allowed to keep the house without paying for any of the construction done prior to the notice. If the buyer had obtained a survey of the property he had contracted to purchase prior to closing and had reviewed it carefully, he could have discovered the error and this case would probably never have arisen.

The seller could attach a survey to a contract which survey shows on its face certain title defects, such as an encroachment. In theory, the seller could attempt to argue that the buyer cannot complain about the title defects, since they were a part of the description of the property. Using the GAR Contract avoids this issue because it specifically provides that the attachment of a survey does not relieve the seller of his responsibility to deliver good and marketable title to the property.[65]

§1.1.9   Use of previous deeds

One method of describing property is to incorporate any previous deed that conveyed the property to the seller into the contract by referring to the deed book and page number of that deed. Assuming that the property was properly and legally described in the seller's deed, this is a valid means of describing property in a contract. Alternatively, a copy of the seller's deed or the legal description from that deed could be attached as an exhibit to the contract.

§1.1.10   "More or less" descriptions may be insufficient

Descriptions of property, which include statements such as "5 acres, more or less", or "running south 75 feet, more or less", or "25 acres +/-", can create problems but are not necessarily invalid.   As long as the property description gives the precise location of the property, the property description will be deemed to be valid. If the description including the term "more or less" or "+/-" is not precise enough to locate the exact property in question, it will be invalid.[66] Again, the parties should strive to provide the most detailed property description possible.

§1.1.11   Attaching property description to contract after execution

Contracts will sometimes provide that a "legal description will be attached later." However, if the contract itself does not contain a sufficient property description to provide a key to the location of the property, a provision stating the intent of the

---

65   GAR Form F20 & 23, paragraph 6C.
66   Dangler v. Rutland, 229 Ga. 439, 192 S.E.2d 156 (1972); Malone v. Klaer, 203 Ga. 291, 46 S.E.2d 495 (1948).

parties to attach a property description later will not be effective. The Court of Appeals of Georgia has aptly described this practice:

> "[A]lthough it may be realized that it is the practice of real estate brokers to merely use this phrase "legal description to be attached later" in order to avoid copying a lengthy legal description into the sales contract, and that many sales are consummated on sales contracts which read this way, it cannot be said that the courts can approve such a practice when neither the sales contract itself, nor the source of the "legal description to be attached later" is definite enough to limit such description to any one tract of property."[67]

Taking the time to have a survey of the property prepared prior to entering into a contract can obviously avoid problems later. However, if this is not possible, the parties should upon obtaining a proper legal description either amend the contract to incorporate it, or terminate the defective contract and enter into a new one.

§1.1.12   Use of preliminary drawings or diagrams to supplement description

Preliminary drawings or diagrams are sometimes attached to a contract to supplement the property description set forth in the contract or to provide the property description when none is set out. The drawing or diagram must be sufficiently definite and precise to identify the property in order for it to constitute a valid property description. If the preliminary drawing or diagram is not sufficiently definite to locate the property, the contract will not be enforceable without some other adequate property description.

In one case, the seller agreed to sell a 32.6 acre tract "less and except for a 25,000 square foot lot, inclusive of Seller's current residence, said exact location to be determined by Purchaser."[68] The contract attached a document that designated the lot, but the buyer redesigned the lot configuration. The seller refused to go through with the contract because, as a result of the buyer's redesign of the lot, the seller's home faced a street sideways and her driveway would have to bisect the front yard to reach the garage. The Court concluded that the contract was void because it did not specifically describe the land to be sold, since the preliminary designation of lots did not accurately reflect the actual site on which the seller's home was to be located.

Similarly, it has been held that a contract describing property to be sold by reference to an attached diagram that did not disclose the location of the property or furnish a key to its description was unenforceable.[69]

---

67   Murphy v. Morse, 96 Ga. App. 513, 100 S.E.2d 623, 625 (1957).
68   Scheinfeld v. Murray, 267 Ga. 622, 481 S.E.2d 194 (1997).
69   Bryan v. Rusk, 89 Ga. App. 125, 78 S.E.2d 853 (1953).

§1.1.13   Occupancy does not cure defective description

Even if the intent of the parties is clear, if the description of property in a contract is not adequate or sufficiently definite to allow it to be located, the contract is void. For example, if the property is not adequately described in a contract, the fact that a proposed buyer has occupied the actual property does not prevent the buyer from contesting the validity of the description of the property and does not cure a deficiency in the property description.[70]

          §1.1.14   Acceptance of a counteroffer may cure defect in property description

If an offer to purchase property contains a defect in the property description, the buyer's acceptance and partial performance (i.e., deposit of earnest money) of a counteroffer cures the defect if the counteroffer incorporates a complete property description. For example, a buyer executed a contract of sale offering to purchase property described as "Oakview Terrace Apartments, 1301 Oakview Road, Decatur, Georgia, as further described in Exhibit 'A' attached."[71] The offer was transmitted without Exhibit "A" attached. The seller signed the contract and attached the property description, which should have been a part of the original offer. When the buyer who neglected to incorporate Exhibit "A" put up a security deposit, that action was deemed to be an acceptance of the counteroffer, which incorporated the Exhibit "A" and the original defective property description issue was remedied. Likewise, if a contract does not contain a sufficient property description can be cured by a subsequent amendment to the contract signed by both parties.

          §1.1.15   Use of owner's name to locate property

As long as there is a sufficient "key", descriptions such as the Robinson Place, the Humphrey Place, or the Anderson Place should be adequate. For example, if a contract describes property sold by name, the Anderson Place, and locates it specifically on a rural road 12 miles out of Augusta, Georgia, the description may be adequate.[72]

Similarly, a property description which identifies the county and the state in which the property is located, states that it is bounded on the north, east, south, and west by certain named owners and states the number of acres in the property is sufficiently definite.[73]

§1.1.16 Description of Condominium and Condominium Units

---

70   Fourteen West Realty, Inc. v. Wesson, 167 Ga. App. 539, 307 S.E.2d 28 (1983)
71   Uitdenbosch v. Gasarch, 160 Ga. App. 85, 286 S.E.2d 63 (1981).
72   Marsh v. Baird, 203 Ga. 819, 48 S.E.2d 529 (1948).
73   Deaton v. Swanson, 196 Ga. 833, 28 S.E.2d 126 (1943).

§1.1.16.1   Description of Property which is part of Condominium

In a condominium, the property which is made a part of the condominium is required to be described in the declaration of condominium. Many condominium developments are phased, meaning that it is being developed in separate steps or phases. The property included in the initial phase of the condominium is described in the declaration. Subsequent phases of the condominium are added by filing an amendment to the declaration in the office of land records. Each amendment must describe the property included in that phase of the condominium.

Sometimes, a condominium can appear to be larger than it truly is because less than all of the physical property in the development has been submitted to or made a part of the condominium. For example, if there are twelve buildings in a development but only six have been submitted to the condominium regime, some purchasers might mistakenly believe that the condominium consists of all twelve buildings.

However, since a description of the property which is a part of the condominium is a matter of public record, it is very difficult for a buyer to successfully sue a condominium developer for misrepresentation or fraud in relation to the property description of the unit. This point was confirmed in a case where the buyer sued the listing agent and seller for misrepresenting the property submitted to the condominium.[74]

When showing the property, the agent told the buyers that some amenities, including the deck, barbecue area and some landscaped area was included in the price. She also said that "you're going to enjoy being out here cooking, using this grill, cooking your fish, and you'll love that deck". The buyers were also given a "Fact Sheet" which listed the amenities. However, the condominium declaration and survey expressly excluded these amenities. The question posed to the court was whether the agent's misrepresentations could be relied upon by the buyers without them being required to prove that they could not have protected themselves through the exercise of due diligence.

The court noted that the buyers did not survey the property or request a copy of the condominium declaration. They also did not make independent inquiries concerning the boundaries of the property. Therefore, the court ruled that the buyers could not as a matter of law justifiably rely on the statements made by the broker to support a claim of misrepresentation. Neither did the agent's statements exempt the buyers' duty to exercise due diligence.

§1.1.16.2   Description of Condominium Units

The Georgia Condominium Act provides that a description of a condominium unit is sufficient if it contains the unit number, condominium name, county, and the

---

74   Brakebill et al. v. Hicks et al., 259 Ga. 849, 388 S.E.2d 695 (1990).

deed book and page number where the declaration of condominium is recorded in the land record office.[75] This information will enable a buyer to easily make an independent inquiry regarding the boundaries of a condominium unit. This is because the declaration of condominium for the condominium sets out the vertical and horizontal boundaries of the unit and references the survey and floor plans of the condominium, which are also recorded.

To comply with the Georgia Condominium Act, the floor plans of a condominium unit must contain the following information:

(1)   Square footage or dimensions of the unit;
(2)   Seal and signature of the preparing architect;
(3)   A statement by the preparing architect indicating how measurements were made;
(4)   The following statement printed on each floor plan:
       "These floor plans and the dimensions and square footage calculations shown hereon are only approximations. Any Unit Owner who is concerned about any representations regarding the floor plans should do his/her own investigation as to the dimensions, measurements and square footage of his/her Unit."
(5)   Each limited common element ("LCE");
(6)   Identification on the floor plans the name of the condominium and
(7)   Identification of the unit type and unit number on each floor plan.

§1.2   Fixtures and Personal Property

§1.2.1   What is considered a fixture

A Georgia statute provides that anything permanently attached to land or to the buildings is part of the property.[76] It further provides that "anything which is intended to remain permanent in its place even if it is not actually attached to the land is a fixture which constitutes part of the realty and passes with it."[77]

The term "fixture" includes all movable things, which, because they are annexed to the property, have the nature of both personalty and realty, regardless of whether they are removable.[78] Whether an item attached to property becomes a fixture depends on the circumstances under which the item was placed upon or attached to the property, the uses to which it is adapted, and the parties who are at issue.[79]

---

75   O.C.G.A. § 44-3-73.
76   O.C.G.A. § 44-1-2.
77   O.C.G.A. § 44-1-6.
78   Burpee v. Athens Production Credit Ass'n, 65 Ga. App. 102, 15 S.E.2d 526 (1941).
79   Wolff v. Sampson, 123 Ga. 400, 51 S.E. 335 (1905); State v. Dyson, 89 Ga. App. 791, 81S.E.2d 217 (1954).

There is limited case law in Georgia to assist in determining whether an item is a fixture. This is likely because the cost of litigating whether an item is a fixture outweighs the cost of simply replacing an item which has been removed from the property. Georgia courts have held that whatever is placed in a building to carry out the purpose of the building, or to permanently increase its value for such purpose, and is not intended to be removed but to be permanently used, becomes part of the building.[80] Generally, items such as mailboxes, light fixtures, and ceiling fans are considered fixtures.[81] Georgia courts have said that sewer lines[82] and sheds[83] are fixtures, while mobile homes[84] are not. Courts in other states have found that furnaces[85] and garbage disposals[86] are fixtures, and stereo systems, gas grills, satellite dishes,[87] and track lighting[88] are not fixtures. While court decisions from other states may be looked to for guidance, they do not establish binding precedent in Georgia.

In one case, a seller of land allegedly sold a shed to a third party *after* entering into a contract for the sale of the land on which the shed was located but before the closing of the sale of the land.[89] The purchaser of the shed did not remove the shed before the closing of the sale of the land. The buyer of the land contended that the shed was a fixture that could not be removed. The court did not determine who owned the shed as it sent the issue back to the trial court, but noted that it was within the power of the seller to detach fixtures before sale, or to reserve them by contract or deed. If the seller does not do so, the strict rule of the common law controls and all fixtures actually or constructively annexed to the land pass by conveyance of the property even though the contract may describe only the land. Therefore, unless there is some contractual agreement to the contrary, all items should be removed from the property prior to the closing.

The best way to eliminate a dispute over whether a beloved item, such as an heirloom chandelier is a fixture, is to remove the item before listing the property for

---

80   Waycross Opera-House Co. v. Sossman et al., 94 Ga. 100, 20 S.E.252 (1894); Brigham v. Overstreet, 128 Ga. 447, 10 L.R.A.N.S. 452.
81   Equibank v. U.S., 749 F.2d 1176 (5th Cir. 1985) (the court noted that any electrical unit detachable by pulling out a socket will generally be treated as personalty, but where the article is permanently connected to the building's wiring, it is a fixture). Using this analysis, a wired security system in a house would probably be considered a fixture.
82   Adams v. City of Macon, 204 Ga. 524, 505 S.E.2d 598 (1948).
83   Hargrove v. Jenkins, 192 Ga. App. 83, 383 S.E.2d 636 (1989). Since a playhouse is similar to a shed, it would also likely be considered a fixture.
84   Homac, Inc. v. Fort Wayne Mtg. Corp., 577 F. Supp 1065 (N.D. Ga. 1983).
85   Rose v. Marlowe's Cafe, Inc., 68 Ohio Misc. 2d 9, 646 N.E.2d 271 (1994).
86   First Nat'l Bank in Dallas v. Whirlpool Corp., 517 S.W.2d 262 (Tex. 1974).
87   Marshall v. Bostic, 1995 WL 115971, Tenn. Ct. App. (Mar. 15, 1995).
88   Rose v. Marlowe's Cafe, Inc., 68 Ohio Misc. 2d 9, 646 N.E.2d 271 (C.P. 1994). In Georgia, track lighting may be considered the same as any other light fixture; however, this issue has never been litigated before a Georgia appellate court.
89   Hargrove v. Jenkins, 192 Ga. App. 83, 383 S.E.2d 636 (1989).

sale. If this is not possible, it is important to be as specific as possible in the sales contract as to items the seller intends to remove or items that the buyer wants to ensure remain with the property. For example, in today's world of built-in refrigerators or stereo speakers as opposed to the more easily removable type, it is not at all clear whether such refrigerators or speakers would be considered fixtures or personal property. A contract provision could be added which would read as follows:

Special Stipulation #1-4: Credit for removed fixture at closing

Prior to closing Seller shall have the right to remove the following fixture from the Property:_____
The parties agree that the value of the fixture being removed is $_____.
At closing, this amount shall be credited towards the purchase price of the Property.

§1.2.2   What is removable personal property

Items such as removable appliances and window treatments are not generally regarded as fixtures, but rather are personal property. The seller may elect to include certain personal property such as the refrigerator, washer or dryer, or window treatments in the sale. Those items of personal property should be identified in the sales contract. The seller also may wish to list items of personal property that could arguably be considered fixtures but that he does not want to remain with the property:

Special Stipulation #1-5: Listing personal property which will remain with property

Notwithstanding any provision to the contrary in this Agreement, the following appliances and items shall remain with the Property as part of the purchase price, and Seller warrants that at closing, said appliances and items shall be in good working order and repair: (i.e., all window treatments, refrigerator, washer and dryer, all built-in appliances, and grill).

§1.2.3   Use of bills of sale and financing statements

If the contract between the parties includes the sale of personal property that would not be considered part of real property under the statutory definitions outlined above, the parties may want to have a bill of sale prepared. The bill of sale identifies the value of the personal property transferred from the seller to the buyer. If the buyer is not financing the purchase of the personal property, the bill of sale is simply evidence of the value of the property transferred. The Georgia Association of REALTORS® has an exhibit to use when a bill of sale is needed.[90]

---

90   GAR Form F136, Personal Property Agreement.

In the event the seller is financing the sale of the personal property, the seller may want the buyer to execute a security agreement and UCC Financing Statement and file the same in the county records where the property is located. The UCC Financing Statement is used to document the lender's interest in that property. An example of when such a statement would be useful is in the case of a seller who sells a furnished house and finances the entire transaction. A security agreement and properly filed UCC Financing Statement would secure the seller's interest in the furniture and appliances sold with the real estate. In the event the buyer defaults in making required payments, the seller could then bring an action to foreclose on the real property and recover the personal property covered by the security agreement.[91] Generally, institutional lenders do not file UCC Financing Statements in residential transactions. However, in commercial transactions, it is common for a lender to file a UCC Financing Statement for certain fixtures and personal property. It should also be noted that UCC Financing Statements have to be refilled at regular intervals to remain effective.

§1.2.4   Fixtures Checklist and Seller's Property Disclosure Statement

The GAR Seller's Property Disclosure Statement includes a fixtures checklist so that sellers can identify the fixtures and other personal property that will remain with the real estate.[92] The idea behind the checklist is to minimize disputes between buyers and sellers by having the seller clearly disclose to the buyer what fixtures and personal property will remain with the property prior to the parties entering into a contract. The GAR Contracts for residential property provide that the Seller's Property Disclosure Statement is attached to the contract and incorporated therein.[93]

If fixtures or other items identified on the Seller's Property Disclosure Statement checklist are not checked as remaining with the property, they can be removed. If, however, the property contains a fixture or other item that is not on the fixtures checklist, the common law of fixtures would apply in determining whether the fixture may be removed from the property. As noted above, the common law provides that, generally, personal property can be removed while fixtures remain with the property.

If the property contains an item that is not listed on the GAR Property Disclosure Statement, and it is unclear whether the item is a fixture or personal property, the seller wishing to retain the item should include language in the contract to exclude the item from the sale. The GAR Property Disclosure Statement provides a space where such items can be listed.

---

91   The seller also may include the personal property in the security deed to secure the seller's interest in the property transferred.

92   GAR Form F50, Seller' Property Disclosure Statement, paragraph 12 and Form 51, Seller's Property Disclosure Statement (New Construction), paragraph 11.

93   GAR Form F20, paragraph 5.

While the GAR Contract in paragraph 1 states that the "Property" includes "all fixtures, landscaping, improvements and appurtenances", this is nothing more than a statement of the common law with respect to fixtures. While this provision is inconsistent with the fixtures checklist in the Seller's Property Disclosure Statements (since it allows the Seller to remove certain fixtures) the exhibit would control over the main body of the GAR Contracts.

§1.2.4.1   When there is more than one of a particular type of fixture

If an item is checked on the fixtures checklist as remaining with the property, all of that particular type of item remains. For example, if light fixtures are identified as staying with the property, all light fixtures stay. If "refrigerator" is identified as staying, all refrigerators stay.

The fixtures checklist includes two spaces where the seller can make modifications, additions or deletions to the checklist immediately below the checklist. So, for example, if a seller wants to remove one light fixture but leave the rest, the seller should indicate this in the appropriate space.

§1.2.4.2   Seller's Property Disclosure Statement not attached to contract

The GAR Contract for residential property assumes that the Seller's Property Disclosure Statement is attached. What should the purchaser do if the Disclosure Statement is not available to be attached to an offer?

The preferred way of handling this would be for the buyer to contact the seller and request that a disclosure statement be provided before an offer is made. In practice, however, this may not always be an option. In such situations the buyer should both (1) include a statement of what fixtures and other items he wants to remain with the property and (2) use a special stipulation such as the following:

Special Stipulation #1-6: Additional time to attach Seller's property disclosure statement

The Seller's Property Disclosure Statement is not attached hereto. Seller shall have three days from the Binding Agreement Date to provide Buyer with a properly and fully completed Seller's Property Disclosure Statement. In the event that Seller fails to timely provide the Statement then Buyer may terminate this Agreement by providing written notice to Seller.

The special stipulation above however, does not give the buyer any recourse to terminate the contract should the buyer be dissatisfied with a condition revealed in the Seller's Property Disclosure Statement. A buyer who wishes to have some protection against such a possibility should only use the special stipulation above if the property is being sold subject to a right to terminate the contract.[94]

§1.2.5   Failure to timely remove a fixture

Under common law, in the absence of an agreement to the contrary, all fixtures, whether actually or constructively attached to the property, pass to the purchaser upon the execution of the deed.[95]

The fixtures checklist contained in the GAR Property Disclosure Statement provides that the seller must remove fixtures or other items that are not included in the sale of the property prior to closing or the transfer of possession of the property to the buyer, whichever is later. Therefore, sellers with large items to remove such as a play-set, must make their removal plans in advance or include a special stipulation in the contract allowing for the fixtures to be removed after closing. The following is an example of such a stipulation:

Special Stipulation #1-7: Allowing seller access to remove personal property and fixtures after closing

Notwithstanding any provision to the contrary contained herein, Seller reserves the right within _____ days from the date of closing to enter upon the Property upon notice to Buyer and remove the following fixture(s) and item(s): _____. Buyer agrees to permit Seller to remove the above referenced fixture(s) and item(s) and specifically grants Seller the right to come onto the Property within the above time frame to do the same. If any fixture or item Seller has a right to remove is located within any residential dwelling on the Property, Seller shall not enter any such dwelling without first notifying the Buyer and arranging a mutually convenient time for the item or fixture to the removed. If Seller has not removed the fixture(s) and item(s) in a timely manner (except where the failure to remove is due to the fault of the Buyer or an inability of the parties to arrange a mutually convenient time for the Seller to remove the item or fixture), Seller shall lose the right to thereafter remove said fixture(s) and item(s). In removing the above referenced fixture and/or item, Seller shall have no obligation to repair the specific area where the above-referenced fixture and/or item was attached to the Property. However, Seller agrees to indemnify and hold Buyer harmless from any damage caused in physically removing the above referenced fixture and/or item from the Property and any claims involving personal injury arising out of or related to the above referenced fixture and/or item from the Property. This provision shall specifically survive the closing.

---

94   See Chapter 8 regarding "free look" issues.
95   Burpee v. Athens Production Credit Ass'n, 65 Ga.App. 102, 15 S.E.2d 526 (1941).

In the absence of such a provision, the seller will lose the right to take the fixture or personal property after the closing or transfer of the property.

§1.2.6 Duty to restore after the removal of a fixture.

What is the seller's obligation to restore or repair the property after the removal of a fixture? Under common law the seller could remove fixtures so long as they did not materially injure the value of the real estate.[96]

The GAR Contracts provide that the seller shall deliver the property clean and free of debris[97]. The GAR Property Disclosure Statement provides that in removing fixtures the seller shall use reasonable care to prevent damage and, if necessary, to restore the property to its original condition. It is clear, therefore, that if the seller removes a light fixture and in the process pulls down a large portion of the ceiling, he must fix the damage.   There can, however, still be room for disagreement between the purchaser and the seller. If the seller removes a light fixture is he entitled to leave the wires and junction box exposed or must he patch the ceiling? Must the seller replace the light with another fixture? If so, must it be of a similar design or value of the one removed? These are questions that clearly should be addressed in the contract. The special stipulations below are examples of some of the different approaches which can be taken in this area.

Special Stipulation #1-8: Limiting seller's obligation to repair damage while removing fixtures

Seller, in removing the _____ from the_____ is not required to replace the said item or fixture or to patch, paint or repair the area from which the item or fixture was removed. Notwithstanding the above, Seller shall use reasonable care to prevent damage to the Property in removing the item or fixture.

Special Stipulation #1-9: Seller's obligation to replace removed fixtures

Seller, in removing the _____ from the Property, shall replace the said item or fixture prior to closing at Seller's cost with a fixture / item readily available at _____ [store] identified by Buyer at least ____ days prior to the date of closing, provided that the cost of said fixture / item shall not exceed $_____ excluding the cost of any labor to install the same. In the event Buyer fails to close on the purchase of the Property due to no fault of Seller, Buyer agrees that the fixture or item selected by Buyer shall become the property of Seller and Buyer hereby relinquishes any interest in the same. The cost of labor, if any, to install the replacement fixture or item shall be paid for by the Seller.

---

96 Lasch v. Columbus Heating & Ventilating Co., 174 Ga. 618, 163 S.E. 486 (1932).
97 GAR Form F20 & F23, paragraph 4A and F27, paragraph 5A.

Special Stipulation #1-10: Increasing seller's obligation to repair damage while removing fixtures

Seller, in removing the _____ from the Property, shall prior to closing, patch, paint, or otherwise repair the portion of the Property to which the said item or fixture was attached in a good and workmanlike manner such that there is no obvious evidence that the said item or fixture was previously affixed to the Property. The repair work shall be performed by _____.

Special Stipulation #1-11: Seller to use reasonable efforts to patch or repair damage while removing fixtures

Seller, in removing the _____ from the Property, shall use reasonable care to patch, paint, or otherwise repair the portion of the Property to which the said item or fixture was attached. The parties acknowledge that the area in which the repair work shall be performed shall extend no further than ____ feet from where the fixture / item was physically attached to the Property and that Seller's obligations shall only be to use reasonable efforts to have the patch and repair work blend in with the existing improvements. The repair work shall be completed in a good and workmanlike manner prior to closing.

CHAPTER 2
PURCHASE PRICE AND METHOD OF PAYMENT

OVERVIEW

This chapter on purchase price and method of payment is perhaps the most detailed in the book. The various methods by which the purchase price can be stated in the contract are discussed first. The main focus of the chapter, however, is on the different ways a buyer can finance the purchase of property and the buyer's obligations to pursue financing.

This chapter discusses FHA and VA loans, commercial loans, financing contingencies, seller financing, loan assumptions, and tax-free exchanges. This chapter also addresses issues such as the requirement that the buyer have sufficient cash at closing, the seller's right to provide financing or buy down the interest rate on a loan on behalf of the buyer, whether the buyer can receive a credit for repairs at closing, and the effect of the buyer applying for a different loan than what is described in the contract.

§2.1   What the GAR Contracts provide

A contract for the sale of real property should always state the purchase price either (a) as a definite and specific amount, or (b) in a manner in which the purchase price can easily be determined.[98] The GAR Contract provides that the purchase price be a definite and specific amount which may be subject to certain financing contingencies. However, other GAR form agreements and stipulations discussed below allow the parties to state the purchase price in other ways. This is permissible provided the purchase price can be easily determined.

§2.2   Purchase price based on acreage

In some transactions the exact purchase price is determined after execution of the contract by the buyer and seller. For example, in contracts for the purchase of raw land, the purchase price is often stated as an amount to be paid per acre with the total acreage to be determined by a survey prepared at a future date. Courts in Georgia have held that so long as the property is clearly defined, such contracts are enforceable even though an exact dollar price for the property is not specified.[99]

The GAR Lot/Land Purchase and Sale Agreement provides for a purchase price based on acreage as an alternative to a specific total dollar amount.[100] If the purchase price is based on acreage, a contingency may be included in the contract giving the buyer the right to terminate the contract if the property is more or less than a

---

98   Carroll v. Jones, 206 Ga. 332, 57 S.E.2d 173 (1950).

99   Bowles v. Babcock and Wilcox Co., 209 Ga. 858, 76 S.E.2d 703 (1953). It is important that even if the actual acreage is not known and is to be determined on the basis of a survey, the location of the property must be clearly defined. See Chapter 1 for a detailed discussion of the sufficiency of the property description.

100   GAR Lot/Land Purchase and Sale Agreement, Form F27, paragraph 2B.

specified number of acres. An example of such a contingency is set out in Special Stipulation #1-3.

§2.3 Purchase price based on appraisal

Contracts contingent on the property appraising at a certain price or providing that the purchase price of the property will be based on an appraisal prepared by a licensed appraiser are generally recognized as being sufficiently definite, and, therefore, enforceable. In one case, a Georgia Court held that an option contract was legally sufficient when the purchase price was "the appraised value of the property based on an MAI Appraisal" because the contract provided a key by which the purchase price could be determined.[101]

On the other hand, the following phrase within an exclusive listing contract which did not specify the method of appraisal or of determining the amount of consideration resulted in an unenforceable contract: "w/option to accept appraised in 60 days."[102] The Court found that the phrase was not sufficiently certain to provide a "key" or "mode" to determine the sales price. Specifically, the Court found that the phrase was incomplete as to the manner in which the property was to be appraised. In another case, the parties agreed that the property would be sold at an appraised value. The Court stated that "appraised value" was too indefinite to create a binding contract. However, the court did note that a price based on an appraised value might be enforceable if there is a "key" by which a definite price can be ascertained.[103]

If the parties agree to have the purchase price determined by an appraisal, the following provision may be incorporated in the contract:

Special Stipulation #2-1: Purchase price based on appraisal

The Purchase Price of the Property shall be determined by an appraisal of the Property prepared by the following appraiser _____, who holds a certified residential or better designation from the Georgia Real Estate Appraiser's Board, no later than _____ days from the Binding Agreement Date. The appraisal shall be jointly arranged by the Buyer and Seller, and the parties agree to instruct the appraiser to immediately provide a copy of the appraisal to both parties upon its completion. Buyer and Seller shall each pay the following percentage of the costs of the appraisal: Buyer _____%, Seller _____%. If the Property appraises for more than $_____, then within _____ days of Buyer's receipt of the appraisal, Buyer may terminate this Agreement by written notice to Seller and all earnest money shall be promptly refunded to Buyer. If Buyer fails to timely exercise

---

101   Miller v. McCullough, 236 Ga. 666, 224 S.E.2d 916 (1976).
102   Wiley v. Tom Howell & Associates, Inc., 154 Ga. App. 235, 267 S.E.2d 816 (1980).
103   Pettigrew v. Collins, 246 Ga.App. 207, 539 S.E.2d 214 (2000).

this termination right, it shall be deemed waived. If the Property appraises for less than $_____, then within _____ days of Seller's receipt of the appraisal, Seller may terminate this Agreement by written notice to Buyer and all earnest money shall be promptly refunded to Buyer. If Seller fails to timely exercise this termination right, it shall be deemed waived.

§2.3.1   Types of appraiser classifications

In Georgia, anyone who appraises real property for a fee must have an appraiser classification unless that person falls under the exceptions to the classification requirements.   There are four types of real estate appraiser classifications in Georgia. Appraisers may either be state registered, state licensed, state certified residential or state certified general. An appraiser is only permitted to appraise what is within the scope of his or her classification. Therefore, before engaging an appraiser, it is important to know how the appraiser is classified and its restricted activity.

Generally, registered appraisers are not permitted to appraise real property. Licensed appraisers are permitted to appraise residential property up to a certain value depending on whether it is a complex transaction, and commercial property or land of up to $250,000. Certified residential appraisers are permitted to appraise any residential property, and commercial property or land of up to $250,000 in value. Certified general appraisers are permitted to appraise all kinds of real estate. Detailed information about what type of classification is required for a particular appraisal can be obtained from the Georgia Board of Real Estate Appraisers.

§2.4   Termination of agreement if property does not appraise for purchase price

The GAR Special Stipulations include language that contemplates that the contract can be subject to the property appraising for at least the purchase price. If the property does not appraise for at least the purchase price, the buyer has an option to terminate the contract. This means that a buyer can make the contract contingent on the property appraising for not less than the purchase price to avoid overpaying for the property. An example of such a contingency is set out below:

Special Stipulation #2-2: Buyer has right to terminate if property does not appraise for contract price

This Agreement is contingent upon the Property appraising for an amount equal or greater than the purchase price of the Property. The appraisal shall be performed by a certified Georgia real estate appraiser holding a certified residential or better designation from the Georgia Real Estate Appraiser's Boar selected by _____ and paid for by _____. The appraisal shall be performed on or before the closing date. In the event the appraisal is not performed in a timely manner, this contingency shall be deemed waived.

An alternative to the above special stipulation is where the appraiser is selected by the buyer's mortgage lender as set forth below:

Special Stipulation #2-3: Buyer has right to terminate if appraisal performed by Buyer's mortgage lender is less than the purchase price

If an appraisal of the Property prior to the closing by a certified Georgia appraiser holding a certified residential or better designation from the Georgia Real Estate Appraiser's Board performed as part of the process of the mortgage lender determining whether to make a mortgage loan on the Property that the appraisal value of the Property is less than the Purchase Price set forth herein, the Buyer may at the Buyer's option terminate this Agreement upon written notice to Seller given prior to the closing.

Rather than incorporating the above type of special stipulation in a commercial real estate purchase and sale agreement, most buyers simply give themselves a sufficiently long due diligence period during which time the buyer can terminate the contract without cause. Buyers of residential real estate can also give themselves a sufficiently long free look period to determine whether and on what terms the property can be financed.

§2.5   Effect of failure to state full purchase price

Parties to a contract should ensure that the full purchase price is stated in the written contract and should not rely on oral promises or side agreements of the buyer to pay additional amounts. When a written contract for the sale of property includes a merger clause[104] (i.e., provides that it is the sole and entire agreement of the parties) and makes no mention of additional sums due from the buyer, the buyer's alleged verbal promise to pay an additional sum is generally unenforceable.

The effect of failure to state the full purchase price in the written contract is demonstrated in a case in which the buyer delivered a letter to the sellers agreeing to purchase the property for $135,000.00 plus an additional $5,000.00 if the buyer was able to sell all of the lots which were to be subdivided from the property within six months from the date of closing.[105] The sellers accepted this proposal and entered into a contract for the sale of the property for $135,000.00 and did not make any reference to the payment of the additional $5,000.00 outlined in the letter. The contract also contained a provision that it constituted the sole and entire agreement between the parties (i.e., a merger clause). The sellers sued the buyer when the buyer refused to

---

104   GAR Form F20 & F27, paragraph 11A; F23, paragraph 12A; and CF2, paragraph 15A.

105   <u>Kiser v. Godwin</u>, 90 Ga. App. 825, 84 S.E.2d 474 (1954).

pay the sellers the additional $5,000.00 after all of the subdivided lots was sold within six months from the closing date. The court concluded that because the contract stated that it was the sole and entire agreement, the parties expressly excluded the use of any evidence outside the contract to show the intent of the parties. Therefore, the buyer's promise to pay the additional $5,000.00 was unenforceable.

More recently, a court concluded that a buyer's oral promise to pay an additional $24,740.00 to a seller was unenforceable.[106] The seller argued that the buyers fraudulently induced her to enter the contract using an oral promise; however, the merger clause in the contract precluded the seller's recovery. The seller's alternative would have been to rescind the contract and sue for the alleged fraud and deceit. Such an action would need to be brought immediately upon the discovery of the fraud.[107]

§2.6 Payment of purchase price in all cash

The GAR Contract for residential property gives the buyer an option to specify that the purchase price will be paid in all cash or its equivalent at closing without a financing contingency. However, even if a contract for the purchase and sale of property does not specify the method for paying the purchase price, it is presumed that the purchase price will be paid in full at closing.[108]

Even if the contract provides for financing, the purchaser can waive the financing contingency in most cases. The general rule that the buyer may waive a financing contingency is based on the theory that the contingency is for the buyer's benefit.[109] However, if the financing terms call for the seller to finance the transaction, the financing contingency may also be for the seller's benefit in which case, the buyer may be precluded from waiving the financing contingency and paying all cash.[110]

§2.6.1 Payment of closing costs in all cash transactions

The GAR Contract provides that the buyer pays all closing costs in "all cash" transactions. There have been some disputes between buyers and sellers over what constitutes and who pays closing costs in all cash transactions. The following special stipulation can be used to try to allocate costs between the buyer and the seller in such a transaction.

---

106   Mitchell v. Head, 195 Ga. App. 427, 394 S.E.2d 114 (1990).

107   See Chapter 11for a more detailed discussion on rescission

108   M.M. Allen, Sr. v. Home Service and Constr., Inc., 93 Ga. App. 438, 92 S.E.2d 36 (1956).

109   Edwards v. McTyre, 246 Ga. 302, 271 S.E.2d 205 (1980); Blanton v. Williams, 209 Ga. 16, 70 S.E.2d 461 (1952).

110   Sikes v. Markham, 74 Ga. App. 874, 41 S.E.2d 828 (1947). See Section 2.10.9 for a discussion of waiver of financing contingency.

Special Stipulation #2-4: Allocating closing costs in all cash transactions

In this transaction, the following costs and charges shall be paid for by either the Buyer or Seller as indicated below:

1. Preparation of Survey	_____*Buyer*	_____*Seller*
2. Preparation of Warranty Deed	_____*Buyer*	_____*Seller*
3. Preparation of Seller's Affidavit	_____*Buyer*	_____*Seller*
4. Preparation of Settlement Statement	_____*Buyer*	_____*Seller*

All other costs and charges necessary to close the transaction shall be paid for by the _____.

§2.6.2   Selection of closing attorney in all cash transactions

The GAR Contract does not specify who selects the closing attorney in an all cash transaction. The following special stipulation can be used to address this issue.

Special Stipulation #2-5: Selection of closing attorney

In this transaction, the closing attorney shall be selected by the _____. The closing attorney shall be responsible for the preparation of all legal documents necessary to consummate this transaction.

§2.7   Financing provisions generally

The financing section of a real estate sales contract is critical to both the buyer and seller of residential property. It is an economic necessity for most buyers to make the contract contingent on their ability to obtain a loan. In the majority of cases, the buyer will pay a portion of the purchase price in cash and finance the balance with the proceeds of a loan.

The seller has an interest in ensuring that the financing provision is not used as a basis for invalidating the contract if the buyer becomes dissatisfied with the property for other reasons. However, once the earnest money is paid, the buyer cannot argue that a contract for sale that is subject to a financing contingency is unenforceable for lack of mutuality of obligation.[111] Therefore, each party has an interest in ensuring that the purchase price and method of payment are clearly stated in the agreement. Georgia courts require that the terms of the contract, including the financing terms, be sufficiently definite so as to ascertain the intent of the parties.[112] If the financing provision is vague and indefinite, the contract may be unenforceable.

---

111   Brack v. Brownlee, 246 Ga. 818, 273 S.E.2d 390 (1980).
112   Denton v. Hogge, 208 Ga.App. 734, 431 S.E.2d 728 (1993).

With commercial loans, the main underwriting criteria are the value and the income potential of the property. For these reasons, the commercial sale and purchase agreement provides for a due diligence period during which time the buyer can determine the availability of financing.

§2.7.1   Pre-qualification letters

Sometimes, a seller will require the buyer to provide the seller with a letter from the buyer's mortgage lender indicating that the buyer is qualified to obtain a mortgage loan in a particular amount. While the buyer normally provides these letters to the seller prior to the buyer making an offer to purchase the property, they are sometimes required in the sales contract to be provided shortly after the binding agreement date.

Pre-qualification letters were originally intended to give the seller a sense of comfort that the buyer had the financial means to complete the purchase of the property. If there were two prospective buyers of a property, the buyer who provided a letter to the seller that he or she was qualified to buyer the property was seen as having a competitive advantage over the other prospective buyer. Unfortunately, these letters over time became less of an accurate prediction of whether the buyer had the financial means to complete the transaction. This is because mortgage lenders tend to issue these letters without doing a credit check on the buyer. As a result, the letters have only become as reliable as the information provided by the buyer to the lender.

Pre-qualification letters would have far greater value if the lender did a full credit check of the buyer prior to issuing such a letter. An example of a special stipulation requiring the same is set forth below.

Special Stipulation #2-6: Provision of pre-qualification letters

Within _____ days from Binding Agreement Date, Buyer shall provide Seller with a letter from an institutional mortgage lender confirming that the Buyer is qualified to obtain a _____ type mortgage loan in the principal amount of _____ with an interest rate at par of not more than _____ to be repaid in monthly payments over a term of _____ years. The lender shall warrant in the letter that the lender in issuing the letter has done a full credit check on and income verification of the Buyer and understands that the letter may be relied upon by prospective sellers in deciding whether or not to sell their properties to Buyer.

§2.8   Mechanics of financing

In a financed transaction a buyer will execute a promissory note in favor of the lender in which the buyer promises to repay the lender the amount financed. The buyer also executes a deed to secure debt in which the buyer grants the lender a security interest in the property being sold to secure the amount of the note due to the lender. By executing the deed to secure debt, the buyer pledges the property being purchased to the lender as security or collateral for the loan.

§2.8.1 The promissory note

The promissory note is a contract between the buyer and lender in which the buyer "promises" to repay the lender the amount of the loan plus interest. It sets out the amount of the loan, maturity date, interest rate, payment terms, default provisions and pre-payment rights. As in the case with most other contracts, the promissory note must be in writing and be signed by all parties obligated under its terms. In addition to personally obligating the buyer to repay the loan, the note also outlines the terms and method of repayment.

While a promissory note in a residential transaction is usually a straightforward repayment of the amount borrowed, a commercial loan is more complex. There may be special payment terms or even a sharing of the revenue from the property. Further, the loan may be disbursed incrementally, as is often the case with construction loans. Another issue in a commercial loan is whether the loan will be a recourse or non-recourse loan. With a non-recourse loan, the borrower is released from liability and the lender looks solely to the property or other collateral in the event of a loan default.

With an institutional lender, loan approval is conditioned on the buyer's acceptance of the terms outlined in the note, which will normally include a requirement that the note be secured by a deed to secure debt on the property. In a seller-financed transaction, however, it is important for the seller to include a requirement in the sales contract that the property being sold shall serve as security for the repayment of the indebtedness due under the note. If the contract provides only that the buyer is to execute a note and does not require that the note be secured by a deed to secure debt on the property, the loan will merely be a personal obligation of the buyer and the seller/lender will not have a security interest in the property.[113]

Most notes also provide that if more than one buyer executes a note, each individual buyer will be jointly and severally liable for repayment of the debt. This means that if both a husband and wife sign a note, they are each individually liable for the entire debt and not just for their respective share. This remains the case even if the husband and wife later file for divorce. Any agreement between the ex-spouses as to who is responsible for the repayment of the note is not binding upon the lender.

§2.8.2 The deed to secure debt

Different states have different laws regarding the use of security instruments. In Georgia, lenders obtain a security interest in the property being sold through execution of a deed to secure debt, which is also known as a security deed or mortgage

---

113   Rumph v. Rister, 211 Ga. 312, 85 S.E.2d 768 (1955).

deed. A buyer executing a deed to secure debt conveys legal title in the property to the lender; however, the buyer retains equitable title to the property. This means that the buyer retains the usual rights of ownership such as possession and use of the property as long as the buyer is not in default on the loan. The deed to secure debt, which is executed by the buyer in favor of the lender, is filed in the land records of the county in which the property is located.

Because the security deed transfers legal title to the lender, Georgia is known as a "title theory" state. Other states, such as Florida, are known as "lien theory" states. Lien theory means that the security instrument (usually a mortgage) acts as a lien on the property rather than actually transferring title.

The deed to secure debt is a separate and distinct document from the promissory note. While the note serves as evidence of the buyer's personal obligation for the debt, the deed to secure debt provides the lender with a mechanism for recovering the property, which serves as collateral in the event that the note is not paid. The collateral or security provided under a deed to secure debt may include personal property as well as real property. A deed to secure debt without an underlying note, however, may be held to be unenforceable.[114] Therefore, most lenders have the borrower execute both a promissory note and a deed to secure debt to protect their interests as much as possible.

For commercial loans, additional documents are often necessary either due to the nature of the transaction or the need for additional security. For example, it is usual to have a separate security agreement against inventory or accounts receivables. The lender may also require loan guarantees. In the case of a construction loan, the construction loan agreement will set out the terms of the loan, the conditions required before the bank advances any part of the loan and the lender's rights relating to the construction project.

§2.8.3   Power of sale in deed to secure debt

In Georgia, most deeds to secure debt contain a "power of sale" clause. This clause entitles the lender upon default to accelerate and call due the entire outstanding loan balance. If the default continues, the lender may invoke the power of sale clause and sell the property in accordance with state foreclosure laws and apply the proceeds from the sale to the payment of the debt.[115] For the most part, Georgia foreclosure laws are lender-friendly in that the lender does not have to initiate a lawsuit in order to foreclose on the property. Instead, under Georgia law, if and when a default occurs, a lender may typically rely on what is referred to as "non-judicial foreclosure" in accordance with state law.[116] A non-judicial foreclosure is a legal procedure in which the lender is authorized under the deed to secure debt to sell the property serving as

---

114   Bramblett v. Bramblett, 252 Ga. 21, 310 S.E.2d 897 (1984).
115   Smith v. Bukofzer, 180 Ga. 209, 178 S.E. 641 (1935).
116   O.C.G.A. § 44-14-160, et seq.

collateral for the loan upon default and apply the proceeds to the debt. The sale must be advertised and the property sold in accordance with state law requirements. In the event the sale does not yield enough money to satisfy the debtor's outstanding balance to the lender, the lender must obtain judicial confirmation of the sale prior to initiating a lawsuit against the debtor seeking what is referred to as a "deficiency judgment."[117] The lender's failure to obtain judicial confirmation of the sale is a bar to any later action against the borrower for a deficiency.

§2.9   Terms of loan must be definite

As noted above, the terms of a financing contingency must be sufficiently certain and definite to create an enforceable contract. The GAR Contract for residential property has blanks for the amount, type, term and interest rate of the loan to be obtained by the buyer.[118] The GAR Contract also requires the buyer to make an application for the loan within a specified number of days from the Binding Agreement Date. The buyer is also required to notify the seller of having applied for the loan, the name of the lender and name and telephone number of the loan originator. Furthermore, the buyer authorizes the buyer's lender to release to the seller the amount and terms of any loan for which the buyer has applied.

The GAR Contract also obligates the buyer to pursue qualification for the loan diligently and in good faith. If the buyer fails to timely apply for a loan the seller can terminate the contract. However, the seller must first give the buyer five (5) day's notice during which time the buyer can cure the default. If the seller has knowledge of the buyer's failure to timely apply for a loan and fails to object to the same, the buyer will likely be deemed to have waived his or her right to object at a later time.

At the time the buyer makes an offer to purchase he or she may not know under what specific terms a loan will be available. The goal in preparing the financing section of the contract is to set forth loan requirements which are acceptable to the buyer but which are not so restrictive so as to give the buyer an automatic or easy way out of the contract. For example, if interest rates are on the rise, it may be advisable to state an interest rate somewhat higher than the prevailing rate or give the seller the option of buying down the interest rate for the buyer.

§2.9.1   Meaning of "ability to obtain" loan

The GAR Contract is contingent upon the buyer's ability to obtain the loan based upon the lender's customary and standard underwriting criteria. However, the GAR Contract also provides that if the basis of the loan denial is either or both of the following, the buyer is deemed to have the ability to obtain the Primary Loan: 1) the buyer lacks sufficient cash to close or 2) the buyer is required to lease or sell other real property as a condition of obtaining the Primary Loan.

---

117   O.C.G.A. § 44-14-161.
118   GAR Form F20 & F23, paragraph 2 and F27, paragraph 3.

These two qualifiers are part of the definition of "ability to obtain" because the buyer warrants elsewhere in the GAR Contract that the buyer has sufficient cash to close the transaction and does not need to sell or lease other real property as a condition to obtaining a loan. By providing that the buyer is deemed to have the ability to obtain the loan if either of these is the basis of the loan denial, the buyer cannot use either of these reasons as an excuse not to close.

§2.9.2   Amount and type of loan

The amount of the loan to be obtained from a third party must be clearly stated in the financing section of the contract, or, in the alternative, the contract must provide a method by which the amount of the loan can be calculated. For example, it would be legally acceptable and, in fact it is often provided, that a contract will be contingent upon a buyer's ability to obtain a loan in an amount equal to 80% of the purchase price.[119] Since the amount of the loan is directly tied to the purchase price, the amount of the loan is easily ascertainable.

In one case, a contract to purchase property for $36,900.00 was made contingent upon the buyer applying for and accepting, if available, "a 2/3 first mortgage loan . . . with interest at the current prevailing rate with principal and interest payable monthly for 20 years, and the balance in cash at closing."[120] The buyer refused to accept a loan in the amount of $24,600.00 at 8% and terminated the contract. When the seller sued, the buyer argued that the contract was void because the financing provision was vague and uncertain. In ruling against the buyer, the Court stated that the language in the contract, which referenced a "2/3 first mortgage loan", obviously referred to 2/3 of the purchase price of $36,900.00 and the prevailing interest rate was readily ascertainable. Therefore, the court concluded that the contract was neither vague nor uncertain as to the terms of purchase and sale.

§2.9.2.1   Applying for different loan than stated in contract

The GAR Contract requires the buyer to apply for the specific loan described in the Contract (known as the "Primary Loan") or any other loan for which the Buyer may qualify more easily. So, for example, let's assume that the buyer agrees to apply for an adjustable rate mortgage with an initial interest rate of 5% and a loan term of 15 years. The buyer could fulfill the requirements of this contingency by applying for an adjustable rate mortgage with a 30-year term since such a loan is easier for the buyer to qualify. However, the buyer could not fulfill the requirement of the loan contingency by applying for a fixed rate mortgage with the same interest rate and term since it would be more difficult to qualify for such a loan.

---

119   The purchase price, of course, must be clearly stated.
120   <u>Barto v. Hicks</u>, 124 Ga. App. 472, 184 S.E.2d 188 (1971).

If the buyer only applies for the Primary Loan and the loan is not approved, the buyer is entitled to terminate the contract. For example, let's assume that the contract is conditioned upon the buyer's ability to obtain a fixed rate loan "in the principal amount of 80% of the purchase price listed, with an interest rate at par of not more than 8½% per annum on the unpaid balance." The mortgage lender later informs the buyer that while he will not be approved for a fixed rate loan, he can be approved for an adjustable rate loan. In this situation, the buyer is still entitled to terminate the contract due to the failure of the financing contingency because he has not applied for a different loan. However, if the buyer applies for the adjustable rate loan, the buyer would then be obligated to accept the loan if the buyer is approved for the same. Of course, proving whether the buyer actually applied for a loan in this situation is sometimes difficult. The GAR Contract also provides that if the buyer applies for any other type of loan (regardless of whether it is harder or easier to obtain than the Primary Loan), and is approved for the same, the buyer must accept the loan.

§2.9.2.2   *Requirement of sufficient cash at closing*

In the GAR Contract, the buyer warrants that he will have sufficient cash at closing, which when combined with the amount of any loans, will allow the buyer to complete the transaction.[121] In other words, the buyer is warranting that if he or she is approved for a loan, he or she will have the rest of the money needed to close. The phrase "sufficient cash to close" was specifically used instead of the phrase "downpayment" to emphasize that the buyer is warranting that he or she will have all monies needed to close other than the loan proceeds. So, for example, if a lender requires a buyer to fund certain escrows at closing, this amount would be part of the funds to close the buyer is warranting that he or she will have. If the buyer does not have these funds, the buyer will be in default under the contract.

So, for example, let's assume that the buyer is required under the contract to obtain a loan equal to 80% of the purchase price at an interest rate of not more than 9% payable over 30 years. After making loan application, the buyer is approved for such a loan. If the buyer cannot then close the transaction because he does not have the funds to close (i.e., the additional 20% of the purchase price plus closing costs, lender required escrow amounts, and any other fees or charges associated with the closing), the buyer would be in default of the contract.

Since buyers may not be aware of how much cash they will need in order to close or obtain loan approval, it is prudent for the buyer to speak with a mortgage lender about these issues prior to entering into a sales contract.

§2.9.3   Interest rate should be specifically identified

As a general rule, the interest rate at which the loan is to be repaid must be specifically identified in the contract. So, for example, a contract which contained a

---

121   GAR Form F20 & F23, paragraph 2, Form F27, paragraph 3.

provision that "[t]he within sale is contingent upon purchaser's ability to secure a conventional loan of $10,000.00 for ten (10) years" was held unenforceable because the contract failed to specify both the interest rate at which the loan was to be repaid and the terms of repayment.[122]

In another case the contract was contingent upon the buyer's ability to obtain a loan of 80% of the purchase price to be paid in monthly installments over a term of at least 30 years.[123] The preprinted financing contingency contained a blank space where the interest rate on the loan could be filled in and another blank space in which a monthly payment amount could be written. Neither of these blanks was filled in. The Court of Appeals held that the contract was missing critical terms and was, therefore, unenforceable. The Court would likely have ruled the same way had the phrase "TBD" or "to be determined" been used instead of a specific interest rate.

Contracts that specify the type of loan should also identify whether the interest rate on the loan is a fixed rate, adjustable rate or interest only. The buyer should identify a maximum interest rate on the loan to protect against interest rates rising between the Binding Agreement Date and the date of closing.

Our courts have viewed the inclusion of a maximum rate of interest above which the buyer does not have to close as being for the protection and benefit of the buyer. As such, in one case, a buyer entered into a contract contingent on the ability to obtain a fixed rate mortgage loan with an interest rate of not more than 10⅓% per annum on the unpaid principal balance.[124] The contract provided (as do the GAR Contracts) that "ability to obtain" meant that the buyer was qualified to receive the loan described in the contract based on lender's customary and standard underwriting criteria. The contract also gave the buyer, "at its option" the right to apply for a loan with different terms and conditions and close the transaction. There was nothing in the contract, however, which required the buyer to close if she applied for and was approved for a different loan. The buyer was approved for an adjustable rate mortgage with an initial rate of 9-7/8%. The court found that the buyer was required to close only if she was able to obtain a fixed rate loan with an interest rate of not more than 10⅓%.

It should be noted that this case would likely have had a different result had the current GAR Contract been used since the GAR Contract now requires the buyer to close if the buyer applies for and is approved for the Primary Loan or any other loan for which it is easier to qualify or any other loan for which the buyer has applied for and is approved, irrespective of whether it is easier to obtain than the Primary Loan.

---

122   Scott v. Lewis, 112 Ga. App. 195, 144 S.E.2d 460 (1965).
123   Homler v. Malas, 229 Ga.App. 390, 494 S.E.2d 18 (1997).
124   Carroll v. Harry Norman, Inc., 198 Ga. App. 614, 402 S.E.2d 357 (1991).

§2.9.3.1 "Prevailing Rate" exception

A contract contingent on the buyer being able to obtain a loan for two-thirds (2/3) of the purchase price with interest payable "at the current prevailing rate" is generally enforceable. In an era of fluctuating interest rates, such a provision is common in general business usage and does not render a contract void for uncertainty.[125] Therefore, once the buyer is approved for a loan with an interest rate at the then current prevailing rate, he is obligated to accept such a loan even if the interest rate exceeds his expectations. Purchasers should pay particular attention to agreeing to accept a loan at the "current prevailing rate" when there is a lengthy period of time between the date of contract and the date of closing since there is more of a risk of interest rates rising.

The other risk in defining the interest rate on the loan as the prevailing rate is that it can lead to disputes between buyers and sellers over what is meant by the term "prevailing rate" since there can be significant variations in the pricing of mortgage loans. So for example, a buyer could argue that he does not qualify for a loan at a prevailing interest rate of 7.25%, when at the same time the seller is arguing that the prevailing rate is 6.75%.

§2.9.3.2 Setting an interest rate range

Another approach in this area is to define the interest rate which will be accepted by a buyer in terms of a range. The following special stipulations illustrate this type of provision.

Special Stipulation #2-7: Buyer to accept stipulated interest rate plus two percentage points

With respect to the Primary Loan, Buyer agrees to accept an interest rate at par of _____% (or less) or an interest rate at par of no more than two percentage points higher than the above-stated interest rate. All other terms of the Primary Loan shall remain the same.

This type of provision is sometimes used by builders when the home closing is still many months away. In addition, the buyer may want to include a provision in the contract in which the buyer contemplates and accepts some increase in interest rates which might occur between the Binding Agreement Date and the date of closing. An example of this special stipulation is as follows:

---

125   Barto v. Hicks, 124 Ga. App. 472, 184 S.E.2d 188 (1971); Southern Prestige Homes, Inc.v. Moscoso, 243 Ga. App. 412, 532 S.E.2d 122 (2000).

Special Stipulation #2-8: Interest rate fluctuations prior to closing

Buyer and Seller acknowledge and agree that interest rates on first mortgage loans may fluctuate between the date of this Agreement and the date of closing. Accordingly, Buyer agrees that, notwithstanding anything to the contrary contained herein, a loan with an interest rate not more than two percent (2%) higher than that interest rate set forth herein, shall be acceptable to Buyer and shall satisfy the new loan contingency.

If the buyer is unwilling to assume the risk of an increase in interest rates above the rate stated in the contract, the seller may want to incorporate the following special stipulation, which gives the seller the flexibility to buy down the loan to ensure that the contract closes:

Special Stipulation #2-9: Seller's right to buy down interest rate

Notwithstanding any provision in this Agreement to the contrary, Buyer and Seller agree that if Buyer is unable to obtain the Primary Loan, Seller shall have the right, but not the obligation, at Seller's sole expense (and in addition to any amounts Seller is contributing towards Buyer's costs to close) to buy down the loan for which Buyer has applied to the agreed-upon interest rate at par by paying additional discount points, provided that the loan otherwise conforms to the requirements set forth in this Agreement. Buyer shall notify Seller immediately if Buyer is unable to obtain the Primary Loan. If Seller intends to buy down the loan, Seller shall notify Buyer of the same no later than within one day of receiving notice from Buyer that Buyer was unable to obtain the Primary Loan.

Additionally, the special stipulation below can be used by the seller to require that his contribution to the closing costs and discount points first be applied to the payment of such discount points as are necessary to buy down the loan to the agreed-upon interest rate. Under this option, the seller will not pay any more at closing but will have somewhat greater protection against the financing contingency not being fulfilled:[126]

---

126   Fannie Mae guidelines will not permit a seller to contribute more than a certain percentage of the purchase price or appraised value of the property (whichever is less) toward closing costs (not to include pre-paids). Therefore, the buyer and seller should consult a mortgage loan officer when completing the above and below stipulations because they may be completed in such a manner to prohibit the buyer from obtaining loan approval.

Special Stipulation #2-10: Seller's contributions to be first used to purchase discount points

Notwithstanding any provision to the contrary contained in this Agreement, at closing, Seller shall pay a sum not to exceed $_____ which shall first be used by Buyer to pay for any discount points necessary to buy down or reduce the interest rate on the loan to the highest rate at which the financing contingency will be fulfilled by Buyer. Any portion of the above amount not used for discount points shall be used at Buyer's discretion to pay for closing costs, survey costs, insurance relating to the Property or mortgage and, if allowed by lender, other costs to close, including escrows and prepaid items. Buyer shall pay any additional closing costs, insurance premiums, or escrow amounts to fulfill lender requirements or to otherwise close this transaction.

§2.9.3.3 Relationship between interest rate and discount points and meaning of the phrase "at par"

While most form real estate contracts provide for identifying the maximum interest rate above which the buyer does not have to close, some are silent on whether the buyer is obligated to close on a purchase if a particular interest rate can be obtained by paying discount points. A discount point is 1% of the amount of the loan. Therefore, on a $200,000 loan, one discount point would be $2,000. The GAR Contract provides that the interest rate ceiling is calculated "at par" or without reference to discount points. This is the rate at which the mortgage broker does not have to pay a fee in order to "buy down" the loan. An interest rate lower than the par rate would cost the broker money; an interest rate higher than the par rate would pay the broker a commission. Therefore, if the buyer wants a loan at an interest rate which is lower than the par rate, the broker will have to "buy down the interest rate" at a cost which is passed on to the buyer in the form of discount points.

Under the GAR Contract, the buyer is not obligated to close on the purchase unless the buyer can obtain a loan at the interest rate specified in the contract without the buyer having to buy down the interest rate on the loan by paying discount points.

For example, let's assume a buyer agrees to purchase a home contingent upon the buyer obtaining a loan of 80% of the purchase price of $100,000.00 for a term of 30 years, with an interest rate at par not to exceed 8%. The buyer applies for financing and is told that he can only get a 30-year fixed rate loan at 8% only by paying two discount points. In this example, the financing contingency has not been met because the buyer cannot obtain the 8% loan at par or without paying discount points. Therefore, the buyer does not have to accept the loan and purchase the property.

§2.9.3.4 Locking in an interest rate

Interest rates may fluctuate between the Binding Agreement Date and the date the buyer "locks in" a particular interest rate on a loan. For example, let's assume that the contract provides that the buyer will not have to purchase the property if the buyer cannot obtain an adjustable rate mortgage with an initial interest rate of 5%, which is the then prevailing market rate. The closing is set 90 days from Binding Agreement Date. The buyer, thinking that the rates are likely to decrease, does not do anything to assure that he can get the 5% rate (i.e., the buyer does not "lock in" the rate). Ten days before the closing the market rate increases to 5.5%. Can the buyer terminate the contract on the basis that he is unable to obtain the specified financing? While arguments can be made on both sides of this issue, the answer is likely "yes".

In times of rapidly changing rates, a seller may therefore want to require the buyer to "lock-in" an interest rate shortly after the Binding Agreement Date. In this way, the buyers cannot tie up the property while gambling that rates may go lower. An example of such a special stipulation is set forth below.

Special Stipulation #2-11: Buyer must lock in rate early

Buyer agrees to "lock in" the interest rate on the Primary Loan within _____ days from Binding Agreement Date. The "lock-in" period shall run for at least through the date of closing referenced in this Agreement plus 7 additional days. The interest rate on the Primary Loan shall be the best available interest rate offered by the mortgage lender with whom Buyer has applied. Upon "locking in" the interest rate Buyer shall immediately give notice to Seller of having done so and the interest rate Buyer has "locked in".

§2.9.4   Term of loan must be identified

The time period in which the loan will be repaid must be identified. As with other terms of the contract, the GAR Contract, if properly completed, identifies the period over which the loan is to be repaid.

The effect of failing to describe when installments of principal and interest are due under a loan is demonstrated in the following case. A buyer entered into a contract conditioned upon the buyer obtaining a loan of $5,400.00.[127] The court stated that the contract was deficient because it failed to set forth not only the amount of the interest rate of the loan to be obtained but also when the installment payments of principal and interest would be due. Similarly, a court held that a contract which stated that $11,000.00 of the purchase price was to be paid in three equal installments was too vague and indefinite because it did not state when the installments were to be paid.

---

127   Brown v. White, 73 Ga. App. 524, 37 S.E.2d 213 (1946).

§2.10 Financing contingencies

§2.10.1 Purchase contingent on sale of current residence

A contract is often made contingent upon a buyer being able to sell or lease other property. Under the GAR Contracts, the buyer warrants that he does not need to sell or lease other real property to complete the purchase of seller's property.[128] Accordingly, the buyer would be in breach of contract in the event the loan was denied solely because of a failure to sell or lease a current residence. However, if there are multiple reasons for the loan denial such that they buyer would have been disapproved for the loan even if the buyer had sold or leased his current residence, the buyer would not likely be found to have breached his or her warranty.

If the buyer must sell other property to complete the transaction, the buyer should include a sale of other property contingency in the purchase contract.[129] As an extra measure of protection, buyers may also wish to include a special stipulation similar to the one set forth below:

Special Stipulation #2-12: Purchase contingent on sale of buyer's property

Notwithstanding any provision to the contrary contained herein, the purchase of the Property is contingent upon the sale and closing of Buyer's property located at _____ on or before the closing date (or any permitted extension thereof) in the Agreement. Buyer agrees to pursue and seek to complete the sale and closing of the above-referenced property diligently and in good faith. Buyer shall immediately notify Seller upon entering into any contract to sell the property and shall immediately provide Seller with a copy of the same. Buyer shall also keep Seller fully and immediately informed of any changes in the status of the contract and facts which could adversely affect the likelihood of the property being closed.

§2.10.2 Purchase contingent on sale or lease of buyer's property

A second approach is to make the sale of the property contingent upon the buyer selling or leasing other property. An example of this approach is set forth below:

---

128   GAR Form F20 & F23, paragraph 2, Form F27, paragraph 3.
129   GAR Form F90, Sale or Lease of Buyer's Property Contingency. If a buyer is using this GAR form because his purchase of the seller's property is going to be contingent upon the sale (and not the lease) of his own property, the buyer should be careful to strike the "or lease" language from the form. If such language is not removed, the seller could conceivably agree to lease the buyer's property in order to force the buyer to close.

Special Stipulation #2-13: Purchase contingent on sale or lease of buyer's property

This Agreement is contingent upon Buyer's ability, acting diligently and in good faith, to close the sale or to lease certain real property owned by Buyer and located at (address) on or before (date). In the event said property is not closed or leased by this date due to no fault of Buyer, this Agreement shall be null and void. For purposes of this Agreement, the term "leased" shall mean that the parties to the lease have executed the same whether or not the actual lease term has commenced   Buyer shall immediately notify Seller upon entering into any lease or contract to sell the property and shall immediately provide Seller with a copy of the same. Buyer shall also keep Seller fully and immediately informed of any 1) changes in the status of the lease or contract to sell and 2) facts which could adversely affect the likelihood of the property being sold or leased.

§2.10.3   Sale of property subject to Kick-Out provision

Another approach is to allow the seller to continue to market the property for sale while the buyer is attempting to sell or lease other property. If the seller receives an acceptable offer from another buyer, the seller must give written notice to the buyer. The buyer then has a specified number of hours to remove all contingencies including any financing contingency, thereby making the contract an "all cash" contract. This type of provision in real estate vernacular is referred to as a "kick-out" clause. Under this approach, the buyer may also be required to deposit additional earnest money with the Holder. An example of this type of provision is set forth below.

Special Stipulation #2-14: Purchase contingent on sale or lease of buyer's property, with kick-out right to Seller and removal of all contingencies

(1)   This Agreement is contingent upon Buyer's ability, acting diligently and in good faith, to close the sale or to lease certain real property owned by Buyer and located at (address), on or before (date). Seller shall have the right to continue to offer and actively market Seller's Property for sale. In the event that Seller receives another acceptable offer to purchase the property, Seller shall give written notice to Buyer or Selling Broker that Seller has received another acceptable offer. Seller shall not be obligated to provide the terms of said offer to Buyer.

(2)   Buyer shall then have (number) hours after receipt of Seller's Notice to deliver to Seller a signed written amendment to this Agreement signed by Buyer in which Buyer agrees to remove all contingencies set forth in this Agreement, including, without limitation, the contingency provided for in this Exhibit, any inspection contingency and any financing contingency, thereby making this an "all cash" transaction, without any contingency whatsoever. Furthermore, Buyer shall deposit with Holder additional earnest money of

$_____ and said earnest money to be delivered to Holder with the amendment. Upon Seller timely receiving the amendment signed by Buyer, Seller shall promptly sign the same and return a copy to Buyer.

(3)   All notices hereunder shall be delivered to the parties or representatives of the parties permitted to receive notice on their behalf in accordance with the notice requirements of this Agreement.

The above provision refers to the Amendment, which is the GAR Amendment to Remove Contingency of Sale or Lease of Buyer's Property[130]. If the buyer chooses this option, the buyer must complete this form, which sets out 1) the additional earnest money payment, 2) the removal of all contingencies and 3) the removal of the sale contingency.

If the buyer wishes to proceed with the purchase after receiving the seller's notice of another offer but to only waive the financing contingency, the buyer should use the following stipulation:

Special Stipulation #2-15: Purchase contingent on sale or lease of buyer's property with kick-out right to Seller and removal of financing contingency

(1)   This Agreement is contingent upon Buyer's ability, acting diligently and in good faith, to close the sale or to lease certain real property owned by Buyer and located at (address), on or before (date). Seller shall have the right to continue to offer Seller's Property for sale. In the event that Seller receives an acceptable offer, Seller shall give written notice to Buyer or Selling Broker.

(2) Buyer shall then have (number) hours after receipt of Seller's Notice to deliver to Seller a signed written amendment to this Agreement signed by Buyer in which Buyer agrees to remove all contingencies set forth in this Agreement, including, without limitation, the contingency provided for in this Exhibit, any inspection contingency and any financing contingency, thereby making this an "all cash" transaction, without any contingency whatsoever. Furthermore, Buyer shall deposit with Holder additional earnest money of $_____ and said earnest money to be delivered to Holder with the amendment. Upon Seller timely receiving the amendment signed by Buyer, Seller shall promptly sign the same and return a copy to Buyer.

(3)   All notices hereunder shall be delivered to the parties or representatives of the parties permitted to receive notice on their behalf in accordance with the notice requirements of this Agreement.

---

130   GAR Form F103.

The GAR Sale or Lease of Property Contingency obligates the buyer to act diligently and in good faith to sell or lease buyer's property. Some sellers may, on occasion, want to incorporate the following provision by which the parties agree to the listing price of the buyer's property to be sold or leased:

Special Stipulation #2-16: Parties agree as to listing price of buyer's property

Seller and Buyer agree that Buyer shall list Buyer's property located at _____for a price not to exceed $_____ and shall list the property with a real estate broker licensed in Georgia for a term of at least _____days.

§2.10.3.1   Seller's notice of kick-out

If the seller receives an acceptable offer from another buyer, the seller must give written notice of the same to the buyer. The buyer then has a specified number of hours to remove all contingencies.

Under the GAR Contract, notice to the broker representing a party as a client is notice to that party.[131]   Therefore, the time that the buyer has to remove all contingencies from the contract begins to run the earlier of when either the buyer receives the notice or the broker representing the buyer as a client receives the notice.

§2.10.4   Buyer's good faith obligation to pursue loan approval

The GAR Contract expressly provides that the buyer shall pursue "qualification for and approval of such loan diligently and in good faith."[132]   As a result, if the buyer, for example, fails to provide the lender with necessary documents, the buyer can be found to have breached the contract for failing to diligently pursue financing. The GAR Contract is tied to the buyer's "ability to obtain" a loan as opposed to the buyer "obtaining" a loan. "Ability to obtain" as defined in the GAR Contract means that the buyer is qualified to obtain the loan based on the lender's customary and standard underwriting criteria.

Some older case law attempted to distinguish between obtaining a loan versus having the ability to obtain a loan, concluding that the former was invalid for lack of mutuality. Case law now indicates that the buyer's obligation to diligently pursue financing eliminates this distinction.[133] However, to avoid any question about whether the financing contingency has been fulfilled, it is better practice to follow the GAR

---

131   GAR Form F20, paragraph 11G2.
132   Brack v. Brownlee, 246 Ga. 818, 273 S.E.2d 390 (1980).
133   Benveniste v. Koets, 252 Ga. 520, 314 S.E.2d 912 (1984), overruling F & C Investment Co. v.Jones, 210 Ga. 635, 81 S.E.2d 828 (1954).

model in any contract and use "ability to obtain" a loan as the standard for the buyer's obligation in this area.

From the seller's perspective, the problems inherent in determining good faith are demonstrated in the following case. The contract had a financing contingency that obligated the buyer to "promptly make application and pursue said application with reasonable diligence to obtain said loan when it is available."[134] The buyer applied for a loan, and it was granted with conditional approval of payment in full of an outstanding credit card account. The lender received information that the buyer had sufficient funds available in various bank accounts to pay off the debt, but the buyer refused to do so. The buyer stated that although her boyfriend was not named on the accounts or listed as a co-owner of the funds on the loan application, the monies in the account also belonged to him. The buyer also stated that her boyfriend had recently lost his job and might need the money. The trial court concluded that the buyer's actions were reasonable and exhibited good faith and diligence implied in the contract.

§2.10.4.1   Must buyer apply for loan to satisfy financing contingency?

One frequently asked is whether the buyer must actually apply for a loan the buyer has no hope of obtaining or which is unavailable? While the safe answer to this question is "yes", there is case law precedent for the opposite conclusion. Specifically, in one case, a buyer verbally inquired about a loan that would comply with the terms of the contract from two savings and loan associations, an insurance company, and a bank.[135] In each instance, the lender did not offer any loan under the terms provided for in the contract. In allowing the buyer to recover earnest money paid under the contract, the court found that there was sufficient evidence produced at trial to authorize the finding that the buyer had sought in good faith to obtain a loan, which was required of him under the contract, even though he did not make a written application for the loan.

However, since questions of whether the buyer acted in good faith to satisfy the financing contingency are questions of fact, applying for a loan and receiving a written letter of loan denial helps to eliminate any factual disputes over whether the buyer fulfilled his or her contractual obligations.

The GAR Contract requires the buyer to make the application for the mortgage loan within a specified number of days from the binding agreement date. Moreover, the buyer must give notice to the seller of having applied for the loan and any subsequent loans and provide the name and telephone number of the lender and the loan originator. The idea behind this provision is to keep the seller fully informed as to the buyer's progress in obtaining loan approval. All notices under the GAR Contract are required to be in writing, including the notice of having applied for a loan.

---

134   Century 21 Mary Carr & Assoc., Inc. v. Jones, 204 Ga. App. 96, 418 S.E.2d 435 (1992).

135   Carmichael v. Gonzales, 111 Ga. App. 695, 143 S.E.2d 190 (1965).

The GAR Contract provides that if the buyer fails to timely apply for the Primary Loan, the seller may terminate the contract if the buyer does not cure the default within five days after receiving written notice thereof by providing the seller with written evidence of having applied for such loan. This provision requires the seller to give the buyer an opportunity to cure any default before the seller can terminate the contract for cause. If a seller fails to give this notice, the seller will not likely be able to terminate the contract even if the buyer has not fulfilled his loan obligations.

Under the GAR Contract, the buyer authorizes the buyer's lender to release information to the seller and the seller's broker verifying the amount and terms of any loan for which the buyer has applied. The idea behind this provision is for the buyer to authorize the release of basic information regarding the loan so that the seller can verify that the buyer is fulfilling his or her loan obligations.

In some situations, the seller may want more than basic information about whether the buyer is fulfilling his or her loan obligations. In such cases, the following special stipulations can be used:

Special Stipulation #2-17: Release of loan information to Seller

Buyer hereby authorizes, directs and agrees to cause Buyer's mortgage lender to provide Seller upon Seller's request, with verification of the amount and type of loan or loans for which Buyer has applied, the status of the application (including whether it is complete, whether it has been approved and whether, if it is not complete, the terms which remain outstanding) and whether there is anything in Buyer's credit history and/or in other information provided to Buyer's mortgage lender as part of Buyer's loan application which could negatively affect Buyer's ability to be approved for the Primary Loan.

§2.10.4.2   Buyer deemed approved for a mortgage loan unless buyer gives notice of disapproval.

Some sellers have grown frustrated with the delays of either the buyer in applying for a loan or the lender in approving the loan. As a result, some sellers have shifted the burden to the buyer to provide notice of loan denial to the seller within a defined time frame. Failure by the buyer to provide the seller with a letter of loan denial within the required time frame is deemed an approval of the loan.

The provision below is an example of such a special stipulation.

Special Stipulation #2-18: Buyer deemed to receive loan approval if buyer does not provide lender's loan denial letter within a stipulated date

If Buyer does not provide Seller with a letter from Buyer's mortgage lender within ___ days from the Binding Agreement Date indicating that Buyer is unable to qualify for the loan described in Paragraph _____, then Buyer shall be deemed to have received loan approval and this Agreement shall no longer be subject to a financing contingency. Upon the removal of the financing contingency, Buyer shall immediately upon the request of Seller provide written notice to Seller verifying the source of Buyer's funds to close on the purchase of the Property. If Buyer does not provide this information to Seller within 3 days of being requested to do so, Buyer shall be in default of this Agreement

Another approach to this issue is to give the seller a right to terminate the contract unless the buyer fails to submit an amendment to the contract to remove the financing contingency within a defined period of time. The special stipulation below is an example of this type of provision.

Special Stipulation #2-19: Seller may terminate contract if buyer does not timely remove financing contingency

If Buyer does not present Seller within _____ days from the Binding Agreement Date an amendment signed by Buyer permanently removing any and all financing contingencies to which this Agreement is subject and agreeing to purchase the Property for all cash, Seller may but shall not be obligated to terminate this Agreement upon notice to Buyer. If Buyer presents the amendment in accordance with the above referenced requirements, Seller shall promptly sign the amendment and return a fully executed copy of the same to the Buyer.

If Buyer does not timely present the amendment meeting all the above-referenced requirements, Seller shall have ten (10) days from the last date the amendment removing any and all financing contingencies was to have been delivered from Buyer to Seller to terminate the Agreement. If Seller does not terminate the Agreement in a timely manner, the obligation of Buyer to provide the above-mentioned amendment to Seller shall thereafter be deemed to be waived by the Seller and shall no longer be an obligation of the Buyer to perform under this Agreement. All other terms and conditions of the Agreement shall remain in full force and effect.

§2.10.4.3   Financing contingency removed upon buyer obtaining loan commitment

Some sellers have argued that once the buyer is approved for a loan, the buyer should bear the risk if there is a change in the buyer's financial status such that the loan is later disapproved. For example, let's assume that the buyer is approved for a loan. Two days before the closing, the buyer is fired from his job and no longer is qualified to purchase the property.

Under the GAR Contract, the financing contingency would fail and the buyer would be entitled to a full refund of his or her earnest money. Some sellers have argued that this is not a fair result and that since the buyer is in a better position to control the risk of losing his or her loan approval than the seller, the buyer's earnest money should be given to the seller to help the seller offset any moving or storage expenses incurred by the seller.

One way to give the seller this type of protection is to provide that the financing contingency is removed from the contract once the loan is approved. An example of this type of provision is set forth below. Note that the seller's remedy in the event of a default by the buyer is limited to keeping the earnest money as liquidated damages. The thought here is that if the buyer loses his or her financing and cannot close on the property, the fair penalty should be for the seller to keep the buyer's earnest money rather than for the seller to bring some other type of claim against the buyer.

Special Stipulation #2-20: Financing contingency removed upon buyer obtaining loan commitment

Buyer shall have ten (10) days from the Binding Agreement Date to provide Seller with letters from a mortgage lender confirming that Buyer has been approved for the Primary Loan subject only to the lender's standard conditions. In the event Buyer fails to present this letter to Seller, this Agreement may be terminated by Seller upon notice to Buyer given within ten (10) days from the date the letter was due. If Seller fails to provide this notice to Buyer in a timely manner, this provision shall be deemed to be waived. Upon the receipt of these letters by Seller, the financing contingency referenced herein shall be deemed to be fulfilled and shall no longer be a part of this Agreement. This Agreement shall at the time no longer be subject to any financing contingency. In the event this Agreement is terminated due to the default of Buyer, Seller's sole remedy against Buyer shall be to retain Buyer's earnest money as liquidated damages. All parties agree the precise amount of Seller's damages is unknown and that this amount constitutes a reasonable estimate of Seller's actual damages and is not a penalty.

§2.10.5   Obligation to apply for loan with second lender

Appellate courts in Georgia have not addressed the question of whether the buyer's good faith obligation to pursue financing requires the buyer to apply for a loan with a different lender if the buyer's initial loan application is denied. Whether such a duty exists will likely depend on the facts and circumstances of the transaction. The chances that a buyer will be found not to have acted in good faith in diligently pursuing a loan are greater if (a) there was sufficient time between the initial loan denial and the closing date to apply for and be approved for a loan, and (b) the reasons for the initial loan denial were such that there was some reasonable likelihood the buyer would be approved for a loan the second time around.

If the GAR Contract is not used, sellers may want to incorporate a special stipulation to address the buyer's obligations in pursing a loan with a second mortgage lender if the initial lender denies the loan. Set forth below is an example of a contract provision that obligates the buyer to apply for a loan with a second lender if the buyer's initial loan application is denied:

Special Stipulation #2-21: Buyer's obligation in pursuing second loan (if GAR Contract not used)

Notwithstanding any provision to the contrary contained in this Agreement, in the event Buyer is notified that his loan is disapproved and more than _____ days remain until the scheduled date of closing in the Agreement, Buyer shall immediately notify Seller of such fact and shall be required to submit a loan application to another lender, to pursue said application diligently and in good faith, to execute all papers, to provide all documents, to perform all other actions necessary to obtain said loan, and to accept said loan if approved by lender. Upon written request by Seller, Buyer shall provide the name and telephone number of any such additional lender to whom Buyer has submitted a loan application.

§2.10.6   Buyer's obligation to apply for second mortgage

Some buyers need to apply for both a first and second loan in order to purchase the property. If this is acceptable to the seller, the buyer must complete GAR Form 66, which sets out the buyer's obligations when applying for a second mortgage. Essentially, the buyer under this form is given a time frame within which he or she must apply for a second mortgage and pursue the application diligently and in good faith. If the buyer does not timely apply for the second mortgage, the seller has the right to void the contract after giving the buyer written notice. Instead of applying for the second mortgage, the buyer may also apply for any other loan for which the buyer may more easily qualify.

§2.10.7   Obligation to accept seller financing or allow seller to buy down rate

The seller may offer to finance all or a portion of the sale if the buyer is unable to obtain a conventional loan. Alternatively, the Seller may agree to buy-down the interest rate on the buyer's loan if it exceeds the rate called for in the contract. While some buyers might appreciate such offers, can the seller force these options on a reluctant purchaser?

Our appellate courts have not yet ruled on these issues. It is likely, however, that a seller could force the buyer to accept his offer to buy down the interest rate on the buyer's loan This makes sense because, from the buyer's perspective, the loan will be on the exact terms for which he applied. For example, let's assume that the buyer applies for an 80% loan at 9% interest and is offered an 80% loan at 10% interest. If the seller agrees to buy down the loan by paying one point (i.e., 1 % of the loan) the net result to the buyer is an 80% loan at 9% interest. The buyer likely would have difficulty arguing that he was not obligated to accept such an offer. Any such offer by the seller would need to be in addition to any sums the seller already agreed in the contract to pay towards closing costs, discount points, etc. If the seller wanted to avoid any uncertainty he could use the special stipulation #2-10.

It is far less clear whether the GAR Contract permits the seller to force seller financing upon the buyer. The seller may argue that the buyer's good faith obligation to diligently pursue financing includes accepting an offer of seller financing (after the buyer's initial loan application has been denied) if the loan is on the same terms and conditions as are set forth in the financing contingency. The better argument, however, is that the buyer is only obligated to pursue or accept financing from an institutional lender. This is because the phrase "ability to obtain" as used in the GAR Contract, is defined to mean a loan "based upon lender's customary and standard underwriting criteria".[136] If the buyer was unable to obtain such a loan, the buyer can make a good argument that he or she did not have the "ability to obtain" the loan and that the financing contingency thereby fails. Moreover, the typical seller of residential property does not have any customary or standard loan underwriting criteria. The buyer may, therefore, argue that seller financing was not the intent of the parties. If the terms of a note or security deed proposed by the seller differ in any material respects from those used by the lender to whom the buyer initially applied, the buyer can additionally argue that she would not be in the same legal position as with an institutional loan.

Again, the seller can use a special stipulation in anticipation of this:

Special Stipulation #2-22: Seller's right to provide seller financing

In the event that Buyer is not able to obtain Primary Loan, then Seller, at Seller's option, may agree to make a loan to Buyer on terms identical to those contained herein and Buyer shall be obligated to accept the loan. Seller may elect this option by giving written notice to Buyer within three (3) days of Seller's receipt of notice from Buyer that Buyer's loan application was denied. Seller and Buyer agree to use a standard FNMA Note and Deed to Secure Debt to evidence Buyer's obligation in such a loan transaction.

---

136   GAR Form F20 & F23, paragraph 2C and Form 27, paragraph 3C.

Another issue is raised when the seller offers to finance a portion of the purchase price. For example, let's assume the purchase price is $100,000 and the contract calls for a 90% loan. The property appraises for $90,000 and the lender is only willing to make a loan based upon the appraised value (i.e., 90% of $90,000). Assuming that the contract is not contingent upon the property appraising for the purchase price, can the seller insist upon giving the buyer a $10,000 loan, thereby reducing the outstanding amount for which the buyer needs financing to $90,000? The answer should be "no". This is because the buyer can again argue that the financing contingency was not fulfilled because the buyer was not able to obtain a loan based upon the lender's customary and standard underwriting criteria.

Additionally, the GAR Contracts specify that the loan to be obtained by the buyer will be secured by a first lien security deed on the property.[137] Since a second mortgage is not a first lien security deed, a good argument can be made that the express requirements of the financing contingency were not fulfilled.

§2.10.8   Inability to procure or have ability to procure loan

§2.10.8.1   Involuntary change in financial condition

Problems may arise when a buyer is approved for a loan but prior to the closing, the buyer's financial condition changes. For example, let's assume a buyer enters into a contract that is made contingent upon the buyer's ability to obtain a loan. Shortly after receiving notification from a lender that his loan is approved, the buyer learns that he has been laid off from his job. Generally, loan approval by an institutional lender is subject to being withdrawn if the buyer's financial condition substantially changes before closing. If the buyer no longer has the ability to obtain a loan due to changed financial circumstances beyond his control, he would be relieved from performing his obligations under the contract and would be entitled to a return of his earnest money.

Similarly, if a lender will only approve a mortgage loan based on the combined income of a husband and wife, the death of a spouse resulting in the loan being disapproved would be an involuntary change in financial condition.

A buyer would probably not be relieved from his contractual obligations simply because his job transfer to an area in which he contracted to purchase a home is changed or canceled by his employer. If this is a possibility, the buyer should include a special stipulation in the contract allowing him to terminate the contract in the event this occurs.[138]

---

137   GAR Form F20 & F23, paragraph 2C and Form 27, paragraph 3C.
138   The buyer may still have an out, however, if as a result of the canceling of the job transfer the lender was no longer willing to make the loan because the property would no longer be the buyer's principal place of residence.

Special Stipulation #2-23 Buyer's right to terminate due to change of employment

Seller recognizes that Buyer is being transferred to (___City___) by his employer. Should Buyer's transfer be changed or canceled by Buyer's employer, such that Buyer will no longer be moving to (___City___), then Buyer may terminate this Agreement by giving written notice to Seller. Buyer's right to terminate this Agreement under this special stipulation shall expire if not exercised prior to (___Date___).

§2.10.8.2   Voluntary change in financial condition

If a buyer intentionally changes his financial condition the buyer may not be able to use failure of the financing contingency to avoid his obligations under the contract. The GAR Contract provides that from the binding agreement date through the closing, the buyer shall not intentionally make any material changes to the buyer's financial condition that would adversely affect the buyer's ability to obtain a loan.[139]   For example, if after signing a sales contract the buyer purchases an expensive new car on credit and, as a result, cannot obtain loan approval, the buyer will likely be deemed to have breached his duty not to make material changes in his financial condition which adversely affect the buyer's ability to obtain a loan. Similarly, if the buyer quits his or her job without having a new job at a similar salary in place, and the buyer loses his or her ability to obtain a mortgage loan, the buyer will likely have breached his obligation not to intentionally alter his or her financial condition. While the courts have yet to decide this issue, a deliberate discretionary change in financial condition may make it difficult for the buyer to prove that he pursued the loan in good faith. As noted above, whether the buyer acted in good faith is generally a question of fact rather than a question of law.

§2.10.9   Buyer may waive financing contingency

As noted above, Georgia courts have held that since the financing contingency is typically for the benefit of the buyer, the buyer may generally waive the contingency and pay the purchase price in all cash.[140]   However, the buyer must notify the seller that the buyer is waiving the financing contingency and that he is ready, willing, and able to pay for the property without financing.[141]

The following case affirms the buyer's right to waive a financing contingency. The contract for the purchase of property provided that the sales price was to be paid in

---

139   GAR Form F20, paragraph 2C(4).

140   <u>Edwards v. McTyre</u>, 246 Ga. App. 302, 271 S.E.2d 205 (1980); <u>Blanton v. Williams</u>, 209 Ga. 16, 70 S.E.2d 461 (1952).

141   <u>Covington v. Countryside Investment Co., Inc.</u>, 263 Ga. 125, 428 S.E.2d 562 (1993).

all cash at the time of closing.[142] However, the contract was also made contingent on the buyer applying for and being approved for an FHA-insured loan in the amount of $27,000.00 to be amortized in equal monthly payments over a 30-year period. The seller apparently changed his mind and called off the deal. At trial, the seller argued that the sales contract was too uncertain to be enforced because the terms of the loan were vague and indefinite. The court ruled that even if the terms of the loan to be obtained were uncertain, if the buyer actually had the purchase price in cash to pay the seller as required by the contract, then it should not make any difference to the seller how the cash is obtained. The court went on to say "since under the terms of the contract, the sales price was stated to be all cash at time of closing, the provision as to the procurement of a loan was merely for the protection of the buyer and could be waived by him."[143]

§2.10.10 Exceptions to buyer waiving financing contingency

Under the GAR Contract the buyer will be precluded from waiving the financing contingency if the buyer fails to timely apply for a loan, and the seller terminates the contract before the buyer has an opportunity to waive the financing contingency. The likelihood of this arising is remote since the seller cannot terminate the contract unless he first gives the buyer written notice and the buyer fails to cure the default (failing to timely apply for a loan) by providing the seller with written evidence of loan application.

The buyer also may be precluded from waiving the financing contingency if the contingency is for the seller's benefit. For example, if the contract provides that the purchase price is to be paid to the seller in deferred payments, the seller may have incorporated this provision for tax reasons and the buyer may not be able to force the seller to accept payment of the entire purchase price in cash.[144]

§2.11   Married persons and financing contingencies

Generally, if both spouses sign a contract containing a financing contingency, then both will be obligated to apply for and pursue the loan in good faith. However, if only one spouse signs the contract containing a financing contingency clause and that spouse fails to qualify for a loan, the spouse who did not execute the contract will not be obligated to apply for a loan. Therefore, it is generally in the seller's best interest to get both spouses to sign the contract.

---

142   Edwards v. McTyre, 246 Ga. 302, 271 S.E.2d 205 (1980); Blanton v. Williams, 209 Ga. 16, 70 S.E.2d 461 (1952).
143   Edwards v. McTyre, 246 Ga. App. 302, 271 S.E.2d 205 (1980).
144   Sikes v. Markham, 74 Ga. App. 874, 41 S.E.2d 828 (1947).

§2.12 FHA loans

The Federal Housing Administration ("FHA") was created by the federal government to provide mortgage lenders with insurance against losses in the event a borrower defaults on a loan. The FHA is not a lending institution, but functions as an insurance company by insuring loans made by banks, mortgage companies, and savings and loan associations. Because FHA insures 100% of the loan amount, the lender's risk is eliminated. FHA's single-family programs are limited to owner-occupied principal residences. A principal residence is defined as a property that will be occupied by the borrower for a majority of the year.[145]

§2.12.1   Maximum loan amount and appraisal

FHA establishes the maximum loan amount for which it will provide insurance coverage. The maximum mortgage loan limits vary by program and number of family units within a dwelling. Generally, the maximum insurable mortgage is the lesser of the statutory loan limit for the area (typically a county or metropolitan statistical area) or the applicable loan-to-value limit. The statutory limit for each program changes on a regular basis. In high cost areas, the maximum amount can be increased by the local FHA office to 95% of the median one-family house price in an area or 87% of the FHLMC limit, whichever is less.[146] FHA mortgage limits for all areas can be obtained on the Internet at the HUD website.

As stated, the maximum mortgage loan limits will change depending on the county in which the property is located. Therefore, to determine the maximum FHA loan permitted in a given area in Georgia, a mortgage loan officer or the U.S. Department of Housing and Urban Development should be contacted.

In addition to the statutory loan limits, there are certain loan-to-value limits. These limits vary depending on occupancy status, value,[147] and stage of construction. For purposes of determining the loan-to-value limit for a particular property, all property will be considered either "proposed or existing construction" if it meets one of the following criteria: (1) construction is completed more than one year prior to the borrower's application; (2) the dwelling site, plans, and materials were approved before construction began by VA, eligible DE underwriter, or a builder under FHA's builder certification procedures or by an "early start" letter; (3) the dwelling is covered by the builder's 10-year insured warranty which is acceptable to FHA; or (4) the dwelling is

---

145   Transmittal Handbook No: 4155.1, REV-5, CHG-1, Section 1.2 (October 2003).

146   Transmittal Handbook No: 4155.1, REV-5, CHG-1, Section 1-6 (October 2003),citing 203(b) of the National Housing Act, as updated by the U.S. Department of Housing and Urban Development Mortgagee Letter 2003-23, December 31, 2003.

147   The applicable value is the lesser of the appraised value plus allowable closing costs or the adjusted sales price of the property in Transmittal Handbook No: 4155.1, REV-5, CHG-1Section 1-8F (October 2003).

being moved to a new location and has been approved for mortgage insurance. For example, the loan-to-value limit for owner-occupied principal residences for proposed and existing construction with values of $50,000.00 or less is 98.75%. The maximum loan-to-value limit for owner-occupied residences with values of more than $50,000.00 and up to $125,000.00 is 97.65%. The limit for properties with values of more than $125,000.00 is 97.15%. Owner-occupied residences under construction or less than one year old are limited to 90%, unless the property meets one of the above-listed criteria and can be considered a "proposed or existing construction" property. In that situation, the maximum loan-to-value rating will be greater than 90%.[148]

Contributions and inducements to purchase from the seller or repair and similar expenses to be borne by the buyer may result in either an increase or decrease in the maximum loan amount. The following expenses result in a dollar for dollar reduction in the sales price before applying the appropriate loan-to-value ratio: decorating allowances, repair allowances, moving costs, and certain gift funds. Certain items of personal property may serve to reduce the appraised value of the property. Therefore, in computing the maximum loan amount available under an FHA loan, the value of any personal property items being conveyed from a seller to a buyer will be deducted from the sales price which will generally result in a reduction of the appraised value. Typically, under an FHA loan, personal property items such as cars, boats, riding lawn mowers, furniture, and televisions are not included as part of the sales price. Depending on local custom, FHA will not deduct some items of personal property such as refrigerators, stoves, dishwashers, washers, dryers, carpeting, and window treatments; provided, however, no cash allowance is given to the borrower.

In some cases, the maximum mortgage amount may be increased. However, this is generally permitted only when the appraised value exceeds the sales price and only the amount that the value exceeds the sales price may be added. For example, repairs and improvements required by the appraiser, which are essential for property eligibility and are to be paid by the borrower, may be included in the mortgage amount. If such repairs are not to be paid by the borrower, they cannot be included.

A buyer of property whose obligation to close is contingent on the buyer's ability to obtain an FHA loan may cancel the contract if the appraisal of the property is less than the amount set forth in the contract.[149] The GAR FHA loan exhibit allows the parties to identify a minimum appraised value.[150] Presumably, the appraised value does not have to be the same as the purchase price. However, as a matter of practice, the minimum appraised value is generally identified as the purchase price.

---

148   For more detail, refer to Transmittal Handbook No: 4155.1, REV-5, CHG-1,Section 1-7 to 15 (October 2003).
149   Purchasers not applying for FHA loans who wish to have this same protection may do so by using special stipulation 2-3.
150   GAR Form F63, FHA Loan Exhibit.

§2.12.2   Limitation on contributions to closing costs and discount points

Under an FHA loan, the seller may not pay more than 6% of the sales price towards a buyer's actual closing costs, prepaid expenses, discount points, and other financing concessions.[151] Included in the 6% limitation are interest rate buy-downs, payments of mortgage interest (but not principal), mortgage payment protection insurance, and payment of the up-front mortgage insurance premium. Items typically paid by the seller such as real estate commissions, pest inspections, and fees for the release of a deed to secure debt are not considered contributions by the seller because they are customarily seller expenses. Since the FHA regulations do not allow the buyer to pay the underwriting, document preparation, and tax service fees, these fees are not included in the 6% limitation. Each dollar exceeding the 6% limitation is subtracted from the property's sale price before applying the appropriate loan-to-value ratio.

The GAR FHA exhibit also allows the parties to provide whether the buyer or seller shall pay certain prepaid items including the following: the amount of money necessary to establish an escrow account as required by the lender, the interest adjustment on the new loan as required by the lender, and the first year homeowners hazard insurance. Although the seller may pay these costs, the buyer generally pays them. If the seller pays the above-referenced costs, they will be subtracted from the total amount seller has agreed to pay in the closing costs and discount point subparagraph of the contract and will count toward the 6% maximum contribution.

§2.12.3   Certain lender fees cannot be paid by buyer

FHA guidelines prohibit a buyer from paying the following lender fees: underwriting, document preparation, and tax service fees. The GAR FHA loan exhibit expressly provides that the seller pays these costs and that these costs are not included in any closing costs that the seller may have agreed to pay in accordance with the closing costs subparagraph of the contract. Therefore, the seller could be required to contribute toward the buyer's cost an amount more than anticipated. If the seller wants to limit his obligation to the buyer for payment of costs associated with the buyer's loan, the parties may modify the GAR FHA loan exhibit to include underwriting, document preparation, and tax service fees in any closing costs the seller may have agreed to pay. If this paragraph is rewritten, the following special stipulation may be used:

Special Stipulation #2-24: Seller to pay stipulated sum to be first applied towards FHA fees that buyer is not allowed to pay

Notwithstanding any other provision contained herein, at closing, Seller agrees to pay a sum not to exceed $_____ to be used by Buyer in obtaining an FHA loan, which sums shall be applied first toward the payment

---

151   Transmittal Handbook No: 4155.1, REV-5, CHG-1Section 1.7A (October 2003).

of any fees FHA prohibits Buyer from paying, including, but not limited to, any underwriting, document preparation, and tax service fees charged by lender in connection with any such FHA loan. The balance of the sum Seller agrees to pay may be used at Buyer's discretion to pay for other closing costs, loan discount points and survey costs. Buyer shall pay any additional closing costs, insurance premiums, or escrow amounts to fulfill lender requirements or to otherwise close this transaction.

It is essential for the buyer that the FHA loan exhibit is included as part of the contract in all transactions in which the buyer anticipates obtaining FHA financing. Even though FHA guidelines prohibit the buyer from paying the underwriting, document preparation, and tax service fees, the seller is not obligated to pay these fees unless he has contractually agreed to do so. The seller may elect to void the contract rather than pay fees that he is not contractually obligated to pay.

§2.12.4   Mortgage insurance premium

Because FHA loans typically do not require a large down payment, FHA charges a mortgage insurance premium to ensure against the higher risk of default, which is inherent when a low down payment is made. The GAR FHA loan exhibit provides that the premium can be paid in its entirety by buyer at closing or may be financed by the buyer into the loan. The premium is collected in an amount based on a percentage of the loan amount. Under FHA guidelines, the seller may pay the up-front mortgage insurance premium, but if such an election is made, it will be counted toward the 6% maximum seller contribution. Further, the seller must pay the entire premium at the time of closing and not just a portion of the premium. If the parties desire to have the seller pay the up-front mortgage insurance premium, the following special stipulation may be used:

Special Stipulation #2-25: Seller to pay part of up-front FHA mortgage insurance premium

The FHA up-front ___% mortgage insurance premium shall be paid by Seller in full at closing.

In addition, an annual premium for mortgage insurance is charged and added to the buyer's monthly loan payment. The amount of the up-front mortgage insurance premium as well as the annual premium vary based on the term of the loan as well as the loan to value ratio. It should be noted that there is no FHA up-front mortgage insurance premium for condominiums.

§2.12.5   Prohibition against buyer receiving credit for repairs at closing

Generally, a buyer may not receive a cash payment or credit at closing for repairs, renovations, and decorating allowances. Typically, if the necessary repairs are not completed prior to closing, a check will be cut out of the seller's proceeds and made payable to the contractor in an amount representing the estimated cost of repairs. In the alternative, a portion of the seller's proceeds may be put in escrow pending satisfactory completion of the repairs. [152] Upon satisfactory evidence that the required repairs have been completed, a check in the amount of the repairs will generally be issued directly to the contractor. To the extent the amount due for the final repairs is less than the amount put in escrow, the seller is entitled to a refund. Under no circumstances can any portion of the funds that were escrowed for repairs be disbursed directly to the buyer.

§2.12.6   Assumption of FHA loan

Buyers could assume FHA loans prior to December 15, 1989, without having to qualify with the respective lender. However, all FHA loans closed since December 15, 1989, require that a buyer's creditworthiness be independently reviewed prior to assuming an FHA loan.

In most instances, an individual may be eligible to receive only one FHA-insured loan at a time. Therefore, if a seller wants to ensure that he remains eligible for a subsequent FHA loan, it may be necessary to make the contract contingent on the seller obtaining a release of liability from the lender. Even if the seller is not concerned about obtaining another FHA loan, it is in his best interest to obtain a release of liability so that the FHA cannot later pursue him for repayment of any amounts due if the buyer later defaults. Set forth below is an example of a provision, which makes the contract contingent on the seller being released from liability by the lender:

Special Stipulation #2-26: Contract contingent on buyer's assumption of seller's FHA loan

This Agreement is contingent on Buyer's ability to assume Seller's existing FHA loan, ability to assume Seller's liability for repayment of the FHA loan, and Seller being released from liability from repayment of said loan. Buyer agrees to immediately apply to FHA and submit any and all documents necessary for Buyer to qualify for loan approval. If Buyer fails to obtain loan approval from FHA within thirty (30) days from the Binding Agreement Date, or if Buyer fails to obtain approval to assume Seller's liability under the FHA loan, Buyer shall give Seller written notice of such denial within five days of its receipt. Seller may, at his option, terminate this Agreement within five days of receipt of Buyer's notice and all earnest money shall be immediately returned to Buyer. If Seller fails to timely exercise this termination right, it shall be deemed waived.

---

152   Transmittal Handbook No: 4155.1, REV-5, CHG-1, 1.7(C)(1) (October 2003).

§2.12.7   FHA financing for condominium units

FHA will not insure a loan for the purchase of a condominium unit unless a certain percentage of the properties are owner-occupied, as opposed to leased. The property must be at least 70% owner-occupied in order for FHA to insure loans in such a community. In the event a real estate contract contemplates that the buyer will obtain FHA-insured financing, but the community in which the property is located does not meet the permitted owner-occupied ratio and the buyer cannot obtain spot approval from FHA for his particular transaction, the buyer may desire to terminate the contract. The following special stipulation can be used for such purpose:

Special Stipulation #2-27: Contract contingent on property approval by FHA

Seller acknowledges and agrees that if Buyer is unable to obtain an FHA-insured loan because the condominium in which the Property is located is not on the FHA approved property list, does not meet the permitted owner-occupied ratio, or the Buyer's lender cannot obtain spot approval from FHA for this transaction, Buyer may terminate this Agreement by written notice to Seller, in which case all earnest money shall be immediately returned to Buyer.

§2.13   VA loans

The Veterans Administration ("VA") was formed immediately after World War II to provide housing, medical and education assistance, and aid to veterans.[153] The VA is an independent agency of the federal government, which guarantees repayment of a portion of a loan made by a conventional lender such as a bank or mortgage company. The VA loan program was established to encourage traditional lenders to make mortgage loans to veterans.

§2.13.1   Eligibility requirements and entitlement

Certain active members of the armed services, discharged members of the armed services (so long as the discharge was not dishonorable), and certain members of the Selected Reserve or National Guard are eligible for VA loans.[154] A veteran determines his eligibility by applying for a Certificate of Eligibility from the VA.[155] Once obtained, the Certificate evidences the maximum entitlement that the veteran is qualified to receive.

The maximum loan amount a qualified veteran may be eligible to receive changes frequently. A VA loan may permit a buyer to finance 100% of the purchase

---

153   38 U.S.C.A. § 3701, et seq.
154   Veteran's Administration Lender's Handbook Pamphlet 26-7, Chapter 2, 2.01.
155   Veteran's Administration Lender's Handbook Pamphlet 26-7, Chapter 2, 2.03.

price of the property.[156] However, a buyer as a qualified veteran is not permitted to finance certain closing costs into a VA loan. Any closing costs payable in connection with a VA loan must be paid out-of-pocket at closing. Computing the maximum loan entitlement available to veterans under a VA guaranteed loan can be complicated and is beyond the scope of this book.

The VA guidelines provide that a buyer is not required to complete the purchase of the property or forfeit his earnest money if the contract purchase price exceeds the appraised value established by the Veterans Administration. This provision is somewhat different from the FHA provision, which allows the parties to establish the minimum appraised value. However, as with an FHA loan, the buyer has the privilege to proceed to close the transaction without regard to the appraised value.

§2.13.2   Funding fee

Veterans are not required to purchase mortgage insurance under VA loans; however, subject to a few specific exceptions, a veteran must pay a VA funding fee at closing as a condition to obtaining a VA loan.[157] The VA funding fee varies depending on the type of loan obtained.

The funding fee may be paid either by the seller or buyer and is intended to offset and replenish losses resulting from veterans who have previously defaulted on VA-guaranteed loans. Either buyer or seller may pay the funding fee in full at closing or the buyer may finance the funding fee into the loan.[158] If the funding fee is financed into the loan, it will be included in the total loan amount for purposes of determining the maximum amount a qualified veteran is entitled to borrow.

§2.13.3   Certain lender fees cannot be paid by buyer

VA guidelines, like FHA guidelines, prohibit a buyer from paying certain fees, which include the following: underwriting, document preparation, and tax service fees.[159] The GAR VA loan exhibit[160] expressly provides that these costs are not included in any closing costs that the seller may have agreed to pay in accordance with the closing costs subparagraph of the contract. (See discussion above for implications and for special stipulation.)

---

156   Veteran's Administration Lender's Handbook Pamphlet 26-7, Chapter 3, 3.03.

157   Veteran's Administration Lender's Handbook Pamphlet 26-7, Chapter 8, 8.02 (VA Funding Fee Requirement).

158   Veteran's Administration Lender's Handbook Pamphlet 26-7, Chapter 8, 8.07.

159   Veteran's Administration Lender's Handbook Pamphlet 26-7, Chapter 8, 8.02.

160   GAR Form F65, VA Loan Exhibit.

§2.13.4   Prohibition against buyer receiving credit for repairs at closing

As in the case of FHA loans, a buyer may not receive a cash payment or credit at closing for repairs, renovations, and decorating allowances. (See discussion above.)

§2.13.5   Assumption of VA loan

A VA loan closed prior to March 1988 may be assumed without the buyer qualifying. On VA loans closed after March 1, 1988, the new buyer must qualify to assume the loan.[161] Also, the veteran selling the property may not be entitled to obtain another VA loan. In general, the seller will want to obtain a release of liability when he permits a buyer to assume his loan.[162] Obtaining a release of liability serves two purposes. First, a release may enable the seller to have his VA loan guarantee entitlement restored, thereby allowing the seller to receive another VA loan.[163] Second, a release will ensure that the VA cannot later pursue the seller for repayment of any amounts due if the buyer later defaults. The special stipulation set forth above may also be used if the contract is contingent on the buyer obtaining a release of the seller's liability.

§2.14   Seller Financing

There are benefits for both seller and buyer in a transaction that provides for seller financing. Seller financing may afford a motivated seller an opportunity to sell his property more quickly. A seller may also offer to finance the purchase of the property because he would rather receive payments over time rather than a lump sum. On the other hand, buyers who may not be able to qualify for a loan with a conventional lender often find seller financing attractive. Additionally, closing costs associated with a seller-financed transaction are typically much lower than when a buyer secures financing from a traditional lender.

A seller will normally secure his loan by taking back a promissory note and deed to secure debt on the property. If there is no lender involved in the transaction, the deed to secure debt of the seller will normally be in a first priority position, which in real estate parlance is commonly referred to as a first mortgage. A seller may also agree to finance a portion of the purchase price by taking back a note and second priority deed to secure debt on the property. This is usually done when the down

161   Veteran's Administration Lender's Handbook Pamphlet 26-7, Chapter 3, 3.12.
162   Veteran's Administration Lender's Handbook Pamphlet 26-7, Chapter 2, 2.06.
163   Restoration of a previously-used entitlement may be applied for if the following conditions are met: (a) the property has been sold and the loan has been paid in full, or (b) a qualified veteran transferee has agreed to assume the outstanding balance on the loan, agrees to substitute his entitlement of the same amount of entitlement originally used for the loan, and the assuming veteran meets the occupancy, income, and credit requirements of the law. Veteran's Administration Lender's Handbook Pamphlet 26-7, Chapter 2, 2.06.

payment of the buyer plus the loan from an institutional lender do not add up to the purchase price. Keep in mind that this type of secondary financing must have the prior approval of the buyer's first mortgage lender.

§2.14.1 Special issues regarding seller financing

As in the case of a buyer obtaining a loan from an institutional lender, it is equally important for a contract which contemplates seller financing to set forth in specific detail the essential terms of the note and deed to secure debt. A contract was found to be vague and unenforceable when it referred to additional terms to be agreed upon at a later date.[164] As noted above, in a seller-financed transaction, the contract should incorporate the provisions to be stated in the note and provide that it will be secured by a deed to secure debt on the property.[165]

The GAR Purchase Money Note First Mortgage exhibit[166] includes the following protection for the seller: the obligation of the buyer to provide the seller with credit information; a due on sale clause; the right to impose a late charge; the obligation of the buyer to provide hazard insurance; and the obligation of the buyer to pay for any charge associated with the preparation of the note and deed to secure debt (if prepared by the buyer's attorney), the intangible tax, and the recording fee.[167] The GAR form also provides certain protection for the buyer including a prepayment privilege and the right to cure a default.

The GAR Purchase Money Note Second Mortgage exhibit[168] also provides additional protection for the seller by including a cross-default clause which states that a default under the terms of the first priority deed to secure debt and note constitute a default under the terms of the second mortgage authorizing the seller to accelerate the entire indebtedness and foreclose on the property.

The Brokerage Relationships in Real Estate Transactions Act ("BRRETA") (codified at O.C.G.A. § 10-6A-1 et seq.) also attempts to protect sellers offering purchase money financing or allowing loan assumptions by requiring the real estate broker representing the buyer as a client to:

> disclose to a prospective seller . . . all material adverse facts actually known by the broker concerning the buyer's financial ability to perform the terms of the sale, and in the case of a residential transaction, the buyer's intent to occupy the property as a principal residence.[169]

---

164   Rush v. Autrey, 210 Ga. 732, 82 S.E.2d 866 (1954).
165   Rumph v. Rister, 211 Ga. 312, 85 S.E.2d 768 (1955).
166   GAR Form F67, Seller Financing (First Mortgage) Exhibit.
167   GAR Form F67, Seller Financing (First Mortgage) Exhibit.
168   GAR Form F68, Seller Financing (Second Mortgage) Exhibit.
169   O.C.G.A. § 10-6A-7(b).

§2.14.1.1   Satisfactory credit report

Seller financing should always be contingent on the buyer providing the seller with a satisfactory credit report, particularly if the buyer is making only a small down payment.

The GAR Purchase Money Note First Mortgage and Second Mortgage exhibits[170] give the seller the right to terminate the contract if the buyer's financial statement and past credit listings do not meet underwriting guidelines as established by the Federal National Mortgage Association ("FNMA" or "Fanny Mae"). These exhibits also provide that the seller shall not unreasonably withhold the approval of a buyer's credit.

§2.14.1.2   Excessive or unlawful interest rates

A seller agreeing to provide financing must be careful to ensure that the rate of interest to be charged under the promissory note does not exceed the rate permitted by applicable law. The permissible rate of interest that can be charged under a loan is set by statute. Georgia law provides for civil and criminal liability for any lender, including an individual, who makes a loan with an excessive interest rate.[171] Other restrictions on lender fees and charges are contained in the Georgia Fair Lending Act.[172]

§2.14.1.3   Ability of buyer to resell or transfer interest in property

The GAR forms include a due on sale clause to protect the seller who takes back a first or second deed to secure debt on a property.[173] Under a due on sale clause, the buyer is obligated to pay the entire principal balance outstanding on the note and deed to secure debt if the buyer transfers the property to a third party. Such a provision protects the seller against the buyer selling the property to an unreliable or unknown third party buyer who then assumes the loan.

If the seller desires for tax or other reasons to have the proceeds of the sale payable over an extended term, the seller may incorporate a provision that allows a qualified successor buyer to assume the loan. If the seller desires to offer a qualified assumable loan, the following language may be used:

---

170   GAR Form F67 paragraph 7 and Form 68 paragraph 8.
171   O.C.G.A. § 7-4-18(a) prohibits a lender from collecting any rate of interest greater than 5% per month.
172   O.C.G.A. § 7-6A-1 et seq.
173   GAR Form F67 paragraph 7 and Form 68 paragraph 8.

Special Stipulation #2-28: Qualified assumption by subsequent buyer of seller-financed property

Notwithstanding any other provision in this Agreement to the contrary, Buyer and Seller agree that the promissory note and deed to secure debt to be executed by Buyer in favor of Seller shall contain a provision that Buyer may sell the Property and have the subsequent purchaser assume the promissory note and deed to secure debt, provided that: (1) the subsequent purchaser is determined by the Seller to be creditworthy based upon the underwriting guidelines as established from time to time by the Federal National Mortgage Association ("FNMA"), and (2) the subsequent purchaser provides all information requested by Seller which is reasonably necessary to determine the creditworthiness of such purchaser.

Seller agrees not to unreasonably withhold approval of credit to the intended transferee. In the event the subsequent purchaser is determined by Seller to be creditworthy and assumes all of Buyer's obligations and liabilities under the promissory note and deed to secure debt, Buyer shall thereafter immediately be relieved of any further obligations and liabilities under the note and deed referenced herein.

§2.14.1.4   Ability of buyer to assign rights

The seller and buyer may have different interests with regard to the ability of the buyer to assign his obligations under the contract, note, and deed to secure debt. From the seller's perspective, the seller may want to limit the buyer's ability to assign his obligations because the seller's willingness to provide financing may be based on the seller's evaluation of the financial ability of the buyer to fulfill the terms of the financing obligation.

The GAR Contract provides that there shall be no assignment of the contract unless signed by all parties. Therefore, the buyer will be unable to assign the contract unless the seller approves the assignment. The seller is not under any legal obligation to be reasonable in granting or denying approval for an assignment.[174] Accordingly, the buyer contemplating a possible assignment of the contract may wish to use the following special stipulation:

Special Stipulation #2-29: Seller's consent to assignment cannot be unreasonably withheld

Buyer may assign this Agreement to a third party with the consent of the Seller which consent shall not be unreasonably withheld.

---

174   Vaswani v. Wohletz, 196 Ga.App. 676, 396 S.E.2d 593 (1990).

The buyer, of course, may want to have the absolute right to assign a contract to a third party. The following provision allows the buyer to assign the contract to a third party without the seller's consent:

Special Stipulation #2-30: Buyer's right to assignment without seller consent

Notwithstanding any provision to the contrary, this Agreement and all obligations required hereunder, including but not limited to the obligation of Buyer to execute a promissory note and deed to secure debt in favor of Seller, may be assigned by Buyer without the consent of Seller, provided, however, that Buyer shall remain jointly and severally obligated with the assignee on the promissory note and deed to secure debt.

§2.14.1.5   Personal obligation for repayment

Generally, when a buyer executes a promissory note and a deed to secure debt, the promissory note becomes the personal obligation of the buyer. Therefore, if the seller is forced to foreclose on the property and the proceeds from the sale are not adequate to satisfy the indebtedness, the buyer remains personally obligated for the deficiency[175].

The buyer may attempt to include a provision in the contract to limit his personal liability by providing that the note and deed to secure debt to be executed by the buyer shall contain what is commonly referred to as an exculpation clause.[176] This means that the seller may look only to the real property to satisfy the debt and cannot hold the buyer personally responsible for its repayment.

Further, such a clause eliminates the ability of the seller to proceed against the buyer on the personal obligation in lieu of foreclosing the seller's interest in the property. Set forth below is an example of an exculpation clause that relieves the buyer from personal obligation for the debt:

Special Stipulation #2-31: Exculpation clause relieving buyer from personal liability

Buyer and Seller acknowledge and agree that the promissory note and deed to secure debt to be executed by Buyer in connection with this Agreement shall each contain an exculpation clause, which limits Buyer's responsibility for repayment of the secured indebtedness on the Property. Seller acknowledges and agrees that Buyer shall be fully released from any and all personal

---

175   Provided, however, that the seller has obtained judicial confirmation of the foreclosure so as to allow the seller to pursue the deficiency.

176   Another way to describe such a situation is that the note and security deed are "non-recourse".

liability for repayment of the indebtedness under the promissory note and deed to secure debt and that in the event of a default on the promissory note and deed to secure debt, Seller's sole remedy shall be against the Property.

§2.14.1.6   Personal property as additional collateral

In addition to obtaining a security interest in the real property being sold, the seller may be able to further protect his interest by obtaining a security interest in personal property owned by the buyer.

To obtain a valid security interest in personal property that is not considered a fixture, it is necessary for the buyer to execute a security agreement and a financing statement in accordance with the Uniform Commercial Code (UCC). The seller needs both a security agreement, in which the personal property is actually pledged as security, and a UCC Financing Statement, which gives notice of the security interest. It is possible for a single document to serve as both a security agreement and a UCC Financing Statement, so long as sufficient language is contained therein. The UCC Financing Statement is filed in the land records of the county where the property is located and identifies the personal property being pledged as additional collateral for the indebtedness.[177] If the seller does not properly file a UCC Financing Statement, he may not be able to enforce his security interest in the personal property against a third-party purchaser who does not have knowledge of the security agreement.   UCC Financing Statements must be refiled from time to time to remain in effect. Set forth below is an example of a contract provision, which contemplates that the buyer will pledge personal property as additional collateral for the loan:

Special Stipulation #2-32: Buyer pledge of personal property as additional collateral for seller financing loan

Buyer hereby agrees to execute any and all instruments and documents necessary to grant and perfect in favor of Seller a security interest in the following personal property owned by the Buyer which is not deemed to be a part of the real property_____. During the term of Seller's loan to Buyer, Buyer shall be entitled, upon written notice to Seller and prior written approval by Seller, to substitute certain items of personalty for those items, which secure the indebtedness.

§2.14.1.7   Proof of payment of taxes

A seller's security interest can be jeopardized if the buyer fails to pay any ad valorem property taxes. Most institutional lenders reduce this risk by requiring the buyer to set up an escrow with the lender for payment of taxes. If the seller who agrees to accept a note and purchase money deed to secure debt does not require the buyer to

---

177   O.C.G.A. § 11-9-401.

escrow taxes, the seller may want to include provisions in the contract as well as in the note and deed to secure debt which require the buyer to provide to seller proof of payment of property taxes. An example of such a contract provision is set forth below:

Special Stipulation #2-33: Buyer's obligation to provide proof of payment of property taxes to seller

Buyer agrees that any promissory note and deed to secure debt to be executed in favor of Seller in connection with Seller agreeing to finance a portion of the purchase price of the Property shall contain the following provision: Each year as long as the indebtedness due to Seller remains unpaid, Buyer agrees to furnish a copy of a paid tax receipt evidencing that the ad valorem taxes for the Property securing the promissory note have been fully paid for the year in question.

Buyer hereby further agrees to submit to Seller such fully paid receipt within thirty (30) days from the date that such taxes become fully due and payable. If Buyer fails to produce such fully paid receipt within the aforementioned time period, Buyer shall be deemed to be in default under the terms of the promissory note and deed to secure debt. Alternatively, Buyer, in his sole discretion, may pay any delinquent ad valorem taxes and the amount of such payments will be added to and become additional amounts due under the terms of the promissory note and deed to secure debt.

§2.14.1.8   Third party guarantee for repayment of loan

In some instances, the seller may desire to have a third party execute a guarantee agreement. The person executing a guarantee agreement agrees to satisfy the debt of the buyer only if the buyer fails to repay the debt. By obtaining the guarantee of a third party, the seller has additional recourse if the buyer defaults on repayment of the loan. An example of such a contract provision is set forth below:

Special Stipulation #2-34: Contract and seller financing contingent on 3rd party guarantee

Buyer agrees that _____ ("Guarantor") shall execute a Guarantee Agreement as consideration for Seller agreeing to accept a promissory note and deed to secure debt from Buyer. Guarantor, after receiving written notice from Seller, agrees to immediately satisfy the debt of Buyer if Buyer is deemed to be in default. If Guarantor fails to execute the Guarantee Agreement attached hereto as Exhibit "__" and deliver the same to Seller at least ten days prior to the date of closing, Seller may terminate this Agreement upon written notice to Buyer.

§2.14.2   Assignment of rents and leases

The seller may want to have the buyer execute what is commonly referred to as an assignment of rents and leases. Under an assignment of rents and leases, if the buyer has leased all or any portion of the property to a third party, any rents received by the buyer would be pledged to the seller as additional security collateral for the debt. If the buyer is in default and the seller has obtained an assignment of rents and leases, then the seller may require the tenant under the lease to make rental payments directly to the seller and not the buyer. The seller could then apply the rent proceeds to any indebtedness of the buyer that is currently outstanding and due. The following provision which may be included in the contract, as well as the note and deed to secure debt, requires the buyer to assign to the seller any rental income generated on the property being sold:

Special Stipulation #2-35: Buyer's assignment of all rents to seller/holder

Buyer and Seller hereby agree and acknowledge that the promissory note and deed to secure debt executed by Buyer in connection with this Agreement shall contain the following provision: Borrower (Buyer) hereby assigns to Lender (Seller) all of the rents of Property. Seller shall forebear from collecting such rents so long as Borrower is not in default in payments to Lender (Seller). All rents collected by Lender shall be applied first to the costs of management of the Property and then to sums secured by the promissory note and deed to secure debt.

§2.14.3   Alterations to property

Some form deeds to secure debt expressly prohibit the buyer from making any alterations to the property.   Since it is not uncommon for a buyer to make improvements, the contract should expressly provide that the deed to secure debt shall permit the buyer to make alterations to the property without constituting default. Failure to include such a provision may result in unusual and unjust results. For example, in one case, a buyer executed a deed to secure debt that obligated the buyer to obtain permission from the seller prior to buyer making any improvements or alterations to the property. The buyer undertook a small amount of demolition and made improvements to the property without obtaining prior consent of the seller. The court held buyer to be in default under his deed to secure debt even though buyer was able to show that he had spent $50,000.00 in making such improvements.[178] Set forth below is a contract provision that entitles the buyer to make repairs and improvements to property without triggering a default under the deed to secure debt:

---

178   Tybrisa Co., Inc. v. Tybeeland, Inc., 220 Ga. 442, 139 S.E.2d 302 (1964). (The court noted that there was conflicting testimony as to whether the property altered, changed, or removed was an "improvement" or a "detriment" and that there was no question of failure of title.)

Special Stipulation #2-36: Buyer's right to renovate without seller approval

Buyer and Seller hereby expressly agree that the deed to secure debt to be executed by Buyer in favor of Seller in connection with this transaction shall include the following provision: Buyer shall not be required to obtain permission from Seller prior to undertaking any improvements, repairs, or demolition on the Property which serves as security for this Promissory Note so long as such improvements, repairs, or demolition do not reduce the value of the Property. Any such improvements, repairs, or demolition undertaken by Buyer shall not constitute a default under the terms of the Deed to Secure Debt.

§2.14.4   Costs associated with preparing and recording documents

The GAR Seller Financing (First Mortgage) and Seller Financing (Second Mortgage) exhibits require that the buyer pay any charge for preparation of the note and deed to secure debt as long as the buyer's attorney prepares them.[179] These GAR exhibits also provide that if the seller chooses to have these documents prepared by seller's attorney and the seller reserves the option to do so, then the seller shall bear the expense of such document preparation. There may be instances where the buyer and seller's interests diverge as to the language to be incorporated in the note and deed to secure debt. An argument can be made that the seller has the greater risk since his money is at stake and that the seller therefore may want his attorney to prepare the note and deed to secure debt in a way that favors him. However, if the parties agree, the buyer may pay the seller's expenses for having the note and deed to secure debt prepared. A special stipulation allowing the buyer to reimburse the seller for his expenses follows:

Special Stipulation #2-37: Buyer pays for seller's attorney to prepare promissory note and deed to secure debt

Seller's attorney shall prepare the promissory note and deed to secure debt and Buyer shall reimburse Seller for the costs and expenses of such preparation.

Under Georgia law, the holder of a long-term promissory note[180] secured by real property is obligated to pay the intangible tax and any fee charged for recording

---

179   GAR Forms F 67 and F68.

180   A long-term promissory note is defined as any note representing credits secured by mortgages, deeds to secure debt, purchase money deeds to secure debt, bonds of title, or other form of security instrument, when any part of the principal of a note falls due more than three years from the date of the note or from the date of any instrument executed to secure the note and conveying or creating a lien or encumbrance on the real estate. O.C.G.A. § 48-6-60(3).

the deed to secure debt.[181] The GAR Seller Financing (First Mortgage) and Seller Financing (Second Mortgage) exhibits all obligate the buyer to pay the intangible tax.[182] However, if the GAR forms are not used and if the real estate contract is silent as to which party shall be responsible for the payment of taxes and recording fees, the seller, as holder of the note, will be obligated to pay these costs.

§2.14.5   Note and deed to secure debt made in favor of more than one seller

Problems and confusion may arise when a buyer executes a note and purchase money deed to secure debt in favor of more than one seller. Unless the contract provides otherwise, a deed to secure debt must be canceled by all the sellers who are payees under the note and deed to secure debt. Various issues may arise when there is more than one seller to whom the buyer should make payments, for instance, and what happens if all the sellers are unavailable to execute a cancellation of the note and deed to secure debt upon satisfaction of the same by the buyer. If there are multiple sellers, an example of a contract provision that addresses these potential problems is set forth below:

Special Stipulation #2-38: Note and deed to secure debt authorizes named payee to accept payment on behalf of all payees

Buyer and Sellers hereby agree that the promissory note and deed to secure debt shall provide that any one of the named payees may accept payment on behalf of all payees. Buyer and Seller further agree that the promissory note and deed to secure debt shall provide that upon payment of the indebtedness under the note in full, any one of the named payees may execute a valid cancellation of the deed to secure debt on behalf of all named payees and such cancellation shall be binding and enforceable against all payees and serve as conclusive proof of payment in full of the debt by Buyer.

§2.14.6   Additional issues if seller takes second priority security interest

A seller who takes a second priority note and deed or other subordinate note and deed is not afforded the same degree of protection as the lender who holds the first priority interest. For example, if the buyer defaults under the first priority deed to secure debt, that lender would be able to foreclose on the property and extinguish the seller's second priority deed to secure debt.

If the buyer does not default on the first mortgage, but defaults on the seller's mortgage, the seller may be able to foreclose on the property serving as collateral for the loan. However, the seller will be responsible for making payments to the first

---

181   O.C.G.A. § 48-6-61.
182   GAR Form F67 paragraph 9B and Form 68 paragraph 10B.

priority holder. Therefore, it is important for a seller to consider the following issues when granting a second or other subordinate security interest.

§2.14.6.1   Default under first priority deed to secure debt

The GAR Seller Financing (Second Mortgage) exhibit includes a cross-default clause.[183] This means that a default under the terms and conditions of the first position deed to secure debt or note constitutes a default under the terms and conditions of the second position deed to secure debt and note and the seller may declare the entire indebtedness secured by the note due and payable at once (i.e., the seller may accelerate the debt). Upon default of the buyer, this provision allows the seller to foreclose on his deed to secure debt and thereby protect his interest by foreclosing and paying the first mortgage.

However, the holder of a first priority deed to secure debt is not required to give junior lien holders notice of default. A seller who holds a second or other subordinate deed to secure debt may protect his interest by obligating the holder of a superior deed to secure debt to notify him of the default under the first priority deed. To legally obligate the first priority holder to provide the requisite notice, there must be an agreement between the first priority holder and the buyer. An example of a contract provision that affords the seller holding a second or other subordinate deed such added protection is set forth below:

Special Stipulation #2-39: Contract contingent on first mortgage holder agreeing to notify seller of buyer's default

Buyer and Seller agree that this Agreement is contingent on the holder of the first priority promissory note and deed to secure debt incorporating a provision in their promissory note and deed to secure debt which legally obligates the first priority holder to provide written notice to Seller in the event of a default by Buyer under the first priority deed to secure debt. If the holder of the first position promissory note does not include such a provision in the promissory note and deed to secure debt, Seller may terminate this Agreement upon written notice to Buyer.

The seller should also be aware that many priority security deeds include what is known as a cross default provision, such that a default under the terms of seller's secondary security deed constitutes a default under the terms of the first deed. Under such a cross default provision, the holder of a first priority mortgage could declare a default in the event the buyer defaults on the second mortgage. Once the holder of the first mortgage is notified that the buyer has defaulted on a second mortgage, the holder could initiate its own foreclosure proceeding that would extinguish the seller's second priory security deed.

---

183   GAR Form 68 paragraph 3.

§2.14.6.2   *Payment to reinstate first priority loan*

The holder of the second priority security interest may want to include a provision in the contract that stipulates that any payments made by seller to cure a default under the first priority loan will be added to the debt secured under the second priority loan. An example of such provision follows:

Special Stipulation #2-40: Seller may cure buyer's default of first priority mortgage

Buyer and Seller hereby agree that the following provision will be included in the promissory note and deed to secure debt to be executed by Buyer in favor of Seller: Seller shall be entitled, at his sole discretion, to cure any default under Buyer's first priority Promissory Note and Deed to Secure Debt; however, Seller shall have no obligation whatsoever to do so. Any amounts expended by Seller to reinstate such first priority Promissory Note and Deed to Secure Debt shall be added to and become additional amounts due under the indebtedness secured by the second priority deed to secure debt held by Seller.

§2.14.6.3   *Excess proceeds to second priority deed holder*

The seller who accepts the second priority note and deed to secure debt may want to provide that any excess proceeds paid under an insurance claim, condemnation award, or by virtue of foreclosure of the first priority deed to secure debt go directly to the seller as the holder of the second priority deed. An example of such provision follows:

Special Stipulation #2-41: Seller entitled to excess proceeds from first priority mortgage foreclosure/condemnation/statement of insurance claim

Buyer and Seller agree that any promissory note and second priority deed to secure debt to be executed by the Buyer shall contain the following provision: In the event there are any excess proceeds remaining pursuant to a foreclosure of Buyer's first priority holder's Promissory Note and Deed to Secure Debt, condemnation award, or settlement of an insurance claim, then after the first priority holder has received payment in full of its debt, Seller, as the second priority holder, shall be entitled to the balance thereof, prior to any distribution to Buyer.

§2.14.7   Wrap mortgage

To further protect the seller who accepts the second priority note and deed to secure debt, the seller may consider a wrap mortgage. Under a wrap mortgage, a seller accepts a note from the buyer, the amount of which represents the balance owed to the seller's lender under the first priority note and deed to secure debt and any additional amounts being loaned by the seller to the buyer. Under this arrangement, the buyer pays the seller, who in turn makes his regular payments to the holder of the first priority loan. This permits the buyer to purchase property when the buyer may not be able to obtain his own loan and the seller does not have sufficient cash to pay off the first mortgage.

Whether such an option is feasible depends on whether the seller's current loan contains a due on sale clause. If the seller's loan contains a due on sale clause, a wrap mortgage would be in violation of the terms of the seller's existing financing. However, if the seller's present loan does not have a due on sale clause (i.e., the seller's present loan is assumable), or if the seller's lender so permits, a wrap mortgage may be possible. The buyer would be well advised to require that the seller produce written confirmation from his first mortgage holder that the wrap mortgage will not trigger a due on sale clause. The buyer may use the following stipulation:

Special Stipulation #2-42: Buyer's right to terminate contract if seller cannot obtain seller's lender's confirmation that wrap mortgage will not trigger due on sale clause or constitute default

This Agreement is contingent upon Seller providing to Buyer written confirmation from Seller's first mortgage holder that a wrap mortgage will not trigger a due on sale clause or otherwise constitute a default under the terms of Seller's first mortgage. If Seller does not provide such confirmation to Buyer within thirty (30) days of the Binding Agreement Date, Buyer may terminate this Agreement upon written notice to Seller and Buyer's earnest money shall be immediately returned to Buyer.

Although the seller is provided additional protection under a wrap note, the buyer has some risks if the seller collects the money from the buyer but fails to remit the amount due on the first mortgage. The GAR Seller Financing (Wrap Around Mortgage) exhibit outlines both the seller and buyer's obligations.[184] The seller's obligations include the obligation to make payments of principal, interest and escrow deposits to the present lender during the life of the wrap loan as long as the buyer is not in default under the terms of the wrap loan and no other default exists under the seller's present loan other than with respect to payments of principal, interest and escrow deposits. To provide additional protection to the buyer, the buyer may want to incorporate a provision in the contract and note that requires the holder of the seller's present loan to notify the buyer if there is a default on that loan.

Special Stipulation #2-43: Seller's right to terminate if unable to obtain notice of default of buyer's loan

Buyer and Seller agree that Seller shall obtain an agreement from the holder of Seller's present loan that Buyer shall be notified in the event of any default

---

184   GAR Form F70.

under said loan. If Seller does not provide a copy of this agreement to Buyer within thirty (30) days of the Binding Agreement Date, Buyer may terminate this Agreement upon written notice to Seller and Buyer's earnest money shall be immediately returned to Buyer.

§2.15 Third party assisting with financing

On occasion, a third party will help a buyer acquire property by helping the buyer with the cash, guaranteeing the mortgage loan or by applying for the mortgage loan along with the buyer. Such third parties are usually a parent, relative or significant other of the buyer. In many cases, the third party will sign the purchase contract and be a co-owner of the property. In other cases, the third party will merely lend his or her good name and hopefully credit to the mortgage application or help the buyer with the needed cash to close the transaction. These are times when a buyer will not want to warrant that the buyer has sufficient cash to close the transaction without getting a commitment from a third party that they will provide some portion of the necessary cash to close. The following special stipulation can help the buyer in this situation.

Special Stipulation #2-44: Contract contingent upon third party contributing funds to close

This Agreement is contingent upon Buyer receiving from _____ the sum of $_____ within _____ days of the Binding Agreement Date which monies shall give Buyer the necessary funds to close (along with the proceeds of the mortgage loan for which Buyer has applied). If Buyer does not provide written evidence that these funds have been deposited into the following account of Buyer: Account #_____ with [_____ name of financial institution_____], within _____ days from the Binding Agreement Date, then this Agreement may thereafter be terminated by Seller.

It is important that any loaned or gifted funds be reported by the buyer to his or her lender. Many lenders have limitations on the amount of gifted funds that the buyer can receive for the closing. If the third party is agreeing to guarantee a mortgage loan to be obtained by the buyer, the following special stipulation may be of benefit to the seller:

Special Stipulation #2-45: Ability of buyer to obtain a loan based on credit of buyer and third party

For all purposes hereunder, the Buyer's ability to obtain the mortgage loan described herein shall be based upon the financial ability of both the Buyer and _____ as co-borrowers to qualify for said loan.

§2.16   Assuming or taking subject to existing loan

Assuming an existing loan can be advantageous to the buyer because there are little or no closing costs and very few loan documents to execute. Further, in some instances, a buyer may find this method of financing to be attractive because he may be able to assume a loan with a lower interest rate than the current prevailing rate. Although there remain some non-qualifying assumable loans, most lenders now require a new party assuming a loan to independently qualify for that loan. In addition, some lenders retain the right to adjust the interest rate upon assumption.

There is some distinction between taking subject to an outstanding loan and assuming an outstanding loan. A buyer is not generally personally liable for indebtedness under the deed to secure debt if the contract specifies that the property be sold "subject to" an existing deed to secure debt.[185] This means that the lender may foreclose on the property if the buyer defaults but will not be able to obtain a personal judgment against the buyer. Therefore, when a buyer takes the property "subject to" a loan without expressly agreeing to pay the seller's debt to the lender, the buyer pays the remaining loan payments as they come due, but the seller continues to be personally liable to the lender for the repayment of the loan in accordance with the terms of the original promissory note.

Most contracts provide that the buyer "assumes" the loan rather than takes "subject to" the loan. A buyer who assumes a loan will be personally liable for the payment of the mortgage debt.[186] If there is a default and the amount realized on the sale of the property at the foreclosure sale does not equal the amount of the debt due under the loan, the lender will normally attempt to obtain a deficiency judgment against any party who is personally liable under the note. If there is no express release of liability for the seller, the seller as the original party to the note and deed to secure debt will continue to be personally liable to the lender as well.[187]

Buyers and sellers should also be mindful that the lender is generally not required to foreclose prior to attempting to obtain a money judgment. In some cases, such as where the value of the real estate has decreased substantially or the property is found to contain hazardous material, the lender will simply ignore the security deed and sue for monetary damages against the buyer under the terms of the promissory note. This may be a preferred option for a seller who has taken back a second mortgage on property in which there is very little or no equity. If the purchaser wishes to force the seller to foreclose prior to obtaining a monetary judgment he should use language such as the following in the contract:

---

185   Alsobrook v. Taylor, 181 Ga. 10, 181 S.E. 182 (1935).
186   Smith v. Kingsley, 178 Ga. 681, 173 S.E. 702 (1934).
187   Federal Land Bank of Columbia v. Conyer, 55 Ga. App. 11, 189 S.E. 567 (1936).

Special Stipulation #2-46: Holder of first security deed must proceed against property before pursuing monetary judgment against buyer

Buyer and Seller agree that any promissory note and deed to secure debt to be executed by the Buyer shall contain the following provision: In the event of any default by the maker hereof, the holder must, prior to bringing any legal action against the maker for monetary damages, foreclose on the Property described herein by judicial, or if permitted by the terms hereof, non-judicial foreclosure, and obtain judicial confirmation of such foreclosure.

§2.16.1   Identifying the loan

The GAR Loan Assumption Exhibit[188] and the GAR Loan Assumption Cash to Control Exhibit[189] provide that the parties identify the loan by the loan number, servicer, original date, original principal amount, and monthly installments. If the GAR exhibits are used and fully completed, the loan will be adequately described.

Failure to adequately describe the loan with specificity may render the contract unenforceable. The following cases address the enforceability of the contract based on specificity of the loan description. In one case, the court held the contract to be enforceable even though it failed to state the date of maturity and the outstanding balance of the loan to be assumed.[190] The contract in that case described the loan as being the "loan outstanding against that property." The court concluded that the contract offered a method for identifying the loan with definite terms contained therein through examination of the real estate records. In two other cases, the court concluded that a loan description was inadequate and, therefore, the contract was unenforceable.[191] In one case, the court held that a contract, which provided for the buyer to assume a loan of $9,500.00, was unenforceable because it failed to completely identify the specific loan, which was to be assumed.[192] Similarly, a contract, which recited that the purchase price was to be paid subject to terms of an existing loan "which is approximately $30,000" was too indefinite to identify the loan referenced.[193]

These cases indicate that if the loan description provides some sort of key for identifying the loan, the contract may be enforceable. Generally, reference to the recorded loan and deed documents will be adequate since the recorded documents contain additional information to supplement the loan description in the contract. However, to avoid any question about the enforceability of a contract based on a loan

---

188   GAR Form F61, Loan Assumption Exhibit.
189   GAR Form F62, Loan Assumption Cash to Control Purchase Price Exhibit.
190   Massell R. Co. v. Hanbury, 165 Ga. 534, 141 S.E. 653 (1927).
191   However, in both of the following cases, the loans were not against the property. Since there were no documents of public record, the terms of the loan could not be determined with reasonable specificity.
192   Trust Co. of Georgia v. Neal, 161 Ga. 965, 132 S.E.2d 385 (1926).
193   Morgan v. Hemphill, 214 Ga. 555, 105 S.E.2d 580 (1958).

description, the parties should at a minimum include all the information set forth in the GAR form.[194] In addition to the information set forth in the GAR form, if the parties have a copy of the note and deed to secure debt being assumed, they should attach those documents to the contract as exhibits.

§2.16.2   The purchase price and loan assumptions

There are potential pitfalls that await an unwary draftsman when setting forth the purchase price of the property under a contract that provides for the property to be taken subject to an existing loan or under a loan assumption. Identification of the purchase price under such a contract is complicated by the fact that the balance of the loan to be assumed or taken subject to is constantly changing as payments are made by the seller. Consequently, the loan balance will generally change between the time the contract is entered into and the time the property is conveyed to the buyer on the date of closing.

If the purchase price is not properly expressed, there is a risk that the contract will be deemed void for uncertainty. For example, in one case, a Georgia court held that a contract was not enforceable because it referred to the purchase price as $57,000.00 net with buyer paying $18,500.00 in cash and agreeing to assume a loan with the balance of approximately $39,000.00.[195]

The Court held the contract to be unenforceable as being too vague when the loan, which was to be assumed, actually had a balance of more than $39,000.00 as referenced in the contract. In this instance, the court stated that the purchase price could not be increased without simultaneously decreasing the down payment, which would essentially require the court to write an entirely new contract. As explained below, there are two commonly used methods to determine the purchase price when the buyer assumes the seller's loan.

§2.16.2.1   *Purchase price set in contract*

The GAR Loan Assumption exhibit[196] contemplates that the purchase price will be set forth in the contract and that the buyer will assume the seller's loan. This exhibit also provides that the balance of the purchase price in excess of the principal balance assumed at closing by the buyer, less the amount of interest accrued on the loan to the date of closing, will be paid by the buyer to the seller in cash at closing.[197] This approach has the advantage of establishing the exact purchase price at the time the contract is entered into. However, the disadvantage to the buyer is the uncertainty as to the amount of cash that the buyer will have to provide at closing.

---

194   GAR Form F61, Loan Assumption Exhibit.
195   Austin v. Willis, 229 Ga. 193, 190 S.E.2d 532 (1972).
196   GAR Form F61, Loan Assumption Exhibit.
197   GAR Form F61, Loan Assumption Exhibit, paragraph 4.

For example, buyer and seller enter into a contract in which the purchase price is $48,000.00 with the buyer to assume an existing loan on the property and pay the balance of the purchase price to the seller in cash at closing. The loan to be assumed has a balance of $35,250.00 on January 15, the Binding Agreement Date. The sale of the property occurs on March 15. If the closing was to have occurred at the same time the contract was entered into, the buyer would have had to bring $12,750.00 in cash ($48,000.00 - $35,250.00). However, if the balance of the loan is reduced by the February and March monthly payments made by the seller, then the buyer will have to bring more cash to closing.

Under this example, if the balance of the loan as of the date of closing is $34,195.00, the buyer would have to bring a cash payment of $13,805.00 ($48,000.00 - $34,195.00), as opposed to the $12,750.00 he may have thought would be required when he executed the contract.

§2.16.2.2   Cash to control price

The alternative GAR Loan Assumption Cash to Control Purchase Price Exhibit[198] contemplates that the buyer will pay an identified amount of cash at closing plus the seller's outstanding principal loan balance as of the date of closing.[199] The total of these two amounts shall be the purchase price. Although the exact purchase price is not identified in the contract, the contract is enforceable because, like a contract which establishes purchase price based on cost per acre, this contract will establish purchase price based on a specified amount of cash plus the outstanding principal of the loan at closing (i.e., the agreement provides a method for calculating the purchase price). Under this approach, the purchase price may actually decrease between the date the contract is entered into and the date of closing.

For example, buyer and seller enter into a contract which provides that the buyer will pay $10,000.00 in cash to seller and the buyer will agree to assume the loan balance as of the date of closing. If the loan balance were $35,250.00 on January 15, the Binding Agreement Date, then the total purchase price of the property would be $45,250.00 ($35,250.00 + $10,000.00). If by March 15, after the seller has made two more payments, the loan balance is $34,195.00, then the total purchase price of the property will be $44,195.00 ($34,195.00 + $10,000.00). Regardless of whether the loan balance changes between the time the contract is entered into and the date of closing, the buyer's cash at closing remains the same ($10,000.00).

---

198   GAR Form F62, Loan Assumption Cash to Control Purchase Price Exhibit.
199   The seller's outstanding principal loan balance will be the last loan balance after the last payment from the seller plus any accrued interest up to the date of closing.

§2.16.3   Special issues regarding loan assumptions

Many of the issues with regard to loan assumptions are the same as issues in any other type of financing. These provisions include, but are not limited to, due on sale clauses, prepayment penalties, and restrictions in the use of property. In addition, there are several special issues with regard to loan assumptions.

§2.16.3.1   Release of seller liability on loan

It is in the seller's best interest to obtain a release of liability from the lender by substituting the buyer's liability for that of the seller. When the original borrower, the seller in this case, is relieved of his personal obligation under the note and deed to secure debt, there has been what is commonly called a "novation" of the seller's liability, and the lender can look only to the buyer to repay the loan. Because the novation operates to absolve the seller from liability for the debt, the lender will generally require that the buyer qualify for the loan. Therefore, in most instances, the seller will not be able to obtain a release of liability if the loan is a non-qualifying assumable loan. If the seller wants to make the contract contingent on the seller obtaining a release of liability, the following special stipulation may be incorporated in the agreement:

Special Stipulation #2-47: Agreement contingent upon seller being released from loan liability

This Agreement is contingent upon Seller obtaining a release of liability from the holder of the above-referenced promissory note and deed to secure debt. Buyer agrees to take any and all steps necessary to qualify for the loan herein. If Seller is unable to obtain the aforementioned release of liability, then Seller may, upon written notice to Buyer, terminate this Agreement, in which case all earnest money shall be immediately returned to Buyer.

§2.16.3.2   Protection of seller where there is no release of liability

If the seller is unable to obtain a release of liability from the holder of the loan but elects to go forward with the sale, he may want to enter into an agreement with the buyer giving him a security interest in the property. For example, buyer and seller could execute a note and deed to secure debt for $500.00 which would be payable at a specified date in the future. The note and deed to secure debt would also provide that a default on the loan assumed by the buyer would constitute default under the buyer's note and deed to secure debt and authorize the seller to foreclose on the property to protect his interest. In conjunction with this agreement, the real estate sales contract could also be contingent on the holder of the loan being assumed agreeing to provide the seller with notice of any default by buyer. In the alternative, the agreement between the buyer and seller could provide that if payments to the holder of the loan being assumed remain current for a specified period of time, the seller's note and deed to secure debt would be canceled. Presumably, after the buyer has an adequate amount of equity in the property, the likelihood of a deficiency in the event of foreclosure would be reduced or eliminated. In either example described above, the buyer would not have the right to pre-pay and satisfy the seller's note or deed to secure debt. An example of contract language using these means to protect the seller follows:

Special Stipulation #2-48: Cross default provision in secondary seller financing

In addition to assuming the loan as provided for in this Agreement, Buyer and Seller agree that Buyer shall execute a promissory note and deed to secure debt in favor of Seller in the amount of $_____ which shall be payable in full on __(date)__ (Buyer shall not have an option to pre-pay such amount to Seller unless such pre-payment is concurrent with Buyer's satisfaction and full repayment of the loan identified in this Agreement to be assumed by Buyer); provided, however, if there has been no default by Buyer under the terms of the loan identified in this Agreement to be assumed by Buyer on or before such date, Seller shall cancel his promissory note and deed to secure debt and Buyer shall not be obligated to pay Seller $_____. Seller's promissory note and deed to secure debt shall contain a cross-default provision and acceleration provision substantially in the form attached hereto as Exhibit "A."[200] Buyer and Seller further agree that Buyer shall obtain from Lender an agreement that Lender shall notify Seller of any default under the loan identified in this Agreement to be assumed by Buyer. If Buyer is unable to obtain an agreement from Lender regarding the notice requirement set forth herein, Seller may terminate this Agreement upon written notice to Buyer, in which case all earnest money shall be immediately returned to Buyer.

§2.16.3.3   *Increase in interest rate on loan assumption*

The note to be assumed may include a provision that entitles the holder to increase the interest rate when the property is sold without the loan being paid off. Both the GAR Loan Assumption Exhibit[201] and the Loan Assumption Cash To Control Exhibit[202] provide that if the loan is a qualifying loan, it will be contingent on the "ability to obtain" approval with an interest rate not to exceed a specified amount which is to be identified by the parties. If the underlying loan agreement authorizes the lender to increase the interest rate, it is in the seller's interest to set forth an interest rate as high as the lender may increase its rate. On the other hand, if the buyer has particular concerns about the total cost of the loan to him, it may be in his interest to limit the increase in the interest rate to an amount acceptable to the buyer.

---

200   GAR Form F67, Seller Financing (Second Mortgage) paragraph 3, contains cross default clause.
201   GAR Form F61, Loan Assumption Exhibit.
202   GAR Form F62, Loan Assumption (Cash to Control Purchase Price) Exhibit.

§2.16.3.4   Dragnet or open end clauses

The deed to secure debt may contain what is called an open end or dragnet clause. Such a clause typically states that the deed to secure debt secures not only the debt referred to in the original note but also secures any and all other present and future debts or liabilities of the original borrower to the lender.

A case in Georgia serves to highlight how such an open end or dragnet clause can have particularly severe consequences for a buyer. In this case, a buyer purchased property subject to a loan in the amount of $1,000.00.[203] The deed securing the loan contained a clause, which stated that it was made to secure the debt of $1,000.00 and any other present or future indebtedness or liability of such borrower to the holder. The buyer subsequently decided to pay off the loan and submitted to the lender a check in the amount of $1,000.00 plus interest. The lender refused to accept the payment based on the fact that there was an additional $5,032.05 that was still outstanding on the open account that the original borrower owed at the time of the loan.

The Court found in favor of the lender on the basis that the deed to secure debt secured not only the face amount of the loan which the buyer agreed to assume, but also any other present or future indebtedness or liability of the original borrower to the lender. If a dragnet clause is contained in a deed to secure debt of a loan being assumed by a buyer, the buyer may be able to reduce his risk by using the following special stipulation in the contract:

Special Stipulation #2-49: Seller's warranty that loan assumed by buyer is seller's entire debt to lender

Seller hereby warrants that as of the Binding Agreement Date, Seller's only outstanding indebtedness or liability to the holder of the debt identified in this Agreement to be assumed by Buyer equals $_____. Seller further agrees and warrants that on or after the Binding Agreement Date and continuing as long as the loan identified in this Agreement to be assumed by Buyer remains outstanding. Seller will not increase the balance of said loan by virtue of requesting or accepting any future advance, renewal, or extension of the aforementioned loan. Buyer and Seller agree that Seller shall obtain an executed agreement between Seller and Lender providing that Seller will not increase the balance of said loan and that Lender will not authorize any increase in the balance of said loan. If it is determined that as of the Binding Agreement Date, Seller's outstanding indebtedness or liability to the holder of Seller's promissory note and deed to secure debt exceeds the amount specified above or if Seller fails to obtain an agreement from Lender as described herein, Buyer may terminate this Agreement upon written notice to Seller, in which case all earnest money shall be immediately returned to Buyer.

---

203   Decatur Lumber & Supply Co. v. Baker, 210 Ga. 184, 78 S.E.2d 417 (1953).

The buyer should have the seller's promissory note and security deed carefully reviewed to determine whether a dragnet clause is contained in these documents.

In another case, the Court held that a future advance made to the original borrower after the property was sold to the buyer was still secured by the original deed to secure debt assumed by the buyer.[204] If a future advance clause is contained in a deed to secure debt of a loan being assumed by the buyer, the buyer may be able to reduce the potential risk inherent in such a clause by including the following provision in the contract:

Special Stipulation #2-50: Seller agrees not to increase loan amount after loan is assumed by buyer

Seller hereby agrees that on or after the date of closing and continuing as long as the loan identified in this Agreement to be assumed by Buyer remains outstanding, Seller will not increase the balance of said loan by virtue of requesting or accepting any future advance, renewal, or extension of the aforementioned loan. Buyer and Seller agree that Seller shall obtain an executed agreement between Seller and Lender providing that Seller will not increase the balance of said loan and that Lender will not authorize any increase in the balance of said loan to Seller. If Seller fails to obtain such an agreement from Lender, Buyer may terminate this Agreement upon written notice to Seller, in which case all earnest money shall be immediately returned to Buyer.

§2.16.4   Costs associated with loan assumption

In most cases, the holder of the seller's loan will require the payment of a loan transfer fee when a contract stipulates that the purchase price will be paid in part by the buyer assuming or taking subject to the seller's existing loan. The GAR Loan Assumption Exhibit provides that the buyer shall pay all usual and customary closing costs, assumption fees, and loan transfer charges.[205]

On the other hand, the GAR Loan Assumption Cash to Control Exhibit provides for the parties to allocate between themselves who shall pay all usual and customary closing costs, assumption fees and loan transfer charges.[206]

In addition, it is necessary to determine how reserves such as taxes and insurance that have previously been paid into an escrow account are to be treated. The GAR Loan Assumption and Loan Assumption Cash to Control exhibits provide that the buyer will reimburse the seller in cash for any escrow deposit being assumed by the buyer that the seller has made to the holder and that seller will transfer the escrow

---

204   A. Leffler Co. v. Lane, 146 Ga. 741, 92 S.E. 214 (1917).
205   GAR Form F61, Loan Assumption Exhibit.
206   GAR Form F62, Loan Assumption Cash to Control Purchase Price Exhibit.

deposit to the buyer. The buyer is generally responsible for purchasing the funds in the escrow account because he receives the benefit when future payments are made out of the account for taxes or insurance, which represent amounts owed during the period that the buyer owns the property.

If the buyer is concerned about the amount of up-front cash he will need at closing, the buyer may want to request that the seller transfer the escrow accounts to the buyer in lieu of prorating the taxes and insurance. Set forth below is an example of such a provision:

Special Stipulation #2-51: Seller's obligation to transfer lender's escrow account to buyer at closing

Notwithstanding any other provision to the contrary contained in this Agreement, Seller shall transfer the escrow account held by Seller's Lender to Buyer at closing at no additional cost to Buyer. This transfer shall occur in lieu of proration of taxes, hazard insurance, and private mortgage insurance, if applicable. In the event there is an escrow account deficit, the Seller shall be responsible for the payment of the deficit at closing. Any future escrow accrual shortage shall be the responsibility of Buyer. In the event there is an escrow account overage, Seller shall be entitled to the overage.

§2.17   Tax-free exchanges

The Internal Revenue Service recognizes and sanctions the exchange of real property for other real property instead of cash. Specifically, Internal Revenue Code Section 1031, commonly referred to as the tax-free or tax-deferred exchange provision, provides as follows:

> No gain or loss shall be recognized if property held for productive use
> in a trade or business or for investment purposes is exchanged solely
> for property of like-kind which is to be held either for productive use
> in a trade or business or for investment.[207]

An individual will most often use a tax-free exchange when the property being sold or purchased is investment or income-producing property such as rental property. The reason for using a tax-free exchange in such a situation is because federal and state laws tax income realized on the sale of personal residences differently from the income realized on the sale of income-producing or investment property.

The sale of real property is taxed as a capital gain. A capital gain is calculated by taking the difference between the seller's "basis" (usually what the seller paid for the property) in the property and the amount the seller recognized on the sale of that property. In certain circumstances, an individual may defer the payment of capital

---

207   I.R.C. § 1031.

gains taxes realized on the sale of his personal residence. Generally, an individual will not have to pay taxes on any capital gain received from the sale of his personal residence as long as he purchases another home for residential purposes of equal or greater value as the home being sold within 24 months of the sale.[208]

However, if an individual sells investment property, any profit or gain realized from that sale is usually subject to being taxed. By using a tax-free exchange, an individual can often postpone or defer the recognition of any gain realized on the sale of such investment or income-producing property.

There are many issues to be considered in structuring a tax-deferred exchange. While a number of issues are discussed below, a fully detailed analysis of the tax issues involved in such an exchange is beyond the scope of this book.

§2.17.1   Sale of property versus exchange of property

A sale occurs when real property is exchanged for the payment of cash. Therefore, as discussed above, if the property being sold is not the personal residence of the seller, the seller may have to pay taxes on any profit (cash) realized on the sale. A tax-free exchange, on the other hand, occurs when one parcel of real property is traded for another parcel of real property. A properly conducted exchange may therefore be treated as a non-taxable event. Anyone considering a tax-deferred exchange should consult with a CPA or tax attorney for advice specific to the transaction.

§2.17.2   Property being acquired must be exchanged for property of like kind

To qualify as a tax-free exchange, the property being exchanged must be considered of a "like kind." What property is considered to be like kind? A common misconception is that the properties being exchanged must be exactly the same type of property. An example of such a misconception is that unimproved property would have to be exchanged for other unimproved property. However, this is simply not true. Under Internal Revenue Code Section 1031, an apartment building may be exchanged for a shopping center or even unimproved property.[209] Like kind does not refer to the type, nature, or character of the property but instead refers to the owner's intended use of the property. Therefore, if the apartment building was acquired and held for business or investment purposes then it may be exchanged for a shopping center, which will be held for the same purposes.

Even though the definition of like kind is extremely broad, some property is clearly not considered to be like kind. Some examples of properties which are not considered to be like kind under the regulations are: (1) stocks, bonds, or notes;

---

208   I.R.C. § 1034; O.C.G.A. § 48-7-27.
209   I.R.C. § 1031; 26 U.S.C.A. § 1031.

(2) interests in a partnership; (3) other property held primarily for sale; and (4) property not within the United States.[210]

A tax-free exchange must be structured so that an individual has an equal or greater amount of debt and equity in the property being acquired as that of the property being exchanged. Failure to do so may result in the individual paying taxes on the property received in the exchange that is not considered to be "like-kind." Property received in an exchange which is not deemed to be like kind, is commonly referred to as "boot." Therefore, to ensure favorable tax treatment, a tax-free exchange must be structured to reduce or eliminate "boot." An example of a tax-free exchange that eliminates taxable boot altogether is set forth below.

A seller exchanges an apartment building with a sales price of $200,000.00 for a shopping center that has a sales price of $250,000.00. The seller has $75,000.00 of equity in the apartment building. After the exchange, the seller will also have $75,000.00 of equity in the shopping center. There is a loan on the apartment building for $125,000.00 and a loan on the shopping center for $175,000.00. In this case, the seller who is known as the exchanger would not realize any taxable "boot" because not only does he have the same amount of equity in the properties being exchanged, but he also has incurred a debt that is equal to or greater in the acquired property.

§2.17.3   Exchange of properties does not have to occur simultaneously

Prior to 1979, to accomplish a tax-free exchange both properties being exchanged had to close on the same day. The Internal Revenue Service now recognizes that a "delayed" exchange can be eligible for a tax deferral.[211] In order for a delayed exchange to be recognized as valid, the property to be acquired must be designated within 45 days of the property being sold. During this 45-day period, the exchanger can identify up to three properties to be exchanged and must then close on one of these three properties within 180 days from the date of closing on the property being sold.[212]

§2.17.4   Use of qualified intermediary in tax-free exchanges

A person or company called a "Qualified Intermediary" is used in most tax-free exchange transactions. There are a number of companies and accounting firms that regularly serve as qualified intermediaries. Certain individuals may not serve as qualified intermediaries. For example, close family members or individuals such as brokers who are considered agents of the seller are disqualified from functioning as intermediaries. Also, the closing attorney handling the sale or purchase of the property that is the subject of the exchange is prohibited from serving as a qualified intermediary.

---

210   I.R.C. § 1031.
211   Starker v. U.S., 602 F.2d 1341 (1979).
212   I.R.C. § 1031(a)(3).

§2.17.4.1   The Tax-Free exchange process

A tax-free exchange usually begins when a contract entered into by a buyer and seller for the purchase of real property is assigned to a qualified intermediary. Internal Revenue Service regulations require that the seller referred to as the exchanger give notice to the buyer and to all other parties under the sales contract on or before the date of transfer, that the exchanger intends to assign the contract in accordance with a tax-free exchange. The exchanger enters into what is called an Exchange Agreement with a qualified intermediary. Under this Exchange Agreement, the qualified intermediary will hold the proceeds received from the sale of the property until such time as the exchanger can locate suitable replacement property. The property being sold is then conveyed to the buyer directly by the exchanger. This may also be accomplished by the exchanger conveying the property to the qualified intermediary, who then transfers the property to the buyer. In both instances, the sales contract must be assigned to the qualified intermediary.

The exchanger will have 45 days to identify suitable replacement property. The exchanger then notifies the qualified intermediary once the replacement property has been identified. The exchanger will enter into a contract to purchase the replacement property. As in the case above, the contract will then be assigned to the qualified intermediary. The qualified intermediary may acquire title directly and transfer title to the exchanger, or the exchanger may acquire title directly. Once again, the sales contract must be assigned to the qualified intermediary and the other respective parties must be notified of the intent to use a tax-free exchange.

Set forth below are two examples of contract provisions to be included in a sales contract when it is contemplated that a tax-free exchange may be utilized by either a buyer or seller or both:

Special Stipulation #2-52: Buyer obligated to cooperate in seller's tax-free exchange

In selling the Property, Seller may elect to utilize an I.R.C. Section 1031 tax deferred exchange where the proceeds from the sale of the Property are used by a qualified intermediary to purchase like/kind property, and the Property may be: 1) conveyed by Seller directly to Buyer, or 2) conveyed by Seller to the qualified intermediary who shall then transfer the Property to Buyer. In such event, Buyer agrees to cooperate with and assist Seller in connection with Seller's like/kind exchange and execute an assignment of this Agreement to the qualified intermediary, provided that Buyer shall not be obligated to incur any additional expense or liability in connection with Seller's exchange of property.

Special Stipulation #2-53: Seller obligated to cooperate in buyer's tax-free exchange

In purchasing the Property, Buyer may elect to utilize an I.R.C. Section 1031 tax deferred exchange by trading Property with a qualified intermediary. In such event, Seller agrees to cooperate with and assist Buyer in connection with Buyer's like/kind exchange and execute an assignment of this Agreement to the qualified intermediary, provided that Seller shall not be obligated to incur any additional expense or liability in connection with Buyer's exchange of property. In the event Buyer so elects to utilize I.R.C. Section 1031, Seller shall convey the Property to the qualified intermediary designated by Buyer.

It may be possible to eliminate the necessity of having either party consent to an assignment of the contract with respect to a contemplated exchange by including the following contract provision:

Special Stipulation #2-54: Assignment of contract limited to qualified intermediary for tax-free exchange

This Agreement may not be assigned by either party hereto except in connection with an Assignment to a Qualified Intermediary in accordance with an I.R.C. Section 1031 tax-deferred exchange.

§2.18   Costs associated with purchase and sale

There are a number of costs associated with a purchase and sale transaction. Many of these charges are defined as closing costs. Other costs will be expenses of either the buyer or the seller. Although identified below as typically buyer or seller expenses, the parties may reallocate these expenses by an agreement between themselves.

§2.18.1   Closing costs

A major component of the closing costs are the lender charges which include, but may not be limited to, the following: the loan origination fee; the underwriting fee; the processing fee; courier fees; tax service fee; document preparation fees; escrow waiver fee, if applicable; mortgage broker fee; commitment fee; appraisal fee; appraisal review fee; credit report fee; flood certification fee; Georgia Residential Mortgage Loan Fee; and loan assumption fee, if applicable.

In addition to these lender fees, the following costs are customarily considered to be closing costs: the intangible tax; the title examination; the lender's title insurance; and attorneys fees and costs, including miscellaneous fees such as courier fees, recording fees, and tax report fees.

§2.18.1.1   Seller's contribution at closing

Since the costs associated with closing a loan are for the benefit of the buyer, in the absence of an agreement to the contrary, the buyer will be responsible for these costs. However, the GAR Contracts, as well as most other form contracts, include a section in which the seller can make some specified contribution toward the closing costs.

The GAR Contract provides that the seller's contribution is towards closing costs, discount points, surveys, and insurance relating to the Property or loan and, if allowed by buyer's lender, escrows and prepaid items.[213] The buyer then pays all other costs or fees required to close the transaction. This provision eliminates the need for any interpretation or calculation as to the manner in which closing costs and discount points are to be allocated between the parties and provides the parties with greater certainty as to the amount of their respective cost obligations at closing.

With the buyer having so much discretion to spend any contribution to closing costs made by the seller, the likelihood of the seller getting some type of refund of an unused portion of the contribution is remote.

If the seller is contributing to the closing costs, the seller may wish to ensure that the buyer selects a reputable lender who can deliver the mortgage and provide the closing firm the information and funds in a timely manner, instead of a lender who quotes the lowest interest rate. The seller may include the following financing contingencies in the contract for this purpose:

Special Stipulation #2-55: Buyer to seek loan from list of lenders

> *Seller agrees to contribute at the time of closing the sum of $_____ which sum may be used by Buyer for any of the costs, fees and charges specified in Paragraph 2(c)(3) of the Agreement, provided that Buyer seeks a mortgage loan from only one of the following mortgage lenders:*
>
> _____
>
> _____
>
> *In specifying the above list of mortgage lenders, Seller is making no representations or warranties regarding the qualifications or capabilities of any of these mortgage lenders. Seller is merely trying to ensure that Buyer obtains mortgage financing from a lender who is actively involved and well known in the mortgage lending industry.*

Provisions such as the above are often used in new construction contracts where the builder or seller agrees to pay certain closing costs if the buyer utilizes the seller's preferred lender.

---

213   GAR Form F20, paragraph 2C(2).

Parties should be very careful when deciding the amount of the seller's contribution to closing costs because FHA, VA, and conventional loans will not be approved for a buyer if the seller is contributing too much money toward closing costs. An in-depth discussion about this as it relates to FHA loans appears in section 12 of this chapter.

As to conventional loans, Fannie Mae guidelines state that for property that will be occupied as a principal residence, the seller cannot contribute more than 3% of the purchase price or appraised value of the property, whichever is less, toward closing costs if the buyer is obtaining a loan for more than 90% of the purchase price. This limitation is raised to 6% if the buyer's loan will be 90% or less of the property purchase price.[214]

The parties may wish to utilize the following special stipulation if there is any question regarding whether the lender will approve the amount of closing costs to be paid by the seller.

Special Stipulation #2-56: Seller's contribution to closing costs to be reduced to meet FHA/VA rules

The parties agree that the closing costs to be paid by Seller shall, if necessary, be reduced to the highest amount permitted to be paid by Seller by applicable FHA, VA or Fannie Mae rules and regulations (but not exceeding the original amount set forth in the Agreement).

For commercial properties, what is paid by seller and buyer should be clearly set out in the contract, which, in the case of the GAR Commercial Contract, allows the parties to allocate who is to pay for the survey, title examination and title insurance premium.[215]

§2.18.1.2   *Seller's contribution to closing costs must be used for specified purposes*

The seller's contributions at closing must be first used to pay for the preparation of the warranty deed and owner's affidavit by the closing attorney. The remainder of any contribution can then be used to pay for the list of items at the discretion of the buyer. This change was made because in many parts of Georgia (outside the metro Atlanta area), closing attorneys charge the seller a separate fee for preparing a warranty deed and owner's affidavit. The idea behind this provision was that if there is a separate charge for the deed and affidavit, it should be paid out of the seller's contribution to closing costs.

---

214   Fannie Mae Seller Servicer Guide, Selling Part VI, Chapter 2, 203.01.
215   GAR Form CF2, paragraph 9

If there are excess funds from the seller's contribution after all closing costs and survey costs have been paid, the buyer can always use the excess funds for discount points to buy down the interest rate, since this is what is contemplated in the contract.

§2.18.1.3   Buyer may use seller's contribution to "buy down" Interest Rate

Interestingly, the GAR Contracts also provide that the seller may agree to pay a specific sum to be used at the buyer's discretion for closing costs, insurance relating to the property or loan and, if allowed by the lender, escrows and prepaid items, discount points, survey costs and other expenses.

§2.18.1.4   Choice of closing attorney

Older versions of the GAR Contract provided that the parties were allowed to specify the closing attorney so long as the attorney is approved by the lender. The current GAR Contract provides that if the specified attorney is listed on the lender's approved list and the buyer is given the choice of law firms on the list, the buyer agrees to select the specified closing attorney. If the specified attorney is not on the lender's list, the buyer may then select another closing attorney who is on the lender's approved list. This complies with the Georgia Fair Lending Act[216], which classifies a home loan as a high cost loan under a "points and fees" test.

If the lender wishes not to include attorneys' fees in the "points and fees" test, then the borrower must be given the right either to select an attorney to conduct the title search and closing from an approved list, or to select an attorney acceptable to the lender. This new provision will also enable the buyer to make an informed choice by consulting with his or her real estate agent on selecting a capable closing attorney.

§2.18.2   Other buyer and seller expenses

Unless otherwise provided in the contract, the following pre-paid items are typically considered to be the buyer's expense: insurance, including hazard insurance, flood insurance, if required, and mortgage insurance, if required; escrows for taxes and insurance; and prepaid interest. In addition, the owner's title insurance is a buyer's expense.

Unless otherwise provided in the contract, the following expenses are generally considered to be seller expenses: transfer tax; termite letter; the broker's commission; and if the seller is a non-resident, the withholding tax.

---

216   O.C.G.A. § 7-6A-2(13)(b)/(HB 1361)

§2.18.2.1   Flood insurance issues

One of the costs usually associated with obtaining a mortgage loan is a fee for a flood certification. Lenders retain third-party providers to examine the Federal Emergency Management Administration ("FEMA") flood maps and determine whether the property that is to secure the lender's loan is located in a federally designated flood hazard area. If the flood certification provided to the lender discloses that the property is located within a flood hazard area, the lender will usually require the borrower to obtain a flood insurance policy naming the lender as a loss payee. The GAR Contracts provide that the buyer will pay this premium as part of the buyer's obligation to pay any "insurance premiums (including flood insurance, if applicable)…to fulfill lender requirements or otherwise close the transaction."[217]

Buyers should be aware that in some instances, the flood certification obtained by the lender will indicate that the property is located in a flood hazard area, but a current survey of the property will disclose that either: (a) the property is not located within a flood hazard area, or (b) a portion of the property is located within a flood hazard area, but the improvements which have been constructed on the property are located outside the flood hazard area. The buyer may be able to convince the lender to waive the flood insurance requirement based on this survey information. It should be noted that FHA will not insure a loan on a property on which construction is proposed, a property under construction, or a property with a dwelling less than one year old if any portion of the property is located in a flood plain.

Sellers should be cautious in making any representations regarding whether their properties are in a flood plain because flood maps can change over time. Likewise, the fact that a property is not shown to be in a flood hazard area on a FEMA map is no guarantee that the property does not flood. FEMA can take years to update its maps. The rapid pace of development in many parts of Georgia in recent years has resulted in a substantial increase in water runoff. As a result, many properties that do not appear on the current FEMA maps as being in flood hazard areas may be located in flood hazard areas once FEMA updates its maps.

Purchasers of property located adjacent to streams, creeks, or in close proximity to recently developed areas should be certain that their homeowner's insurance provides adequate coverage for flood damage even if the property is not located in a FEMA designated flood hazard area.

§2.18.2.2   Mortgage insurance

Lenders may require the borrower to obtain private mortgage insurance (PMI), which protects the lender against losses due to borrower default or in the event of foreclosure. A lender will be able to sell a PMI-backed loan, which would otherwise be considered too risky, to third party investors like the Federal National

---

217   GAR Form F20 & F23, paragraph 2C and Form 27, paragraph 3C.

Mortgage Association (FNMA) and the Federal Home Loan Mortgage Corporation (FHLMC). It is common business practice for lenders to sell loans to these investors as a way to maintain their liquidity so that they may continue to provide new loans.

Usually, a portion of the premium is paid up front at closing and the rest is paid as part of the monthly mortgage payment. The lender will usually collect 14 months premium at closing and pay twelve months of the premium to the PMI provider. The remaining two months is placed in the escrow account to start the collection for the next year. The lender then collects 1/12 of the renewal every month thereafter.

The mortgage insurance only covers the lender for a percentage that the lender will designate. This percentage is usually based on what the investors (often, Fannie Mae or Freddie Mac) require. The insurance does not cover the whole loan. Instead, it covers only the difference between the loan amount and 80% value of the property. Generally, a lender will require the borrower to obtain private mortgage insurance unless the borrower is able to make a 20% down payment for the purchase of the home. By buying private mortgage insurance, the buyer may need to only make a 3%-5% down payment.

The Homeowners Protection Act of 1998, which became effective in 1999, establishes rules for mortgage lenders to cancel PMI when certain criteria are met.[218] These protections apply to certain home mortgages signed on or after July 29, 1999 for the purchase, initial construction, or refinance of a single-family home. These protections do not apply to government-insured FHA or VA loans or to loans with lender-paid PMI.

These rules provide for two cancellation options. The first option is known as automatic cancellation, which will occur when the loan-to-value (LTV) ratio reaches 78% based on the original market value of the home. This may take some time. For example, for a home mortgage signed on or after July 29, 1999, the PMI must be terminated automatically when the borrower accumulates 22% equity in the property based on the original property value.

The second option, called owner-initiated cancellation, occurs at 80% LTV. This option allows a lender and a borrower to agree to cancel PMI before automatic cancellation occurs at 78% LTV. The exceptions to the above provisions are: 1) the loan is "high-risk"; 2) the mortgage payments have not been current within the year prior to the time for termination or cancellation; and 3) there are liens on the property.

---

218   12 U.S.C.A. § 4901

The law does not provide for automatic cancellation for mortgages before July 29, 1999. Instead, the borrower must request for PMI cancellation once he or she has 20 percent equity in the property.

§2.18.2.3   *Properties serviced by septic systems and wells*

If the property that is being purchased has a septic system, the mortgage lender will usually require the buyer to provide a letter verifying that a visual inspection of the septic system site has been conducted and that the system appears to be in proper working order.

If there is a well on the property, certain bacteriological and/or organic tests may be required by the buyer's lender to ensure the acceptability of this private water system. In some counties, a branch of the local government, usually the health department, conducts these inspections. If the local government does not provide this function, the lender will usually require that a licensed plumber or qualified septic inspector make the inspection.

Any expense associated with a letter regarding the septic system or well is typically a buyer expense because the buyer's lender imposes the requirement. Under the GAR Contract, if this cost is not covered by the seller's contribution to closing costs, discount points, and survey, the buyer would normally pay the fee for this letter as part of the buyer's obligation to pay "any additional fees, closing costs, insurance premiums or escrow amounts to fulfill lender requirements and otherwise close this transaction."[219] To avoid any confusion on the point, however, the following special stipulation can be included in the contract for property containing a septic system:

Special Stipulation #2-57: Allocation of fees for septic system clearance letter

Notwithstanding any provision to the contrary contained herein, _____ shall pay the fee associated with obtaining any Lender-required septic system clearance letter meeting the requirements of Lender. Such letter shall generally provide that a visual inspection of the septic system site has been conducted and shall provide the results of such visual inspection.

The following special stipulation can be used in a contract for property on which a well is located:

Special Stipulation #2-58: Allocation of fees for well clearance letter

Notwithstanding any other provision to the contrary contained herein, _____ shall pay the fee associated with obtaining any Lender-

---

219   GAR Form F20 & F23, paragraph 2C and Form 27, paragraph 3C.

required well clearance letter meeting the requirements of the Lender. Such letter shall generally provide that the necessary bacteriological and/or organic tests of the well have been conducted and shall provide the results of such tests.

It should be noted that under the FHA Loan Exhibit, the seller is obligated to provide proper certification that the property is connected to and serviced by a public sewer system.[220]

Buyers should keep in mind that these inspections are, in most instances, only visual inspections to verify that sewage is not escaping from the septic field and that the accompanying reports will not include any sort of warranty as to the soundness of the septic system. Buyers should therefore consider having a thorough inspection of the septic system performed by a licensed plumber as part of their inspection of the property. Buyers should also verify the condition of the septic system with the county health department even if a private clearance letter has been obtained. Unfortunately, some buyers have received private septic approval letters only to learn, too late, that the county health department had determined the system to be substandard.[221]

§2.18.2.4   Credits at closing

Buyers and sellers will in some instances want to include contract stipulations that provide for the seller to give the buyer a credit at closing for items such as repairs, renovations, or decorating allowances. While this arrangement is frequently desirable to the parties in that it relieves the seller of making certain repairs or improvements requested by the buyer and provides the buyer with a source of funds to undertake the requested repairs or improvements, it is generally not permitted by mortgage lenders due to Fannie Mae guidelines.[222]

The rationale for this lender prohibition is that these types of credits or concessions are actually just reductions in the purchase price and should be reflected as such. For example, a contract reflects a purchase price of $100,000.00 and includes a stipulation for a $3,000.00 repair credit to be given by the seller to the buyer and also includes a financing contingency providing for the buyer to obtain a loan of 90% of the purchase price. What the parties have actually done in providing for the $3,000.00 repair credit is to reduce the purchase price to $97,000.00, and the lender is now willing to lend only 90% of this amount, which is a smaller loan than was called for in the financing contingency.

Lenders will in some instances allow these types of credits with transactions in which there is a low loan-to-value ratio. If the above-referenced contract included a

---

220   GAR Form F63, FHA Loan Exhibit, paragraph 10.
221   <u>Georgia Real Estate Commission v. Peavy</u>, 229 Ga.App. 201, 493 S.E.2d. 602 (1997).
222   Fannie Mae Seller Servicer Guidelines, Part VI, Chapter 2, 203.01.

financing contingency providing for the buyer to obtain a loan of 60% of the purchase price, the lender may be willing to allow the repair credit to remain in the contract, since the loan of $60,000.00 would still be adequately secured by the collateral with an actual purchase price of $97,000.00.

The alternative to these types of credits or concessions which is preferred by lenders is to have the seller undertake any requested repairs prior to closing and have any invoices for this repair work paid either prior to closing or from the sale proceeds at the closing. In instances where the repairs cannot be completed prior to closing, the lender may authorize a portion of the sale proceeds to be held in escrow for a limited period of time following the closing and disbursed directly to a vendor upon the completion of any requested repairs.

As a practical matter, buyers should contact their mortgage lenders regarding any contract provisions concerning proposed credits, allowances, or repairs in order to resolve any potential loan underwriting issues.

§2.19   Mortgage fraud

§2.19.1   What is mortgage fraud

In its broadest sense, mortgage fraud occurs when one or more parties misrepresent facts in a real estate transaction to obtain mortgage financing. Normally, the financing allows the borrower to fraudulently "cash out" phantom or non-existent equity in a property. Mortgage fraud usually falls into one or both of two categories: (1) information and/or documents are falsified to make the property look more valuable than it really is in order to trick the lender into loaning too much money on an overvalued property, and (2) information and/or documents are falsified to get a loan application approved for a buyer who would not otherwise be qualified for a loan. The participants in mortgage fraud include fraudulent buyers, mortgage brokers, real estate appraisers, closing attorneys and real estate agents.

§2.19.2   Types of mortgage fraud

§2.19.2.1   *"Property Flipping"*

Perhaps the best-known example of mortgage fraud is known as "property flipping." Flipping is a form of fraud that involves the purchase and quick resale of a property for more than its true value. Some property flips are perfectly legal and involve sophisticated buyers who purchase real estate that is simply undervalued. Because values in real estate can increase quickly due to legitimate market forces, it is sometimes difficult to know if the transaction is fraudulent or merely savvy business.

For a "property flip" to work, the perpetrators usually have to work in concert with one another or with settlement service providers who will at least look the other way when this type of criminal activity occurs. In other words, the crime of mortgage fraud is typically a team sport. For example, a scheme may need the help of a dishonest mortgage broker who will hire the "right" appraiser for a property that is being flipped or to help get a phony buyer or buyer who is not credit worthy qualified. Another type of scheme may need the help of a shady closing attorney who will not ask questions about suspect transactions or who is willing to actually participate in the mortgage fraud. In one extreme case, it was reported that the closing attorney allowed the buyer to refinance a property at a grossly inflated price before the buyer actually purchased the property so that the buyer essentially purchased the property from the proceeds of the refinance. The paperwork was then recorded in a different order to make it look like the sale of the property took place before the refinance.

To further complicate matters, fraudsters become more and more savvy and sophisticated, they may develop schemes in which some of the participants have no idea that anything untoward is transpiring. Also, some lenders fail to utilize sufficient safety measures to help identify potential fraud.

§2.19.2.2   *Qualifying for a loan by fraud*

Some buyers commit identity theft to obtain other people's personal information, such as social security numbers, in order to qualify for a loan. Buyers may also lie about their income, job, or credit history by falsifying their pay stubs, forging their income tax returns, or falsifying their credit reports. The easy availability of programs, such as TurboTax®, make it easier than ever to produce falsified documents that are very authentic-looking. Other times, unscrupulous mortgage brokers may simply falsify this information and submit it to the actual lender without the buyer's knowledge.

§2.19.2.3   *Inflating the property price*

Another example of mortgage fraud is the situation in which the buyer cannot come up with the down payment for the home and the seller, without the approval or knowledge of the actual lender, agrees to give the buyer the down payment and to inflate the sales price of the house by a corresponding amount so that the lender finances the down payment.

Yet another situation is where the buyer wants to close on a new house before his current residence is sold, but does not qualify for a loan until his first house has sold. The buyer creates a fake lease under which a "friend" is said to be leasing the house and making the payments on the old mortgage so that the buyer appears to be making more money than he really does.

§2.19.3   Preventing mortgage fraud

§2.19.3.1   Identifying mortgage fraud

When should one suspect mortgage fraud? Below are examples of some situations, which do not prove mortgage fraud conclusively, but deserve more attention:

1. Transactions in which large sums of money are going back to the buyer at closing;
2. The HUD-1 does not reflect the "true" transaction;
3. The purchase price is being modified via a special stipulation or amendment as a part of the original contract or the "real" contract is different from the one supplied to the lender;
4. The purchase price exceeds the listing price and there is no "bidding war.";
5. There is a "phantom" second mortgage;
6. The seller is paying some of their proceeds to the buyer for a contractor from whom there is no contract or estimate;
7. The buyer/mortgage broker objects to showing a breakout of an increased price in the contract;
8. The seller is doing extremely short term financing and commissions are held until a "refinance" by the purchaser; or
9. Some unknown person appears at the closing for no apparent reason.

§2.19.3.2   Role of REALTORS®

The GAR Exclusive Seller Listing/Brokerage Agreement[223] now includes a section that would help REALTORS® report mortgage fraud without fearing whether reporting suspicious activity will violate some duty to their clients if it causes the transaction to fall apart and create potential liability to them.

The GAR Listing Agreement provides that the broker is given permission, by the seller, to report any suspicious, unusual and/or potentially illegal or fraudulent activity to governmental officials, agencies and/or authorities and any mortgage lender, mortgage insurer, mortgage investor and/or title insurance company which could potentially be harmed by fraudulent activity. This will give REALTORS® clear authority to report suspicious mortgage activity.

Further, the GAR Listing Agreement contains a provision which allows the REALTOR® to report potential fraud even though the REALTOR® is not completely sure that fraud is occurring. Specifically, the seller expressly acknowledges that the broker does not have special expertise in detecting fraud in real estate transactions. Therefore, the broker may not detect any activity which is fraudulent or illegal, and may report any lawful activity as suspicious or fraudulent.

---

223   GAR Form F1, paragraph 11.

This provision attempts to protect the REALTOR® in the event that the REALTOR® is wrong in his or her assessment that mortgage fraud is occurring. The idea behind placing this language in the brokerage engagement agreements is that it allows the REALTOR® to get the client's permission to report suspicious activities at the outset of the broker-client relationship, before the client might be tempted by the lure of making easy money on a transaction (regardless of whether it is legal or illegal to do so). The objection to this language by a potential client should send warning signals to the REALTOR® and whether to represent this client.

§2.19.3.3   Reporting mortgage fraud

Suspicious activities can be reported to the District Attorney's office for the county in which the property is located, the Georgia Attorney General's Office or the Assistant United States Attorney in Atlanta. Other relevant authorities are the Georgia Department of Banking and Finance, Legal and Consumer Affairs Division in Atlanta. Complaints about appraisers can be submitted to the Georgia Real Estate Appraisers Board in Atlanta. Other federal contacts can be accessed by visiting www.stopmortgagefraud.com, a website developed by the Mortgage Bankers Association. However, the best first step for REALTORS® may well be to contact the various settlement service providers involved in the transaction to express the concern and clarify whether mortgage fraud is or is not occurring.

For example, if the appraisal seems completely out of line with what the appropriate property valuation should be, the REALTOR® may call the appraiser for clarification. Before doing so, the REALTOR® should first confirm with the appraiser the property values on your copy of the report to make sure they are the same as on the appraiser's copy. This is because in many cases criminals have altered the valuations on otherwise legitimate appraisals without the appraiser even knowing it has occurred. In other cases, criminals have stolen letterhead from an appraiser and created completely fictitious appraisals of which the appraisers are unaware. The REALTOR® should take care not to make any accusation of wrongdoing, particularly to third parties, to avoid any claims of libel or slander. If the appraiser is hostile or uncooperative, the REALTOR® can verify with the Georgia Real Estate Appraisers Board that the appraiser is indeed licensed. If the appraiser is licensed and the REALTOR® has serious unanswered concerns, the REALTOR® can also file a complaint with the Appraisers Board explaining his/her concerns and request an investigation.

Similarly, if a mortgage broker tells a REALTOR® that the ultimate lender has approved a large cash out payment to the buyer on the purchase of an existing home, the REALTOR® may ask what lender the mortgage broker is acting on behalf of and indicate that he or she intends to verify the information. If the broker is uncooperative, a complaint can be filed with the Georgia Department of Banking and Finance. The REALTOR® can also provide the closing attorney with a copy of the "true" sales contract to be sure it is the same as the copy provided to the lender.

§2.19.4 Consequences of committing mortgage fraud

Persons committing mortgage fraud can be charged with any number of state and federal crimes. At a state level, the more obvious crimes include criminal fraud, theft by taking, forgery, identity theft, criminal solicitation, criminal conspiracy and racketeering. At a federal level, persons committing mortgage fraud can, among other things, be charged with wire fraud, mail fraud, use of false identification documents, use of false social security numbers, conspiracy to defraud the United States government and racketeering.

§2.19.4.1 Consequences for REALTORS®

In addition to the penalties under state and federal law, real estate agents and brokers who participate in mortgage fraud can also be sanctioned by the Georgia Real Estate Commission, up to and including the revocation of their licenses, for engaging in any number of unfair business practices including the following:

(a) Making substantial misrepresentations[224];

(b) Having demonstrated incompetence to act as a real estate licensee in such manner as to safeguard the interest of the public or any other conduct ... which constitutes dishonest dealing[225];

(c) Failing to keep for a period of three (3) years a true and correct copy of all sales contracts, closing statements, or other documents relating to real estate closings[226]; and

(d) Being or becoming a party to any falsification of any portion of any contract or other document involved in any real estate transaction.[227]

Even if no specific charges are brought by the Georgia Real Estate Commission against a licensee for violating any of the above license law provisions, if a licensee is convicted of a state or federal crime involving mortgage fraud, they can also lose their real estate license as a result of the criminal conviction. Licensees are required to immediately report to the Georgia Real Estate Commission any felony conviction or any crime involving moral turpitude. The term "conviction" means a guilty finding, a verdict or plea, a sentencing to first offender treatment without a determination of guilt or a plea of nolo contendere.[228] Upon such a conviction, the licensee's license is automatically revoked 60 days after the conviction unless the licensee timely requests a hearing to determine whether the licensee remains fit to hold a real estate license.

---

224 O.C.G.A. §43-40-25(a)(21).
225 O.C.G.A. §43-40-25(a)(25).
226 O.C.G.A. §43-40-25(a)(27).
227 O.C.G.A. §43-40-25(a)(28).
228 O.C.G.A. §43-40-15(b)(1).

§2.19.4.2   Brokers' liability for the fraud of their agents

Brokers may also have exposure to sanctions before the Georgia Real Estate Commission for mortgage fraud committed by their licensees if the Commission determines that the broker did not properly supervise his or her licensees. This may be the case even though the broker may not even be aware of the licensee's fraud. The Georgia real estate licensing law specifically provides that the broker or qualifying broker is responsible for any licensee whose license is affiliated with the broker's firm unless the broker can prove all of the following:

(1)   the broker is able to show that he/she had in place reasonable procedures for the supervision of the licensee,

(2)   the broker did not participate in the violation, and

(3)   the broker did not ratify the violation.[229]

To avoid a sanction, the broker must also show that he or she had reasonable procedures in place to supervise the agent's actions. Georgia license law sets out numerous substantive areas in which brokers are required to establish and implement procedures to supervise affiliated licensees. Specifically, the law requires brokers to establish and implement procedures for reviewing "all listing contracts, leases, sales contracts, management agreements, and offers to buy, sell, lease or exchange real property secured or negotiated by the firm's associates" for compliance with the License Law and Regulations. This review must be performed within thirty (30) days of the date of the offer or the contract.[230]

To fulfill the duties to supervise affiliated licensees, brokers should look deeper into the transactions of licensees whom they supervise. During the review of each document, the broker should keep in mind other transactions in which the affiliated licensee has been involved. Brokers need to be on the lookout for patterns of quick re-sales of the same property and if a property is involved in a rapid resale, the broker should ask the licensee about the circumstances surrounding the parties to the sales, the loan, and the appraisal until the broker is satisfied that the transaction is legitimate. Brokers should also be sure that their office procedures manual includes a discussion of mortgage fraud and the consequences for licensees who participate in or abet mortgage fraud.

---

229   O.C.G.A. §43-40-18(b).
230   O.C.G.A. §43-40-18(c)(3).

CHAPTER 3
EARNEST MONEY

OVERVIEW

This chapter will address the broker's duties in holding earnest money and the right of the broker under the GAR Contracts to disburse earnest money based upon a reasonable interpretation of the contract. In addition, this chapter discusses the mechanics of interpleader actions and the legal standard for when a real estate broker may interplead disputed earnest money funds.

§3.1   What the GAR Contract provides

It is customary for a buyer to deposit a sum of money to show the buyer's commitment to purchasing the property. This is commonly referred to as earnest money, although some new construction contracts may refer to it as a construction deposit. The nature of the payment will be determined by the intent of the parties rather how it is labeled. A contract to buy and sell property is still valid even when it does not provide for payment of any deposit.

Paragraph 3 of the GAR Contract contemplates the payment of earnest money to a third party known as a "Holder." It also sets out the type of account into which the earnest money must be deposited, what the earnest money may be used for, when and how the Holder may disburse the earnest money, and what the Holder should do in the event of a dispute about the earnest money.

§3.2   Payment of earnest money

The GAR Contract requires that the earnest money be deposited in an escrow account within five banking days from the Binding Agreement Date. The earnest money may be paid by check, wire transfer or in cash.

§3.2.1   Payment by check

If the earnest money check is not honored for any reason, the Holder is required to immediately notify all parties, even if he or she believes that the bank has made a mistake. The buyer then has three banking days after notice from the Holder to deliver good funds to the Holder. If the buyer does not timely deliver good funds, the seller has the right to terminate the agreement upon written notice to the buyer.[231]

§3.2.2   Payment in cash

While most earnest money is paid by check or wire transfer, there are circumstances when earnest money is paid in cash. For obvious reasons, the broker should not accept any cash without giving a receipt for the funds and keeping a copy of the same for the record.

---

231   GAR Contract, paragraph 3.

§3.2.3   Payment of earnest money when buyer has a right to terminate

When the buyer has a right to terminate the agreement, some thought should be given to whether any special stipulation needs to be made for the handling of earnest money. If the payment of the earnest money is made by check, the GAR Contract provides that the Holder of the earnest money is not required to return the earnest money until the check has cleared. If the buyer terminates the agreement shortly after it is entered into, the buyer may have to wait several weeks to get the earnest money beck. If the buyer wants to ensure that all or a portion of the earnest money is repaid sooner, the buyer may want to provide in the contract that the earnest money check will not be deposited until the buyer's right to terminate expires or is waived. The special stipulation below is an example of this type of provision.

Special Stipulation #3-1: Delayed deposit of earnest money

Buyer and Seller expressly agree that Buyer's earnest money check of $_____paid pursuant to this Agreement shall be held by Holder and not deposited into Holder's trust account until after Buyer's right to terminate this Agreement has expired or otherwise ended without Buyer electing to terminate this Agreement. Upon the occurrence of this event, Holder shall deposit the earnest money check into Holder's trust account within five (5) business days thereafter. If Buyer elects to terminate this Agreement, Holder shall return the earnest money check to Buyer.

An approach which will likely be more acceptable to a seller is for a portion of the earnest to be deposited and for the buyer to provide a check for the remainder of the earnest money to be deposited when the buyer's termination right has either been waived by the buyer or has expired. The following stipulation may be used for such situations.

Special Stipulation #3-2: Delayed payment of additional earnest money

In addition to the earnest money of $_____ held by Holder, Buyer shall deposit additional earnest money of $_____ by check with Holder no later than three (3) days from the date that Buyer's right to terminate this Agreement expires or terminates without Buyer terminating this Agreement. Holder shall deposit this check for additional earnest money in Holder's trust account within five (5) business days of the receipt of said check.

§3.3   Defining Banking Day in earnest money section

As discussed above, the GAR Contract requires that the Holder deposit the earnest money into the Holder's escrow account within "five banking days" from the Binding Agreement Date. If for some reason, the earnest money check is dishonored, the buyer has "three banking days" after notice to deliver good funds to the Holder.

How are the timeframes calculated? The meaning of "within" is "no later than" [232] and a day means an entire 24-hour day beginning immediately after midnight and ending 24 hours later. Therefore, if the Holder receives a check on the 2nd January and must deposit the same within five banking days, the end of January 3rd would be the first banking day, the end of January 4th would be the second banking day and so on until five banking days have elapsed. The time starts to run midnight on January 2nd for 24 hours for each banking day.

What is meant by a banking day? A banking day is defined under Georgia law as "a part of a day on which a bank is open to the public for carrying on substantially all of its banking functions."[233] Therefore, what constitutes a banking day will vary from one financial institution to another. For most banks, Saturdays, Sundays, and holidays are not banking days because even if certain branches are open, the bank is not open to the public for carrying on substantially all of its banking functions. There are some banks, however, where Saturdays are banking days because they carry on substantially all of their banking functions. An officer of the bank should be able to answer questions regarding which days the bank treats as official banking days.

The requirement in the GAR Contract to deposit the earnest money within five banking days would be calculated based on the practices of the bank in which the Holder has established its escrow/trust account. For example, if Saturday were a day when substantially all of the bank's functions are performed, this day would count toward the requirement that the earnest money be deposited within five banking days.

What is unfortunately unclear is whether the practices of the buyer's bank or the Holder's bank would be used in counting the three banking days the buyer has to make good on a dishonored earnest money check. With there being no Georgia case on this issue, sellers and real estate brokers are well advised to evaluate the banking practices of both banks and decide any variances between the two banks' practices in favor of the buyer. So, for example, if Saturday is not a banking day at the buyer's bank but is a banking day at the Holder's bank, the safe approach is to not count Saturday as a banking day for the purpose of determining a buyer's default. The following special stipulation can be used to clarify the buyer's obligation:

Special Stipulation #3-3: Definition of "Banking Day" for replacing dishonored check

In the event Buyer's earnest money check is dishonored for any reason whatsoever, Buyer shall have three banking days, to provide good funds to the Holder. For purposes of this special stipulation, a banking day is a day on which the bank upon which the check is written carries on substantially all of its banking functions.

---

232   Wall v. Youmans, 223 Ga. 191, 154 S.E.2d 191 (1967); Head v. Williams, 269 Ga. 894, 506 S.E.2d 863 (1998)
233   O.C.G.A. § 11-4-104.

§3.4 Contract may be enforceable even if buyer fails to pay earnest money

A contract may still be enforceable even if the earnest money referenced in the contract is not paid. Georgia courts have held that failure to make down payment or pay escrow money does not make the contract void for lack of consideration.[234] In one case, a buyer and seller signed a contract for land. Although the contract required the buyer to deposit $3,000.00 as earnest money, the buyer failed to do so. The seller argued that the contract was invalid due to a failure of consideration. The court rejected this argument and stated that "the agreement on the part of one to sell for a stipulated amount is a good consideration for a promise of the other to buy."[235]

If a contract does not expressly allow the seller to terminate if the earnest money is not paid, the courts will not give the seller the right to do so. Instead, the seller can sue the buyer to recover the earnest money contemplated by the contract.[236] As discussed in greater detail below, in order to help avoid costly and timely litigation, the GAR Contract gives the seller an express right to terminate the contract if the earnest money check is dishonored and the buyer does not make good the funds within three banking days after notice.

Mutuality is generally required for a valid contract. Mutuality of obligation requires that unless both parties to a contract are bound, neither is bound. That is, if a contract provides that a contingency is wholly within the discretion of one party, the contract lacks mutuality.

Although earnest money is not required as consideration for a real estate sales contract, if a party pays some form of consideration (such as earnest money), then the contract will generally not lack mutuality. In evaluating mutuality, one court held that a financing contingency in a contract did not render the contract void for lack of mutuality because the exchange of earnest money and the buyer's showing of good faith and cooperation in trying to obtain a loan evidenced her "consideration."[237] Also, obtaining a loan is not usually in the sole discretion of one party to the contract, because the buyer's lender is usually a third party making such a decision.

---

234 Mangum v. Jones, 205 Ga. 661, 54 S.E.2d 603 (1949); Atlanta Six Flags Partnership v. Hughes, 191 Ga. App. 404, 381 S.E.2d 605 (1989).

235 Mangum v. Jones, 205 Ga. 661, 666, 54 S.E.2d 603, 607 (1949).

236 Stone Mountain Abstract Co. v. Valcovy Realty Co., 141 Ga. App. 875, 234 S.E.2d 705 (1977).

237 Brack v. Brownlee, 246 Ga. 818, 273 S.E.2d 390 (1980); Koets, Inv. v. Benveniste, 169 Ga. App. 352, 312 S.E.2d 846 (1983), aff'd, 252 Ga.520, 314 S.E.2d 912 (1984).

§3.5 Seller holding earnest money

Most contracts for the sale of property, including the GAR Contract, allow the real estate broker or some other party to serve as the Holder of the earnest money. There is nothing that prohibits the seller from holding the earnest money if that is what the parties agree.[238] This is often the case where the seller is also the builder, such as in new home sales or in new condominium sales.

§3.5.1 Earnest money on condominium sales

The Georgia Condominium Act requires that any payment of money in respect of the first sale of a residential condominium unit that is paid before the closing be held in escrow until the unit is delivered at closing. If the sale is not closed, the funds must be held in escrow until it is paid to the persons entitled to the funds.

The funds must be deposited in a separate account designated to hold the earnest money. However, if the deposit is held by a REALTOR®, the funds may be placed in the broker's escrow account instead of a separately designated account.[239] A GAR exhibit is available for cases where the parties agree to have the seller hold the earnest money.[240]

§3.6 Buyer or seller modifying earnest money provision

On occasion, a buyer or seller will present an offer or counteroffer in which the rights of the Holder of the earnest money have been modified. Normally, this is done to limit the ability of the Holder to recover its costs and attorneys fees in the event a dispute about the earnest money is litigated or to delete the Holder's ability to disburse the earnest money based upon a reasonable interpretation of the contract. The real estate broker is obligated to present such offers even when they contain modifications to the earnest money section, which the Holder might find objectionable.[241] Of course, nothing requires the listing or selling broker to serve as the Holder of the earnest money if the terms of the escrow in the contract are not acceptable to such broker. In a situation like that, the real estate broker can simply decline to serve as the Holder of earnest money, unless it is on terms acceptable to him or her.

§3.7 Rights and duties of escrow agent under GAR Contract

§3.7.1 Holder of earnest money is agent for both parties

---

238   Cloud v. Jacksonville National Bank, 239 Ga. 353, 236 S.E.2d 587 (1977).
239   O.C.G.A. § 44-3-112.
240   GAR Form F80, Earnest Money Held by Seller.
241   O.C.G.A. § 43-40-25(a)(19).

In Georgia, a party holding earnest money is considered an escrow agent.[242] As such, when the Holder acts as a trustee of an express trust with duties to perform for each of the parties. The broker's powers with regard to the earnest money are strictly limited to those set forth in that part of the contract (or other agreement) establishing the terms upon which the earnest money will be held.[243]

Therefore, even though the real estate broker may be representing the buyer or the seller in any given transaction, the broker serving as the Holder of earnest money owes duties to both parties. These duties are limited, however, to the handling of earnest money and do not create a client relationship. For example, if the broker represents the buyer as a client, the broker's agreement to act as the Holder has no bearing upon whether the broker has a client relationship with the seller. Such relationship would need to be created by an express written agreement between the broker and the seller.[244]

> §3.7.2 Broker who is escrow agent must account for and remit earnest money

To establish a valid escrow with regard to earnest money, the following criteria must be met: (a) there must be a valid, lawful contract between the parties; (b) there must be an absolute deposit of the earnest money with the escrow agent (normally the real estate broker); and (c) the earnest money must pass beyond the control of the buyer to unilaterally withdraw.[245]

A licensee must account for and remit any money coming into the licensee's possession that belongs to others.[246] If a broker serving as an escrow agent fails to account or remit the earnest money, the broker may lose his or her real estate license.[247] The associate broker or licensee must place, as soon after receipt as practically possible, the earnest money in the custody of the broker who must deposit the money in a trust or escrow account.[248] A broker cannot generally commingle the earnest money with the broker's own money.[249] Further, the broker must maintain and deposit in a separate, federally insured checking account all money received by the broker, acting as escrow agent of the funds of others, unless all the parties having an interest in the money have agreed otherwise in writing.[250]

---

242   Carter v. Turbeville, 90 Ga. App. 367, 83 S.E.2d 72 (1954).
243   Fickling & Walker Co. v. Giddens Constr. Co., Inc., 258 Ga. 891, 376 S.E.2d 655 (1989).
244   O.C.G.A. § 10-6A-3(1).
245   O.C.G.A. § 44-5-42; Brown v. Brown, 192 Ga. 852, 16 S.E.2d 853 (1941).
246   O.C.G.A. § 43-40-25(b)(3)
247   Land v. Georgia Real Estate Commission, 142 Ga. App. 860, 237 S.E.2d 243 (1977).
248   O.C.G.A. § 43-40-20(h).
249   O.C.G.A. § 43-40-25(b)(4)
250   O.C.G.A. § 43-40-25(b)(5).

If the broker deposits funds into an interest-bearing account, the broker must obtain a written agreement of the parties indicating to whom the broker will pay any interest earned prior to depositing the funds into such an account.[251] The GAR Contract provides that the earnest money will be deposited in the Holder's escrow/trust account with the Holder retaining the interest if the account is interest-bearing.[252]

§3.7.3   When Holder can disburse earnest money

The GAR Contract obligates a Holder to disburse earnest money as follows:[253]
at closing;
(a)   upon a subsequent written agreement signed by all parties with an interest in the funds. The agreement must be separate from the contract directing the broker to hold the funds, which in most cases is the sales contract;
(b)   upon order of a court or arbitrator[254] with jurisdiction over a dispute involving the earnest money; or
(d)   upon the parties' failure to enter into a binding agreement.

The Contract also allows the Holder to disburse the earnest money upon a reasonable interpretation of the contract.[255] The Holder in these situations must give 15 days' notice stating to whom the disbursement of disputed earnest money will be made. This provision was included in the GAR Contract to give the parties an opportunity, within the 15-day period, to provide the Holder with any objections they may have to the disbursement, any disputed questions of fact or law to justify an interpleader action, or any additional facts or laws to support a proposed disbursement of the earnest money. It is important to note, however, that in Georgia, only a licensed attorney is authorized to represent a corporation in a proceeding in a court of record. This means that the qualifying broker of an incorporated real estate brokerage firm may not file an interpleader without retaining the services of a licensed attorney.[256]

Before the Holder disburses earnest money based on a reasonable interpretation of the contract, the Holder must give all parties 15 days' notice as to whom the disbursement will be made. Any party may object in writing to the proposed disbursement, provided the Holder receives the objection within the 15-day period. All objections not raised in a timely manner are waived. In the event a timely objection is made, the Holder must consider the objection and choose either to (a) hold the earnest money for a reasonable period to allow the parties to resolve the dispute; (b) disburse

---

251   O.C.G.A. § 43-40-25(b)(30).
252   GAR Contract, paragraph 3A.
253   GAR Contract, paragraph 3C.
254   See section 11.6 regarding arbitration. Arbitration is being used more and more frequently to resolve earnest money disputes.
255   The Georgia Real Estate Commission has similar provisions, see Rule 520-1.08(3)(b).
256   Eckles v. Atlanta Technology Group, Inc., 267 Ga. 801, 485 S.E.2d 22 (1997).

the earnest money and notify all the parties; and/or (c) interplead the earnest money into the appropriate court. The GAR Contract requires the Holder to send a new 15-day notice if the Holder changes his or her mind and intends to disburse the earnest money in a manner different from what was stated in the first 15-day notice.

Does a disbursement that is based on a specific provision of the purchase and sale contract require the Holder to send a 15-day notice? An example is the provision in the GAR Contract, in which the buyer has the right to terminate the agreement if a new survey is materially different from any survey attached to the contract, in which event the earnest money shall be returned. The answer is "yes", unless the seller signs a termination and release agreement permitting the funds to be returned to the buyer. Even though the contract clearly states that the earnest money be refunded, the Holder would still be making an interpretation of the contract, which requires that notice be sent prior to a disbursal of the funds. If a real estate broker does not disburse the earnest money according to the provisions of the contract, the Georgia Real Estate Commission may consider that the broker has acted incompetently.[257]

§3.7.4 Interpreting the GAR Contract

To assist the Holder in deciding which party is entitled to the earnest money, the GAR Contract has been amended to include a section setting out when the buyer or the seller is entitled to the earnest money.[258]

The GAR Contract provides that the buyer is entitled to the earnest money upon the following events:

(a)   failure of the parties to enter into a binding agreement;
(b)   failure of any contingency or condition of the agreement
(c)   termination of the agreement due to the default of seller;
(d)   termination of the agreement according to a right to terminate contained in the agreement; or
(e)   upon closing.

The GAR Contract also provides that the seller is entitled to the earnest money if the Agreement is terminated due to the default of Buyer.

§3.7.5 What is a reasonable period for broker to hold earnest money

The Georgia Real Estate Commission and the courts have not defined a particular time as a "reasonable period" for the real estate broker to hold the earnest money in the event of a dispute between the parties. The intent of the provision in the GAR Contract was to give the real estate broker the time to do any or all of the

---

257   Georgia Real Estate Commission Rule 520-1.08(3)(a).
258   GAR Contract, paragraph 3B.

following: (a) impose a "cooling off" period on the parties to an earnest money dispute; (b) have time to thoroughly investigate which party is entitled to receive the earnest money; or (c) otherwise attempt to resolve the dispute.

The time by which the earnest money must be disbursed by the Holder will likely depend on the facts in each case. The Holder should have the right to hold the earnest money if there is some realistic hope that the parties may resolve their earnest money dispute or if the Holder is waiting on information, which will make it possible to disburse, based upon a reasonable interpretation of the contract. The period of time that disputed earnest money can legitimately be held, however, is probably measured in months rather than years.

Earnest money should not be held for an extended period of time merely because the broker would rather not deal with the dispute. Brokers should also be aware that, if the earnest money is a large sum and is placed in an interest-bearing account with the Holder, the longer it is kept, the greater the likelihood the parties will claim the Holder is breaching her duty by retaining the earnest money for her own financial gain.

§3.7.6 Commencing an interpleader lawsuit

§3.7.6.1 What is an interpleader action?

The Holder of earnest money may file what is known as an interpleader action when there are competing claims to the earnest money and the Holder is unsure how to disburse the funds. An interpleader is a lawsuit where the Holder deposits the earnest money into the registry of the court and asks the court to make a decision with regard to its disbursement.[259]

The Earnest Money paragraph of new F20 was modified to change the word "interpleader action" to "interpleader lawsuit." Many buyers and sellers do not realize that an interpleader action is a lawsuit in which the broker sues both the seller and the buyer. When the suit is filed, the broker deposits the earnest money into the registry of the court and the judge is asked to make a judicial determination with respect to which of the parties is entitled to the earnest money. The change in terminology may help educate buyers and sellers more clearly as to what they are getting themselves into when they encourage a broker interplead the funds.

§3.7.6.2 The cost of interpleading

Brokers should also remind buyers and sellers that the GAR Contract provides that "The prevailing defendant in the interpleader lawsuit shall be entitled to collect its attorney's fees and court costs and the amount deducted by Holder from the non-prevailing defendant." In other words, if the attorney representing the brokerage firm

---

259   O.C.G.A. § 9-11-22.

charges the broker $500 to prepare and file the interpleader lawsuit, this amount can be assessed against the losing party in the interpleader lawsuit.

The GAR Contract gives the Holder the right to deduct from the funds interplead its costs and expenses, including reasonable attorneys fees. In addition, it provides that the prevailing party has a right to be reimbursed for any funds paid to the Holder from the losing party. This procedure, although untested in the appellate courts, gives the Holder the advantage of being reimbursed for the costs and expenses of the interpleader immediately rather than having to wait for a final determination by the court as to the dispute between the buyer and seller. Therefore, there is a monetary risk in insisting that disputed earnest money be interpleaded into court.

The idea that prevailing parties can recover their costs and attorneys fees is designed to encourage parties to be cautious in demanding that earnest money be interpleaded into court. The risk of additional costs and charges being assessed against a buyer or seller is often used as leverage to negotiate resolutions of earnest money disputes. A great many earnest money disputes involve sums in the $1,000 to $2,000 range. Disputes over sums in this range would normally be considered small by most litigation standards. While these disputes can be extremely contentious, they rarely justify the significant attorney's fees usually expended on the part of the buyer and seller and real estate broker to litigate. Like it or not, it is often in the parties best financial interest to reach a settlement rather than risk spending even larger arguing over who is entitled to the earnest money.

§3.7.6.3   When interpleader is appropriate

As a condition of interpleading the funds into court, the Holder must show that the conflicting claims create a reasonable doubt as to whom the funds shall belong.[260] A petition for interpleader will be denied if the escrow agent is in possession of all the facts and the questions of law are not intricate or debatable. In other words, an interpleader is not available if there is no bona fide controversy between the parties.

A broker who files an interpleader inappropriately may incur liability, which is illustrated in the following case.[261] The earnest money provision in the contract stated: "If the sale, due to buyer's default, willful or otherwise, is not consummated, then said earnest money shall be refunded." The sale was not consummated and after a period of unsuccessful negotiations to save the deal, the buyers demanded return of the deposit. When the money was not returned to the buyers, they sued the escrow agent and the seller for conversion, claiming that the escrow agent had wrongfully refused to return the earnest money in accordance with the contract. The escrow agent responded by interpleading the earnest money into the registry of the court asserting that it was "in great doubt" as to whether the buyers or sellers were entitled to the funds.

---

260   O.C.G.A. § 9-11-22.
261   Panfel v. Boyd, 187 Ga. App. 639, 371 S.E.2d 222 (1988); Callahan v. Panfel, 195 Ga.App. 891, 395 S.E.2d 80 (1990).

After the interpleader was filed, the trial court and the parties agreed to have the earnest money returned to the buyers. The trial court also denied the buyers' claim against the escrow agent for wrongfully refusing to return the escrow before litigation ensued and judgment was entered in favor of the escrow agent on that issue. The buyers appealed the trial court's ruling on that issue, claiming they should be entitled to money damages from the escrow agent for all their expenses, costs, and attorney's fees in trying to get their earnest money back. The Court of Appeals agreed with the buyers and held that the escrow agent should not have been entitled to interplead the money in order to withhold the disposition of the funds, because the terms of the contract were clear. The Court of Appeals then returned the case to the trial court for a determination of the amount of damages the buyers were entitled to recover. The jury ultimately found against the escrow agent for general damages, punitive damages, and litigation expenses. Then, the escrow agent appealed the jury award. The Court of Appeals concluded that evidence of the buyer's litigation expenses and attorney's fees could be heard by the jury because the escrow agent had no basis for withholding the earnest money in the first place (since the contract terms were clear). Additionally, the Court authorized punitive damages and general damages even though the earnest money had been refunded with interest.

The case discussed above is different from a situation in which the broker gives the earnest money to a third party when there is a legitimate issue as to whether the earnest money is an unenforceable penalty. For example, the Court in one case had to decide on a dispute over the allocation of earnest money where the seller sought, among other things, an award of punitive damages for breach of fiduciary duty, fraud, and conversion as a result of the escrow agent's refusal to agree to an unconditional release of the escrowed funds on seller's demand.[262] In this case, there were questions about the enforceability of the liquidated damages provision in the contract and the court ultimately concluded that punitive damages against the broker as escrow agent were not appropriate.

§3.7.6.4   *Practical advice on when to interplead or disburse*

While the courts in Georgia have clearly stated that it is inappropriate to interplead earnest money when there is no bona fide dispute between the parties, this does not mean that the real estate broker must sit as a judge and jury in all cases of disputed earnest money. Instead, the courts merely require that there be a bona fide dispute before an interpleader action is brought. A bona fide dispute is more than a dispute where both sides claim the funds. To be a bona fide dispute, there must be some legitimate question of fact or law, which makes it unclear to whom the earnest money should rightfully be disbursed. A bona fide dispute is illustrated in a case where the contract was unclear as to when the Holder can disburse the earnest money, as illustrated in the recent case of Ali v. Aarabi.[263] In this case, the buyer

---

262   Fickling & Walker Co. v. Giddens Constr. Co., Inc., 258 Ga. 891, 376 S.E.2d 655 (1989).

263   Ali v. Aarabi, 264 Ga. App. 64, 589 S.E.2d 827 (2003)

had paid $5,000 earnest money to the broker as required under the contract. Subsequently, the buyer paid the seller an additional $60,000 earnest money to buy more time to complete an environmental report that the lender required before it would provide financing.

The contract provided that the $5,000 earnest money be refunded "upon the failure of any contingency or failure of either party to fulfill its obligations as set forth in this Agreement". When the buyer paid the $60,000 to the seller, the parties agreed in an addendum that the $60,000 is non-refundable except if the property becomes irreparably damaged and that the earnest money provisions in the original contract 1) shall remain in full force and effect and 2) apply to both broker and seller. The environmental report was unsatisfactory and the lender refused to finance the purchase. The buyer requested the refund of the earnest money on the basis of a failure in the financing contingency. The seller objected, presumably on the basis that he was entitled to keep the earnest money unless the property was destroyed.

Since the language of the contact was uncertain, the court stated that it was necessary to look at the agreement between the buyer and the seller as a whole to ascertain the intention of the parties. The contract stated that the earnest money could be disbursed only at 1) closing; 2) upon written agreement signed by all parties having an interest in the funds; 3) upon court order; 4) upon the failure of any contingency or failure of either party to fulfill its obligations under the contract; and 5) as otherwise may have been provided in the contract. Further, in the event of a dispute, the broker was authorized to disburse the earnest money based upon a reasonable interpretation of the contract, or, in the alternative, could interplead the disputed sum into the court.

The contract between the parties also contained a default provision stating that if the transaction did not close due to the buyer's default, the seller could retain the earnest money and vice versa. Further, the seller warranted in the contract that the subject property was not used for the handling, storage or disposal of toxic chemicals creating an environmental hazard. Lastly, the purchaser's obligation to purchase the subject property was subject to an inspection of the property and the ability of the purchaser to obtain financing.

Taking these contractual provisions into consideration, the court held that the buyer did not waive, amend or modify the financing or the inspection contingencies provided in the original contract. These contingencies were required to be satisfied as a condition precedent to the contract, and the earnest money was nonrefundable only if these contingencies were met. Since the buyer could not obtain financing due to the environmental conditions revealed through an inspection of the property, these contingencies were not met. The buyer was therefore entitled to a refund of the earnest money. The lesson in this case is to make the intention of the parties absolutely clear in the contract.

As a further example, a bona fide dispute would not exist in a situation where the buyer has been legitimately declined for a loan and the contract contains a loan contingency. If the seller wants the earnest money simply because she is angry that her house has been off the market, the Holder should disburse the money to the buyer upon a reasonable interpretation of the contract.. However, if there is an issue about whether the buyer was declined for a loan because she failed to provide all necessary information to the lender, a factual question arises which could justify an interpleader action. Similarly, if the loan contingency fails because the buyer cannot obtain a loan with a 7% fixed interest rate and the buyer rejects the seller's offer to pay the amount necessary to buy the loan down to 7%, a question might arise as to whether the seller's offer to buy down the interest rate was legal. Such a question might justify interpleading disputed earnest money.

The Holder should take a close look at the whole contract and not rely solely on the earnest money provision when considering whether to file an interpleader action. In one case, the earnest money provision stated that "disbursement of earnest money held by Holder, escrow agent, can occur only as follows…upon failure of any contingency or failure by either party to fulfill his obligations contained in this Agreement".[264] The contract was contingent upon the buyer's ability to obtain a 75% mortgage loan. The buyers did not even apply for a loan and had clearly breached the contract. Since the buyer was clearly in breach, the Holder had correctly disbursed the $50,000 earnest money to the seller. The buyer then sued the seller for the $50,000 and the seller counterclaimed against the buyer for lost profits.

However, the brokerage provision of the contract stated: "…Buyer shall forthwith pay Broker the full commission immediately; provided that Broker may apply one-half of the earnest money toward payment of, but not to exceed, the full commission and *may pay the balance thereof to Seller as liquidated damages to Seller, if Seller claims balance as Seller's liquidated damages in full settlement of any claim for damages* [Emphasis added]". The Court held that since the seller had accepted the $50,000 as liquidated damages, it precluded the seller from seeking additional liquidated damages. However, if the seller had wanted the earnest money but made it clear to the Holder that he was unwilling to accept the funds as liquidated damages, the Holder should file an interpleader action.

§3.7.7   Broker's entitlement to earnest money as commission

Georgia law provides that a broker is not entitled to any part of the earnest money or other money paid to the broker in connection with any real estate transaction as part or all of the broker's commission or fee until the transaction has been consummated or terminated.[265] Once the transaction has been consummated or terminated, the contract will determine the broker's entitlement to the earnest money. Otherwise, the

---

264   Hawkins et al. v. GMAC Mortgage Corporation, 241 Ga. App. 234, 526 S.E.2d 421 (1999).

265   O.C.G.A. § 43-40-20(e).

Georgia Real Estate Commission prohibits a broker from taking any part or all of the earnest money as commission or a fee unless the broker has secured a written agreement to such an arrangement that is separate from the sales contract and signed by all parties having an interest in the transaction.[266]

Earlier versions of the GAR Contract provided that the Holder had the right to apply one-half of the earnest money to the payment of the broker's commission.[267] However, newer versions of the GAR Contract eliminate the broker's entitlement to any portion of the earnest money as commission. The rationale for this change is that if the broker is to serve in a disinterested role as escrow agent, removing the broker's interest in the escrow money will better ensure that the broker holding earnest money is not accused of disbursing the earnest money for financial gain

§3.7.8 Parties to contract cannot sue Holder for damages

The GAR Contract provides that all parties agree to indemnify the Holder against all claims, causes of action, suits and damages arising out of or related to the performance of the Holder's duties under the earnest money paragraph.[268] This sentence protects the Holder from claims made against her for actions she performs in accordance with the contract. However, it does not protect a Holder from claims against her for failing to perform in accordance with the express terms of the contract.

Also, a broker who disburses trust funds from the broker's designated trust or escrow account contrary to the terms of a contract for the sale or rental of real estate, or other contract creating the escrow, or who fails to disburse trust funds according to the terms of any contract creating the escrow, will be considered by the Georgia Real Estate Commission to have demonstrated incompetence to act as a real estate broker in such manner as to safeguard the interest of the public.[269]

§3.8 Application of earnest money when contract breached

If a buyer breaches a real estate sales contract, the existence of an earnest money provision in the contract will have one of three effects: (a) the money may be considered partial payment of any actual damages incurred by the seller if it can be proven that such damages resulted from buyer's breach; (b) the money can be applied as part payment of the purchase price of the property in a lawsuit against the buyer for specific performance of the contract; or (c) the money may be considered liquidated damages[270] for buyer's breach of the contract. However, under Georgia law, a

---

266 Georgia Real Estate Commission Rule 520-1.08(3)(d)4
267 GAR Purchase and Sale Agreement, paragraph 3 (1995 Printing).
268 GAR Contract, paragraph 3.
269 Georgia Real Estate Commission Rule 520-1.08(3)(a)
270 A liquidated damages provision in a real estate contract is a specific sum of money that has been stipulated by the parties as the amount of damages to be suffered by either party for a breach of the contract.

provision for earnest money cannot be used for all three results.[271] The effect of the earnest money will depend on the language used in the contract and the intent of the parties.[272]

As discussed below, the GAR Contract provides that if the buyer is in default the Holder may pay the earnest money to the seller by check. If the seller accepts the check then the funds are deemed to be liquidated damages in full settlement of all claims.[273] Accordingly, if the seller wants to be able to pursue additional claims against the buyer, the seller should reject the tender of an earnest money check from the Holder.

§3.8.1   Partial payment of actual damages

If a buyer breaches the real estate sales contract, courts will look to the terms of the contract to determine how the earnest money should be applied. If the contract limits a seller's damages to the earnest money and if the seller does not terminate the contract because of the buyer's breach, the seller's recovery will be limited to the amount of the earnest money, even though the seller may have incurred additional expenses in preparing to sell the property.[274] Alternatively, if the contract does not expressly limit the seller's remedy to the earnest money as liquidated damages, the seller may terminate the contract and sue the buyer for any actual damages incurred by the seller.[275]

§3.8.2   Partial payment in suit for specific performance

Unless the contract limits the seller's recovery to the earnest money as liquidated damages, the seller may forego money damages and seek specific performance of the contract. In seeking specific performance, the seller asks the court to require that the buyer purchase the property. Even if the contract does not expressly say that the seller can seek specific performance, case law holds that a seller may seek this general remedy for a breach of contract.[276] In one case, the Court concluded that the following language did not prevent the seller from seeking specific performance of the contract: "If said sale is not consummated because of Purchaser's default, then the Seller shall be entitled to retain the Purchaser's earnest money for liquidated damages of such default by the Purchaser."[277]

---

271   Southeastern Land Fund, Inc. v. Real Estate World, Inc., 237 Ga. 227, 227 S.E.2d 340 (1976).

272   Everett Associates v. Gardner, 162 Ga. App. 513, 291 S.E.2d 120 (1982).

273   GAR Contract, paragraph 3.

274   New York Ins. Co. v. Willett, 183 Ga. App. 767, 360 S.E.2d 37 (1987).

275   New York Ins. Co. v. Willett, 183 Ga. App. 767, 360 S.E.2d 37 (1987).

276   Laseter v. Brown, 251 Ga. 179, 304 S.E. 2d 72 (1983); Southeastern Land Fund, Inc. v. Real Estate World, Inc., 237 Ga. 227, 227 S.E.2d 340 (1976).

277   Laseter v. Brown, 251 Ga. 179, 304 S.E.2d 72 (1983).

The GAR Contract provides that if the buyer breaches the obligations or warranties under the contract, the Holder may pay the earnest money to the seller by check. If the seller accepts and deposits the check, the seller accepts the earnest money as liquidated damages and waives all other claims.[278] Therefore, under the GAR Contract, the seller will not be entitled to specific performance if the earnest money is accepted.

A GAR special stipulation addresses earnest money as liquidated damages.[279] Under this special stipulation, the parties agree that in the event of buyer's breach, the seller may claim the earnest money as liquidated damages. However, this special stipulation also allows the seller to proceed with an action for actual damages or specific performance in lieu of liquidated damages. If the parties want to limit remedies, the following special stipulations can be used:

Special Stipulation #3-4: Seller's damages limited to earnest money as liquidated damages

Notwithstanding any provision to the contrary contained herein, Buyer and Seller hereby agree that in the event of Buyer's breach of this Agreement, Seller's sole remedy shall be receipt of the earnest money as liquidated damages, which is a reasonable estimate of the probable loss, and that Seller shall not be entitled to actual damages or specific performance.

Special Stipulation #3-5: Buyer and seller agree not to seek specific performance or actual damages

Notwithstanding any provision to the contrary contained herein, Buyer and Seller hereby agree that in the event of a breach of this Agreement by either party, Seller's sole remedy shall be receipt of the earnest money as liquidated damages, which is a reasonable estimate of probable loss and Buyer's sole remedy will be a refund of the full earnest money. Seller and Buyer agree that neither party shall seek any action for specific performance or for actual damages.

§3.8.3   Earnest money designated as liquidated damages cannot be penalty

Courts will not allow a seller to keep earnest money as liquidated damages for a buyer's breach of a real estate contract if the buyer can show that doing so would be a penalty. The distinction between an enforceable liquidated damages provision and an unenforceable penalty can be slight and, in many cases, there will be no clear answer. The courts have, however, repeatedly cited a three-part test for the enforceability of liquidated damages. First, the injury caused by the breach must be difficult or

---

278   GAR Contract, paragraph 3B2.
279   GAR Form SS 43.

impossible to accurately estimate. Second, the parties must intend to provide for damages rather than for a penalty. Third, the sum stipulated as liquidated damages must be a reasonable pre-estimate of the probable loss.[280]

The courts will look at the facts, the contract, and the intent of the parties in determining whether the liquidated damages provision is enforceable. In one case, the Court reviewed whether a $10,000.00 earnest money payment on a contract of sale for a $111,000.00 condominium unit was intended as liquidated damages in the event of the buyer's default. The buyer argued that $10,000.00 was a penalty and since such penalties are not enforceable, recovery should be limited to the seller's actual damages shown. The court noted that it must decide if the injury caused by the breach is difficult or impossible to accurately determine, if the parties intend to provide for damages rather than a penalty, and whether the sum stipulated is a reasonable pre-estimate of the probable loss. In that case, the Court concluded that the amount of earnest money demanded was a reasonable pre-estimate of the probable loss, especially in light of the seller's uncertainty of the real estate market in the early 1980's and staggered payments called for in the earnest money provision.[281]

On the other hand, the court in another case reviewed the payment of $50,000.00 as earnest money on an $800,000.00 purchase price. In correspondence, the president of the realty company had set out revised terms of payment and added that they would deposit the $50,000.00 non-refundable earnest money with the escrow agent which would apply in full against the purchase price. When the parties failed to close, the buyer demanded return of the earnest money. In testimony before the Court, the real estate agent testified that, "the $50,000 figure bore no relation to estimated damages; rather it was an arbitrary number--high enough to insure that the buyer would go through with the deal."[282] The Court concluded that at least two of the three factors required for a finding of liquidated damages were missing: the intention to provide for damages and the estimate of the probable loss. Therefore, the non-refundable earnest money was found to be an unreasonable and unenforceable penalty.[283]

Generally, the label the parties place on the payment does not determine whether the liquidated damages are an unreasonable penalty.[284] However in one case, the Court concluded that use of the term "forfeited" in the addendum to the sales contract showed an intent of the parties to impose an unenforceable penalty rather than a reasonable pre-estimate of the seller's probable loss should the buyer fail to close the

---

280   Southeastern Land Fund, Inc. v. Real Estate World, Inc., 237 Ga. 227, 227 S.E.2d 340 (1976); citing Calamari & Perillo, The Law of Contracts, 367 (1970).
281   Everett Associates v. Garner, 162 Ga. App. 513, 291 S.E.2d 120 (1982).
282   Budget-Luxury Inn of Dayton, Ltd. v. Kamash Enterprises, Inc., 194 Ga. App. 375, 390 S.E.2d 607 (1990).
283   Budget-Luxury Inn of Dayton, Ltd. v. Kamash Enterprises, Inc., 194 Ga. App. 375, 390 S.E.2d 607 (1990).
284   Martin v. Lott, 144 Ga. 660, 87 S.E. 902 (1916).

transaction. Therefore, the seller was not entitled to the earnest money as liquidated damages.[285] While there is no "magic" number that will ensure that a certain sum will be found to be valid liquidated damages rather than a penalty, the Georgia Supreme Court in one case appears to have indicated that a liquidated damages clause in the amount of ten percent (10%) of the purchase price is per se reasonable.[286]

§3.9   Deductions from earnest money

In some instances, the seller and buyer may agree that the seller can use part of the earnest money paid for the buyer's benefit. For example, in one case, the parties agreed that the seller would use the earnest money to prepare plans for building a home. The seller drew two sets of plans at the request of the buyer. The seller was also contractually obligated to initiate the loan process. When the loan process was not timely initiated, the buyers demanded return of their full earnest money. The Court concluded that even though the seller breached the contract, the seller was entitled to retain the amounts that were spent for the buyer's benefit (i.e., the expense of preparing the plans) with the balance refunded to the buyers.[287] If the parties agree that the seller will use a portion of the earnest money to do work expressly authorized for and benefiting the buyer, the following language can be used:

Special Stipulation #3-6: Seller may deduct from earnest money amount spent on work done for buyer's benefit

If the sale is not consummated for reasons other than the default of Buyer, the total amount of earnest money paid to Holder, less amounts as may be expended on Buyer's request and for Buyer's benefit and account, shall be returned to Buyer.

Of course, the risk to the buyer of having difficulty in obtaining a refund of earnest money in the event of seller's breach may be greater if the seller, rather than a third party, holds the earnest money. Therefore, a broker may want to include the following language in a real estate sales contract if the seller will be holding the earnest money:

---

285   Fickling & Walker Co. v. Giddens Constr. Co., Inc., 258 Ga. 891, 376 S.E.2d 665 (1989). The addendum to the contract read as follows: "It is expressly understood and agreed to by all parties that, if for any reason this sale is not consummated by November 30, 1985, the $1,000 earnest money and the $400 security deposit shall be forfeited as liquidated damages and the sale contract shall become null and void."
286   Oran v. Canada Life Assur. Co., 194 Ga. App. 518, 390 S.E.2d 879 (1990).
287   Jeff Goolsby Homes Corp. v. Smith, 168 Ga. App. 218, 308 S.E.2d 564 (1983).

Special Stipulation #3-7: Buyer's acknowledgement of risk in seller holding earnest money

Buyer recognizes and accepts the risk of depositing earnest money with Seller. Buyer acknowledges that he has not relied upon the advice of Broker or Broker's Affiliated Licensees in deciding to pay such earnest money to Seller.[288]

§3.10   Disbursement of earnest money if contract void

If a determination is made that a contract is void, the prospective buyer will be entitled to a return of the earnest money. In one case, a real estate contract included a special stipulation stating that the contract was conditioned upon getting the property rezoned.[289]   The contract was silent as to whose duty it was to have the property rezoned. The Court refused to enforce the contract on such vague terms and concluded that since the contract was void for vagueness, it required that the buyer's earnest money be returned. The same principle should apply to any contract ultimately determined to be unenforceable.

§3.11   Making earnest money non-refundable in a contingent contract

Most real estate sales contracts contain contingencies. When a real estate sales contract is subject to a contingency, it means that the condition must be satisfied before the contract is becomes enforceable.[290]   In other words, the condition must be met before the parties are bound to carry out their obligation to buy and sell the property. [291] Therefore, if earnest money had been paid in respect of a sale that is contingent upon a condition being fulfilled, and the condition is not met, the earnest money must be refunded in full unless the sale contract has provided otherwise.

However, if a contract contains a contingency, it does not mean that a party to the contract is not bound until the contingency is removed or is fulfilled. The Georgia Court of Appeals has stated that a contingency does not defeat the existence of a valid contract.[292]   Therefore, every party to a contract has an implied duty to act in good faith and fair dealing in performing his or her obligation.[293] For example, the seller cannot rescind the contract during the contingency period to sell the property to a third party who has offered a higher price. The Georgia Court of Appeals stated:

"...many real estate contracts contain...financing conditions. If a vendor could successfully utilize this contract term (which is unquestionably for the

---

288   See GAR Form F80, Earnest Money Held by Seller for more complete disclaimer.
289   Hit v. Lord, 194 Ga. App. 655, 391 S.E.2d 681 (1990).
290   D. Parker et al. v. R.L. Averett, 114 Ga. App. 401, 151 S.E. 2d 475 (1966).
291   Grier V. Brogdon, 234 Ga. App. 79, 505 S.E. 2d 512 (1998)
292   Grier V. Brogdon, 234 Ga. App. 79, 505 S.E. 2d 512 (1998)
293   Patel v. Burt Development Company, 261 Ga. App. 436, 582 S.E.2d 495 (2003)

buyer's protection) to rescind the contract at any time prior to the occurrence of the condition (presumably whenever the vendor received a better offer), a purchaser would never be able to rely on the contract while he sought financing. Any vendor could rescind such a contract with impunity. This result would be intolerable and would destroy the good faith reliance among individuals which permits them to act in accordance with their agreements."[294]

Likewise, when the contract is subject to a financing contingency, the buyer has a duty to seek financing diligently.

§3.12 Brokerage company not liable for agent's misrepresentations with regard to earnest money

The general practice in Georgia is that real estate licensees are independent contractors and not employees of the real estate brokerage firms for which they work. The Court has upheld the independent contractor relationship between the broker and the licensee.[295] This should be the case so long as the broker does not attempt to control the licensee's time, manner, or method of work but merely instructs the agent as to the desired outcome (i.e., obtain listings and/or purchasers, etc.).

As an independent contractor, the broker and his or her real estate company cannot be held liable for the tortious acts of the licensee unless the broker takes an active role in the wrongful act or subsequently affirms the licensee's misdeed. In one case, the Court reviewed a situation in which the real estate licensee falsely represented that he had received an earnest money check from the prospective buyer.[296] The seller continued with the contract, thereby keeping the property off the market and causing the seller harm when the transaction did not close. Because the seller did not have the earnest money as liquidated damages, the seller sued the real estate company as well as the agent. The Court concluded that the realty company was not responsible for the tortious acts of its independent contractor affiliated licensee.

In at least one reported case, however, the broker went too far and was found to have created an employer/employee relationship with the licensee.[297] In this case the Court described what it found to be the "more typical business arrangement" between a broker and agent as one in which the agent "clearly occupies the position of an independent contractor". In such "typical" situations, "great care is taken by the [broker] to refrain from exercising control over the manner in which individual salespersons conduct their work. No particular working hours are set. The salespersons exercise personal initiative to obtain "listings," or the opportunity to sell existing houses, from individual owners. Duties that could be considered "control" by

---

294   Brack et al. v. Brownlee et al., 246 Ga. 818, 273 S.E. 2d 390 (1980).
295   Ross v. Ninety-Two West, Ltd., 201 Ga. App. 887, 412 S.E.2d 876 (1991).
296   Ross v. Ninety-Two West, Ltd., 201 Ga. App. 887, 412 S.E.2d 876 (1991).
297   Mark Six Realty Associates, Inc. v. Drake, 219 Ga.App. 57, 463 S.E.2d 917 (1995)

the [broker], such as attending sales meetings or assisting in the broker's office, are clearly designated as "optional." Items such as form contracts, telephones, and office supplies are either paid for by the salesperson or provided as a convenience with no requirement that they be used."

In this case, however, "evidence was presented that [the agent] was by no means a 'typical' real estate salesperson". The agent was assigned by the broker to work in a new home subdivision as her sole and exclusive employment during certain specified business hours or "staff duty schedule." She was required to be "on duty" during these hours. She was required to use certain procedures when negotiating the sale of a lot in the subdivision. She was required to use standard forms. The agent was also subject to quarterly performance reviews. In light of the nature and degree of these controls, the Court found that there was a true employer/employee relationship. As such, the Court found that the broker could be liable for the wrongful acts of her employee.

§3.13   Law against money laundering

Federal and state law requires financial institutions and other money service businesses to report transactions exceeding $10,000.00 and transactions deemed suspicious for any reason. The law also prohibits any party from structuring a transaction where the transaction is divided into two or more transactions, which if considered as a whole, would be reportable.[298] Under federal law, property that is involved in a transaction or attempted transaction or offense in violation of the money laundering statutes is subject to forfeiture to the government.[299]

For example, the Court ordered forfeiture in one case where the mortgage on the property had been paid by checks drawn on 3 accounts funded by 33 cash deposits, each in an amount less than $10,000 and made over a period of 2 days in 3 financial institutions.[300] The federal government argued that the property was involved in, facilitated, or represented proceeds of deposits structured to avoid the currency reporting requirements.

In another case, the Court found that the property was involved in a transaction or attempted transaction in violation of federal reporting and structuring law when the $95,000 down payment on the property was made by way of 10 cashier's checks ranging in amount from $7,500 to $10,000, and where the checks were obtained on 5 different dates and from 5 different banks. The Court noted that the owners failed to prove that the property was not involved in the structuring or other violations.[301]

---

298   31 U.S.C.A. § 5313(a), 31 U.S.C.A. § 5324(a) and O.C.G.A. § 7-1-912
299   18 U.S.C.A. §981(a)(1) and §982(a)(1)
300   United States v 5709 Hillingdon Rd. (1996, WD NC); 919 F Supp 863
301   United States v 874 Gartel Drive (1996, CA9 Cal) 79 F3d 918, 96 CDOS (1945)

CHAPTER 4
CLOSING AND POSSESSION

OVERVIEW

This chapter discusses the closing and the transfer of possession of the property to the buyer. Among the issues which are addressed include how closings work generally, who pays for various charges at closing such as transfer tax and intangible tax, how items like property taxes are prorated, under what circumstances the closing date may be extended and what happens when one party fails to close as required under the contract.

This chapter also discusses issues regarding possession of the property, such as buyers moving in early and sellers and tenants remaining in possession after closing. An explanation of what happens if the property is destroyed or damaged after the contract has been signed but prior to closing is also included.

§ 4.1   Closings generally

§ 4.1.1   Only attorneys can conduct closings

The closing of the sale of property in Georgia consists of the conveyance of title to the property from the seller to the buyer and payment of the purchase price for the property by the buyer to the seller. In Georgia, unlike some other states, only an attorney can conduct a closing of a real estate purchase and sale transaction.

The Georgia Supreme Court recently confirmed that anyone other than a Georgia licensed attorney who prepares or executes a deed of conveyance on behalf of another, or facilitates its signing is engaged in the unauthorized practice of law.[302] The Court stated, "we have consistently held that it is the unauthorized practice of law for someone other than a duly-licensed Georgia attorney to close a real estate transaction or to prepare or facilitate the execution of such deed(s) for the benefit of a seller, borrower or lender." This confirms the approach taken in an earlier opinion, where the Court stated, "it would be ethically improper for a lawyer to aid non-lawyers to 'close real estate transactions' or for a lawyer to delegate to a non-lawyer the responsibility to close the real estate transaction without the participation of the attorney."[303]

The Court's reasoning is that the public is best protected when such work is limited to attorneys. Unlike a purely commercial enterprise, attorneys are trained to protect the rights of the party they represent. Further, attorneys are held accountable through a malpractice or bar disciplinary action. Therefore, anyone other than an attorney licensed in Georgia who conducts any real estate closings, which include real estate transaction loan closings and "witness-only" closings, is engaging in the unauthorized practice of law and may be guilty of a misdemeanor. The punishment

---

302   Advisory Opinion 2003-2, No. S03U1451, Nov. 10, 2003 (2003 WL 22533156)
303   Formal Advisory Opinion 86-5

extends to every officer, trustee, director, agent, or employee of a corporation or voluntary association who directly or indirectly engages in the unauthorized practice of law. [304]

§ 4.1.2   Closing process

The closing is the final step in buying or selling property. It is during a closing when the seller signs the deed transferring title to the property and affidavits required for title purposes. If the buyer obtains a loan, it is also the time when the buyer will sign the promissory note, deed to secure debt, and other lender-required documents.

All costs and prorations provided for under the contract will be stated on a settlement or closing statement, using a form specified by the Department of Housing and Urban Development and often called a "HUD-1." This form has separate columns for the buyer and seller and itemizes each cost or credit showing the amount owed by the buyer and the net proceeds to be paid to the seller.

The closing attorney deposits the funds from the purchaser and the loan funds into the law firm's escrow account and disburses checks from the escrow account to pay all the costs of the closing, including the net proceeds check to the seller and the commission to the real estate brokers. All special stipulations and other contract obligations should be fulfilled at the closing, unless the contract terms provide for a later date of completion.

§ 4.2   Property condition

§ 4.2.1   Risk of property loss before closing on buyer

The general rule of law in Georgia is that before the seller conveys title to the buyer, the risk of loss falls upon the buyer if a substantial part of the property is destroyed and neither party is at fault. However, the seller and buyer must have entered into a binding contract and the seller must be willing and able to consummate the sale.[305]

This rule, established in England in 1801, is based on the principle that the buyer is, in fact and substance, the effective owner of the property (if the seller is prepared to convey clear title and is not in default) and the seller retains only the legal title to the property during the contract period in order to secure the purchase money. The exception to the general rule is when the parties agree that the seller will bear the risk of loss.

---

304   O.C.G.A. § 15-19-56
305   Bleckley v. Langston, 112 Ga. App. 63, 143 S.E.2d 671 (1965); Phillips et al. v Bacon et al., 245 Ga. 814, 267 S.E.2d 249 (1980).

§ 4.2.2 Contract provisions alter general rule on risk of loss

The GAR Contract provides that if the property is destroyed or substantially damaged prior to closing, the seller must promptly notify the buyer of the amount of any insurance proceeds available to repair the damage.[306] The GAR Contract also provides that either the buyer or the seller may terminate the contract by giving written notice to the other party not later than fourteen days from the seller's notice regarding the insurance proceeds. Under older versions of the GAR Contract, if the buyer or seller did not terminate the contract, the buyer received at closing the insurance proceeds which had not been spent to repair the damage. However, this provision was somewhat problematic for buyers because few mortgage lenders will lend money on seriously damaged property until the damage had been fixed.

Therefore, the new GAR Contract provides that if neither the seller nor the buyer chooses to terminate the contract, the seller then has up to one year to restore the property to substantially the same condition it was in at the binding agreement date. The new closing date will then be the earlier of one (1) year from the original closing date or seven days from the date the property is restated to substantially the same condition as on the Binding Agreement Date, and if required, a new certificate of occupancy is issued.

Most preprinted form contracts include a provision to relieve the buyer of the obligation to purchase the property when the improvements thereon have been substantially destroyed. The reason for shifting the risk of loss to the seller is illustrated by a case decided by the Georgia Court of Appeals.[307] A buyer entered into a contract with a seller for the sale of property for $120,000.00, which property included pecan trees. The contract did not contain any language shifting the risk of loss to the seller. An ice storm damaged all the pecan trees, and the fair market value of the property decreased by at least $32,000.00. The buyer sought to terminate the contract, and a lawsuit was filed. The court concluded that under the general rule, the contract could not be terminated and the risk of the loss fell on the buyer.

The GAR Contract does not define how much damage is necessary before the property "has been destroyed or substantially damaged." In all cases, this question is one of fact, and the outcome will vary from case to case. Examples of the factors a court will consider in deciding whether property has been destroyed or substantially damaged include the condition of any improvements to the property before and after the loss[308] and any change in the fair market value of the property.[309]

---

306   GAR Form F20, para. 4A.
307   Bleckley v. Langston, 112 Ga. App. 63, 143 S.E.2d 671 (1965).
308   Bruce v. Jennings, 190 Ga. 618, 10 S.E.2d 56 (1940).
309   Bleckley v. Langston, 112 Ga. App. 63, 143 S.E.2d 671 (1965).

§ 4.2.3   Property condition at closing to be same as at Binding Agreement
             Date

The GAR Contract provides that the property will be in the same condition on the date of closing as on the Binding Agreement Date except for normal wear and tear and items the seller has agreed to repair. This means that the seller would be responsible for any changes to the condition of the property, except for changes due to normal wear and tear. For example, if the dishwasher is broken on the Binding Agreement Date and the buyer does not request its repair during the inspection period, the buyer cannot complain about its broken condition at a later time. An alternative approach is for the buyer to request that the seller affirmatively warrant that specific appliances and/or systems in the property will be in good working order and repair as of the date of closing (regardless of their previous condition) An example of such a special stipulation is as follows:

Special Stipulation #4-1: Seller warrants that appliances and systems will be in good working order on date of closing

Seller warrants that all appliances remaining with the Property and all portions of the heating and air conditioning, plumbing and electrical systems will be in good working order and repair as of the date of closing.

§ 4.2.3.1   Property being in same condition includes conditions revealed in Seller's Property Disclosure Statement

The seller's warranty that at the time of closing or upon the granting of possession if at a time other than at closing the property will be in substantially the same condition as on the Binding Agreement Date includes conditions revealed by the seller in the Seller's Property Disclosure Statement. For example, let's say a seller discloses in his Seller's Property Disclosure Statement that a portion of his property periodically floods during periods of heavy rain. If the property did not flood on the Binding Agreement Date, but flooded on the date of closing, this provision means that the buyer could not avoid his contractual obligations to close by arguing that the condition of the property had changed because the condition was revealed in the Seller's Property Disclosure Statement.

§ 4.2.3.2   What is normal wear and tear

"Normal wear and tear" is also often referred to as "ordinary wear and tear", "fair wear and tear" or "reasonable wear and tear". Legally, 'normal wear' means the deterioration caused by the reasonable use of the property. It does not include damage caused by negligence, carelessness, accident, or abuse.[310] It means the deterioration caused by the ordinary operation of natural forces.[311] Normal

---

310   By analogy to Landlord and Tenant law, O.C.G.A. § 44-7-34.
311   Blacks Law Dictionary 8th edition (2004)

wear and tear also includes what are commonly referred to as "Acts of God". Georgia statute defines acts of God to mean accidents produced by physical causes which are irresistible or inevitable, such as lightning, storms, perils of the sea, earthquakes, inundations, sudden death, or illness, but excludes all causes due by human intervention.[312] Therefore, if a tree limb fell on the house because of strong winds during a storm between the time of contract and closing, the damage would qualify as normal wear and tear because the cause was a natural force and the buyer would have to bear the loss.

If the tree limb fell on the house because it was diseased, and the seller knew or should have known about the condition of the tree, the seller would be negligent in not treating the tree. Since fair wear does not include damage caused by negligence, the seller would be responsible for the damage to the house. The seller may also be responsible if the tree had dangerous characteristics (the species is known to have weak limbs) or if the danger was visible and apparent and the seller did not take any steps to remove the danger.

It is unclear, however, whether the seller would have to repair damage not due to the seller's negligence, carelessness, accident, or abuse. Assume, for example, that prior to the closing but after the inspection contingency has lapsed, the dishwasher breaks, or the hot water heater springs a leak, or a leak develops in the roof. With each of these items, the seller can argue that he is not responsible for making repairs because the damage was not caused by his negligence, carelessness, accident, or abuse and therefore falls within the exception for normal wear and tear.

The problem with the result is that it flies in the face of the expectation of many buyers that the seller will maintain the property right up until the day of closing. The buyer can initially argue that the landlord-tenant definition of "wear and tear" is inapplicable. Additionally, the buyer can argue that, in any event, that definition is not exclusive of the term "wear and tear" and can be interpreted more narrowly to limit the applicability to the normal changes in the condition of the property one would reasonably expect, even when all routine maintenance is being performed (e.g., an occasional nick or scratch). Under such an interpretation, the seller would be obligated to make all reasonable repairs to the property up until closing that one would expect to see if the seller were remaining in the property.

There is some case support for the notion that courts are not limited by the statutory definition.[313] The law remains unclear in this area, however, and arguments can be made both ways with regard to the seller's duties. The best solution for concerned buyers is to add a special stipulation to the contract to impose a duty upon the seller to make repairs up until closing:

---

312   O.C.G.A. § 1-3-3
313   Fincher v. Bergeron, 193 Ga. App. 256, 387 S.E.2d 371 (1989), cert. denied.

Special Stipulation #4-2: Seller shall repair defects until closing

Notwithstanding any provision to the contrary contained herein, Seller shall be obligated during the time period commencing with the Binding Agreement Date and ending with the closing, or granting of possession if at a time other than the closing, to repair and/or replace all defects in the Property, regardless of cause, that (1) develop in the Property, including all improvements located thereon and appliances contained therein that are to be transferred to the Buyer and (2) are discovered or should reasonably have been discovered by the Seller during said time period. Such defects shall be repaired and/or replaced by Seller in a good and workmanlike manner prior to closing.

§ 4.2.4   Risk of loss with a "tear-down" home

Some buyers purchase property with the idea of tearing down the existing home and building a new one. In other words, the buyer is purchasing the property for the value of the land. In such cases, the buyer would not want the seller to have the right to terminate the contract in the event the same is destroyed or substantially damaged prior to closing. The buyer would also not want the seller to repair or rebuild a damaged or destroyed property since the destruction of the improvements would likely expedite the process for the buyer of having the existing house torn down. Of course, some agreement would need to be reached as to who would receive any insurance proceeds and whether the seller would be obligated to remove the debris caused from the destruction of the improvements. The special stipulation below is an example of how these issues might be addressed.

Special Stipulation #4-3: Seller not to repair in the event of casualty

Buyer and seller acknowledge that Buyer may tear down or substantially alter the house and other improvements on the Property after closing on the Property. Therefore, Seller shall not have a right under any circumstances to terminate this Agreement in the event the Property (or any improvements located thereon) is destroyed or substantially damaged.

If the Property (or the improvements located thereon) is destroyed or substantially damaged prior to the closing of the Property so as to render the Property uninhabitable (and not capable of being lawfully occupied prior to the date of closing), then Seller agrees not to repair or rebuild the improvements which were destroyed or substantially damaged. Seller shall be entitled to keep all insurance proceeds, if any, received by Seller as a result of the casualty. However, Seller shall be obligated to the extent required by law to promptly remove from the Property, at the sole expense of Seller, all damaged or destroyed improvements and all other trash and debris on the Property resulting from the casualty or the clean-up thereof. Seller shall use its best efforts to complete the removal of the damaged and destroyed property prior to closing or as soon thereafter as is reasonably practicable. The obligation of Seller referenced herein shall specifically survive the closing.

§ 4.3 Taxes, utilities, and homeowners association dues

§ 4.3.1 Proration of property taxes

Since real estate taxes are a lien on property, they must be paid at closing to convey clear title. Although property taxes are assessed on a calendar year basis and are based on the condition of the property on January 1st, they are not billed until later in the year and generally are not due until the third or fourth quarter of the year.

Each city or county in Georgia sets the due date for taxes for property located in its jurisdiction. Because the taxes are assessed for the calendar year, once billed, they become a lien against the property, regardless of the due date. Therefore, once the tax bill is issued, it must be paid at closing in order for the seller to convey clear title to the property. In other words, the seller is responsible for payment of property taxes from January 1 up to the date of closing, and the buyer is responsible for the payment of property taxes from the date of closing through December 31.

The allocation of property taxes between the seller and the buyer will be determined by the contract. Most contracts, including the GAR Contract, provide that the real estate taxes will be prorated as of the date of closing. However, if the closing takes place before the tax bills have been issued, the proration will be based on the prior year's taxes. Most settlement statements provide that the parties agree to account to one another for any differences between what is charged based on an estimate from the previous year's bill and what is actually billed.

For example, if the actual taxes are substantially higher than the estimated amount charged at closing based on the previous year's taxes, the buyer has the right to re-prorate the taxes and seek reimbursement from the seller. Similarly, if the actual taxes are lower than the estimated amount charged at closing based on the previous year's taxes, the seller has the right to re-prorate the taxes and seek reimbursement from the buyer. Further, the buyer may want to request an assignment from the seller of the right to appeal the valuation of the property for taxes since the record owner on January 1st is treated as the owner for tax purposes.

If the buyer knows that property taxes will be based on an estimate and wants to incorporate a provision in the contract to address adjustments when actual bills are issued, the following special stipulation may be used:

Special Stipulation #4-4: Proration of taxes after closing and assignment of right to appeal tax assessments

Buyer and Seller understand that the allocation of ad valorem property taxes is based on last year's actual taxes because the tax bill(s) for the current year have not been issued. If the actual bill is greater or less than the estimated amount allocated at closing, Buyer and Seller agree to prorate the taxes among themselves. Further, Seller does hereby agree to assign to Buyer any rights Seller may have to appeal the tax assessment effective as of the date of closing.

If the seller wants to eliminate responsibility for paying additional funds for taxes, the following special stipulation may be incorporated in the contract:

Special Stipulation #4-5: No further proration of taxes after closing and assignment of right to appeal tax assessments

Buyer and Seller understand that the allocation of taxes is based on last year's actual taxes because the tax bill(s) for the current year have not been issued. Buyer and Seller agree that neither party shall have any obligation to the other in the event that actual taxes are greater or less than paid at closing; provided, however, that Seller agrees to assign any rights Seller may have to Buyer to appeal the tax assessment effective as of the date of closing.

A problem that occasionally arises in the new construction context is when the taxes for the prior year are based upon the unimproved value of the property, but the taxes for the year in which the sale occurs are based upon the improved value of the property. For example, assume that as of January 1, 1999, (the date upon which the property is valued for the 1999 taxes) the property is unimproved and is taxed at a value of $25,000.00. A house is subsequently built on the property and, as a result, the property is valued at $150,000.00 as of January 1, 2000. The property is sold on March 15, 2000. The 2000 tax assessments and bills are not yet available and the 1999 assessment will substantially understate the year 2000 taxes. In this instance the parties may wish to make a "best guess" estimate of what the new taxes will be and set the tax proration accordingly. Additionally, the parties may wish to have funds held in escrow to cover anticipated tax increases.

Special Stipulation #4-6: Proration of taxes after closing with Seller depositing funds into escrow

Buyer and Seller recognize that the ad valorem property taxes for the Property for the year in which this transaction is scheduled to close may not be available as of the Closing Date. The parties agree that in this event the ad valorem taxes will be prorated at closing based upon the prior year's ad valorem taxes and Seller shall deposit the sum $_____ with the closing attorney. The funds shall be held in escrow until such time as the ad valorem *property taxes are available, at which time the funds shall be disbursed based upon the actual tax bill. Any overage shall be paid to the Seller. In the event the escrowed funds are insufficient to pay Seller's prorated portion of the taxes then Seller shall pay any remaining difference to Buyer.*

§ 4.3.2   Selling property during pending tax appeal

A buyer will sometimes contract to purchase property that is subject to a tax appeal. In such cases, the questions, which should be addressed in the contract, are whether the appeal will continue after the property is sold, who will be responsible for handling the appeal and who will receive any tax refund. The following stipulation may be used to address such a situation:

Special Stipulation #4-7: Proration of taxes in a pending tax appeal

Buyer and Seller acknowledge that the Property is currently the subject of an appeal of ad valorem property taxes for the following tax years: _____.

Seller hereby assigns to Buyer upon the closing of the Property all of Seller's right, title and interest in said appeal. Buyer shall have the right to proceed with said appeal either in Buyer's own name or in the name of Seller. Upon the closing of the Property, Seller does hereby authorize Buyer to act as Seller's power of attorney with respect to said appeal.

Upon the closing of the Property, Seller shall have no further responsibility for any ad valorem property taxes on the Property and Buyer does hereby agree to indemnify Seller from and against any and all claims arising out of or relating to the same.

Special Stipulation #4-8: Seller may continue with tax appeal after closing

Buyer and Seller acknowledge that the Property is currently the subject of an appeal of ad valorem property taxes for the following tax years: _____.

Seller shall have the right to continue with the appeal after the closing of the Property and to retain any tax refund resulting therefrom. Seller agrees to be fully responsible for the payment of any additional taxes owing as a result of the appeal for the tax years referenced above and agrees to indemnify and hold Buyer harmless arising out of or relating to the same.

§ 4.3.3   Payment of transfer tax

A real estate transfer tax is not a property tax. It is an excise tax levied by statute on the sale of property for the privilege of selling that particular property and is customarily paid by the seller. Since the seller transfers the property, absent a contract provision to the contrary, the seller will pay the transfer tax. The GAR Contract provides that the seller pays the transfer tax. This is a separate provision unrelated to any agreement regarding closing costs.

The amount of the transfer tax is based on the sales price of the property.[314] Georgia law provides that the transfer tax is calculated as follows:

> $1.00 for the first $1,000.00 or fractional part of $1,000.00 and at the rate of $.10 for each additional $100.00 or fractional part of $100.00 on each deed, instrument, or other writing by which any lands, tenements, or other realty sold is granted, assigned, transferred, or otherwise conveyed to or vested in the purchaser or purchasers, or any other person or persons by his or their direction, when the consideration or value of the interest or property conveyed (exclusive of the value of any lien or encumbrances existing prior to the sale and not removed by the sale) exceeds $100.00.[315]

For example, the transfer tax on property sold for $100,000.00 would be $100.00. However, if the buyer assumed a loan already securing the property in the principal amount of $65,000.00, then the value of the loan is subtracted from the purchase price and the transfer tax owed would be $35.00.

The tax must be paid to the clerk of the superior court of the county where the property is located. The clerk certifies the amount and the date of payment on the face of the recorded deed or other instrument. This tax must be paid as a pre-requisite to recording the deed, and no deed is to be recorded without payment of the transfer tax.

Recording of the following do not require payment of a transfer tax[316]:

(1)   any deed to secure debt;

(2)   any deed of gift;

(3)   any deed, instrument, or other writing to which any of the following is a party: the United States, Georgia, any agency, board, commission, department, or political subdivision of either the United States or Georgia, any public authority, or any nonprofit public corporation;

(4)   any lease of lands, tenements, standing timber, or any realty or any lease of any estate, interest, or usufruct in any of the foregoing;

---

314   City of Columbus v. Ronald A. Edwards Constr. Co., 155 Ga. App. 502, 271 S.E.2d 643 (1980).
315   O.C.G.A. § 48-6-1.
316   O.C.G.A. § 48-6-2.

(5)   any transfer of real estate between husband and wife in connection with a divorce case;

(6)   any order for year's support awarding an interest in real property;

(7)   any deed in lieu of foreclosure for a purchase money deed to secure debt in existence and properly executed and recorded for a period of 12 months;

(8)   any deed from the debtor to the first transferee at a foreclosure sale;

(9)   any transfer of property which is acquired for transportation purposes;

(10)   any deed of assent or distribution by an executor, administrator, guardian, trustee, or custodian or other instrument carrying out the exercise of a power of appointment and any other instrument transferring real estate to affirm a fiduciary (this exemption applies only if the transfer is without valuable consideration); and

(11)   any deed which effects a division of real property among joint tenants or tenants in common if there is no consideration other than the division of the property.

§ 4.3.4   Payment of intangible tax

Georgia law provides that every holder of a long-term note secured by real estate must, within 90 days from the date the instrument is executed, record the security instrument in the county where the property is located and pay an intangible recording tax at the rate of $1.50 for each $500.00 or fraction thereof of the face amount of the note. The maximum amount of any intangible tax payable on a single note is $25,000.00.[317]

A long-term note secured by real estate is defined as any note representing credits secured by mortgages, deeds to secure debt, purchase money deeds to secure debt, bonds of title, or other form of security instrument, when any part of the principal of a note falls due more than three years from the date of the note or from the date of any instrument executed to secure the note and conveying or creating a lien or encumbrance on the real estate.[318] For example, a buyer obtains a 30-year loan evidenced by a note and security deed which will be recorded in the county land records. Since payment is not required in less than three years, intangible tax must be paid upon the recording of the security deed.

---

317   O.C.G.A. § 48-6-61.
318   O.C.G.A. § 48-6-60(3).

A short-term note is defined as a note secured by real estate where the whole of the principal of the note falls due within three years from the date of the note or from the date of any instrument executed to secure the note.[319] For example, a seller grants a short-term loan payable in 30 months to a buyer as evidenced by a note and security deed. Since payment is due within three years, no intangible tax is due upon recording the security deed. This would be true regardless of the number of years over which the payments are amortized. The only factor considered is whether or not the note matures within three years.

As with the transfer tax, payment of the intangible recording tax is a prerequisite to the recording of the security instrument. The collecting official (the tax commissioner or, in counties of 50,000 or more, the clerk of the superior court) must determine the amount of intangible tax owed and collect the tax before the security instrument is recorded.

Georgia law also provides that no intangible tax shall be collected on that part of the face amount of a new instrument securing a long term note secured by real estate which represents a refinancing by the original lender of unpaid principal on a previous instrument securing a long term note if all intangible recording tax due on the previous instrument had been paid or was exempt from intangible recording tax.

As a prerequisite, either the new instrument must contain a statement of what part of its face amount represents a refund of the unpaid principal on the previous instrument or the holder of the new instrument must submit an affidavit identifying what part of the face amount of the new instrument represents a refinancing of unpaid principal on the previous instrument.[320]

For example, if a buyer refinances a 30-year fixed rate $100,000.00 loan with the same lender for a new $100,000.00 loan at a better interest rate, no additional intangible tax would need to be paid, since the new loan is for the same or a lesser principal amount. If the new loan is for $110,000.00, then intangible tax is owed on only the additional $10,000.00 in principal. Note that this only applies when the same lender is involved in both loans.

§ 4.3.5   Water bills, utility bills, and sanitation bills

An unpaid or delinquent water bill is not a lien against the property unless a lien is filed in the county records by the water supplier. However, by statute, a public or private water supplier cannot file a lien for unpaid water bills against property unless the owner is the person who incurred the charges.[321] The same is true for gas, sewer, or electricity.[322]

---

319   O.C.G.A. § 48-6-60(4).
320   O.C.G.A. § 48-6-65(d).
321   O.C.G.A. § 36-60-17(c).
322   O.C.G.A. § 36-60-17(d).

By a law which became effective in April 1994, a water supplier cannot refuse to supply water to a single or multi-family residential property with separate meters for each unit upon application of an owner or tenant because of a delinquent bill of a prior owner, occupant, or tenant.[323] Even though these statutory protections now exist, the best practice is to verify prior to closing that the water bill has been paid through the date of closing. To further protect the buyer, the contract should include a provision regarding prorating all utility bills after final bills are received.

Most cities and counties include a sanitation tax as part of the property tax bill. However, in a few counties and cities, separate bills or periodic bills (i.e., quarterly) are sent to owners of property for sanitation (garbage pickup) services. At closing, any outstanding sanitation bills should be paid and prorated between the seller and buyer.

§ 4.3.6 Changes in prorations after final bills received

Changes in prorations must be addressed by contract. Most form real estate contracts, including the GAR Contract, provide that the seller and the buyer agree to prorate between themselves as of the date of closing or the date of possession of property by the buyer, whichever is later, all utility bills which are issued after closing. This would apply only to utility bills that include service for any period of time the property was owned or occupied by the seller or any other person prior to the buyer.

§ 4.3.7 Withholding tax on sale of Georgia property

§ 4.3.7.1 Requirements under Georgia law

Georgia law requires withholding of up to 3% of the purchase price on any sale or transfer of real property and related tangible personal property located in Georgia from non-residents of the state of Georgia.

The burden to withhold and remit this tax to the Commissioner is placed on the buyer. The buyer must file the required return and remit payment on or before the last day of the month after the month in which the sale has occurred. If the tax payable is more than the sale proceeds, the buyer must withhold the entire sale proceeds.

Any buyer who fails to withhold the 3% when required is personally liable for this tax, and the state revenue commissioner may collect any unpaid withholding tax in the same manner as all other withholding taxes are collected. This means the commissioner may file a lien for any unpaid withholding tax which lien attaches to all the buyer's property.[324]

---

323   O.C.G.A. § 36-60-17(a).
324   O.C.G.A. § 48-7-128(b).

For purposes of this statute, the seller or transferor of property will not be considered a non-resident of Georgia if he executes an affidavit affirming that all of the following conditions have been met:

(1)   the seller or transferor has filed Georgia income tax returns or appropriate extensions have been received for the two income tax years immediately preceding the year of sale;

(2)   the seller or transferor is in business in Georgia and will continue substantially in the same business in Georgia after the sale or the seller or transferor has real property remaining in the state at the time of closing equal to or greater in value than the withholding tax liability as measured by 100% property tax assessment of such remaining property;

(3)   the seller or transferor will report the sale on a Georgia income tax return for the current year and file it by its due date; and

(4)   if the seller or transferor is a corporation or limited partnership, it is registered to do business in Georgia.[325]

The withholding requirement does not apply to the following types of transactions:

(1)   sale or transfer of principal residences;

(2)   deeds in lieu of foreclosure with no additional consideration; or

(3)   when the transferor or transferee is an agency or authority of the United States, the state of Georgia, the Federal National Mortgage Association (Fannie Mae) or Federal Home Loan Mortgage Corporation (Freddie Mac) or the Government National Mortgage Association (Ginny Mae), or a private mortgage insurance (PMI) company.[326]

If the seller is a partnership, S corporation or unincorporated entity, and there are non-resident owners of such entity, the buyer is not required to withhold if the entity certifies to the buyer that a composite return is being filed on behalf of the non-resident owners and that the entity will remit the tax on behalf of the non-resident owners.

---

325   O.C.G.A. § 48-7-128(a).
326   O.C.G.A. § 40-7-128(d).

Federal law requires that the buyer to deduct and withhold a tax equal to 10 percent of the sale proceeds from a foreign seller in respect of any sale of an interest in United States real property. The exemptions are:

(1)   Seller provides to buyer an affidavit by the transferor stating, under penalty of perjury, the seller's United States taxpayer identification number and that the transferor is not a foreign person; or

(2)   If the seller is a privately held U.S. corporation, it provides to the buyer an affidavit stating, under penalty of perjury, that it is not and has not been a United States real property holding corporation or as of the date of the sale, the interests in such corporation are not United States real property interests; or

(3)   Buyer receives a statement by the Secretary of State that the seller has reached agreement with the Secretary for the payment of any tax imposed by the law on any gain recognized by the transferor on the disposition of the United States real property interest, or is exempt from any such tax and either the buyer or seller has satisfied any of the seller's unsatisfied withholding liability or has provided adequate security to cover such liability; or

(4)   the property is acquired by the buyer for use by him or her as a residence and the sale proceeds do not exceed $300,000; or

(5)   the sale of the real property interest comprise of a share of a class of stock that is regularly traded on an established securities market.

§ 4.3.8   Condominium and homeowner association dues

When property is located in a condominium or mandatory membership homeowners or property owners association, the dues owed to the association must be prorated at closing and any past due amount paid by the seller, absent a contract provision to the contrary.

The closing attorney should contact the board of directors or the manager of the association and obtain a written statement of all past due assessments and related charges on the property.[327] However, since the closing attorney does not normally represent the buyer, the buyer would be well advised to independently confirm whether there are any outstanding assessments and other charges due against the property.

---

327   The charges include the prorated liability insurance and casualty insurance policy for all structures within the condominium, which the association was required to obtain under the Georgia Condominium Act (O.C.G.A. § 44-3-107).

The seller generally pays all assessments owed to the date of closing and the dues are prorated for the month, or other time period, between the parties. If a special assessment has been adopted which is being paid in increments, then confirmation must be obtained from the association as to whether the assessment is structured as a one-time assessment with periodic payments or is split and due only on the periodic payment dates. This will determine whether the full amount is due at closing and whether or not it is all owed by the seller. See the chapter on title for a discussion of liens created by unpaid association dues.

§ 4.4   Closing date and possession

§ 4.4.1   What the GAR Contract provides

The GAR Contract requires that all amendments to the closing date be in writing and that this requirement shall be strictly construed. This was added to prevent the closing date from being extended verbally.

§ 4.4.2   Effect of time of essence clause on closing date

Many real estate contracts, including the GAR Contract, specifically provide that time is of the essence. Such a provision serves to require that actions to be taken by a certain date or within a certain time period must be performed in a timely manner.

If the sale does not close on the date specified in the contract and one of the parties is injured thereby, the injured party has the right to terminate the contract and to file a claim. The GAR requires that all notices, including termination notices, be in writing, signed by the party giving the notice and delivered either: (a) in person; (b) by an overnight delivery service, prepaid; (c) by facsimile transmission (FAX); or (d) by the United States Postal Service, postage prepaid, registered or certified return receipt requested.[328]

The GAR Contract also provides that notice to the broker shall for all purposes be deemed to be notice to the party being represented by the broker as a client, except in transactions where the Broker is practicing designated agency. In transactions where the broker is practicing designated agency, notice to the designated agent shall be deemed to be notice to the party being represented by the designated agent. There are also specific provisions governing faxed notices. Lastly, all notices shall be deemed to be given as of the date and time they are received. The GAR Contract provides that its notice requirements shall be strictly construed.

---

328   GAR Contract, paragraph 11G.

Absent contract provision, time not of essence

If a contract does not have a time is of the essence provision, then the general rule is that time is not of the essence in a contract of sale and merely providing a certain time within which the transaction will be closed does not require tender of the purchase price within that time.[329] However, delay must not be willful, must not be unreasonably long, and must not result in damages that cannot be compensated. Further, if there has been a failure to comply within the time stipulated, the other party may, by notice, assign a reasonable time for completing the contract and may require the defaulting party to perform within the time specified.[330]

§ 4.4.2.2   *Timely performance when time is of the essence*

Georgia courts have held that if the contract specifies that time is of the essence, the court will require timely performance. The facts in the following lease purchase case are illustrative.

The buyer brought an action against the seller for specific performance of a contract.[331] After hearing the evidence, the trial Court concluded that the buyer had not tendered the contract price before the date specified in the contract. The Court also implicitly found that there was not sufficient evidence to prevent enforcement of the time requirement in the contract. The contract provided that a down payment was to be made November 10, 1975 and the balance of the purchase price paid on or before November 10, 1976. The buyer paid rent in the interim. The buyer was to assume the seller's loan and pay for the equity in the property in cash. On November 10, 1976, the buyer tendered a check for the equity in the property and informed seller's counsel that due to a misunderstanding, the loan assumption had been disapproved but that the assumption would be approved in a few days. On November 15, 1976, counsel for the seller returned the uncashed check for the equity and refunded a fee for title and deed services not performed. The seller took the position that the contract expired and the buyer was required to vacate the property. The buyer argued that time was not of the essence; however, the preprinted portion of the form contract stated that time was of the essence. The Court concluded that with time being of the essence, the seller was justified in returning the down payment and refusing to close at a subsequent date.

In another case, the buyer failed to provide the purchase money by the closing date. Five days later, the buyer sent the closing attorney the payment to buy the property. The seller refused to accept the money and the buyer sued for specific performance. The Georgia Supreme Court stated that when a contract provides that

---

329   It should be noted that the rule with reference to options is the reverse. An option is peculiarly an agreement of which time is of the essence. Belk v. Nance, 232 Ga. 264, 206 S.E.2d 449 (1974).

330   Gulf Oil Corp. v. Wilcoxon, 211 Ga. 462, 86 S.E.2d 507 (1955).

331   Dulock v. Shiver, 239 Ga. 604, 238 S.E.2d 397 (1977).

time is of the essence and the buyer failed to close, the buyer could not then apply for specific performance.[332]

The parties through their conduct may waive the requirement of timely performance before or after the date of closing. On one case, the seller, who was also the mortgage lender, prepared and processed a loan application for the buyers after the closing date had passed. The Court stated that the seller should not, after the time of closing, act in a manner as to lead the buyer to believe that it will not insist upon the date set for closing.[333]

§ 4.4.2.3   Contract does not automatically terminate when closing date passes

In Georgia, real estate sales contracts do not automatically expire if the transaction fails to close. This is the case even if there is a "time of the essence" clause in a contract. The injured party must serve a notice of termination to the other party. If written notice of termination is not given, the contract does not actually terminate.

The GAR Contract, like the contract in the above-referenced case, contains a clause stipulating that time is of the essence, and it does not expressly provide that the contract expires if not closed by the date specified or the date of any authorized extensions. Therefore, if the sale is not closed by the date specified or by the date of any authorized extension, the non-breaching party may terminate the contract by giving written notice to the breaching party, and the non-breaching party has a cause of action for breach of contract.

If the parties wish to provide for automatic termination of the contract following the closing date set forth in the contract, the following alternative language may be used:

Special Stipulation #4-9: Automatic termination of contract following closing date

In the event the closing does not occur on or before the date set forth in this Agreement, including any permitted extensions, then this Agreement shall automatically terminate and the non-defaulting party shall have the right to pursue all available claims at law or in equity against the defaulting party.

§ 4.4.3   Timing of date of closing and possession

Some contracts for the sale of land may provide that parties may have "until" a certain date to close, or that closing will take place "on or before", "within" or "by" a specified date. Such language may raise an issue as to whether the buyer can

---

332   Benedict v. Snead, 253 Ga.App. 749, 560 S.E.2d 278, 2 FCDR 437, (2002)
333   Frank et al. v. Fleet Finance, Inc., 227 Ga. App. 543, 489 S.E.2d. 523 (1998)

unilaterally demand that the closing take place before the specified date, thereby forcing the seller to vacate the property before the anticipated outside closing date. It also creates ambiguity as to the exact date of the closing.

For example, use of the word "until" has resulted in a number of lawsuits, even though Georgia statute states that when "until" is used with reference to a certain day, it includes that day.[334] This meaning of "until" was applied in one case where the court stated that the word "until" includes such day, term or time.[335]

In another case, the court held that a statutory meaning given to a word should be applied to contracts unless there is a good reason not to.[336] However, in other cases, the courts have looked at the context in which the word was used in the contract and the intention of the parties. Based on this approach, the court in one case decided that "until December 1993" meant up to "midnight, November 30th", instead of up to 31st December.[337]

To prevent any uncertainty, it is best to avoid using ambiguous words. Instead, parties should state an exact closing date. For example, the GAR Contract provides that closing will be on a specified date "or on such earlier date as may be agreed to by the parties in writing."[338]

As with the date of closing, time of possession will be dictated by the contract. The GAR contract provides for the seller to remain in possession either until the closing, for a specified number of hours after the closing or at a specified time after a specified number of days after the closing.[339]

§ 4.4.3.1   Indefinite closing date generally construed as reasonable date

Even if a contract is missing a provision identifying time of performance, a reasonable time for performance will be implied.[340] Therefore, if the closing date is specified as 15 days after completion of construction, the contract will not necessarily be void for indefiniteness. Failure to include a time for performance should not be a violation of the rule against perpetuities,[341] because a reasonable time will be implied.

---

334   O.C.G.A. §1-3-3

335   Rogers v. Cherokee Iron and Railway Company, 70 Ga. 717, 1883 WL 3058 (1883)

336   Brooks v. Hicks et al., 230 Ga. 500, 197 S.E.2d 711 (1973)

337   Burns et al. v. Reeves, 217 Ga. App. 316, 457 S.E.2d 178 (1995).

338   GAR Form F20, paragraph 4C.

339   GAR Form F20, paragraph 4D.

340   Read v. GHDC, Inc., 254 Ga. 706, 334 S.E.2d 165 (1985), citing Whitley v. Patrick, 226 Ga. 87, 172 S.E.2d 692 (1970); Brown v. McInvale, 18 Ga. App. 375, 163 S.E.2d 854 (1968)

341   The rule against perpetuities is a legal principle that a property interest is void unless it vests within 21 years of a life in being plus gestation period.

§ 4.4.3.2 Date of closing can be extended by verbal agreement

Even when the contract states that time is of the essence, this provision can be waived and conduct by a party either before or after the deadline may show waiver. As stated by the Georgia Court of Appeals, "[t]imely performance may be waived orally when acted upon by one or both of the parties."[342]

The following case illustrates how an oral agreement may waive timely performance. The buyer entered a contract, which expressly stipulated that time was of the essence and which included a financing contingency for the buyer's benefit.[343] Before obtaining financing, the buyer told the seller that financing was not a problem and that the seller was to proceed with customizing work on the home. The seller proceeded with the work. Approximately three weeks after the stipulated closing date, the buyer notified the seller that the transaction would not close and demanded full return of the earnest money. The Court concluded that there was a question of fact for jury determination on whether the buyer waived the financing contingency before or after the date specified, thereby precluding the buyer from having a right to a full refund of the earnest money as a matter of law. The Court also noted that a contract provision requiring all modifications to the contract to be in writing does not preclude waiver of the financing contingency or its timely expiration.

In another case decided by the Georgia Court of Appeals, the Court concluded that evidence that one of the parties expressly agreed to an extension of the closing date and both parties continued to make arrangements for closing after the originally scheduled closing date would authorize the jury to conclude that strict compliance with the time provisions of the contract were waived.[344]

Therefore, even where a contract provides that amendments must be in writing and that time is of the essence, the conduct of the parties may be sufficient to waive a time requirement. Parties to a contract must be careful not to conduct themselves in a manner that could be interpreted as waiving the timeliness of performance of obligations under the contract.

§ 4.4.3.3 Closing on a Sunday

When preparing a contract, the parties may elect to close on a particular date without considering the day of the week on which it falls. If the contract states a closing date which falls on a Sunday or a legal holiday, Georgia law provides that the

---

342   Edwards v. McTyre, 246 Ga. 302, 271 S.E.2d 205, 206 (1980). In this case, the court concluded that an issue of fact remained as to whether or not timely performance was waived. Frank et al. v. Fleet Finance, Inc.,227 Ga. App. 543, 489 S.E.2d. 523(1998)

343   Koets v. Benveniste, 169 Ga. App. 352, 312 S.E.2d 846 (1983).

344   Ferris v. Hill, 172 Ga. App. 599, 323 S.E.2d 895 (1984); Edwards v. McTyre, 246 Ga. 302, 271 S.E.2d 205 (1980).

closing will extend to the following business day, even if time is of the essence.[345] If the contract does not state that closing shall take place on a specific date but it is to take place either "by" or "on or before" a certain date, and that date falls on a Sunday or legal holiday, closing will extended to the next business day.[346]

A similar conclusion would likely be reached when an act of God interferes with performance of the contract terms. Under Georgia law, an "act of God" is an accident caused by physical forces that are irresistible or inevitable, such as lightning, earthquakes, and sudden death.[347] Similarly, the bad ice storms which periodically paralyze Georgia would be considered an act of God. Such an event protects a person against responsibility for non-performance of a contract.[348] Where an act of God does not destroy the property but interferes with the closing, equity would allow the parties to reset the closing to a different date.

§ 4.4.3.4   Extending closing date unilaterally

Although parties by their conduct can waive their right to require timely performance of contract terms, courts have held that one party cannot unilaterally modify the terms of the contract for reasons other than the default of a party. Addressing termination of a contract, the Georgia Court of Appeals held that absent evidence of a mutual intention to terminate a contract, one party cannot unilaterally terminate a contract.[349] In that case, the Court also cited a case in support of the general rule that an oral agreement to modify a written contract for the sale of land is unenforceable.[350]

§ 4.4.3.5   Contract may authorize party to extend closing date

The GAR Contract provides that if the loan described in the contract is unable to be closed or if the seller fails to satisfy valid title objections, either party may, by notice to the other party, extend the contract's closing date up to seven days from the original date. The provision allowing for the closing date to be extended if the loan is unable to be closed is broadly written and does not require any particular showing that the delay was for reasons beyond the control of the buyer or the lender. While there has been some discussion in the GAR Forms Committee of limiting the circumstances for which the closing date can be extended, this has not occurred so far. To unilaterally extend the GAR Contract, notice of the same must be received on or before the closing date.[351] GAR has a Notification form which may be use to provide such notice.[352] The

345   Brooks v. Hicks, 230 Ga. 500, 197 S.E.2d 711 (1973).
346   Target Properties, Inc. V. Gilbert, 192 Ga. App. 161, 384 S.E.2d 188 (1989).
347   O.C.G.A. § 1-3-3(3).
348   Sampson v. General Electric Supply Corp., 78 Ga. App. 2, 50 S.E.2d 169 (1948).
349   Atlanta Six Flags Partnership v. Hughes, 191 Ga. App. 404, 381 S.E.2d 605 (1989).
350   Sanders v. Vaughn, 223 Ga. 274, 154 S.E.2d 616 (1967).
351   GAR Contract, paragraph 4C(3).
352   GAR Form F133, Notice to Unilaterally Extend Closing Date Up To Seven Days.

same provisions are included in the GAR New Construction Purchase and Sale Agreement.[353]

In one recent case, a Georgia court gave effect to such a provision and allowed the buyers to extend the closing date.[354] The standard form contract provided for a closing on April 20, 2000. The contract also contained a standard unilateral extension of the closing for seven days to remedy either (1) that the mortgage cannot close before the closing date or (2) that the seller fails to satisfy a valid title objection prior to the closing date. Otherwise, the contract provided that all the parties in writing must agree to any extension of the closing date. The buyers could not complete the loan documents prior to the April 20 closing date which allowed them to unilaterally extend the closing date.

A question which sometime arises is whether a buyer has the right to extend the closing date for the seven-day period under the GAR Contract if the loan is unable to close because of lack of cooperation by the buyer in the processing of the loan. Although the GAR Contract requires that the buyer pursue loan qualification and approval diligently and in good faith, in a practical sense, it is hard to provide evidence that the buyer has breached this obligation. Thus, the likelihood is that the buyer will be able to unilaterally extend the closing date for up to seven days, even if the buyer has caused or partially caused the delay in loan approval.

If either the buyer or seller wants to limit the unilateral ability of either party to extend the closing date, the following alternative language may be used:

Special Stipulation #4-10: No right to unilaterally extend contract

This transaction shall be closed on _____, 20___ or such earlier date as may be agreed to by the parties in writing. Notwithstanding any other provisions of this Agreement, no further extensions of the closing date shall be authorized except as may be agreed to in a separate writing by the Seller and Buyer.

For new construction, builders may wish to select a closing date, depending on the anticipated completion date and provide for automatic extensions to take into account construction delays. The following stipulation may be used:

Special Stipulation #4-11: Automatic extensions for construction delays

The closing of this transaction shall be during normal business hours on a date and time selected in the discretion of Seller upon substantial completion of the improvements on the Property ("Closing"). Such date

---

353   GAR Form F23
354   <u>Yargus v. Smith,</u> 254 Ga.App. 338, 562 S.E.2d 371 (2002)

shall be on or before (in the discretion of Seller)
_____, 20___ *("Final Closing Date").*
Substantial completion shall be deemed to occur when a certificate of occupancy, temporary certificate of occupancy or final inspection certificate covering the Property has been issued by the applicable governmental agency. Should the closing date change from the above date, Seller shall give Buyer advance notice of the date and time of the closing. Seller shall have the right (and in addition to all other rights therein) upon notice to Buyer to extend Final Closing Date unilaterally for two (2) periods of thirty (30) days each OR two (2) extension periods of up to sixty (60) days for each extension period [CHOOSE ONE].

If the construction project consists of more than 99 units, the Interstate Land Sales Full Disclosure Act requires the seller to construct the property within two (2) years of the date of this Agreement.

§ 4.4.3.6   Closing date extended if Defect Resolution Period extends beyond closing date

In one recent case, the Defect Resolution Period did not end until after the original contract closing date. The Court of Appeals resolved this conflict by extending the closing date not only to after the Defect Resolution Period, but also to a reasonable time period thereafter during which the seller could complete the repairs in a good and workmanlike manner.[355] The Court ruled that to do otherwise would frustrate the intent of the parties to have a time frame of a specific duration during which the parties could agree on the defects to be repaired and the seller could then complete the repairs.

The obvious lesson of this case is for REALTORS® to insure that the closing date is after the Inspection and Defect Resolution Periods have lapsed.

§ 4.4.3.7   Damages for failing to close

The measure of damages is the difference between the contract price and the market value of the property at the time of the breach.

The Georgia Court of Appeals ruled on such a case. A seller who was a builder brought an action against a buyer, claiming that the buyer breached a contract to purchase a house and lot.[356] The seller contracted to construct a house and after completion of the house, to sell the house and lot to the buyer. The contract provided that time was of the essence. There were various modifications of the contract including increasing the price and extending the closing date. However, the closing did not take place as specified in the modified contract, and the parties did not agree to

---

355   Yargus v. Smith, 254 Ga.App. 338, 562 S.E.2d 371 (2002)
356   Separk v. Caswell Builders, Inc., 209 Ga. App. 713, 434 S.E.2d 502 (1993).

further extend the contract. The buyer refused a demand to close on a certain date, and the seller sold the house to a third party.

Subsequently, the seller sued the buyer for damages in an amount constituting the difference between the price the buyer agreed to pay and the price for which the house ultimately sold. The buyer argued that such a measure of damages was contrary to law because there was no contract between the parties. The buyer based his contention on the theory that when there is a time of the essence clause, the contract terminates when the sale does not close on the date specified. The Court concluded that this argument was without merit because there was no expiration date in the contract and no clause imposing a condition of closing by the date specified. Rather, the contract provisions merely bound the parties to perform certain actions by the dates specified or the contract would be breached. The Court also noted that the measure of damages in a breach of contract case is the difference between the contract price and the market value of the property on the date of the breach. In this case, since testimony established a range of damages in excess of the amount awarded, the damages were within the range authorized.

§ 4.5   Transfer of warranties

Contracts for the sale of property should address transfer of the seller's interest in any manufacturers' warranties, service contracts, termite bonds, treatment guarantees, and/or other similar warranties which by their terms may be transferable to the buyer. The GAR Contract provides that the seller agrees to transfer to the buyer, at closing, subject to the buyer's acceptance thereof, the seller's interest in any of the above-referenced warranties. The "subject to the buyer's acceptance thereof" language was added in the 1997 and later GAR Contracts so that buyers were not forced to accept undesirable service contracts. Since warranties are generally of a personal nature, they will not transfer without an express agreement to do so.

The new GAR Contract provides that if there are any costs associated with transferring a warranty service contract or termite bond, such costs shall be paid for solely by the buyer. This change was made because some security companies are now charging a fee to transfer security systems and some termite companies are charging a fee to transfer a termite bond.

§ 4.6   Seller remaining in possession after closing

It is important that the provisions regarding the seller remaining on the property be certain and definite. A contract provision that the seller would be allowed to remain in a house for rent not to exceed $300.00 per month "as long as necessary until seller finds a new home," was found to be uncertain by its terms so as to render the entire contract unenforceable.[357]

---

357   Farmer v. Argenta, 174 Ga. App. 682, 331 S.E.2d 60 (1985).

To best protect the buyer, the parties should enter into a temporary occupancy agreement. Most standard deeds to secure debt and standard FNMA and FHLMC requirements provide that the buyer must occupy the property as her principal residence on or before 60 days from the date of closing. In addition to identifying the period of occupancy and the payment for remaining on the property, the occupancy agreement should specify that the seller will leave the property in the same or better condition than at the date of closing and that the seller will be responsible for any damage to the property. If the buyer wants additional protection, the buyer may require that the seller pay a security deposit to the buyer which will be refunded if the property is turned over in the same condition as existed on the date of closing. The occupancy agreement may also provide that the seller will continue to pay utilities until occupancy is terminated. As owner of the property, the buyer will maintain insurance on the structure; therefore, the occupancy agreement should also provide that the seller is responsible for the seller's personal property. The buyer may also want to specify that the seller is responsible for any costs of legal action necessary to enforce the occupancy agreement.[358]

The GAR Temporary Occupancy Agreement stipulates that it does not create the relationship of landlord and tenant but merely gives the Seller a right to occupy the property until the date specified in the Agreement. This is because the Agreement specifically provides that the rights of the temporary occupant of the property are those of a "licensee" who has been given the mere right to use the property for a short period of time. This was done to avoid the parties having to comply with numerous statutory requirements applicable to landlord and tenant relationships that may be burdensome to follow when the occupancy of the property is only for a short period of time. The Agreement provides that if the temporary occupant holds over, he or she becomes a tenant at sufferance. This will allow the new owner to dispossess the occupant in a matter of weeks rather than having to bring a much more time-consuming action for eviction.

The Agreement further provides that the occupant will be liable for the cost of any action instituted by the buyer to enforce the terms of the Agreement. The buyer should not, however, use "self-help" or forcibly remove or lockout the seller. Such action could lead to claims by the seller for wrongful eviction. Georgia law requires a landlord to obtain a writ of possession before the landlord is entitled to dispossess a tenant. Essentially, this means filing a lawsuit against the tenant.

§ 4.7   Buyer obtaining possession before closing

Many sellers are reluctant to allow a buyer to move in prior to closing out of fear he will discover something undesirable about the house or neighborhood and refuse to close the sale. The terms of any occupancy agreement allowing the buyer to occupy the property before closing should be definite and certain. Many of the same

---

358   GAR Form F140, Temporary Occupancy Agreement for Seller After Closing.

issues identified in the previous section should be addressed. In addition, the seller may want to provide that the buyer may not make any alterations to the property without the seller's prior written consent, and if changes are permitted, the buyer will be responsible for their cost without reimbursement if the sale does not close. If the buyer makes alterations and does not pay the contractors performing the work, a lien may be placed on the seller's property. Therefore, it is important to specify that the buyer will be responsible for the cost of improvements and will indemnify the seller for any damages arising from modifications or alterations to the property. If the seller has concerns about the condition of the property during the buyer's occupancy, the seller may require a security deposit. Since the seller is the owner of the property, the seller will maintain property insurance on the structure, and the buyer should be responsible for insuring personal property. The GAR has a form occupancy agreement that can be used for these purposes.[359]

As noted above, the occupancy agreement may specify that it is for temporary occupancy and does not create the relationship of landlord and tenant. However, it is not clear that such a provision exempts the seller from pursuing statutory dispossessory procedures if the sale does not close and the buyer fails to vacate the property. Such a provision has not been ruled on by a Georgia appellate court and the safest course of action is for the seller to file a dispossessory action.

§ 4.8   Tenant remaining in property after closing

If there is a tenant in the property prior to closing, the buyer should request a copy of the lease agreement. If the lease agreement does not provide for early termination by the lessor, the buyer will be bound to allow the tenant to remain on the property for the balance of the lease term. If the lease is on a month-to-month basis and the buyer wants possession as close to the closing date as possible, the buyer may include the following provision in the contract:

Special Stipulation #4-12: Termination of seller's lease

Seller agrees that within 5 days of the Binding Agreement Date, Seller shall notify in writing Seller's tenant in the Property, by U.S. mail, certified, return receipt requested, that his or her lease agreement shall be terminated sixty days from the date of the notice. Seller's notice to tenant shall inform tenant that if tenant remains in possession of the Premises after expiration or earlier termination of the lease without buyer's agreement, tenant shall be a tenant at sufferance and commencing on the date following the date of such expiration or termination, the monthly rental payable by tenant shall be twice the monthly rental for each month or fraction thereof during which tenant so remains in possession of the premises.

The law requires the sixty-day provision and the parties should not reduce

---

359   GAR Form F139, Temporary Occupancy Agreement for Buyer Prior to Closing.

this time period unless a shorter period is provided under the terms of the lease. Of course, the risk to the seller in agreeing to such a provision is that if the transaction does not close, the seller may not have a tenant after the sixty days pass.

CHAPTER 5
PROPERTY DISCLOSURE STATEMENT

The Seller's Property Disclosure Statement is a unique tool developed by GAR to help sellers disclose defects in their properties. A seller of residential property owes a duty to disclose defects in a property to prospective buyers that the seller knows of or should have known about and which could not be discovered upon a reasonably diligent inspection of the property by the buyer. While sellers owe a duty to disclose hidden or latent defects, there is no state law requirement that the disclosure be made using the GAR Seller's Property Disclosure Statement. By disclosing defects, the seller protects himself or herself against claims of misrepresentation or fraud.

Among other things, this chapter includes an explanation of why the GAR Seller's Property Disclosure Statement is incorporated into the GAR Contracts, the seller's obligation to disclose defects, the delayed delivery of the property disclosure statement and the need for the statement to be complete and accurate as of the Binding Agreement Date.

§ 5.1   What the GAR Contract provides

The Seller's Property Disclosure Statement[360] referenced in the GAR Contract is a list of questions relating to the physical condition of the property. The GAR Seller's Property Disclosure Statement was amended in 2004 for the seller to disclose historical information about the property, past problems and current problems with the property. Additional changes include disclosures about 1) the cost of transferring and maintaining a termite bond, 2) mold infestation, 3) recreational facilities and the cost of use (if the property is within a condominium), 4) name of the house inspector and purpose of inspection and 5) the number of property insurance claims made by the seller.

The GAR Contract attaches and incorporates the Seller's Property Disclosure Statement.[361] The GAR Contract also assumes that the buyer has received a Seller's Property Disclosure Statement prior to making an offer to purchase a property. Listing brokers and agents should therefore ensure that their sellers complete the Seller's Property Disclosure Statement as soon as possible (preferably at the time of listing). Copies should also be made available to potential buyers for them to review and attach to any purchase offer.

§ 5.2   Incorporating the Property Disclosure Statement in the contract

§ 5.2.1   Rationale for Property Disclosure Statement being part of contract

Prior to 1997, the GAR Contract did not incorporate the Seller's Property Disclosure Statement into the contract. Buyers were often confused on this point,

---

360   GAR Form F50.
361   GAR Form F20, paragraph 5

because the Seller's Property Disclosure Statement was usually attached to the contract and was therefore assumed by many to be a part of it. Since the Seller's Property Disclosure Statement was not actually a part of the contract, buyers had difficulty asserting claims for breach of contract against sellers when sellers answered questions inaccurately on the Seller's Property Disclosure Statement.

In one case where the Seller's Property Disclosure Statement was not incorporated into the contract, the sellers did not disclose the rupture and subsequent repairs that they had made to the bottom of the swimming pool.[362] The contract had a provision where the buyer acknowledged receipt of the property disclosure statement, but it did not contain a provision stating that it incorporated the property disclosure statement into the contract. The Court stated that the provision was not sufficient to incorporate the statement into the contract. Since the false statement was made outside the contract and the contract contained an "entire agreement" clause, the buyers could not sue the sellers for fraud.

The solution of the Georgia Association of REALTORS® was to make the Seller's Property Disclosure Statement a part of the contract and to have sellers warrant that the information contained therein is accurate and complete to the best of the seller's knowledge as of the Binding Agreement Date. In this way, buyers using the 1997 and later GAR Contracts should be able to bring successful claims against sellers for breach of contract or breach of warranty if sellers make material misrepresentations in the Seller's Property Disclosure Statements. With this new potential for liability, sellers should use care to accurately complete their Property Disclosure Statements and should provide buyers with additional written explanations about issues which might otherwise be unclear to buyers.

For example, in a case where the Seller's Property Disclosure Statement was incorporated into the contract, the sellers checked the "yes" box on the disclosure statement to the question on whether the septic tack had been professionally serviced.[363] They also stated on the disclosure statement that they were not aware of any past or present leaks or problems relating to the plumbing or sewer system in the property. In fact, the sellers had the system repaired instead of merely serviced as indicated on the disclosure statement. The court held that the sellers were liable for fraud.

A breach of contract claim brought by the buyer against the seller for answering questions inaccurately in a Seller's Property Disclosure Statement is often easier to prove than a claim for fraud and misrepresentation. This is because in order to prevail in a claim for fraud and misrepresentation, the buyer must prove that he or she exercised due diligence to protect themselves against the fraud. This normally requires buyers to show that they attempted to independently verify all of the representations made by the seller or seller's agent or broker instead of just blindly

---

362   Ainsworth et al. v. Perreault et al., 254 Ga. App. 470, 563 S.E.2d 135 (2002).
363   Hudson v. Pollock et al., 267 Ga. App. 4, 598 S.E.2d 811 (2004)

relying on the representations.[364] This high standard often leaves buyers without an effective remedy to pursue sellers for failing to disclose defects in the property.

§ 5.2.2   Effect of Property Disclosure Statement being part of contract

When a seller discloses a defect relating to the property in the Property Disclosure Statement, the buyer is put on notice of the same and cannot then bring a claim against the seller for failing to disclose the defect. A buyer should never blindly rely upon the seller's property disclosure statement but should instead independently inspect the property to determine if there are additional defects and to better understand the nature and extent of the defects being disclosed. This is because when the seller discloses a defect, the buyer in bringing a claim for fraud is not only put on notice of the defect but also any other condition that the disclosure of the defect would normally lead a reasonably prudent person to examine. In this way, the Property Disclosure Statement protects sellers.

An example is the case where the sellers stated in the Property Disclosure Statement that the property's exterior contained untreated stucco.[365] The sellers also provided a letter from a stucco inspector, which stated that the hard-coat stucco was in good condition. However, the letter reference an earlier letter also provided by the same inspector, which stated that the trim was made of synthetic stucco. The contract provided that the buyers had the right to void the contract if a stucco inspection revealed major defects in the property. However, the buyers did not conduct a separate stucco inspection or obtain a copy of the letter referred to in the stucco inspection letter provided to the buyers. The Court held that the buyers failed to exercise due diligence and therefore could not prove fraud.

The Georgia Court of Appeals recently held that buyers could successfully sue the sellers for facts falsely stated in the Property Disclosure Statement even if the Statement was not made part of the contract if the sellers actively concealed the damage. In this case, the seller gave the buyers a property disclosure statement (which was not made a part of the contract) in which he stated that he was not aware of any damage due to termites or structural defects in the home.[366] A few months after the closing, the buyers saw termites swarming in the house and called an inspector who found that putty and paint that had been used to conceal holes and gaps in the wood caused by termite infestation. The buyers then sued the seller alleging that he was defrauded by the seller's active concealment of the damage. The Court held that the seller was liable for fraudulently concealing d the termite damage even though the contract used in selling the property did not make the property disclosure statement a part of the contract (unlike the current GAR Purchase and Sale Agreement) and contained an "entire agreement" clause,

---

364   Copeland v. Home Savings of America, F.A., 209 Ga. App. 173, 433 S.E.2d 327 (1993).

365   Meyer et al. v. Waite et al., 270 Ga.App. 255, 606 S.E.2d 16 (2004).

366   Browning v. Stocks, 265 Ga. App. 803, 595 S.E.2d 642 (2004).

specifically stating that it *"constitutes the sole and entire agreement between the parties"* and *"[n]o representation, promise, or inducement in the Agreement shall be binding upon any party thereto."*

§ 5.2.3   Broker's liability for false statements in Property Disclosure Statement

In Georgia, a buyer has no claim against the listing agent for false statements made by the seller in the Seller's Disclosure Statement unless the listing agent knows the representations to be false.[367] Neither can the buyer sue the seller's agent for fraud when the seller fails to disclose concealed defects in the property.[368] A good example is the following case, where the buyers sued the sellers, the real estate agent and the brokerage firm for fraud, conspiracy to defraud, breach of contract and breach of BRRETA.[369]

The buyers and sellers had entered into a contract of sale, which contained a disclaimer provision stating that they did not rely on any statements made by the broker. The contract also contained an "entire agreement clause" stating that the contract represented the entire agreement between the parties and any representations made that is not included in the contract shall not be binding. Finally, the contract incorporated by reference the sellers' disclosure statement. Before the parties signed the sales contract, the sellers gave the buyers the Property Disclosure Statement, which referred to past and present termite damage, but stated that the damage had been taken care of. It also stated that there were problems with the walkways and water intrusion, but that there had been no water in the basement since 1989. Shortly after the closing, the homeowners found termite and rodent infestation, water intrusion, and soil settlement problems.

The Court held that with respect to the buyer's claims against the agent and the broker, there was no evidence that the agent knew about the home's defects apart from what was stated in the Seller's Disclosure Statement. Therefore, the agent and the broker could not be held liable for the seller's false statement.

§ 5.3   Seller's duty to disclose without providing Property Disclosure Statement

Sellers are not obligated by law to complete the GAR Seller's Property Disclosure Statement or any other written property disclosure statement. If the seller refuses to complete the Property Disclosure Statement, the section about the Property Disclosure Statement should be deleted from the contract that is executed by the parties. When deciding not to provide a Property Disclosure Statement, sellers should be aware that since the use of a property disclosure statement is becoming increasingly customary in the real estate industry, buyers may be reluctant to purchase property for

---

367   O.C.G.A. §10-6A-5(b).
368   <u>Remax North Atlanta v. Clark,</u> 244 Ga.App. 890, 537 S.E.2d 138 (2000).
369   <u>Bircoll et al. v. Rosenthal et al.</u>, 267 Ga.App. 431, 600 S.E.2d 388 (2004).

which no such document has been completed. Sellers should also be aware that failure to complete a disclosure statement does not relieve the seller from disclosing defects in the property of which the seller knows or should know and which are not discoverable by a prospective purchaser upon a reasonable inspection of the property.[370] Answering "I don't know" to all questions on the Seller's Property Disclosure Statement would similarly not protect the seller from the above disclosure obligations. For example, if the seller checks "I don't know" about any roof damage, but in fact does have knowledge that the roof leaks, the seller could be held liable for his failure to accurately and honestly disclose this information.

While *caveat emptor*, or buyer beware, is still generally the law in Georgia, there are three circumstances in which sellers of residential property can be held liable for failing to disclose defects in the property. The first is when the seller knowingly lies about the existence of a concealed defect. In one case, the buyer asked the seller about the septic system, and the seller replied that the system had been serviced and was in perfect working condition. The truth was that the septic system was repaired as opposed to being merely serviced and the system should have been replaced rather than repaired.[371]

The second situation involves active concealment where the seller does not discuss the defect, but takes steps to prevent its discovery by the prospective buyer. A good example is the case where the seller concealed termite damage by filling holes with putty and fresh paint.[372]

The third circumstance is when the seller knows of a concealed material defect and does not attempt to hide the problem but simply keeps quiet and makes no disclosure of its existence. In such cases of passive concealment, the seller can also be liable if the seller fails to disclose special knowledge he has of a defect which would not be reasonably apparent to the buyer.[373] An agent may be liable for passive concealment if the agent had actual knowledge of the defect but did not disclose the defect.[374]

A great many disputes arise regarding items contained in the Seller's Property Disclosure Statement. Sellers should take the time necessary to fully and completely fill in the Disclosure Statement. Buyers should insist that they receive a fully completed Disclosure Statement and should ask any and all questions they have related thereto. This is oftentimes the buyer's only chance prior to closing to receive information concerning the property directly from the seller.

---

370   Wilhite v. Mays, 140 Ga. App. 816, 232 S.E.2d 141 (1976), aff'd, 239 Ga. 31, 235 S.E.2d 532 (1977).

371   Hudson v. Pollock et al., 598 S.E.2d 811 (2004)

372   Browning v. Stocks, 265 Ga.App. 803, 595 S.E.2d 642 (2004).

373   Fincher v. Bergeron, 193 Ga. App. 256, 387 S.E.2d 371 (1989).

374   Ikola v. Schoene et al., 264 Ga. App. 338, 590 S.E.2d 750 (2003).

§ 5.4 Disclosure to be accurate and complete as of Binding Agreement Date

The GAR Contract requires the seller to warrant that the information contained in the Seller's Property Disclosure Statement is accurate and complete as of the Binding Agreement Date. This means that listing agents should always inquire of their seller clients, before they accept an offer, whether any information on the Seller's Property Disclosure Statement has changed since it was first completed. Obviously, if it has, the Seller's Property Disclosure Statement should be updated to ensure that the information is accurate and complete as of the Binding Agreement Date. To the extent the seller revises the Seller's Property Disclosure Statement after it is included as part of an offer to purchase, the revisions would constitute a counteroffer to which the buyer would need to agree.

Listing agents should also confirm that all questions on the Seller's Property Disclosure Statement have been answered to avoid a later claim for breach of warranty for incompleteness. Of course, listing agents should avoid answering any of the questions on the Seller's Property Disclosure Statement on behalf of the seller because: (1) it is the seller's statement to make, and (2) to answer questions could expose the listing broker to significant legal liability. Agents should also avoid the temptation to ask the seller the questions and then fill in the blanks on the form on behalf of the seller. Even though the seller will ultimately sign the Disclosure Statement, the seller could still claim that the agent checked the wrong box, either intentionally (a fraud claim) or by mistake (a negligence claim).

The seller has an ongoing obligation to promptly update the GAR Disclosure Statement and provide any such revised copy to the buyer.

While the GAR Contract contemplates that a property disclosure statement be attached, there is nothing which prevents builders or other sellers from using their own form disclosure statement, so long as it has been completed in full and is accurate as of the Binding Agreement Date. Therefore, for example, a builder using the GAR Contract could develop his own disclosure statement which either addresses fewer questions or has more specific questions than the GAR Seller's Property Disclosure Statement. Of course, if there is a house on the property for which an alternative property disclosure statement has been prepared and which was constructed prior to 1978, the listing broker should confirm that the property disclosure statement contains the disclosures and acknowledgments regarding lead-based paint.

§ 5.5 Delayed delivery of Seller's Property Disclosure Statement

If the Seller's Property Disclosure Statement is unavailable at the time of contract, the buyer and seller can agree that it be provided after the contract is signed. Samples of special stipulations dealing with this issue are set forth below:

Special Stipulation #5-1: Buyer's right to terminate for delayed delivery of property disclosure statement

Seller shall provide Buyer with a complete and accurate Seller's Property Disclosure Statement on the GAR form within _____ days from Binding Agreement Date. If Buyer has not received the Seller's Property Disclosure Statement within such time period, Buyer may terminate this Agreement provided that written notice of termination is delivered to Seller within _____ days from the Binding Agreement Date. If the Property is being sold with the right to request repairs, Buyer may request, in Buyer's inspection amendment, that Seller repair, among other things, any defects revealed in the Seller's Property Disclosure Statement.

Special Stipulation #5-2: Buyer's right to terminate for defects revealed in property disclosure statement delivered late

Seller shall provide Buyer with a complete and accurate GAR Seller's Property Disclosure Statement within _____ days from Binding Agreement Date. If Buyer has not received the Seller's Property Disclosure Statement within such time period, or if the Seller's Property Disclosure Statement reveals defects in the property, Buyer may terminate this Agreement provided that written notice of termination is delivered to Seller within _____ days from Binding Agreement Date.

It is also possible that the Disclosure Statement will be available at the time an offer is made, but that the buyer still has questions regarding the seller's responses. For example, the seller may indicate on the Disclosure Statement that he has knowledge of damage to the property from termites. Even though the Seller's Property Disclosure Statement provides that the seller is to give a detailed explanation of the damage, not all sellers will do so. A prudent purchaser would want to know more about the damage before binding himself to purchase the property. The purchaser can always simply ask the seller to more fully complete the Disclosure Statement. Alternatively, the buyer could insert a special stipulation similar to the following:

Special Stipulation #5-3: Explanation of specific items in seller's property disclosure statement

Seller shall provide Buyer with a complete and accurate written statement, including all related and pertinent documents, regarding Seller's response to item(s) _____ in the Seller's Property Disclosure Statement within _____ days from Binding Agreement Date. If Buyer has not received such statement within such time period Buyer may terminate this Agreement provided that written notice of termination is delivered to Seller within _____ days from Binding Agreement Date. If the Property is being sold with the right to request repairs, Buyer may request, in Buyer's inspection amendment, that Seller repair, among other things, any defects revealed in the statement.

§ 5.6   Other matters addressed in the Seller's Property Disclosure Statement

The GAR Seller's Property Disclosure Statement also contains a list of fixtures and other items that the seller is including with the property in the sale and a Lead-Based Paint Warning Statement and Disclosure. If the seller fails or refuses to provide a GAR Seller's Property Disclosure Statement prior to an offer being made by the buyer, then the buyer must take care to identify in his offer those fixtures and other items he wishes to have remain with the property. These items are addressed in detail in section 1.2 concerning fixtures. [375] The following discussion focuses on the disclosure requirements regarding lead-based paint.

§5.6.1   Residential Lead-Based Paint Hazard Reduction Act of 1992

On September 6, 1996, the Residential Lead-Based Paint Hazard Reduction Act of 1992[376] ("Act") went into effect. Owners with four or fewer dwelling units had until December 6, 1996, to comply with the new law. The Act imposes lead-based paint disclosure requirements on sellers, real estate brokers, and landlords for all sales and rental transactions if the dwelling was built before 1978. (This book addresses the Act only as it relates to brokers, agents, sellers, and buyers of real property. The obligations of landlords and their agents in complying with the Act will not be discussed herein.)

Although the law was adopted in 1992, it did not go into effect until the fall of 1996 because the Department of Housing and Urban Development had to issue regulations to implement the new law. The regulations are referred to as The Requirements for Disclosure of Known Lead-Based Paint Hazards in Housing.

The legislation was passed to protect consumers, particularly children, who may suffer health problems because of inadvertent exposure to lead-based paint. The risk of exposure to lead-based paint is especially great if the paint is chipping or flaking. Additionally, sanding of lead-based paint occurring during renovation can result in lead particles in the air.

The Act requires disclosure of lead-based paint in the purchase of what is referred to as "target housing." The term "target housing" covers most forms of residential property which were constructed prior to 1978; construction on the dwelling must have been competed by December 31, 1977 to qualify as target housing. In other words, if the house was started in December of 1977 and finished in March of 1978, it is not considered "target housing." The types of properties classified as target housing are most single and multi-family dwellings, including detached housing, apartments,

---

375   Section 1.2.
376   42 U.S.C. § 4852, et seq.

condominiums, co-ops, and townhouses. The law does not apply to commercial, office, or other properties used for non-residential purposes.

The disclosure requirements are for homes built before 1978 because that was the year lead-based paint was banned from further use. The focus of the law is on disclosure rather than repair. If lead-based paint exists in a dwelling, the purpose of the law is to let consumers know about it when they buy such property. Owners of residential dwellings built after 1977 have no special obligations, unless they know their property contains lead-based paint or lead-based hazards, in which case they must disclose this information.

§5.6.2   Pre-1978 residential properties exempt from Act

Certain types of residential properties constructed before 1978 are exempt from the Act. The exempt properties include the following:

(1)   Property sold at foreclosure (however, the Act applies when the property is later resold);

(2)   The purchase, sale, or servicing of a mortgage;

(3)   Zero-bedroom dwellings where the sleeping area is not separated from the living area (such as studio apartments, efficiencies, dormitories, military barracks, and individual rooms rented in residential dwellings);

(4)   Housing for the elderly or disabled, where children under the age of six are not expected to reside.

§5.6.3   Responsibilities for advising sellers of disclosure obligations

Under the lead-based paint disclosure law, real estate licensees, when selling target housing, must advise sellers of their obligation to disclose their actual knowledge of lead-based paint or lead-based paint hazards in the property. Moreover, the law requires that real estate licensees ensure that the seller has performed all activities required of him under the law, or the licensee must personally ensure compliance on the seller's behalf. The law further provides that by informing sellers of their obligation to disclose, the licensee will not be held liable for failing to disclose to a purchaser that lead-based paint and/or lead-based paint hazards exist on the property, when such hazards are known to the seller but were not disclosed to the licensee.

Therefore, determining whether the dwelling was constructed prior to 1978 and advising the seller of his disclosure obligations should be standard operating procedure on all listing calls. Licensees should require that the seller sign the "Disclosure of Information and Acknowledgment of Lead-Based Paint and/or Lead-

Based Paint Hazards," prepared by the National Association of REALTORS®, in which sellers acknowledge being advised of their disclosure obligations.[377]

§5.6.4   Sellers' disclosure obligations

Before a buyer executes a contract with a seller, the regulations require the seller of target housing to do the following:

(1)   Disclose to the buyer any actual knowledge he has regarding the presence of known lead-based paint and/or lead-based paint hazards in the property being sold. Actual knowledge means any information that the seller received through first-hand account. While a rumor is not actual knowledge, the law even requires a seller to disclose knowledge of the rumor to the buyer;

(2)   Provide the buyer with copies of all available records or reports that relate to the presence of lead-based paint and/or lead-based paint hazards in the property being sold;

(3)   Provide the buyer with a federally approved lead-based paint hazard information pamphlet entitled "Protect Your Family From Lead in Your Home;"

(4)   Provide the buyer with a period up to ten days (or some mutually agreed time period), prior to becoming obligated under the contract, during which time the buyer may conduct a risk assessment or inspection for the presence of lead-based paint and/or lead-based paint hazards (the buyer may agree to waive this testing opportunity); and

(5)   Include in each contract to sell target housing an attachment containing a specific warning about lead-based paint. The warning in the GAR Lead-Based Paint Exhibit is as follows:

Every purchaser of any interest in residential property on which a residential dwelling was built prior to 1978 is notified that such property may present exposure to lead from lead-based paint that may place young children at risk of developing lead poisoning. Lead poisoning in young children may produce permanent neurological damage, including learning disabilities, reduced intelligence quotient, behavioral problems, and impaired memory. Lead poisoning also poses a particular risk to pregnant women. The Seller of any interest in residential real property is required to provide the Buyer with any information on lead-based paint hazards from risk assessment or inspections in the Seller's possession and notify the

---

377   See GAR Form F54, Lead-Based Paint Exhibit, and Form F55, Lead-Based Paint Pamphlet.

Buyer of any known lead-based paint hazards. A risk assessment or inspection is recommended prior to purchase.[378]

§5.6.5   When to disclose that property is target housing

The disclosure obligation does not extend to all prospective buyers, regardless of their degree of interest. Only the actual buyer must receive information on target housing. The disclosure must be made before a purchaser is obligated under any contract to purchase target housing. Under the new law, sellers are required to permit buyers a ten-day period to have the property tested for lead-based paint or lead-based paint hazards unless the inspection period is waived in writing by the buyer. The ten-day inspection period does not apply to lease transactions.

§5.6.6   Seller's right to copy of buyer's lead-based paint test results

Pursuant to the GAR Contract, the buyer submitting an amendment requesting repairs (pursuant to the Property Sold with Right to Request Repairs portion of the GAR contract paragraph 8B(1) is obligated to give a copy of the lead-based paint test results to the seller along with the amendment. Absent this or some other specific contractual provision requiring that the report be provided to the seller, there is no obligation in the lead-based paint law that a buyer give the report to a seller. If a buyer includes a special stipulation giving him an absolute right to terminate the contract if lead-based paint is found, and the seller agrees to such a provision, the seller should require the buyer to give him all test reports involving lead-based paint.

§5.6.7   Record-keeping requirements

The real estate broker, agent, and the seller must sign and retain a completed copy of certain information contained in the National Association of REALTORS'® "The Disclosure of Information and Acknowledgment Form," along with its accompanying documents.[379] The information must be kept for three years from the date the sale of the property was completed. The form can be found in the National Association of REALTOR'S'® publication, "Lead-Based Paint--A Guide to Complying with the New Federal EPA/HUD Disclosure Regulations."

§5.6.8   Penalties for violating Act

The consequences for violating the federal regulations are severe. Sellers and licensees who knowingly violate the regulations may be subject to civil and criminal penalties. The civil penalties can range up to $10,000.00 per violation. Violators may also be liable for three times the damages incurred by the buyer. These damages often include costs of correcting lead-based paint hazards and medical costs related to lead-based paint. The criminal penalties are fines of

---

378   GAR Form F53, Lead-Based Paint Exhibit.
379   24 CFR § 35.92.

$10,000.00 per violation and/or up to one-year imprisonment. Brokers and their affiliated licensees may face additional liability under the Brokerage Relationships in Real Estate Transactions Act ("BRRETA") if they knowingly fail to disclose any adverse material facts relating to lead-based paint in the dwelling.

§5.6.9   Level at which lead-based paint becomes hazardous

The existence of lead-based paint in a dwelling is not necessarily dangerous. Whether the lead-based paint is hazardous often depends on the condition of the structure or object covered with lead-based paint. For example, lead-based painted walls of a child's bedroom that are chipping pose a greater threat to the health of the occupants of the property than a non-chipping lead-based painted pipe under the kitchen sink. Buyers should be advised to seek expert advice about whether the existence of lead-based paint in a residential property is hazardous.

CHAPTER 6
TITLE

OVERVIEW

This chapter discusses the closing and the transfer of possession of the property to the buyer. Among the issues which are addressed include how closings work generally, who pays for various charges at closing such as transfer tax and intangible tax, how items like property taxes are prorated, under what circumstances the closing date may be extended and what happens when one party fails to close as required under the contract.

Possession of the property is also discussed including buyers moving in early and sellers and tenants remaining in possession after closing. An explanation of what happens if the property is destroyed or damaged after the contract has been signed but prior to closing is also included.

§ 6.1   What the GAR Contract provides

The GAR Contract requires the seller to convey good and marketable title (with certain exceptions that will be discussed below) to the property. The buyer has, until closing, to examine title and furnish the seller with a written statement of objections that affects the marketability of title. The seller must satisfy all valid title objections prior to closing or the buyer may terminate the contract by giving written notice to the seller.[380] In addition, if a survey of the property is attached to the contract, and a new survey obtained by the buyer is materially different from the one attached to the contract, the buyer may terminate the contract by giving written notice to the seller.[381]

The GAR Contract for residential property requires the buyer to notify the seller of title defects prior to closing.[382] This means that the buyer has up to and excluding the date of closing to give the notice of termination. There is no requirement that notice must be given in reasonable time, which is the case with some contracts. This helps the buyer because the title examinations may not be completed until days before closing. If the seller fails to satisfy valid title objections prior to closing, the buyer may terminate the contract upon written notice to the seller, in which case the earnest money must be refunded to the buyer. Alternatively, the buyer or seller may unilaterally extend the closing date by no more than seven days for the seller to satisfy valid title objections.[383]

For commercial property, the buyer has a specified timeframe within which to make title objections, which must be given to the seller in writing[384]. If the title objection is a lien or other monetary encumbrance, the seller can cure the objection be

---

380   GAR Contracts, paragraph 6

381   GAR Contracts, paragraph 6C

382   GAR F20, paragraph 6B

383   GAR F20, paragraph 4C(3). GAR F133 may be used to extend the closing date.

384   GAR CF2, paragraph 5B

making payment on or before closing. The seller must cure all other title objections within the timeframe specified in the GAR contract. If the seller fails to do so, the buyer has the right to the exercise the following remedies within 5 days of the expiration of the seller's 'cure period': 1) rescind the contract and obtain a refund of the earnest money; 2) waive the objection without any reduction in the purchase price or 3) extend the closing date for up to 15 days for the seller to cure any title objection. If the buyer fails to act within the 5-day window, the buyer will be treated as having waived these rights.

If the GAR Contract is not used, parties should state clearly when the buyer is entitled to terminate the contract due to title defects. For example, in one case, the contract provided that the buyers had "until" the closing date to examine title defects and "…in the event the Purchaser concludes in its sole discretion that Seller's title is such that Seller will be unable to or will elect not to cure the defects herein in with accordance to the Agreement, Purchaser may so notify the Seller…" to terminate the contract.[385]

The contract also contained a termination provision, which stated the purchaser might terminate "if any or more of the following conditions or states of fact exist at the time of Closing…" The buyers argued that their right to terminate existed for the period until closing, while the seller argued that the buyer only could exercise the right to terminate at closing. The court looked at the contract as a whole and held that the buyer's right to terminate refers to the time prior to the closing date.

§ 6.2   Notice requirements for title defects

The GAR Contract requires that title objections be given by written notice to the seller. The objections must affect the marketability of title, which should be specifically stated in the notice so that the seller can verify their validity and have sufficient information in order to satisfy the objections. All notices shall be deemed to be given as of the date and time they are received. The GAR Contract sets out the requirements for sending notices and that these requirements shall be strictly construed.[386]

Parties are expected to comply strictly with the notice provisions in the contract. In one case, two corporate real estate entities represented by attorneys entered into a contract for the purchase of property.[387] The contract required the seller to convey marketable fee simple title in accordance with Georgia law and the Title Standards of the State Bar of Georgia.[388] The buyer was required to give the seller written notice of objections affecting the marketability of the title. Those objections

---

385   Thornton et al. v. Kumar et al., 525 S.E.2d 735, 240, Ga. App. 897 (1999).
386   GAR Contract, paragraph 11G.
387   Real Estate World, Inc. v. Southeastern Land Fund, Inc., 137 Ga. App. 771, 224 S.E.2d 747 (1976), overruled on other grounds.
388   See below for separate discussion of Title standards.

were to be mailed by registered or certified mail to a specific partner in a law firm representing the seller. On the final day for examination of title, the buyer's attorney hand-delivered a letter to an associate of the law firm representing the seller regarding "difficulty with chain of title" to 70 acres of the total acreage of 3,613. The letter asked for an opinion of that associate as to the title issues and indicated that he would continue to contact other parties to resolve his questions.

The buyer failed to appear at closing, and the seller kept $45,000.00 in earnest money. The Court concluded that the letter did not comply with the specific provisions of the contract. It was hand-delivered, not mailed, and it was not addressed to the party specified in the contract. In addition, the letter did not qualify as a notice of defect nor was it an objection raising an issue of marketability of title that would defer a sale of this magnitude. The Court noted that neither the word "objection" nor the phrase "marketability of title" was mentioned in the letter.

In another case, the contract provided that notice of termination must be sent to the sellers by hand or federal express to a specified address.[389] The buyers sent the notice of termination to only one of the sellers, and to an address other than the one indicated in the contract. The buyers also sent the notice to the sellers' agent. The Court held that the sellers could retain the earnest money because the buyers failed to give proper notice. Since the contract did not contain any provision that the agent was authorized to receive notice, the notice to the agent was also invalid.

§ 6.3   Seller has obligation to convey marketable title

If the property has defective title, the seller has an obligation to provide clear title even when the buyer fails to give written notice of the title defect. The buyer, by giving written notice of a title defect, gets the right to declare the contract null and void based on the failure to satisfy the stated title objection.

For example, in one case, the closing on a contract to purchase property never occurred because the title examination revealed the existence of a deed to secure debt on the property creating an indebtedness greater than the purchase price.[390] The sellers argued that the buyer's failure to present a written statement of objection to title as contemplated by the terms of the contract excused their failure to consummate the sale. In that case, the Court noted that it was undisputed that the sellers were unable to remove the encumbrance created by the deeds to secure debt since their proceeds were insufficient to pay the full amount of the indebtedness and they were unwilling or unable to pay the difference. The Court held that it would not have made any difference if the sellers had been given written notice of the existence of the encumbrance, because they still would not have been able to convey clear and marketable title to the buyers.

---

389   Thornton et al. v. Kumar et al., 525 S.E.2d 735, 240, Ga. App. 897 (1999).
390   Hill v. McGarity, 179 Ga. App. 788, 347 S.E.2d 679 (1986), cert. denied.

In another case, the Court similarly held that the seller was required to convey marketable title even though written notice of the title problems was given after the date of closing.[391] In that case, the sales contract provided for closing within 31 days, but gave the sellers 90 days after written notice from buyer to cure any title defects. The day before closing was to take place, the buyer's attorney informed the sellers that there was several title problems. The sellers insisted that the sale be closed the following day. The day after the closing was to have taken place, the buyer's attorney responded with a letter in which he detailed eight title problems, including outstanding deeds to secure debt and interest, unpaid taxes, and a judgment lien. At the end of the 90 days, the sale was not closed and the buyer demanded a return of the earnest money. The sellers argued they were entitled to the money on the theory that the buyer failed to give timely notice of any alleged title defects.

The trial court concluded that because the sellers were not able to tender marketable title as was required by the contract, the buyer was entitled to judgment as a matter of law. The appellate court noted the contract, which did not state that time was of the essence and merely specified a closing date, did not obligate the buyer to tender notice of title objections prior to the time set for closing.

§ 6.4 Definition of good and marketable title

Even where title is not mentioned in a real estate sales contract, the law implies that the seller agrees to furnish "good and marketable title." Good title generally means one which is clear of defects and encumbrances. Good title has been defined as "not merely a title valid *in fact*, but a marketable title which can be again sold to a reasonable buyer or mortgaged to a person of reasonable prudence as security for the loan."[392]

The GAR Contract requires that:

> Seller will convey good and marketable title to said Property by general warranty deed, subject only to (1) zoning; (2) general utility, sewer, and drainage easements of record on the Acceptance Date upon which the improvements do not encroach; (3) subdivision and/or condominium declarations, covenants, restrictions, and easements of record on the Acceptance Date; and (4) leases and other encumbrances specified in this Agreement.[393]

---

391   Pollard v. Martin, 191 Ga. App. 681, 382 S.E.2d 720 (1989).
392   Atlanta Title & Trust Co. v. Erikson, 67 Ga. App. 891, 21 S.E.2d 548 (1942), cert. denied.
393   GAR Contract, paragraph 6A.

§ 6.4.1   Marketable title and economic marketability

Title marketability relates to defects affecting legally recognized rights of ownership, such as liens or other types of encumbrances. Economic marketability generally relates to physical conditions affecting the use of property. For example, location of property in a flood plain may affect the economic marketability of property, but it does not affect the marketability of title.[394]

Covenants applying to the use of property may affect the economic marketability rather than the title marketability of the property. Case law in Georgia defines marketable title as title that is not merely a title valid in fact, but a marketable title that can again be sold to a reasonable purchaser or mortgaged to a person of reasonable prudence as security for the loan of money.[395]

This standard was applied in a case in which a religious organization exercised an option to purchase certain property intending to use it as a church or a school.[396] One of the conditions of the option was that if the property were not zoned for church or school purposes, the option money would be refunded. The title search revealed a recorded survey containing a restriction prohibiting use of the property for schools or churches. The organization sought the return of its option money on the basis that the seller could not give good and marketable title to the property.

The court concluded that while the property had covenants running with the land which prevented it from being used as a site for a church or school, this would not prevent the title to the property from being marketable, because it could not be said that a reasonable man would neither purchase nor loan money on the property because of these restrictions. However, if the religious organization had argued that its option money should be returned because the seller did not meet the conditions of the option agreement, the court's decision probably would have been different.

It should be noted that statutory provisions set forth in covenants for certain types of communities (e.g., pursuant to the Georgia Condominium Act and Georgia Property Owners' Association Act) must be complied with by the seller in order to convey marketable title.

§ 6.4.2   Marketable title and insurable title

The Official Code of Georgia Annotated defines title insurance as follows:

---

394   Chicago Title Ins. Co. v. Investguard, Ltd., 215 Ga. App. 121, 449 S.E.2d 681 (1994).
395   Ardex, Ltd v. Brighton Homes, 206 Ga. App. 606, 426 S.E.2d. 200 (1992).
396   Swinks v. O'Hara, 98 Ga. App. 542, 106 S.E.2d 186 (1958). For a more comprehensive discussion on the impact of covenants on the use of property, see chapter 14.

[I]nsurance of owners of real property or others having an interest in such real property, or liens or encumbrances on such real property, against loss by encumbrance, defective titles, invalidity, adverse claim to title, or unmarketability of title by reason of encumbrance or defects not excepted in the insurance contract, which contract shall be written only upon evidence or opinion of title obtained and preserved by the insurer.[397]

Title insurance is issued after a thorough examination of title and an analysis of any claims or encumbrances. An insurer can make the business decision to insure title that is not marketable or even not to insure marketable title. Consequently, marketable title and insurable title are not synonymous. Nevertheless, most buyers equate the two.

Although marketable title does not necessarily mean one that a title insurance company will insure, the parties can agree to define marketable title in such a fashion.[398] The GAR Contract recognizes this common requirement and defines good and marketable title, as "title which a title insurance company licensed to do business in Georgia will insure at its regular rates, subject only to standard exceptions."[399] If the GAR Contract is not being used, the following special stipulation can be included in another real estate contract:

Special Stipulation #6-1: Good and marketable title must be insurable

Notwithstanding any other provision in this Agreement to the contrary, in order for Seller to meet his or her obligation to convey good and marketable title to Buyer, title to the Property that is the subject matter of this Agreement must be insurable by a title insurance company licensed to do business in the State of Georgia at the title insurance company's regular rates and subject only to standard title exceptions.

§ 6.4.3   Agreement to provide title acceptable to buyer

Some purchasers may attempt to avoid the issue of marketable versus insurable title by having the contract provide that title must be acceptable to the buyer. Buyers should be careful with such language, however, for a contract that bases acceptance on the subjective decision of one party is known as an illusory contract and may be void for lack of mutuality. Although language providing that title must be acceptable to the buyer has the potential to render the contract void, so long as the title is not rejected for capricious reasons or is fraudulently made, rejection by the buyer should be upheld. For example, a court upheld a buyer's rejection of title because his attorney failed to approve title for reasons that were specified in the attorney's written

---

397   O.C.G.A. § 22-7-8.
398   Green v. Sams, 209 Ga. App. 491, 433 S.E.2d 678 (1993), cert. denied.
399   GAR Contract, paragraph 6B.

report. The Court concluded that since there was nothing in the report to indicate that it was capriciously or fraudulently made, the rejection by the buyer was valid.[400]

§ 6.4.4   Threats of litigation affect title marketability of property

Potential litigation concerning title to property may render the property unmarketable:

> A title which exposes the [buyer] to litigation is not a good and merchantable one if the danger thereof is apparent and real, not merely imaginary or illusory, which may be apprehended upon the basis of some fact or truth as to which there can be no ascertainment with reasonable certainty.[401]

An example of a situation where conveying title to property would be uncertain enough to become a threat of litigation to the buyer is described in the case discussed below. In this case, the description of the property in previous conveyances referenced marble monuments and iron pins. However, no one could recall what the marble monuments referred to and the iron pins had been removed. The adjacent landowner disagreed with the seller on the location of the property lines, and the buyer refused to close. The court concluded that acquiring property under such circumstances is likely buying a lawsuit with the adjacent landowner in order to ascertain just where the boundary lines between the two properties lie. Accordingly, the court did not require the buyer to purchase the property, because, "[t]he law will not compel a party to purchase a lawsuit or accept a conveyance which a reasonably prudent man would refuse."[402]

§ 6.4.5   Some survey defects do not affect title marketability of property but may affect economic marketability

When a property description refers to monuments actually erected as the boundaries of property and the distance between such monuments is also part of the property description, Georgia law holds that if there is a discrepancy between the distances stated and the actual distance between the monuments, the actual distances between the monuments will prevail.

For example, if a property description states that the distance between monument 1 and monument 2 is 125 feet, but when measuring, the actual distance between the monuments is discovered to be only 120 feet, the seller of the property will be warranting title obligated to only 120 feet to the buyer.

---

400   Youngblood v. Schwan, 72 Ga. App. 86, 33 S.E.2d 26 (1945).
401   Mrs. E. B. Smith Realty Co. v. Hubbard, 130 Ga. App. 672, 204 S.E.2d 366 (1974), citing Cowdery v. Greenlee, 126 Ga. 786, 791, 55 S.E. 918 (1906).
402   Mrs. E. B. Smith Realty Co. v. Hubbard, 130 Ga. App. 672, 204 S.E.2d 366, citing Horne v.Rodgers, 113 Ga. 224, 228, 38 S.E. 768, 770 (1901).

A monument is a permanent landmark, natural (trees or water bodies) or artificial (fences, walls, stakes, pins, or roads) established for the purpose of indicating boundaries of property. In a case where the length of a call line did not meet the buyer's expectations, but the monuments cited were accurate, a court held that the buyer received good and marketable title to the property in question based on the monuments and that the error in the call lines was of no consequence.[403] However, the buyer also argued that the title insurance company insured more than the marketability of title. The buyer claimed that the title insurance covered the length of the property lines as set forth in the property description and not just the property as measured between the monuments and as shown on the survey. Although the title insurance policy in this case did not contain an exception for defects in the survey, the court held that such defects were not insured. This situation was distinguished from a case in which the title insurance policy affirmatively stated that the survey was insured.

In situations where a current survey dated within six months of the closing is prepared, title insurance policies will insure the property subject to only the specific exceptions disclosed on the survey. If a current survey is not obtained, the title policy will contain an exception for matters which would be disclosed by a comprehensive survey of the property. It is almost always in the buyer's best interest to obtain a survey, even if the buyer's lender does not impose such a requirement.

§ 6.5   Incorporating survey into contract

In earlier versions of the GAR Contract, buyers had the right to survey the property, but the survey itself was not a part of the contract. The legal description of the property was defined as "the same as is recorded with the Clerk of Superior Court of the county in which the Property is located."[404] Since most buyers do not have a title examination of the property performed prior to entering into a contract, they were contracting to purchase property based on a legal description they had never seen or examined.

The current GAR Contracts contain a section which provides in part as follows:

> Any survey of the Property attached hereto by agreement of the parties prior to the Binding Agreement Date shall be a part of this Agreement. Buyer shall have the right to terminate this Agreement upon written notice to Seller if a new survey performed by a surveyor licensed in Georgia is obtained which is materially different from any

---

403   Lynburn Enterprises, Inc. v. Lawyers Title Ins. Corp., 191 Ga. App. 710, 382 S.E.2d 599 (1989), cert. denied, citing Stewart v. Latimer, 197 Ga. 735, 742, 30 S.E.2d 633 (1944).

404   GAR Purchase and Sale Agreement, paragraph 1 (1995 printing).

attached survey with respect to the Property, in which case Buyer's earnest money shall be returned.[405]

Under this provision, buyers can request that sellers provide a copy of their surveys of the property which the buyers can review prior to executing the contract. It should be noted, however, that the seller is not required to attach a survey to the contract absent an affirmative agreement between the parties to do so.

Even if there are no material differences between the survey and the legal description of the property found in the county land records, the GAR Contract provides that the seller will convey good and marketable title subject to all general utility, sewer, and drainage easements of record on the Acceptance Date upon which improvements do not encroach. Therefore, if the survey and the legal description in the county land records are the same, but the survey shows an improvement encroaching on an easement (like a house built on top of a county sewer line), the seller must remedy this title defect in order to convey good and marketable title to the buyer. In order to avoid this, the seller may incorporate the following alternative language in the contract:

Special Stipulation #6-2: Buyer agrees to take title subject to survey matters

Notwithstanding the warranty of title provisions of Paragraph 6C of this Agreement, Buyer agrees to take title to the Property subject to all matters shown on the attached survey.

§ 6.5.1   Why attaching survey important

A survey will show the actual boundary lines of the property being conveyed and will show easements and encroachments which may affect the buyer's interest in purchasing the property. Therefore, if a survey is presented as part of the legal description of the property, the buyer can determine if there is any issue reflected on the survey which would affect the buyer's decision to purchase the property before signing the contract.

For example, a buyer signs a contract for the purchase of property, intending to put a pool in the rear yard. The contract states that the property description is the same as what is found in the county land records. The buyer believes that the rear boundary of this property is a hedge. However, a survey obtained later shows that the rear yard is 20 feet closer to the dwelling than the hedge and that there is a county drainage easement running through the area in which the buyer intends to put the pool. Since the property being conveyed is the same as described in the land records, the buyer will be obligated to purchase it even though she thought the property extended all the way to the hedge. However, if a survey were part of the legal description, she

---

405   GAR Contract, paragraph 6C.

would have discovered the easement that would prevent her from building a pool prior to executing the contract.

From a legal perspective, a contract that incorporates a recorded survey which provides the metes and bounds description is treated as proof that what is being conveyed is what is stated on the survey. In other words, the buyer will be treated as having actual knowledge of the property being conveyed.

Further, the buyer will be considered as having actual knowledge of any encumbrance, easement or other defect that is shown on the recorded survey, since a recorded survey gives notice of any encumbrances to title, whether or not the buyer knows of the record. Therefore, the buyer will take title to the property subject to any defect that is stated on the recorded survey.[406]

§ 6.5.2   Guidelines for one survey "materially different" from another

The GAR Contract states that, if a new survey which the buyer obtains is materially different from the seller's survey, the buyer can terminate the contract.[407] Alternatively, the buyer can use the threat of termination as a basis to negotiate some mutually satisfactory resolution to the discrepancy. This provision gives a buyer the ability to terminate a contract based on concerns with the economic marketability of the property.

The GAR Contract does not define the term "materially different." Generally, a matter is considered "material" if it relates to a matter which is so substantial and important as to influence a party. Whether a difference in surveys will be considered material is a question of fact. It is likely that if a new survey shows the property in a flood plain, the difference will be considered material, particularly if it means the buyer will be obligated to purchase flood insurance.

Similarly, if a fence or other structure has been erected which constitutes an encroachment, the difference may be material. If boundary lines vary between the surveys, the difference may or may not be material. For example, a one-foot difference along a 100-foot call of a 100-acre tract may not be material. On the other hand, a one-foot difference on a 1/4-acre lot may be material, particularly if it affects the setback and placement of the dwelling.

§ 6.5.3   Protection for buyer if no existing survey available

As noted above, many contracts identify the property as set forth in the county land records. However, a metes and bounds description will not show the buyer

---

406   Security Union Title Insurance Co. et al. v. RC Acres, Inc., 269 Ga.App. 359, 604 S.E.2d 547 (2004)

407   GAR Contract, paragraph 6C.

whether a fence is within the boundary of the property or the driveway encroaches onto a neighboring property.

Further, a metes and bounds description does not show where easements of record may be located or indicate whether the property is in a flood hazard area. Additionally, a metes and bounds description does not enable most buyers to readily determine the shape of the property they are considering purchasing.

One possible solution to this problem is to provide in the contract that a survey acceptable to the buyer is attached by the seller. However, Georgia courts have held that a sales contract is voidable for lack of mutuality if the buyer is the sole judge of her satisfaction.[408] Below are several special stipulations that can be used in cases where a survey is unavailable at the time of contract but the buyer still wants protection against possible survey problems in the future:

Special Stipulation #6-3: Seller warrants no easements, encumbrances or septic tanks on property

Notwithstanding any provisions in this Agreement regarding title, Seller warrants that there are no easements or other title encumbrances on the Property nor any septic tanks or septic fields which would preclude Buyer from placing a pool on the Property in the location identified on Exhibit "__" to this Agreement and incorporated herein.

Special Stipulation #6-4: Seller warrants property is not in a floodplain

Seller warrants that no portion of the Property is in a flood plain. If any portion of the Property is in a flood plain, Buyer may terminate this Agreement, in which case all earnest money shall be immediately returned to Buyer.

Special Stipulation #6-5: Seller warrants no setback violations or encroachments onto adjacent property

Seller warrants that there are no existing setback violations or encroachments onto adjacent properties. If a survey reveals any such violations or encroachments, Buyer may terminate this Agreement, in which case all earnest money shall be immediately returned to Buyer.

Special Stipulation #6-6: Seller warrants minimum acreage of property

Seller warrants that the Property contains at least _____ acres. If a survey reveals that the Property contains less than _____ acres, Buyer may terminate

---

408   Nalley v. Harris, 176 Ga. App. 553, 336 S.E.2d 822 (1985), citing Stone Mountain Properties, Ltd. v. Helmer, 139 Ga. App. 865, 867, 229 S.E.2d 779 (1976).

this Agreement, in which case all earnest money shall be immediately returned to Buyer.

Special Stipulation #6-7: Seller warrants size of front and rear boundaries

Seller warrants that the front and rear boundaries of the Property are a minimum of _____ feet in length and the side boundaries are a minimum of _____ feet in length. If a survey reveals boundaries of lesser dimensions, Buyer may terminate this Agreement, in which case all earnest money shall be immediately returned to Buyer.

§ 6.6   Zoning matters do not affect marketability or quality of title

It is generally recognized that the zoning status of property does not relate to title and does not create a breach of a warranty of title. Georgia case law provides that the zoning status of property does not concern title.[409] Zoning ordinances are legislative enactments, thus the uses which may be made of land under the applicable law or ordinance is a matter of law and a buyer is presumed to know what zoning regulations do or do not permit on a certain property.[410]

The Georgia Title Standards state that "a title examiner must be careful to disclaim in his or her opinion any coverage as to the applicability of effect of zoning because it is settled in Georgia that such matters do not implicate the locus or quality of title."[411] That section of the Title Standards also states that title insurance companies operating in Georgia are not permitted to issue insurance as to "zoning matters," broadly conceived. Therefore, title opinions do not refer to "zoning matters" as exceptions. Although a seller is obligated to deliver marketable title to a buyer under the GAR Contract, zoning issues are specifically listed as an exception in this area because by law, such issues do not affect title. If the buyer is purchasing the property for a particular use and wishes to make the contract conditional upon rezoning, the buyer should include the following stipulation in the contract:

Special Stipulation #6-8: Seller warrants zoning and rezoning contingency

Buyer understands and agrees that Property is zoned _____ and that the improvements thereon may not meet Buyer's zoning requirements. The Buyer's obligation hereunder in conditional upon the Property being rezoned to _____ by the appropriate (County/City) authorities by _____, 20___. The Buyer/Seller shall be responsible for pursuing such

---

409   Sachs v. Swartz, 233 Ga. 99, 209 S.E. 2d 642 (1974).

410   Gignilliat v. Borg, 131 Ga. App. 182, 205 S.E.2d 479 (1974), citing Barton v. Atkinson, 228 Ga. 733), 187 S.E.2d 835 (1972) and Maloof v.Gwinnett County, 231 Ga. 164, 166,200 S.E.2d 749 (1973).

411   State Bar of Georgia Title Standards, section 34.1(a). See section below on Title Standards.

rezoning and paying all affiliated cost. In the event the said rezoning is not obtained by said date, then this Agreement shall become null and void and all earnest money shall be refunded to the Buyer. All rezoning applications shall be submitted to Seller for Seller's approval prior to filing, which approval shall not be unreasonably withheld. All parties agree to cooperate, to sign the necessary documentation and to support the rezoning application.

The buyer may want the seller to provide proof of zoning, in which case the buyer may include the following stipulation:

Special Stipulation #6-9: Seller to provide proof of zoning

This Agreement is conditional upon Seller providing a letter from the city or county zoning authority stating that the Property is presently zoned for _____use. Seller shall have two weeks from the date of acceptance to present said letter to Buyer. Should the Seller not present the letter within the above-stated time period, Buyer must, within forty-eight hours past the time period, declare this Agreement null and void or this contingency shall be removed as a condition of this Agreement. If Buyer elects to declare this Agreement null and void, said declaration shall be on a GAR Termination and Release Agreement with all earnest money being promptly refunded to Buyer. All parties agree to sign promptly all documentation.

§ 6.6.4   Violations of zoning ordinances not matters affecting title

Zoning matters are not included with the general warranty of title contained in a general warranty deed. Therefore, the conveyance of land which is in violation of a zoning ordinance is not a breach of the covenants included in a general warranty of title.

This is illustrated in a case where a large parcel of property was subdivided and the one-acre lot conveyed to the buyer was in violation of the zoning ordinance regarding the minimum acreage of property. The buyer argued that the seller had breached his warranty of title because an existing violation of a zoning ordinance subjected the buyer to litigation and, therefore, resulted in title which was not marketable.[412] In that case, the Court of Appeals concluded that even though zoning is not a matter of title, the conveyance of land in violation of a municipal ordinance is an encumbrance and constitutes a breach of warranty of title because the buyer is exposed to litigation. However, the Georgia Supreme Court reversed the Court of Appeals, declining to extend the traditional scope of a general warranty of title to include zoning matters.[413] Likewise, the commentary in the Title Standards states that even if a survey reveals that a building violates a "zoning" setback line, the title examiner may ignore

---

412   Decatur v. Barnett, 197 Ga. App. 459, 398 S.E.2d 706 (1990).
413   Decatur v. Barnett, 261 Ga. 205, 403 S.E.2d 46 (1991)

the violation on the theory that "zoning matters" are not title matters and title examiners may certify such titles as marketable.

For this reason, buyers should check if the relevant zoning ordinance permits the present use of the premises, as well as any other different uses. A buyer should not simply assume that the existing use is permitted violation because the authorities can enforce zoning laws despite that the violation has been in existence for a long time. Buyers should review ordinances, statutes, or regulations, and the zoning map to determine the zone and the permitted use. Buyers should also enquire about any proposed amendments to the ordinances.

If the buyer wishes to make the contract subject to there being no setback violations, the contract should contain Special Stipulation #6-5 set forth in § 6.5.3 above.

§ 6.6.5   Special stipulations warranting zoning status are enforceable

Although zoning provisions do not affect title, the parties to a real estate contract can agree that a buyer may terminate the contract if the property is not zoned for a particular purpose.[414] The following special stipulation could be used for that purpose:

Special Stipulation #6-10: Right to terminate if property not zoned for particular purpose

Notwithstanding any other provision in this Agreement to the contrary, if it is determined that the Property subject to this Agreement is not zoned as_____ (i.e., multi-family residential, office/industrial), Buyer shall have the right, within five business days of such determination, to terminate this Agreement by written notice to Seller. In such case, all earnest money shall be immediately returned to Buyer.

Since warranty of the zoning status of the property is not a title issue, the notice requirements in the contract as to non-performance of a condition relating to title would not be applicable.[415] Thus, the buyer would need to add a provision to the contract such as one of those that follow.

Special Stipulation #6-11: Seller warrants property will be properly zoned by closing

Notwithstanding any other provision in this Agreement to the contrary, Seller warrants that at the time of closing, the Property shall be zoned for multi-family residential development. If by the commencement of the closing, the

---

414   Sachs v. Swartz, 233 Ga. 99, 209 S.E. 2d 642 (1974).
415   Sachs v. Swartz, 233 Ga. 99, 209 S.E. 2d 642 (1974).

Property is not so zoned, this Agreement may be terminated in Buyer's sole discretion, in which case all earnest money shall be immediately returned to Buyer.

Special Stipulation #6-12: Seller's warranty that there are no zoning or building violations at closing

Notwithstanding any other provision in this Agreement to the contrary, Seller warrants that at closing, Seller shall deliver Property free from all violations of zoning and building ordinances.

§ 6.7 Common encumbrances on property

§ 6.7.1 Encroachments

An encroachment is generally defined as an illegal intrusion or projection of improvements either from or onto property. There are three general classifications of encroachments which may affect title to property: (1) encroachments upon abutting property; (2) encroachments upon the subject property; and (3) encroachments upon streets and alleys.

For title insurance purposes, encroachments related to property boundary lines, easements, minimum building setback lines, or restricted areas without authority are generally listed as title exceptions. This means that title insurers will not insure such encroachments on an owner's title policy. Additionally, the extent of the encroachment and the length of time it has existed may impact an insurer's willingness to insure over such encroachments for lenders.

For example, title insurers generally distinguish between minor and major encroachments. Minor encroachments may be defined as improvements less than 10% over the minimum building setback lines and improvements onto public utility drainage easements. Encroachments of fences and gravel driveways onto easement areas or over boundary lines may be considered minor if they are less than three feet.[416] The length of time the encroachment over a building line has existed affects the enforcement of the violation. Georgia law provides that actions which may accrue as a result of the violation of a building setback line must be brought within two years after the right of action accrues.[417]

§ 6.7.2 Boundary line agreements

The purchaser of property on which an encroachment exists or which encroaches on abutting property may want to obtain a boundary line agreement, even if

---

416   United General Title Insurance Company Underwriting Guidelines.
417   O.C.G.A. § 9-3-29(a).

not required by the title insurer, to avoid disputes in the future as to boundary lines or authority to move or remove improvements.

A boundary line agreement permits the encroachment and has each owner acknowledge the boundary line and acknowledge that neither owner will claim any interest in the other owner's property. It is recorded in the land records of the county where the property is located and should be cross-referenced to the deeds of both property owners. Once the agreement is recorded, it is enforceable against all future owners of both properties. The party having actual possession of property under a boundary line agreement for more than seven years will acquire title to that property.[418]

In the absence of a boundary line agreement, an owner with an improvement encroaching on another's property may be required to remove the improvement. For example, a property owner built a concrete garage which extended more than 11 feet over the property line. Neither party was aware of the encroachment, and it was not discovered for 17 years. After it was discovered, the neighboring owner brought an action to have the garage removed. The court concluded that the garage owner did not have a boundary line agreement and did not have title to the property on which the garage was located, so the garage owner was obligated to remove the trespassing improvement from the neighboring property.[419]

Boundary line agreements can be used to address a variety of encroachments including, but not limited to, fences, walls, garages, and other improvements.

§ 6.7.3   Easements and licenses

An easement is " an interest in land owned by another person, consisting in the right to use or control the land, or an area above or below it, for a specific limited purpose."[420] On the other hand, a license is merely a "permission, usually revocable, to commit some act that would otherwise be unlawful."[421]

It is sometimes difficult to distinguish between an easement and a license. Easements are generally distinguished from licenses in that easements are interests in property which: (1) are related to the property; (2) pass with the property from one owner to the next; (3) can be created only in writing or by the actions of the parties over time; and (4) are not revocable.

Licenses are a right given by the owner of property to do an act on her property which is created either orally or by implication. Also, under Georgia law, a

---

418   O.C.G.A. § 44-4-7.
419   Roe v. Doe, 233 Ga. 691, 212 S.E.2d 854 (1975).
420   Black's Law Dictionary (8th ed. 2004); Brown v. Tomlinson, 246 Ga. 513, 272 S.E.2d 258 (1980).
421   Black's Law Dictionary 9 (8th ed. 2004).

parol or verbally granted license to do something on another's property is revocable at any time if its revocation does no harm to the person to whom it has been granted. However, a parol license can become a non-revocable easement if the licensee has acted in reliance on the license and has incurred expense.[422] For example, if a property owner verbally grants a person the right to construct a road over her property, and the person purchases an adjoining property in reliance upon such a parol license and spends money and labor to build and improve the road, the person holds an executed license which becomes an easement running with the land.[423]

§ 6.7.3.1   Recorded easements

The GAR Contract provides that recorded easements on which improvements do not encroach are exceptions to title.[424] In other words, the buyer cannot claim that such easements title defects. However, if an improvement encroaches on the recorded easement, then a title defect does exist.

In some cases, easements may affect the buyer's use of the property purchased. For example, if an abutting owner has a landscape easement on the buyer's property, the buyer may be precluded from putting a fence where he intended to put one. Similarly, a utility easement for a sewer line may preclude a buyer from placing an improvement (such as a pool) on a portion of the property. Since recorded easements are identified on the survey, these problems may be avoided if the survey is part of the contract.

§ 6.7.3.2   Unrecorded easements

On the other hand, the GAR Contract does not list unrecorded easements or licenses as permitted exceptions to title. Therefore, if a buyer discovers an unrecorded easement or license after examining the property, the buyer may object to these matters as title defects, and the seller will have to remedy the defect before closing.

An example of an unrecorded easement is an easement acquired by prescription.[425] This means that title to an easement was acquired after a period of twenty years' use that was public, continuous, uninterrupted, and peaceable. The general law on title acquired by prescription applies to easements.[426] Private ways (i.e. a road, path or driveway across property belonging to another party) are protected after seven years' use, which must be constant and uninterrupted.[427] The private way must not exceed 20 feet during the prescribed period and must be kept

---

422   O.C.G.A. § 44-9-4.
423   Jordan v. Coalson, 235 Ga. 326, 219 S.E.2d 439 (1975); Waters v. Pervis, 153 Ga. App. 71, 264 S.E.2d 551 (1980).
424   GAR Contract, paragraph 6A.
425   O.C.G.A. §44-5-175.
426   See §5.15 for a discussion of title by prescription.
427   O.C.G.A. § 44-9-54.

open and in repair by the applicant. Further, there must be an adverse claim and actual notice of the claim to the other party.[428]

Another example of an unrecorded easement is an implied easement. An easement is implied in favor of one owner by law when the easement is necessary, such as for light and air. In one case, the buyer bought property that was land-locked by a tract retained by the seller. However, the buyers used a private way across the retained tract. The court held that although there was no written record of the private way or easement, the buyers had an implied easement in the private way for access to and exit from their property.[429]

§ 6.7.4   Judicial liens

Money judgments against an owner of property entered on the General Execution Docket of the county in which that owner's property is located constitute a lien on all property owned by the owner in that county.[430] It should be noted that judgment creditors might file their judgments in counties other than the counties where the judgments are obtained in order to perfect their lien rights on any property owned by the defendant in those counties. A judgment against a seller constitutes an encumbrance on the seller's property and must be satisfied before or at closing in order to convey clear title to a buyer.

In some cases, a seller may have a name which is the same as, or very similar to, a judgment defendant, but the seller may not be the defendant. In such cases, the closing attorney will have to be satisfied that the judgment defendant and the seller are not the same person, and the seller will usually have to execute an affidavit to that effect.

If there is a judgment recorded against a buyer, the judgment may affect the buyer's ability to obtain an approved loan for financing the transaction. In some cases, the buyer may be required to satisfy a judgment in order to obtain financing. If the buyer cannot do so, the contract may terminate because the buyer is unable to obtain a loan and therefore meet the financing contingency.

§ 6.7.5   Special assessment liens

The costs of grading, curbing, paving, laying sewer and water pipes, etc., are generally required to be assessed in some part against abutting landowners.[431] Such special assessments are not a tax but are a lien on the property.

---

428   Greer v. Piedmont Realty Investments, Inc., 248 Ga. 821, 286 S.E.2d 712 (1982)
429   Burk v. Tyrell, 212 Ga. 239, 91 S.E.2d 744 (1956)
430   O.C.G.A. § 9-12-80.
431   O.C.G.A. § 36-39-3, 36-39-7, and many municipal ordinances.

§ 6.7.6   Ad valorem tax liens

Ad valorem tax Fi.Fa.'s (writs of Fieri Facias) are general liens against all property owned by a taxpayer in addition to being a special lien on the taxed land.[432] Therefore, even if ad valorem taxes are not owed on the property being sold to a buyer, if the seller owes taxes on another property in the same county, those taxes will constitute a lien on the property being sold. However, unpaid taxes on other property will usually be waived by the title insurance company insuring the property being sold because payment of the taxes is secured by the other liened property.

§ 6.7.7   Federal tax liens

Federal tax liens include liens for federal estate taxes, unpaid income taxes, gift taxes, excise, and other taxes. Such liens attach on the date of assessment to all the taxpayer's property, but a federal tax lien does not gain priority over other liens or interests until a notice or lien is filed in the public records. When property subject to a federal tax lien is sold at a foreclosure sale, the United States has 120 days from the date of the sale to redeem the property.[433]

§ 6.7.8   Mechanics' and materialman's liens

Under Georgia law, mechanics, contractors, subcontractors, materialmen furnishing material and labors furnishing labor, architects, surveyors, and engineers are given statutory liens for their contributions toward the improvement of real property.[434] These liens must be filed in the county land records where the property is located within three months after completion of the work or furnishing of services. In addition, the lien claimant must start an action for recovery of the amount of the claim within 12 months from the time the amounts became due.[435]

Since these liens are valid for three months before they are required to be recorded, they are an unrecorded encumbrance on the property during that period. For that reason, sellers will generally be asked by a closing attorney to sign an affidavit stating that no work has been performed on the property which may result in a lien being filed against the property in the three months preceding the closing and that all construction costs have been paid in full.

§ 6.7.9   Liens under Georgia Condominium Act and Georgia Property Owners' Association Act

The Georgia Condominium Act and the Georgia Property Owners' Association Act both provide that condominium or homeowner assessments not paid

---

432   O.C.G.A. § 48-3-5.
433   26 U.S.C. § 7425.
434   O.C.G.A. § 44-14-361(a).
435   O.C.G.A. § 44-14-361.1.

when due constitute an automatic lien against the property.[436] Since these liens are not recorded in the county land records, it is incumbent on the closing attorney, or the party charged with ensuring that title is clear, to contact the management company or the board of directors for the association to determine if assessments are due. Both statutes provide that a written statement can be requested from the association setting forth amounts due and that successors are not liable for any amounts in excess of the amounts set forth in the statement.[437]

§ 6.7.10   Deeds to secure debt

A deed to secure debt, also referred to as a security deed, constitutes an absolute conveyance of the property by the buyer to the lender with the lender having an obligation to reconvey the property back to the buyer upon payment of the debt.[438] It is commonly said that the lender has legal title to the property and the buyer has equitable title while the debt or mortgage is being paid off by the buyer.

§ 6.7.10.1   *Three methods to cancel deed to secure debt*

Unless the seller's loan or loans are being assumed by the buyer at closing, all loans to the seller secured by deeds to secure debt encumbering the property should be paid in full at closing and subsequently released by the lender. Georgia law sets forth three methods to cancel a deed to secure debt: (a) a cancellation upon the original deed to secure debt; (b) a quitclaim deed from the record holder of the deed to secure debt to either the current holder of record title, the person to whom title is to be conveyed, or the original grantor of the security; or (c) a cancellation document, in the event that the original deed to secure debt has been lost, stolen or mislaid.[439]

§ 6.7.10.2   *Reversion of title to grantor without cancellation*

Although Georgia law requires that the grantee of a deed to secure debt cancel the deed of record within 60 days of full payment of the debt,[440] there are cases where this does not happen. To address the problem of locating grantors of old deeds to secure debt, Georgia law provides that after a certain amount of time, title will revert to the grantor or her successors, even if the debt has not been satisfied of record.

Title to real property conveyed to secure a debt reverts to the grantor or her heirs, personal representatives, successors, and assigns at the expiration of seven years from the maturity of the debt or debts or the maturity of the last installment of the debt as stated in the record of the conveyance; provided, however, when the parties affirmatively state in the record of conveyance that they intend to establish an

---

436   O.C.G.A. § 44-3-109, 44-3-232.
437   O.C.G.A. § 44-3-80(e), 44-2-225(c).
438   O.C.G.A. § 44-14-60.
439   O.C.G.A. § 44-14-67.
440   O.C.G.A. § 44-14-3.

indefinite security interest, title reverts at the expiration of the later of (a) seven years from the maturity date of the debt or the maturity of the last installment as fixed in the record of conveyance, or (b) twenty years from the date of the conveyance as stated in the record.[441]

§ 6.7.11   Covenants

Covenants are restrictions on the way property may be used. In the 1970's, more elaborate sets of covenants began to be used as part of the development of condominiums and HOAs. The covenants in these planned communities are contained in separate recorded legal documents typically known as a "declaration of condominium" in a condominium and a "declaration of covenants, conditions, and restrictions" ("CC&R") in a HOA. In addition to restrictions on the use of the property, the declarations typically address whether the owner must belong to the association of owners and pay assessments. They also generally give a developer special rights to develop the community and control the association.

Covenants are generally considered an encumbrance on property. However, as noted above, although such covenants are in the chain of title to the property and may affect the economic marketability of title, they do not generally affect title marketability as that term is defined in the GAR Contract.

Under the GAR Contract, the seller must convey marketable title to the buyer, with the exception that subdivision and/or condominium declarations, covenants, restrictions, and easements of record are permitted to be on the property, so long as they were recorded on the property on or before the Acceptance Date of the contract.[442] The rationale for providing that such encumbrances are of record on the Acceptance Date is to ensure that the seller does not place covenants or restrictions on record between the Acceptance Date and the Binding Agreement Date.

Earlier versions of the GAR Contract did not include subdivision covenants, condominium declarations, and the like within the warranty exceptions. Therefore, under previous versions of the GAR Contract, if subdivision covenants were recorded against the property, the buyer could raise the existence of the covenants as a title defect.

In any event, since an owner of such property has to comply with the covenants, it is important that a buyer obtain a copy of the covenants to review. Buyers are on legal notice of recorded covenants, whether or not they read them and regardless of whether they agree to them in the contract. This is a concept known as constructive notice, and it applies to all documents recorded in the county land records. The declaration reviewed by a potential purchaser should be stamped by the clerk of court as having been recorded in the land records. This avoids the problem of

---

441   O.C.G.A. § 44-14-80(a)(1).
442   GAR Contract, paragraph 6A.

purchasers being given an early unrecorded draft of a declaration which is later changed to include provisions they find unacceptable.

Real estate brokers representing buyers as clients are well advised to ensure that the buyer reviews the covenants prior to signing a purchase contract. If a buyer signs the contract and then finds an unacceptable provision in the covenants, the buyer cannot use the provision as a basis for terminating the contract (unless the contract specifically provides for this). A special stipulation affording the buyer time to obtain and review the covenants is as follows:

Special Stipulation #6-13: Agreement subject to acceptance of covenants

For and in consideration of the sum $10.00 and other good and valuable consideration, the receipt and sufficiency of which is hereby acknowledged, Purchaser shall have _____ days from the Binding Agreement Date in which to review any declaration of covenants or declaration of condominium to which the Property is subject. Purchaser may terminate this Agreement if the terms of such declaration of covenants or declaration of condominium are not satisfactory to Purchaser by providing written notice thereof to Seller within the stated time. In such event the earnest money shall be returned to Purchaser.

§ 6.7.11.1   Duration of Covenants

Georgia law generally limits the term that covenants apply to a piece of property in counties or municipalities that have adopted zoning laws to no more than 20 years,[443] subject to three exceptions. The first two exceptions relate to covenants on property subject to the Georgia Condominium Act[444] and the Georgia Property Owners' Association Act, which are perpetual.[445] The third exception is for subdivisions of 15 or more lots (that are not subject to the Georgia Property Owners' Association Act), where the covenants will automatically renew unless a majority of the lot owners execute and record an instrument terminating the covenants prior to their expiration.[446] This applies only to covenants recorded after 1993. Covenants recorded prior to 1993 would likely expire after 20 years.

In one case, a property owner sold property in a subdivision subject to covenants recorded on a plat. The covenants stated they would expire in 30 years. The covenants did not provide for renewal in any way. The purchaser acquired the property in 1973 after the covenants were recorded. The purchaser intended to develop the property that was shown on the plat as the recreation property for office or

---

443   O.C.G.A. § 44-5-60(b).
444   O.C.G.A. § 44-3-116.
445   O.C.G.A. § 44-3-234.
446   O.C.G.A. § 44-5-60.

commercial use.[447] The court first held that the covenants expired in 20 years, not 30. The court further held that the purchaser relied on the plat and the law at the time of the purchase that the covenants would expire, and application of the statute would take away the purchaser's right to use the property. Therefore, the court held the statute would not apply retroactively to covenants recorded before 1993.

Many covenants recorded before 1993 limited the term to 20 years but also contained provisions for automatic renewal for consecutive ten-year terms. The court's decision did not address the enforceability of such automatic renewal provisions in covenants recorded prior to the 1993 statute.   When buying a lot adjacent to or near undeveloped property designated by a developer for future recreational use, the buyer may want to consider adding the following provision to the sales contract to protect against the undeveloped property being used for non-recreational purposes in the future.

Special Stipulation #6-14: Seller to provide covenant against property being developed for non-recreational purposes

This Agreement shall be contingent upon Seller, prior to closing, filing a restrictive covenant limiting the use of the property described on Exhibit "A" (legal description of recreation property) hereto to recreational use only for the use and enjoyment of the owners in _____ subdivision.

The provision and the requested restrictive covenant will be valid and enforceable only if the developer with whom the buyer is contracting also owns the undeveloped property.

§ 6.8   Title Standards

The Title Standards adopted by the State Bar of Georgia are described as a "crystallization of the practice of title attorneys" and their purpose is to eliminate technical objections to title which do not impair marketability.

A title standard is a statement officially approved by a bar association, which declares the answer to a question or a solution for a problem involved in the process of title examination. It is not a law, but acquires its authority from voluntary compliance by attorneys.

The Title Standards address a number of issues, including, but not limited to, the following: name variances; conveyances by co-tenants; instruments executed by corporations; conveyances involving limited partnerships, general partnerships, and limited liability companies; title through decedents' estates; foreclosures; planned unit developments; bankruptcy; mineral rights; environmental issues; surveys; marital

---

447   Appalachee Enterprises, Inc. v. Walker, 266 Ga. 35, 463 S.E.2d 896 (1995).

rights; conveyances by and to trustees; assessments for governmental improvements and services; federal tax liens; commercial real estate broker liens; zoning; and condemnation.

§ 6.9   Title insurance against losses arising through defects in title

Even if the title search is done perfectly, there may be encumbrances recorded between when the title examination is performed and the dates on which the warranty deed and deed to secure debt are recorded. This is called the "gap period" and is insured routinely by some, but not all, title insurers. Whether or not the gap is routinely insured may depend on the county in which the property is located and the county's timeliness in recording documents. Title insurance also protects against encumbrances not properly satisfied at closing and other claims of ownership caused by forged deeds, deeds by minors or incompetent persons, or the like.

Rather than a guarantee of marketable title, title insurance is generally described as an indemnity against unmarketability. Even though title insurance will not protect the owner against all risks associated with the purchase of property, buyers are well advised to purchase title insurance. It is a one-time expense that, if needed, can prove to be invaluable.

§ 6.9.1   Lender's title policy does not protect owner

Lenders require a title policy for their protection. The lender's policy insures against loss by the lender and its successors. It ensures that the lender has an enforceable, valid lien on the property securing the loan. Since the lender's title insurance policy does not protect the buyer, the buyer should obtain a separate insurance policy, known as an owner's policy, to protect the buyer's ownership interest in the property.

Georgia courts have held that the duty of the insurer is only to its insured, not to one who is not a party to the contract, even though the buyer pays the premiums on the policies.[448] The cost of the title insurance policy is a closing cost which is often paid by the buyer. If the owner's title insurance is written at the same time as the lender's policy, a simultaneous issue rate is charged and the expense is less than if the buyer purchased an owner's title policy at a later date.

---

448   Gaines v. American Title Ins. Co. etc, 136 Ga. App. 162, 220 S.E.2d 469 (1975); Sherrill v. Louisville Title Ins. Co., 134 Ga. App. 322, 214 S.E.2d 410 (1975).

§ 6.9.2   Title insurance does not insure against all risks of ownership of property.

The standard ALTA owner's policy covers the following risks:

1. Loss or damage resulting from title to the property being vested in someone other than the person listed on the policy;
2. Loss or damage resulting from a lien or encumbrance on the title;
3. Loss or damage resulting from a lack of right of access to the property;
4. Loss or damage resulting from unmarketable title.

Title insurance is not the answer to every problem relating to property. There are five standard exceptions, which are:

1. Assessments and taxes from the year the policy is purchased;
2. Rights or claims of parties in possession not shown by public records;
3. roadways, streams or easements not shown by public records, riparian rights and title to any filled-in land;
4. Encroachments, overlaps, boundary line disputes and other matters that would be disclosed by an accurate survey or inspection and
5. Liens or rights to a lien for services, labor or material imposed by law and not shown in the public records.

An example where the title insurance did not cover the costs to correct the error in a faulty survey is a case where the buyer brought an action against a title insurance company that denied coverage for what was described only as "2727 Spalding Drive" in the purchase contract.[449] The buyer walked the boundaries of the property with the seller, and the seller represented that he owned title to parcels one through four, but in fact, because of faulty surveys by predecessors in title, he owned only parcels two and three. The buyer claimed that he was led to believe that he was purchasing four parcels of land, but in reality, he paid for parcels two, three, and four and received a warranty deed describing only parcels two and three. The title insurance company reached a settlement with the buyer on parcel two because the warranty deed containing the property description insured included that parcel. The buyer then brought legal action against the title insurance company (among others), contending that the title policy did not include parcel four, which the parties intended to convey. Even though the court eventually found that the buyer had title to parcel four, the title insurance company was not responsible for any of the expenses, because its policy did not insure that parcel.

Purchasers of title insurance should exercise caution in determining what is covered and what is excepted from the policy. For example, matters of survey are frequently excepted. Therefore, if the warranty deed correctly describes the metes and bounds of the property, but the survey inaccurately shows more acreage than actually

---

449   White v. Lawyers Title Ins. Corp., 197 Ga. App. 780, 399 S.E.2d 526 (1990).

conveyed, the title insurance policy will not insure the shortage in area. On the other hand, if the survey is included under the policy, the shortage in area will be insured.[450] However, standard practice is for title insurers to specifically provide an exception that the exact acreage of the property is not insured.

Other excluded risks are:

1. Matters relating to building or zoning ordinances or regulations, environmental protection laws or any improper subdivision of property either current or back in the chain of title, and exercise of other governmental police power, unless there is notice in the "public records" at the date of the policy;
2. Loss or damage relating to exercise of eminent domain;[451]
3. Defects, liens, encumbrances, adverse claims or other matters including those resulting from those created, suffered, assumed or agreed to by the insured, those not known to the insurer or not recorded but known to the insured and not disclosed in writing to the insurer by the insured; those resulting in no loss or damage to the insured; those created after the policy date and those resulting in loss and damage because the insured did not pay value for the interest insured by the policy.
4. Any fraud or preferential claim that is based on the current transaction and arising from the operation of federal bankruptcy, state insolvency or other creditors rights laws.

§ 6.9.3   Enhanced title policy

An enhanced title policy provides coverage for a range of different items that are not covered by the standard policy. First, an enhanced policy may offer coverage for items that cannot be insured at all under a standard policy. A standard title policy excludes any encroachments, overlaps, boundary line disputes and other matters that would be disclosed by an accurate survey or inspection. Therefore, a standard title policy gives only limited protection for a buyer who does not obtain a survey. On the other hand, an enhanced policy will cover some, but not all, matters that would show up on a survey.

Second, an enhanced policy insures some matters that occur after the policy is issued, such as forgery, easements, liens for labor and material, encroachment by neighbors, supplemental tax assessments and/or limitations on use of the land.

---

450   U.S. Life Title Ins. Co. of Dallas v. Hutsell, 164 Ga. App. 443, 296 S.E.2d 760 (1983), cert. denied.

451   The right of the state to reassert its dominion over property for public exigency and public good.

§ 6.9.4 Title to property can be marketable and still be worthless in economic sense

Title insurance is not a guarantee that the property is worth what the buyer paid for it, and it does not protect against a drop in fair market value of the property. As noted above, the fact that property is in a flood plain is not considered a title defect.[452] However, the price the buyer paid for the property may be in excess of its worth if the buyer was not aware of the fact that the property was in a flood plain.

§ 6.10 Difference between "tenants in common" and "joint tenants with right of survivorship"

Tenancy in common is created whenever two or more persons are entitled to the simultaneous possession of any property. Tenants in common may have unequal shares in the property, but they will be held to be equal unless otherwise stated.[453] If parties hold property as tenants in common and one of the parties dies, the decedent's interest in the property will be transferred through her will or as provided by the intestacy laws. For example, if Joe and Mary own property as tenants in common and Mary dies with a will that designates her daughter Sally as her sole beneficiary, Sally will acquire Mary's interest in the property and will become a tenant in common with Joe.

The Joint Tenancy Act of 1976 provided for joint tenancy in Georgia. Joint tenancy means that parties can take title to property jointly and when one party dies, the surviving party will have title to the entire property automatically without the property having to pass through the decedent's estate.[454] Any instrument of title in favor of two or more persons which expressly refers to the takers as "joint tenants," "joint tenants and not as tenants in common," or "joint tenants with survivorship" or as taking "jointly with survivorship," or language essentially the same as these phrases creates a joint tenancy estate or interest.[455] If the instrument does not contain such language, no joint tenancy is created. This form of ownership is typically used when property is titled in the names of spouses or others with close relationships. For example, if Joe and Mary own property as joint tenants with right of survivorship and Mary dies with a will that designates her daughter Sally as her sole beneficiary, Joe will take Mary's interest in the property because title to the property passes to Joe outside the will.

---

452   <u>Chicago Title Ins. Co. v. Investguard</u>, 215 Ga. App. 121, 449 S.E.2d 681 (1994).

453   O.C.G.A. § 44-6-120.

454   Prior to 1976, Georgia law did not recognize joint tenancy. However, parties in Georgia could still create a right of survivorship. A right of survivorship meant that property could be owned by two persons so that they would hold the property as tenants in common until one of them died and then the survivor would take title to the whole in fee simple. <u>Williams v. Studstill</u>, 251 Ga. 466, 306 S.E.2d 633 (1983), citing Agnor,"Joint Tenancy in Georgia," 3 Ga. St. Bar J. 29 (1966).

455   O.C.G.A. § 44-6-190.

The statute as drafted in 1976 stated that if a joint tenant transferred all or part of her interest in the property to a third party during her lifetime, the joint tenancy would be severed. However, the Code section was amended in 1984 to protect bona fide purchasers from a severance by any lifetime transfer which is unrecorded. Survivorship deeds are not subject to these severance problems and have been upheld by case law.[456]

§ 6.11   Bankruptcy by seller can affect title

Bankruptcy proceedings affect the conveyance and encumbrance of property and the enforceability of liens against property but do not automatically extinguish all judgments and liens against a debtor's property. To convey marketable title, a seller will have to follow certain procedures outlined in the Bankruptcy Code.[457] These procedures may vary depending on the type of bankruptcy action filed. Bankruptcy actions may fall under several chapters as follows: a Chapter 7 is a liquidation; a Chapter 11 is a reorganization for an individual with unsecured debt in excess of $250,000.00 and secured debt in excess of $750,000.00 as of the date of filing of a bankruptcy or for a corporation; a Chapter 12 is family farmer bankruptcy; and a Chapter 13 is an individual reorganization for all other individuals.

Whenever property to be sold is owned by a person or entity in bankruptcy, the closing attorney should be notified as soon as possible to give her time to verify that all necessary documentation is available so that the parties can be assured that marketable title can be conveyed. Additionally, the conveyance will likely be subject to the approval of the bankruptcy judge, which approval may take time. Many bankruptcy issues can be complex and are beyond the scope of this book. Outlined below is a brief review of issues involved when property to be sold is part of a bankruptcy action.

§ 6.11.1   Property of debtor that is part of bankruptcy

The property of a bankrupt individual or entity is known as the bankruptcy estate or property of the estate. The bankruptcy estate consists of all property of the debtor at the commencement of the case.[458] Inheritance, property received through a property settlement or divorce decree and life insurance benefits the debtor receives or is entitled to receive within 180 days from the date the bankruptcy action is filed are also property of the estate.[459] Additionally, in a Chapter 13 case, property of the estate includes property the debtor acquires after commencement of the case but before the case is closed.[460]

---

456   Epps v. Wood, 243 Ga. 835, 257 S.E.2d 259 (1979).
457   11 U.S.C.A. § 101, et seq.
458   11 U.S.C.A. § 541(a)(1).
459   11 U.S.C.A. § 541(a)(5).
460   11 U.S.C.A. § 1306.

§ 6.11.2   Purchase and sale agreement can be rejected in bankruptcy

If property is listed or a contract for sale of property is entered into before the bankruptcy is filed, the Bankruptcy Code allows the bankruptcy trustee to assume or reject any contract which has been signed, but not yet carried out (i.e., an executory contract). In a Chapter 7 bankruptcy action, the contract is deemed rejected if not assumed (specifically agreed to) by the bankruptcy trustee within 60 days of the filing of the petition.[461] In Chapter 11 and 13 cases, the debtor generally retains possession of the property and has the power to assume or reject an executory contract at any time before confirmation of the bankruptcy reorganization plan.[462]

Since a listing agreement is an executory contract, the real estate broker may request an order directing the debtor to decide within a specified time whether to assume or reject the listing agreement.[463] The attorney for the broker would normally file this request. In addition, the broker should file a motion with the bankruptcy court for approval of employment of a professional person. If the broker does not verify that the debtor has affirmed the listing agreement and if the broker does not apply to the court for appointment as a professional person, there is a risk that the broker could lose the commission. In the alternative, the broker may have to file a lawsuit and make an equitable argument for entitlement to the commission.

To avoid this situation, the broker should ensure that the listing agreement is affirmed or the broker should have a new listing agreement signed after the bankruptcy action is filed. The broker's motion for approval of employment of a professional person, if granted, will ensure that when a motion to sell the property is filed with the court, the commission will be paid to the broker directly out of closing.[464]

If the listing agreement or real estate contract is entered into after the petition is filed, the issues above regarding executory contracts do not exist. However, as explained below, in most cases, the court must approve the sale.

§ 6.11.3   Impact on real estate transaction if one co-owner files for bankruptcy but other does not

If one co-owner of property files a petition in bankruptcy, the property that is jointly owned will be affected, but any other property owned by the non-filing co-owner, individually or jointly with some other third party, will not be affected. Additionally, if only one spouse files a bankruptcy action, property owned solely by the spouse who has not filed bankruptcy will not be affected. That is, if a wife owns

---

461   11 U.S.C.A. §365(d)(1).
462   11 U.S.C.A. §365(d)(2).
463   11 U.S.C.A. §365(d)(2).
464   11 U.S.C.A. §327.

property in her own name and her husband does not have any interest in the property, the property will not be affected if the husband files the bankruptcy petition.

However, if husband and wife own the property jointly, either as joint tenants or as tenants in common, the bankruptcy petition of the husband will affect the property, even if the wife does not file. In some instances, the property may be released from the bankruptcy estate due to an exemption which the debtor may claim.

In certain cases where the non-bankrupt owner does not agree to the sale, the bankruptcy trustee has the authority to sell the entire property anyway, including the interest of the non-bankrupt owner. This can happen when: partition of the property between the bankruptcy estate and co-owner(s) is impracticable; the sale of the estate's undivided interest in the property would realize significantly less for the estate than sale of the property free of the interest of such co-owner(s); and the benefit to the estate of a sale of such property free and clear of the interests of co-owner(s) outweighs the detriments, if any, to such co-owner(s).[465]

In such cases, co-owner(s) may purchase the property at the price at which the sale is to be consummated.[466]

§ 6.11.4   Sale of property under protection of bankruptcy

In a Chapter 7 case, the bankruptcy trustee is the party that would sign a deed of conveyance, unless the trustee abandons her interest in the property because it has little or no value to the estate. If the trustee sells the property, marketable title may be conveyed if there is an order authorizing the sale of the property filed in the bankruptcy court showing notice given to all creditors and an opportunity for hearing, documentation of the appointment of the trustee, and proof that the property is property of the estate.[467]

If the trustee abandons the property in a Chapter 7 bankruptcy, the debtor may sell it; however, it is subject to all liens and encumbrances. In some cases, the debtor may avoid a judicial lien on property to the extent that it impairs an exception;[468] however, the debtor may not avoid statutory and certain other liens against the property. The debtor may convey marketable title upon proof showing the trustee has abandoned the property and upon satisfaction or release of liens which are not avoided under the Bankruptcy Code.[469]

Chapter 11 reorganization cases are generally more complex than Chapter 7 and Chapter 13 cases. In many Chapter 11 cases, a trustee is generally not appointed.

---

465   11 U.S.C.A. § 363(h).
466   11 U.S.C.A. § 363(i).
467   State Bar of Georgia Title Standards, §21.2(B); 11 U.S.C.A. § 363.
468   11 U.S.C.A. § 522(f).
469   State Bar of Georgia Title Standards, §21.2(C).

In such a case, a debtor may sell the property subject to certain notice requirements to creditors and an opportunity for a hearing.[470] If the sale is to be considered in the "ordinary business" of the Chapter 11 debtor, notice to creditors may not be necessary.[471] In addition, if the sale is authorized as part of the confirmed plan, marketability of the title to the property will not be impaired.[472]

In a Chapter 13 case, marketability of the title to the property will not be impaired if the debtor has obtained a final order authorizing the sale after notice to creditors and the opportunity for a hearing.[473] As in a Chapter 7 case where the debtor may sell the property, the sale of the property will be subject to outstanding liens and encumbrances unless the order from the court specifically provides that the sale is "free and clear of all liens."[474]

In most instances, the trustee or debtor conveying the property will obtain an order that the sale is free and clear of all liens. Generally, in order to obtain an order authorizing the sale, the sales contract must provide for sales proceeds to be used to pay liens that have not been avoided.

§ 6.12   Effect of divorce on title

Property owned by a spouse prior to marriage remains the separate property of that spouse.[475] However, both spouses acquire an equitable interest in property acquired after the marriage, even if the property is titled in the name of only one of the spouses. Such property is subject to later equitable division.[476] Third parties are not affected by the equitable interest of a spouse until an order or petition for divorce is filed in the county in which the property is located.[477]

§ 6.12.1   Transferring title during divorce proceedings

If a notice of lis pendens has been filed in the superior court of the county where the land is located after a petition for divorce has been filed, neither party may transfer the property to avoid the vesting of title according to the final verdict in the divorce, except for a bona fide transfer in payment of preexisting debts.[478] The Title Standards further provide that even if a notice of lis pendens is not recorded, both spouses' signatures should be obtained on real property transfers which occur while a

---

470   11 U.S.C.A. §363.
471   11 U.S.C.A. §363(c)(1). A determination of what is in the "ordinary course of business" is not always plain and may require an order of the court.
472   State Bar of Georgia Title Standards, §21.2(d).
473   11 U.S.C.A. §363, State Bar of Georgia Title Standards, §21.2(e).
474   11 U.S.C.A. §363(f) and (g).
475   O.C.G.A. § 19-3-9; Bailey v. Bailey, 250 Ga. 15, 295 S.E.2d 304 (1982).
476   O.C.G.A. § 19-5-13; Stokes v. Stokes, 246 Ga. 765, 273 S.E.2d 169 (1980).
477   State Bar of Georgia Title Standards, §27.2(a).
478   O.C.G.A. § 19-5-7.

divorce or separate maintenance action is pending.[479] When the broker is aware that property is being sold when a divorce is pending, they should advise their client to consult with their divorce attorney to determine if the property will be in dispute in the divorce and whether the client's spouse will need to consent to the sale.

§ 6.12.2   Title by decree

Georgia law provides that a decree for specific performance operates as a deed to convey land or other property without any conveyance being executed by the vendor, if the decree is recorded in the superior court of the county where the property is located, and the decree "shall stand in the place of a deed."[480] Even when the decree is not recorded, the decree transfers the title to the property.[481]

The State Bar of Georgia Title Standards also provide that a divorce decree declaring title to be vested in one spouse is sufficient to vest title without the need of a deed, provided the decree contains a sufficient description of the property.[482] The Title Standards further provide, however, that if the decree calls for a deed but does not contain vesting language, then a deed must be obtained.[483]

Georgia case law provides that when one spouse receives a percentage of the net proceeds, such award is not an interest in property and it is not necessary to obtain a quitclaim deed from the other spouse.[484]

§ 6.13   Title through decedent's estate

When a person dies, the procedure for administering the estate is similar to the liquidation process that takes place when a corporation goes out of business. First, a personal representative is appointed to wrap up the affairs of the person who has died ("decedent"). If the decedent dies with a will, the representative is called the executor and may be named in the will. If the person dies without a will (in testate), the representative is called the administrator and is appointed by the court according to a statutory procedure.

The duties of the personal representative are to collect, conserve, pay claims of creditors, and distribute assets of the decedent. The representative is under the control

---

479   O.C.G.A. § 19-5-7.
480   O.C.G.A. § 9-11-70. This code section also provides remedies against a party who fails to comply with an order for specific performance (i.e., a requirement to execute a deed).
481   Richardson v. Park Avenue Bank, 173 Ga. App. 43, 325 S.E.2d 455 (1984).
482   State Bar of Georgia Title Standards, § 27.2; Elrod v. Elrod, 231 Ga. 222, 200 S.E.2d 885(1973).
483   State Bar of Georgia Title Standards, § 27.2.
484   Sisk v. Sisk, 214 Ga. 223, 104 S.E.2d 103 (1958); Lawrence v. Smith, 213 Ga. 57, 96 S.E.2d 579 (1957).

of and accountable to the Probate Court. "To go through probate" means to have an estate administered by the Probate Court.

The State Bar of Georgia Title Standards set forth the criteria that must be met in order to have marketable title conveyed from an estate.[485] The methods used to determine what is necessary to convey title through a decedent's estate will depend on a number of factors including, but not limited to the following: (1) whether the decedent died intestate or with a will; (2) how long ago the decedent died; and (3) if the decedent died with a will, how the will was probated and whether or not it authorizes sale of the property.

A surviving spouse or minor children may apply for a year's support, which is defined as that property or money set apart and assigned to the spouse and children, or children only, for their support and maintenance for 12 months from the date of death.[486] An application for a year's support will affect the ability of an administrator or executor to transfer property.

It is important to ascertain that the party executing the contract has proper authority to act on behalf of the estate. If the party does not have such authority, the contract will be null and void. The ability to convey good and marketable title to property out of an estate may be time-consuming and somewhat involved and goes beyond the scope of this book. Even if the party executing the contract has authority to enter the contract, the closing attorney should always be made aware, as soon as possible, that the property is being sold by an estate to give the attorney time to resolve issues and obtain the necessary verification that title is marketable. For example, in some cases, the Georgia Title Standards require the heirs to execute an affidavit renouncing their interest in the property. In many cases, obtaining such affidavits may be time-consuming because of the number of heirs. In some cases, the closing attorney will refer certain situations to a probate attorney to handle certain unresolved issues before the closing may take place.

§ 6.14   Title through trustee

To ensure that marketable title is conveyed from a trust, the existence of the trust and the authority of the trustee must be verified.[487] Georgia law provides that an express trust must be in writing and must have each of the following elements, ascertainable with reasonable certainty: (1) an intention by a settlor to create a trust; (2) trust property; (3) a beneficiary; (4) a trustee; and (4) active duties imposed on the trustee.[488] A trustee has no authority to sell or convey the property of the trust estate unless expressly authorized by the instrument creating the trust or pursuant to an order

---

485   State Bar of Georgia Title Standards, §§ 13.1-13.14.
486   O.C.G.A. § 53-5-2.
487   See chapter 12 on Parties to the Contract for capacity of trustee to execute a contract.
488   O.C.G.A. § 53-12-20.

of the superior court.[489] In many cases verification as to the existence of the trust and authority of the trustee must be made by reference to facts or documents outside the record.

If a decedent conveys property to a trust, the provisions of the Testamentary Additions to Trusts Act should be considered.[490] This statute governs how property conveyed by a testator under a will shall be part of the trust to which it is given and shall be administered and disposed of in accordance with the provisions of the instrument or will setting forth the terms of the trust.[491]

§ 6.15   Title by prescription or adverse possession

A possessor of property may acquire title to the property by prescription if the possession extends over the period of time prescribed by statute, commonly referred to as adverse possession. Georgia law provides that   possession of real property for a period of 20 years shall confer good title against everyone with a few exceptions.[492]

In order to acquire title by prescription, the claimant must be the party in possession of the property and the possession must be public, continuous, exclusive, uninterrupted, peaceable and not obtained by actual fraud. If the possession is by permission of the owner, the possession cannot amount to title unless the claimant has given actual notice of the claim to the owner.[493]

The prescribed time period is reduced to seven years if there is some written evidence of title, legally referred to as "color of title", which does not actually pass title but is sufficient evidence of the claim to title.[494]   "Color of title" means a document that on its face appears to transfer title, but which fails to do so because the transferee does not have title or because the conveyance was defective in some way. In other words, that there is some form of written evidence showing a transfer of title of property to the claimant.

The conditions are that the property must be described so that it can be identified with certainty and the claimant must have claim to the property in good faith. The rationale of allowing a claimant to have good title despite only having "color of title" is to make a bad title good when the claimant has bought the property in good faith, and believing he has obtained good title, enters into possession and remains there uninterruptedly and peaceably. The date of the seven-

---

489   O.C.G.A. § 53-12-257.
490   O.C.G.A. § 53-12-70, et seq.
491   O.C.G.A. § 53-12-71.
492   O.C.G.A. § 44-5-163. Title by prescription cannot be acquired in respect of public property. City of Marietta v. CSX Transportation, Inc., 272 Ga. 612, 533 S.E.2d 372 (2000). Other exceptions listed in O.C.G.A. § 44-5-170
493   Love v. Love, 259 Ga. 423, 383 S.E.2d 329 (1989)
494   O.C.G.A. § 44-5-164

year period begins to run from the date of the written color of title and not from the time of possession.

Set forth below are examples of documents which qualify as "color of title", which ripen into good title:

1. A deed from a partnership signed only by one partner;[495]
2. A sheriff's deed that is based on a void judgment;[496]
3. A deed transferring the marital home from the wife to husband which was void because she did not obtain the order of the superior court;[497]
4. A quitclaim deed;[498] and
5. A deed from a seller who did not have title to the property.[499]

The following are documents which were held not to be "color of title":

1. A void mortgage;
2. The payment of taxes is not evidence of title but is admissible as a circumstance tending to prove adverse possession;[500] and
3. A deed lacking a good legal description from which the property could not be identified.[501]

§ 6.16   Effect of foreclosure

Foreclosures in Georgia may be either by judicial procedure or by non-judicial procedure. Judicial foreclosures may be conducted pursuant to statutory procedures[502] or equitable procedures.[503] However, the method of foreclosure used by virtually all lenders in Georgia is foreclosure by non-judicial power of sale which is exercised under a deed to secure debt.[504] Although there is no statutory procedure for conducting non-judicial foreclosure sales, such sales must be advertised and conducted in the same manner as sheriff's sales[505] and notice must be provided to the debtor.[506]

To convey marketable title through a foreclosure sale, all statutory and contractual requirements must be complied with and there must be no outstanding rights of redemption. In a non-judicial foreclosure sale, the security instrument and

---

495   Tarver v. Depper, 132 Ga. 798, 65 S.E. 177, 24 L.R.A.N.S. 1161 (1909)
496   Rogers v. Smith 91 S.E. 414 (1917)
497   Carpenter v. Booker 62 S.E. 983 (1908)
498   Warlick v. Rome Loan & Finance Co. 194 Ga. 419, 22 S.E.2d 61 (1942)
499   Gitten v. Lowry, 15 Ga. 336 (1854)
500   Chamblee v. Johnson 200 Ga. 838, 38 S.E.2d 721 (1946)
501   Donaldson v. Nichols 223 Ga. 206, 154 S.E.2d 201 (1967)
502   O.C.G.A. § 44-14-180, 44-14-210.
503   O.C.G.A. § 44-14-49.
504   O.C.G.A. § 23-2-114.
505   O.C.G.A. § 44-14-162.
506   O.C.G.A. § 44-14-162.1-162.4.

succession of transfers to the current holder should be recorded. This allows the examining party to verify the instrument under which the property was foreclosed and to verify that all contractual requirements are met.

For example, failure to pay intangible recording tax applicable to a security instrument is a bar to foreclosure.[507] However, this bar to foreclosure may be removed by payment of the tax plus penalty and interest. In addition, the security instrument should outline the terms and procedures for conducting the foreclosure sale and these terms and procedures must be followed. Finally, the instrument must contain a valid power of attorney empowering the grantee to conduct the foreclosure sale and execute the deed under power of sale as attorney in fact for the grantor.[508]

Prior to commencing foreclosure, the foreclosing party should also ensure that, if applicable, the Soldiers' and Sailors' Civil Relief Act[509] has been complied with. This statute provides protection to people in the military service from loss of certain interests in property during the period in which they are involved in a military conflict and can preclude foreclosure.

Generally, a valid foreclosure sale terminates the debtor's interest in the property and there is no right of redemption in favor of the debtor or junior lien holders. If an IRS tax lien is properly filed more than 30 days prior to the foreclosure sale date, written notice of the foreclosure sale must be given to the Internal Revenue Service at least 25 days prior to the sale date. If such notice is not given, a federal tax lien is not eliminated by the foreclosure sale of a senior security instrument. If a federal tax lien is eliminated by the foreclosure sale, the United States has a period of 120 days from the date of the sale to redeem the property.

In addition, if the owner of the property filed a bankruptcy action which was pending on the date of foreclosure, there must be evidence that the foreclosing party complied with the provisions of the Bankruptcy Code.[510] An automatic stay precluding creditors from proceeding against the debtor's property arises upon commencement of the bankruptcy case.[511]

Generally, a foreclosing party must obtain from the bankruptcy court an order for a relief from stay to proceed with foreclosure. Oftentimes the homeowner is at the bankruptcy court on the morning of the foreclosure. Even though the foreclosing lender is not aware of the filing of the bankruptcy, the automatic stay is nonetheless effective and renders the foreclosure void.

---

507   O.C.G.A. § 48-6-77(a).
508   State Bar of Georgia Title Standards, § 17.1.
509   50 U.S.C. § 464.
510   11 U.S.C.A. § 101, et seq.
511   11 U.S.C.A. § 362.

As an alternative to foreclosure, a conveyance of property in lieu of foreclosure may be made by quitclaim deed, limited warranty deed, or general warranty deed from the debtor to the lender. However, a deed in lieu of foreclosure does not eliminate junior security interests. Therefore, most lenders will not accept a deed in lieu of foreclosure and will choose to exercise their rights under the deed to secure debt.

§ 6.17 Transfer of title by deed

A deed is a written instrument, the purpose of which is to convey the ownership of property from one party to another. A party who executes a deed and relinquishes her interest in the property is called the grantor. The person receiving the grantor's interest in the property is the grantee.

§ 6.17.1 Requirements for valid deed

To be valid, a deed must contain the following:

a. A written instrument purporting to convey title to the land.[512] Title to real estate cannot be conveyed orally but must be conveyed in writing.[513]

b. A grantor, that is, a person or legal entity possessing the property and having the legal ability to convey title.[514]

c. A grantee, which must be a person or a legal entity capable of holding title to the conveyed property.[515]

d. Words of conveyance or granting clause. Although a deed must contain language which has the effect of conveying title, no particular form of words is necessary. However, the granting clause must clearly express the grantor's intent to make a present or immediate conveyance of title to the grantee, not a future conveyance.[516] Phrases most commonly used are: "bargain, sell, and convey," "give, grant, and convey," "demise, quitclaim, and release," "transfer and assign."[517]

e. A description of the property sufficient to identify it. The property being conveyed must be described so that it can be clearly distinguished from all

---

512   O.C.G.A. § 44-5-30.
513   O.C.G.A. § 13-5-30.
514   McCollum v. Loveless, 187 Ga. 262, 200 S.E. 115 (1938).
515   State Highway Dept. v. Williams Lumber Co., 222 Ga. 23, 148 S.E.2d 426 (1966); Handy v. Handy, 154 Ga. 686, 115 S.E. 114 (1922).
516   Caldwell v. Caldwell, 140 Ga. 736, 79 S.E. 853 (1913).
517   Woodward v. LaPorte, 181 Ga. 731, 184 S.E. 280 (1935).

other parcels of land. If the description is so indefinite that it cannot be identified with certainty, the deed is void.[518]

f. Signature of the grantor. Although the names of both the grantor and grantee appear in the deed, only the grantor is required to sign it since it is the grantor who is conveying the title.[519]

g. Delivery and acceptance. Title to real estate is conveyed when a properly executed deed is delivered to and accepted by the grantee or grantee's agent.[520] The grantee's acceptance need not be by express words, but may be by acts, conduct, or words showing an intention to accept the conveyance.[521] Acceptance may be inferred from such facts as retention of the deed, assertion of title, subsequent sale or encumbrance of the property, or bringing suit on the deed.[522]

There are two other elements that are usually included in a deed, even though the deed is valid between the parties in their absence:[523]

a. A good or valuable consideration. This is defined as the inducement to a contract and must be something of value moving from the grantee to the grantor. As between parties, a deed without actual consideration may be valid if a nominal consideration is recited, or if the conveyance was intended as a gift.[524] Conveyances without actual consideration are termed "voluntary deeds" and are recognized as recordable.[525] A deed which recites the payment of a consideration is valid, even though it is a nominal amount, and may not in fact have been paid, since it could be sued for and recovered.[526]

b. Attestation and/or acknowledgment is required in order for the deed to be recorded.[527] An acknowledgment is different from an attestation. An attestation is the act of witnessing the actual execution of the paper and

---

518   Allen v. Smith, 169 Ga. 395, 150 S.E. 584 (1929); Furney v. Dukes, 226 Ga. 804, 177 S.E.2d 680 (1970). See chapter 1 on Property Description for an in-depth discussion of this topic.
519   O.C.G.A. § 44-5-30.
520   Domestic Loans of Washington, Inc. v. Wilder, 113 Ga. App. 803, 149, S.E.2d 717 (1966).
521   Domestic Loans of Washington, Inc. v. Wilder, 113 Ga. App. 803, 149 S.E.2d 717 (1966); McKenzie v. Alston, 58 Ga. App. 849, 853, 200 S.E. 518 (1938).
522   Widincamp v. Brigman, 166 Ga. 209, 143 S.E. 149 (1928).
523   O.C.G.A. § 44-5-30.
524   Dodson V. Phagan, 227 Ga. 480, 181 S.E.2d 366 (1971).
525   O.C.G.A. § 44-2-3.
526   Thornton V. North American Acceptance Corp., 228 Ga. 176, 184 S.E.2d 589 (1971).
527   O.C.G.A. § 44-2-14.

signing one's name as a witness to the execution. An acknowledgment is the act of a grantor going before a notary public and declaring the paper to be her deed. The deed is then accompanied by a certificate of the notary public stating that the acknowledgment was made.[528] In order to record a deed, it must be attested to by at least two witnesses, one of who must be a notary, or attested to by two witnesses and acknowledged by a notary.[529] This requirement goes only to the recordability of the deed, and a deed will not be invalid between the parties simply because there is no attestation.[530]

§ 6.17.2   Types of deeds

All deeds serve the same basic function, which is to convey the grantor's interest in property. This function is accomplished after a deed has been properly executed, delivered, and accepted. The distinctions between deeds are found in the extent of title protection the grantor promises the grantee, the identity of the grantor, and the circumstances under which the property is conveyed.

§ 6.17.2.1   General warranty deed

A general warranty deed offers the most comprehensive title protection of any deed. It contains covenants of title which are promises by the grantor that certain conditions of title exist. Typical covenants of title include: covenant of seisin, covenant against encumbrances, covenant of quiet enjoyment, covenant of warranty forever, and covenant of further assurances.[531] The covenants of warranty apply not only to title defects occurring during the grantor's period of ownership but also to those occurring before she took title.

§ 6.17.2.2   Limited warranty deed

A limited warranty deed is distinguished from a general warranty deed in that the grantor warrants the property's title only against defects occurring during the grantor's ownership and not against defects existing before that time.[532]

For example, the purchaser in one case had purchased a property by way of a limited warranty deed.[533] The seller was the bank, which became the owner after foreclosing on the loan and obtaining a power of sale. The warranty provided that the " . . . Grantor will warrant and forever defend the right and title to the above

---

528   White & Co. v. Magarahan, 87 Ga. 217, 13 S.E. 509 (1891), overruled on other grounds.
529   O.C.G.A. §§ 44-2-14, 44-2-15, 44-5-30.
530   Budget Charge Accounts v. Peters, 213 Ga. 17, 96 S.E.2d 887 (1957).
531   O.C.G.A. § 44-5-62.
532   McDonough v. Martin, 88 Ga. 675, 16 S.E. 59 (1892).
533   Creek v. First Nat. Bank of Atlanta, 154 Ga.App. 266, 267 S.E.2d 872 (1980)

217

described property unto the said Grantee against the claims of all persons claiming by, through or under Grantor, and not otherwise." The bank was not aware that there were unpaid taxes on the property, which constituted a lien on the property. The lien existed before the bank became the owner of the property.

The tax authority claimed the unpaid taxes against the buyer, who then sued the bank for reimbursement. The Court stated that the limited warranty only protects the buyer against claims made after the conveyance by the bank or by some person claiming through or under the bank. The bank did not warranty anything else except as against itself and its own acts, or acts of third parties affecting the right to possession, which occur during the time of when the bank owned the property. Since the tax lien was imposed by the tax authority and not the bank or anyone claiming under the bank, the tax lien did not fall within the limited warranty.

§ 6.17.2.3   Quitclaim

A quitclaim is intended to pass any title, interest, or claim which the grantor may have in the property, but it does not guarantee the title is valid and does not contain any warranty or covenants of title.[534]

§ 6.17.2.4   Gift deed or voluntary deed

A gift deed conveys title without the exchange of valuable consideration.[535] Generally, the phrase "For love and affection" is stated in the deed and is sufficient to make the conveyance valid.[536]

§ 6.17.2.5   Deed to secure debt

This is a loan instrument used in Georgia in lieu of a mortgage or trust deed found in other states. It conveys equitable title as security for the debt as compared with a mortgage, which conveys merely a lien, not title.[537]

6.17.2.6   Deed in foreclosure or deed under power

A deed under power is used to convey title when the holder of a deed to secure debt forecloses on the property and sells the property to satisfy a lien.[538]

---

534   Black's Law Dictionary (8th ed. 2004).
535   Clayton v. Tucker, 20 Ga. 452 (1856).
536   Hobbs v. Clark, 221 Ga. 558, 146 S.E.2d 271 (1965).
537   O.C.G.A. § 7-1-1000; Pusser v. Thompson, 132 Ga. 280, 64 S.E. 75 (1909).
538   O.C.G.A. § 44-14-160.

6.17.2.7　Tax deed

A tax deed is used to convey title to property that has been sold by the government because of non-payment of taxes.[539] The method of sale is the same as a judicial sale.[540] The sale is advertised for a public sale, which is published weekly for four weeks preceding the sale. Sales are made at public outcry at the courthouse of the county where the levy was made, on the first Tuesday in each month, between the hours of 10 A.M. and 4 P.M. At the sale, the purchaser must pay by cash or cashier's check and will take title at his/her own risk. A purchaser who acquires property in a tax sale does not acquire fee simple title to the property. Instead, the purchaser will only acquire title that was vested in the owner.[541]

A title under a tax deed executed pursuant to a valid and legal tax sale before July 1 1989 will ripen into fee simple title by prescription after a period of seven years from the date of execution of that deed. Similarly, a title under a tax deed executed on or after July 1, 1989, but before July 1, 1996 will ripen into fee simple title after four years from the execution of that deed. For tax deeds executed on or after July 1, 1996, title will ripen by prescription after a period of four years from the recording of that deed in the land records in the county in which said land is located.[542]

A tax deed which has ripened by prescription as described above will convey a fee simple title to the property described in that deed, which will vest absolutely in the grantee in the deed or in the grantee's heirs or assigns.[543] Until then, any person having any right, title, or interest in or lien upon such property may redeem the property from the sale by the payment of the redemption price or the amount required for redemption.[544] The right of redemption may be exercised at any time within 12 months from the date of the sale or at any time after the sale until the purchaser bars the right to redeem. The purchase can bar the right to redeem by the giving notice after 12 months from the date of a tax sale giving the requisite notice required by statute.[545]

539　O.C.G.A. § 48-5-359.
540　O.C.G.A. § 48-4-1
541　For example, a widow's life estate that was sold by a sheriff's deed was held to convey only her life estate and hence the purchasers were subject to ejectment subsequent to her death. Allen v. Lindsey, 1913, 139 Ga. 648, 77 S.E. 1054
542　O.C.G.A. § 48-4-48.
543　O.C.G.A. § 48-4-48c
544　O.C.G.A. § 48-4-40
545　O.C.G.A. § 48-4-45

§ 6.17.2.8   Survivorship deed

A survivorship deed is a deed conveying property to several grantees, often a husband and wife, for their joint lives with the survivor(s) entitled to the deceased party's interest. A survivorship deed conveys interest outside a will.[546]

§ 6.17.2.9   Fiduciary deeds

Fiduciaries who are grantors and are acting in a representative capacity generally have no power to warrant anything. They convey no more title or interest than that owned by the person or estate they represent.[547] Examples of fiduciary deeds are a trustee's deed, a guardian's deed, an executor's deed, and an administrator's deed.

A trustee uses a trustee's deed in her representative capacity to convey property owned by a trust. It contains no warranties of title, as a trustee does not have the power to bind the trust by a warranty of title.[548]

A guardian's deed is used to convey a ward's interest in real property.[549] The property can be sold when it is presumed to be in the best interests of the ward. However, such sales are required to be consummated under supervision and direction of the probate court.[550]

An executor's deed conveys title to property of a decedent who died leaving a valid will.[551] For a decedent who died intestate, or without naming an executor in the will, an administrator's deed is executed to convey title for the purposes of payment of debts or for distribution.[552]

---

546   See discussion of Joint Tenancy above.
547   Harrison v. Harrison, 214 Ga. 393, 105 S.E.2d 214 (1958); Smith Realty Co. v. Hubbard, 124 Ga. App. 265, 183 S.E.2d 506 (1971).
548   Moss v. Twiggs, 260 Ga. 561, 397 S.E.2d 707 (1990).
549   O.C.G.A. § 29-2-3.
550   Merritt v. DOT, 147 Ga. App. 316, 248 S.E.2d 689 (1978), rev'd on other grounds.
551   Knowles v. Knowles, 125 Ga. App. 642, 188 S.E.2d 800 (1972).
552   Horn v. Wright, 157 Ga. App. 408, 278 S.E.2d 66 (1981).

CHAPTER 7
THE TERMITE LETTER

OVERVIEW

Most contracts require the seller to repair termite damage and provide the buyer with what is known as a termite clearance letter or wood destroying organisms inspection report at closing. This chapter discusses these obligations and includes, among other things, an explanation of the remedies available to the buyer if termite damage is discovered after closing. The difference between a pest control contract, guarantee and bond is also explained in this chapter.

§ 7.1   What the GAR Contract provides

The GAR Contract provides that an Official Georgia Wood Infestation Report be attached to the Contract. The report must: be prepared by a licensed pest control operator; cover each dwelling and garage on the property; and be dated within 180 days of the acceptance date.[553] The termite report can either be attached to the contract or be provided within 7 days of the binding agreement date. If the termite report is not timely provided or if the report indicates present infestation or damage from termites or other wood destroying organisms, the buyer is entitled to terminate the contract within 10 days from the binding agreement date.

Earlier versions of the GAR Contract provided that the seller produce the termite letter to the buyer at closing. The problem with this approach is that if the letter revealed infestation or damage, the parties were forced at the last minute to negotiate a solution to a serious problem, if not resolved, could cause the transaction to fall apart. Additionally, some buyers in the rush of signing closing documents did not carefully review the termite letter and realized only after closing that there was a problem. Unfortunately, closing with knowledge of a termite problem likely waives the buyer's ability to pursue a claim against the seller after the closing.

A recent example of such a case is where the buyers sued the sellers for fraudulently concealing the termite damage. The buyers' inspector had discovered some terminate damage and requested the sellers to have "Arrow check, re-inspect and issue a clearance letter." The buyers then received a Georgia Wood Infestation Report indicating pervious termite damage. Despite notice of the problems, the buyers proceeded to close on the purchase of the property. The court held that the buyers could not claim fraud when they had sufficient notice of the termite damage.[554]

In another case, the buyer received a standard form termite letter which indicated a prior infestation.[555] The termite letter, as all standard form termite letters,

---

553   GAR F20, paragraph 7

554   Meyer et al. v. Waite et al. 270 Ga.App. 255, 606 S.E.2d 16, (2004)

555   Westminster holdings, Ltd. V. Weatherspoon, 237 Ga.App. 819, 517 S.E.2d 80 (1999). See also, Leeuwenburg v. Clark, 226 Ga.App. 615, 492 S.E.2d 263 (1997) and Artzner v. A & A Exterminators, Inc., 242 Ga.App. 766, 531 S.E.2d 200 (2000).

contained a provision stating that the buyer should assume that structural damage could have resulted from the prior infestation. The buyer proceeded to closing without addressing this issue further. The buyer subsequently discovered termite damage and sued the seller. The Court ruled in favor of the seller, holding that the seller's obligation to repair termite damage ceased at closing and the buyer's failure to raise this as an issue waived any claim against the seller.

The current GAR Contract is designed to encourage the seller to provide a report to prospective purchasers prior to their making an offer on the property. By providing a termite letter at the time of the execution of the contract the buyer is much more likely to notice any adverse conditions noted on the clearance letter and can take them into consideration in the terms of her offer. Furthermore, the sale is less likely to fall through at the closing as could happen when terminate damage is revealed at the last minute

In addition to the preliminary clearance letter the GAR Contract provides that the seller will produce a second clearance letter, dated within thirty days of closing. This secondary letter must state that the property has been found to be free of any active infestation of termites and other wood destroying organisms. The seller is responsible for treating any active infestation. The purpose for the second clearance letter is twofold; (1) it is required by most lenders and (2) it provides confirmation that any treatment rendered as a result of the first inspection did, in fact, eliminate any active infestation.

Under the GAR Contract the seller warrants that, to the best of her knowledge and information, the information contained in any termite report supplied to the buyer is accurate and complete and that no inconsistent termite inspection reports have been issued. This provision is designed to help to prevent the seller from "shopping" for termite companies until she finds one that will issue a "clean" report.

§ 7.1.1 Termite letter covers dwelling, garage and attachments thereto

The GAR Contract requires that the termite inspections include each dwelling, including attachments to the dwellings and garages on the property. A "dwelling" is generally defined as a house or other structure in which a person lives. It would include the house and all buildings attached to or connected directly with the house or by an enclosed passageway.[556] If there are multiple structures on the property used as residences, such as a cottage, guesthouse, or separate garage which has been converted into a residence, such structures must be included in the termite letter. Structures attached to any dwelling, such as balconies, porches, or sheds, must also be included in the termite letter.

The GAR Contract provides that the termite inspection applies to "each dwelling (including attachments thereto and garage on the Property." On occasion,

---

556   Black's Law Dictionary, 8th Ed. (2004)

disputes may arise over whether particular structures constitute garages or, for that matter, even residences. When it is unclear whether a building constitutes a garage, the best way to avoid a dispute is to write into the contract whether the particular structure shall be considered a garage for the purposes of the termite section of the GAR Contract. An example of such a special stipulation is as follows:

Special Stipulation #7-1: Outbuilding shall be considered as garage

Buyer and Seller agree that the outbuilding located behind the main dwelling on the Property [and designated as an outbuilding on the survey attached hereto and incorporated herein] shall for all purposes be considered a "garage" under the Termite Letter section of this Agreement.

§ 7.1.2   Limiting seller's obligation to repair termite damage

If the seller agrees to be responsible for damage from termites or other wood-destroying organisms but wants to minimize this obligation, the following provision can be used:

Special Stipulation #7-2: Seller not responsible to repair termite damage

Notwithstanding any other provision in this Agreement to the contrary, including Buyer's right to request repairs, Buyer may not request, and Seller shall not be obligated to make, any repairs of damage caused by termites and other wood-destroying organisms, the total cost of which exceed the sum of $_____. If Seller receives a written estimate from a third party contractor that such repairs will exceed $_____, Seller shall immediately notify Buyer and provide Buyer with a copy of the estimate. Buyer shall have the right, within five (5) days from the delivery of such notice, to terminate this Agreement by written notice to Seller, in which case Buyer's earnest money shall be immediately refunded to Buyer. If Buyer elects not to terminate this Agreement, Seller shall, in Buyer's sole discretion and upon notice from Buyer to Seller either: (a) make the repairs up to the amount specified above prior to closing and provide written documentation to Buyer of the cost and nature of the repairs made by Seller for the above-specified sum, or (b) deduct the amount specified above from the purchase price with Buyer paying the balance at closing.

Buyers should be mindful that most lenders will require all structural damage from termite infestation to be corrected prior to closing (except possibly where the loan already designates a portion of the loan proceeds to be used for the rehabilitation of the property). If the buyer is to be responsible for the repair of structural damage she may not be able to obtain approval for the loan or may be forced to repair the termite damage out of her own funds prior to closing.

Sellers also may negotiate to narrow the scope of their clearance letter obligations under the GAR Contract so that the responsibilities do not include every dwelling, structure, and garage on the property. An example of such a special stipulation is set forth below:

Special Stipulation #7-3: Seller to reduce obligations under termite clearance letter

Notwithstanding any other provision in this Agreement to the contrary, the parties agree that Seller's obligations to provide Wood Infestation Reports shall not extend to the following improvements to the Property: [Examples: any dwelling except the main dwelling; any garage, including the gray outbuilding located behind the main dwelling; the rear deck attached to the main dwelling; etc.]

§ 7.1.3   Broadening seller's obligation to repair termite damage

Buyers may broaden the scope of the seller's repair obligations under the termite section of the GAR Contract. An example of such a special stipulation is as follows:

Special Stipulation #7-4: Seller responsible for structural termite damage

Notwithstanding any other provision in this Agreement to the contrary, Seller shall be obligated to correct all structural damages resulting from termites and other wood destroying organisms, and provide documentation at closing to the Buyer of the treatment of the infestation and the correction of all structural damage for the following improvements on the Property: [Examples: decks, fences, gazebos, outbuildings, carports, playhouses, trash enclosures, sheds, etc.]

§ 7.1.4   Buyer obtaining termite inspection and report

Under the GAR Contracts, the buyer has the right, but not the obligation to have a termite company to do his own inspection report. This is not always case with other standard real estate sales contracts. Set forth below is a special stipulation in which the buyer obtains the termite inspection and report but the seller pays for the report. The idea behind this provision is that if the buyer selects the termite company it can help prevent the seller from shopping for a company, which through incompetence or collusion, fails to identify termite infestation or damage.

Special Stipulation #7-5: Buyer to obtain termite report

Notwithstanding any other provision in this Agreement to the contrary, within _____ days of the Binding Agreement Date, Buyer shall cause to be made an inspection by a licensed pest control operator of each dwelling and garage on the Property for termites and other wood-destroying organisms. Seller shall pay all costs of the inspection up to an amount not to exceed $_____. The inspection shall meet the standards of the Georgia Structural Pest Control Commission. If visible evidence of active or previous infestation is found, Seller agrees at his own expense, prior to the closing, to (a) treat the active infestation, correct all structural damage resulting from any infestation, and provide documentation to Buyer of the treatment of the infestation and the correction of the structural damage, or (b) provide documentation, satisfactory to the lender, if any, indicating that there is no structural damage resulting from any infestation. Seller, at closing, shall provide a standard letter from the licensed pest control operator selected by Buyer to perform the inspection (or such other inspector as may be acceptable to Buyer) meeting the requirements of the Georgia Structural Pest Control Commission stating that each dwelling and garage on the Property has been so inspected and found to be free from visible evidence of active infestation of termites and other wood-destroying organisms.

Finally, some buyers may seek to have the seller repair both structural and cosmetic damage to the property resulting from termites. The following is a special stipulation to the contract which would address this issue:

Special Stipulation #7-6: Seller responsible for structural and cosmetic termite damage

If any repairs, renovations, or excavations to the Property are necessary due to infestation of the Property by termites and/or other wood-destroying organisms, Seller agrees at Seller's sole cost and expense, to repair all damage to the Property, regardless of whether the damage is structural or cosmetic. If there is damage to any wallpaper, the Seller shall seek to replace the wallpaper with matching wallpapers if it can be readily obtained. If Seller does not have and cannot readily obtain such wallpaper, Seller shall replace the wallpaper in the entire room where it appears with wallpaper of equal or better quality and cost and in a design reasonably similar to the existing wallpaper. If there is damage to any wood paneling, Seller shall replace the damaged wood with the same type of wood and stain it to reasonably match the existing wood.

Regardless of who obtains or pays for the termite report, the buyer should coordinate the timing of the termite report with the timing of their property inspection to assure that the report is obtained prior to the expiration of the Inspection Period.

§ 7.1.5 Problems with carpenter ants

Buyers should be aware that the standards of the Georgia Structural Pest Control Commission do not apply to carpenter ants. Therefore, termite inspections and termite bonds do not cover inspection or treatment for carpenter ants. However, carpenter ants can destroy wood. Carpenter ants tend to be more localized in their infestation than termites. They also tend to be easier to treat than termites. Nevertheless, because carpenter ants can cause damage, buyers may want to utilize the following special stipulation to require that the termite inspection include an inspection for carpenter ants and require the seller to repair any damage caused by carpenter ants.

Special Stipulation #7-7: Seller to complete inspection for carpenter ants

Within 30 days prior to closing, the Seller shall cause to be made, at Seller's sole cost and expense, an inspection of each dwelling and garage on the Property for termites and other wood-destroying organisms, including but not limited to carpenter ants. The inspection shall meet the standards of the Georgia Structural Pest Control Commission. If visible evidence of active or previous infestation is found, including but not limited to infestation of carpenter ants, Seller agrees, prior to the closing, to treat the active infestation, correct all structural damage resulting from any infestation, and provide documentation to Buyer of the treatment of the infestation and the correction of the structural damage. Seller, at closing, shall provide a standard letter meeting the requirements of the Georgia Structural Pest Control Commission stating that each dwelling and garage has been so inspected and found to be free from visible evidence of active infestation of termites and other wood-destroying organisms, including but not limited to carpenter ants.

§ 7.2 Termite letter provision and inspection contingency

Although the termite letter provision and the inspection contingency are distinct separate stipulations in the GAR Contract, the two provisions can work together to benefit the buyer. If the buyer has a right in the contract to request that the seller repair defects, this would include a right to request that any termite damage be repaired regardless of its location. For example, the buyer can request that the seller repair termite damage in freestanding fences, gazebos, barns, and other improvements not covered by the seller's termite clearance letter.

If the property is sold "as is," with no right of the buyer to request the repair of defects, the buyer is also waiving any right to request the repair of termite damage. This differs from the older GAR Contracts, which provided that the seller was required to make repairs to the property necessary for the issuance of a "clear" termite letter (i.e., one with no active infestation and no structural damage). Agents representing purchasers should be certain that their clients understand this new contract language.

§ 7.3   Fraud claims relating to termite damage

§ 7.3.1   Actual knowledge of termite damage necessary

To successfully pursue a claim against a seller for termite damage after closing on the purchase of the property, the buyer must show that the seller had actual knowledge of the damage before the closing.[557]

For example, in one Georgia case, a buyer lost when he sued his seller for fraudulent concealment and misrepresentation of termite damage because the buyer could not prove that the seller had actual knowledge of the termite damage.[558]   In that case, the seller hired an exterminator to inspect and issue a termite clearance letter. The exterminator discovered and treated a minor infestation of subterranean termites but reported that the house was free of other wood-destroying insects or fungus, structural damage, or rotten timbers. The exterminator also conducted an inspection after the initial treatment and reported no active infestation or damage.

After the buyer moved into the house, he discovered termites in the kitchen and den. Upon investigation, the buyer's exterminator found termite infestation and damage to the den floor, the sub-flooring, and the frame and jambs of the entrance door. The buyer's exterminator also found that the den floor tiles had been patched and structural repairs had been made during the 33 years that the seller had lived in the house. While the inspector did not find evidence of repairs to termite damage or concealment, the buyer argued that the court should infer such knowledge from the structural repairs that were made during the years that the seller lived in the house. However, the Court held that this alone was not enough to support an action for fraud.[559]

The court may sometimes infer that the seller must have actual knowledge of the damage. This is illustrated in a recent case where a property owner had bought a home that he had completely rebuilt because it was almost completely destroyed by a fire. The seller was the general contractor in the renovation and lived in the property for several years. As such, he was very familiar with the condition of the property. A few months after the closing, the buyers saw termites swarming in the house and began to investigate further. They called the inspector back to the property who had conducted the initial inspection. Upon closer inspection, the inspector found putty and paint that had been used to conceal holes and gaps in the wood caused by termite infestation. The buyers then sued the seller alleging that he fraudulently induced them to buy the house by making false representations about its condition. Based on these facts, the Court held that the

---

557   Bircoll et al. v. Rosenthal et al., 267 Ga.App. 431, 600 S.E.2d 388 (2004); Meyer et al. v. Waite et al., 270 Ga.App. 255, 606 S.E.2d 16 (2004)
558   Webb v. Rushing, 194 Ga. App. 732, 391 S.E.2d 709 (1990).
559   Webb v. Rushing, 194 Ga. App. 732, 391 S.E.2d 709 (1990).

jury was authorized to find that the seller must have known about the termite damage and was therefore liable for fraudulent concealment.

This is a significant case because the Court also held that in cases of active fraudulent concealment, the buyers could rely on verbal representations to show a pattern of deception by the seller even where the contract itself specifically stated that the buyer was not relying on such representations.

In this case, the seller had given the buyers a Seller's Property Disclosure Statement in which he stated that he was not aware of any damage due to termites or structural defects in the home. The contract contained an "entire agreement" clause, stating that the contract "*constitutes the sole and entire agreement between the parties*" and "*[n]o representation, promise, or inducement in the Agreement shall be binding upon any party thereto.*" The contract did not make the Seller's Property Disclosure Statement a part of the contract, unlike the current GAR Purchase and Sale Agreement.

Under Georgia law, when a buyer sues a seller for fraud and monetary damages but plans to keep the house, the buyer is said to "affirm" the purchase and sale contract. As such, the buyer is normally bound by (or stuck with) any disclaimer in the contract which protects the seller. Previously, the "entire agreement" clause would bar the introduction of any representations not included in the contract. The effect of this decision is that in cases of active fraudulent concealment, representations of sellers and REALTORS® may be used against them even if the representations are not written into the contract and if the contract specifically states that the contract reflects the entire agreement of the parties.

The court inferred actual knowledge in another case where the seller had constructed the den, which the buyer discovered was infested with termites after the closing. The buyer sued the seller and the pest control company that had inspected the property. [560] When the buyer moved in, he discovered a "soft spot" in the den's floor. Several months later, he removed the baseboards around two walls, found six holes drilled through the carpet into the wood floor and detected a chemical odor in the carpet at these locations. The buyer removed the carpet to find a linoleum floor, and under the linoleum, he found pieces of flooring, sub-flooring and floor joists. At the trial, the buyer showed evidence of the deteriorated condition of the lumber from the den floor and sub-floor and evidence that the lumber was highly infested with termites. The buyer's expert testified that it would have taken one to three years for the termites to accomplish this level of infestation. Based on this evidence, the court held that the seller could be liable for fraudulently concealing the termite damage from the buyer. [561]

---

560   Allred v. Dobbs, 137 Ga. App. 227, 223 S.E.2d 265 (1976).
561   Allred v. Dobbs, 137 Ga. App. 227, 223 S.E.2d 265 (1976).

§ 7.3.2 Buyer must use due diligence to protect against fraud

Buyers seeking to bring fraud claims against sellers for concealing termite damage must also show that they attempted to protect themselves against the fraud through the exercise of due diligence.

In one case, the buyer sued the seller for fraud and negligent misrepresentation after moving into a house and discovering substantial termite damage.[562] While the buyer was remodeling his kitchen, he discovered that portions of the house were propped up with wood, stacks of stones, bricks, and railroad ties. Before purchasing the property, the buyer knew that some of the wood in the porch area was damaged and the buyer had been given a termite clearance letter reflecting that there had been previous infestations of termites and beetles. However, the buyer never independently investigated the property. The court held that the buyer could not recover against the seller for fraud because of the buyer's lack of diligence in inspecting the property himself.

The general rule is that when purchasing property, a buyer cannot claim that she has been deceived by false representations, if the buyer could have learned the truth had she only exercised due diligence. Issues that frequently arise are whether the buyer could have discovered the truth via due diligence and whether the seller's alleged fraud prevented the buyer from exercising due diligence.

§ 7.3.3 Seller's pest control inspector may be liable to buyer for negligent inspection

If the buyer can show that visible evidence of termite damage or infestation was present at the time of the pre-closing inspection, the exterminator may be liable to the buyer for negligently inspecting and failing to report the damage.[563] Pest control companies are generally required to make a thorough inspection of a home and make a qualified inspection report as to what wood-destroying organisms are visible in the home, including signs of wood-destroying organisms such as previous infestation or subsequent damage, including a graph showing where the problems are located.[564] If these standards are not met, the pest control company may be liable for negligence. Also, even though the seller hires the pest control company for the inspection (and there is no contract between the buyer and the pest control company), the buyer can sue the company for negligently inspecting the property.[565]

---

562   Lester v. Bird, 200 Ga. App. 335, 408 S.E.2d 147 (1991).
563   American Pest Control, Inc. v. Pritchett, 201 Ga. App. 808, 412 S.E.2d 590 (1991); Tabor v. Orkin Exterminating Co., Inc., 183 Ga. App. 807, 360 S.E.2d 34 (1987), cert. denied.
564   Perloe v. Getz Exterminators, Inc., 163 Ga. App. 397, 294 S.E.2d 640 (1982), on appeal after retrial, Getz Services, Inc. v. Perloe, 173 Ga. App. 532, 327 S.E.2d 761 (1985).
565   Perloe v. Getz Exterminators, Inc., 163 Ga. App. 397, 294 S.E.2d 640 (1982), on appeal after retrial, Getz Services, Inc. v. Perloe, 173 Ga. App. 532, 327

For example, a pest control company hired by the seller prepared an infestation report which was presented to the buyer at closing.[566] The report stated that there had been no previous infestation of wood-destroying organisms. One month after closing, the buyers began remodeling the house and discovered extensive structural and other damage caused by infestations of wood-destroying organisms. At the trial of the case, the buyer's expert testified that the damage was present at the time of the inspection because the damage had been present for at least five years. Because the buyer's expert testified that damage was present when the seller's pest control company inspected the house, the Court held that the seller's pest control company might be liable to the buyer for its negligent inspection.

Similarly, in another case, the buyer discovered severe termite infestation in the floor and sub-flooring of his den several months after moving into the house.[567] The exterminator hired by the seller had issued an inspection report prior to closing which certified that the company completed a comprehensive inspection of the property and found that it was completely clear of termite or beetle infestation. The court found that based on the exterminator's report, the company could be liable to the buyer because it guaranteed that the entire property was completely clear of termites. If the termite inspection had been limited only to areas that were accessible to the termite company (as most inspections are), the company might not have been liable to the buyer for this infestation. The damage here was discovered in the lumber of the floor and sub-flooring in the den which was under both carpet and linoleum and was not accessible to the termite company for inspection.

In another case, the seller hired the pest control company that had treated the home for over 20 years to provide a termite clearance letter.[568] The inspection report stated that there had been termite infestation in the past, but that there was no visible evidence of damage to the home. After the sale, the buyers discovered that although there was no active infestation, their home had been severely and extensively damaged by earlier infestations of termites. Support jacks had been installed to shore up the structure, and the damage to the wooden beams had been concealed with black paint.

The Court found that there was evidence of termite damage and the exterminator knew of the prior infestation and damage, yet failed to probe the painted wood which would have revealed the extensive damage. Also, because the company had treated the house for over 20 years and knew of the previous infestation and extensive damage, it was responsible for knowing the contents of its records about the treatment of the house.[569]

S.E.2d 761 (1985); Allred v. Dobbs, 137 Ga. App. 227, 223 S.E.2d 265 (1976).

566 American Pest Control, Inc. v. Pritchett, 201 Ga. App. 808, 412 S.E.2d 590 (1991).

567 Allred v. Dobbs, 137 Ga. App. 227, 223 S.E.2d 265 (1976).

568 WMI Urban Services, Inc. v. Erwin, 215 Ga. App. 357, 450 S.E.2d 830 (1994), cert. denied .

569 WMI Urban Services, Inc. v. Erwin, 215 Ga. App. 357, 450 S.E.2d 830 (1994), cert. denied.

§ 7.3.4   Pest control company may be liable for fraudulently concealing termite damage

In order for the pest control company to be liable for fraudulently concealing termite damage, the buyer must show that the termite company had actual knowledge of the damage.[570]   Also, the buyer must show that the company concealed its knowledge of the damage with the intent and purpose of deceiving the buyer.

For example, in one Georgia case, the seller obtained a wood infestation inspection report in 1982 for his house which a buyer had contracted to purchase.[571] The seller used the company which regularly treated the house for pest control. The report stated that the inspection was conducted by "a qualified inspector" who performed a "careful visual inspection of the readily accessible areas" of the house. The report indicated no active infestation of any sort but reported visible evidence of previous termite infestation and structural damage. After buying the house, the buyer assumed the seller's contract with the pest control company. In 1986, he contracted to sell the house and obtained a second wood infestation inspection report from the company. The 1986 report again indicated no active infestation, but the previous infestation and structural damage was reported to be far more extensive in the crawl space of the house than indicated in the 1982 report.

The buyer then learned that the damage reflected on the 1986 report had existed prior to the 1982 report and, in fact, had existed prior to 1952, all of which the pest control company knew. Also, the inspector who issued the 1982 report was not a licensed termite technician and did not examine any of the crawl space under the house, as is essential for a proper inspection. Under these facts, the court held there was more than sufficient evidence to hold the pest control company liable for fraudulent concealment of the termite damage.

§ 7.4   Verbal promise to provide termite letter at closing unenforceable

Most contracts, including the GAR Contract, specifically provide that only the terms written in the agreement are binding on the parties. This is also a general rule of contract construction and means oral representations, promises, or statements that are not included in the terms of the actual written contract will not bind either party. Additionally, a separate written agreement that is not referenced in the contract and that does not itself reference the contract, will not generally be used by the court for purposes of interpreting the contract.

Therefore, if the contract does not require the seller to provide a wood infestation inspection report or to warrant that the property is free and clear of wood-destroying organisms and/or damage caused by wood-destroying organisms, the seller

---

570   Tabor v. Orkin Exterminating Co., Inc., 183 Ga. App. 807, 360 S.E.2d 34 (1987), cert. denied.

571   Orkin Exterminating Co., Inc. v. Flowers, 187 Ga. App. 270, 370 S.E.2d 29 (1988).

will likely not be liable for any treatment or damage related to such organisms later discovered by the buyer, even if the seller made some related oral promise or representation to the buyer otherwise.

For example, in one Georgia case, the contract for the sale of a house included the statement that, "Buyers waive termite inspection."[572] However, at the closing, the buyers asked the sellers for the termite certificate and the seller responded that he did not have it with him, but "there were definitely no termites on the property." When the buyers discovered termites, they sued the seller for damages. The Court held that the seller was not liable for damages for the termite infestation because nothing in the contract required any information or action by the seller regarding termites.

Buyers should therefore confirm that the contract specifically requires the seller to provide a wood infestation inspection report, treat the infestation, and provide for the repair or negotiation of any resulting structural damage.[573] Most lenders will require a wood infestation inspection report no matter what the terms of the contract state, so if the contract does not provide that the seller must obtain the report, the buyer will most likely have to obtain one at her own expense in order to meet the underwriting requirements for loan approval. It is a common misunderstanding that a termite letter is required by law. It is not. Rather, it is a requirement imposed by most lenders.

§ 7.5   Seller forgets to bring termite letter at closing

What should the buyer do if the seller has not obtained a required termite clearance letter by the closing? The buyer has two options in this situation if the parties have used a standard GAR Contract. First, the failure of the seller to provide the buyer with a termite clearance letter before or at the closing constitutes a breach of the seller's obligations under the contract for which the buyer can terminate the contract.

Alternatively, the buyer and seller can enter into an amendment to the contract in which the seller agrees to provide the termite clearance letter to the buyer after the closing. An example of such an amendment is set forth below:

Amendment for seller to provide termite letter after closing

For and in consideration of the sum of $10.00 and other good and valuable consideration the receipt and sufficiency of which is hereby acknowledged, the buyer and seller do hereby agree to amend the Agreement as follows:

---

572   Hannah v. Shauck, 131 Ga. App. 834, 207 S.E.2d 239 (1974).
573   Lester v. Bird, 200 Ga. App. 335, 408 S.E.2d 147 (1991).

1.   Seller shall provide Buyer with an official Georgia Wood Infestation Report no later than _____ days from the date of the closing.

If the buyer closes on the property without receiving a required termite clearance letter and fails to either amend or terminate the contract, the obligation of the seller to provide the buyer with a required termite clearance letter will likely be deemed to be waived. In one case, the contract provided that the seller shall repair all damage as specified in the termite and wood infestation provisions of the Contract and deliver at closing a clean termite letter in the form specified in the Contract. The seller did not furnish any documentation showing that the structural damage had been corrected as required. The Court held that the buyer could have delayed the closing until the termite problem was under control or choose not to close. Instead, the buyer proceeded to close and therefore waived any right the buyer may have had under the contract pertaining to the termite clearance letter.[574]

§ 7.6   Inspection Standards of Georgia Pest Control Commission

All structural pest control companies and operators must be licensed by the State of Georgia and must comply with Georgia's Structural Pest Control Act[575] ("Act") and the Rules of Georgia Structural Pest Control Commission[576] ("Rules"). Georgia's Department of Agriculture oversees compliance with and enforcement of the Act and Rules.

The Rules require that pest control companies and operators must use the Official Georgia Wood Infestation Report ("Report") when certifying that a structure is apparently free from wood-destroying organisms in conjunction with the sale of real property.[577] This Report provides that if visible evidence of active or previous infestation is reported, it should be assumed that some degree of damage is present. A diagram identifying the structure inspected and showing the location of the active or previous infestation must be attached to the Report. The disclosure that some degree of damage should be assumed to be present if there is visible evidence of active or previous infestation will likely result in more situations where buyers and lenders are concerned about termite damage. As noted, this is one of the reasons the GAR Contract provides for the termite letter to be attached to the contract.

Further, the Report may be issued only by a pest control operator certified in wood-destroying organisms.[578] The Report must carry a guarantee that, if the Report certifies that a structure is apparently free from wood-destroying organisms, and wood-

---

574   Westminster Holdings, Ltd. v. Weatherspoon, 237 Ga.App. 819, 517 S.E.2d 80, (1999)
575   O.C.G.A. § 43-45-1, et seq.
576   Rules of Georgia Structural Pest Control Commission ("Rules"), §620-1-.01, et seq.
577   Rules, § 620-6-.03(2).
578   Rules, § 620-6-.03(1).

destroying organisms are found in the structure within 90 days from the date of issuance, the infested structure will be treated by the pest control operator, free of charge, in accordance with the minimum adequate treatment prescribed by the Rules.[579]

§ 7.7   Pest control contracts, guarantees, and bonds

§ 7.7.1   Pest control contracts and guarantees

Pest control companies must issue a separate written contract to the property owner each time they undertake to control wood-destroying organisms on the property.[580]   The contract must state: 1) the specific type of application to be performed; 2) the effective date and contract period; and 3) a diagram consisting of a reasonable depiction of the structure(s) to be treated, indicating the location of any visible active or previous infestation.[581] Pest control companies are bound to treat the areas depicted on the contract diagram. For example, a Georgia court held that a pest control operator could be liable for breach of contract and fraud when it failed to treat a homeowner's carport where the carport was depicted on the contract diagram and the carport later became infested with termites.[582]

Also, if the pest control company tries to limit its liability for treatment of the property based on any modification or addition to a structure as it is depicted in the contract diagram, the contract must specifically state that the homeowner is obligated to notify the pest control company of any modifications or alterations to any structure on the property during the contract period.[583] The pest control contract must also state the price of the contract.[584] Further, if the pest control company is going to perform repairs, replacement, or excavations on the property which are related to the control of wood-destroying organisms, the contract must give an estimate of such work.[585]

Finally, the contract must provide for the specific terms of any guarantee or warranty and whether it applies to the re-treatment of the structure(s) under the contract and/or the repair of damages to the structure(s) under the contract.[586] If the guarantee or warranty provides only for re-treatment, the type of re-treatment and the details of the re-treatment must be specified in the contract.[587] Most guarantees or warranties in pest control contracts will cover only "new damage" to the structure, that

---

579   Rules, § 620-6-.03(2).
580   Rules, § 620-6-02(1).
581   Rules, § 620-6.02(a) to (c).
582   Woodall v. Orkin Exterminating Co., Inc., 175 Ga. App. 83, 332 S.E.2d 173 (1985).
583   Rules, § 620-6-.03(g).
584   Rules, § 620-6-.02(d).
585   Rules, § 620-6-.02(d).
586   Rules, § 620-6-.02(e).
587   Rules, § 620-6-.03(e).

is, damage caused by wood-destroying organisms <u>after</u> the date of the initial treatment by the company.[588]

The Rules also require that the Inspection Report include a guarantee for the inspection. The Report must guarantee that, if the Report certifies that a structure is apparently free from wood-destroying organisms and wood-destroying organisms are found in the structure within 90 days from the date of issuance, the infested structure will be treated by the pest control operator, free of charge, in accordance with the minimum adequate treatment prescribed by the Rules.[589] Unless the buyer can prove negligence in the pest control operator's inspection, if the buyer finds infestation within the 90-day period and the inspector fulfills its obligations to retreat the structure in accordance with Georgia's minimum adequate treatment standards, the inspector will not be liable for further damages in accordance with the limitations of the Report's guarantee.[590]

§ 7.7.2   Pest control bonds

Unlike the guarantee for treatment in a contract for treatment of wood-destroying organisms or the guarantee of proper inspection in the Report, pest control bonds guarantee actual performance of the extermination. Pest control bonds are written instruments issued by a bonding, surety, or insurance company guaranteeing the fulfillment of a contract between a pest control company and its customer. They are surety bonds issued by a third party insuring the performance of the pest control company. They do not include any warranty or guarantee between the pest control company and the customer.[591]

Pest control companies are not required to maintain performance bonds. However, if a pest control company is bonded, the company must maintain a master or blanket bond in an amount equal to 5% of its previous year's gross sales or gross liability assumed during the previous year, whichever is higher, up to a maximum of $100,000.00, or it must provide a separate bond for each job.[592] In order for a pest control company to advertise that it is bonded, the pest control company must state in writing to each customer that it is bonded, as part of every proposal or contract, whether or not such proposal or contract is covered by the bond.[593] Additionally, the pest control company must submit proof of the existence and type of bonding in force to the Georgia Structural Pest Control Commission.[594]

---

588   <u>Parsells v. Orkin Exterminating Co., Inc.</u>, 178 Ga. App. 51, 342 S.E.2d 13 (1986).
589   Rules, § 620-6-.03.
590   <u>Holbrook v. Burrell</u>, 163 Ga. App. 529, 295 S.E.2d 201 (1982).
591   Rules, § 620-2-.01.
592   Rules, § 620-4-.01(3)(a).
593   Rules, § 620-4-.01(3)(c).
594   Rules, § 620-4-.01(3)(d).

Pest control companies themselves issue two types of bonds to their customers: repair bonds and treatment bonds. Repair bonds provide greater protection to an owner and guarantee treatment of the property for termite infestation and repair of any damage to the property caused by termites. Treatment bonds are limited to the guarantee of treatment of any termite infestation.

Buyers who purchase properties already under bond should consider renewing the seller's bond. In addition to the guaranteed treatment for infestation and/or repair of related damage, bonds provide other cost savings. If an owner decides to sell the property, the wood infestation inspection report will be much less expensive if the house is under bond. Also, the annual renewal charge for bonds is much less expensive than the costs of an annual inspection and repair for a property not under bond. Although a repair bond has more value than a treatment bond, an owner will save money with either type of bond.

Additionally, the buyer can provide in the contract that if termites or wood-destroying organisms are discovered during the inspection or at the time the seller or buyer obtains the necessary closing letter, the seller shall obtain a treatment or repair bond from a pest control company of buyer's choosing. Then, when the buyer takes title to the property after closing, the buyer can assume the bond from the seller. Care must be taken to determine whether there is ay cost associated with the transfer of a bond. Additionally, some repair bonds convert to retreatment bonds upon transfer unless an additional fee is paid.

Alternatively, when the buyer makes an offer on a property, the offered contract could include a provision which would require the seller to obtain a bond from a certain pest control company if it is determined before closing that wood-destroying organisms are or were active on the property. The following special stipulation can be used for either of these two purposes:

Special Stipulation #7-8: Seller to obtain termite bond

For purposes of obtaining the termite Report at closing, Seller agrees to use either ABC Pest Control Company or XYZ Pest Control Company to inspect for termites and other wood-destroying organisms and provide a termite letter regarding such inspection. If termites or other wood-destroying organisms are found, Seller agrees to purchase from the same pest control company chosen for the termite inspection and letter, a treatment/damage bond (choose one) which will guarantee the property for at least one year and which shall be assumable by Buyer after the closing of this transaction without additional charge during the first year.

In considering from whom and what type of termite bond to purchase, owners should choose a reputable pest control company which offers bonds with reasonable annual renewal charges. Many bonds exclude an obligation to retreat or repair termite infestation and/or damage which is a consequence of moisture. Since termites cannot live without moisture, such an exclusion can arguably be used to reject most, if not all, requests for termite repairs. One solution to this problem is to slightly modify this provision of the pest control contract. The following language should be added to a pest control contract which excludes retreatment or repairs caused by moisture:

Special Stipulation #7-9: No exclusion on termite bond

Notwithstanding any provision to the contrary contained herein, the pest control operator shall not be permitted to limit its obligations to treat and, if applicable, repair and/or replace damage to structures resulting from termites and other wood-destroying organisms caused by excessive moisture in the area of the infestation and/or damage unless the pest control operator has previously identified in writing to Owner any areas with excessive moisture which could contribute to termite infestation and/or damage.

§ 7.8 Amount of damages to which buyer may be entitled

Generally, damages for injury to property equals the cost to restore the property to its condition at the time of the loss. If the seller or pest control inspector is liable to a buyer for damages caused by wood-destroying organisms, the buyer will usually be entitled to recover the costs necessary to restore the property to its condition immediately prior to the damage.[595]

However, if the costs to restore the property to its original condition are much greater than the market value of the property prior to the damage, then the buyer's damages will be measured by the decrease of the property's market value from before the damage to after the damage, unless the property has historical or other intrinsic worth to the owner.

If damaged property has historical or other intrinsic worth to the owner which is not reflected in the fair market value of the improved property, the proper measure of damages is the cost of repair, even though this may result in a recovery which far exceeds the fair market value of the improved property prior to the damage.

Depending on the circumstances, there may be more than one appropriate measure of damages for injury to improved property. For example, in one case, the termite damage was so extensive that the repair costs were estimated to be twice the purchase price of the house. The court held that the jury could consider whether repairing the house was an absurd undertaking or whether the house had intrinsic value

---

[595]   American Pest Control, Inc. v. Pritchett, 201 Ga. App. 808, 412 S.E.2d 590 (1991); Getz v. Perloe, 173 Ga. App. 532, 327 S.E.2d 761 (1985).

to the buyers and thus should be repaired despite the costs.[596] The actual amount of damages to award in a case is usually a question of fact, if the matter is litigated.[597]

§ 7.9   Emerging pest issues

As of the writing of this book a serious pest issue is emerging in the form of Formosan termites ("Formosans"). It is believed that Formosans were first introduced into the United States in the 1950's, when they stowed away onboard ships returning from the Pacific after World War II.[598] Formosans are a particularly hardy species of termite, having a high tolerance to sunlight and air and extremely large colonies. Under the proper conditions Formosans can establish secondary or tertiary nests in walls or the attic. They then proceed to destroy the house both from the ground up and the roof down. While a "normal" termite colony may contain several hundred thousand individuals, Formosan colonies can run into the millions.

Unfortunately, it appears that whatever natural predators or diseases help keep Formosans in check in the Pacific was not also imported to the United States. It is estimated that Formosan termites cause damage in the United States in the amount of $1 billion a year.[599]

The United States Department of Agriculture's Agricultural Research Service has undertaken a comprehensive program to determine the Formosans' natural enemies and hopes to one day eradicate Formosans.[600] In the meantime, Formosans have already become a serious problem in Louisiana, having costs hundreds of millions of dollars in damage.[601]   In the past few years Formosans have started to appear in Georgia. Most, if not all, repair bonds specifically exclude the repair and damage caused by Formosans.

---

596   American Pest Control, Inc. v. Pritchett, 201 Ga. App. 808, 412 S.E.2d 590 (1991); Getz v. Perloe, 173 Ga. App. 532, 327 S.E.2d 761 (1985).

597   American Pest Control, Inc. v. Pritchett, 201 Ga. App. 808, 412 S.E.2d 590 (1991); Getz v. Perloe, 173 Ga. App. 532, 327 S.E.2d 761 (1985).

598   Southern Regional Research Center, Agricultural Research Service, USDA, new Orleans, La. 70179.

599   Southern Regional Research Center, Agricultural Research Service, USDA, new Orleans, La. 70179.

600   Southern Regional Research Center, Agricultural Research Service, USDA, new Orleans, La. 70179.

601   In New Orleans alone, it is estimated that Formosans infest as many as 30 percent of all trees. Southern Regional Research Center, Agricultural Research Service, USDA, new Orleans, La. 70179.

CHAPTER 8
INSPECTION

OVERVIEW

This chapter discusses the buyer's rights to inspect the property. Commonly asked questions, including who may inspect, when they may inspect, how they may inspect, and for what they may inspect will be addressed. The mechanics of the inspection and the procedures for the negotiation and repair of defects are also discussed. Numerous sample special stipulations are provided largely to give the buyer alternatives to the inspection approach set forth in the GAR Contract.

This chapter also discusses other issues, such as how to deal with a bad inspection report, making mistakes in completing the time periods in the inspection section, and inspecting seasonally difficult items such as swimming pools in the winter. Hazardous conditions such as radon and lead-based paint are addressed in detail, including the specifics of the Lead-Based Paint Hazard Reduction Act.

§ 8.1 What the GAR Contract provides about inspections

The inspection provision of the GAR Contract gives the buyer and/or buyer's representatives the right to inspect, examine, test, and survey the property at the buyer's expense. This inspection right also extends to all appliances and equipment remaining with the property. The inspection provision also allows the buyer access to the property (including prior to closing), to confirm that fixtures have not been removed and all agreed upon repairs have been completed.

Earlier versions of the GAR Contract gave buyers two choices regarding inspection. The buyer could either request that the seller repair defects in the property (as that term is defined in the GAR Contract) identified during the inspection process or accept the property in "as-is" condition.

Under the 2005 GAR Contract, the buyer has a third choice, which is to terminate the contract after an agreed upon period of time during which the buyer may inspect the property. This new option is commonly referred to as a "free look".

§ 8.1.1 Buyer's right to inspect generally

The GAR Contract gives the buyer the right to enter and to thoroughly inspect, examine, test, and survey the property. This right exists regardless of whether the property is being sold "as is" with a right to request repair of defects or subject to a right to terminate. The right to inspect has to be exercised at reasonable times, and exists up to the time of closing. It also includes the right to inspect and test for lead-based paint and lead-based paint hazards for not less than ten days from the Binding Agreement Date. All such inspections are at the buyer's expense.

The seller must ensure that all utility services and any pool, spa, and similar items are operational so that the buyer may complete all inspections. The buyer agrees to hold the seller and all brokers harmless from all claims, injuries, and damages arising out of or related to the exercise of these inspection rights. This means, for example, that if the buyer's inspector damages the property as part of inspecting it, the buyer would need to pay for the damages caused by the inspector.

If the buyer or buyer's inspector is injured on the property as the result of owner's failure to exercise ordinary care in keeping the property safe, the owner is liable in damages to the inspector for such injury and the indemnification provision will not shield the seller from liability.[602] So, for example, let's assume that a seller is aware of a broken step leading to the basement. The stairwell is dark and it is hard to see the broken step. The owner knows about the perilous condition of the staircase but does not warn the inspector, who unfortunately trips on the broken stairs and is injured. Even though the buyer has agreed to indemnify the seller for all claims and injuries arising out of the buyer's inspection of the property, this obligation would likely not apply where the seller breached his duty to take ordinary care in keeping the premises safe for invitees.

An owner is only liable if he or she knew about a condition that may expose the invitees to a reasonable risk of harm and the invitee did not have such knowledge.[603] For example, in one case, a meat inspector who slipped and fell on the floor of a breakroom provided by law for the exclusive use of meat inspectors could not claim for his injury because he was generally exposed to the breakroom and had equal, if not superior, knowledge of the slippery condition of floor. [604]

The right to inspect immediately prior to closing clearly gives the buyer the right to do a "walk-through" inspection prior to closing to confirm that repairs have been made in a good and workmanlike manner, to confirm that there have been no changes to the condition of the property, and to confirm that no fixtures have been improperly removed.

The GAR Contract also includes a check box where buyers can select one of three options once the inspection has been completed. These include accepting the property in "as-is" condition, having the right to request the repair of defects and having a right to terminate the contract if the buyer is dissatisfied with the inspection. Each of these options will be discussed below.

While the issue of what constitutes "reasonable times" to inspect has not been decided by the courts, it would likely be interpreted broadly, to allow the buyer ample opportunities to visit the property. So, for example, if the buyer had conducted a very thorough inspection of the basement during dry weather but then wanted to return to

---

602   O.C.G.A. § 51-3-1, § 51-3-2
603   Kitchens v. Keadle Lumber Enterprises, Inc., 249 Ga.App. 831, 549 S.E.2d 781 (2001)
604   Pierce v. Fieldale Corp., 194 Ga.App. 303, 390 S.E.2d 298 (1990)

the property during rainy weather to check for moisture in the basement, such an inspection would clearly be permissible.

Similarly, returning to a property to measure rooms for furniture placement or show the property to a contractor to get a bid on repairs or improvements to be made after closing would all likely be permissible under the GAR Contract. If the seller is concerned about loss of privacy resulting from giving the buyer a right to inspect, the seller may want to limit the right to inspect to specific days and hours. The following special stipulation is an example of such a limitation.

Special Stipulation #8-1: Limiting the time to inspect

Notwithstanding any other provision in this Agreement to the contrary, Buyer and Buyer's representatives shall have no right to inspect, test, survey or otherwise enter or come onto the Property for any other purpose during the following times: (1) on Sundays; (2) on weekdays and Saturdays after 8:00 p.m. or before 8.00 a.m.; and (3) at any time without 24-hour advance notice to Seller.

§ 8.1.2   Property sold with right to request repairs

There are three separate time periods of which buyers should be aware if the property is being sold subject to a right to request repairs. The first is the inspection period during which the buyer can have an inspector or inspectors to inspect the property to determine if it contains any defects. The second is a "Defect Resolution Period" during which the buyer and seller negotiate through offers and counteroffers the defects to be repaired and/or replaced by the seller. If the parties are not able to reach an agreement regarding the defects to be repaired and/or replaced during the Defect Resolution Period, there is then a one-day time period thereafter during which either party can accept the other's last offer of repairs. If neither party does this, the contract then terminates automatically.

To seek the repair of defects, the buyer must provide the seller with the following: 1) a copy of the inspection report prepared by an inspector detailing the defects which the buyer is seeking the seller to repair and/or replace, and 2) an Amendment to Remove Inspection Contingency form[605] requesting that the seller repair and/or replace these defects.

The buyer must present the inspection report and the proposed amendment to the seller within a specified number of days from the Binding Agreement Date. If the buyer does not do this in a timely manner, the buyer is deemed to have accepted the property in "as is" condition. If the buyer timely submits the inspection report and the written amendment, the buyer and seller then have a specified number of days to negotiate, through written offers and counteroffers, the defects to be repaired and/or

---

605   GAR Form F100

replaced by the seller. This time period is called the "Defect Resolution Period". If the buyer and seller agree on what is to be repaired and/or replaced, they must sign a written amendment to reflect their agreement.

If the buyer and seller do not agree on the defects to be repaired and/or replaced by the expiration of the Defect Resolution Period, the buyer or seller may either accept the other party's last offer or counteroffer of repairs (if any) or the buyer may accept the property "as is". The party who accepts the offer or counteroffer must give notice of acceptance by providing to the other party a written agreement stating what is to be repaired and/or replaced. This has to be done within one day of the expiration of the Defect Resolution Period. If neither the buyer nor seller gives this notice in a timely manner, the contract then automatically terminates.

Once the parties agree on which defects the seller will repair and/or replace, the repairs and replacements must be completed in a good and workmanlike manner prior to closing. Finally, if the seller is willing to repair and/or replace all of the defects in the inspection amendment regardless of how numerous they may be, the buyer may not use the inspection contingency as a basis to terminate the contract.

§ 8.1.2.1 Counting time periods correctly when property is sold with right to request repairs

When the property is sold subject to a right to request repairs, the inspection period and the "Defect Resolution Period" are both measured from the original Binding Agreement Date. The Defect Resolution Period is not measured from the end of the inspection period.

There are two blanks in this section of the GAR Contract, the first of which is to be filled in with the length of time the buyer has to do his or her inspection and the second of which is the length of the Defect Resolution Period.

So for example, if the actual inspection period is 10 days and the Defect Resolution Period is intended to be 5 days thereafter, the first blank in this section of the GAR Contract would be filled in with the number "10" and the second blank would be filled in with the number "15". This again is because both time periods are measured from the Binding Agreement Date.

If the buyer and seller cannot come to an agreement within the Defect Resolution Period on the defects to be repaired, either party can then accept the other party's offer of repairs within one (1) day thereafter. Case law defines a day to mean an entire 24-hour day beginning immediately after midnight and ending 24 hours later.[606]

---

606   Southern Trust Ins. Co. v. First Federal Sav. & Loan Ass'n of Summerville, 168 Ga.App. 899, 310 S.E.2d 712 (1983)

Finally, if a buyer has a ten (10) day inspection period and the Binding Agreement Date is January 1st, the inspection period would end upon the conclusion of January 11th. This is because when a party counts days from a specific date, the day after the Binding Agreement Date is the first day and January 11th would be the tenth day from the Binding Agreement Date.[607]

§ 8.1.2.2 Buyer can only request for repairs to "defects" identified by professional inspector

The 2005 GAR Contract contains a major change from the older forms in that the right to request the repair and/or replacement of defects in the property applies only to defects which have been identified by buyer's inspector in a written report. Therefore, while the buyer is still entitled to have anyone inspect the property, the buyer can only ask the seller to repair and/or replace defects identified by a professional inspector.

The 2005 GAR Form defines the term "Inspector" to mean "a person or company with specific, professional expertise in property inspections or in an item, building product, or condition therein, for which the "Inspector" is inspecting, examining, testing and/or surveying.

Georgia law provides for certain requirements with which home inspectors must comply. The law defines "home inspectors" as any person who for consideration inspects and reports on the condition of any home or single-family dwelling or the grounds, roof, exterior surface, garage or carport, structure, attic, basement, crawl space, electrical system, heating system, air-conditioning system, plumbing, on-site sewage disposal, pool, hot tub, fireplace, kitchen, appliances, or any combination of these for a prospective purchaser or seller.[608]

Every home inspector must provide to the person on whose behalf he is inspecting a home or single-family dwelling a written document specifying the following information:

1.   the scope of the inspection, including the structural elements, systems, and subsystems to be inspected;
2.   that the inspection is a visual inspection; and
3.   that the home inspector will notify in writing the person on whose behalf the inspection is being made of any defects noted during the inspection, along with any recommendation that certain experts be retained to determine the extent and corrective action necessary for the defects.[609]

---

607   O.C.G.A. § 1-3-1(c)(3); Brooks v. Hicks, 230 Ga. 500, 197 S.E.2d 711 (1973).
608   O.C.G.A. § 8-3-330.
609   O.C.G.A. § 8-3-331.

Any person who violates any of these home inspector requirements is guilty of a misdemeanor criminal offense.[610] Misdemeanor offenses generally carry a maximum penalty of a $1,000.00 fine and up to 12 months in jail.[611]

The GAR Contract does not require inspections to be done by home inspectors who are members of professional associations such as the American Society of Home Inspectors ("ASHI") for two reasons. [612] First, inspectors with ASHI or other similar certification might not be available in every locale in Georgia. Second and more importantly, with many homes, specialized inspections of roofs, heating and air conditioning systems, swimming pools, and structural components are also needed.

Similarly, there may be the need for specialized inspections for mold, radon, asbestos and other toxic substances. Such inspections are often conducted by engineers or other professionals, who may not be members of a professional home inspection organization but are nevertheless experts in their respective areas. Limiting inspections to only members of ASHI would leave buyers without the legal ability to ask for repairs and/or replacement of defects identified by these experts.

Sellers may want to limit the initial inspection of the property to a member of ASHI to ensure a fairly objective review of the property. If the seller wants to make such a requirement part of the contract, the following special stipulation can be used:

Special Stipulation #8-2: Buyer obligated to employ only an ASHI certified inspector

Notwithstanding any provision to the contrary contained herein, Buyer shall employ only a member of the American Society of Home Inspectors to conduct the initial inspection of the property for defects and prepare the inspection report referenced in this Agreement. If the Inspector recommends that specific follow-up inspections or tests be done to the Property, such inspections do not have to be performed by a member of ASHI provided that such inspector(s) has expertise in the portion of the Property or condition or product therein being inspected or tested.

Builder and developer contracts often require inspections to be done by qualified home inspectors. This normally occurs where the builder has had a bad experience with particular inspectors aggressively claiming that items in a property are defects when such claims are disputed by the builder. Some builders have gotten so

---

610   O.C.G.A. § 8-3-332.
611   O.C.G.A. § 17-10-3.
612   ASHI is a professional organization of home inspectors. Each inspector belonging to ASHI must have a specific level of education and experience in the home inspection field.

frustrated with particular inspectors that they have limited a buyer's right to inspect to certain approved inspectors or provide that they will only pay closing costs if the buyer uses an inspector from an approved list. A detailed discussion of this issue is set out in the chapter 15 of this book.

§ 8.1.2.3 Inspectors can limit their liability

Before signing a contract with a home inspector, parties should carefully read the terms and conditions of the contract. Some inspection contracts may limit any loss for negligent inspection to the cost of the inspection. For example, in one Georgia case, the buyer of a condominium unit sued her inspector for $23,700.00 in damages allegedly resulting from the negligent inspection of her unit.[613] The buyer signed a contract at the time of the inspection, which provided that the inspector's liability was limited to the cost of the inspection. However, the buyer argued that a contract with this type of limitation against liability was void as against public policy. The Georgia Court of Appeals disagreed, holding that such a limitation of the inspector's liability was enforceable and the buyer could only recover the costs she paid for the inspection. This case also serves as the legal basis for the limitation against liability contained in the GAR listing and buyer brokerage agreements.

§ 8.1.2.4 Extending the inspection and Defect Resolution Period

The 2005 GAR Contract gives the buyer a right to extend the inspection period and Defect Resolution Period once for up to seven days in the event the inspector recommends any additional test, study, inspection or evaluation of any product, item or condition in the property. The recommendation of the inspector for a follow-up test must be contained in the inspector's written report. The buyer must provide the seller with the notice to extend the inspection and Defect Resolution Period, along with a copy of the inspector's report recommending the additional test, study or evaluation, prior to the end of the inspection period. In other words, the buyer cannot give notice to extend the inspection period once the Defect Resolution Period has commenced.

The date of closing is not automatically extended along with the inspection period and the Defect Resolution Period. Instead, it is only extended if the new Defect Resolution Period overlaps the original closing date. So, for example, let's assume that the date of closing is May 1st and the Defect Resolution Period is to end on April 15th. If the inspection period and Defect Resolution Period are properly extended by the buyer for 7 additional days, the new Defect Resolution Period would end on April 22nd, since the new date does not overlap the date of closing, the closing date would remain the same. However, if the Defect Resolution Period ends on April 25th and is extended for 7 additional days, it would overlap the original date of closing by 1 day. In such a case, the closing date would then also be

---

613   Brainard v. McKinney, 220 Ga. App. 329, 469 S.E.2d 441 (1996).

extended for 7 additional days until May 8th. There is a special GAR form which can be used to give notice to unilaterally extend the inspection period.[614]

§ 8.1.2.5 Meaning of "last offer or counteroffer"

As described above, the buyer or seller may, within one day after the end of the Defect Resolution Period, accept the other party's last offer or counteroffer. This may be done even if the offer or counteroffer has expired or has been rejected by the party to whom the offer was made. The GAR Contract specifically states that it is intended to override the common law which provides that once an offer has been rejected or has lapsed, it is no longer capable of being accepted. An offer or counteroffer expires when it specifies a time limit for acceptance and that period has passed. An offer or counteroffer is rejected when the receiving party rejects it outright or responds with a counteroffer. The following examples show how the GAR provision works.

Example #1: Buyer timely submits an amendment and a copy of the inspection report asking the seller to repair and/or replace ten defects. During the Defect Resolution Period, the seller submits a counteroffer agreeing to repair seven items. The Defect Resolution Period then expires. Under common law, if the counteroffer has expired, there is no binding agreement. However, the GAR Contract will allow the buyer to accept the seller's offer to repair the seven items within one-day of the expiration of the Defect Resolution Period, even though the time limit on his counteroffer has already expired. Likewise, the seller can agree to the buyer's request to repair the ten defects even though the seller has responded with a counteroffer. The party who accepts the other's offer first creates a Binding Agreement. However, if neither party acts within the one-day period the contract automatically terminates.

Example #2: Buyer timely submits an amendment to remove inspection contingency and a copy of the inspection report asking for ten defects to be repaired. During the Defect Resolution Period, seller submits a counteroffer agreeing to repair seven items. The buyer submits another counteroffer to the seller asking the seller to repair eight of the original ten items. The Defect Resolution Period expires. The buyer can either accept the property "as is", let the contract terminate or accept the seller's counter to repair seven items even though the buyer has rejected that offer by making another counteroffer asking the seller to fix eight items. Likewise, the seller can agree to fix the eight defects identified in the buyer's last counteroffer.

Example #3: Buyer timely submits a repair amendment to remove inspection contingency and a copy of the inspection report asking the seller to repair and/or replace ten defects. During the Defect Resolution Period, seller submits a counteroffer agreeing to repair four items. The buyer submits another counteroffer to the seller asking the seller to repair eight of the original ten items. The seller responds, again

---

614   GAR Form F134

stating that they will only make four repairs. The buyer makes no further counteroffers and the Defect Resolution Period ends. The seller may agree to fix the eight items and force the buyer to purchase the property. Similarly, the buyer may agree to have the seller repair only four items even though the Defect Resolution Period has ended.

If the buyer or seller is no longer anxious to complete the transaction, they may want to make their last offer of repairs less desirable than their previous offers. So, for example, if the buyer originally requested the repair of 15 defects but through negotiations reduced this number to 10, the buyer may want to revert back to his original request of 15 items if he wants to discourage the seller from accepting his last offer of repairs.

§ 8.1.2.6   *Right to request repairs limited to "defects"*

If the property is being purchased subject to the right to request repairs section of the GAR Contract, the buyer is limited to asking the seller to repair "defects" identified by an inspector in a written report. The 2005 GAR Contract defines "defects" as any portion of or item in the Property which:

(1)   is in a condition which represents a significant health risk or an imminent risk of injury or damage to persons or property;

(2)   constitutes a violation of current laws, governmental codes or regulations except if it is "grandfathered" because it was initially installed or constructed prior to or in accordance with all applicable laws, codes or regulations; or

(3)   is not at the present time in good working order and repair, normal wear and tear excepted.

It is important to note that an item is considered as a "defect" if it meets any one of the above definitions rather than all three. One of the admitted weaknesses of the definition is that it is very general and leaves room for the parties to debate whether an item or condition in the property is a defect. Unfortunately, with our housing stock in Georgia being brand new to over 300 years old, it is difficult in a few short sentences to come up with a "one-size fits all" definition of a defect.

The following are examples of what would be considered a defect under the GAR Contract.

Example #1: Buyer hires an inspector to examine a house he has just put under contract. The inspector reports that: (a) the roof is old but still in good working order and repair; (b) the house has lead-based paint in it; and (c) the building code has been changed since the time the house was constructed to now require additional floor bracing. The house has not shown any signs of stress from the lack of bracing, and

251

there is no requirement to retrofit the house with additional bracing. What right does the buyer have to request that these items be repaired?

Answer: Under the current GAR Contract, the buyer does not have a right to request that the roof be replaced. This is because the roof is simply old rather than defective. The same would likely apply to the floor bracing if the original method of construction is grandfathered and there is no present requirement to add the bracing. The buyer should be able to request that the lead-based paint be remedied.

Example #2: The inspector discovers that the house has the following: (a) aluminum wiring which would not be permitted under today's building code but is grandfathered and does not need to be replaced, and (b) no ground fault interrupt outlets in the bathrooms. The inspector believes that the current condition of the aluminum wiring is such that a fire could occur if it is not repaired. He also believes that not having ground fault interrupt outlets is a safety hazard.

Answer: While the buyer has no right to have the aluminum wiring repaired as a code violation, he probably can have it repaired as a condition, which represents an unreasonable risk of injury or damage to persons or property since this is what the inspector concluded. The same argument applies to the lack of ground fault interrupt outlets.

§ 8.1.2.7   "Defects" include products subject to class action lawsuits

The GAR Contract also provides that all parties acknowledge that certain building products are or have been the subject of class action lawsuits and are generally considered by inspectors to be defective. Such a building material is termed as a "Defective Product" in the GAR Contract.

Just because a property contains a Defective Product does not necessarily give the buyer the right to request that it be repaired or replaced. A Defective Product is not considered to be a defect (which the buyer can request be repaired or replaced) if: 1) the Defective Product is disclosed in the Seller's Property Disclosure Statement; 2) the Seller's Property Disclosure Statement is provided to the buyer prior to the acceptance date of the purchase contract; and 3) the Defective Product is functioning according to the manufacturer's specifications and is reasonably fit for the purposes for which it was intended as of the time of the inspection.

If a Defective Product is properly disclosed and is not presently performing in accordance with the manufacturer's specifications, the buyer can request the seller to repair or replace only the currently defective portion of the Defective Product. In the event that either of the first two conditions are not met, the buyer can request the repair or replacement of the entire Defective Product, irrespective of whether it is currently failing or not. This is explained in the following example.

Example: An inspector discovers that the house has certain siding that was the subject of class action lawsuit. The seller is unaware that his house has this defective siding and does not disclose it as a Defective Product the Seller's Property Disclosure Statement. The siding on the southern exposure of the house is swelling and delaminating. The rest of the siding appears to be in good condition. Can the buyer seek to have all of the siding replaced or only those boards which are delaminating?

Answer: If the particular siding is a Defective Product and was not disclosed in the Seller's Property Disclosure Statement, the buyer could request the seller to repair and/or replace the entire siding. This would also be the case if the seller answered "don't know" to the question of whether the property contained any Defective Product. However, if the seller had disclosed this condition in the Seller's Property Disclosure Statement, the buyer would only be able to request the repair and/or replacement of those portions of the siding which are not functioning in accordance with the manufacturer's specifications.

§ 8.1.2.8 Resolving disputes over what is "defect"

As discussed above, the GAR Contract does not allow the buyer to request that the seller repair items that are not defects. What happens however when a buyer and the seller disagree on whether an item is a defect? Suppose, for example, that the buyer requests the seller to, among other things, replace as a defect an old-fashioned electrical circuit box with screw-in fuses because the inspector believes it is a fire hazard. The seller agrees to fix the other items on the buyer's inspection amendment but asserts that the circuit box is old but not defective in any way.

Another example is the buyer who requests that five windows in a ten-year-old house be replaced because the inspection reveals that the seals in these windows are broken, causing them to fog. The buyer maintains that since the inspector noted that the seals are "broken," they fall within the definition of a "defect" under the contract. The seller asserts that the windows are not defective in that the glass is not broken and they open and close properly. The seller takes the position that the fog in the windows is merely cosmetic, and that the alleged broken seals are merely normal wear and tear.

In all of these examples the buyer and seller can argue and even litigate over whether these items constitute defects. If the buyer terminates the contract on the basis that the parties could not agree upon the defects to be repaired, the seller may claim that the buyer wrongfully terminated the contract.

The above examples illustrate that that there may be no clear definition of the term "defect". While there is not yet case law interpreting the definition of the term "defect," courts will likely apply a reasonableness standard when it comes to whether a particular condition is or is not a defect. The courts will likely place heavy reliance on the conclusions of a professional home inspector who at least in theory at least should be able to give more of an objective opinion on whether a particular item in the property is a defect.

Based upon this reasonableness approach, the inspector can conclude that the windows in the above example are not in good working order and repair if the broken seals are not providing the insulating value for which they were designed. Similarly, the inspector can find that the old electrical circuit box is defective if he reasonably believes it constitutes a fire hazard. If it can be scientifically proven, however, that the risk of fire is no greater with old fashioned versus more modern circuit breakers, the likelihood is that the condition would not constitute a defect as defined by the GAR Contract.

There are steps the parties could have taken to prevent the disputes over the meaning of the term "defect" referenced in the above examples. First, buyers should always negotiate in the contract the specific repair of as many items as can be easily identified. For example, if the buyer's offer includes a requirement that the seller replace specific windows with broken seals or the old fashioned circuit breakers, and the offer is accepted, the potential for further disputes on these issues has likely been eliminated. If the seller's disclosure statement indicated synthetic stucco this can be addressed in the initial offer. Cosmetic items, like dings in sheetrock, peeling wallpaper, chips in paint, or stains in the carpet are also items which can be easily identified by the buyer and negotiated at the time of the offer. The following special stipulation can be used in the buyer's initial offer to the seller:

Special Stipulation #8-3: Listing items which seller agrees to repair before inspection

Notwithstanding any other provision in this Agreement to the contrary, Seller agrees prior to closing to repair or replace in a good and workmanlike manner the following items in the Property _____. Seller's obligation herein shall in no way limit Buyer from submitting an inspection amendment in accordance with the section of the Agreement entitled "Property Sold With Right to Request Repairs."

If it is unclear whether an item in the property is a defect, the parties can contractually agree in advance that an item is considered defective. For example, the parties could agree in the contract that a heating or air conditioning system with an efficiency rating below a certain level is a defect. Also, the parties could agree that the presence of polybutylene pipes in the plumbing system is a defect regardless of whether there has been any history of breakage of the pipes on the property. The following is a sample special stipulation which could be used in this situation:

Special Stipulation #8-4: Certain items deemed to be defects

Notwithstanding any other provision in this Agreement to the contrary, Buyer and Seller agree that the following conditions or items if discovered in or on

the Property during the inspection shall be deemed a "defect" pursuant to the
terms   and   conditions   of   this   Agreement:

_____.

The parties may also want to include a special stipulation in the contract which provides that if the parties disagree as to whether an item is a "defect," a mutually agreed upon arbitrator would decide the issue. For example, the parties could decide in advance that should a dispute arise, they would contact the Georgia Chapter of the American Society of Home Inspectors ("ASHI") who would then randomly pick an ASHI-approved inspector to act as an arbitrator and to make a binding decision as to whether the disputed item constitutes a defect. The parties could agree to split the cost of this inspector's services. This would provide a quick and effective resolution to a potential problem. The following special stipulation can be used for this purpose:

Special Stipulation #8-5: Agreement to hire ASHI certified inspector to arbitrate whether item is a defect

Notwithstanding any other provision in this Agreement to the contrary, if Buyer and Seller cannot agree as to whether a certain item is a "defect" as that term is defined in this Agreement, Buyer and Seller agree to immediately contact the American Society of Home Inspectors ("ASHI"), to request that it randomly pick an ASHI-approved inspector to determine whether such item is a "defect" pursuant to this Agreement. Buyer and Seller further agree that: (1) the decision of said inspector shall be binding upon all parties to this Agreement; (2) the cost of obtaining such a determination shall be evenly split between the parties; and (3) the Defect Resolution Period shall be extended until one day after the determination is made to allow the parties to consider the decision of the inspector.

§ 8.1.2.9 Seller does not have to replace defect if it can be repaired

The new GAR Contract provides that the seller does not have to replace a defect if it can be repaired such that at closing it is reasonably fit for the purposes for which it is intended. This language was added to try to resolve one of the more common disputes between buyers and sellers.

While the new language opens the door for buyers and sellers to argue over whether a defect can be repaired such that it is fit for the purposes for which it is intended, it should help give guidance that replacing a defect is not needed if it can be reasonably repaired.

§ 8.1.3   Property sold with right to terminate

The 2005 GAR Contract contains a new option which, if agreed to by the seller gives the buyer a right to terminate the contract without penalty within a negotiated period of time. The right to terminate the contract is often referred by

REALTORS® as a "free look". Prior to the expiration of the right to terminate, the buyer may conduct whatever due diligence on the property the buyer deems appropriate and terminate the contract without obligation. The contract also states that the buyer has paid the seller $10.00 as consideration for the seller granting the buyer a right to terminate.

There was a lot of debate over whether to include a right to terminate in the GAR Contract. Some REALTORS® have argued that including a "free look" gives buyers too much power in the negotiation process. The thought here is that buyers may use a termination right to extract additional concessions from sellers.

Others have said that the price paid by the buyer for a "free look" should be significantly more than $10.00 if a property is to be taken off the market for any period of time. A special stipulation where the money paid by the buyer for the "free look" is significantly more than $10.00 is set forth below:

Special Stipulation #8-6: Larger payment by buyer to seller for right to terminate

Notwithstanding any provisions to the contrary contained herein, the consideration for Seller granting Buyer the right to terminate as set forth herein shall be the payment by Buyer to Seller of the sum of $_____. This payment shall be made no later than within one (1) day from the Binding Agreement Date. In the event the payment is not timely made, the Seller may, but shall not be required to terminate this Agreement upon notice to Buyer. Since this payment is consideration of Seller granting Buyer the right to terminate this Agreement, it shall not be refundable to Buyer and shall not be applied to the purchase price of the Property.

Another approach is for the buyer to give the seller a significant sum for the right to terminate the contract, but then provide that a portion of this payment is applied toward the purchase price of the property if the buyer closes upon the purchase of the property. The special stipulation set for below is an example of such a provision:

Special Stipulation #8-7: A portion of payment for right to terminate to be applied towards purchase price

Notwithstanding any provision to the contrary contained herein, the consideration for the Seller granting Buyer the right to terminate as set forth herein shall be the payment by Buyer to Seller of the sum of $_____. This payment shall be made no later than within one (1) day from the Binding Agreement Date. In the event the payment is not timely made, the Seller may, but shall not be required to terminate this

Agreement upon notice to Buyer. Since this payment is in consideration of Seller granting Buyer the right to terminate this Agreement, it shall not be refundable to Buyer. However, if Buyer elects to close upon the purchase of the Property, _____% of the above-referenced amount shall be applied towards the purchase price of the Property at closing.

The right to terminate was added to the 2005 GAR Contract for several reasons. First "free look" provisions have already found their way into numerous contracts as special stipulations. For example, it is not uncommon to find special stipulations in contracts which state, "If Buyer is dissatisfied with the inspection of the property for any reason whatsoever, Buyer may terminate this Agreement". Unfortunately, since these provisions lack separate consideration and give buyers complete discretion to terminate contracts, an argument can be made that these contracts are void for what is known as a lack of mutuality.

Second, since the inclusion of a "free look" requires the agreement of both the buyer and the seller, the seller cannot be forced to agree to a "free look" against their will.

Third, while a "free look" provision makes it easy for buyers to get out of contracts, buyers can already exploit other provisions in the contract, such as the inspection or financing contingencies to get out of contracts. In many ways, the "free look" enables the seller to assess more quickly whether the buyer is really interested in the property. This is because if the buyer has a right to terminate the contract and elects not to do so, the likelihood of the buyer completing the transaction is probably increased.

Fourth, the requirement that a buyer prove an item is defective before the buyer can request that it be repaired has led to numerous disputes between buyers and sellers over what constitutes a "defect". Giving a buyer a right to terminate for any reason whatsoever should help prevent these types of disputes.

Legally, the "free look" provision functions as an option contract. An option contract is one of the few legal devices available to buyers to give them a discretionary right to buy or not buy property. The GAR Contract recites the sum of $10 as consideration for the free look and include language that the receipt and sufficiency of this amount is acknowledged by the seller.

Therefore, the seller will not likely be able to challenge the failure of the buyer to actually pay the said sum if the seller has signed the contract. If the buyer requires more time and the seller agrees to extend the "free look" period, the parties should execute an amendment to the contract. The amendment should also contain a recital of a small additional fee as consideration for the extension.

§ 8.1.3.1 *Prohibition against buyer contracting for multiple properties*

To avoid buyers being able to tie up multiple properties when the buyer has a right to terminate, the GAR Contract provides that the buyer warrants that he or she does not currently have other property under contract (including property subject to a "free look" or right to terminate) and will not put the property under contract during the right to terminate. If the buyer is a real estate investor who regularly puts multiple properties under contract at the same time, this provision will need to be struck from the GAR Contract.

In other cases, buyers may want to limit the geographical area in which they are agreeing not to execute simultaneous contracts on multiple properties. The special stipulation below is an example of this type of provision.

Special Stipulation #8-8: Buyer to limit geographical area of properties under contract

Notwithstanding any provision to the contrary contained herein, Buyer's warranty not to contract to purchase other real property during the time period when Buyer has a right to terminate this Agreement shall only apply to the following area(s):
[describe city county, etc.] _____

§ 8.1.3.2 *Amendment to Address Concerns with Property*

The "free look" period in the GAR Contract is the time for the buyer to inspect and decide whether or not to purchase the property. The contract is not set up for the buyer to get both a "free look" period and then a separate inspection period and Defect Resolution Period. All inspections and the negotiations of any concerns with the property must be completed prior to the end of the right to terminate. As such, the "free look" period is similar to the buyer's due diligence provision in the GAR Commercial Purchase and Sale Agreement.

Prior to the expiration of the right to terminate, the buyer must notify the seller that he is not going forward with the purchase of the property. If the buyer does nothing and the "free look" period expires, the buyer is obligated to purchase the property in "as-is" condition.

During the "free look" period, the buyer may also propose an amendment to the contract to address any concerns the buyer may have with the property. For example, let's assume the buyer hires an inspector who indicates that the roof is old and will need to be replaced in the next couple of years. Can the buyer request that the seller replace the roof? The answer to this question is "yes". The buyer can submit an amendment requesting the seller to either replace the roof prior to closing or reduce the sales price in an amount sufficient to allow the buyer to do the work after the closing. The amendment should be on the GAR Form F107: "Amendment to Address Concerns with Property".[615]   When the buyer has a right to terminate, the buyer no longer has to prove that items of concern in the property are defective. Instead, the buyer can request the repair of any item in the property and propose any amendment to the Agreement the buyer desires. The seller, of course, can accept, reject or counter any proposed amendment of the buyer. The buyer can also elect to terminate the contract if the seller does not agree to any proposed amendment and the right to terminate has not expired.

The nature of the negotiations between buyers and sellers will likely be much more open-ended with the "free look" option. Unlike the traditional inspection section where the negotiations are restricted to "defects", no such restrictions apply with a "free look". So for example, nothing would prevent a buyer who realizes that she is paying too much for a property to simply go back to the seller and say that she will terminate the contract if the seller does not agree to an amendment reducing the purchase price of the property.

Similarly, it is also likely that buyers will ask for sales price concessions in lieu of repairs, since there is nothing limiting buyers to request only the repair and/or replacement of defects. However, if the seller makes a financial concession without stating in the contract the defects or concerns the price concession is intended to address, the seller runs the risk that an unscrupulous buyer might later assert a claim against the seller for the very defects the concession was intended to address.

This risk is particularly great if the buyer discovers after the closing that the cost of the repairs turns out to be greater than the concession in the sales price made by the seller. To avoid problems in this area, sellers agreeing to reduce the sales price instead of making repairs should state in the contract what repairs the reduction in sales price is intended to cover, or clearly state that the payment is being made in lieu of all repairs. The special stipulation below is typical of this kind of provisions:

Special Stipulation #8-9: Clarification of repairs to be addressed through price concessions

Buyer acknowledges that Seller is agreeing to reduce the sales price of the Property by $_____ to reflect the fact that the Property contains certain problems, conditions and/or defects including the following:

_____

_____

Buyer: 1) acknowledges that Buyer and Buyer's inspectors and/or other experts have had an ample opportunity to inspect and become thoroughly familiar with the above-referenced problems, conditions and/or defects; 2)

---

615   GAR Form F107

agrees to accept the same "as-is"; and 3) covenants and agrees never to sue Seller with respect to the same or with respect to any other problems, conditions or defects that a thorough investigation of the above referenced problems, conditions and/or defects by Buyer and Buyer's inspectors and experts would have revealed.

The new GAR Amendment to Address Concerns with Property form on which amendments can be requested during the "free look" period does provide that if the seller agrees to the buyer's proposed amendment, the right to terminate period automatically terminates.

This change was made to avoid the situation where the seller agrees to the buyer's requested amendment, but the buyer still terminates the contract because the "free look" period has not expired. Therefore, since the buyer may have only one opportunity to negotiate items of concern, the buyer should address all of his concerns with the property in any Amendment to Address Concerns with Property.

§ 8.1.3.3 *Using Amendment to Request Concerns with Property as notice to terminate*

If the buyer is concerned about failing to timely give a notice to terminate when the buyer has a "free look", one option available to the buyer is to use the Amendment to Address Concerns with Property form as a notice to terminate if the Amendment is not accepted. This can be done by adding the following special stipulation to the end of the Amendment to Address Concerns with Property.

Special Stipulation #8-10: Using GAR Amendment to Address Concerns with Property as a notice to terminate.

In the event this Amendment to Address Concerns with Property is not accepted by Seller and delivered back to Buyer prior to the end of the Buyer's Right to Terminate this Agreement set forth herein, this Amendment to Address Concerns with Property shall serve as notice of Buyer's decision to terminate this Agreement.

Of course, the problem with this type of provision is that if it is not accepted, the contract is automatically terminated.

§ 8.1.3.4 *Right to proceed rather than right to terminate*

Another approach to the "free look" is to provide that the contract automatically terminates unless prior to the end of the "free look" period, the buyer gives a notice that he or she will proceed with the purchase of the property. With this approach, if no notice is given to the seller, or if notice is given late, the contract terminates. In this way, the risk of the buyer being forced to buy a property that he or she does not want to buy is minimized. The special stipulation below is an example of this type of provision.

Special Stipulation #8-11: Free look where notice to proceed is required

For and in consideration of ten ($10.00) dollars and other good and valuable consideration the receipt and sufficiency of which is hereby acknowledged, Seller hereby grants to Buyer the option for ____ days from the Binding Agreement Date ("Option Period") to purchase the Property in accordance with the terms and conditions of this Agreement. If Buyer elects to purchase the Property, Buyer must give notice of Buyer's decision to proceed with the purchase of the Property prior to the expiration of the Option Period. If Buyer does not give Seller notice of its decision to proceed with the purchase of the Property prior to the expiration of the Option Period, this Agreement shall automatically terminate and Buyer shall be entitled to the return of his earnest money. During the Option Period, Buyer shall have the right to seek to amend the Agreement to address any concerns of Buyer with the Property.

§ 8.1.3.5 *Combining right to terminate with right to inspect and right to request repairs*

While the GAR Contract contemplates that only one inspection option will be selected, it is possible to combine the right to terminate with a traditional right to inspect and request the repair and/or replacement of defects.

The approach would most likely be used where the buyer needs only a few days to decide whether or not to purchase the property but then wants a longer period of time to inspect for and negotiate the repair and/or replacement of defects. The special stipulation below is an example of this type of provision.

Special Stipulation #8-12: Right to terminate with right to inspect

Buyer has selected to purchase the Property subject to both a Right to Terminate the Agreement and a Right to Inspect and Request the Repair of Defects. Upon the expiration of the Right to Terminate this Agreement, Buyer shall not be obligated to purchase the Property in "as-is" condition. Instead, Buyer shall then have the right to inspect the Property and request the repair of defects in accordance with the Property Sold With Right to Request Repairs section of the Agreement.

§ 8.1.3.6 *Combining right to terminate with seller's right to continue offering property for sale*

The seller may want the right to continue marketing the property while the buyer inspects the property. The special stipulation below is an example of this type of provision.

Special Stipulation #8-13: Right to terminate with kick out provision

This Agreement is subject to Buyer's Termination Right which must be exercised on or before _____, 20_____. Seller shall have the right to continue to offer Seller's Property for sale. In the event Seller receives an acceptable offer, Seller shall give notice of having received such an offer to Buyer in accordance with the Agreement. Buyer shall then have _____ hours, after receipt of such notice to deliver a notice to Seller terminating and ending Buyer's Termination Right. The removal and termination of the Termination Right shall not, however, terminate or affect any other contingencies to which the Agreement may be subject. In the event Buyer does not deliver the required notice within the time period stated above, then the parties agree that this Agreement shall become null and void upon the expiration of said time period, and Holder shall refund the earnest money to Buyer.

§ 8.1.3.7 Buyer exercising right to terminate

If the buyer elects to terminate the contract pursuant to a right to terminate provision set forth in the GAR Contract, the buyer must give written notice of the buyer's decision prior to the expiration of the right to terminate. If the buyer fails to do this, buyer agrees to purchase the property in "as is" condition. This means that buyers must know when the right to terminate period ends, and ensure that any notice of termination is delivered to the seller or the broker representing the seller as a client prior to the expiration of the right to terminate.

Being in the middle of negotiations regarding items of concern will not stop or prevent the right to terminate from expiring. So, for example, if the buyer has a remaining concern regarding the property and the seller is obtaining bids for its repair, the right to terminate will still expire if the parties do not agree and sign off on the Amendment to Address Concerns With Property prior to the expiration of the right to terminate.

Alternatively, the buyer can give the seller a notice of the buyer's decision to terminate the contract or get an amendment to the contract signed extending the right to terminate for some additional time period. An example of an amendment to extend the right to terminate period is set forth below:

Amendment to extend time to exercise right to terminate

For and inconsideration of the sum of $10.00, the receipt and sufficiency of which is hereby acknowledged, Buyer and Seller agree that Buyer's Right To Terminate as set forth in the Agreement shall be extended for _____ additional days from the Binding Agreement Date. All other provisions in the Agreement shall remain the same.

§ 8.1.3.8 Expiration of right to terminate does not affect other contingencies in contract

The GAR Contract specifically provides that the expiration of the right to terminate the contract does not eliminate any other contingencies to which the contract is subject. So, for example, if the contract contains a financing contingency, the expiration of the right to terminate the contract does not eliminate any financing contingency contained in the Contract.

If the seller grants the buyer a right to terminate for a particularly long period of time, the seller may want to provide that all contingencies in the contract are eliminated upon the expiration of the right to terminate. The following is an example of such a special stipulation:

Special Stipulation #8-14: All contingencies in contract eliminated upon expiration of right to terminate

Upon the expiration of the Buyer's Right to Terminate this Agreement as set forth herein, the parties agree that all other contingencies to which this Agreement is subject shall also end. At that time, this Agreement shall no longer be subject to any contingencies.

§ 8.1.4   Inspection special stipulations for buyers

§ 8.1.4.1 Right to terminate based on repair costs

Buyers may on occasion want to include other inspection stipulations to give themselves greater flexibility. For example, the parties could stipulate that the buyer will have the right to terminate the contract if the repair costs for the defects exceed a specified amount. The following sample provision may be used in this instance:

Special Stipulation #8-15: Buyer's right to terminate if repair costs excessive

Notwithstanding any other provision in this Agreement to the contrary, Buyer shall have the right to terminate this Agreement upon written notice to Seller within _____ days of the Binding Agreement Date if the Inspector after inspecting the Property estimates that the cost of repairing and/or replacing any defects (as defined in this Agreement) discovered therein will cost more than $_____.

§ 8.1.4.2   *Right to reduce sales price*

The buyer and seller may also agree that the buyer will accept a certain defect present in or on the property if the sales price of the property is lowered accordingly. The following provision contemplates such an agreement while reserving the buyer's right to request repairs for all other defects in or on the property:

Special Stipulation #8-16: Buyer accepts defects "as is"

Notwithstanding any other provision in this Agreement to the contrary, Buyer and Seller acknowledge that the agreed-upon purchase price of the Property contemplates that the Property contains the following defects_____; Buyer agrees to accept these defects in the Property "as is" and will not request that the defects be repaired or replaced in any inspection amendment submitted on the Property. Other than the defects specified above, the Property is sold with the right of the Buyer to request repairs.

§ 8.1.4.3   *Right to terminate for condition that is not a "defect*

The buyer may want to include a special stipulation to allow for termination of the contract upon discovery of certain conditions on the property or structures which are not considered "defects" under the terms of the contract but which might lower the property value or about which the buyer has special concern. For example, the buyer may not want to purchase the property if it is determined that a portion of the dwelling on the property lies in a flood plain. In this circumstance, the buyer may include the following special stipulation:

Special Stipulation #8-17: Flood plain termination

Notwithstanding any other provision in this Agreement to the contrary, Buyer shall have the right to terminate this Agreement upon written notice to Seller within _____ days of the Binding Agreement Date if it is determined that any portion of the residential dwelling or garage on the Property is located in a flood plain.

§ 8.1.4.4 *Seasonal inspections*

In some circumstances, several months might be required in order for the buyer to obtain a complete inspection of a particular condition or structure in or on the property. For example, even though the GAR Contract requires the seller to have all utility services and any pool, spa, or similar item operational during the inspection period, in reality, if the property has a pool or outdoor spa and a contract is entered into in December, the pool or spa may not be open for inspection. Likewise, the air conditioning may not be properly tested during colder months and the heating system may not be tested in hot weather.

In these situations, the parties may agree that for a specified time period, the seller will ensure that such items are fully and properly operational and if they are not, the seller will agree to make any necessary repairs. The following special stipulation may be used for such an agreement:

Special Stipulation #8-18: Seller's obligation to fix defects not found before closing due to seasonal issues

Notwithstanding any other provision in this Agreement to the contrary, Buyer and Seller acknowledge and agree that the following item or items in or on the Property cannot be properly inspected due to seasonal weather or other conditions: _____. Seller therefore warrants that said items are in good working order and repair as of the Binding Agreement Date and without defect as defined by this Agreement. If, for a period of _____ days from the closing date of this Agreement, Buyer uses such items for the first time and finds that such items are not in proper working order and that such items are, in fact, defective, Seller shall be responsible at Seller's sole expense to repair and/or replace any defect in said items at that time. If Buyer does not use such item for the first time within the period specified above or if the defects of which the Buyer complains were caused by the Buyer or his guests, agents, or representatives, Seller's obligation to repair or replace defects in such items shall terminate.

To protect the seller from having to spend a great deal of money to fix the defect after closing, the above special stipulation could also limit the amount of money the seller would be required to pay for this type of repair.

§ 8.1.4.5 Invasive testing

The GAR Contract permits buyers to perform invasive testing on the property. The GAR Contract specifically allows testing for lead-based paint, which may involve drilling holes in walls and removing paint samples from various rooms. Similarly, a buyer may choose to remove some pieces of siding or synthetic stucco to check for rotten wood and structural damage.

Although the GAR Contract requires the buyer to repair any damage caused by his tests, the seller may want to address this issue in a special stipulation by requiring the buyer to post money, held by one of the brokers, to cover the cost of repairing any damage to the property caused by any invasive testing. The following special stipulation could be used in such a situation:

Special Stipulation #8-19: Buyer posting funds with listing broker for repairs caused by seller's invasive testing

Should Buyer or Buyer's representatives desire to perform any invasive tests or inspections to the Property that involve the removal of siding, stucco, or paint or the drilling, boring, or sampling of the physical dwelling or soil, then Buyer shall notify Seller in writing of the exact nature and extent of the tests to be performed not less than three days in advance of said tests and shall post a sum of money with listing broker as set forth below to insure that the Property is repaired or restored to its original condition.

Buyer shall provide Seller with a written estimate from a contractor to repair the Property according to the type and nature of tests and shall post one and one-half times the amount of the repair estimate with the listing broker. Listing broker shall be entitled to disburse said funds to repair all damage done by invasive testing and to refund any excess to Buyer. All decisions of listing broker with respect to repairing damage caused by invasive testing shall be final and binding upon all parties, and no claims shall be asserted against listing broker for any decisions made hereunder in good faith.

§ 8.1.4.6 Right to terminate if lead-based paint found

The literal language of the law gives the buyer only the opportunity to inspect and test for lead-based paint or lead-based paint hazards; it does not give the buyer a right to terminate a contract if lead-based paint is found in the property. Brokers and licensees representing buyers will therefore want to confirm that the contract protects their buyer clients in the event the testing for lead-based paint is positive.

The inspection provision of the GAR Contract gives buyers only the right to request repairs. Accordingly, if the seller agrees to have the lead-based paint removed, the buyer would be obligated to purchase the property.

Some buyers will want the absolute right to terminate a purchase contract if the property is found to contain any lead-based paint. Buyers with this position may want to include the following special stipulation as a special stipulation to the contract to allow for such a contingency:

Special Stipulation #8-20: Buyer's right to terminate contract on discovery of lead-based paint

Buyer shall have the right to terminate this Agreement upon written notice to Seller if it is determined within _____ days of the Binding Agreement Date that the Property contains lead-based paint or lead-based paint hazards. For the purposes herein, the term lead-based paint shall mean paint or other surface coatings that contain lead equal to or in excess of 1.0 milligram per square centimeter or 0.5 percent by weight.

On the other hand, the parties may want to include the following special stipulation which provides more flexibility and allows the seller an opportunity to correct the problem to avoid terminating the contract:

Special Stipulation #8-21: Lead-based paint testing contingency

This Agreement is contingent upon a risk assessment or inspection of the Property for the presence of lead-based paint and/or lead-based paint hazards at Buyer's expense within _____ days of the Binding Agreement Date. This contingency will terminate at said predetermined deadline unless Buyer (or Buyer's agent) delivers to Seller (or Seller's agent) a written contract amendment listing the specific existing deficiencies and corrections needed, together with a copy of the inspection and/or risk assessment report. Seller may, at Seller's option, within _____ days after delivery of the addendum, elect in writing whether to correct the condition(s). If Seller decides to correct the condition, Seller shall furnish Buyer within _____ days after delivery of Buyer's addendum, a certification from a risk assessor or inspector demonstrating that the condition has been remedied. If Seller elects not to make the repairs, or if Seller makes a counteroffer, Buyer shall have _____ days to respond to the counteroffer or remove this contingency and take the Property in "as is" condition or this contract shall become void. Buyer may remove this contingency at any time without cause.

§ 8.1.4.7   Radon testing

Buyers may be concerned about radon levels in the property they intend to purchase and may want to terminate the contract if radon levels exceed current acceptable levels. Alternatively, the buyer may want to give the seller to lower the radon levels. The following stipulations can be used for these purposes:

Special Stipulation #8-22: Radon testing contingency

This Agreement is contingent upon having the Property inspected for the presence of radon within _____ days from Binding Agreement Date at Buyer's discretion and expense. Said testing shall be conducted by a current National Environmental Health Association ("NEHA") Certified Measurement Provider using an EPA approved testing method and reporting format. Testing device shall be placed and retrieved by a current NEHA Certified Measurement Provider. This contingency shall terminate at said predetermined date unless Buyer or Buyer's agent deliver to Seller or Seller's agent a written amendment stating that said results reveal a radon level within the residential dwelling on the Property equal or higher than the level established by the EPA as being potentially hazardous to human beings. Seller may, at Seller's option and within _____ days of delivery of the amendment, elect in writing to remedy the condition at Seller's sole expense. If Seller decides to remedy the condition, Seller shall undertake all remedial measures necessary to reduce the radon level in the residential dwellings on the Property to a level within the recommended safe level established by the EPA and provide the Buyer with written re-test results performed by current NEHA Certified Measurement Provider confirming such reduction of radon.

Said remediation may include the installation of fans which may increase utility costs to the buyer. If Seller elects not to remedy the condition, makes a counteroffer or does not respond within the time period in which Seller has to respond, Buyer shall have _____ days from the expiration of said time period to respond or remove this contingency or this contract shall become void. Buyer may waive this contingency at any time.

Some buyers may want an absolute right to terminate if the test results show a radon level equal or higher that the action level established by the EPA. The following special stipulation may be used:

Special Stipulation #8-23: Buyer's right to terminate if high radon level

Buyer shall have the right to have the Property inspected for the presence of radon within _____ days from Binding Agreement Date at Buyer's discretion and expense. Testing shall be conducted by a current National Environmental Health Association ("NEHA") Certified Measurement Provider using an EPA approved testing method and reporting format. Testing device shall be placed and retrieved by a current NEHA Certified Measurement Provider. If said radon testing reveal a radon level equal or higher than the level established by the EPA as being potentially dangerous to human beings in the Property, Buyer shall have the right to terminate this Agreement upon written notice to Seller within _____ days of the Binding Agreement Date.

§ 8.1.4.8 Right to remove asbestos

Buyers may be concerned about elevated levels of asbestos present in the property they intend to purchase. If buyers have such concerns, they may want to include special stipulations requiring the seller to take steps to remove all asbestos. The following special stipulation can be used for these purposes:

Special Stipulation #8-24: Asbestos removal

During the inspection period, Buyer shall have the Property inspected for the presence of asbestos. If it is determined within _____ days of the Binding Agreement Date that asbestos is present in the Property, Seller shall remove the asbestos from the Property in a good and workmanlike manner and in accordance with all applicable laws and regulations prior to the closing.

In the alternative, the parties could agree that the presence of asbestos is a defect pursuant to the contract. Adding a stipulation that such conditions constitute defects allows buyers to request that sellers repair the problem as part of the inspection contingency. The following provisions can be used for such stipulations:

Special Stipulation #8-25: Asbestos constitutes defect

During the inspection period, Buyer shall have the property inspected for the presence of asbestos. Notwithstanding any other provision in this Agreement to the contrary, Buyer and Seller agree if the results of said inspection reveal the presence of asbestos in or on the Property, this shall constitute a defect pursuant to the provision of the Agreement entitled "Property Sold With Right to Request Repairs."

On the other hand, buyers may prefer to have the right to terminate the contract if the property contains asbestos. In this event, the parties may include the following special stipulation in the contract:

Special Stipulation #8-26: Buyer's right to terminate if asbestos found

Notwithstanding any other provision in this Agreement to the contrary, Buyer shall have the right to terminate this Agreement upon written notice to Seller within _____ days of the Binding Agreement Date if an inspection for asbestos reveals that asbestos is present in or on the Property.

§ 8.1.4.9   *Right to terminate due to neighborhood conditions*

Under the GAR Contract, buyers are restricted in their inspection amendments from raising defects that are not on or in the property. The buyer cannot raise off-site conditions such as being near an airport, pending rezoning proposals, school districts, or political jurisdictions. Therefore, the buyer should satisfy himself regarding neighborhood conditions prior to signing the contract. In the alternative, the parties can include a provision such as one or more of the samples below, which give the buyer the right to terminate the contract on the basis of the discovery of specified neighborhood conditions.

Special Stipulation #8-27: Buyer's right to terminate because of school district

Notwithstanding any other provision in this Agreement to the contrary, Buyer shall have the right to terminate this Agreement upon written notice to Seller within _____ days from the Binding Agreement Date if it is determined by Buyer that the children living in the Property would attend Elementary School, _____ Middle School, and _____ High School.

Special Stipulation #8-28: Buyer's right to terminate because of rezoning

Notwithstanding any other provision in this Agreement to the contrary, Buyer shall have the right to terminate this Agreement upon written notice to Seller within _____ days from the Binding Agreement Date if Buyer determines that the Property is within 300 feet of any other property subject to a rezoning application to a more intensive land use which was filed prior to the Binding Agreement Date.

Special Stipulation #8-29: Buyer's right to terminate because of political jurisdiction

Notwithstanding any other provision in this Agreement to the contrary, Buyer shall have the right to terminate this Agreement upon written notice to Seller within _____ days from the Binding Agreement Date if it is determined by Buyer that the Property is not located within the incorporated city limits of

_____.

Furthermore, buyers should ensure that the property they are planning to purchase does not contain any violations of the neighborhood covenants, if any such covenants exist. Buyers may want to add the following stipulation to their contract to ensure that if a covenant violation is found, the seller will agree to repair, remove, or abate the violation prior to closing:

Special Stipulation #8-30: Seller's obligation if covenant violation discovered on property

Buyer shall have _____ days from the Binding Agreement Date to determine if a violation of a neighborhood or subdivision covenant exists on the Property. If it is determined that such a violation exists, Buyer shall present Seller with written notice of such violation, which notice shall also include the steps Seller shall take to repair or remove said violation. Seller shall comply with Buyer's written notice and repair or abate the violation prior to closing.

Special Stipulation #8-31: Buyer's right to terminate due to violation of neighborhood or subdivision covenants

Notwithstanding any other provision in this Agreement to the contrary, Buyer shall have the right to terminate this Agreement upon written notice to Seller within _____ days from the Binding Agreement Date if it is determined by Buyer that a violation of a neighborhood or subdivision covenant exists on or with respect to the Property (other than which violation can be cured by the Seller at or before closing through the payment of money)

§ 8.1.4.10   Right to terminate due to inability or high cost of obtaining property insurance

Buyers should note that the possibility of obtaining property insurance on the property he or she is contracting to purchase and its cost might depend on the number of claims that the previous owner filed on the property. Insurers have long used loss histories to underwrite and rate a homeowner's insurance. When a homebuyer approaches an insurance provider for homeowner's insurance for a prospective home purchase, the insurer may obtain information on the buyer's former home to check how responsible the person is as a homeowner. The insurer may also obtain information on the new home to check whether or not that home has had recurring problems that justify higher premiums. Water leaks, for instance, are treated with more caution because of the threat of mold.

An insurer can obtain the loss history of a property from databases, such as CLUE (Comprehensive Loss Underwriting Exchange). If a property has negative marks on its CLUE report, it may be more difficult for a buyer to purchase the property because the buyer may either have to pay a high property insurance premium or may not be able to obtain property insurance at all. Each insurer will use the CLUE report based on its own underwriting and rating criteria. Therefore, while one insurer may qualify a home prone to flooding as high risk, another insurer may refuse insurance altogether.

A buyer may wish to make the purchase contingent upon a satisfactory CLUE report. The following special stipulation can be used for these purposes:

Special Stipulation #8-32: Buyer's right to terminate due to unsatisfactory CLUE or other claims report

Notwithstanding any other provision in this Agreement to the contrary, Buyer shall have the right to terminate this Agreement upon written notice to Seller within _____ days from the Binding Agreement Date if an insurance provider of Buyer's choice determines, based on the Property's CLUE (Comprehensive Loss Underwriting Exchange) report or any other report that 1) it cannot insure the Property or 2) it is able to insure the Property with limitations which is unacceptable to Buyer or 3) is able to provide property insurance at a higher premium than what the insurance provider would normally price.

§ 8.1.5   "As Is" clause

Under the GAR Contract, parties may agree that the property is being sold "as is" with all faults, including lead-based paint, lead-based paint hazards, radon hazards, and/or asbestos hazards. Pursuant to this provision, the buyer must accept the property, with all of its defects, even if the buyer does not know about the defect. The seller will not be obligated to make any repairs to the property, except as may be specially stipulated otherwise in the contract.

For example, in one Georgia case, the buyer sued the seller and the seller's real estate agent to recover the cost of structural repairs necessitated when she discovered, after purchasing a house, that the attic had been damaged by fire. The house in this case was vacant and in a dilapidated condition, not suitable to be lived in. The buyer paid $25,000.00 for the house with the understanding that she would have to undertake substantial repairs. The buyer's agent drafted the contract which contained a special stipulation that the house was being purchased "as is" with no termite certification.[616] After the closing on the purchase of the property, the buyer began to make repairs, during which the contractor installing the HVAC equipment in the attic discovered fire damage to the ceiling joists. The appellate court in ruling against the buyer found that the buyer did not exercise reasonable care to discover the charred timber and thus could not maintain her fraud claim. The Court also ruled that the buyer should have exercised a heightened degree of diligence in inspecting the house because she knew that it was in dilapidated condition with many major defects and was purchasing the house in "as is" condition.

On the other hand, in a different Georgia case, a buyer who purchased a house "as is" recovered damages from the seller who fraudulently concealed insect damage.[617] In this case, a provision in the sales contract required the seller to give the buyer a termite certificate declaring the property free from termite infestation or damage. At the closing, the seller stated that he did not have such a certificate, and when the buyer refused to proceed with the closing, the seller promised to give the buyer a certificate in order to complete the sale. The seller's agent typed into the sales contract the words "The sale is as is condition."

After the buyer took possession of the house, she discovered wood beetle damage. She also discovered that, more than two years before she bought the house, the seller had hired an exterminator to treat an infestation. On this basis, the buyer sued the seller and his agent for fraud in the inducement of the contract and affirmative and willful nondisclosure of the insect damage.

The buyer settled her claim with the seller's agent, and a jury awarded her general damages and punitive damages against the seller. The seller argued that the words "as is" in the sales contract removed any question of fraud as to the condition of the property, on the grounds that the acceptance of a contract with an "as is" clause forces the buyer to undertake an absolute duty of inspection. However, the Court ruled against the seller and found that the "as is" provision does not protect a seller who willfully misrepresents the condition of the property to the buyer.

§ 8.1.5.1   Special disclosure by sellers unfamiliar with condition of property

Some sellers sell property the condition of which they are unfamiliar. In such instances, sellers are well advised to add a special stipulation to the contract informing the buyer of this fact and encouraging them to do a more thorough inspection. The following special stipulation is an example of this type of provision.

---

616   Ben Farmer Realty Co. v. Woodard, 212 Ga. App. 74, 441 S.E.2d 421 (1994), cert. denied.
617   Mulkey v. Waggoner, 177 Ga. App. 165, 338 S.E.2d 755 (1985).

Special Stipulation #8-33: Disclosure to buyer that seller is unfamiliar with condition of property

Buyer acknowledges that Seller has only owned the property [for a short period of time and/or never resided in the Property]. As a result, Seller is largely unfamiliar with the condition of the Property. Buyer is therefore encouraged to do an extra thorough inspection of the Property to satisfy himself as to its condition.

§ 8.2   Seller's duty to repair

The GAR Contract states that the agreed-upon defects shall be repaired or replaced. The seller has the option of repairing or replacing the defective item himself, unless the parties specifically state otherwise in the contract. Moreover, the contract does not specify the type or quality of materials to be used in making repairs to the property, the methods of repair, or whether the repairs will be warranted for any period of time. However, the contract does provide that all agreed-upon repairs shall be made in a good and workmanlike manner prior to closing.

There is implied in every construction contract the obligation to perform the work in a fit and workmanlike manner, which is breached when the contractor fails to exercise a reasonable degree of care, skill, and ability.[618] In other words, repairs must be performed in a good and workmanlike manner whether or not this is stated in the contract. Further, the standard of "good and workmanlike manner" means that the work is to be performed in accordance with industry standards and applicable building codes.[619] It is also implied that the closing date will be automatically extended until the repairs are made in a workmanlike fashion.[620]

The GAR Contract specifically provides that the seller is not obligated to replace a defective item if it can be repaired such that at closing it is reasonably fit for the purposes for which it was intended. So, for example, if some shingles fall off a relatively new roof, the seller would not have to replace the entire rood if it can be adequately repaired by merely replacing the missing shingles. However, if the repair will not leave the repaired item reasonably fit for the purposes for which it was intended, the buyer could demand that the item be replaced.

While a buyer and seller can still vigorously debate whether a defect, if repaired, will be reasonably fit for the purposes for which it was intended at closing, GAR Forms Committee hope that the language will at least give our courts some guidance to resolve disputes of this type.

---

618   Nulite Industries Co., LLC v. Horne, 252 Ga.App. 378, 556 S.E.2d 255 (Ga.App.,2001)

619   Fussell v. Jones, 198 Ga. App. 399, 401 S.E.2d 593 (1991).

620   Yargus v. Smith, 254 Ga.App. 338, 562 S.E.2d 371 (Ga.App.,2002)

§ 8.2.1　　Deciding who should make repairs

Some buyers may want to require that repairs be performed by a particular contractor or with a higher level of skill than what might normally be used by a contractor. The special stipulations below can be used to address these concerns:

Special Stipulation #8-34: Agreement to hire specific company to perform repairs

Seller agrees that all repairs and replacements of defects agreed to by the parties (excepting items the cost of which to repair or replace is less than $10.00) shall be performed by XYZ Contractor prior to closing. Prior to closing, Seller shall present Buyer with a paid invoice from said contractor confirming that the agreed upon repairs have been performed.

Special Stipulation #8-35: Agreement to hire contractor with experience

Seller agrees that all agreed upon repairs to the Property shall be performed by a highly skilled contractor with at least _____ years of full-time experience in the area requiring repairs and who is licensed (where it is possible to obtain a license to perform the repair in question) to make the agreed upon repairs. Seller further agrees that all repairs shall be performed prior to closing in a first quality manner typical of a contractor with the level of expertise described above.

§ 8.2.2　　Deciding who should pay for repairs

The seller may be willing to hire a particular company to perform the work but may be concerned about the cost of the repairs. In this instance, the seller can try to cap the seller's financial obligations to make repairs. The special stipulation below is an example of this type of provision.

Special Stipulation #8-36: Agreement to hire specific company to perform repairs and replacements with cost limitation

Seller shall hire XYZ Contractor to complete the following agreed-upon repairs and replacements: _____.
However, Seller shall not be obligated to pay more than $_____ for said repairs and replacements based on the bid provided by Contractor attached hereto and incorporated herein. Buyer shall be obligated to pay any additional costs in excess of said amount. At or prior to closing, Seller shall provide Buyer with copies of paid invoices to verify that Seller has fulfilled his obligations hereunder.

The parties may also agree to limit only the seller's total costs for repairs and replacements under the contract. The following stipulation provides for such a limitation:

Special Stipulation #8-37: Seller's cost limitation for repairs and replacements

Notwithstanding any other provision in this Agreement to the contrary, Seller shall not be obligated to pay more than $_____ for the agreed-upon repairs and replacements under this Agreement. All costs incurred by Seller in excess of $_____ shall be Buyer's sole responsibility and shall be reimbursed by Buyer to Seller at or before closing. At or before closing, Seller shall provide Buyer with copies of paid invoices to verify that Seller has fulfilled his obligations hereunder.

Buyers may also require the seller to assign to the buyer any warranty for such repairs or replacements:

Special Stipulation #8-38: Seller assigns repair warranties to buyer

Notwithstanding any provision to the contrary contained herein, where the contractor who performs such repairs or replacement offers a warranty for the labor and/or materials, Seller shall either provide that the warranty be issued in the name of the Buyer or assign his interest in the warranty to the Buyer at or before closing.

§ 8.2.3   Repairs with guarantees

There are some repairs which buyers will likely want warranted or guaranteed in order to be comfortable closing on the purchase. This is particularly the case with recurring defects such as roof leaks or leaking basements. While the inspection amendment procedure in the GAR Contract does not give the buyer a right to demand a warranty or guarantee of repairs, such a right can be negotiated as part of an offer. The following is an example of such a provision.

Special Stipulation #8-39: Seller required to use contractor that provides warranty for recurring defects

Should the Inspector's report reveal any roof leaks or moisture damage, flooding or water leakage problems affecting any portion of the residential dwelling on the Property, then all agreed-to repairs shall be performed by a licensed Georgia contractor who has been continuously in the business for at least five (5) years and who will provide an assignable written guarantee or warranty (or written guarantee or warranty in Buyer's name) against failure and defects in labor and materials used in this repair for a period of not less than one year from the date of the repair, which guarantee or warranty shall be assigned by Seller to Buyer at or before closing (if not issued in the Buyer's name).

§ 8.2.4   Specifications on how repairs to be made

Some buyers may want more control over the repair process than to simply have the seller agree to make repairs in a good and workmanlike manner. An example of a special stipulation where the buyer controls the method of repairs is set forth below:

Special Stipulation #8-40: Seller must make repairs according to inspector's specifications

Notwithstanding any other provision to the contrary contained in this Agreement, Buyer shall have the right to require Seller to cause all agreed-upon repairs and replacements of defects to be repaired and/or replaced in accordance with specifications prepared by Buyer's Inspector.

For certain structural repairs, the buyer may require that the seller obtain an engineer's opinion that structural defects on the property were properly corrected in accordance with accepted standards and practices of the construction industry. The special stipulation below is an example of this type of provision.

Special Stipulation #8-41: Seller required to provide engineer's opinion for structural repairs

Notwithstanding any provision to the contrary contained herein, for any agreed-upon repair of a structural defect, Seller shall at Seller's sole expense provide Buyer at or prior to closing with a sealed, written opinion of a licensed Georgia structural engineer that in the professional engineer's opinion, the structural defect was corrected in accordance with sound engineering practices and principles and all applicable building code requirements.

§ 8.3   Buyer's duty to inspect

The buyer's duty to inspect is based on the doctrine of caveat emptor, or "buyer beware". Under Georgia law, this means that the buyer is assumed to know about defects that are obvious and patent. In other words, the buyer is expected to make his own examination and draw his own conclusions as to the condition of the property. There is no confidential or fiduciary relationship between a buyer and seller, even though they are parties to a real estate transaction.[621]

---

621   Duval v. Kidder, 191 Ga. App. 856, 383 S.E.2d 356 (1989); Westbrook v.

As part of the buyer's due diligence, the buyer should determine who resides at the property. If any resident is not a party to the contract, the buyer should inquire of all such persons (such as a tenant) what right or claim they have to the possession of the property.[622] The buyer is charged with notice under the law of how such persons would have replied to the buyer's questions, even if the buyer never fulfills his obligation to speak with them.[623]

A buyer should also carefully inspect the property for defects. The following cases illustrate the importance that the law places on the buyer carrying out independent investigation as to the condition of the property. The buyers sued the sellers for fraudulently concealing the presence of synthetic stucco trim in the property.[624] The sellers had informed the buyers in the Property Disclosure Statement that the property contained untreated stucco cladding. The sellers also gave the buyers a letter from a stucco inspector, which referenced a 1997 inspection. While the letter stated that the stucco was in good condition, the 1997 inspection indicated that there was synthetic stucco trimming. However, the buyers did not request for a copy of the 1997 inspection report. Neither did the buyers conduct a separate stucco inspection. The court stated that the underlying principle of law is that a buyer cannot claim that he has been deceived by false misrepresentations about defects that the buyer could have discovered. This case shows that the law requires that buyers exercise diligence before consummating a real estate contract, and courts will not give buyers relief when the buyer could have discovered by inspection the truth or falsity of a representation made by a seller or an agent. Thus, where a buyer could have learned the truth and avoided later damages, the law will not permit the buyer to claim he had been deceived by false misrepresentations.

In another case, the buyers of a house sued the seller for breach of contract and fraud because of problems with the sewage system that the buyers discovered after moving into the house.[625] The buyers claimed that the seller assured them that "the property was in reasonably satisfactory condition" and did not mention any problems with the sewage system. The contract expressly called for the buyer's prior inspection of the sewage and plumbing system, and although the buyers inspected portions of the property, the evidence was unclear as to how comprehensively they inspected it. Once the buyers moved into the house, they discovered that the sewage "backed up" or "percolated" in the plumbing system.

The court found that the seller was not responsible for the malfunctions of the sewage system. First, the seller was not liable for breach of contract, because it was the buyers who failed to fulfill their contractual obligation to inspect the sewage and

---

Beusse, 79 Ga. App. 654, 54 S.E.2d 693 (1949), cert. denied.

622   Pierce v. Thomas, 258 Ga. 469, 369 S.E.2d 742 (1988).

623   Yancey v. Montgomery & Young, 173 Ga. 178, 159 S.E. 571 (1931).

624   Meyer et al. v. Waite et al., 2004 WL 2102084

625   Duval v. Kidder, 191 Ga. App. 856, 383 S.E.2d 356 (1989).

plumbing system. Also, the Court held that the seller was not responsible for fraud even if the seller represented that she had no problem with the sewage system. The buyers did not show any evidence that the seller had problems with the sewage system prior to the sale or that she should have discovered any problems.

Moreover, the Court found no reason why the buyers could not have discovered the problems with the sewage system "by simple observation upon a prudent inspection." Thus, the Court held that even if the seller had misrepresented the facts, she was not liable for the sewage problems because the buyers failed to show that they were justified in relying on her representations; that they exercised reasonable diligence required of everyone to discover misrepresentations; and that they complied with their own duty to inspect or were excused from this duty for some reason.

§ 8.4   Inspection report

In the inspection report, home inspectors should describe and/or discuss the condition of the property's grounds, roof, exterior surface, garage or carport, structure, attic, basement, crawl space, electrical system, heating system, air-conditioning system, plumbing, on-site sewage disposal, fireplace, kitchen, appliances, and if applicable, pool and hot tub.

The report must state the scope of the inspection, including identification of the structural elements, systems, and subsystems that were inspected. Also, the report should verify that the inspection was visual. In addition, the report should notify the person on whose behalf the inspection is being made of any defects noted during the inspection, and the report should provide appropriate recommendations that certain experts be retained to determine the extent of corrective action necessary for the defects discovered.

Buyers should be aware that they are not entitled to request repairs of defects that are not referenced in the inspection report. The GAR Contract provides that the buyer may request that the seller repair only defects which are included in the inspection report given to the seller. This provision prohibits buyers from raising as a defect any verbal representations of their inspector regarding items not referenced in the inspection report.

§ 8.5   Dealing with bad inspection report

Some contracts fail because the inspection report reveals significant or disputed defects in the property which the seller is unwilling to repair. What is the duty of the seller and the listing agent to disclose a bad inspection report to a subsequent prospective buyer? There is no statute or legislation governing the conduct of the seller in this instance. The listing broker must comply with the Brokerage Relationships in Real Estate Transactions Act ("BRRETA").[626]

---

626   O.C.G.A. §§ 10-6A-1 - 10-6A-14.

Moreover, the GAR Seller's Property Disclosure Statement[627] includes the question, "Have there been any inspections on the Property in the past year?"[628] Answering this question in the affirmative would not necessarily obligate the seller to provide prospective buyers with actual copies of the other inspection reports. Most buyers, however, will request the other inspection reports (if the seller indicates that other inspections have been performed) and not enter into a contract without first reviewing them.

Georgia case law has long held that a seller has a duty to disclose defects in the property of which the seller knew or should have known and which would not have been observable by the buyer upon a reasonable inspection of the property.[629] While a seller may not have a legal obligation to provide prospective buyers with prior inspection reports, the seller does owe a duty to reveal defects in the report which could not have been reasonably discovered by the buyer. The problem is that inspectors sometimes reach different conclusions regarding whether an item or condition is in fact a defect. Therefore, the risk to the seller is relying on the wrong inspector in deciding not to reveal disputed defects in an inspection report. If there are conflicting inspection reports or a disputed inspection report and the seller chooses not to disclose the defects in the report or reports, the seller may still be legally liable if a judge or jury later concludes that the defects could not otherwise have been reasonably discovered.

The listing broker may have a different obligation regarding disclosure. All real estate licensees in Georgia are required to comply with BRRETA, which also places certain duties of disclosure upon the seller's real estate agent. BRRETA requires agents of the seller to timely disclose all adverse material facts pertaining to the physical condition of the property and improvements located on the property which could not be discovered upon a reasonably diligent inspection by the buyer.[630] Moreover, listing brokers must timely disclose to all prospective buyers all material facts pertaining to existing adverse physical conditions in the immediate neighborhood within one mile of the property which are actually known to the broker and which could not be discovered by the buyer upon a diligent inspection.[631]

In light of these legal requirements, the seller and the listing broker may take one of several courses of action in dealing with a bad inspection report. First, the seller can disclose the report to subsequent prospective buyers so that they cannot claim that

---

627   GAR Form F50, Seller's Property Disclosure Statement.
628   GAR Form F50, Seller's Property Disclosure Statement.
629   Wilhite v. Mays, 140 Ga. App. 816, 232 S.E.2d 141 (1976), aff'd, 239 Ga. 31, 235 S.E.2d 532 (1977); Holmes v. Worthey, 159 Ga. App. 262, 282 S.E.2d 919 (1981), aff'd, 249 Ga. 104, 287 S.E.2d 9 (1982).
630   O.C.G.A. § 10-6A-5(b).
631   O.C.G.A. § 10-6A-5(b).

latent defects were concealed from them. Under Georgia law, while hidden defects do not have to be repaired, they do have to be disclosed.

Second, the seller can fix all of the defects listed in the report. In such a situation, it is still recommended that the seller reveal the existence of the bad inspection report but explain that the defects had all been fixed.

Third, if the seller disputes the defects, the seller can hire another inspector and obtain a second report. The seller should then give both reports to a prospective buyer to minimize the negative impact of the first report. Obviously, this approach only makes sense if the second report contradicts the findings of the first report.

Finally, if the bad inspection report was not prepared by an expert, the seller can hire an expert to refute the opinion of the first inspector. It is strongly recommended, however, that sellers and real estate brokers avoid providing buyers with only the expert's report. As discussed above, this is because if it turns out that the expert report is incorrect, the seller may be liable for fraud and the real estate broker may be found to have violated BRRETA.

BRRETA provides that a listing broker is not excused from his duties simply because the seller instructs him to perform in a manner that is in violation of the law.[632] Therefore, the listing broker must make an independent decision with respect to disclosure. BRRETA provides protection to the listing broker from liability to the seller if the listing broker discloses material adverse facts relating to the physical condition of the property even though the seller instructed him not to do so.[633] If the listing broker and the seller cannot agree on what should be disclosed, the listing broker can disclose to the buyer or in the alternative, can terminate his brokerage engagement with the seller.

§ 8.6   Home warranty programs

Several companies offer home warranty programs to buyers purchasing previously occupied homes. Generally, such programs warrant the systems in the home for one year. The purpose of these programs is to give buyers some peace of mind about purchasing a previously occupied home where the systems and appliances in the home are relatively old.

The warranty typically covers the home's plumbing, heating, air conditioning, appliances, and electrical systems. Buyers should read the terms and conditions of the program they select carefully to determine what items are actually covered and to determine all exclusions. Buyers should also determine any additional costs for service calls and deductibles.

---

632   O.C.G.A. § 10-6A-5(b).
633   O.C.G.A. § 10-6A-5(b).

Sellers of older homes with older systems may offer to purchase a warranty program for the buyer as an incentive to the buyer, and the cost of the program can be included in the contract.

For new construction, builders typically provide a one-year warranty with the sale of the home. Buyers should inquire about any warranties available and review carefully the terms and conditions of such warranties. In particular, buyers should be careful to follow exactly the notice requirements contained in a builder's warranty. Many such warranties only provide coverage if notice is sent via certified mail to a specified address, etc. In addition, the systems in a newly constructed home may be under a manufacturer's warranty when the home is purchased by the buyer.

CHAPTER 9
DISCLAIMERS FOR BROKERS

OVERVIEW

This chapter discusses how brokers can limit their legal liability by using appropriate disclaimers. The discussion includes the nature and enforceability of disclaimers, and the rights of buyers and/or sellers to modify or delete the disclaimers and the other provisions designed to protect brokers.

§ 9.1   Limiting liability of brokers

§ 9.1.1   What the GAR Contract provides

The disclaimer provision in the GAR Contract provides: "Buyer and Seller acknowledge that they have not relied upon any advice, representations or statements of Brokers and waive and shall not assert any claims against Brokers involving the same."[634] The disclaimer paragraph of the GAR Contract provides real estate brokers with protection against claims brought by identifying areas in which the broker lacks expertise. So, for example, if a broker represents in a contract that he or she lacks expertise with regard to termites, it becomes difficult for a disgruntled buyer who has bought a house with termites to argue that the brokers involved in the transaction were negligent in not finding the termite infestation.

The disclaimer language in the GAR Contract provides that the buyer and seller waive their rights to assert any claims against the broker relative to any alleged advice, representations, or statements rendered by the broker. Such a waiver arguably constitutes a covenant not to sue, a form of a release wherein one party agrees not to sue the other in the future[635] and which, in the absence of fraud, is generally enforceable under Georgia law.[636]

With respect to disclaimers, Georgia courts have consistently held that parties are free to contract and may act to limit their rights and duties so long as public policy is not violated.[637] In a 1994 case, the Georgia Court of Appeals relied on the disclaimer language in a GAR Contract when it affirmed a trial court decision in favor of a listing broker against a buyer's claim for fraud and misrepresentation involving information provided to the buyer about a road widening project.[638]

---

634   GAR Form F20, paragraph 9.

635   Cash v. Street & Trail, 136 Ga. App. 462, 221 S.E.2d 640 (1975).

636   Brantley Co. v. Briscoe, 246 Ga. 310, 271 S.E.2d 356 (1980); Benford v. RDL, Inc., 223 Ga. App. 800, 479 S.E.2d 110 (1996); Bass v. Citizens & Southern Nat'l Bank, 168 Ga. App. 668, 309 S.E.2d 850 (1983); Cash v. Street & Trail, 136 Ga. App. 462, 221 S.E.2d 640 (1975).

637   West Side Loan Ofc. v. Electro-Protective Corp., 167 Ga. App. 520, 306 S.E.2d 686 (1983).

638   Allen, et al. v. ReMax North Atlanta, Inc., et al., 213 Ga. App. 644, 445 S.E.2d 774 (1994).

In this case, a selling agent was working with Florida residents in the purchase of a home in metro Atlanta. The buyers became interested in a house on a lot in a subdivision, which backed up to Medlock Bridge Road. The buyers asked the selling agent to inquire with the proper highway authority as to whether the road behind the house was going to be widened. The buyers, one of whom was a licensed real estate agent, specifically asked their selling agent not to rely on the subdivision agents for this information.

The selling agent informed the buyers that she made the appropriate inquiries and that the road behind the subdivision was not going to be widened. The selling agent did not tell the buyers that she obtained this information from the subdivision agents and not the Department of Transportation. The buyers bought the house, and the road behind the house was subsequently widened. The buyers discovered that this information was available prior to the time they contracted to buy the house. The buyers sued the selling broker for, among other things, fraud and misrepresentation.

The Georgia Court of Appeals found that the buyers' fraud claim must fail because there was not a fiduciary relationship between the buyers and the selling broker, which would have entitled the buyers to justifiably rely upon her statements. The Court also noted that the disclaimer language in the sales contract provided that the buyers had not relied upon the advice or representations by their broker or its salespersons relative to, among other things, the purchase and ownership of the property. Therefore, the buyers could not show that they justifiably relied upon their broker's statement either.

Under the 2000 revisions to BRRETA the broker is absolved from liability for providing false information if the broker does not know of its falsity and discloses the source of the information. [639]

A list of items about which the broker does not owe any special duty or have special expertise is also included. The list specifies: anything which could be learned through a survey, title search or inspection; the condition of the property; building products and construction techniques; the necessity or cost of any repairs; mold; hazardous or toxic materials or substances; termites and other wood destroying organisms; the tax or legal consequences of the transaction; the availability and cost of utilities or community amenities; the appraised or future value of the property; any off-site conditions; financing; and zoning. The disclaimer states that if buyers and sellers have questions about these areas, they should seek advice from experts in those areas.

This list of items about which brokers do not have special expertise was developed to comply with the real estate broker's obligations under the Brokerage Relationships in Real Estate Transactions Act ("BRRETA") to advise buyers and sellers "to obtain expert advice as to material matters which are beyond the expertise of

---

639   O.C.G.A. § 10-6A-5.

the broker."[640] Each of the items listed above are within the expertise of a professional other than the broker, be it a real estate attorney, surveyor, accountant, appraiser, engineer, or loan officer.

In addition, the disclaimer provides that since every neighborhood has conditions which are objectionable to some buyers, it shall be the responsibility of the buyer to familiarize himself or herself with neighborhood and other off-site conditions, which might be objectionable to the buyer.[641] This language was added to try to alert buyers to their responsibilities in this area.

§ 9.1.2   How disclaimer language in GAR Contract protects brokers

The disclaimer language helps protect brokers against claims for fraud and misrepresentation and claims under BRRETA. In order to sue a broker for fraud or misrepresentation, a party must show, among other things, that she relied upon some misrepresentation of the broker and was justified in so doing. Like the case discussed above, the disclaimer language makes it difficult to prove justifiable reliance, since the parties are acknowledging in the contract that they have not relied upon any representations of the broker. Brokers have successfully made this specific argument in Georgia courts to defend against claims of fraud and misrepresentation.[642] A full discussion of the law on this topic is set out in chapter 11 of this book.

In addition to claims for fraud and misrepresentation, buyers and sellers can also bring claims against real estate brokers based on BRRETA. Specifically, BRRETA provides that brokers timely disclose the following: (a) all adverse material facts pertaining to the physical condition of the property and improvements excluding facts which could have been discovered by the party upon a reasonably diligent inspection of the property and (b) and all material facts pertaining to existing adverse physical conditions in the immediate neighborhood within one mile from the property.[643] BRRETA also states that the law "may serve as a basis for private rights of action and defenses by sellers, buyers, landlords, tenants, and real estate brokers."[644]

The acknowledgment by buyers and sellers in the GAR Contract that they are not relying on any statements of the brokers provides the broker with additional protection against claims filed under the above sections of BRRETA. It would be difficult for parties to argue that they were damaged by false statements upon which they contractually acknowledged they have not relied.[645]

---

640   O.C.G.A. § 10-6A-7, 10-6A-5.
641   GAR Form, F4, paragraph 4e
642   Hanlon v. Thornton, 218 Ga. App. 500, 462 S.E.2d 154 (1995); Allen, et al. v. ReMax North Atlanta, Inc., et al., 213 Ga. App. 644, 445 S.E.2d 774 (1994).
643   O.C.G.A. § 10-6A-5; O.C.G.A. § 10-6A-7.
644   O.C.G.A. § 10-6A-2.
645   See, however, the section on rescission.

§ 9.1.3 Limitation on duties and liability

In addition to the disclaimer language, there is also language in the agency section of the GAR Contract, which provides that the brokers owe no duties other than what is contained in BRRETA and their brokerage engagements.

The GAR Exclusive Listing Agreement and the Exclusive Buyer Brokerage Agreement provide further protection.[646] These documents limit the broker's liability in the case of breach of contract or negligence to the amount of commission actually received by the broker less any amount retained or paid to any other broker. While this provision has not yet been tested in any appellate court it should withstand scrutiny absent fraud since similar provisions in property inspector's contracts have been upheld.[647]

§ 9.1.4 When disclaimer is deleted or modified

There is probably little that real estate brokers can do to prevent a buyer or seller from deleting all or a portion of the disclaimer language from the GAR Contract. The buyer and seller are free to include in their contract any provision they desire with respect to the purchase and sale of property. Real estate brokers are obligated to timely present all offers to buy and sell property even when they include provisions that are not to their liking.[648]

If all or part of the disclaimer language has been deleted from the contract, the broker should inquire why the particular language was struck. If there is a representation a party is relying upon, and the broker has in fact made such a representation, the party and the broker may agree to allow the specific representation to be included in the contract as a special stipulation and otherwise preserve the language of the disclaimer. If a party is insistent on striking the entire disclaimer section, the broker can protect herself somewhat by providing the party with a written statement disclaiming the areas in which she lacks special expertise and stating that she has not made any representations upon which she intended the party to rely. Alternatively, the broker can simply refuse to participate in the transaction or sign the contract.

---

646   GAR Form F1 and F4.
647   Brainard v. McKinney, 220 Ga.App. 329, 469 S.E.2d 441 (1996).
648   O.C.G.A. § 43-40-25(a)(19).

CHAPTER 10
CREATING A BINDING CONTRACT

OVERVIEW

This chapter on creating a binding contract addresses some of the thorniest issues that arise in real estate sales transactions. This includes how various time periods in the contract are calculated, when offers can be withdrawn, the effect of a party making a counteroffer in which the time limit of the offer has already expired, the effect of a party refusing to sign a "clean" copy of the contract and what constitutes proper notice. This chapter also includes a discussion on the basics of contract formation.

§ 10.1   What the GAR Contract provides

As a general rule in real estate, a binding contract is created only when one party presents a signed written offer to purchase or sell property to a second party and that party accepts the same offer in writing and delivers it back to offeror.[649] The GAR Contract refers to the date when the offer is accepted as "Acceptance Date" and the date when it is delivered back to the offeror as the "Binding Agreement Date." There is obviously a need for two separate dates since the date that the contract is accepted is often different from the date it is delivered.

The terms of the offer as proposed by the offeror and accepted by the offeree must be the same in order for the parties to have a binding contract.[650] Also, in making the offer and acceptance, the parties must strictly abide by the time limitations and notice requirements of the contract.[651] Disputes often arise in transactions with multiple offers and counteroffers when the parties either (a) forget to change the time limit of the offer in the contract causing the offer or counteroffer to expire prematurely, or (b) otherwise fail to meet the time and notice requirements in the contract. For these reasons, it is important for parties to understand what makes a binding contract, the principles of offer and acceptance and the time and notice requirements for reaching a binding agreement.

§ 10.2   Creating an enforceable real estate contract

§ 10.2.1   Real estate contract must be in writing

Georgia law requires that any contract for the sale of real estate, or any interest in real estate must be in writing and signed by the person against whom the contract is

---

649   Federal Farm Mortgage Corp. v. Dixon, 185 Ga. 466, 195 S.E. 414 (1938); Holland v. Riverside Park Estates, Inc., 214 Ga. 244, 104 S.E.2d 83 (1958); Smith v. Knight, 75 Ga. App. 178, 42 S.E.2d 570 (1947).

650   Lamb v. Decatur Fed. Sav. & Loan Ass'n, 201 Ga. App. 583, 411 S.E.2d 527 (1991); Harry Norman & Assoc., Inc. v. Bryan, 158 Ga. App. 751, 282 S.E.2d 208 (1981).

651   Holland v. Riverside Park Estates, 214 Ga. 244, 104 S.E.2d 83 (1958); Century 21 Pinetree Properties, Inc. v. Cason, 220 Ga. App. 355, 469 S.E.2d 458 (1996).

being enforced or someone authorized by him.[652] The written contract must also express all of the essential terms of the agreement.[653] These requirements invalidate most verbal land agreements and any written agreement that is incomplete or indefinite. At a minimum, the contract must identify the buyer and seller, describe the property, and state the price to be paid for the property and how it is to be paid.[654] The exceptions to the rule that real estate contracts must be in writing are when:

1.   a contract has been fully performed;
2.   a contract where one party performs his part of the contract which is accepted by the other party in accordance with the contract;
3.   a contract where there is partial performance by one party that would amount to fraud of the party refusing to comply if the court did not give effect to the contract.655

§ 10.2.2   Enforceability of verbal real estate contracts

While Georgia law invalidates most verbal real estate contracts, it will enforce such a contract under the following circumstances:[656]

1.   if both parties admit that there is a verbal agreement;
2.   if one party has performed the contract to such an extent that if the party could not be restored to his or her previous position if the contract is not enforced; or
3.   if the seller has accepted a) full payment, b) partial payment accompanied by the buyer taking possession, or c) the buyer has taken possession and made valuable improvements to the property657.

This is illustrated in the following case. The plaintiff and the defendant were co-owners of a certain property.[658] The co-owner moved out and allegedly entered into a verbal agreement with the other co-owner that he could have the property if he made all the payments for it. Although the co-owner who moved out disputed the existence of any verbal agreement, the co-owner who stayed was able to prove that he paid off the mortgage, made certain improvements to the property and remained in possession

---

652   O.C.G.A. § 13-5-30(4); Fraser v. Jarrett 153 Ga. 441, 112 S.E. 487 (1922)

653   Engram v. Engram, 265 Ga. 804, 463 S.E.2d 12 (1995); Smith v. Cox, 247 Ga. 563, 277 S.E.2d 512 (1981); Stonecypher v. Georgia Power Co., 183 Ga. 498, 189 S.E. 13 (1936).

654   Powell v. Adderholdt, 230 Ga. 211, 196 S.E.2d 420 (1973); Pierce v. Rush, 210 Ga. 718, 82 S.E.2d 649 (1954); A.S. Reeves & Co., Inc. v. McMickle, 270 Ga.App. 132, 605 S.E.2d 857 (2004)

655   O.C.G.A. § 13-5-31

656   O.C.G.A. § 23-2-131

657   Stephens v. Trotter, 213 Ga. App. 596, 445 S.E. 2d 359 (1994); Braddy v. Boynton, 271 Ga. 55, S.E. 2d 411 (1999)

658   Vaughn v. Stoenner 276 Ga. 660, 581 S.E.2d 543 (2003)

of the property after the alleged verbal agreement. The co-owner who moved out did not make any mortgage payments, which was consistent with the alleged verbal agreement. The Court held that based on these facts, there were grounds to support a claim for specific performance.

On the issue of proof, the party trying to enforce the verbal agreement must prove that their actions were done according to the verbal agreement. In addition, the party must show that there was an agreement on the essential terms of the contract.[659] For example, in one case, two partners entered into a verbal partnership agreement to purchase, renovate, and sell properties.[660] One partner's role was to purchase the properties, while the other partner was to supervise the renovation in return for 50 percent of the profits upon the sale of the properties. The court held that the partnership agreement was unenforceable because the parties did not agree on the duration of the agreement, the manner of selecting homes for renovation, the time during which renovations would be completed and compensation for renovations that were unprofitable.

§ 10.2.3   Initialing changes to contract

Any changes in the terms of the contract must also be in writing and agreed to by all of the parties.[661] For this reason, parties should be careful when making changes directly on a written contract. Parties frequently alter the terms of the contract by striking over terms, stating new terms, and initialing the changes on the contract. However, if the parties make such changes, all of the parties should initial and time-date any such alterations to reflect the parties' assent to the changes. If the contract does not clearly reflect that all of the parties agreed to the changes, the changes may not be binding against the parties who did not initial them.[662]

§ 10.2.3.1   Initialing every page of a contract

Many REALTORS® have inquired whether it is a good idea to have their clients and customers initial every page of a contract. There are both pluses and minuses to this approach.

On the plus side, when a party initials every page of a contract, it is an acknowledgement that the party has seen every page of the contract. It also makes it

---

659   O.C.G.A. § 13-5-30; Powell v. Adderholdt, 230 Ga. 211, 196 S.E.2d 420 (1973); East Piedmont 120 Assocs., L.P. v. Sheppard, 209 Ga. App. 664, 434 S.E.2d 101 (1993), cert. denied.

660   Razavi v. Shackelford 260 Ga.App. 603, 580 S.E.2d 253, (2003)

661   Sanders v. Vaughn, 223 Ga. 274, 154 S.E.2d 616 (1967); Re/Max Specialists, Inc. v. Kosakai, 202 Ga. App. 871, 415 S.E.2d 698 (1992).

662   Re/Max Specialists, Inc. v. Kosakai, 202 Ga. App. 871, 415 S.E.2d 698 (1992); Target Properties, Inc. v. Gilbert, 192 Ga. App. 161, 384 S.E.2d 188 (1989), cert. denied.

harder for such a party to be a victim of having new or altered pages to a contract with different terms and conditions substituted for the original by some unscrupulous individual.

Of course, the risk of this occurring is minimized when using a standard GAR Contract because written language of that contract cannot under the GAR licensing agreement be altered without noting all of the changes in the contract itself. On the minus side, the obvious problem with getting a party to initial every page of a contract is whether the validity of a contract can be challenged if a person inadvertently fails to initial every page.

§ 10.2.4   Effect of writing "clean" contract after agreement reached

During contract negotiations, parties frequently use one form contract to make their offer and counteroffers by striking over terms and stating new terms on the initial form. Once the parties reach their binding agreement, one of the brokers often transfers the information to a "clean" form reflecting the final terms of the contract. Creating such a "clean" contract has no effect on the original binding agreement.

The practice of crossing out, adding to, dating and initialing multiple changes to a contract can render the document practically illegible or incomprehensible. The better practice is to use a separate counteroffer addendum to make any changes or modifications. GAR Counteroffer Form F22 provides a convenient method for making and tracking counteroffers. Of course, the GAR Counteroffer Form itself specifically provides that after the parties enter into a binding agreement, all parties will sign a conformed or "clean" copy of the contract is so requested by either party.

The purpose of the conformed contract is to merely have it retyped in a legible form. Therefore, the conformed contract should not change any provision in or the substance of the original contract, even if the original language contains grammatical errors. Since a conformed contract is a "clean" version of the original contract, the date on the conformed contract should be the same as the original contract even though it is signed at a later date. If one party should later refuse to sign the conformed contract, the parties would still have a binding agreement if they had signed the original contract

What happens if the conformed contract is different from the original contract? While the last contract signed by all the parties normally takes precedence over an earlier contract, this may not always be the case. The Courts will review the circumstances of each case to ascertain the intention of the parties. The best way to prevent this problem is to state in the conformed contract that in the event of conflict between the conformed contract and original contract, the original contract will take precedence. An example of this type of special stipulation is set forth below.

Special Stipulation #10-1: Original agreement takes precedence over "clean" or conformed copy

This Agreement is intended to be a conformed copy of the existing contractual agreement of the parties. In the event of any discrepancy, conflict or difference between the original contract and this conformed copy, it is the express intent of the parties that the original contract shall control.

Of course, there are ties when changes and amendments are agreed upon by the parties and intended to be included in a conformed copy of the contract. In such an instance, the conformed copy should control over the original copy. An example of this type of provision is set forth below.

Special Stipulation #10-2: Conformed Agreement takes precedence over original contract

This conformed Agreement contains amended or modified provisions not included in the original Agreement. It is the express intention of the parties that this conformed Agreement shall amend, take precedence over and supercede the original Agreement.

§ 10.2.5   Counteroffers and the GAR Contract

The GAR Counteroffer form[663] provides a convenient method for either the buyer or seller to counter a proposal from the other. The GAR Counteroffer form starts out referencing the specific dated offer to purchase real property made by one of the parties which is the subject of the counteroffer. The Counteroffer form then states that all terms and conditions of the original offer are agreed to and accepted by the parties with the express exception of the following. The party making the counteroffer then spells out in the counteroffer the changes he or she is seeking to make to the original offer.

The Counteroffer form goes on to expressly provide that "the provisions set forth in this counteroffer shall control over any conflicting or inconsistent provisions set forth in the Agreement or any counteroffer. By signing below, all parties agree and acknowledge that they are accepting the Agreement subject to the terms and conditions set forth herein." The terms of the original Agreement are also incorporated into the counteroffer form by reference. Accordingly, the parties need only sign the Counteroffer form in order to create a binding contract.

So, for example, assume that the GAR Contract is signed only by the buyer and states a purchase price of $110,000.00. The seller signs and delivers a counteroffer, changing only the purchase price to $115,000.00. If the purchaser signs the counteroffer a binding contract will be created, irrespective of whether both parties

---

663   GAR Form F22.

have signed the original Purchase and Sale Agreement. The GAR Counteroffer form provides, however, that the parties agree, if requested, to sign a conformed copy of the Purchase and Sale Agreement incorporating therein the terms of the counteroffer.

Frequently a number of counteroffers are exchanged between the parties before a binding contract is created. It is important that the party making the latest counteroffer state therein all the terms she wishes to modify. This is because the GAR Counteroffer form does not incorporate the terms of any prior counteroffers. The following examples illustrate this point.

The buyer's initial offer states a purchase price of $150,000, with a closing date of June 1, and is contingent upon the buyer obtaining an 80% loan. The seller does not accept this offer, but rather, transmits a GAR Counteroffer form showing a purchase price of $160,000, a closing date of May 15, and no financing contingency (i.e., an "all cash" transaction). The buyer then submits her own GAR Counteroffer form, stating a purchase price of $155,000.00 and a closing date of May 15. This counteroffer is silent as to financing. If the seller accepts this counteroffer the terms of the contract will be a purchase price of $155,000.00, a May 15 closing date, and the contract will be contingent upon the buyer obtaining an 80% loan. This is because the financing contingency was a part of the original offer and no modification was made to this term in the final counteroffer.

It is, of course, possible to incorporate the terms of prior counteroffers into subsequent counteroffers by reference. This is not recommended as a general rule because the terms of the contract can become quite confusing, particularly in transactions involving more than two counteroffers. Once a term has been agreed by the parties, there is no need to incorporate previous counteroffers into later counteroffers. The Counteroffer form clearly states that all terms and conditions of the agreement are agreed to and accepted by the parties with the express exception of what is listed in the Counteroffer form.

§ 10.2.6   Making counteroffers to more than one prospective buyer

In a "hot" real estate market, a seller may receive multiple offers to buy the seller's property. Sometimes, the seller will want to counter more than one of these offers at the same time. Can the seller do this? While the answer to this question is "yes", this must be done very carefully to avoid selling the property to two different buyers. This is because if more than one prospective buyer accepts the seller's counteroffer, the seller could end up being contractually obligated to sell the property to more than one party. How can the seller protect himself in these situations? There are a variety of different options set forth below.

1.   Invitation to Bid

One approach for dealing with multiple buyers is for the seller to contact all of the buyers and give them all an opportunity to make their best and final offer by a particular date. Since the seller is requesting to receive offers rather than making an offer, there is no risk of creating an enforceable contract without some further action by the seller. The risk of inviting prospective buyers to make their best offer is that some buyers may have no interest in being placed in competition with other buyers and may withdraw from making any further offers.

2.   Making counteroffers to multiple buyers

The second approach is to make the same counteroffer to all of the buyers who made an offer but restrict the terms under which it can be accepted. The following is an example of such a special stipulation:

Special Stipulation #10-3: Counteroffer offer to multiple buyers

This Agreement constitutes a counteroffer. It is being made to more than one prospective buyer. Acceptance of this Agreement will not create an enforceable contract unless it is accepted and delivered back to the Seller prior to the following: 1) the expiration of the time limit of the offer, and 2) prior to the acceptance and delivery back of this Agreement by any of the other prospective buyers.

This Agreement may only be accepted in writing delivered to Seller's Listing Broker by facsimile at the following number: _____. Notice to Seller's Listing Broker shall be deemed to be notice to Seller. Listing Broker shall maintain a list of the prospective buyers and determine which prospective buyer, if any, is the first to accept and deliver back this Agreement. All parties agree that the determination of the Listing Broker in this regard shall be final and binding upon Seller and all prospective buyers. Upon the receipt by the Listing Broker of the first acceptance of this Agreement meeting the terms and conditions specified above, the Listing Broker shall promptly notify said buyer:

a)   that a binding agreement has been formed between said Buyer and Seller; and

b)   the binding agreement date. The Listing Broker shall also promptly notify the other prospective buyers that a binding agreement has been formed with another party.

3.   Making a counteroffer to one buyer and taking back-up contracts

The other approach with multiple buyers is for the seller to negotiate with the best prospect and to take a back-up offer on any other buyer interested in being in this position.

§ 10.2.7 Signing contract in counterparts

There may be some circumstances where a buyer and seller cannot sign the same original contract, for instance, where the buyer is in another state. It is possible to have two original contracts, which contain the same terms where the buyer signs one, and the seller signs the other. The GAR Contract provides that it may be signed in multiple counterparts.[664]

Georgia courts have also made it clear that the offer and acceptance of a contract do not have to be in the same document and that one document does not have to expressly incorporate the others. The Supreme Court of Georgia has expressly rejected the notion that the whole agreement must be contained in one writing signed by all of the parties.[665] Additionally, the Court specifically ruled, "as long as all the necessary terms are contained in signed contemporaneous writings, the statutory requirements and purpose of the Statute of Frauds have been met, whether or not the writings are cross referenced.

In another case, the Georgia Court of Appeals explained, "[w]hen an agreement consists of multiple documents that are executed at the same time and during the course of a single transaction, those documents should be read together."[666] In using the Counteroffer form, the parties are agreeing to all of the provisions in the original offer subject to what the parties have additionally agreed to in the Counteroffer form.

Georgia law allows multiple documents to be considered together as a single contract as long as all the necessary terms are contained in signed contemporaneous writings.[667] The law states that binding contracts may consist of several writings provided there is no conflict between the various parts.[668] Thus, if one party signs one form and the other party signs another form, but the terms contained in each form are the same, the parties have entered a binding and enforceable contract. To avoid any confusion the parties may wish to add a special stipulation where multiple counterparts are anticipated.

---

664   GAR Form F20, paragraph 11c

665   Baker v. Jellibeans, 252 GA 458, 314 S.E. 2d 874 (1984).

666   Sofran Peachtree City LLC v. Peachtree City Holdings L.L.C., 250 GA App 46, 550 S.E. 2d 249 (2001).

667   Board of Regents of the Univ. Sys. of Ga. v. Tyson, 261 Ga. 368, 404 S.E.2d 557 (1991); Baker v. Jellibeans, Inc., 252 Ga. 458, 314 S.E.2d 874 (1984). Georgia courts have interpreted one thing to be contemporaneous with a given transaction when it is so related in point of time as reasonably to be said to be a part of such transaction. Contemporaneous does not necessarily mean perfect or absolute coincidence in point of time. Manry v. Hendricks, 66 Ga. App. 442, 18 S.E.2d 97 (1941).

668   Cassville-White Assoc., Ltd. v. Bartow Assoc., Inc., 150 Ga. App. 561, 258 S.E.2d 175 (1979).

Special Stipulation #10-4: Signing contract in multiple counterparts

This Agreement may be executed in any number of counterparts, each of which shall be deemed an original and any of which shall be deemed to be complete in itself and be admissible into evidence or used for any purpose without the production of the other counterparts.

§ 10.2.8   Reconciling conflicts between the contract, special stipulations and exhibits

The GAR Contracts create a hierarchy for resolving disputes between the contract, special stipulations and exhibits. Specifically, exhibits control over the contract in the event of a conflict between the contract and an exhibit. Special stipulations control over exhibits and any other portion of the contract in the event of a conflict between the special stipulation and either the contract or an exhibit. Since special stipulations are at the top of the hierarchy, persons using the GAR forms should always include provisions as special stipulations if they are at all concerned about whether they will take precedence over inconsistent provisions contained anywhere else in the contract.

In addition to the rules for resolving conflicts within the GAR Contracts, our courts also apply their own rules for the resolution of conflicts. First, the court has to decide if the contract is ambiguous. If the contract is clear, the court will enforce the contract as stated. If the contract is ambiguous, the court will try to ascertain the intention of the parties.[669] The court will look at the whole contract when deciding on the meaning of any part of the contract. Further, the courts will also favor an interpretation of the contract that will uphold the entire contract as a whole. If the contract is still ambiguous, then it must be resolved by jury. Typewritten provisions in a contract prevail over printed provisions.[670]

§ 10.2.9   Effect of mistakes in the contract

The types of mistakes made in real estate contracts can be grouped into two categories: unilateral mistakes and mutual mistakes. The legal consequences of a mistake will depend on its type. A unilateral mistake is a mistake made by only one party to a contract. An example of such a mistake is where a buyer contracts to purchase a property on the mistaken belief that he will be able to build a single-family home on the property when it is not possible due to its lot size. Generally, a party is not able to cancel a contract based on a unilateral mistake.

A mutual mistake is a mistake that is shared and relied on by both parties to a contract. A court will often revise or nullify a contract based on a mutual mistake

---

669   Grier v. Brogdon, 234 Ga. App. 79, 505 S.E. 2d 512 (1999); Ali v. Aarabi, 2003 W. 22403390 (2003)

670   Hibbard v. P.G.A., Inc., 251 Ga.App. 68, 553 S.E.2d 371 (2001)

involving a material term in the contract. The legal effect of each type of mistake is discussed below.

§ 10.2.9.1 Effect of a mutual mistake

If both the buyer and the seller entered into a sale contract under a mistake as to the subject matter of the contract so that the contract does not express the true intention of the parties, the court may reform the contract to correct the parties' mutual mistake.[671]

The parties can also rescind the contract based upon a mutual mistake. In one case, both the seller and the buyer were unaware at the time the contract was signed that the wall and patio attached to the house were situated on an adjoining property instead of the property that was being sold.[672] When the buyer's lawyer informed the seller's lawyer of the encroachment, the seller offered either to move the wall and patio over to the land being conveyed, or to place a certain sum of money in escrow to pay any damages that might result from the defect in title. The buyer refused both proposals. The seller then entered into negotiations with the adjoining landowner to acquire the land on which the encroachment existed in exchange for footage at the rear of the property to be conveyed, but at no time did the seller offer to consummate the contract as executed. Eventually, the seller sold the property to a third party and the buyer sued the seller for the return of the buyer's earnest money. The Court held that since there was a mutual mistake, the buyer was entitled to sue for rescission of the sale contract and obtain a refund of the earnest money. Georgia law provides that if the consideration upon which a contract is based was given as a result of a mutual mistake of fact or of law, the contract cannot be enforced.[673]

In another case, a grandmother instructed her attorney to prepare a deed conveying the home place lot to her grandson.[674] When she signed the deed, the space for the property description was blank. The attorney made a mistake in describing an adjoining lot instead and delivered the deed to her grandson. Neither the grandmother nor the grandson read the deed at any time. The grandson recorded the deed and built a mechanic shop on the property. After the grandmother was declared incompetent, her son was appointed as her guardian and sought to eject the grandson. The Georgia Court of Appeals held that the grandson was entitled to reformation of the deed because any error in the deed was a mutual mistake of both parties.

---

671   W. P. Brown & Sons Lumber Co. v. Echols, 200 Ga. 284, 36 S.E.2d 762, (1946); Timeless Architectural Homes, Inc. v. Jones, 606 S.E.2d 635 (2004)

672   Lundin v. Hill, 105 Ga.App. 449, 125 S.E.2d 105, (1962)

673   O.C.G.A. § 13-5-4

674   Curry v. Curry, 267 Ga. 66, 473 S.E.2d 760 (1996)

A buyer who has entered into a contract based on a genuine, mutual mistake has basically two choices. The buyer can keep the property and recover damages by reason of the defects, in addition to suing for reformation of the contract if necessary. Alternatively, the buyer can sue for rescission or cancellation, which means that the buyer wishes to return the property to the seller and recover the amount paid. The factors that the buyer should consider when making the choice is the value of the property in its present state compared to the purchase price, the cost of correcting any defect, the possible use of the property and the likelihood of recovering any money from the seller.

However, not all contracts made under a mutual mistake can be rescinded. In a purchase and sale transaction, the buyer is still required to exercise due diligence to try to prevent a mistake from occurring. So, for example, in one case, the Georgia Court of Appeals refused to allow the contract to be rescinded even though there was mutual mistake as to the size of the property because the mistake could have been easily discovered had the buyer exercised due diligence.[675] The seller's sign had mistakenly listed the size of the property as 1.5 acres. However, a plat listed property as 0.8 acres, the description of property in contract made specific reference to plat, and the contract was given to the buyer to read before its execution. The Court stated that if the buyer had given the contract more than a cursory review, he could have discovered the discrepancy. The Court stated the buyer could not seek rescission of the contract based on mutual mistake of fact if he failed to exercise due diligence to protect himself against the mistake.

§ 10.2.9.2   Effect of a unilateral mistake

A party will not normally be granted a reformation or rescission of the contract based on a unilateral mistake unless there has been some fraud, misrepresentation or other wrongful act by the seller. For example, in one case, the buyers claimed that when they and the seller entered into the contract, they all thought that the property was free from termite damage.[676] In other words, the buyers claimed that the sales contract was the product of mutual mistake of fact. The Court found that the seller knew about the termite damage and if there was any mistake, it was only a unilateral mistake by buyers in that the buyers did not know there was any damage to the property from wood destroying insects at the time they signed the contract for sale. The Court stated that relief is not available to a buyer on the basis of a unilateral mistake in the absence of fraud, inequitable conduct or other special circumstances.

A unilateral mistake, even if it pertains to a material term, will generally not support the reformation or rescission of the contract. There are exceptions, such as when one party knows that the other acted under a mistaken belief or was the cause of the mistake. Another ground for reformation or rescission is when the

---

675   Simmons v. Pilkenton, 230 Ga.App. 900, 497 S.E.2d 613 (1998)
676   Lester v. Bird, 200 Ga.App. 335, 408 S.E.2d 147 (1991)

300

mistake goes to the substance of the transaction and both parties must either know, or should know that the mistake was the principal reason for making the contract.

§ 10.2.10 Enforceability of an "agreement to agree"

If a contract fails to establish an essential term and allows the parties to agree on that term at a later date, the contract is an "agreement to agree" and is not a valid contract. For example, an agreement to transfer assets where "[d]ivision to be by mutual agreement" was held to be unenforceable.[677] Likewise, an agreement where a loan officer assured a borrower that "something will be worked out" in respect of additional loans was held be a mere agreement to agree in the future. The Court held that unless an agreement is reached as to all terms and conditions and nothing is left to future negotiations, a contract to enter into a contract in the future is of no effect.[678]

The same principle applies to option contracts. In one case, the landlord granted an option to a tenant to renew the lease where "[t]he rental rate for the renewal term shall be the fair market rental with fair market escalations. Fair market rental rate and fair market escalations being that rate and escalation found within comparable premises in comparable properties within the Northwest office submarket, taking into account any concessions being offered at that time."[679] The Court held that the above provision did not contain a specific rental rate because the fair market value would have to be determined by an undesignated party. The provision did not define an objective method of ascertaining the fair market rental rate, comparable premises, comparable properties, nor the Northwest office submarket. The rent was an essential part of the contract upon which there must be a meeting of the minds and even though the negotiations showed a complete willingness or determination to agree in the future upon such term, there was no binding contract. The Court stated that unless all the terms and conditions are agreed on, and nothing is left to further negotiations, an agreement to reach an agreement in the future is of no effect.

In another case, an option contract to purchase improved real property in five years for "the appraised value of the property at time of purchase based on an MAI Appraisal," was held to be valid because the contract defined an objective method by which the value could be ascertained.[680]

In addition to the price of the contract, the obligations of the parties must be clearly set out for a contract to be enforceable. If any essential term is left open for future consideration, there is no binding contract. For example, in one case, a buyer

---

677   Kreimer v. Kreimer, 274 Ga. 359, 552 S.E.2d 826 (2001)
678   Bridges v. Reliance Trust Co., 205 Ga.App. 400, 422 S.E.2d 277 (1992)
679   Insurance Industry Consultants, Inc. v. Essex Inv., Inc., 249 Ga.App. 837, 549 S.E.2d 788 (2001)
680   Miller v. McCullough, 236 Ga. 666, 224 S.E.2d 916 (1976)

sued the seller to obtain specific performance of a provision in a real estate purchase contract requiring the seller to execute a restrictive covenant.[681] The provision clearly stated that the restrictive covenant would survive the closing and would not be subject to merger. The Court of Appeals held that such an obligation was not a mere "agreement to agree" but an enforceable contract.

§ 10.3 Offer and Acceptance

To form a binding contract, there must be mutual agreement by all of the parties to all of the terms.[682] Such mutual agreement is established when one party makes an offer which the other party accepts unconditionally without any changes.[683] A qualified or conditional acceptance, or one that adds a new material term, is a counteroffer. Therefore, if a party accepts all of the terms of the offer, but places a condition or adds a new term in the acceptance, mutual agreement is not established and there is no binding contract.[684] The response of a party to a proposed contract that varies even one term from the original offer is a counteroffer.[685] Thus, where a party returns a proposed contract to the offeror with everything originally offered the same except for one term, the offeree has made a counteroffer, not an acceptance.[686]

For example, in one Georgia case, the seller made an offer to sell certain property in which the closing would take place no later than July 30, 1981.[687] The buyer attempted to accept the seller's offer but stipulated that the closing would take place by August 25, 1981. The seller treated the buyer's offer as a counteroffer and refused to accept it. The court held that no contract existed between the parties because the buyer made a counteroffer, not an acceptance, when he changed the closing date of the original offer.

---

681 Neely Development Corp. v. Service First Investments, Inc., 261 Ga.App. 253, 582 S.E.2d 200 (2003)

682 O.C.G.A. § 13-3-1.

683 Lamb v. Decatur Fed. Sav. & Loan Ass'n, 201 Ga. App. 583, 411 S.E.2d 527 (1991); Harry Norman & Assoc., Inc. v. Bryan, 158 Ga. App. 751, 282 S.E.2d 208 (1981); Butler v. Household Mortg. Services, Inc., 266 Ga.App. 104, 596 S.E.2d 664 (2004).

684 Harry Norman & Assoc., Inc. v. Bryan, 158 Ga. App. 751, 282 S.E.2d 208 (1981).

685 Benton v. Shiver, 254 Ga. 107, 326 S.E.2d 756 (1985) (varying closing date); Stubbs v. Tattnall Bank, 244 Ga. 212, 259 S.E.2d 466 (1979) (varying original price offered); Panfel v. Boyd, 187 Ga. App. 639, 371 S.E.2d 222 (1988); Harry Norman & Assoc., Inc., 158 Ga. App. 751, 282 S.E.2d 208 (1981); Clover Realty Co. v. Gouyd, 153 Ga. App. 64, 264 S.E.2d 547 (1980); Frey v. Friendly Motors, Inc., 129 Ga. App. 636, 200 S.E.2d 467 (1973) (varying means of acceptance).

686 Panfel v. Boyd, 187 Ga. App. 639; 371 S.E.2d 222 (1988) (holding that original contract had expired where closing date was past and changed to new date from original contract).

687 Benton v. Shiver, 254 Ga. 107, 326 S.E.2d 756 (1985).

When a party makes a counteroffer, intentionally or not, the counteroffer operates to reject the offer and terminates the party's power of acceptance of the original offer.[688] In order to reach a binding agreement between the parties, the party making the original offer must formally accept the counteroffer.[689] Alternatively, the party who originally made the offer may renew it.[690] Thus, once an initial offer is rejected, the negotiations end, unless the party who made the original offer renews it or agrees to any counteroffer suggested.[691]

§ 10.3.1   Time limit of offer

Most form contracts include a provision by which the offeror can limit the time during which the offeree may accept the offer or the offer will expire. The time limit of offer section of the GAR Contract provides that the offer will remain open for acceptance until a stipulated time and date. If the offer is silent as to time given for acceptance, the offer will be considered open for a "reasonable time."[692] The law does not define what constitutes a reasonable time, and it will likely vary with the facts and circumstances of different transactions.

One scenario, which occurs frequently in real estate sales transactions, is for the party making a counteroffer to forget to change the time limit of the offer. Sometimes, this means that the counteroffer is made after the time for it to be accepted has already expired. While there is no case law on this point, courts will allow such counteroffers to be accepted for a reasonable time thereafter on the theory that the party would not have made a counteroffer which was incapable of being accepted.

Where the contract contains an express time limit for acceptance of the offer, if the offer is not accepted within the stated time, no contract is formed. However, if the offer is accepted after the stated time,[693] the late acceptance is considered a counteroffer which the original offeror may accept or not.[694] If the original offeror timely accepts this counteroffer and delivers it back to the original offeree, a contract is formed. For example, in one Georgia case, the time limit of the offer expired on March 10, 1956, but the offeree did not accept the offer until March 27, 1956.[695]

---

688   Duval & Co. v. Malcom, 233 Ga. 784, 214 S.E.2d 356 (1975); Lamb v. Decatur Fed. Sav. & Loan Ass'n, 201 Ga. App. 583, 411 S.E.2d 527 (1991).

689   Lamb v. Decatur Fed. Sav. & Loan Ass'n, 201 Ga. App. 583, 411 S.E.2d 527 (1991).

690   Duval & Co. v. Malcom, 233 Ga. 784, 214 S.E.2d 356 (1975); Lamb v. Decatur Fed. Sav. & Loan Ass'n, 201 Ga. App. 583, 411 S.E.2d 527 (1991).

691   Lamb v. Decatur Fed. Sav. & Loan Ass'n, 201 Ga. App. 583, 411 S.E.2d 527 (1991).

692   Simpson & Harper v. Sanders & Jenkins, 130 Ga. 265, 60 S.E. 541 (1908).

693   Century 21 Pinetree Properties, Inc. v. Cason, 220 Ga. App. 355, 469 S.E.2d 458 (1996); Crawley v. Sexton, 207 Ga. App. 360, 427 S.E.2d 804 (1993), cert. denied.

694   Century 21 Pinetree Properties, Inc. v Cason et al., 220 Ga. App. 355, 469S.E.2d 458 (1996);
Achour v. Belk & Co., 148 Ga. App. 306, 251 S.E.2d 157 (1978); B. L. Montague Co., Inc. v. Somers, 94 Ga. App. 860, 96 S.E.2d 629 (1957).

695   W.B. Leedy & Co. v. Shirley, 97 Ga. App. 801, 104 S.E.2d 580 (1958).

However, even though the offeree did not timely accept the offer, the parties operated under the contract for several months. For this reason, the court found that the offeror had waived the deadline for acceptance of the offer by his actions and the parties had formed a valid and binding contract.

Likewise, in another Georgia case, the time for acceptance of the buyer's offer expired on February 23, 1976.[696] The seller rejected the buyer's offer on February 23, but submitted a counteroffer which the buyer accepted on March 9, 1976. The buyer later tried to back out of the contract and argued that the contract was not binding because it was entered after the time limit of the offer expired. However, the court held that the buyer waived the February 23 limitation when the buyer accepted the seller's counteroffer on March 9 and, thus, the contract on the accepted counteroffer was binding and enforceable.

§ 10.3.2   Acceptance Date

The Binding Agreement Date is the date the accepted offer is delivered back to the offeror. For example, if a buyer makes an offer to a seller which is accepted by the seller on a Sunday but not delivered back to the buyer until Wednesday, the Binding Agreement Date would be Wednesday. The obligations of the buyer to apply for financing or inspect the property are all measured from the Binding Agreement Date. The GAR Contract requires the offeror to notify the offeree when notice of acceptance has been received. In other words, if the buyer receives the signed contract back on Wednesday, the buyer is then obligated under the contract to notify the seller that Wednesday is the Binding Agreement Date.[697] This was included to avoid disputes between the parties regarding the Binding Agreement Date.

As discussed above, to be binding, the notice of acceptance must be pursuant to the specific terms of the contract. For the GAR Contract, this means that notice must be actually received by either the party to the contract, the party's broker if the broker represents the party as a client, or the party's designated agent in the case of designated agency. Therefore, if the seller accepts the buyer's offer and delivers the signed contract to the buyer, the notice of acceptance is valid.

Likewise, if the buyer is represented by a broker as a client, the seller may deliver the signed contract to the buyer's broker. However, if the broker working with the buyer is only a transaction broker and is representing the buyer as a customer and not as a client, the seller may not effectively deliver notice to the buyer via notice to the transaction broker. Only when notice of acceptance is delivered properly pursuant to the terms of the contract will the Binding Agreement Date be established. This can, however, be modified with the following special stipulation.

---

696   Achour v. Belk & Co., 148 Ga. App. 306, 251 S.E.2d 157, 158 (1978).
697   It is a violation of Georgia law for a real estate broker to fail to deliver within a reasonable time, a completed copy of the purchase agreement. O.C.G.A. § 43-40-25(a).

Special Stipulation #10-5: Notice to broker working with customer is notice to party

Notwithstanding anything contained in this Agreement to the contrary, notice to _____ (insert name of broker or agent) shall be deemed to be good notice to (seller/buyer) for all purposes herein provided it is delivered in accordance with the requirements set this Agreement.

Until delivery is complete, the buyer's time-restricted obligations under the contract do not commence. One question which occasionally arises is whether a binding contract is created if the offeror does not fill in the Acceptance Date in the GAR Contract upon the receipt of a signed acceptance. There is no case law in Georgia on this point. The likelihood is, however, that a binding contract will be found to exist even without filling in the Acceptance Date. This is because under general principles of contract law, the requirements to create a binding agreement are fulfilled as soon as the accepted contract is delivered back to the offeror. Since this is an open question of law, however, it is always good practice to fill in the Acceptance Date on the contract and notify the offeree of the same as required under the GAR Contract.

§ 10.3.3   Delivery of acceptance required

Under the GAR Contract, the party accepting an offer must deliver written notice of the acceptance to the offeror <u>before</u> expiration of the time limit of the offer. This means that the notice must be received by the offeror before the time limit of the offer expires.[698]   A party cannot privately accept an offer and form a binding agreement until the acceptance has been delivered to the offeror.[699]

For example, if a buyer makes an offer and states that the time limit of the offer expires at 11:00 a.m. on May 1, the seller must deliver the acceptance to the buyer by 11:00 a.m. on May 1. If the seller decides to accept the contract before 11:00 a.m. on May 1 and signs the contract, but does not deliver the acceptance to the buyer (or the buyer's authorized agent) by 11:00 a.m. on May 1, there is no binding agreement.

A phone call to the other party or a note saying that the contract will be forwarded shortly is generally not sufficient. For example, in one Georgia case, the buyer submitted an offer to the seller which provided that the offer would be open for acceptance by the seller until 3:00 p.m. on July 5, 1957 "by which time written acceptance of such offer must have actually been received by the purchaser."[700] The seller orally agreed by telephone with his broker that he should accept the offer and he

698   Holland v. Riverside Park Estates, Inc., 214 Ga. 244, 104 S.E.2d 83 (1958).
699   Federal Farm Mortgage Corp. v. Dixon, 185 Ga. 466, 195 S.E. 414 (1938); Hartford Fire Ins. Co. v. Steenhuis, 115 Ga. App. 625, 155 S.E.2d 690 (1967).
700   Holland v. Riverside Park Estates, 214 Ga. 244, 104 S.E.2d 83 (1958).

authorized the broker to accept the offer on his behalf. However, the seller never gave his broker or the buyer <u>written</u> acceptance of the offer. The broker wrote the buyer a letter on July 2, 1957 stating, "Your offer to purchase the [seller's] property has been accepted," and further stated that the "signed contract will be forwarded to you shortly." However, the court found that these communications did not constitute written acceptance pursuant to the terms of the contract, and because the seller did not deliver to the buyer the signed contract by July 5, there was no mutually binding contract.

Many parties may rely on their real estate brokers to complete delivery of the contract for them. Brokers are required to deliver all offers or counteroffers entrusted to them within a reasonable time to the purchaser or seller.[701] A broker's license may be revoked or suspended for failing to do so and the broker may also be subject to a fine or other sanctions.[702]

§ 10.3.4 Sample problems regarding time limit of offer

Brokers can help prevent disputes over whether there has been compliance with the time limit of the offer section by reviewing this section each time an offer or counteroffer is made to confirm that a reasonable time period has been included and then reminding the client of the relevant time requirements. However, disputes are bound to arise. The following hypothetical situations illustrate some of the common problems related to the time limit of the offer.

<u>Problem #1</u>: The buyer makes an offer to the seller, which provides that the time limit of the offer expires at 10:00 a.m. on May 1. At 8:30 a.m. on May 1, the seller delivers the buyer the offer, with several terms changed, but fails to change the time limit of the offer from 10:00 a.m. Does the buyer have to accept the counteroffer by 10:00 a.m. in order to reach a binding agreement?

<u>Answer</u>: Yes. While the time period to accept the contract is short, the buyer will have to accept it and deliver the acceptance back to the seller before 10:00 a.m. pursuant to the express terms of the counteroffer submitted by the seller which has incorporated the time limit of the original offer. However, in all likelihood, the seller's failure to change the time limit of the offer is due to an oversight (since in most cases but not all, the seller would give the buyer more than one and one-half hours to accept the counteroffer). The buyer may want to contact the seller to discuss increasing the time period in which the counteroffer may be accepted. If the buyer accepts the counteroffer after the time limit expires, however, the acceptance becomes a counteroffer by the buyer, and the seller would be entitled to reject it or would have to formally accept it in order for a binding contract to be created. If the parties, however, operate under the contract as if it were binding, they would likely be deemed to have waived any objections to the validity of the contract.

---

701   O.C.G.A. § 43-40-25(a)(19); O.C.G.A. § 10-6A-5; O.C.G.A. § 10-6A-7.
702   O.C.G.A. § 43-40-25(a).

Problem #2: The buyer makes an offer to the seller which provides that the time limit of the offer expires at 10:00 a.m. on May 1. At 3:00 p.m. on May 1, the seller delivers a signed acceptance back to the buyer. Does the seller's acceptance after the expired time limit of the offer create a binding agreement?

Answer: No. The seller's acceptance after the time limit of the offer had expired operates as a counteroffer which the buyer may accept or reject.

Problem #3: The buyer makes an offer to the seller which provides that the time limit of the offer expires at 10:00 a.m. on May 1. At 3:00 p.m. on May 1, the seller makes a counteroffer, but fails to change the original time limit of the offer from 10:00 a.m. In other words, the seller makes a counteroffer which is incapable of being accepted within the time limit of the offer provided. If the buyer accepts the seller's counteroffer and delivers it back to the seller, has a valid contract been formed?

Answer: While arguments can be made on both sides of this question, the answer is probably yes. Presumably, the seller would not have made a counteroffer which the buyer was incapable of accepting. A court in this case would likely look to what the intent of the seller was in making the counteroffer with an expired time limit on the offer. If the court concluded that the intent of the seller was to make a counteroffer, the court would likely effectuate the intent of the seller and reform the contract to give the buyer a reasonable time period to accept the seller's counteroffer.

Problem #4: The buyer makes an offer to the seller which provides that the time limit of the offer expires at 10:00 a.m. on May 1. At 3:00 p.m. on May 1, the seller delivers a signed acceptance back to the buyer. The seller does not object to the buyer having delivered the acceptance after the time limit expired; the parties begin operating under the contract; and, the buyer has an inspection done and applies for financing. The parties also begin negotiating over what repairs are to be made to the property through a series of offers and counteroffers during the Defect Resolution Period. Several days later, the seller receives a better offer. The seller looks for a way out of the contract and argues that she and the buyer never reached an enforceable contract because the seller accepted it after the time limit of the offer expired. Can the seller escape the contract with the buyer?

Answer: While arguments can be made on both sides of this question, the best answer is probably no. Once the seller delivered the executed contract back to the buyer and the parties began acting upon it as a binding agreement, the seller likely waived her right to object to the acceptance having been made after the time limit of the offer had expired.

§ 10.3.5   When offer can be withdrawn

A binding contract is formed only when the parties mutually agree to all the terms of the contract. Until then, each party may withdraw her offer or counteroffer.[703] This means that there is no binding contract between the parties until the contract is accepted, and the offeror may withdraw her offer at any time before that even if the time limit of the offer has not expired.[704] For example, if a seller makes a counteroffer to a buyer which expires at 5:00 p.m. on May 1, but on April 29 the seller gets a better offer for her property, the seller may withdraw the counteroffer if the first buyer has not yet accepted it.

Also, a party may withdraw an offer before actual delivery is made to the offeree or the offeree's broker who is representing that party as a client. For instance, if a seller accepts a buyer's offer and the seller gives the executed agreement to her broker, the seller can withdraw her acceptance anytime before her broker delivers the acceptance to the buyer or the buyer's broker.

Likewise, pursuant to the delivery requirements, even if a party attempts to accept an offer by telephone or by sending a note saying that acceptance will be delivered soon, the offeror may still withdraw the offer until actual delivery of acceptance is complete.[705]

§ 10.3.6   Option contracts to prohibit withdrawal of offer

In order to avoid having an offer withdrawn before the time limit of the offer expires, the parties may enter into what is called an option contract where the seller absolutely commits to sell the property to the buyer during a certain time period and the buyer may buy or not.[706] By agreeing to the option, the seller may not withdraw the offer during the stated time period. The buyer must pay a sum of money for such a privilege, called an option. The following special stipulation may be added to the GAR Contract in order to provide for such an option:

Special Stipulation #10-6: Seller not to withdraw offer for a stipulated period

Notwithstanding any other provision in this Agreement to the contrary, in consideration of the payment by Buyer to Seller of $_____ which shall be nonrefundable and immediately paid to Seller, this Agreement shall operate as an irrevocable option to purchase the Property on terms and conditions set forth in the Agreement for a period of _____ days until _____, 20___ ("Option Period"). During the Option Period, Buyer may convert this option to purchase into a purchase and sale agreement upon

---

703   Harry Norman & Assoc., Inc. v. Bryan, 158 Ga. App. 751, 282 S.E.2d 208 (1981); Vlass v. Walker, 86 Ga. App. 742, 72 S.E.2d 464 (1952).

704   Camp Realty Co., Inc. v. Jennings, 77 Ga. App. 149, 47 S.E.2d 917 (1948); Blanchard v. Sachs, 74 Ga. App. 727, 41 S.E.2d 326 (1947).

705   Holland v. Riverside Park Estates, 214 Ga. 244, 104 S.E.2d 83 (1958).

706   Mattox v. West, 194 Ga. 310, 21 S.E.2d 428 (1942).

written notice to Seller, in which case the consideration for the granting of the option or the $_____ specified herein shall be applied to the purchase price at closing. If not accepted in writing during the Option Period, all rights hereunder shall lapse.

§ 10.4   Explanation of terms related to time

Many real estate contracts contain time periods within which something has to be done. The most significant time period is the period within which the offer must be accepted. In most real estate transactions, time is of the essence. When the transaction requires something to be done within a specific period, it is critical to state in no uncertain terms exactly when that period ends. This section explains the definitions of words commonly used in reference to time.

§ 10.4.1   Definitions of dates and times

A **day** means an entire 24 hour day beginning immediately after midnight and ending 24 hours later. For example, if the buyer signs the contract at 3 p.m. on January 1 and delivers it back to the seller at 4 p.m. on January 1, the binding agreement date would be January 1. If the seller has 7 days from the binding agreement date to terminate the contract, the time does not end at 4 p.m. on January 8. Instead, it would run through the end of the day on January 8.[707]

A **week** means 7 days. Therefore, a week from Monday is 7 days from Monday, therefore ending on Monday, not Sunday. However, "calendar week" means the specific period of time starting on Sunday and ending on Saturday.

A **month** means calendar month, regardless of whether the month consist of 28, 29, 30 or 31 days. Therefore, if a tenant wishes to renew the lease by giving 1 month's notice, that means 1 calendar month, even though there are only 28 days in that month.

A **year** usually means January 1 to December 31, inclusive.[708] However, if a contract states that offer to open for acceptance for a year commencing, say January 1, 2004, the term ends on January 1, 2005.

---

707   O.C.G.A. §1-3-1(d)(3) provides that when any time (except hours) is prescribed for the exercise of any privilege or the discharge of any duty, the first day shall not be counted but the last day shall be counted.

708   O.C.G.A. § 1-3-3

§ 10.4.2   Definitions of other words commonly used for time

There are words, such as "from", "within", "until", "continue through" that are sued when referring to time. For example, the GAR Contract provides that the offer is open for acceptance "until" a specified time and date. Georgia statutes state that "until" a certain date includes that day when used in a statute.[709] The Supreme Court of Georgia held that the same meaning should be used in contracts unless the parties to the contract clearly intended otherwise.[710] Therefore, the word "until" as used in the GAR Contract includes the stated date.

If there is any ambiguity, the courts will look to the intention of the parties to decide when the time expires. An example is in the case where the tenants had a lease commencing December 1990 and continued "until December 1993", and were given an option to purchase the property for the same period.[711] The court held that since the lease terminated in November, the option would be ineffective beyond the term of the lease. Therefore, the time period of "until December 1993" for the tenants to exercise the option terminated at midnight on the last day of November. To avoid any ambiguity, it is best to specify an exact time and date in which something has to be done.

If a contract states that the seller has 30 days "from" the offer date to accept the offer, it most probably means 30 days exclusive of the offer date.[712] If the contract states that the seller has to accept the contract "by" July 1st, the time period includes July 1st. The meaning of "within" is "no later than". Therefore, if the seller has to accept the offer within 15 days from January 1st, the seller 15 complete days from midnight of January 1st. This expires on midnight January 16. When the contract states the tenant has 15 days' prior to the expiration of the lease to exercise the option to purchase, the notice to exercise the option has to be given 15 whole days before sale of the property, excluding the date of lease expiration.

§ 10.4.3   Meaning of banking day

What is meant by a banking day? A banking day is defined under Georgia law as "a part of a day on which a bank is open to the public for carrying on substantially all of its banking functions. "Therefore, what constitutes a banking day will vary from one financial institution to another. For most banks, Saturdays, Sundays, and holidays are not banking days because even if certain branches are open, the bank is not open to the public for carrying on substantially all of its banking functions. There are some banks, however, where Saturdays are banking days because they carry on substantially all of their banking functions. An officer of the bank should be able to answer questions regarding which days the bank treats as official banking days.

---

709   O.C.G.A. § 1-3-3
710   D. Brooks v. Hicks et al., 230 Ga. 500, S.E.2d 711 (1973)
711   Burns et al. v. Reves, 217 Ga.App. 316, 457 S.E.2d 178 (1995)
712   Dobbs v. Conyers et al., 36 Ga.App. 511, 137 S.E.298 (1927)

§ 10.4.4   Time expiring on a Sunday or public holiday

What happens if the last day falls on a Sunday or a public holiday? The general rule is that if the last day falls on a Sunday or public holiday, then the last day will be extended to the next business day. For example, if a lease requires the tenant to give notice of extension by certified mail by a certain date, which happens to be a Sunday, it would be impossible to send a certified letter on Sunday. Therefore, the tenant can send the notice on Monday.[713] However, this is only the case if the performance cannot take place on a Sunday.[714] Accepting an offer only requires notice to be delivered pursuant to the contract, which is possible on a Sunday or public holiday. On the other hand, if the closing date falls on a Sunday or public holiday, it will be postponed to the next business day when lenders can disburse funds and attorney firms are open.

§ 10.5   Notice

§ 10.5.1   Notice must be in writing

An offer must be accepted according to the notice requirements of the contract. The GAR Contract provides that all offers, counteroffers and acceptances must be in writing, signed by the party giving the notice and delivered either:

(a)   in person;
(b)   by an overnight delivery service, prepaid;
(c)   by facsimile transmission (FAX); or
(d)   by the United States Postal Service, postage prepaid, registered or certified return receipt requested.[715]

This requirement that notices be in writing was included in the GAR Contract to minimize disputes between the parties as to the substance of the notice and whether it was actually delivered. Giving verbal notice when the GAR Contract requires notice to be in writing creates a significant risk that the notice will be deemed to be ineffective.

If acceptance is made in a manner inconsistent with the terms of the contract, it may also be considered a counteroffer. For instance, in one Georgia case, the court held that an attempted oral acceptance of an offer constituted a counteroffer because

---

713   Target Properties, Inc. v. Gilbert, 192 Ga. App. 161, 384 S.E.2d 188 (1989) cert. denied, 192 Ga. App. 903 (1989). The contract in Target Properties also provided that notice could be hand-delivered; however, the address for notice was post office box, making hand-delivery impossible.

714   Brooks v. Hicks, 230 Ga. 500, 197 S.E.2d 711 (1973).

715   GAR F20, paragraph 11G

such an oral acceptance would have varied the terms of the offer which required the acceptance of the offer to be in writing.[716]

§ 10.5.2   Notice to broker is generally notice to broker's client

The GAR Contract provides that notice to the broker shall be deemed to be notice to the party being represented by the broker as a client. In cases where the broker is practicing designated agency, notice to the designated agent shall be deemed to be notice to the party being represented by the designated agent. Under the terms of the GAR Contracts, notice to the broker is not notice to the broker's customer.

For example, let's assume that a buyer wants to notify the seller that he or she has decided to terminate the contract. If the seller is represented by a listing broker, delivering notice to the listing broker is the same thing as delivering it directly to the seller. The notice is deemed to be delivered to the seller as of the time it is received by the listing broker, even though the listing broker has yet to deliver the notice to the seller. However, if the seller is not being represented by a listing broker, the notice would have to be received directly by the seller to be considered good notice.

§ 10.5.3   Notice by facsimile

Under the GAR Contract, notice by facsimile is deemed to have been given as of the date and time it is transmitted, so long as the sending facsimile machine produces a written confirmation with the accurate date, time, and telephone number to which the notice was sent. In other words, the sending of a facsimile is good notice provided that the sending facsimile machine produces the required information and it is accurate. The requirement that the facsimile machine produce a written confirmation with the accurate date and time was added in the 2005 version of the GAR Contracts. This change was made to discourage brokers from sending notices using facsimile machines that not properly calibrated as to date or time. While notice will likely be deemed to be good notice if, for example, the facsimile machine is off by a few minutes. If the facsimile machine is off by several hours or displays the wrong day, the notice will likely not be deemed to be good notice.

A faxed signature of a party shall constitute an original signature binding upon that party. Any party sending notice by fax will have to send an original copy of the notice if the receiving party so requests. The 2005 GAR Contract provides for fax notices to the listing or selling broker to be sent to the fax numbers set out in the signature page of the contract. When a brokerage firm is acting in a designated agency capacity, a fax notice to the designated agent for the seller is only good notice if it is sent to the fax number of the listing broker. Similarly, fax notices to the designated agent for the buyer must be sent to the fax number of the selling broker.

---

716   Frey v. Friendly Motors, Inc., 129 Ga. App. 636, 200 S.E.2d 467 (1973).

There is also a section for fax numbers to be filled in where the buyer or seller is unrepresented. If an unrepresented buyer or seller includes a facsimile number at which he or she can receive notice, a notice sent to that facsimile number is deemed to be received by the unrepresented party when the notice is faxed, provided that the fax machine produces a written confirmation showing the correct date and time it was sent.

Further, the GAR Contract provides that any party may change the fax number by sending a notice of the change to the party sending the fax. These changes to the GAR Forms were largely made to avoid having faxes sent to the wrong office of a brokerage firm with multiple offices.

One question which was left purposefully vague in the notice section of the GAR Contracts is whether an agent can fill in his or her home facsimile number instead of the broker's telephone number on the signature page of the GAR Contracts. While the GAR Forms Committee intended to discourage such a practice, it is most likely permissible if the agent's broker authorizes the use of the home facsimile number. To avoid disputes over this issue, agents should consider including one of the special stipulations set forth below:

Special Stipulation #10-7: Facsimile notices shall be sent to agent's home facsimile telephone number

All parties agree that unless notice to use a different facsimile telephone number is given by the [Listing/Selling] Broker, all facsimile notices sent to the [Listing/Selling] Broker shall be sent to_____, an affiliated licensee of Broker, at the following facsimile telephone number: _____.

An alternative to this approach is to require that notices by facsimile be sent to both the broker's facsimile number and the agent's facsimile number. The special stipulation below is an example of this type of provision:

Special Stipulation #10-8: Facsimile notices shall be sent to facsimile numbers of both broker and agent

All parties agree that all facsimile notices sent to the [Listing/Selling] Broker shall also be sent at the same time to the facsimile telephone number of _____, an affiliated licensee of Broker at the following facsimile telephone number: _____. Notice hall be deemed received when it is first received at either of the above referenced facsimile telephone numbers.

§ 10.5.4   Notice delivered in person

The GAR Contracts also permit notices to be delivered in person by a party. The delivery of the notice should also be able to be effected by the broker representing a party as a client although the GAR Contract is silent on this point. To avoid any dispute on this issue, the following special stipulation can be used:

Special Stipulation #10-9: Broker may give notice in person

All parties agree that notices can be delivered in person by a party or the Broker (and the Broker's affiliated licensees) representing that party in a client relationship.

While the GAR Contracts permit notices to be delivered in person, there is no requirement that the person to whom the notice is given be present to receive the notice. However, if this were anticipated to be the case, it would be a good idea for the party giving the notice to have another person present who can witness the delivery of the notice. Hopefully, this will minimize evidentiary disputes as to whether notice was properly given by fax. If no witness if present, the party delivering the notice should note in writing the time, date and manner of the delivery of the notice.

If the notice is delivered in person and a party is there to receive the notice, it is always good practice to have that party sign an acknowledgement that he or she received the notice along with the date and time of delivery.

If the notice is delivered in person, for example, to a broker's office and the licensee (or his or her broker) are not present to receive the notice, the party delivering the notice should get the receptionist or the agent on duty to acknowledge in writing the date and time of delivery.

§ 10.5.5   Limiting form of notice

There are times when a party will only want notice given in one particular way, such as by facsimile. This is most often the case when there are time critical deadlines in a transaction and the parties want to know the specific means by which notice will be delivered. The special stipulation below can be used to limit the form of notice.

Special Stipulation #10-10: Limited form of notice

All parties agree that all notices hereunder shall be only given by facsimile and through no other means.

CHAPTER 11
DISPUTES ARISING FROM THE CONTRACT

OVERVIEW

A variety of problems and disputes arise in residential real estate transactions. Buyers sometimes get cold feet and do not want to go through with their purchases. Sellers occasionally get better offers and look for ways to avoid their obligations. Buyers and sellers often fight with one another over what personal property stays with the real estate, whether the buyer is being reasonable in requesting that defects be repaired, or whether the buyer is diligently pursuing financing. Other disputes arise when the buyer discovers hidden defects in the property after the closing and accuses the seller or listing broker of knowing about the defects and not disclosing the same. With newly constructed homes, some buyers often assert claims against the builder for negligent construction.

Parties are often able to resolve such disputes by themselves, with the help of their brokers or through mediation. Parties who do not resolve their differences often end up suing each other and sometimes the real estate broker or brokers involved in the transaction. The two most common legal claims arising out of real estate sales contracts are for: (a) breach of contract when a party does not close and/or refuses or fails to comply with the terms of the contract, and (b) fraud where the buyer alleges that the seller and/or the seller's broker knew about hidden defects in the property but failed to disclose to the buyer or concealed them in order to encourage the buyer to purchase the property.

This chapter discusses disputes between the parties including the kinds of claims that are asserted, the relevant statute of limitation periods, and the damages available to parties. This chapter also discusses alternatives to going to court, including arbitration and mediation.

§ 11.1   What the GAR Contract provides

The parties to a contract owe a duty of good faith and fair dealing in performing their obligations under the contract.[717] When a party breaches a contract, courts have the power to order the breaching party to perform as agreed in the contract or pay for the damages caused by the breach.[718] The possible remedies will depend on the facts and circumstances of the dispute. Although the law provides for several remedies that the injured party may have, the contract may limit what remedies are available.

The GAR Contract does not limit the rights of either buyer or seller to pursue any claim against the other for an alleged breach of the contract. If one party breaches the contract, the other can sue for specific performance, monetary damages, or any other remedy provided by law.

---

717   Brack v. Brownlee, 246 Ga. 818, 273 S.E.2d 390 (Ga., 1980)
718   Baker v. Jellibeans, Inc., 252 Ga. 458, 314 S.E.2d 874 (1984).

The GAR Contract provides that in the event of a breach by the seller, the buyer would be entitled to the return of the earnest money.[719] The buyer would also be entitled to sue for specific performance or for damages. If the buyer breaches the contract, the seller would be entitled to receive the earnest money from the Holder. If the seller accepts and deposits the earnest money from the Holder, the earnest money will be considered liquidated damages accepted in full settlement of all claims that the seller may have against the buyer.[720] This means that the seller could not then pursue other claims against the buyer.[721] If, on the other hand, the seller does not accept the earnest money from the Holder, the seller may pursue any other legal remedies against the buyer. Alternatively, the buyer can sue for specific performance, rescission or damages.

One issue not squarely addressed by the GAR Contract is what happens if the buyer breaches the contract, but the seller is the Holder of the earnest money. If the seller accepts and deposits the earnest money from the Holder after a buyer's breach, this is considered liquidated damages taken in full settlement of all claims. However, if the seller is the Holder, then he is already in possession of the earnest money. If he does not return the earnest money to the buyer, will he be deemed to have accepted and deposited the funds as liquidated damages? There is no definitive answer to this, but it makes little sense to require a seller who is already in possession of funds to return them to a defaulting purchaser whom the seller claims owes him even more money. Also, it is difficult to conclude that the seller affirmatively accepted and deposited the earnest money as liquidated damages, since the funds were deposited prior to the buyer's breach. The safest course of action for a seller in this situation is to immediately notify the defaulting buyer that he is claiming additional damages and is not holding or accepting the earnest money as liquidated damages.

§ 11.2   Breach of contract prior to closing

Generally, the remedies for breach of contract prior to closing include claims for monetary damage and/or rescission (cancellation) or specific performance (enforcement) of the contract. These different remedies are discussed in detail below.

§ 11.2.1   Monetary damages

If a party to the contract refuses to complete the sale (i.e., breaches the contract), the other party may choose to sue for monetary damages for the breach.[722] An obvious precondition to a claim for breach of contract requires that the contract be binding and valid in the first place.[723] Also, the party seeking to recover must not himself be in breach, as this might excuse the other party's non-performance.

---

719   GAR Contract, F20, paragraph 3b(1).
720   GAR Contract, F20, paragraph 3b(2).
721   Everett Assoc. v. Garner, 162 Ga. App. 513, 291 S.E.2d 120 (1982), cert. denied.
722   O.C.G.A. § 13-6-1.
723   Covington v. Countryside Inv. Co., Inc., 263 Ga. 125, 428 S.E.2d 562 (1993);

The general rule for the measure of damages for breach of a contract to purchase or sell real estate is the difference between the contract price and the fair market value of the land at the time of the breach.[724] Questions of value are typically questions of fact and must be decided by a judge or jury.[725] Additional damages (that is, damages other than general damages) recoverable for breach of contract are only those that arise naturally from the breach. They must also be expenses or costs contemplated by the parties when the contract was made and must be the probable result of a breach.[726]

Recoverable damages are frequently far less than the parties to the contract imagine. Most purchasers will not knowingly pay more for property than its fair market value. Accordingly, it is the rare case where there are any meaningful differences (i.e., damages) between the contract price and the fair market value of the property at the time of the breach. For example if the contract sales price was $100,000, and the property was worth $103,000 on the date of breach, a non-defaulting buyer would be entitled to $3,000.00 in damages. A non-defaulting seller may have no recoverable damages, since he would still have ownership of the property, which is worth more than the price for which he was selling it. Alternatively, if the purchase price was $100,000 but the property was worth only $95,000 as of the date of breach, the non-defaulting buyer might have no damages because the property was worth less than he was paying for it. The non-defaulting seller would presumably have a $5,000 damage claim. Interestingly, however, if the contract was contingent upon the buyer's ability to obtain financing or was contingent upon the property appraising for the contract price, the purchaser may attempt to justify his breach on that basis.

There are some incidental damages that may be recoverable. For example, the court allowed one buyer to recover increased interest costs when the closing was delayed because the seller failed to comply with the contract.[727] However, unless the language of the contract expressly authorizes it, the non-breaching party may not recover many other additional damages, such as utility bills, insurance coverage, ad valorem taxes, repair and maintenance costs, or "lost opportunity" costs (such as the non-breaching seller's loss of another house, which was contingent upon the sale of his current home or the non-breaching purchaser's need to rent an apartment because he already sold his prior home). [728]

McMicheal Realty & Ins. Agency, Inc. v. Tysinger, 155 Ga. App. 131, 270 S.E.2d 88 (1980).

724   Mills v. Parker 267 Ga.App. 334. 599 S.E.2d 301 (2004); Quigley v. Jones, 255 Ga. 33, 334 S.E.2d 664 (1985), aff'd; SePark v. Caswell Builders, Inc., 209 Ga. App. 713, 434 S.E.2d 502 (1993), cert. denied, 209 Ga. App. 915 (1993); CCameron v. Frazier, 172 Ga. App. 794, 324 S.E.2d 773 (1984).

725   Croft v. Kamens, 171 Ga. App. 105, 318 S.E.2d 809 (1984).

726   O.C.G.A. § 13-6-2; Quigley v. Jones, 255 Ga. 33, 334 S.E.2d 664 (1985).

727   Executive Constr., Inc. v. Geduldig, 170 Ga. App. 560, 317 S.E.2d 564 (1984).

728   Quigley v. Jones, 255 Ga. 33, 334 S.E.2d 664 (1985); Baker v. Jellibeans, Inc., 252 Ga. 458, 314 S.E.2d 874 (1984).

As discussed above, the GAR Contract contains a mandatory "liquidated damages" provision whereby the seller's monetary damages is limited to the earnest money if the seller accepts and deposits the earnest money from the Holder. If the seller wants to avoid this limitation, he should decline to accept the earnest money.

§ 11.2.2   Specific performance

The non-defaulting party to a contract may sue for specific performance to compel the defaulting party to purchase or sell, as the case may be, the property as agreed in the contract.[729] In order for a party to be entitled to specific performance, the contract must be clear and definite in its terms and entered into without fraud. [730] The contract must have provided the seller with an adequate price for the real estate[731] which the buyer typically must have already tendered for the property.[732] The non-defaulting party must have fully performed as required by the contract and must have waived or satisfied any contractual contingencies or conditions.[733] This is why buyers often send written notice to reluctant sellers declaring that they are "ready, willing, and able to perform" and go to closing even if they believe the sellers will not show up.

In one case the sellers of property in Dalton, Georgia, contracted to sell their house to a couple who planned to move to Dalton from West Virginia but who changed their plans and failed to close on the property.[734] The sellers sued the buyers for specific performance and, at trial, the court found that the contract had been signed by all parties and had been complied with by the sellers who were "ready, willing and able to perform." The court ordered the buyers to complete the sale. On appeal by the buyers, the Georgia Supreme Court upheld the trial court's ruling that "[s]o long as the contract for the sale of land is in writing, signed by the other necessary parties, is certain and fair, for adequate consideration, and capable of being performed," the court can order that it be specifically performed. Therefore, the buyers were compelled to comply with the terms of the contract and purchase the house.

While the above case involved a successful specific performance claim by a seller against a buyer, sellers rarely file such claims. The seller must keep the property off the market and remain "ready, willing, and able to sell" the property while the suit,

---

729   Baker v. Jellibeans, Inc., 252 Ga. 458, 314 S.E.2d 874 (1984).
730   Pridgen v. Saville, 237 Ga. 49, 226 S.E.2d 905 (1976) (terms of payment not stated); Fourteen West Realty, Inc. v. Wesson, 167 Ga. App. 539, 307 S.E.2d 28 (1983) (property description inadequate); McMichael Realty & Ins. Agency, Inc. v. Tysinger, 155 Ga. App. 131, 270 S.E.2d 88 (1980).
731   Baker v. Jellibeans, Inc., 252 Ga. 458, 314 S.E.2d 874 (1984) (holding that court will grant specific performance only if contract price is "fair, just and not against good conscience," Baker at 461, 314 S.E.2d at 877); Walker v. Bush, 234 Ga. 366, 216 S.E.2d 285 (1975).
732   Covington v. Countryside Inv. Co., Inc., 263 Ga. 125, 428 S.E.2d 562 (1993); Gallogly v. Bradco, Inc., 260 Ga. 311, 392 S.E.2d 529 (1990).
733   Stribling v. Ailion, 223 Ga. 662, 157 S.E.2d 427 (1967).
734   Golden v. Frazier, 244 Ga. 685, 261 S.E.2d 703 (1979).

including any appeals, is pending. This can take years. Even if the seller eventually wins the suit, a judgment ordering the buyer to purchase the property does little good if the buyer lacks sufficient cash with which to close. Lenders may be unlikely to lend to someone who does not want the property and who explains they are only purchasing the property because a court ordered them to do so.

In another case, the trial court refused to order the specific performance of a contract to sell land where the terms were too indefinite.[735] In that case, the contract provided that the buyer would pay 29% of the price by August 1, but the contract did not provide for how the balance of the purchase price was to be paid. The Georgia Supreme Court affirmed the trial court's ruling that the payment terms were not definite or specific. The Court reasoned that the terms of a real estate contract must be such that neither party can misunderstand them. The Court stated that it would be inequitable to carry a contract into effect where the Court is forced to guess the intent of the parties, because it might erroneously decree what the parties never intended or contemplated.

§ 11.2.3   Rescission or cancellation

Another option for a non-defaulting party is to simply cancel or rescind the sales contract. As with other remedies, the non-defaulting party must not himself be in breach.[736] Rescission, or cancellation, of the contract is a remedy in which neither party is held liable for damages for breach of the contract.[737] Rather, the contract is treated as no longer binding between the parties, and the court proceeds to restore the *status quo ante* (putting the parties in the positions they were in prior to entering into the contract).[738] The parties may cancel the contract by simple agreement through conduct, writing, or words.[739] All earnest money should be returned to the buyer and the seller should be compensated for any extraordinary costs (e.g., the cost of removable upgrades made at the buyer's insistence).

Rescission can be based upon the mutual agreement of the parties where they both effectively conclude that they simply want to "call the deal off". Additionally, rescission can be based upon a mutual mistake of a material fact. For example, the parties are both under the mistaken belief that the property is zoned for residential use.

---

735   Pridgen v. Saville, 237 Ga. 49, 226 S.E.2d 905 (1976).

736   Sulejman v. Marinello, 217 Ga. App. 319, 457 S.E.2d 251 (1995); McLeod v. McLatcher, 201 Ga. App. 17, 410 S.E.2d 144 (1991).

737   Once a contract has been rescinded, there is no liability for a breach of that contract. However, as is discussed in the next section, a party may still be liable for fraud arising out of the transaction.

738   Martin v. Rollins, Inc., 238 Ga. 119, 231 S.E.2d 751 (1977); Ardex, Ltd. v. Brighton Homes, Inc., 206 Ga. App. 606, 426 S.E.2d 200 (1992), cert. denied, 206 Ga. App. 899 (1992).

739   Hennessy v. Woodruff, 210 Ga. 742, 82 S.E.2d 859 (1954); Shoup v. Elliott, 192 Ga. 858, 16 S.E.2d 857 (1941); Seaboard Coast Line R.R. Co. v. Metzger, 126 Ga. App. 178, 190 S.E.2d 156 (1972).

They are surprised when the discovery that the property is actually zoned for light commercial use. The seller does not want to sell because he thinks the property might be worth more that the contracted for purchase price. The buyer does not want to purchase because he is interested in building a residence, not a commercial building. Finally, rescission can be based upon a unilateral mistake as to a material fact, but only if the other party was aware of the mistake, knew it was a material condition to the sale, and the truth could not have been discovered by the exercise of due diligence.[740]

In one Georgia case a builder entered a contract with a buyer for the purchase and sale of a house and lot in Fulton County, Georgia.[741] The buyer paid $5,000.00 earnest money. The house was to be completed by June 30, and the parties agreed to close on July 1. On June 30, the buyer and an inspector went to the house and found 40 items that needed attending to by the builder, and the builder agreed to address 35 of the items. A disagreement arose as to the date of closing. The builder wanted to close immediately, while the buyer wanted to wait until the house was totally completed. The builder advised the buyer that they could either close on the house or the buyer could take back his earnest money because the builder had the house ready and he wanted to close. The buyer's attorney called the builder to tell him that the deal was off and the buyer wanted his earnest money back. The builder then offered to compromise, but the buyer wanted to accept the earnest money and rescind the contract. The builder then put the house up for sale and returned the earnest money.

The house later sold for $4,450.00 less than the original contract and the builder had to pay points and additional interest on his construction loan. The builder also had to incur considerable painting and redecorating expenses in order to sell the house and pay for utilities, maintenance, and upkeep. The builder sued the original buyer to recover these expenses. The buyer counterclaimed for expenses the buyer had incurred because of the builder's refusal to complete the house as required by the contract. The trial court ruled against both parties' claims and did not award either party any damages. The Court found that the parties canceled the contract by mutual consent. Once the builder offered to return the buyer's earnest money and the buyer accepted this offer, the parties effectively rescinded the contract, thereby barring any recovery by either party.[742]

§ 11.3 Breach of contract after closing

Generally, the remedies for breach of contract after the closing include claims for monetary damage and/or specific performance (enforcement) of some unfulfilled provision of the contract.

---

740   Lester v. Bird, 200 Ga.App. 335, 408 S.E.2d 147 (1991).
741   Johnson Ventures, Inc. v. Barkin, 141 Ga. App. 810, 234 S.E.2d 340 (1977), cert. denied.
742   Johnson Ventures, Inc. v. Barkin, 141 Ga. App. 810, 234 S.E.2d 340 (1977), cert. denied.

§ 11.3.1   Monetary damages

The measure of damages for breach of contract after the sale has closed is the difference between the value of the property as contacted for and the value of the property as delivered. Damages may also be proven by showing the cost to repair or restore the property to the condition in which it was supposed to be delivered.[743]

Typically, post-closing breach of contract claims involve allegations that the property was not in the condition in which it was warranted to be (i.e., claims against a builder for failing to deliver the property in a good and workmanlike manner, claims against a seller for failing to have the roof properly repaired, etc.). In the case of new construction, such claims may be covered under the builder's warranty. In that event, the terms of the warranty should be followed.[744]

§ 11.3.2   Specific performance

As with pre-closing contracts, specific performance is an available remedy for breach of contract. Since the property would have already been conveyed, such claims would involve compelling the breaching party to perform some other act contracted for. For example, a buyer might bring a specific performance claim if the seller contracted to leave certain furniture in the house but failed to do so.

§ 11.3.3   The GAR Contract

The GAR Contract makes no specific references with regard to breach of contract claims. It does, however, contain a "survival clause" as follows: "All conditions and stipulations in this Agreement, which the parties agree shall be performed or fulfilled after the closing, shall survive closing until such time as said conditions or stipulations are performed or fulfilled.[745] The parties need to be certain that any conditions or stipulations are fulfilled at the closing or that a new agreement is created to address any unfulfilled matters. The following example illustrates this point.

Assume that the sales contract contains a special stipulation that "seller shall replace the loose roof shingles identified on the attached inspection report, will replace the water heater, and, within 5 days after closing shall cause he rusty swing set to be removed from the back yard.." The parties appear for closing and the seller presents an invoice from a roofer indicating that the shingles have been replaced. The seller does not, however, provide any proof that the water heater has

---

743   <u>Ryland Group v. Daley</u>, 245 Ga.App. 496, 537 S.E.2d 732 (2000); <u>Rose Mill Homes, Inc. v. Michell</u>, 155 Ga.App. 808, 273 S.E.2d 211, (1980)

744   See Chapter 15 regarding new construction contracts and Georgia's Right to Repair law.

745   GAR Contract, F20, paragraph 11B.

been replaced or that the swing set has been removed. After the closing the buyer discovers that neither of these matters have been addressed by the seller.

Under the GAR Contract, the buyer can still maintain an action against the seller for the cost to remove the rusty swing set. This is because the sales contract clearly specified the parties' intent that the swing would be removed after closing. However, since the parties did not agree that the seller's obligation to replace the water heater would remain after the closing, this requirement is likely waived and the buyer could not successfully maintain an action against the seller.

The following special stipulation can be used to address matters that the parties wish to have survive the closing:

Special Stipulation #11-1: Survival of conditions

Notwithstanding anything else contained herein to the contrary, the parties specifically intend and agree that the following conditions and stipulations shall survive the closing until such time as said conditions or stipulations are performed or fulfilled: _____ .

What happens if the parties discover at the closing that certain obligations or conditions have not been met? Using the example above, what if the buyer learned at the closing that the seller had not replaced the water heater? In that event, the buyer has three options.

First, he can simply refuse to complete the closing on the basis that the seller has failed to fulfill the terms of the sales contract. Obviously, a seller may be reluctant to do this if for no other reason than he may have no place to live if he can't move into the subject property.

Another option is for the buyer and seller to amend the contract or enter into a side agreement, whereby additional time is given during which to complete the unfulfilled contractual obligations. Such an agreement may look like the following:

Special Stipulation #11-2: Unfulfilled conditions discovered at closing

The attached Purchase and Sale Agreement requires that the (Seller / Buyer) complete the following prior to closing: _____ .
For and in exchange of ten dollars and other good and valuable consideration, the receipt and sufficiency of which is hereby acknowledged, it is agreed that these items may be completed within _____ days after the closing. It is the intent of the parties that these items shall survive the closing until such time as said conditions or stipulations are performed or fulfilled

§ 11.4 Fraud

Many times a party to a contract believes that the other party had knowledge of a defect or unfavorable condition related to the property, which knowledge they lied about, did not share, or actively concealed. These circumstances can give rise to claims of fraud. As a practical matter, most fraud claims in real estate sales transactions are brought by the buyer and typically include claims against the seller and/or real estate broker(s).

§ 11.4.1   Elements of fraud

There are two general types of fraud recognized by our courts in Georgia: active fraud and passive fraud.

Active fraud requires proof that:
(1)   The offending party lied or actively conceals a defect by taking steps to prevent the buyer from discovering the defect;
(2)   The offending party intended to lie or was reckless as to the truth of the matter asserted;
(3)   The lie was told to induce the buyer or seller to act (or not act, as the case may be);
(4)   that the buyer or seller justifiably relied on the misrepresentation; in other words, the buyer or seller could not have protected himself or herself against the fraud through the exercise of due diligence; and
(5)   The lie was the proximate cause of the buyer or seller being damaged.

With passive fraud, the party committing the fraud does not affirmatively tell a lie or actively conceal a defect. Instead, he or she simply possesses knowledge of a hidden or latent defect in the property and does not reveal what he or she knows.[746] In most cases, it is difficult to prove all five of the elements of fraud. It is particularly difficult for buyers to show that the seller or broker had <u>actual</u> knowledge of the material fact.[747] Another area of difficulty is that buyers must prove that they justifiably relied on the seller or real estate broker.[748] Buyers are required to

---

[746]   <u>Fincher v. Bergeron</u>, 193 Ga. App. 256, 387 S.E.2d 371 (1989), <u>cert.</u> <u>denied</u>; <u>Wilhite v. Mays</u>, 140 Ga. App. 816, 232 S.E.2d 141 (1976), <u>aff'd</u>, 239 Ga. 31, 235 S.E.2d 532 (1977).

[747]   <u>Lively v. Garnick</u>, 160 Ga. App. 591, 287 S.E.2d 553 (1981), <u>cert. denied</u>; <u>Wilhite v. Mays</u>, 140 Ga. App. 816, 232 S.E.2d 141 (1976), <u>aff'd</u>, 239 Ga. 31, 235 S.E.2d 532 (1977); <u>Ainsworth et al. v. Perreault et al.</u>, 254 Ga. App. 470, 563 S.E. 2d 135 (2002); <u>Bircoll et al. v. Rosenthal et al.</u>, 267 Ga.App. 431, 600 S.E.2d 388 (2004); <u>Resnick v. Meybohm Realty Inc. et al.</u>, 269 Ga.App. 486, 604 S.E.2d 536 (2004); <u>Ikola v. Schoene et al.</u>, 264 Ga. App. 338, 590 S.E.2d 750

[748]   <u>Real Estate Int'l, Inc. v. Buggay</u>, 220 Ga. App. 449, 469 S.E.2d 242 (1996), <u>cert. denied</u>; <u>Hill v. Century 21 Max Stancil Realty</u>, 187 Ga. App. 754, 371 S.E.2d 217 (1988).

prove that they exercised "ordinary and reasonable care" or "due diligence" to protect themselves in order to be able to recover for fraud. Generally, this means that if the buyer could have discovered the problem if he had inspected the property or neighborhood, or noticed signs of the problem, and the seller did not prevent the inspection, then the buyer cannot recover.[749]

§ 11.4.1.1   Cases where buyers' fraud claims denied

The legal requirement that buyers prove that they exercised "due diligence" or "ordinary and reasonable care" to protect themselves before they can succeed in an action for fraud decreases the legal risks faced by sellers and real estate brokers in selling real property. As seen in the following discussion of cases, this single element often prevents a buyer's recovery for fraud or misrepresentation. Courts will not allow buyers to merely rely on what they are told about the condition of the property; instead, buyers must independently investigate problems and defects of which they are aware.

For example, in one Georgia case, a buyer sued the real estate agent with whom she was working (although the agent was representing the seller) for fraud, alleging that the agent concealed that the house was subject to flooding.[750] The buyer inspected the house several times before closing and noticed a creek adjacent to the property. She also noticed that the basement was dank and smelled musty. The buyer asked the agent whether the property had flooding problems. The agent allegedly denied that there had been previous flooding. Moreover, the surveyor reported that the property was not in a flood hazard area. The trial court ruled in favor of the agent, because the buyer could not prove that she justifiably relied on any representations. The buyer appealed, and the Court held that the buyer was unable to establish the five elements necessary to maintain an action for fraud. The Court noted that the buyer neglected to adequately investigate the risk of flooding, in spite of her many inspections of the property and her ability to check with the county records or her homeowner's insurance agent. Without such an investigation, the Court did not believe the buyer could establish the fourth element of fraud, that her reliance on alleged false representations was justifiable. The Court emphasized that the law does not offer relief to buyers who make no attempt to ascertain the condition of the property.

A buyer in another case raised similar issues of fraud where the buyer purchased a dilapidated, vacant, residential property for $25,000.00.[751] The buyer inspected the property twice with a real estate licensee working with her but representing the seller, and she understood that she needed to make substantial repairs.

---

749   A buyer may be able to recover if it can be shown that the seller had "special knowledge" about the alleged defect that would require disclosure. Brookshire v. Digby, No. 224 Ga.App. 512, 481 S.E.2d 250 (1997).

750   Copeland v. Home Sav. of America, F.A., 209 Ga. App. 173, 433 S.E.2d 327 (1993)

751   Ben Farmer Realty Co. v. Woodard, 212 Ga. App. 74, 441 S.E.2d 421 (1994), cert. denied, 212 Ga. App. 897 (1994).

The sales contract, which was prepared by the licensee, stated that the house was being sold "as is," without a termite inspection, and that purchaser did not rely on any representations made by seller or his agents. During her inspections, the buyer made no attempt to inspect the attic. After the closing, she discovered structural damage in the attic caused by a fire which had occurred prior to the sale. She stated that, using a flashlight, she could see the damage through the access hole to the attic. The buyer sued the seller and the listing and selling agents, claiming they fraudulently induced her to enter the sales contract by passively concealing the fire damage. The agents claimed they had no knowledge of the fire damage. The court held that in cases of passive concealment, the buyer must prove that the concealment of the defect was fraudulent or deceitful, including evidence that the defect could not be discovered by the due diligence of the buyer and that the seller or agent was aware of the defect and did not disclose it. inceSince the buyer had failed to use due diligence to discover the fire damage, her claim for fraud was barred.

In one case, the buyers sued the sellers, the sellers' agent and broker for fraud, conspiracy to defraud, breach of contract and breach of BRRETA.[752] The buyers and sellers had entered into a contract of sale, which contained a disclaimer provision and an "entire agreement" clause. The contract also incorporated by reference the seller's disclosure statement. The buyers knew that the house they were contracting for had a synthetic stucco exterior and that such houses were more likely to attract termites. Before the parties signed the sales contract, the sellers gave the buyers a Seller's Disclosure Statement, which referred to past and present termite damage, but stated that the damage had been taken care of. It also stated that there were problems with the walkways and water intrusion, but that there had been no water in the basement since 1989. After the parties signed the contract, the sellers' agent sent a detailed termite treatment history report to the buyers' agent. The report stated that existing conditions of the property might lead to future infestation. The buyers also conducted a professional visual inspection, which revealed possible water intrusion and stucco repairs. However, the buyers did not conduct a stucco or termite inspection. Just before the closing, the sellers obtained a detailed infestation report, which the buyers signed at closing.

The Court held that the buyers' claim against sellers for misrepresentation must fail because the buyers had affirmed the contract and were therefore bound by the disclaimer and merger clause. As for the claim against the agent and the broker, the Court ruled that there was no evidence that the agent knew about the home's defects apart from what was stated in the Seller's Disclosure Statement. As for the claim against the seller, the Court found no evidence that the sellers knew of any current problems with the property. Further, although the buyers' inspection listed problems with the stucco exterior and water intrusion, the buyers did not conduct a separate stucco or termite inspection. Therefore, the buyers could not claim justifiable reliance on the property disclosure statement.

---

752   Bircoll et al. v. Rosenthal et al., 267 Ga.App. 431, 600 S.E.2d 388 (2004)

In another case the buyer sued claiming the property had been advertised as being 1.5 acres but was actually only 0.8 acres.[753] The Court ruled that even though the seller misstated the true acreage, this did not relieve the buyer of his obligation to independently confirm the size of the property. This could have been accomplished, for example, by looking at a plat or survey. Similarly, in another case, the buyers contracted to buy a new home in a subdivision that was "the same house on Lot 74 as on Lot 65", which was the model home. However, the different lot size allowed a smaller foundation, which caused some design changes and a reduction in area. The buyers were informed of that the foundations were different and the rooms had to be redesigned. However, they did not take any steps to discover the change in area. In their claim against the broker for fraud in failing to disclose the reduced area, the Court stated that since the buyers knew about the differences, the buyers were required to exercise due diligence to determine area of their redesigned property before relying on the representations of the broker.

In a case involving an "as is" clause, the Court of Appeals defined the scope of a broker's liability in the sale of a house with substantial defects.[754] The case involved a buyer who decided to purchase a house "as is," despite the fact that he had knowledge that the roof was leaking, water was running down the walls, the carpet was mildewed, the fireplace had moisture all over it, and the house was in general disrepair. Prior to closing, the buyer hired a home inspector to inspect the house. The home inspector's report found that the house was built on a sloping lot with inadequate grade and that there was water in the crawl space. While the inspector recommended that a drainage specialist examine the property, the buyer did not heed the inspector's advice. The listing agent allegedly informed the buyer that the water under the house was run-off from a hill in the backyard, the drainage problems could be repaired, and the house was structurally sound. However, the buyer was aware that prior repairs by the sellers had not been successful in correcting the drainage problems. At closing, the buyer was told that the termite inspection was not completed because the termite inspector could not get into the crawl space due to flooding. The house eventually closed but the buyer later discovered that the water problems stemmed from an underground spring beneath the house. The buyer sued all parties to the transaction for fraud and negligent misrepresentation[755]

In the buyer's suit against the listing broker, the Court of Appeals determined that the buyer's reliance upon the alleged misrepresentations regarding the water problems was not justified as a matter of law. The Court held that the buyer failed to exercise due diligence to protect himself in light of evidence that would have caused most people to investigate further. The Court emphasized that the law does not afford relief to one who does not use ordinary means of information to protect him. It should be noted that under the 2000 revisions to BRRETA, the agent could also avoid liability by disclosing to the buyer the source of their information, which in this case was the

---

753   Simmons v. Pilkenton, 230 Ga.App. 900, 497 S.E.2d 613 (1998).
754   Real Estate Int'l, Inc. v. Buggay, 220 Ga. App. 449, 469 S.E.2d 242 (1996).
755   Real Estate Int'l, Inc. v. Buggay, 220 Ga. App. 449, 469 S.E.2d 242 (1996).

seller.[756]   The GAR Disclosure of Information form[757] should be used whenever the broker has been asked to research or investigate information on behalf of his client. The Disclosure form provides a statement of the question asked, the answer, and the source of the information. So long as the source of the information is disclosed and the broker did not know that the information was incorrect at the time it was given, there will be no liability.

Here is a quick reference to other cases where the buyers' fraud claims were denied: buyers could not claim fraud based on misrepresentations that the recreational amenities were included in planned community when they did not attempt to independently verify the boundaries of the property[758]; buyer who made no attempt to discover the boundaries of the property could not justifiably rely on a misrepresentation by the seller regarding those boundaries[759]; buyer could not claim against a broker for misrepresentations regarding financing on an assumed loan because the buyer failed to exercise ordinary and reasonable care to independently confirm the accuracy of the information[760]; buyer could not assert claim against seller/broker for misrepresentations regarding zoning because buyer failed to exercise ordinary and reasonable care by inquiring about zoning himself[761]; buyer's failure to examine title barred fraud claim for portion of property previously sold to Department of Transportation[762].

§ 11.4.1.2   Cases where sellers found responsible for fraud

Of course, the seller would be liable for fraud if the buyer were able to prove the five requisite elements. One case involved a four-year old house equipped with an inadequate septic tank that overflowed during rainy weather.[763] Whenever it rained heavily, surface water would collect under the house, which caused it to deteriorate. Further, the septic tank and drainage lines were inadequate, which resulted in an overflow of raw sewage from the septic tank into the front yard of the home after a heavy rain. The Court held that the buyer could not have discovered these defects by the exercise of due diligence at any time except after a heavy rain. The seller, however, was aware of the defects and failed to disclose them. The Court held that the seller is obligated to disclose situations where he has special knowledge not apparent to the buyer and is aware that the buyer is acting under a misapprehension as to facts which would be important and would probably affect his decision in the purchase of

---

756   O.C.G.A. § 10-6A-5; O.C.G.A. § 10-6A-7.

757   GAR Form F55.

758   Brakebill v. Hicks, 259 Ga. 849, 388 S.E.2d 695 (1990)

759   Crawford v. Williams, 258 Ga. 806, 375 S.E.2d 223 (1989)

760   Bennett v. Clark, 192 Ga. App. 698, 385 S.E.2d 780 (1989)

761   Hill v. Century 21 Max Stancil Realty, 187 Ga. App. 754, 371 S.E.2d 217 (1988)

762   Jim Royer Realty v. Moreira, 184 Ga. App. 848, 363 S.E.2d 10, cert. denied, 184 Ga. App. 910 (1987)

763   Wilhite v. Mays, 140 Ga. App. 816, 232 S.E.2d 141 (1976), aff'd, 239 Ga. 31, 235 S.E.2d 532 (1977).

the property. Therefore, the Court found that the seller was liable to the buyer for fraud by "passively concealing" defects.

In another passive concealment case, the Court held that the seller was liable for failing to inform the buyers of several concealed defects in the house which were not noticeable upon a reasonable inspection[764]. The buyer's inspection could not have revealed the defects which existed in the utility systems and the structural integrity of the dwelling house and pool house. The seller had actual knowledge of all of the defects and supervised a major renovation project on the main house. Moreover, the defects in the property were not as a result of typical wear and tear, and none were noticeable on a visual examination.

Likewise, a seller was found responsible for fraudulently concealing numerous structural and hidden defects in a house which he built and in which he had lived for 12 years.[765] In that case, the seller failed to reveal that the house had an unusual framing and roof structure which was concealed by a drop ceiling. The seller urged the buyer to go look at other houses he was currently building to see the framing and type of work, quality of materials, and workmanship present in the house the buyer was purchasing. However, none of the houses to which he referred the buyer were constructed in the same way. Also, the seller lied about the age of the well pump and he lied about previous termite infestation and damage. The Court found that the seller acted with the intention of misleading the buyer and that the buyer could not have discovered the defects by exercising due diligence.

An example of an active fraud case involved a house which was infested with termites.[766] The seller had completely rebuilt the property because it was destroyed by a fire. The seller acted as a general contractor in the renovation and the property was his personal residence for several years. As such, the seller was very familiar with the condition of the property. The seller gave the buyers a Seller's Property Disclosure Statement in which he stated that he was not aware of any damage due to termites or structural defects in the home. The buyers' inspection did not reveal any termite damage. A few months after the closing, the buyers saw termites swarming in the house and began to investigate further. They called the inspector back to the property who had conducted the initial inspection. Upon closer inspection, the inspector found putty and paint that had been used to conceal holes and gaps in the wood caused by termite infestation. The Court held that the seller was liable for fraud by concealing the termite-damaged wood.

---

764   Fincher v. Bergeron, 193 Ga. App. 256, 387 S.E.2d 371 (1989), cert. denied.
765   Brookshire v. Digby, 224 Ga.App. 512, 481 S.E.2d 250, 97 FCDR 453 (1997)
766   Browning v. Stocks et al., 265 Ga.App. 803, 595 S.E.2d 642 (2004)

§ 11.4.2   Remedies for fraud claims against seller and/or broker

When a buyer alleges fraud against a seller and/or real estate broker, the buyer has various options to address the wrong. However, the buyer must choose which legal tool to use. This choice is referred to as an "election of remedies."[767] First, the buyer may rescind the contract upon the discovery of fraud, and, after offering to restore any benefits received under the contract, sue in tort for recovery of the purchase price and any additional damages resulting from the fraud.[768] If the buyer fails to timely rescind, he will be deemed to have affirmed the contract, including the merger clause, and his fraud claim will be barred.[769] Offering to restore any benefits means that the buyer must offer to deed the property back to the seller. The buyer must also offer to restore any benefits received under the contract.

The buyer's other remedy is to affirm the contract upon discovery of the fraud and to sue for damages resulting from the fraud.[770] Unlike the first remedy, this remedy allows the buyer to keep the "fruits" of the contract.[771] The buyer's damages would be the difference in value of the property as sold to him and the real value of the property. [772]

If the buyer elects to affirm the contract, the buyer would generally be bound by the terms of the contract, including the "merger" clause. The GAR Contract includes a merger clause which provides that:

> This Agreement constitutes the sole and entire agreement between the parties and shall be binding upon the parties and their successors, heirs and permitted assigns. No representation, promise or inducement not included in this Agreement shall be binding upon any party hereto.[773]

This type of provision is also commonly referred to as an "entire agreement" clause and is contained in most real estate contracts. The effect of this clause is to

---

767   Hightower v. Century 21 Farish Realty, 214 Ga. App. 522, 448 S.E.2d 271 (1994).
768   Ben Farmer Realty Co. v. Woodard, 212 Ga. App. 74, 441 S.E.2d 421 (1994),
        cert. denied, 212 Ga. App. 897 (1994); Price v. Mitchell, 154 Ga. App. 523, 268
        S.E.2d 743 (1980), cert. denied.
769   Ben Farmer Realty Co. v. Woodard, 212 Ga. App. 74, 441 S.E.2d 421 (1994),
        cert. denied, 212 Ga. App. 897 (1994).
770   Ben Farmer Realty Co. v. Woodard, 212 Ga. App. 74, 441 S.E.2d 421 (1994),
        cert. denied, 212 Ga. App. 897 (1994); Price v. Mitchell, 154 Ga. App. 523, 268
        S.E.2d 743 (1980), cert. denied; Weaver v. ABC Bus, Inc., 191 Ga. App. 614, 382
        S.E.2d 380 (1989), cert. denied, 191 Ga. App. 923 (1989).
771   Tuttle v. Stovall, 134 Ga. 325, 67 S.E. 806 (1910); Carpenter v. Curtis, 196 Ga.
        App. 234, 395 S.E.2d 653 (1990).
772   Ben Farmer Realty Co. v. Woodard, 212 Ga. App. 74, 441 S.E.2d 421 (1994),
        cert. denied, 212 Ga. App. 897 (1994).
773   GAR Contract, paragraph 11A.

merge all agreements between the parties during negotiations into the single written contract. It also excludes any "representation, promise, or inducement" that the seller or broker may have made during the contract negotiations that are not expressly written into the contract.[774] For example, in a case where the contract did not incorporate the seller's property disclosure statement, the court held that the "entire agreement" clause in the contract precluded the statements made by the sellers on the property disclosure statement.[775] The GAR Contract specifically incorporates the Seller's Property Disclosure Statement.

A clarification to the rule regarding rescission and merger clauses was made in a recent decision where the Court of Appeals held that affirming a contract that contains an entire agreement clause does not necessarily bar a claim based upon active concealment.[776] In that case, the seller actively covered up extensive termite damage with wood putty and paint. No seller's disclosure statement was incorporated into the sales contact. The contract contained an entire agreement clause. The seller argued, unsuccessfully, that the presence of the clause barred the buyer's fraud claim because the buyer failed to rescind the contract. The Court disagreed, holding that the seller was liable to the buyer based on his affirmative acts of fraud, and the merger language in the contract does bar such a claim.

§ 11.4.3   Malpractice claims against real estate broker/agent

Georgia courts have made it clear that the "entire agreement" clause applies in a malpractice claim against the broker in the same way it does in a fraud action to exclude any representations made outside the contract. Therefore, if the buyer elects to affirm rather than rescind a contract containing a merger clause, the buyer would generally not be able to rely on any statement that the broker or agent has made as a basis for a malpractice claim.

This is illustrated in a case where the buyers brought a professional malpractice action against a real estate agent who represented the seller after they discovered that their house was infested with bats.[777] The buyers argued that the seller and the listing broker knew about the problem and failed to disclose it to the buyers. There was evidence that the broker knew something about a bat problem, although he apparently did not know how severe the problem was. The buyers argued that they were suing for malpractice and all they had to prove was that (1) the listing broker had a duty to disclose; (2) the listing broker breached the duty by failing to carry out the duty according to the required standard of care and (3) the breach caused injury to the buyers.

---

774   American Demolition, Inc. v. Hapeville Hotel Ltd. Partnership, 202 Ga. App. 107, 413 S.E.2d 749 (1991), cert. denied, 202 Ga. App. 905 (1992); Carpenter v. Curtis, 196 Ga. App. 234, 395 S.E.2d 653 (1990).

775   Ainsworth et al. v. Perreault et al. 254 Ga. App. 470, 563 S.E.2d 135 (2002).

776   Browning v.Stocks et al. 265 Ga.App. 803, 595 S.E.2d 642 (2004)

777   Pennington v. Braxley, 224 Ga. App. 344, 480 S.E.2d 357 (1997), cert. denied

The Georgia Court of Appeals stated that in a fraud claim, the buyer has an election of remedies: to rescind the contract or affirm the contract and sue for damages for the fraud. However, the fraud claim would be barred if the buyer affirmed the contract. The reason was because the buyer needed to prove that he relied on the misrepresentations, which would be impossible since the "entire agreement" clause provided that the buyer had not relied on any representations not in the contract. The buyer argued that reliance is not an element required to prove a malpractice claim and the presence of the merger clause should not bar a malpractice claim. The Court rejected this argument, holding a malpractice claim was the same thing as a fraud claim and required the same proof as a claim for fraud.

This rationale was followed in a recent case where the buyer brought a breach of duty claim against her own agent. Like the previous case, the Court of Appeals held that the "entire agreement" clause prevented the buyer from proving that she relied on misrepresentations made outside the contract and therefore barred her claim of breach of professional duty.[778]

In another case, the buyers brought a malpractice claim against their own agent and the sellers for fraudulently concealing a water problem in the property.[779] The seller had noticed a sump pump in the basement when she first saw the property. Her agent allegedly told her that she would never have to worry about flooding because of the pump. The agent allegedly urged the buyer to accept the property "as-is" and discouraged her from conducting a professional inspection. The agent also allegedly had been given a Seller's Property Disclosure Statement that indicated a prior water leak, but the agent did not provide this document to her client.

The Court of Appeals held that, the "entire agreement" clause in the contract did not bar the buyer's breach of duty claim against their agent. Notably, this case was decided based upon the pre-2000 revisions to BRRETA.[780] As amended, BRRETA provides that no broker or agent will be held liable for failures to disclose without proof that the broker or agent committed fraud.

§ 11.5   Court action

§ 11.5.1   Use of lis pendens

Under some circumstances a lis pendens may be filed in conjunction with a lawsuit. Lis pendens is a legal doctrine which describes the power or control which courts acquire over property involved in a lawsuit pending the outcome of the case and

---

778   Resnick v. Meybohm Realty Inc. et al., 269 Ga.App. 486, 604 S.E.2d 536 (2004)
779   Ikola v. Schoene et al., 264 Ga. App. 338, 590 S.E. 2d 750 (2003)
780   O.C.G.A. § 10-6A-1 et seq.

until final judgment is entered.[781] The purpose of the doctrine of lis pendens is to keep any property which is the subject of litigation within the power of the court until the judgment is entered so that the court can ensure itself that it can enforce its judgment.[782] A lis pendens is a notice that an action is pending in which someone claims an interest in the subject real estate. This notice is filed in the court public records and would reveal the pending litigation to any potential buyer or lender. The doctrine also has the effect of protecting innocent purchasers of property involved in pending litigation.[783]

§ 11.5.1.1   Lis pendens notice

The Lis Pendens Act requires that for any action seeking legal and/or equitable relief as to any property in Georgia, a notice must be filed and recorded in the lis pendens docket in the office of the clerk of the superior court of the county where the property is located.[784] The notice must contain the names of the parties to the pending suit,[785] the date that the legal action commenced, the name of the court in which it is pending, a description of the real property involved, and a statement of the relief sought regarding the property.[786]

A lis pendens notice is required only for property that is actually and directly brought into litigation by the pleadings in a pending lawsuit and as to which some relief is sought in the lawsuit respecting that particular property.[787] Lis pendens notices apply only to actions which affect title to property and are not properly filed where the underlying litigation seeks only a money judgment.[788] So, for example, it would not be proper for a broker seeking a real estate commission to file a lis pendens.[789] If a notice of a claim of lien on the property is properly and timely filed and recorded, a notice of lis pendens is neither necessary nor applicable.[790]

---

781   Coleman v. Law, 170 Ga. 906, 154 S.E. 445 (1930).

782   Carmicheal Tile Co. v. Yaarab Temple Bldg. Co., 177 Ga. 318, 170 S.E. 294 (1933).

783   Patent Scaffolding Co. v. Byers, 220 Ga. 426, 139 S.E.2d 332 (1964).

784   O.C.G.A. § 44-14-610, 44-14-611.

785   Federal Deposit Ins. Corp. v. McCloud, 478 F. Supp. 47 (N.D. Ga. 1979).

786   O.C.G.A. § 44-14-610.

787   Hill v. L-A Management Corp., 234 Ga. 341, 216 S.E.2d 97 (1975); Evans v. Fulton Nat'l Mortgage Corp., 168 Ga. App. 600, 309 S.E.2d 884 (1983).

788   Alcovy Properties, Inc. v. MTW Inv. Co., 212 Ga. App. 102, 441 S.E.2d 288 (1994); South River Farms v. Bearden, 210 Ga. App. 156, 435 S.E.2d 516 (1993) (stating that classic example of suit requiring lis pendens is one which seeks to have a prior conveyance of the property set aside or declared null and void); Evans v. Fulton Nat'l Mortgage Corp., 168 Ga. App. 600, 309 S.E.2d 884 (1983).

789   See Chapter 13 regarding real estate commissions.

790   Grand Atlanta Corp. v. Chenggis, 142 Ga. App. 375, 235 S.E.2d 779 (1977).

§ 11.5.1.2 Effect of lis pendens on sale

A lis pendens does not prevent the sale of property, and it does not constitute a lien.[791] However, buyers should be extremely cautious before purchasing property as to which a lis pendens notice has been filed and recorded. The lis pendens puts the buyer on notice of the underlying lawsuit and that the buyer therefore will be bound by any judgment entered and will be required to comply therewith.[792] Also, title companies will in all likelihood not insure title to properties on which a lis pendens notice has been filed and recorded. Even if the title examiner does not find a lis pendens notice recorded for a property a buyer intends to purchase, as an added precaution the buyer may ask the seller to swear by affidavit that there are no suits pending against him as to the property. This is done by the seller signing an owner's affidavit which usually includes certifications regarding loan deeds, work done by contractors, labor and supplies, suits and bankruptcies, taxes, assessments, and other liens against the property.

§ 11.5.1.3   Duration of notice

A valid notice of lis pendens remains effective as notice to prospective purchasers of land until a final judgment has been entered in the pending litigation and the time for appeal of the case has expired.[793] Lis pendens notices need not be canceled so long as the underlying lawsuit is satisfactorily terminated.

§ 11.5.2   Time limit for filing suit

Parties should be aware that any claim arising out of or related to a real estate contract must be brought within a legally prescribed time period, called the statute of limitations. If a claim is not filed in the appropriate court within the required time frame, the court may dismiss the claim. The applicable statute of limitations for a claim depends on the specific facts of the claim. Parties who believe they may have a claim arising out of or related to a real estate transaction should seek legal advice to determine the applicable statute of limitations for their claim in order to ensure that suit is timely filed, otherwise the claim may be lost.

Typically, a suit for breach of a real estate contract must be brought within six years after the time required for performance.[794] Parties may contract to a lesser time

---

791   Bell v. King, Phipps & Assoc., 176 Ga. App. 702, 337 S.E.2d 364 (1985), cert. denied.

792   Wilson v. Blake Perry Realty Co., 219 Ga. 57, 131 S.E.2d 555 (1963); Walker v. Houston, 176 Ga. 878, 169 S.E. 107 (1933).

793   Vance v. Lomas Mortgage USA, Inc., 263 Ga. 33, 426 S.E.2d 873 (1993).

794   O.C.G.A. § 9-3-24. However, if the contract was executed under seal, the suit may be brought within 20 years after the right of action has accrued. O.C.G.A. § 9-3-23. No instrument is considered "under seal" unless the body of the instrument contains a recital that it is given under seal and there is a seal affixed to the instrument after the signatures of the parties. O.C.G.A. § 9-3-23. Chastain v.

limit within which an action may be brought, so long as the period fixed is not unreasonable so as to raise a presumption of undue advantage.[795]

The statute of limitations for breach of contract begins to run from the time that the contract is broken, not from the time the actual damage results or is ascertained.[796] For example, if a buyer sues a builder for breach of contract for design defects in the construction of a home, the statute of limitations for the action commences when the defective construction is substantially complete and not when the defects become apparent.[797]

In some circumstances, certain factors may "toll" or stop the calculation of the period of limitation. For example, if there is fraud by the breaching party which prevents the non-breaching party from filing a lawsuit, the statute of limitations may be tolled and the right of action may not begin to run until the time the fraud is or should have been discovered.[798] Promises by the breaching party to remedy the problem will not toll the statute of limitations.[799] However, the parties can enter into a written tolling agreement in which they contractually agree that a statute of limitations will not run for some period of time.

An action for fraud and misrepresentation in inducing the purchase of property, which is an action in tort, must be brought within four years after the right of action accrues.[800] Generally, in a tort action, the statute of limitations begins to run when the damage from the tortious act is actually sustained.[801] For example, if a buyer sues a builder in tort for damages for negligent construction involving a defective roof, the claim must normally be brought within four years from the date that the roof was constructed.[802]

L. Moss Music Co., 83 Ga. App. 570, 64 S.E.2d 205 (1951).

795   Rabey Elec. Co. v. Housing Auth., 190 Ga. App. 89, 378 S.E.2d 169 (1989); General Elec. Credit Corp. v. Home Indem. Co., 168 Ga. App. 344, 309 S.E.2d 152 (1983), cert. denied.

796   Mobley v. Murray County, 178 Ga. 388, 173 S.E. 680 (1934); R.L. Sanders Roofing Co. v. Miller, 153 Ga. App. 225, 264 S.E.2d 731 (1980).

797   Space Leasing Assoc. v. Atlantic Bldg. Sys., 144 Ga. App. 320, 241 S.E.2d 438 (1977), cert. denied.

798   O.C.G.A. § 9-3-96.

799   Mullins v. Wheatley Grading Contractors, 184 Ga. App. 119, 361 S.E.2d 10 (1987).

800   O.C.G.A. § 9-3-31; Kerce v. Bent Tree Corp., 166 Ga. App. 728, 305 S.E.2d 462 (1983); Phipps v. Wright, 28 Ga. App. 164, 100 S.E. 511 (1922).

801   Hunt v. Star Photo Finishing Co., 115 Ga. App. 1, 153 S.E.2d 602 (1967).

802   Corporation of Mercer Univ. v. National Gypsum Co., 258 Ga. 365, 368 S.E.2d 732 (1988); Wellston Co. v. Sam N. Hodges, Jr., & Co., 114 Ga. App. 424, 151 S.E.2d 481 (1966). If a party has a cause of action (1) for any deficiency in a survey or plat, planning, design, specifications, supervision or observation of construction, or construction of an improvement to real property; (2) for any injury to property, real or personal, arising out of any such deficiency; or (3) for injury to the person or for wrongful death arising out of any such deficiency, the lawsuit to

The Georgia Legislature, however, carved out an exception to this rule in the 2000 session. It amended the Georgia Code to provide that the recovery of damages to a "dwelling due to the manufacture of or the negligent design or installation of synthetic exterior siding shall accrue when the damage to the dwelling is discovered or, in the exercise of reasonable diligence, should have been discovered".[803]

If a seller, builder, or broker fraudulently conceals a defect in the house or fraudulently misrepresents information about the house which the buyer cannot discover because of the fraud, it is possible for a court to extend the statute of limitations for an additional limited time to allow the injured party to assert his claim.[804]

For example, in one Georgia case, a buyer sued a builder for damages in tort for negligently constructing a house with a substandard foundation and fraudulently misrepresenting that the foundation was built in accordance with current home-building standards.[805] The buyer did not file his lawsuit within the statutory limit (in this case, four years after the house was built); however, the court held that because of the builder's alleged fraud, the buyer could file his lawsuit within four years from the date that he discovered that the house's foundation was not constructed as the builder represented.[806]

Where the cause of action is for fraudulent inducement in the execution of the contract, the period of limitation begins to run from the date of the execution of the contract.[807]

---

recover damages must be filed against the person performing or furnishing the survey or plat, design, planning, supervision or observation of construction, or construction of such an improvement within eight years after substantial completion of such an improvement. O.C.G.A. § 9-3-51(a). In the case of such an injury to property or the person or such an injury causing wrongful death, which injury occurred during the seventh or eighth year after such substantial completion, an action in tort to recover damages for such an injury or wrongful death may be brought within two years after the date on which such injury occurred, irrespective of the date of death, but in no event may such an action be brought more than ten years after the substantial completion of construction of such an improvement. O.C.G.A. § 9-3-51(b).

803   O.C.G.A. § 9-3-30.
804   Hahne v. Wylly, 199 Ga. App. 811, 406 S.E.2d 94 (1991).
805   Gilmore v. Bell, 223 Ga. App. 513, 478 S.E.2d 609 (1996), cert. denied.
806   Gilmore v. Bell, 223 Ga. App. 513, 478 S.E.2d 609 (1996), cert. denied; Ramey v. Leisure, Ltd., 205 Ga. App. 128, 421 S.E.2d 555 (1992), cert. denied, 205 Ga. App. 901 (1992) (statute of limitation tolled until buyer's discovery of defect in footing).
807   Kerce v. Bent Tree Corp., 166 Ga. App. 728, 305 S.E.2d 462 (1983).

§ 11.5.3   Action to take upon breach of contract

What should you do when you learn that the other party to the contract has or is going to breach the contract? The answer is going to depend upon the specific facts of any given situation. There are, however, several broad rules of thumb.

§ 11.5.3.1   Notice of breach

Usually the first action the non-breaching party should take is to give the breaching party notice of his breach or anticipated breach. Giving such notice provides the breaching party the opportunity to return to a position of compliance with the terms of the contract. This also gives the other party an opportunity to clarify any misperception in the event there has been no actual breach. The best practice is to give notice of breach in writing. If time is a critical factor the notice may, as a practical matter, need to be given verbally. This should, however, be followed by a written confirmation of the notice.

§ 11.5.3.2   Attending the closing

Must the non-breaching party attend the closing in order to preserve his rights? While the answer is "not always"[808], the safest course of action is for the non-breaching party to be present at the closing, ready, willing and able to hold up their end of the bargain.

In one case the buyer informed the seller that he (the buyer) would not purchase the property because the seller had not repaired certain structural defects.[809] As a result, no closing was scheduled and the seller did not obtain a termite letter as required by the contract. The seller subsequently sued the buyer, claiming breach of contract. The buyer argued that he had no liability because the seller failed to provide a termite letter at the closing (which was never scheduled). The Court noted that the contract required the termite letter to be provided at closing and that, as such, it was not due until well after the buyer's repudiation of the contract. The Court went on to state that because the buyer repudiated the contract prior to the time the seller was obligated to perform, the seller was relieved of his responsibilities under the contract.

The risk a party runs by not attending the closing is demonstrated in the following case. The seller was required to make numerous repairs to the property prior to the time of the closing.[810] The buyer inspected the property the afternoon before

---

808   A.G. Nikas v. W.F. Hindley, 98 Ga.App. 437, 106 S.E.2d 335 (1958) (holding that
        if the other party has clearly breached or repudiated the contract, the non-
        breaching party is excused from the necessity or performing or being ready to
        perform on his own part unless the repudiating party withdraws his repudiation).
809   McLeod v. McLatcher, 201 Ga.App. 17, 410 S.E.2d 144 (1991).
810   Clark v. Cox, 179 Ga.App. 437, 347 S.E.2d 4 (1986).

closing and found that not only were the repairs not made, but the yard was overgrown and a "pigsty", the carpeting was soiled, and there was water in the basement and in the main floor. The buyer declared that there was "no way that the items could be remedied" in time and, accordingly, he (the buyer) would not appear for the closing. The seller subsequently sued the buyer for breach of contract. The buyer argued that he did not need to appear for closing since the seller could not possible have lived up to his end of the deal. The Court, however, disagreed. The Court held that the buyer's declaration that he would not attend the closing actually acted as a repudiation by the buyer, and that this relieved the seller of his obligation to make to repairs prior to the time of the scheduled closing. As demonstrated here, and as noted above, it is almost always best for the non-breaching party to attend the closing.

§ 11.6   Alternatives to going to court

Parties should be aware that going to court to resolve a dispute could be a very time-consuming and expensive process. Some litigation can take years to resolve, particularly if a party appeals the initial ruling in the case. Attorney's fees can mount and the expenses of suing can be very high. In addition, many people find that protracted litigation is emotionally draining. For these reasons parties who have disputes which they cannot settle among themselves, but for which they do not want to go to court, may want to utilize alternative methods of settling their dispute. Alternative dispute resolution ("ADR") procedures are available to parties in this event. ADR has become increasingly common as individuals look for more cost-effective, time-efficient ways to resolve disputes rather than going to court.

§ 11.6.1   ADR procedure for residential construction disputes

Before a residential homebuyer can file a claim for a construction defect against a "contractor", the buyer must comply with the ADR procedure set out in the "Right to Repair Act" ("Act"). Its purpose is to resolve residential construction disputes, thereby avoiding legal proceedings. If a claimant files a legal action (suit or arbitration) "without first complying with the requirements" of the Act, the court or arbitrator is required, if requested by the contractor or other party to the action, to stay the action until the claimant has complied.

The Act requires that a sales contract between a residential homebuyer and a "contractor" contain the following notice:

> CONTRACTOR DISPUTES DISCLOSURE. GEORGIA LAW CONTAINS IMPORTANT REQUIREMENTS YOU MUST FOLLOW BEFORE YOU MAY FILE A LAWSUIT OR OTHER ACTION FOR DEFECTIVE CONSTRUCTION AGAINST THE CONTRACTOR WHO CONSTRUCTED, IMPROVED, OR REPAIRED YOUR HOME. NINETY DAYS BEFORE YOU FILE YOUR LAWSUIT OR OTHER ACTION, YOU MUST SERVE ON THE CONTRACTOR A WRITTEN NOTICE OF ANY

338

CONSTRUCTION CONDITIONS YOU ALLEGE ARE DEFECTIVE. UNDER THE LAW, A CONTRACTOR HAS THE OPPORTUNITY TO MAKE AN OFFER TO REPAIR OR PAY FOR THE DEFECTS OR BOTH. YOU ARE NOT OBLIGATED TO ACCEPT ANY OFFER MADE BY A CONTRACTOR. THERE ARE STRICT DEADLINES AND PROCEDURES UNDER STATE LAW, AND FAILURE TO FOLLOW THEM MAY AFFECT YOUR ABILITY TO FILE A LAWSUIT OR OTHER ACTION.

Therefore, a residential sales contract where the seller qualifies as a "contractor" as defined under the Act must contain the notice set out above. This is the case even if the seller is merely an investor who has not made any improvements to the property, since the investor may be considered to be "in the business of …selling" residential property.

§ 11.6.2   What the GAR Contract provides

Previous versions of the GAR Contract advised buyers and sellers that arbitration and mediation are available to them to resolve disputes. However, since most people are now familiar with ADR, the current GAR Contract does not reference the availability of these procedures. If parties to the GAR Contract wish to agree to want to add an agreement to arbitrate or mediate any disputes, they may use the under the contract, GAR has an Arbitration or Mediation Agreement form.[811] Alternatively, the following provision can be added to the contract to provide for such an agreement:

Special Stipulation #11-3: Agreement to arbitrate

_____ *Buyer Initials*   _____ *Seller Initials*

Buyer and Seller agree that any unresolved claim arising out of or relating to this Agreement, or the breach thereof, shall be settled by arbitration in accordance with the Commercial Arbitration Rules of the American Arbitration Association. The decision of the arbitrator shall be final and the arbitrator shall have authority to award attorneys' fees and allocate the costs of arbitration as part of any final award. The arbitration shall be conducted in accordance with O.C.G.A. § 9-1-1, et seq., and with the rules and procedures of the arbitrator.

If parties want to arbitrate disputes only as to certain matters, they can include the following special stipulation and specify which matters must be submitted to arbitration:

---

811   GAR Form F121, Arbitration/Mediation Agreement.

<u>Special Stipulation #11-4: Agreement to arbitrate particular dispute</u>

_____ *Buyer Initials* _____ *Seller Initials*

Buyer and Seller agree that any unresolved claim arising out of or relating to_____ regarding this Agreement shall be settled by arbitration in accordance with the Commercial Arbitration Rules of the American Arbitration Association. The decision of the arbitrator shall be final and may be enforced by any court having jurisdiction thereof. The arbitration shall be conducted in accordance with O.C.G.A. § 9-1-1, et seq., and with the rules and procedures of the arbitrator. Notwithstanding the above, Buyer and Seller are not obligated to arbitrate any dispute involving _____, and Buyer and Seller may pursue any and all available legal and/or equitable remedies as to such disputes.

§ 11.6.3   Agreement to arbitrate must be initialed

In order for a binding arbitration provision to be enforceable, the parties must initial it on the contract. If both parties do not initial the provision, it will be void and unenforceable. This initialing requirement is a requirement of Georgia law. [812] The purpose of this requirement is to ensure that purchasers of residential property do not give up their common law right of access to the courts unless they specifically acknowledge this intent by initialing the arbitration provision.

Therefore, if a buyer and seller desire to arbitrate any disputes which may arise between them, it is critically important that their agreement to arbitrate be initialed on the sales contract.

§ 11.6.4   Right to insist on arbitration may be waived

Parties should be aware that an agreement between them to arbitrate a dispute is waived by any action of a party which is inconsistent with the right of arbitration.[813] This means that even if parties have entered into a valid arbitration agreement, by certain conduct they can waive their right to insist on arbitration as the means to settle a dispute. For example, if a party files a lawsuit despite the existence of an arbitration agreement, the opposing party must formally ask the court by written motion to order arbitration rather than participate in the litigation.[814]

---

812   <u>Pinnacle Constr. Co., Inc. v. Osborne</u>, 218 Ga. App. 366, 460 S.E.2d 880 (1995).

813   <u>Tillman Group, Inc. v. Keith</u>, 201 Ga. App. 680, 411 S.E.2d 794 (1991);
<u>McCormick-Morgan, Inc. v. Whitehead Elec. Co.</u>, 179 Ga. App. 10, 345 S.E.2d 53 (1986), <u>cert. denied</u>.

814   O.C.G.A. § 9-6-6(a); <u>Tillman Group, Inc. v. Keith</u>, 201 Ga. App. 680, 411 S.E.2d 794 (1991).

In one Georgia case, a builder waived his right to enforce an arbitration agreement with the buyers of a house he built.[815] The buyers filed a lawsuit against the builder for breach of warranty asserting certain construction defects. The warranty agreement contained an arbitration provision specifying that any dispute arising out of the warranty would be settled by binding arbitration. After the buyers filed the lawsuit for breach of warranty, the builder responded to the lawsuit and asserted that any dispute as to the warranty must be settled by arbitration. However, the builder never filed a formal motion with the court to compel arbitration and the court heard the case and entered a judgment for the buyers. On appeal, the Georgia Court of Appeals held that the builder waived his right to enforce the arbitration agreement because rather than filing a motion to compel arbitration he participated in the litigation.

§ 11.6.5 Arbitration versus mediation

Arbitration is the most traditional form of ADR and can be either binding or nonbinding. Binding arbitration is a process in which the parties choose a neutral person or persons to hear their dispute and to render a final and binding decision or award after hearing the evidence. Nonbinding arbitration uses the same process as binding arbitration except that the decision by the arbitrator is advisory only. If either of the parties is dissatisfied with the decision they are not bound by it and may resort to litigation.

An arbitration can be arranged in a variety of different ways. In its simplest form, the parties can agree to have any neutral party hear both sides of the dispute and render a decision. Arbitrations can also be arranged through dispute resolution organizations, such as the American Arbitration Association. There are both nonprofit and for-profit organizations that provide alternative dispute resolution services. Nonbinding arbitrations are also sometimes ordered by a court, as will be explained below.

Mediation is a process in which a neutral party tries to help the parties resolve their dispute. The mediator does not have authority, however, to make a decision or impose a settlement. The mediator guides discussions and clarifies issues with the intent of producing settlement proposals which are nonbinding and which may help bring the parties closer together. The purpose of mediation is to help the parties work together to come to a mutually agreeable resolution. The most significant difference between mediation and arbitration is that the arbitrator decides for one side or another with respect to the dispute and the mediator facilitates discussion but does not render a decision.

---

815   O.C.G.A. § 9-6-6(a); Tillman Group, Inc. v. Keith, 201 Ga. App. 680, 411 S.E.2d 794 (1991).

§ 11.6.6   Selecting arbitrator

The parties' agreement to arbitrate may provide for a method of selecting an arbitrator. However, if it does not, a court may appoint an arbitrator pursuant to the Georgia Arbitration Code.[816] The arbitration provision of the GAR New Construction Purchase and Sale Agreement[817] provides that the arbitration must be settled by an arbitrator mutually agreed upon by the parties.

Typically, the parties are given a list of names and resumes of potential arbitrators. The potential arbitrators usually have some experience in the matter about which the parties have a dispute. So, for example, if the parties have a dispute about construction defects, it would not be surprising to see that most of the potential arbitrators have some type of construction background. The parties can mutually agree on an arbitrator to hear the matter, or an arbitrator will be appointed from the list they have been given. If the parties do not mutually agree on an arbitrator, each party must strike from the list the names of the arbitrators to which they object.

The rules of the organization conducting the arbitration will govern how many names each party can strike from the list of arbitrators. Once these lists are returned to the organization, it will assign an arbitrator to the case whose name was not struck from the list by either party. Some agreements between parties can require arbitration to be conducted by three arbitrators. In that circumstance, usually each party selects one arbitrator and then the two arbitrators select the third.

Buyers should be aware that contracts used by builders may contain an arbitration provision which requires that the arbitration of any disputes be conducted by a specific arbitrator or arbitration company with which the builder has a long standing or close relationship. This does not, of course, indicate that the arbiter will therefore rule in favor of the builder. However, buyers should review all arbitration provisions carefully to determine the terms and conditions of the provision and should pay particular attention to the requirement that a particular arbitrator or arbitration company be named at the execution of the agreement.

§ 11.6.7   The arbitration process

The procedures for private arbitration are also controlled by written rules and regulations of the organization conducting the arbitration. Normally, the procedure is similar to a shortened and less formal version of what would happen if the parties litigated their dispute in court.

A hearing is usually scheduled at the office of the arbitrator or at the office of the organization conducting the arbitration. At the hearing each party has an

---

816   O.C.G.A. 9-9-7.
817   GAR F23 New Construction Purchase and Sale Agreement.

opportunity to present evidence supporting his side of the story. While formal rules of evidence are not necessarily followed, each party can usually make an opening statement, present and cross-examine witnesses, and make a closing statement. If the arbitrator is experienced in the subject matter of the dispute, he may know as much as or more than the witnesses and may play an active role in asking questions about the dispute. Ultimately, the arbitrator will issue a ruling according to his own interpretation of the law and findings of fact.

§ 11.6.8   The mediation process

In the case of mediation, the process is that of negotiation with the assistance of a neutral facilitator. The mediator tries to help the parties communicate more clearly with one another rather than to focus on their "positions." The goal of mediation is to clarify the issues so as to enable parties to resolve their own differences. The mediator will usually do this by meeting with the parties together and separately to help them find some common ground.

§ 11.6.9   Advantages of ADR procedures

The most commonly cited advantages of settling disputes through ADR rather than in court include the following:

(1)   Resolving a dispute through ADR is often less time-consuming and costly than if the dispute were resolved through the traditional court system. Some arbitration companies have expedited procedures which can resolve the dispute from start to finish in as few as 45 days.

(2)   Private ADR allows the parties to select the person or persons who will arbitrate or mediate their dispute. This allows the parties to select persons who are experienced in the field.

(3)   Private ADR may also be scheduled at the convenience of the parties rather than at the convenience of the court.

(4)   Private ADR is generally private and confidential. Many parties find this aspect of ADR an appealing alternative to litigation, which makes the dispute a matter of public record.

(5)   ADR is more likely than litigation to result in relationships being preserved. In many cases, the less formal procedures create a less hostile environment.

(6)   Mediation allows the parties to reach a mutually agreeable resolution instead of having a third party decide the case.

343

§ 11.6.10   Disadvantages of ADR procedures

Although there are many advantages of ADR over lawsuits, in some cases ADR may not be desired.

(1)   Arbitration, more so than mediation, can become an expensive and time-consuming process. In addition, if the ADR method is nonbinding and the parties do not resolve their dispute, the process can actually become more expensive and time-consuming, because the expense and time of ADR is then added to the resulting litigation.

(2)   There may be cases where one of the parties would prefer to have the case heard by a jury. For example, a buyer with fraud claims for serious hidden defects may want to have the case heard by a jury, which may be more sympathetic to the emotional nature of the claims than an arbitrator.

(3)   A decision rendered in binding arbitration is not subject to review, except in limited circumstances.818 The finality of the process can be seen as an advantage or disadvantage. The successful party may see it as a speedy way to resolve a dispute with finality. The losing party may honestly believe that the award was inequitable and want "another bite at the apple." Our traditional justice system allows for such appeals.

§ 11.6.11   Enforcement of binding arbitration

If a party refuses to comply with a binding arbitration award, a court must still be called upon to enforce the award. Fortunately, if a party has to resort to the courts to enforce an award, the judicial process is limited to confirming the order of the arbitrator, which does not involve a retrial of the dispute.

---

818   An application to a court to vacate an arbitration award must be made within three months after the delivery of a copy of the award to the applicant. O.C.G.A. § 9-9-13(a). The court may vacate an award only if it finds that the rights of the petitioning party were prejudiced by "(1) corruption, fraud, or misconduct in procuring the award; (2) partiality of an arbitrator appointed as a neutral; (3) an overstepping by the arbitrators of their authority or such imperfect execution of it that a final and definite award upon the subject matter submitted was not made; (4) a failure to follow the procedure of [the Georgia Arbitration Code], unless the party applying to vacate the award continued with the arbitration with notice of this failure and without objection; or (5) the arbitrator's manifest disregard of the law." O.C.G.A. § 9-9-13(b).

§ 11.6.12   Court-ordered ADR

After the filing of a lawsuit the courts in Georgia may refer cases to nonbinding processes of either arbitration or mediation, depending on the county. A number of counties in Georgia already have various procedures for what they refer to as "court-annexed ADR," and others that do not currently have such programs are planning to institute them. These programs are being developed to try to resolve as many cases as possible outside of the traditional litigation process. Court-ordered ADR does not usually prevent the parties from continuing on with their lawsuit and having their day in court if they are unable to resolve the dispute.

§ 11.6.13   When ADR is recommended

Whether a party will want to try to resolve a dispute through litigation, arbitration, or mediation will depend on the facts and circumstances of the case and the objectives of the party. As a result, many individuals will want to wait until a dispute arises before committing to a particular method for resolving the dispute.

Real estate brokers should be comfortable explaining how ADR works generally. However, they should be extremely cautious in advising clients to seek one legal method of resolving a dispute over another. Under BRRETA, brokers have a duty to advise their clients to obtain expert advice on matters which are beyond the expertise of the broker and which they are not licensed to provide. Unless a licensee has legal training, he will probably want to avoid potential liability for giving potentially bad advise concerning ADR. Rather, he should refer the client to an attorney to help make the decision on how best to resolve the dispute.

CHAPTER 12
PARTIES TO THE CONTRACT

OVERVIEW

This chapter explains the effect of a buyer or seller not signing a real estate sales contract or signing the contract in the wrong capacity.

The technical requirements for signing real estate sales contracts by different types of entities are also discussed. Sample signature blocks are provided to illustrate how corporations, partnerships, and limited liability companies should sign contracts. Signature blocks are also included to show how persons acting in representative capacities such as executors, administrators, trustees, guardians and persons holding powers of attorney should sign contracts.

Finally, this chapter discusses whether persons who are mentally incapacitated, intoxicated, or minors have the legal capacity to enter into real estate sales contracts. Issues including the death of a party to a contract are also discussed.

§ 12.1   Parties who must sign the contract

§ 12.1.1   All buyers and sellers must sign contract

In order for a real estate sales contract to be valid, the parties must sign the contract.[819] Courts will not enforce a real estate sales contract unless there is a definite and specific statement of the terms of the contract and the parties to the contract are clearly defined.[820]

The names of all of the parties to the contract should be clearly printed or typed in the body of the contract or beneath the signature lines identifying each person as a buyer or seller. If two or more persons own the property, each name should be listed as a seller and each owner should sign the contract. Likewise, each individual buyer whose name will be listed on the title must be listed as a buyer on the contract and each should sign the contract.

§ 12.1.2   Recourse against owner who signs contract

If property is owned by more than one person and only one owner signs the sales contract and the other owners do not or will not sign the contract, the party who signed the contract may be liable for damages to the buyer for failure to convey the whole property. For example, in one Georgia case, a husband contracted to sell property that he and his wife owned as co-tenants.[821] The wife never signed the sales contract. At the time of the scheduled closing, the wife refused to convey her one-half

---

819   O.C.G.A. § 13-3-1.
820   Brega v. CSRA Realty Co., 223 Ga. 724, 157 S.E.2d 738 (1967); Harris v. Porter's Social Club, Inc., 215 Ga. 687, 113 S.E.2d 134 (1960).
821   Deal v. Mountain Lake Realty, Inc., 132 Ga. App. 118, 207 S.E.2d 560 (1974).

undivided interest to the buyer. The court held that the husband was liable for money damages to the buyer because the husband failed to convey title to the whole property.

Likewise, under the GAR Contract, the seller would be liable for failure to convey good and marketable title. The GAR Contract provides that the seller warrants that at the time of closing, the seller will convey good and marketable title to the buyer by general warranty deed.[822] The seller would be liable for money damages to the buyer if she breaches this warranty and does not convey good and marketable title at closing.

Real estate brokers may avoid some of the problems that arise by requesting the seller to produce a copy of the deed by which they obtained title to the property. This will help determine who needs to sign the sales contract.

§ 12.1.3   No recourse against owner who does not sign contract

Owners who do not sign a real estate contract as sellers will not be required by the courts to convey their interest in the property.[823] For example, in the case discussed above where the husband signed the contract but his wife did not, the court required the husband to convey his one-half undivided interest in the property to the buyer. However, the court could not require the wife to convey her interest, because she had not signed the sales contract.

In a similar case, the husband signed a sales contract to convey a piece of property to a buyer.[824] However, at the time of conveyance, the property was titled solely in his wife's name. The wife had not signed the sales contract and she would not convey the property to the buyer. The court would not order her to convey the property to the buyer because she never signed the contract. In this situation, like the others discussed above, the husband could be liable for money damages to the buyer.

§ 12.1.4   Protecting buyers when sellers not properly listed on contract

The GAR Contract allows buyers to conduct a title search on the property and to present to the seller a written statement of objections affecting the marketability of the title. Pursuant to the GAR Contract, the seller must satisfy all valid title obligations prior to closing, or the buyer can terminate the contract and obtain a refund of all her earnest money.[825] The buyer may also be able to recover additional money damages from the seller. A buyer should obtain a title search to determine, among other things, the identity of the current legal owner(s) of the property.

---

822   GAR Contract, paragraph 6
823   Smith v. Tippins, 207 Ga. 262, 61 S.E.2d 138 (1950); Sandison v. Harry Norman Realtors, Inc., 145 Ga. App. 736, 245 S.E.2d 37 (1978).
824   Pryor v. Cureton, 186 Ga. 892, 199 S.E. 175 (1938).
825   GAR Contract, paragraph 6B

If all of the current title holders of the property are not listed as sellers to the contract, the buyer can request that the contract be re-executed to properly identify the sellers and/or the buyer can request that the sellers listed in the contract obtain legal title to the property before closing.

§ 12.1.5   Recourse against Buyer who signs contract

Sellers may enforce the terms of the contract against all buyers who sign the contract.[826] This means that if a buyer signs a real estate contract and later decides (improperly) not to purchase the property, the seller can sue the buyer for specific performance seeking to require her to purchase the property. However, courts will not enforce a real estate sales contract against a buyer who did not sign the contract. So, if a seller sues an individual to require her to purchase the property, the court will not require a closing on the property if the person being sued did not sign the contract to purchase the property.[827]

As a practical matter, however, specific performance claims against purchasers are difficult to maintain unless the buyer has sufficient cash to close. Irrespective of what any court may order, a purchaser may simply refuse to make a loan application. A lender may, likewise, be reluctant to issue a loan on behalf of someone whom the court has "forced" to purchase the property against her will. Accordingly, the seller's remedy is more often than not, a claim for monetary damages.

§ 12.2   Parties must sign in the right capacity

§ 12.2.1   Owner signing in wrong capacity

If an individual owns a piece of property, she should execute the sales contract by signing just her name. If a corporation or some other entity owns the property, the person signing the contract on behalf of the company must reflect her representative capacity in the signature block of the contract. However, parties will sometimes sign a contract in the wrong capacity. In one Georgia case, the buyer entered into a contract to purchase certain property from Holiday Builders, Inc.[828] The president of Holiday Builders, Inc. signed the contract on behalf of the corporation in his capacity as an officer of the corporation. The buyer later learned that the president owned the property individually and the corporation had no interest in the property.

The buyer sued both the corporation and its president to convey the property (i.e., a claim for specific performance). The court held that neither the corporation nor its president was required to convey the property to the buyer. The court ruled this way because even though the corporation signed the contract, it did not own the property and the individual who did own the property signed the contract, but in the

---

826   Golden v. Frazier, 244 Ga. 685, 261 S.E.2d 703 (1979).
827   O.C.G.A. § 13-5-30; Golden v. Frazier, 244 Ga. 685, 261 S.E.2d 703 (1973).
828   Jolles v. Holiday Builders, Inc., 222 Ga. 358, 149 S.E.2d 814 (1966).

wrong capacity. Therefore, the true and proper owner of the property had never signed the sales contract. It is likely, however, that the corporation would be liable for monetary damages even though the purchaser could not maintain an action for specific performance.

§ 12.2.2   Authorized agents or representatives

There are instances when someone other than the named party to the contract can sign the contract on the party's behalf.   Additionally, authorized representatives may sign on behalf of corporations, partnerships, limited partnerships, and limited liability companies.   In particular circumstances, executors, administrators, trustees, and guardians may sign real estate contracts for the estate, trust, or individual they represent.

The contract must identify the capacity in which a person is signing. It is important that when an agent, representative, trustee, guardian, or the like signs a contract on behalf of another, the representative names the person or entity being represented on the face of the contract and shows that she is signing the contract in a representative capacity. If the representative relationship is not clearly disclosed on the contract, the contract could be enforced against the individual acting as the agent, representative, trustee, or guardian and not against the person or entity being represented.

§ 12.3 Using a power of attorney

§ 12.3.1   Requirements for a power of attorney

An individual who has been given a power of attorney may sign a contract on behalf of any individual party who has the capacity to enter into a contract   Since a contract for the sale of land must be in writing, the power of attorney giving someone the authority to sign a real estate contract on someone else's behalf also must be in writing.[829] This is known in the law as the "equal dignity rule".[830] Oral authority will not be sufficient. Additionally, the standard Georgia form for a power of attorney as it appears in the Official Code of Georgia requires that the power of attorney be signed and sealed by a notary public if the power of attorney is being given to buy or sell land.[831]

Furthermore, if a power of attorney to sign a contract is executed after the real estate sales contract, the power of attorney will not have a retroactive effect, unless the power of attorney contains an express intention to make the power of attorney

---

829   Turnipseed v. Jaje, 267 Ga. 320, 477 S.E.2d 101 (1996); Jones v. Sheppard, 231 Ga. 223, 200 S.E.2d 877 (1973); Dover v. Burns, 186 Ga. 19, 196 S.E. 785 (1938).

830   Augusta Surgical Center, Inc. v. Walton & Heard Office Venture, 235 Ga. App. 283, 508 S.E.2d 666 (1998).

831   O.C.G.A. § 10-6-142.

retroactive.[832] For example, if the power of attorney is executed after the real estate contract is signed, the power of attorney must specifically provide that the representative had the authority to enter that specific real estate contract on behalf of the named party.

The recommended practice is for a party to grant the representative a formal power of attorney that expressly empowers the representative to execute a sales contract for a particular piece of property. If such a power of attorney is executed, the terms of the power of attorney should describe the property with the same specificity as the contract itself. Although the power of attorney may include only a general description of the property, title insurance companies are reluctant to accept such general authority for a representative to act. Therefore, merely having a general description of the property is not recommended.

The power of attorney does not have to set out the terms of the sale in detail. Instead, the law provides that representatives with a power of attorney are given the power to sell or buy property on such terms and conditions as the representative deems appropriate.[833] Nevertheless, it is best if the power of attorney states that the representative has the express power to buy and sell property on credit.

§ 12.3.2   Consequences of an insufficient power of attorney

A party who signs a contract with an insufficient or ineffective power of attorney is not bound to the contract. Therefore, individuals who deal with representatives in real estate contracts should carefully examine the representative's authority to act. If there is a written power of attorney, the party giving the power of attorney should be contacted, if possible, to confirm its authenticity. The parties may also attach a copy of the power of attorney to the sales contract.

A power of attorney must be effective at the time of exercise. If the power of attorney is very old, it is best to verify that it is still valid. The power of attorney must be signed by the property owners on record. Further, the power of attorney must contain a provision which allows the agent to execute a deed of transfer of ownership to the property as well as the power to negotiate the terms of the sale. A power of attorney terminates by express revocation, by the appointment of a new agent or by the death of the principal or agent.

If a representative signs a contract with a power of attorney when the power of attorney does not actually give the representative the authority to enter into the contract, the other party to the contract cannot sue the representative for a breach of authority if that other party could have protected herself by taking ordinary care, such

---

832   Hubert Realty Co. v. Bland, 79 Ga. App. 321, 53 S.E.2d 691 (1949).
833   O.C.G.A. § 23-2-115, 23-2-116.

as reviewing the power of attorney or contacting the party who gave the power of attorney.[834]

§ 12.3.3   Real estate brokers with power of attorney

Although real estate brokers can enter into contracts on behalf of their clients if the broker is given a power of attorney, doing so is not recommended. Brokers have a financial interest in the real estate transaction, and if they were to execute sales contracts on behalf of their clients, this might give an appearance of conflicts of interest, which could be challenged later. It is a better practice to have a third party, with no financial interest in the transaction, hold the power of attorney and execute the contract on behalf of the party.

§ 12.3.4   Spouse has no implied power of attorney to sign for other spouse

One spouse des not have a power of attorney by virtue of marriage to sign a real estate sales contract for the other spouse. Therefore, if a spouse is going to be unavailable to sign a real estate sales contract, it is best to have that spouse execute a power of attorney in favor of the other spouse.

Some builders will include a provision in their contracts that once the contract is initially signed by both spouses, the signature of one spouse thereafter on any amendment or addendum to the contract will automatically bind the other spouse. This type of provision is particularly helpful to builders when the buyers need to make multiple design selections for a new home after signing a contract. An example of this type of provision is set forth below:

Special Stipulation #12-1: One signatory has power to sign for other signatories

If two or more persons are named as Purchaser herein, any one of them is authorized to act as agent and power of attorney for, with the right to bind, the other(s) in all matters related to this Agreement, and by affixing their signatures to this Agreement, each shall be deemed to appoint the other as his or her attorney-in-fact for purchasing the Property and making revisions to this Agreement. This appointment and grant of power-of-attorney may only be terminated upon written notice to Seller, and shall only be effective upon actual receipt of said notice.

---

834   Nalley v. Whitacker, 102 Ga. App. 230, 115 S.E.2d 790 (1960); Millender v. Looper, 82 Ga. App. 563, 61 S.E.2d 573 (1950), cert. denied.

§ 12.4   When corporations sign contracts

§ 12.4.1   Individuals signing on behalf of a corporation

A contract with a corporation as a party should identify the corporation as the buyer or seller of the property and fully identify the officer executing the contract on behalf of the corporation and clearly specify that the officer is acting as a representative for the corporation and not in an individual capacity. In order for the officer's signature to clearly reflect her representative capacity, the name of the corporation must precede or follow the name and office of the corporate representative.

If the corporation and its executing officers are not fully identified, the contract may not be enforceable. For example, in one Georgia case, Porter's Social Club, Inc. owned a piece of property and the potential buyer of the property sued Porter's Social Club, Inc. asking the court to order the club to convey the property to him.[835] The buyer had signed a contract that had been executed by "Ezekiel Harvery" and "C. T. Brinson Treas." who were identified in the contract as the "Sellers." Nothing in the contract reflected that the sellers were acting on behalf of the club, and the name of the club was never mentioned in the contract. Thus, the court held that the contract was too indefinite to support an order requiring the club to convey the property.

In another case, a corporation owned a piece of property and an individual named Williamson represented to a buyer that he was the vice president of the corporation and was authorized to execute a sales contract for such property on the company's behalf.[836] The contract specified that the corporation was the seller of the property, but nothing in the body of the contract or at the signature line reflected that Williamson was acting as an agent for the company. When the buyer sued the company for conveyance of the property, the court found that Williamson had executed the contract in his individual capacity because he was not identified as an agent of the corporation anywhere in the contract and the court refused to order the company to convey the property.[837] As discussed below, if Williamson had been identified as vice president but the contract did not include the signature of a secretary or a corporate seal, then unless other actions or conduct were present, there would not be apparent authority.[838] However, the signature by an identified chief executive officer or president would bind the company absent a provision in the corporate documents taking away such authority.

§ 12.4.2   Apparent authority

Georgia law provides that a principal may authorize an agent to act on his

---

835   Harris v. Porter's Social Club, Inc., 215 Ga. 687, 113 S.E.2d 134 (1960).

836   Brega v. CSRA Realty Co., 223 Ga. 724, 157 S.E.2d 738 (1967).

837   Brega v. CSRA Realty Co., 223 Ga. 724, 157 S.E.2d 738 (1967).

838   See section 12.4.3

behalf merely by a course of conduct whereby the principal holds that person out as an agent and induces others to rely on the agent's statements.[839] Such authority is called apparent authority and it can become an issue when an agent so authorized signs a real estate contract in her capacity as agent for a corporation or other principal. When a principal's conduct leads third parties to believe that its agent has apparent authority, those third parties may bind the principal to the agent's acts.[840] Accordingly, where a corporation holds out a particular party as its agent, authorized to bind it in contract, the agent's execution of a real estate contract as corporate agent binds the corporation.

Apparent authority is based on the conduct of the principal, not of the agent, and on the reasonableness of third parties' reliance thereon.[841] A party trying to show an agent's apparent authority must establish that he relied in good faith on the principal's conduct which would lead a reasonable person to believe that a principal-agent relationship existed.[842] A principal cannot deny that its agent has authority reasonably deduced from its conduct.[843] If a corporation's actions reasonably induce a third party to believe its agent is authorized to enter into a real estate contract, and the agent does so in its capacity as corporate agent, the corporation is bound. The lesson here is that you need to be very careful about who you allow to act on your behalf and explain very clearly the limits on any representative's authority.

§ 12.4.3   President may sign for corporation

The chief executive officer or president (if there is no chief executive officer) of a corporation has the authority to sign real estate contracts on behalf of the corporation if the sale does not require approval by the board of directors or share-holders.[844] However, when all or substantially all of the assets of a solvent corporation are involved, stockholder approval is required.[845] Also, the articles of incorporation, bylaws, or a resolution of the board of directors of a corporation may authorize other officers to execute contracts on behalf of the corporation.[846] Parties may rely on resolutions of the board of directors permitting other officers to execute contracts, unless all or substantially all of the assets of a solvent corporation are involved.[847] In order to protect themselves, parties should make a full inquiry as to what percentage of the corporation's assets are involved in the sale. Assets are deemed to be all or

---

839   Ampex Credit Corp. v. Bateman, 554 F.2d 750 (5th Cir. 1977).

840   Morris v. Williams, 214 Ga. App. 526, 448 S.E.2d 267 (1994).

841   Addley v. Beizer, 205 Ga. App. 714, 423 S.E.2d 398 (1992), cert. denied, 205 Ga. App. 899 (1989).

842   APCOA, Inc. v. Fidelity Nat'l Bank, 703 F. Supp. 1553, aff'd, 906 F.2d 610 (1988).

843   Addley v. Beizer, 205 Ga. App. 714, 423 S.E.2d 398 (1992), cert. denied, 205 Ga. App. 899 (1989).

844   O.C.G.A. §§ 14-2-841, 14-2-1202.

845   O.C.G.A. § 14-2-841.

846   O.C.G.A. § 14-2-841.

847   O.C.G.A. § 14-2-1201.

substantially all of a corporation's property if they exceed two-thirds of the fair market value of all of the assets of the corporation.[848]

Although the chief executive officer or president of a corporation may have the authority to sign contract acting alone, it is better practice to have real estate sales contracts signed by two officers. Georgia law provides that the execution of a real estate contract on behalf of a corporation by the president or vice president and attested to or countersigned by the secretary, an assistant secretary, or other officer authorized to authenticate records of the corporation, conclusively establishes that: (1) the president or vice president of the corporation executing the document does in fact occupy the official position indicated; (2) the signature of such officer on the contract is genuine; and (3) the president or vice president is properly authorized to execute the document on behalf of the corporation.[849] The signature block below is an example of how a contract should be signed by a president on behalf of a corporation:

SMITH REALTY CO., INC.

By: *John Smith*_____
John Smith, President

Attest: *Jane Jones*_____
Jane Jones, Secretary

§ 12.4.4   Effect of corporate seal affixed to contract

If the board of directors of a corporation has passed a resolution authorizing an officer other than the president of its corporation to execute real estate contracts on behalf of the corporation, the corporate seal, or a facsimile thereof, should be affixed to the contract. Additionally, it is preferable and provides further authority if the signature of the secretary, assistant secretary, or other authorized officer of the corporation is also included.

This second signature called an attestation, provides evidence that: (1) the corporate seal or facsimile thereof affixed to the document is, in fact, the seal of the corporation or a true facsimile; (2) any officer executing the document does in fact occupy the official position indicated in the signature block; (3) an officer in that position is duly authorized to execute such document on behalf of the corporation; (4) the signature of the officer signing the contract is genuine; and (5) the person signing the contract on behalf of the corporation has been properly authorized by the board of directors.[850]

---

848   O.C.G.A. § 14-2-1201.
849   O.C.G.A. § 14-2-151.
850   O.C.G.A. § 14-2-151.

When the corporate seal is affixed to the contract or when the contract is executed by the president or vice president and attested by the secretary, assistant secretary, or officer authorized to authenticate corporate records, a buyer or seller entering a contract with that corporation may rely on the document and the signatures to the document as being valid unless the buyer or seller has knowledge or reason to know otherwise.[851] Although the corporate seal may be affixed to any document executed by a corporation, the absence of the seal does not automatically invalidate the document or invalidate any actions taken by a party in reliance on the contract.[852]

Where an officer of the corporation other than the president signs the contract, all necessary parties should complete the following signature block:

SMITH REALTY CO., INC.

By: ___*Ed White*_____
      Ed White, Vice-President

Attest: *Jane Jones*_____
       Jane Jones, Secretary

[CORPORATE SEAL]

§ 12.4.5   Unformed corporations have no authority to contract

Buyers and sellers should be careful not to enter a contract with an entity that may become a corporation, but that is not yet a corporation. Corporations cannot act until they are chartered and organized. If a buyer or seller enters a contract with an entity she believes to be a corporation but the corporate entity is never properly created, the buyer or seller can still enforce the contract, but not against the non-existent corporation.

The buyer or seller's only recourse is against the individuals who represented and acted on behalf of the unformed corporation. Such individuals could be personally and individually liable under the real estate contracts they sign.[853]

While parties entering contracts with purported corporations must be careful, people who intend to incorporate should also be wary of attempting to enter contracts on behalf of a corporation they have not yet formed.

For example, in one case, the owner of a theater offered to lease the theater to a corporation once the corporation was organized.[854] The theater owner and

---

851   O.C.G.A. § 12-2-151(c).

852   O.C.G.A. § 14-2-151(d).

853   O.C.G.A. §§ 14-2-204, 14-2-841; Gifford v. Jackson, 115 Ga. App. 773, 156 S.E.2d 105 (1967).

incorporators drew up a written lease. Relying on the offer to lease the theater, the individual expended money and formed the corporation. Before the final incorporation of the company and before the company could legally accept the theater owner's lease offer, the theater owner withdrew his offer.

When the corporation sued for enforcement of the lease, the court held that the corporation was not entitled to enforcement because there was no enforceable lease contract. Although the theater owner had made an offer to lease, the corporation could not have accepted the offer until it had attained the legal status of a corporate entity, by acquiring a charter and organizing the corporation. This did not occur until after the theater owner's offer was withdrawn. Because the offer was never legally accepted before it was withdrawn, no enforceable contract was ever created.[855]

In order to avoid problems with corporations that are not yet formed, parties intending to form a corporation should sign contracts in their individual capacity with the right to assign the contract to the corporation once it is created. If the future corporation enters a contract through an individual as a buyer, the contract should specify that the sale will be for cash (or the corporation must pay cash upon the transfer of the property), because the corporation will not likely be able to assume the credit terms of the individual.[856] Also, when the contract is assigned from the individual to the corporation, the assignment must be executed in the same way as a deed for an original conveyance of property.[857]

Additionally, individuals signing a contract that will later be assigned to a corporation should try to limit their personal liability if the contract is terminated. A good way to do this is to limit the other party's recourse to the earnest money deposited in the transaction.

The following special stipulation allows for an assignment of the contract but limits the recourse of the other party to the contract to the earnest money:

Special Stipulation #12-2: Limitation of liability upon assignment of contract

If Buyer assigns this Agreement to a third party and this Agreement is later terminated, for any reason whatsoever, Seller's recourse against Buyer and

---

854   R.A.C. Realty Co. v. W.O.U.F. Atlanta Realty Corp., 205 Ga. 154, 52, S.E.2d 617 (1949).

855   R.A.C. Realty Co. v. W.O.U.F. Atlanta Realty Corp., 205 Ga. 154, 52, S.E.2d 617 (1949).

856   Sims v. Cordele Ice Co., 119 Ga. 597, 46 S.E. 841 (1904).

857   O.C.G.A. § 44-5-32; Pawn World, Inc. v. Estate of Sam Farkas, Inc., 218 Ga. App. 334, 461 S.E.2d 295 (1995). The assignment must be: (1) in writing; (2) signed by the party making the assignment; (3) signed by at least two witnesses; (4) delivered to the assignee; and (5) made for good or valuable consideration; O.C.G.A. § 44-5-30.

Buyer's assignees shall be limited to the Earnest Money held by _____ (Holder) as full liquidated damages, it being acknowledged that it is impossible to more precisely estimate the specific damages to be suffered by Seller, but that the sum herein stipulated is a reasonable amount and the parties hereto expressly acknowledge and intend that this provision shall be a provision for the retention of the Earnest Money as liquidated damages and not as a penalty pursuant to the provisions of O.C.G.A. § 13-6-7, whereupon all rights, liabilities, and obligations created under the terms and provisions of this Agreement shall be deemed null and void and of no further force or effect.

Alternatively, the following special stipulation can be used in contemplation of an assignment to a yet to be formed corporation.

Special Stipulation #12-3: Seller's consent to assign to yet to be formed corporation

Seller acknowledges that Buyer intends to form and incorporate a corporation (or limited liability company) and that this Agreement will be assigned to the said corporation. For and in consideration of the sum $10.00 and other good and valuable consideration, the receipt and sufficiency of which are hereby acknowledged, Seller agrees that should Buyer form said corporation Seller shall permit the assignment of this Agreement from Buyer to said corporation (provided that Buyer is a principal thereof) and Buyer will thereafter be released from and have no further personal liability under this Agreement.

§ 12.5   When partnerships sign contracts

Pursuant to the Uniform Partnership Act, (the "Act")[858] it is not necessary to have all partners sign a real estate contract to convey partnership property, but it is best to do so. Generally, every partner is an agent of the partnership for the purpose of its business, including execution of real estate contracts.[859]

In some circumstances, however, a partner has no authority to act for the partnership.[860] Whether a partner has authority to act on behalf of the partnership can be ascertained from the statement of partnership that may be recorded in the office of the clerk of the superior court of one or more counties.[861] Although statements of partnership are not required, if filed, they may state, among other things, what

---

858   O.C.G.A. §§ 14-8-1 - 14-8-64.
859   O.C.G.A. §§ 14-8-9; 14-8-10(a).
860   O.C.G.A. § 14-8-12.
861   O.C.G.A. § 14-8-10.1(a). The statement of partnership can be filed in any county in Georgia or in more than one county. However, Georgia law does not require that a statement of partnership be filed at all.

authority the partners have or if the partners' authority differs from what is listed in the Act.[862]

According to the Act, any partner may convey title to property held in the partnership name by a contract executed in the partnership name.[863] However, if the statement of partnership or other partnership documents does not give the contracting partner the authority to convey partnership property, the partnership may be able to regain title to its property.[864]

In order to recover its property, the partnership will have to show that the contracting partner did not have the authority to convey the property and that the buyer and any subsequent purchaser knew this.[865] Where title is held in all of the individual names of the partners, all the partners must execute the contract in order to transfer all of their rights in the property.[866]

In order to avoid problems regarding a partner's authority to sign a real estate contract, when entering real estate contracts with general partnerships, a party should require all partners in the partnership to sign a Consent and Authorization.

Below is an example of a signature block to be used when an individual partner signs a real estate sales contract on behalf of her partnership:

SMITH REALTY, a Georgia Partnership

By: ___*Janet Smith*_____
Janet Smith, its Partner

§ 12.5.1   When limited partnerships sign contracts

Property owned by a limited partnership (including limited liability limited partnership) is titled in the partnership name and not the names of the individuals or entities that make up the limited partnership. Only the general partners of a limited partnership may execute real estate contracts on behalf of the limited partnership.[867] The Georgia Revised Uniform Limited Partnership Act[868] provides that general partners who sign a contract to convey property on behalf of limited partnerships are presumed to have the authority to do so, if the property is located in Georgia.

---

862   O.C.G.A. §§ 14-8-10.1(b)(5).
863   O.C.G.A. § 14-8-10.
864   O.C.G.A. § 14-8-10(a).
865   O.C.G.A. § 14-8-10(a).
866   O.C.G.A. § 14-8-10(d).
867   O.C.G.A. § 14-9-106(b).
868   O.C.G.A. § 14-9-106.

An exception to this presumption is when the general partner's authority is limited and the limitation is properly recorded in a certificate of limited partnership. To be valid, a copy of the certificate of limited partnership must be certified by the secretary of state and filed with and recorded in the superior court clerk's office in the county where the property is located.[869] The certificate can be obtained by searching the land records of the county in which the property is located. Once the certificate is obtained, the other party to the contract can confirm the general partner's authority.

If the general partner does not have the necessary authority, the contract may not be enforceable against the limited partnership. Like with general partnerships when entering real estate contracts with limited partnerships, a party should require that all partners sign a Consent and Authorization.

Below is an example of a signature block to be used when a general partner signs a real estate contract on behalf of the limited partnership:

> SMITH-JONES HOMES,
> a Georgia Limited Partnership (or Limited Liability Limited Partnership)
>
> By: SMITH BUILDERS, INC., its General Partner
>
> By: *John Smith*_____
>   John Smith, President
>
> Attest: *Jane Jones*_____
>   Jane Jones, Secretary

§ 12.6   When limited liability companies sign contracts

Unless the articles of organization provide otherwise, every member of a limited liability company is an agent of the company and may execute real estate contracts on its behalf.[870] Contracts signed by a member of a limited liability company on behalf of the company are binding on the company unless the contracting member of the company has, in fact, no authority to act for the company and the other party to the contract knows this.[871] The members' rights or limitations to bind the company in a real estate contract can be found in the company's articles of organization which are filed with the secretary of state.[872]

---

869   O.C.G.A. § 14-9-106(c).
870   O.C.G.A. § 14-11-301.
871   O.C.G.A. § 14-11-301(a).
872   O.C.G.A. § 14-11-203.

The articles of organization of a limited liability company may provide that all powers of management of the company are vested only in one or more manager(s).[873] If this is the case, no member, acting solely in her capacity as a member, may execute a real estate contract on behalf of the limited liability company. Instead, only the manager(s) may enter real estate contracts on behalf of the limited liability company.[874]

Parties who deal with limited liability companies should be aware that if any limitations on the authority of any or all of the members or managers are set forth in the articles of organization and properly recorded with the secretary of state, the limitations will be conclusively binding against the party dealing with the limited liability company.[875] For example, if a member of a limited liability company contracts to sell property owned by the company to a buyer, and the articles of organization (which are properly filed in the secretary of state office) prohibit the members from conveying property on behalf of the limited liability company, the buyer would not have any recourse against the limited liability company for conveyance of the property. In a situation like this, the buyer is deemed to have known that the member had no authority to sign the contract because the buyer could have obtained and reviewed the articles of organization.

In order to ensure that the party signing a contract on behalf of the limited liability company has the authority to do so, a copy of the company's articles of organization can be obtained from the secretary of state.

Additionally, for restrictions on members' or managers' authority to be conclusively presumed against a grantee, a copy of the articles of organization certified by the secretary of state must be filed with and recorded in the superior court clerk's office where the property is located.[876] In such cases, anyone searching the land records can obtain a copy of the articles of organization and confirm the authority of the person contracting on behalf of the limited liability company. A sample of the signature block for a contract being executed by a limited liability company is shown below:

SMITH REALTY SERVICES, L.L.C.

By: *John Smith*
John Smith, its Manager

§ 12.7 Fiduciaries: executors, administrators, trustees, and guardians

With the permission of the appropriate probate court, an executor, administrator, trustee, or guardian who has the power to sell property held by the estate

---

873   O.C.G.A. § 14-11-301(b).
874   O.C.G.A. § 14-11-301(b).
875   O.C.G.A. § 14-11-302.
876   O.C.G.A. § 14-11-302.

of a deceased person, the trust, or the minor she represents may sell the property privately instead of through auction, as is otherwise required.[877] So long as she has the consent of the probate court, the executor, administrator, trustee, or guardian may execute a real estate contract to sell the property or sign a power of attorney authorizing someone else to sell the property.[878]

In order to ensure that an executor, administrator, trustee, or guardian has the authority to sell property, a search of the court records should be conducted in the appropriate probate court. The probate judge should have signed an order of the court permitting the sale of the property and the signed order should be filed with the probate records. If no order is found, the other party to the contract should require that such an order be obtained prior to closing.

If the executor, administrator, trustee, or guardian sells property at a public sale, the contract to buy or sell the property becomes binding and subject to enforcement "upon the fall of the auctioneer's hammer."[879]

§ 12.7.1   When executors sign contracts

Executors of an estate may sell property owned by the estate upon the approval of the appropriate probate court judge.[880] Where there is more than one executor, each one should sign the real estate contract.[881] Unless the terms of a will provide otherwise, one executor cannot bind the estate to a real estate contract unless the co-executor(s) has also signed the contract.[882]

If an executor enters a contract on behalf of the estate without the signature(s) of the other executor(s), even though the estate might not be bound to the contract, the contracting executor could be obligated individually for the contract.[883] The signature block below should be used when contracting with an estate's executor. More than one of the following signature blocks should be drafted at the end of the contract if there is more than one executor:

---

877   O.C.G.A. § 23-2-115, 23-2-116, 53-8-34.
878   O.C.G.A. § 10-6-4, 29-2-21.
879   Stanley v. Whitmire, 233 Ga. 675, 212 S.E.2d 845 (1975); Smith v. Tippins, 207 Ga. 262, 269, 61 S.E.2d 138, 143 (1950).
880   O.C.G.A. § 53-8-34.
881   First Nat'l Bank & Trust Co. v. McNatt, 141 Ga. App. 6, 232 S.E.2d 356 (1977); Harrison v. Carpenter, 72 Ga. App. 149, 33 S.E.2d 274 (1945).
882   First Nat'l Bank & Trust Co. v. McNatt, 141 Ga. App. 6, 232 S.E.2d 356 (1977).
883   First Nat'l Bank & Trust Co. v. McNatt, 141 Ga. App. 6, 232 S.E.2d 356 (1977).

Jane Jones, Executor

Jane Jones
As Executor under the Last Will and
Testament of Mary Brown, Deceased

§ 12.7.2   When administrators sign contracts

Administrators of an estate may also sell property belonging to the estate with a court order entered by the probate judge. A sale without an order from the probate court is void and conveys nothing to the buyer.[884] When an administrator signs a contract, the signature block should look like the following:

John Smith, Administrator

John Smith
As Administrator under the Last Will
and Testament of Mary Brown, Deceased

Additionally, neither an administrator nor an executor can bind the estate to any type of warranty in any real estate contract (including warranty of title) made on behalf of the estate. This means that in conveying property, an executor or administrator does not sign a warranty deed or limited warranty deed. Rather, she signs a special executor's or administrator's deed to convey title to a buyer. Similarly, the administrator or executor will not be personally bound by any such warranty unless the intent to create personal liability is expressly stated in the contract.[885]

§ 12.7.3   When trustees sign contracts

Trustees may be expressly authorized by the instrument creating the trust to sell or convey property of the trust. However, if no statement of such authority is included in the documents, the trustee may sell the trust's property only upon an order issued by the appropriate superior court permitting the sale.[886]

Like executors and administrators, trustees may not be personally liable on any warranty made in any conveyance of property lawfully sold, unless the trustee expressly undertakes such liability.[887] In conveying property from a trust, the following signature block should be used:

---

884   Porter v. LaGrange Banking & Trust Co., 187 Ga. 528, 1 S.E.2d 441 (1939).

885   O.C.G.A. § 53-8-48.

886   O.C.G.A. § 53-12-257.

887   O.C.G.A. § 53-12-1912.

Jane Jones, Trustee

Jane Jones
As Trustee for Samuel Brown

§ 12.7.4   When guardians sign contracts

A guardian may sell, lease, encumber, or exchange her ward's property only by order of the appropriate probate court and upon such terms as the court may order.[888] To avoid personal liability, the guardian should sign a real estate contract in the following manner:

Janet Smith, Guardian

Janet Smith
As Guardian of the property of
Dick Brown, a minor child

§ 12.8 Capacity of the parties to enter into contracts

For a valid sale of land, there must be a seller and buyer who must be persons or legal entities capable of contracting. The parties must have the legal capacity to act. Parties without the legal capacity to act include minors and mentally incompetent persons.

§ 12.8.1   Minors

The age of legal majority for all Georgia residents is 18 years; until that age, all persons are minors.[889]

§ 12.8.1.1   Students residing in Georgia

An individual is not automatically a resident of Georgia when she is in Georgia for the purpose of attending school.[890] In fact, a person in Georgia only to attend school may be considered a minor in Georgia (even though she may be 18 years old) if the student's home state has a legal age of majority that is beyond 18.

The student's home state residence will be the state in which her parents reside if under the laws of that state she would still be considered a minor and if she is incapable of proving her emancipation.[891]

---

888   O.C.G.A. § 29-2-3.
889   O.C.G.A. § 39-1-1.
890   O.C.G.A. § 39-1-1.
891   O.C.G.A. § 39-1-1.

§ 12.8.1.2 Contract of minor voidable upon majority

The age upon which a person reaches majority is significant because generally, when a minor reaches majority age, she can choose to void any contract she entered while still a minor.[892] Similarly, a minor may disaffirm a deed, security deed, bill of sale to secure debt, or any other conveyance of property or interest in property when she reaches majority.[893] However, if a minor receives property through a contract and after she reaches age 18, she retains possession of the property or interest in the property, she shall have ratified or affirmed the original conveyance and it shall continue to be binding on her.[894]

Similarly, upon reaching majority, minors may take back property from certain purchasers that they had conveyed during minority.[895] Minors must reclaim such property within a reasonable time after attaining majority. If the minor fails to reclaim her property within a reasonable time, the right to do so will be lost. What constitutes a reasonable time depends on the facts and circumstances of each situation, but it will not be longer than seven years after the minor reaches majority.[896]

§ 12.8.1.3 Contracting with a minor

The right of a minor to disaffirm a contract is a personal privilege[897] that the other party to the contract does not have. In addition, the other party to the contract cannot use the fact that she contracted with a minor to get out of the contract herself unless she did not know of the person's minority status at the time of the contract.[898] Accordingly, contracts by adults or other entities made with minors are generally enforceable against the adults or legal entities, but not against the minors.[899]

Before entering a real estate contract with a minor, parties should seek legal advice in order to determine how best to protect themselves from future loss as a consequence of the transaction.

§ 12.8.2 Mentally incompetent persons

The status of contracts entered into by persons who are insane, mentally ill, mentally retarded, or mentally incompetent varies. The status depends on whether a

---

892 O.C.G.A. § 13-3-20; Clemons v. Olshine, 54 Ga. App. 290, 187 S.E. 711 (1936).

893 O.C.G.A. § 44-5-41.

894 O.C.G.A. §§ 13-3-20, 44-5-41.

895 Ware v. Mobley, 190 Ga. 249, 9 S.E.2d 67 (1940).

896 Holbrook v. Montgomery, 165 Ga. 514, 141 S.E. 408 (1928); McGarrity v. Cook, 154 Ga. 311, 114 S.E. 213 (1922).

897 O.C.G.A. §§ 13-5-2, 13-5-3.

898 O.C.G.A. § 13-5-3; Smith v. Smith, 36 Ga. 184, 91 Am. Dec. 761 (1867).

899 Hughes v. Murphy, 5 Ga. App. 328, 63 S.E. 231 (1908).

court has made a legal determination about the individual's mental competency and capability of managing their affairs and whether the court has appointed a guardian to handle the person's affairs.[900]

A person is mentally incompetent if she has a total deprivation of reason.[901] If someone is mentally incompetent, contracts which she enters are voidable,[902] which means that they are not automatically void, but they are capable of being declared void at a later time, even if the other party to the contract had no notice of the person's incompetence.[903]

Additionally, the contract of a person who is mentally incompetent, even though not legally adjudged so, is voidable after her death upon the instance of her legal representative[904] or heirs at law.[905] Conversely, contracts entered into by a mentally incompetent person could be determined enforceable at a later date.

§ 12.8.2.1 *Contracting with a mentally incompetent person with guardian*

Once a person is legally declared mentally incompetent and the affairs of the person are vested in a guardian, the power of the person to contract, even though the person is later restored to sanity, is lost. Any contracts made by the mentally incompetent person are absolutely void until the guardianship is dissolved.[906] However, the guardian may enter contracts on the mentally incompetent person's behalf.

§ 12.8.2.2 *Contracting with a mentally incompetent person without a guardian*

The validity and enforceability of a contract with someone adjudicated mentally incompetent, but without a guardian, is dependent upon the person's sanity at the time of the execution of the contract.[907] The law presumes that such a person continues to be mentally incompetent and the contract is void. It is the obligation of the person who contracts with someone who has been adjudicated as mentally incompetent to prove that the individual was sane at the time the contract was executed or that the person entered the contract during a lucid interval.[908]

---

900 O.C.G.A. § 13-3-24.
901 Slaughter v. Heath, 127 Ga. 747, 57 S.E. 69 (1907).
902 Sewell v. Anderson, 197 Ga. 623, 30 S.E.2d 102 (1944).
903 Sewell v. Anderson, 197 Ga. 623, 30 S.E.2d 102 (1944); Herrin v. George, 183 Ga. 77, 187 S.E. 58 (1936).
904 Morris v. Mobley, 171 Ga. 224, 155 S.E. 8 (1930).
905 Dean v. Goings, 184 Ga. 698, 192 S.E. 826 (1937); Warren v. Federal Land Bank, 157 Ga. 464, 122 S.E. 40 (1924).
906 O.C.G.A. § 13-3-24.
907 Strickland v. Chewning, 227 Ga. 333, 180 S.E.2d 736 (1971).
908 Strickland v. Chewning, 227 Ga. 333, 180 S.E.2d 736 (1971); Georgia Power Co. v. Roper, 201 Ga. 760, 41 S.E.2d 226 (1947).

Additionally, a contract with a mentally incompetent person will automatically be considered valid and binding whenever it is shown that the terms of the contract have been subsequently ratified either expressly or by implication by words or conduct of the mentally incompetent person during a lucid interval, or if the mentally incompetent person's personal representative later confirms the contract.[909]

If you are unsure about a person's mental capacity to contract, you could request that a doctor examine the person. If it is determined that the person is sane, the doctor's report can be used later to prove the validity of the contract. Short of a doctor's examination, you may want to ask the person some questions at the time the person is executing the contract.[910] The questions should be asked and answered in front of two or three witnesses who are not related to the transaction. The witnesses could also sign the contract under a statement showing that they attest to the sanity or lucidity of the party being questioned.

§ 12.8.2.3 Voiding a contract with a mentally incompetent person

A party with whom an incompetent person contracts cannot get out of the contract simply because the other person is incompetent. Even though a party did not know the other party was mentally incompetent and entered the contract in good faith, the party may not be relieved of her obligations under the contract on the basis of the other party's incompetence. Parties contract at their own peril and must bear the loss if necessary.[911]

§ 12.8.2.4 Voided contracts may require restitution from mentally incompetent person

Generally, when the contract is voided by a mentally incompetent person, such person must restore the other party to the position she was in prior to entering into the contract. However, if the other party was aware that the person was incompetent at the time of the contract, such restoration is not required.[912]

---

909   Norfolk Southern Corp. v. Smith, 262 Ga. 80, 414 S.E.2d 485 (1992); Bunn v. Postell, 107 Ga. 490, 33 S.E. 707 (1899); Watkins v. Stulb & Vorhauer, 23 Ga. App. 181, 98 S.E. 94 (1919).
910   Questions to ask the party you believe could be mentally incompetent should include the following: What is your birth date? Do you know how old you are? Do you know what the date is today? Do you want to sell your house? Do you understand that if you sign this document, you will be forced to sell your house? Where do you live now?
911   Norfolk Southern Corp. v. Smith, 262 Ga. 80, 414 S.E.2d 485 (1992); Williford v. Swint, 183 Ga. 375, 188 S.E. 685 (1936); Watkins v. Stulb & Vorhauer, 23 Ga. App. 181, 98 S.E. 94 (1919).
912   Metter Banking Co. v. Millen Lumber & Supply Co., 191 Ga. App. 634, 382 S.E.2d 624 (1989).

Before entering a real estate contract with a person whose mental capacity is at issue, parties should obtain legal advice in order to determine how to best protect themselves from future loss as a consequence of the transaction.

§ 12.8.3   Intoxicated persons

A contract made by a voluntarily intoxicated person is valid, unless the intoxication was so great that the person was deprived of all reason and the other party had notice of this condition.[913]

If the other party brought about the intoxication, the intoxicated person can avoid the contract. Alternatively, the intoxicated party can approve or ratify the contract either expressly or by acting in a way consistent with the terms of the contract.[914]

§ 12.8.4   Persons who do not speak (or read) English

What should be done when the buyer or seller does not speak or read the English language? It is incumbent upon someone who does not read English to arrange for a translator to truly and accurately convey to them the terms of the sales contract and any other documents related to the transaction.

A real estate agent proficient in the seller's or buyer's native tongue may be tempted to act as the translator. While the agent can certainly assist in this regard, it is strongly recommended that the agent advise his or her client to have someone else, perhaps a friend, attorney, or professional translator, perform this function. English does not translate easily into some languages, and it is not unheard of for an unhappy buyer or seller to claim that the real estate agent either failed to accurately translate the contract or neglected to include some important point in the translation.

If a buyer or seller does not speak or read English but refuses to obtain the services of a qualified translator, it may be a good idea for the real estate agent to have the following warning translated into the client's native language and have it signed by the client:

> The sales contract you are about to enter into concerns your legal rights and liabilities related to the purchase and sale of _____(property address). Because this document is written in English, you are strongly encouraged to retain the services of an independent qualified translator. By signing below, you acknowledge that you have not relied upon _____ (name of agent or broker) to act as your translator in this matter.

---

913   Weldon v. Colquitt, 62 Ga. 449, 35 Am. Rep. 128 (1879); Abbeville Trading Co. v. Butler, Stevens & Co., 3 Ga. App. 138, 59 S.E. 450 (1907); .

914   O.C.G.A. § 13-3-25.

§ 12.9 Substitution of parties to contract

Real estate sales contracts may provide for the future substitution of new parties.[915] The GAR Contract provides that it is binding upon the parties to the contract, their heirs, successors, legal representatives, and permitted assigns. Any assignment must be signed by all of the parties to the contract, and all of the terms and conditions of the contract will be binding upon the assignee.

§ 12.10 Death of a party to contract

The GAR Contract provides that it shall be for the benefit of and binding upon the parties and their heirs, successors, legal representatives, and assigns. Therefore, when either a buyer or seller dies before the real estate contract she executed is consummated and where there is no administrator or executor appointed to represent the estate, the heirs at law may enforce the contract.

For example, in one Georgia case, an individual contracted to purchase property and died before the closing.[916] There was no legal representative or administrator for the decedent's estate. The court held that the heirs of the decedent could sue the seller and force the seller to execute a warranty deed to the decedent's estate for the property which the decedent had contracted to buy before his death.[917]

Similarly, Georgia law allows the seller of property to enforce a real estate contract against a decedent's estate through the decedent's heirs at law, unless the contract executed by the seller and the decedent states otherwise.[918] For instance, when a person contracts to sell her property and dies before the closing, the buyer may sue the heirs of the decedent/seller to force them to convey the property.[919] In one Georgia case, a seller entered an option contract with a buyer for certain property owned by the seller.[920] The seller died before the sale was consummated, and the buyer sued the seller's surviving heirs because the seller died without a will. The court held that the contract was enforceable against the seller's heirs and they were required to comply with the terms of the contract and convey the property to the buyer.[921]

---

915   Pearson v. Courson, 129 Ga. 656, 59 S.E. 907 (1907).

916   Gaskins v. Vickery, 234 Ga. 833, 218 S.E.2d 617 (1975).

917   O.C.G.A. § 53-7-98; Gaskins v. Vickery, 234 Ga. 833, 218 S.E.2d 617 (1975).

918   O.C.G.A. § 53-3-1, 53-3-8 to 53-3-14, 53-3-19, 53-3-20.

919   O.C.G.A. § 53-7-9; Harper v. Georgian Villa, Inc., 222 Ga. 130, 149 S.E.2d 90 (1966).

920   Harper v. Georgian Villa, Inc., 222 Ga. 130, 149 S.E.2d 90 (1966).

921   Harper v. Georgian Villa, Inc., 222 Ga. 130, 149 S.E.2d 90 (1966).

§ 12.11 Selling property not yet owned

The GAR Contract provides that the seller warrants that at the time of closing, the seller will convey to the buyer good and marketable title to the property. Thus, a seller is not prevented from contracting to sell property for which she does not have title at the time the contract is executed, so long as the seller obtains title before the specified time of conveyance in order to complete the sale.[922]

If the seller fails to obtain title to the property before the closing date, the seller will be liable in damages to the buyer for failure to convey the property.[923] In such a situation, the seller cannot be required to sell the property to the buyer, because the seller does not own the property, but the seller could be liable to the buyer for money damages.[924]

Additionally, the GAR Contract provides that prior to closing, the buyer may examine the title and furnish the seller with a written statement of objections affecting the marketability of the title. The seller must satisfy all valid title objections prior to closing, or the buyer may terminate the contract and obtain a refund of all of her earnest money.

For this reason, some sellers will want to limit their liability in the event they are unable to convey good and marketable title to the buyer. The first special stipulation below limits the seller's liability to the return of the buyer's earnest money if the seller cannot convey good and marketable title to the buyer at closing. The second special stipulation listed below limits the seller's liability to the return of the buyer's earnest money and the reimbursement of any and all of the buyer's actual expenses.

Special Stipulation #12-4: Seller's liability limited to return of earnest money if Seller cannot convey title at closing

Buyer has paid to _____ ("Holder") earnest money of $_____ check, which has been received by Holder, as set forth in Paragraph 3 of this Agreement. In addition to all other terms and conditions of said Paragraph 3, in the event that Seller cannot convey good and marketable title to Buyer at closing, Holder shall return to Buyer said earnest money, which shall constitute liquidated damages in full settlement of all claims of Buyer.

---

922   Northington-Munger-Pratt Co. v. Farmers Gin & Warehouse Co., 119 Ga. 851, 47 S.E.200 (1904); Williams v. Bell, 126 Ga. App. 432, 190 S.E.2d 818 (1972).

923   Northington-Munger-Pratt Co. v. Farmers Gin & Warehouse Co., 119 Ga. 851, 47 S.E.200 (1904); Williams v. Bell, 126 Ga. App. 432, 190 S.E.2d 818 (1972).

924   Smith v. Hooker/Barnes, Inc., 253 Ga. 514, 322 S.E.2d 268 (1984).

Special Stipulation #12-5: Seller's liability limited to return of earnest money and reimbursement of actual expenses if Seller cannot convey title at closing

Buyer has paid to _____ ("Holder") earnest money of $_____ check, which has been received by Holder, as set forth in Paragraph 3 of this Agreement. In addition to all other terms and conditions of said Paragraph 3, in the event that Seller cannot convey good and marketable title to Buyer at closing, Holder shall return to Buyer said earnest money and Seller shall pay to Buyer all of Buyer's actual expenses associated with this Agreement up to $_____, which shall constitute liquidated damages in full settlement of all claims of Buyer.

The contract may be entered into conditionally upon the seller's ability to acquire title prior to closing. However, as discussed above, if the contract is not conditional, the seller will be liable in damages for breach of contract if she is unable to secure title to the property in time to make delivery of it at the closing.[925]

Special Stipulation #12-6: Contract contingent on Seller obtaining title to property

The parties hereto acknowledge that the Seller does not presently have good and marketable title to the Property. This Agreement is contingent upon the Seller obtaining good and marketable title to the Property prior to the closing date or any extension thereof. In the event the Seller is unable to timely obtain good and marketable title to the Property then Buyer, in his or her sole discretion, may terminate this Agreement upon notice to Seller, in which case Holder shall promptly disburse all earnest money in accordance with the Earnest Money paragraph of this Agreement.

In many of the cases cited in this chapter, the buyers could have protected themselves at the beginning of the contract period by conducting a title search on the property they were planning to purchase. The title search would have disclosed the identity of all legal owner(s) of the property and/or whether the contracting party had the authority to execute a contract for the conveyance of the property. In all situations where the buyer contracted with incorrect parties, the buyer could have raised title obligations, which the seller would have been obligated to remedy before closing. If the title objections were not remedied by closing, the buyer would then have a good claim for breach of contract against the individual who represented that she owned the property. In Georgia, most buyers do not take these steps to protect themselves, but a

---

925   Northington-Munger-Pratt Co. v. Farmers Gin & Warehouse Co., 119
       Ga. 851, 47 S.E.200 (1904); Horn v. Wright, 157 Ga. App. 408, 278
       S.E.2d 66 (1981); Williams v. Bell, 126 Ga. App. 432, 190 S.E.2d 818 (1972).

little work before entering a real estate contract could save a great deal of time and heartache later.

§ 12.12 Facsimile copies and signatures

Georgia law provides that any contract for sale of real estate, or any interest in, or concerning real estate must be in writing and signed by the party against whom it is being enforced. Does a real estate sale contract which contains only faxed signatures satisfy this requirement? The answer is yes. Georgia law provides that when the law requires something to be in writing, an electronic record satisfies that legal requirement.[926] The law also recognizes the legality of electronic signatures.[927]

The GAR Contract states that all notices, including demands, pursuant to the contract, shall be in writing signed by the party giving the notice and may be delivered by facsimile transmission.[928] When sending notices by fax, the notice is deemed to have been given as of the date and time it is transmitted, if the sending facsimile produces a written confirmation with the date, time and telephone number to which the notice was sent.

When sending notice to a party by way of the real estate broker with whom that party is working, care should be taken to note whether a client or customer relationship exists. This is because notice to a broker is deemed to be notice to a party with whom the broker is working as a client. It is not, however, deemed to be notice to a party with whom the broker is working as a customer.

---

926   O.C.G.A. § 10-12-4(c)
927   O.C.G.A. § 10-12-4(a)
928   GAR Contract, paragraph 11G

CHAPTER 13
REAL ESTATE COMMISSIONS

OVERVIEW

This chapter discusses the broker's right to claim a commission contractually and under the doctrines of procuring cause and quantum meruit. It also discusses how the GAR Contract and other form contracts provide for the broker's commission.

§ 13.1 What the GAR Contract provides about commissions

§ 13.1.1 Amount of commission to be set out in a separate agreement

The GAR Contract does not state the amount of the commission to be paid to the broker. Instead, it provides for the seller to pay the broker's commission pursuant to a separate agreement or agreements.[929] The amount of the commission is typically stated in the listing agreement. If the commission is to be shared between brokers, the sharing arrangement is controlled by an agreement to cooperate between the brokers. In listing property in a multiple listing service ("MLS") the listing broker is offering to cooperate with other members of the MLS (on the terms stated in the MLS) if they procure the buyer who purchases the property.

It is important that the amount of the commission actually be set out in at least one document.[930] As noted, in most cases this document will be the listing agreement. There are, however, situations where no listing agreement exists. In one case the broker used a generic "listing sheet" instead of a listing agreement.[931] The listing sheet contained all the critical information regarding the property, but did not state the amount of commission to be paid. The court reviewed the GAR Contract and noted that it referenced that the amount of the commission was to be stated in a separate agreement or agreements. The court then scrutinized the listing sheet and several other documents submitted by the broker, but could not find the amount of the commission spelled out in any of these documents. Accordingly, the court denied the broker's claim.

A similar situation could arise if owner lists the property for sale and the broker does not obtain confirmation from the seller as to the amount of commission that will be paid. Brokers should use the GAR Authorization to Show Unlisted Property form[932] in these situations to avoid a commission dispute with the FSBO seller.

---

929 GAR F20, paragraph 10B. Brokers may use the appropriate brokerage contracts, such as GAR forms F1-F10.
930 See section 13-1-8.
931 Mitchell Realty Group, LLC. v. Holt, 266 Ga.App. 217, 596 S.E.2d 625 (2004)
932 GAR F3

§ 13.1.2   Brokerage provision ensures payment of commission

The GAR Contract provides for the seller to pay the commission to the listing broker, which is the custom in Georgia. It goes on to state that the selling broker will receive a portion of the Listings Broker's commission pursuant to a cooperative brokerage agreement.[933] Since the GAR Contract provides for the seller to pay the broker's commission, a buyer will generally not be liable for the commission. The courts will, however, enforce provisions in the sales contract or other agreements[934] stating that the buyer has agreed to be liable for the payment of the broker's commission.[935]

The GAR Contract also provides that if the sale is not closed due to the default of the buyer or seller, then the defaulting party is liable for the broker's commission.

§ 13.1.3   The GAR Exclusive Buyer Brokerage Agreement

The GAR Exclusive Buyer Brokerage Agreement[936] is used by real estate brokers representing buyers as clients.[937] The GAR Buyer Brokerage Agreement provides that the selling broker will seek to be paid a commission from the listing broker or from the seller in any transaction. However, in the event that neither the seller nor listing broker pays a commission, then the buyer will be liable to the selling broker for its commission in an amount stated in the GAR Buyer Brokerage Agreement.

It is important to note, however, that the commission stated in the GAR Buyer Brokerage Agreement applies only if no other commission is paid. For example, a GAR Buyer Brokerage Agreement may state that the buyer will pay the broker representing the buyer a commission equal to 3% of the purchase price if he or she is not otherwise paid a commission. The broker for the buyer finds a property for the buyer where the commission due to the broker for the buyer equals 2.5% of the purchase price of the property. Once the broker for the buyer has accepted the commission from the listing broker, no further commission is owed. This remains the case even though the broker received a commission smaller than the 3% of the purchase price commission.

Selling brokers should be certain to complete the commission amount in the GAR Buyer Brokerage Agreement. If this provision of the Agreement is left blank or

---

933   GAR F20, paragraph 10B.
934   The GAR Exclusive Buyer Brokerage Engagement is an example of an agreement
        in which the buyer obligates himself to pay a commission under limited
        circumstances when the seller or listing broker does not pay the commission.
935   Milton v. Austin, 124 Ga. App. 657, 185 S.E.2d 551 (1971); Harling v. Tift, 43 Ga.
        App. 94, 157 S.E. 914 (1931).
936   GAR F4.
937   See Chapter 16 on the types of agency relationships under BRRETA.

contains "N/A" or "0", then the selling broker will not be able to recover anything from the buyer in the event that no commission is paid by the seller or listing broker.

§ 13.1.4   Brokers may pursue independent commission claims

The GAR Contract provides that each broker in a cooperative transaction may pursue an independent claim for a commission in the event of a breach by either the buyer or seller. This means that either broker may, independently or jointly, pursue the defaulting party for its commission. Therefore, each broker can make an independent business decision as to whether to file suit for his commission in a given situation. The following example explains the value of such a provision.

Example: The listing agreement provides that the total commission to be paid is 7% of the purchase price of the property, with the selling broker to receive 50% of the total commission and the listing broker to receive the other 50%. The buyer gets cold feet, refuses to close on the purchase of the home, and thereby defaults under the contract. The buyer tells the selling broker that he has enjoyed working with him and wants his help in locating another home. In such a situation, the selling broker may not want to pursue his commission under this contract because he wants to continue to work with this buyer. The listing broker, however, may wish to pursue his commission and may do so under the language of the GAR Contract.

§ 13.1.5   Terms of sales contract can control listing agreement

If the broker signs a sales contract which recites a reduced commission amount, a court would probably interpret this as a concession by the broker to be paid the lower amount and would preclude any action on the listing agreement for the higher commission amount. This is because the terms of the sales contract will generally control over the listing agreement as to the commission rights, assuming the real estate broker has signed the contract.[938] The broker should therefore be careful to review the sales contract and confirm that the parties have not inserted any reduced commission amount into the contract.

The broker who is faced with a sales contract that includes a reduction in commission can take the position that the commission is non-negotiable. If that does not resolve the matter, the broker may decide not to sign the contract or to sign the contract but include a written caveat that the broker is not agreeing to any reduction in commission contained therein.

The GAR Contract also contains a provision that "[n]o representation, promise, or inducement not included in this Agreement shall be binding upon any party hereto." Therefore, absent the broker signing a GAR Contract that has been modified

---

938   Parr Realty Co. v. Carroll, 131 Ga. App. 549, 206 S.E.2d 550 (1974); Blount v. Freeman, 94 Ga. App. 110, 93 S.E.2d 820 (1956).

to reflect a lower or reduced commission, the seller will be obligated to pay the commission amount set forth in the listing agreement.[939]

§ 13.1.6   When commission rights are disputed

A question which frequently arises in the brokerage area is whether a listing broker loses any of his rights by agreeing in the contract or in a GAR Instructions to Closing Attorney form to include another broker for a commission whom the first broker does not believe is entitled to one. This issue often arises when a broker "parachutes" into the transaction at the last minute to assist the buyer in consummating the transaction.

Whether broker #1 includes broker #2 for what broker #1 believes is an undeserved commission will depend in large measure on whether the brokers are REALTORS®. This is because REALTORS® are required to submit all contractual disputes regarding real estate commissions to arbitration.[940]   REALTORS® are ethically bound to make the interests of their clients primary and ahead of their own personal financial interests.[941]   Therefore, they should not let a commission dispute disrupt the transaction. If the dispute cannot be resolved amicably, a REALTOR® will generally include another REALTOR® in the contract for a commission and then arbitrate the dispute after closing. The GAR Instructions to Closing Attorney form specifically states that including another broker for a commission on the form does not prevent either broker from arbitrating any dispute over the commission after closing.

If the broker with whom a commission dispute arises is not a REALTOR® or a member of a multiple listing service which requires the arbitration of commission disputes as a condition of membership, no obligation to arbitrate exists. Including broker #2 for a commission in the contract would likely constitute a waiver of any claim to recover the commission from broker #2 after closing. Efforts should therefore be made to resolve the dispute without including broker #2 for a commission in the contract.

§ 13.1.7   Deferred payment of real estate commission

On occasion, brokers are forced to accept a deferred payment of a real estate commission. This tends to occur when there is little equity in the property and the seller is not receiving any profits from the sale. When this occurs, brokers should always get a promissory note signed by the seller and, if possible, have it secured with a deed to secure debt on some other property owned by the seller.

---

939   Jones v. Trail Cities Realty, Inc., 160 Ga. App. 533, 287 S.E.2d 588 (1981).
940   Article 17 of the Code of Ethics and Standards of Practice of the National Association of REALTORS®, 2005 edition.
941   Article 1 of the Code of Ethics and Standards of Practice of the National Association of REALTORS®, 2005 edition.

§ 13.1.8   Terms of Brokerage agreement must be clear

The terms of the brokerage agreement must be clear in order for the agreement to be enforceable. This is illustrated in the following case.[942]

The property was listed with a broker. The prospective buyer, who was looking for a site for a car dealership, saw the 'for sale' sign and called the broker. The broker then acted as dual agent in the transaction. The buyer later decided that the property was not a suitable site for a car dealership and the broker sued the buyer for the alleged 10% commission.

The broker, buyer and seller had entered into a contract of sale, which provided that:

> "The Broker(s) identified herein have performed valuable brokerage service and are to be paid a commission pursuant to a separate agreement or agreements. Unless otherwise provided for herein, the Seller will pay the Listing Broker a commission, and the Selling Broker will receive a portion of the Listing Broker's commission pursuant to a cooperative brokerage agreement.... In the event the sale is not closed because of Buyer's and/or Seller's failure or refusal to perform any of their obligations herein, the non-performing party shall immediately pay the Broker(s) the full commission the Broker(s) would have received had the sale closed, and the Selling Broker and Listing Broker may jointly or independently pursue the non-performing party for their portion of the commission."

This is the same provision as that provided in the GAR Contract.

The issue was whether the parties had entered into an enforceable brokerage agreement establishing the amount of commission to be paid. The broker argued that a separate commission agreement existed, in the form of a document entitled "Highway 515 Properties Ellijay, Georgia,". The document listed four properties, their price per acre, and their total sales price. The court ruled that this document did not constitute a brokerage agreement because it did not name the parties to the agreement; was not signed, and did not clearly establish that a commission was to be paid. Instead, the document merely stated: "*10 Acre Site is an Exclusive Right to Sell Listing--Others are Unlisted, but Seller is offering a 10% Commission on any Contract with 5% to Selling Broker.*" In reading this language, the court ruled that the seller offering a 10% commission did not apply to the 10-acre site but only to the unlisted property. Therefore, the court found that no specific commission agreement existed on the 10-acre parcel. The broker also produced another document entitled "listing sheet" which described the property but was silent on the 10% commission.

---

942   Mitchell Realty Group, LLC. v. Holt, 266 Ga.App. 217, 596 S.E.2d 625 (2004)

The Court stated that BRRETA requires a "brokerage engagement" to be in the form of "a *written* contract wherein the seller [or] buyer ... becomes the client of the broker and promises to pay the broker a valuable consideration or agrees that the broker may receive a valuable consideration from another" for brokerage services.[943] Therefore, the written brokerage engagement must, among other things, include a provision that states clearly the amount of the broker's compensation. Since there was no such document, the broker could not recover the commission.

§ 13.2 Other methods of claiming a commission

Brokers may, in certain circumstances, be entitled to a commission even if there is no written brokerage agreement. However, since this issue is currently the subject of much litigation in our courts, the safe approach should always be to get a written commission signed with a party. The law[944] should hopefully continue to recognize a broker's claim for a commission if the broker can show that he or she is the procuring cause of the sale or if the claim is justified based on the principle of quantum merit.

The Georgia Court of Appeals confirmed this recently in the case of a broker who sued for commission when the broker did not enter into a written brokerage agreement with the client.[945] The client had purchased a substantial piece of property. Instead of a written brokerage agreement, the broker claimed that there was an understanding that the broker would be paid "an amount not less than Seven Percent (7%) of the value...for the transaction." When the sale closed, the client refused to pay and the broker sued for the commission.

The broker claimed that it was entitled to a commission because it acted as the buyer's real estate agent, pursued the transaction, undertook a feasibility study of the purchase and performed other significant professional services.

The buyer argued that since state law requires a broker and his or her client to have a written brokerage agreement, the broker was not entitled to a commission in a transaction in which there was no written agreement. This argument was based on a provision under BRRETA, which defines "brokerage engagement" to mean a

---

943   O.C.G.A. § 10-6A-3
944   As this book went to press the Georgia Supreme Court granted a petition for
        certiorari in Killearn Partners, Inc. et al. v. Southeast Properties, Inc., 266 Ga.App.
        508, 597 S.E.2d 578 (2004). This issue being addressed by the Supreme Court is
        whether "the Brokerage Relationships in Real Estate Transactions Act (BRRETA),
        as amended in 2000, forecloses a broker from seeking a common-law remedy (i.e.,
        procuring cause, quantum meruit) when no written engagement agreement has been
        executed".
945   Killearn Partners, Inc. et al. v. Southeast Properties, Inc., 266 Ga.App. 508, 597
        S.E.2d 578 (2004), on appeal.

written contract.[946]   Therefore, since there was no written contract, there was no brokerage relationship, and therefore no commission was owed.

The Court of Appeals disagreed with the client's argument and stated that BRRETA does not regulate the payment of commissions. Instead, the primary purpose of BRRETA is to set out the duties and standards of skill owed by a broker. The court ruled that there is nothing in BRRETA which prevents a broker from suing for breach of an express oral contract. Neither does BRRETA eliminate the legal principles of procuring cause and quantum meruit that would allow a broker to state a claim for payment for services rendered.   Therefore, the court held that the broker could sue for its commission even without a written brokerage agreement. As noted, however, the Georgia Supreme Court recently granted certiorari in this case and is taking the issue up as this book goes to press. Readers should, therefore, check to determine whether the Court of Appeal's decision is upheld or reversed.

§ 13.2.1   Procuring Cause

The "procuring cause doctrine" entitles a broker to commission as soon as he or she is able to find a buyer who is ready, able and willing. When a broker has an exclusive right to sell listing agreement with the seller, the terms and conditions by which the broker will earn a commission are typically set out in the agreement.   The Georgia Court of Appeals have stated that where a contract expressly provided for how commissions are to be paid, the "procuring cause" doctrine does not apply.[947]

There are, however, situations where the terms of the commission are not established. This could happen, for example, under an open listing where the owner generally indicates a willingness to sell, but does not have an exclusive listing arrangement with any broker. Alternatively, there are situations where the broker and seller sign a general commission agreement that sets forth the amount of the commission, but is silent as to the circumstances upon which the commission will be deemed earned.

Under these circumstances, a real estate broker would have difficulty establishing a claim for his commission on a breach of contract theory, because no contract exists detailing how a commission is earned.   In the absence of an express contract governing the conditions under which a commission is to be paid, the real estate broker may pursue a claim as the procuring cause of the sale.[948]

However, merely locating a prospective purchaser and attempting to make a sale, without more, is generally insufficient to entitle a broker to a commission.[949] This is true even if the broker locates the ultimate purchaser of the property.[950]

---

946   O.C.G.A. § 10-6A-3
947   D.R. Horton, Inc.-Torrey v. Tausch, 2005 WL 288831 (Ga.App.)
948   B&B Realty, Inc. v. Carroll, 245 Ga.App. 44, 537 S.E.2d 183 (2000).
949   Christopher Inv. Properties, Inc. v. Cox, 219 Ga.App. 440, 465 S.E.2d 680 (1996)

In determining whether a real estate broker is the procuring cause of a sale where there is no exclusive listing to sell, the broker must prove that there were negotiations still pending between the broker and the prospective purchaser and that the owner was aware that negotiations were sill pending at the time he consummated the sale.[951] However, where the owner knowingly interferes with the negotiations between the buyer and the broker, it becomes unnecessary to show that negotiations were pending when the sale was consummated. The broker can make out a prima facie case by showing that negotiations were set on foot through his efforts, that he performed every service required by his employment which it was possible to perform, and that the failure on his part to personally consummated the sale was due to the interference of the owner.[952]

In one case the owners agreed they would pay the broker a 10% commission if the broker negotiated a sale to the United States Postal Service.[953] The Postal Service conditioned its purchase on the several contingencies, including the removal of an old house and the rezoning of the property. The seller satisfied both contingencies. However, due to intervening budget cuts, the Postal Service could no longer purchase the property. The Sellers, apparently being tired of negotiating with the Postal Service, instructed the broker to cease negotiations. Several years later the Postal Service contacted the owner directly and purchased the property. The broker learned of the sale and demanded a commission. Affirming a jury award in favor of the broker, the Court of Appeals found that the broker was responsible for bringing the buyer and seller together, that the broker was an active participant in the initial negotiations, that the budget problems that previously prevented the sale were merely a "temporary setback", that the broker performed every service he could, and that the only reason he was not part of the consummation of the sale was because the owners told him to cease any involvement.

In another case, the buyer started negotiations directly with the seller.[954] The buyer, mistakenly thinking that broker #1 had acquired the exclusive right to sell the property, ceased direct communications with the seller and began negotiating through broker #1 . After his initial negotiations failed, the buyer learned that broker #1 had only an open listing on the property. The buyer later saw a sign on the property indicating that broker #2 had the exclusive right to sell the property. The buyer started negotiations through broker #2, which led to the

---

950   Cartel Realty, Inc. v. Southern Bearings & Parts Company, 243 Ga.App. 653, 534 S.E.2d 119 (2000).

951   Christopher Inv. Properties, Inc. v. Cox, 219 Ga.App. 440, 465 S.E.2d 680 (1996)

952   Center Pointe Investments, Inc. v. Frank M. Darby Company, 249 Ga.App. 782, 549 S.E.2d 435 (2001).

953   Green v. Bowers, 229 Ga.App. 324, 493 S.E.2d 709 (1998).

954   Cartel Realty, Inc. v. Southern Bearings & Parts Company, 243 Ga.App. 653, 534 S.E.2d 119 (2000).

purchase of the property. The court found that broker #1 was not the procuring cause of the sale because he did not introduce the buyer to the property and there was no evidence that the seller colluded with the buyer to prevent broker #1 from claiming a commission.

§ 13.2.2 Quantum meruit

In cases where there is no express contract for a commission, a broker may still assert a claim under the theory of quantum meruit.[955] "Ordinarily, when one renders services or transfers property which is valuable to another, which the latter knowingly accepts, a promise is implied to pay the reasonable value thereof."[956] "A real estate broker may bring a claim for commission based upon an implied obligation to pay where the broker's services have been rendered and accepted by the beneficiary thereof."[957] It is, therefore, possible for a broker to bring a quantum meruit claim even though he was not the procuring cause of the sale.[958] The amount of his claim will be the reasonable value of his services, which may or may not be the same as the same as the amount of commission he expected to receive.[959]

In one case the broker, acting without a commission agreement, introduced the tenant and landlord, assisted with lease negotiations, and was told by the landlord that it would "be protected" with regards to its commission.[960] The owner and tenant thereafter finalized lease negotiations between themselves. The broker submitted an invoice for service rendered to the landlord, which it refused to pay. The court found that the landlord knew the broker was rendering a valuable service, that the broker expected to be paid, and that the landlord reassured the broker that it would be paid. Under these circumstances, the court held that it would be unjust to allow the landlord to escape paying the fair value of the services that it knowingly accepted.

---

955   United Controls, Inc. v. Alpha Systems, Inc., 195 Ga.App. 331, 393 S.E.2d 694 (1990) (There can be no recovery on quantum meruit when the action is based on an express contract.).

956   O.C.G.A. § 9-2-7.

957   Atlanta Apartment Investments, Inc. v. New York Life Insurance Company, 220 Ga.App. 595, 469 S.E.2d 831 (1996).

958   Christopher Inv. Properties, Inc. v. Cox, 219 Ga.App. 440, 465 S.E.2d 680 (1996); Futch v. Guthrie, 176 Ga.App. 672, 337 S.E.2d 384 (1985) (Although in a suit for a broker's commission a REALTOR® must show that he either effected the sale of property or was the procuring cause of the sale, a REALTOR® may recover in quantum meruit without such a showing for the value of his services received by and of benefit to another party)

959   Centre Pointe Investments, Inc. v. Frank M. Darby Company, 249 Ga.App. 782, 549 S.E.2d 435 (2001)

960   Centre Pointe Investments, Inc. v. Frank M. Darby Company, 249 Ga.App. 782, 549 S.E.2d 435 (2001)

CHAPTER 14
CONDOMINIUMS, HOMEOWNER ASSOCIATIONS AND OTHER FORMS OF PROPERTY OWNERSHIP

OVERVIEW

This chapter discusses some of the more complex forms of property ownership involving common ownership or management of property. These include condominiums, homeowner associations, cooperatives and timeshares. These forms of property ownership are becoming increasingly complex and varied, especially with the growth of mixed-use developments. This chapter discusses the practical and legal issues relevant to different forms of property ownership, particularly to condominiums and homeowner associations.

§ 14.1 Condominiums

§ 14.1.1 What is a condominium?

The condominium form of ownership can exist in all types of housing, including single-family detached houses, townhomes, mid-rise buildings, and high-rise buildings. The condominium form of ownership can also be applied to office and commercial space and to such facilities as parking lots, garages, marinas, and hotels. A condominium is normally created through the filing of a declaration of condominium in which property is submitted to a condominium regime.

A condominium is a form of property ownership in which owners own their individual units in fee simple, together with an undivided (or shared) ownership interest in the common elements.[961] The common elements in a condominium typically include the grounds and recreational facilities for the common benefit of all owners, which they own jointly as tenants-in-common. Limited common elements are common elements that are reserved for the exclusive use of one or more, but less than all, of the units.

In a conveyance of a single family detached home, the property being purchased is defined by the physical boundary lines of the property. These boundary lines are referenced by points or landmarks on the land itself. A condominium is different in that a unit is defined with both vertical and horizontal boundaries.[962] Legal descriptions can therefore be more easily created for stacked residential flats in a multi-family building, where the boundaries of units could not otherwise be easily defined by references on the land.

Typical vertical boundaries of a residential condominium unit might be the centerline of the wall separating a unit from an adjoining unit and the midpoint of a wall between a hallway and a unit) or the unfinished surfaces of the interior walls (i.e.,

---

961   O.C.G.A. § 44-3-71(4). Common elements are defined as all portions of the condominium other than the units.

962   O.C.G.A.§ 44-3-75(a)

the gypsum board or plaster behind the wallpaper). Horizontal boundaries refer to the upper and lower boundaries of a unit.[963] The upper horizontal boundary of a unit might include the unfinished surfaces of the gypsum board comprising the ceiling or it might extend to the underside of the roof materials. In some loft condominiums, the upper horizontal boundaries of the units include the roof joists and cross braces. The lower horizontal boundaries of a unit might be the unfinished surfaces of the interior flooring on the lowest floor of the unit (i.e., the underside of the carpet or hardwood planks) or it may be the subflooring below the interior flooring.

The common elements in a condominium include all of the property that is not a part of the units.[964] This typically includes building exteriors, landscaped areas, roads and recreational facilities. All owners of units in the condominium own a certain percentage of the common elements.[965] Sometimes the percentage of common element ownership is the same for all unit owners in the condominium and sometimes it is weighted to correspond to the size of the unit (bigger units owning a larger percentage of the common elements than smaller units).[966] In most condominiums the amount of assessments paid by the unit owner to the association corresponds to the percentage of ownership interest such owner has in the common elements of the condominium. This does not have to be the case. A condominium declaration can provide that all unit owners pay the same monthly assessment regardless of the size of their unit.[967]

---

963   In certain situations the horizontal boundaries of the units may be left undefined in the declaration. In such a condominium, an owner would hold title to all of the ground underneath his/her unit and all of the air space above it. This situation could only exist in a condominium that does not have stacked, flat units.

964   O.C.G.A. § 44-3-71(4).

965   See O.C.G.A § 44-3-78.

966   The size of the unit usually is based on heated square feet in the unit or based on the unit type. For example, the percentage of ownership interest in the common elements may be based strictly on the square footage of each individual unit. If there are 50 different size units, each unit has a different percentage of ownership in the common elements. However, in some condominiums there may be a number of units that are almost the same size and a number of units that are much bigger or smaller. Instead of dividing the percentage of ownership interest in the common elements by the square footage of each unit, the ownership percentages may be based on categories of units. Basing ownership percentages on unit types allows the developer to assign all of the small units (i.e., studios and one bedrooms) the same percentage of ownership interest, all of the medium size units (i.e., two bedroom units) a higher percentage than the smaller units and all of the large units (i.e., three bedroom or penthouse units) an even greater percentage of ownership interest.

967   In choosing which way to establish the assessment obligations, a developer must think about the realities of the budgeting process. As described in greater detail in infra note 68, the annual condominium budget will include line items for administration, management fees and insurance. Does an owner cause the association to incur more expenses in these areas because his/her unit is larger than other units? If not, is it fair to require the owner of the larger unit to pay more to the association in monthly assessments than the owner of the smaller unit? Juxtapose this with the budget line items for maintenance and reserve funds. For such

Notwithstanding the above discussion regarding percentage of ownership interest in the common elements, each unit usually has one vote.[968]

In a condominium, there also can be "limited common elements." A limited common element is a portion of the common elements reserved for the exclusive use of those entitled to use one or more, but less than all, of the units.[969] Limited common elements usually consist of such things as balconies, patios, entrance stoops, or parking spaces.[970] To some degree limited common elements are something of a legal fiction. They were created because certain property in a condominium (i.e., a balcony or patio) is not truly part of a condominium unit, as defined by its horizontal and vertical boundaries, but not really a part of the common elements, because less than all of the unit owners have the exclusive right to use the area. In order to distinguish such property from the defined unit and from the common elements, the idea of a limited common element was created.

Limited common elements may be assigned to a unit in the initial declaration or may be assigned at a later time, as long as the declaration permits the assignment of common elements to limited common elements.[971] In order to convert common element property to an assigned limited common element, the association, by and through its board of directors, must prepare and sign an amendment to the condominium declaration. Such amendment also must be executed by the unit owner(s) to whose unit the assignment is being made and such owners must pay all reasonable costs for the preparation, execution and recordation of the amendment.[972]

Once assigned, limited common elements may be reassigned (i.e., two unit owners switching parking spaces), so long as the declaration does not prohibit such reassignments.[973] In order to reassign a limited common element the owners

---

expenses it probably does make sense to require the owners of larger units pay more per month than the owners of smaller units. However, the budget is not divided up into those items that will be assessed equally among all of the units and those items that will be assessed based on the ownership percentage of the common elements assigned to each unit. When the condominium declaration is initially drafted, the developer of the condominium must decide how assessments will be allocated in that association. Changing such allocation later requires the consent of the unit owners and their mortgagees and is very difficult to accomplish.

968 There are condominiums that have weighted voting based on the unit's percentage of ownership of the common elements, but such situations are rare. Weighted voting creates logistical problems for the association during board elections and with respect to amending the condominium legal instruments. It is for this reason that most condominium declarations provide for one vote per unit, regardless of unit size or type.

969 O.C.G.A. § 44-3-71(19).

970 O.C.G.A. § 44-3-75(a)(5).

971 O.C.G.A. § 44-3-82(a).

972 See id. § 44-3-82(c).

973 See id.

requesting the reassignment must submit a written application to the association. Thereafter, the association must prepare and sign an amendment to the condominium declaration. Such amendment also must be executed by all of the unit owners affected by the reassignment and such owners must pay all reasonable costs for the preparation, execution and recordation of the amendment.[974] While there is no case law in Georgia on this point, it has long been assumed that an affected unit owner within the meaning of this code section is a party who is directly affected because the reassignment changes the limited common elements assigned to his/her unit.

§ 14.1.2   Creating a condominium

In Georgia, a condominium must be created in accordance with the Georgia Condominium Act ("GCA").[975] The GCA sets forth detailed requirements for the legal documents and disclosures required for creation of a condominium. Condominiums are created by recording a declaration of condominium, a plat of survey, and floor plans in the land records in the county in which the property is located.[976]

The declaration of condominium sets out details about the condominium, which includes the metes and bounds legal description of the unit, the allocation of votes in the association, the sharing of maintenance costs, the maintenance responsibility and the association's rights and restrictions.[977] The declaration also contains numerous covenants which are binding on all owners. The covenants include the obligation to pay assessments to the association and use restrictions defining what the owners may or may not do at the condominium. In a residential condominium, these use restrictions generally limit or regulate such things such as parking, pets, leasing, architectural changes to the exterior of units and the extent that the units can be used for conducting a business.

Further, the declaration may contain other provisions, including granting the developer specific easement rights, procedures to for amending the condominium documents, assigning and reassigning limited common elements, reducing the size or terminating the condominium.

The declaration also includes the bylaws of the association. A condominium association must be incorporated, which may either be a non-profit or a for-profit corporation.[978]

---

974   See id. § 44-3-82(b).
975   O.C.G.A. § 44-3-70, et seq.
976   O.C.G.A. § 44-3-72.
977   O.C.G.A. § 44-3-77 lists the information required for the declaration.
978   O.C.G.A. § 44-3-100(a).

§ 14.1.3 Disclosure package

The Georgia Condominium Act requires specific documents and disclosures (Disclosure Package) be provided to the first bona fide purchaser of each residential condominium unit for residential occupancy by the buyer, any member of the buyer's family, or any employee of the buyer.[979] These requirements do not apply to subsequent sales.

The documents required by the Act include a copy of the floor plan, declaration, the articles of incorporation and bylaws of the association, and the estimated or actual operating budget for the condominium. The documents must be contained in a bound, single package with an index sheet on the cover which lists each item required and shows that either that item is attached or does not exist.

The seller may require a non-refundable deposit not in excess of $25.00 from the recipient of the documents. That deposit must be applied to the purchase price in the event that the recipient purchases the unit. A dated written acknowledgment of receipt of all items required to be provided, executed by the recipient, is evidence that the items were delivered as of the date of delivery.[980]

A contract for the first initial sale referred to in the GCA is a "covered contract."[981] Any covered contract is voidable by the buyer until at least seven days after the seller has furnished to the prospective buyer the documents required by the GCA. This requirement cannot be waived.[982] Within the text of the contract, the following information must be in boldface type or capital letters no smaller than the largest type in the text:

> THIS CONTRACT IS VOIDABLE BY PURCHASER UNTIL AT LEAST SEVEN (7) DAYS AFTER ALL OF THE ITEMS REQUIRED UNDER CODE SECTION 44-3-111 OF THE "GEORGIA CONDOMINIUM ACT", TO BE DELIVERED TO PURCHASER, HAVE BEEN RECEIVED BY PURCHASER. THE ITEMS SO REQUIRED ARE: (1) A FLOOR PLAN OF THE UNIT, (2) THE DECLARATION AND AMENDMENTS THERETO, (3) THE ASSOCIATION'S ARTICLES OF INCORPORATION AND BYLAWS AND AMENDMENTS THERETO, (4) ANY GROUND LEASE, (5) ANY MANAGEMENT CONTRACT HAVING A TERM IN EXCESS OF ONE (1) YEAR, (6) THE ESTIMATED OR ACTUAL BUDGET FOR THE CONDOMINIUM, (7) ANY LEASE OF RECREATIONAL OR OTHER FACILITIES THAT WILL BE

---

979   O.C.G.A. § 44-3-111.
980   O.C.G.A. § 44-3-111(d).
981   O.C.G.A. § 44-3-111.
982   O.C.G.A. § 44-3-111(c)(1).

USED ONLY BY THE UNIT OWNERS, (8) ANY LEASE OF RECREATIONAL OR OTHER FACILITIES THAT WILL OR MAY BE USED BY THE UNIT OWNERS WITH OTHERS, (9) A STATEMENT SETTING FORTH THE EXTENT OF THE SELLER'S COMMITMENT TO BUILD OR SUBMIT ADDITIONAL UNITS, ADDITIONAL RECREATIONAL OR OTHER FACILITIES, OR ADDITIONAL PROPERTY, AND (10) IF THIS CONTRACT APPLIES TO A CONDOMINIUM UNIT WHICH IS PART OF A CONVERSION CONDOMINIUM, A STATEMENT DESCRIBING THE CONDITION OF CERTAIN COMPONENTS AND SYSTEMS, A STATEMENT REGARDING THE EXPECTED USEFUL LIFE OF CERTAIN COMPONENTS AND SYSTEMS, AND CERTAIN INFORMATION REGARDING ANY NOTICES OF VIOLATIONS OF COUNTY OR MUNICIPAL REGULATIONS. A DATED, WRITTEN ACKNOWLEDGEMENT OF RECEIPT OF ALL SAID ITEMS SIGNED BY PURCHASER SHALL BE PRIMA-FACIE EVIDENCE OF THE DATE OF DELIVERY OF SAID ITEMS.[983]

A covered contract must also contain the following provision in boldface type or capital letters no smaller than the largest type on the first page of the contract:

ORAL REPRESENTATIONS CANNOT BE RELIED UPON AS CORRECTLY STATING THE REPRESENTATIONS OF SELLER. FOR CORRECT REPRESENTATIONS, REFERENCE SHOULD BE MADE TO THIS CONTRACT AND THE DOCUMENTS REQUIRED BY CODE SECTION 44-3-111 OF THE "GEORGIA CONDOMINIUM ACT" TO BE FURNISHED BY A SELLER TO A BUYER.[984]

If the covered contract applies to a condominium unit which includes a leasehold estate or estate for years in property such as a ground lease and if upon the expiration of such leasehold or estate, the unit will be deemed to have been withdrawn in accordance with the GCA or the condominium will be terminated, the contract shall contain the following text in boldface type or capital letters:

THIS CONTRACT IS FOR THE TRANSFER OF A CONDOMINIUM UNIT SUBJECT TO A LEASE THAT EXPIRES _____, AND THE LESSEE'S INTEREST WILL TERMINATE UPON EXPIRATION OF THE LEASE.[985]

---

983   O.C.G.A. § 44-3-111(c).
984   O.C.G.A. § 44-3-111(e)(1).
985   O.C.G.A. § 44-3-111(e)(3).

If the covered contract applies to a condominium unit that is subject to a lien for rent payable under a lease of a recreational facility or common use facility, the contract shall contain the following text in boldface type or capital letters:

THIS CONTRACT IS FOR THE TRANSFER OF A CONDOMINIUM UNIT THAT IS SUBJECT TO A LIEN FOR RENT PAYABLE UNDER A LEASE OF A RECREATIONAL FACILITY, AND FAILURE TO PAY THIS RENT MAY RESULT IN FORECLOSURE OF THE LIEN.[986]

It should be noted that long-term leases of recreational facilities in a condominium entered into between the condominium developer and the developer on behalf of a developer-controlled condominium association are uncommon because: (a) they have been attacked as being illegal tying arrangements in violation of the Sherman Antitrust Act, and (b) such contracts can be statutorily terminated by the condominium unit owners during the first year the unit owners take control of the condominium association from the developer in accordance with a procedure set forth in the Georgia Condominium Act.[987]

If the condominium is subject to a statute, ordinance, rule, or regulation which requires the issuance of a certificate of occupancy by any governmental entity, the covered contract must contain an express obligation on the part of the seller to furnish the buyer at or prior to closing, a true, correct, and complete copy of a duly issued certificate of occupancy covering the unit which is the subject matter of the contract.[988]

If a condominium unit is offered for sale before construction or remodeling of that unit is complete, the seller must make available to each buyer for inspection at a place convenient to the site, a copy of the existing plans or specifications for the construction or remodeling of that unit and of the improvements which will be part of the common elements.[989]

§ 14.1.4   Advertising and sales brochure requirements

The Georgia Condominium Act also imposes certain requirements on sellers with regard to the content of sales brochures and advertisements dealing with the first bona fide sale of a condominium unit. Any sales brochure describing such a condominium unit must include a description and location of the recreational facilities proposed to be provided by the seller, the parking facilities, and other commonly used facilities together with a statement providing "which of the facilities will be owned by the unit owners as part of the common elements and which of the facilities will be owned by others; [and] with respect to each such facility, whether the seller will be

---

986   O.C.G.A. § 44-3-111(e)(4).
987   O.C.G.A. § 44-3-101(b).
988   O.C.G.A. § 44-3-111(e)(5).
989   O.C.G.A. § 44-3-111(f).

obligated to complete the facility;" and limitations or conditions, if any, on the seller's obligation to complete the facilities.[990]

On the inside front cover of a sales brochure or on the first page containing text in a sales brochure, the following text must appear in boldface type or capital letters:

ORAL REPRESENTATIONS CANNOT BE RELIED UPON AS CORRECTLY STATING REPRESENTATIONS OF THE SELLER. FOR CORRECT REPRESENTATIONS, REFERENCE SHOULD BE MADE TO THIS BROCHURE AND TO THE DOCUMENTS REQUIRED BY CODE SECTION 44-3-111 OF THE 'GEORGIA CONDOMINIUM ACT' TO BE FURNISHED BY THE SELLER TO A BUYER.[991]

If the condominium unit or units are sold subject to a lease, then all written or printed advertising must contain the following statement in boldface type or capital letters:

THESE CONDOMINIUM UNITS WILL BE TRANSFERRED SUBJECT TO A LEASE.[992]

§ 14.1.5   Developer Control

A successful condominium community adequately balances the interests of individual owners and the interests of the condominium as a whole. The document that attempts this balancing act is the declaration of condominium, which sets forth an owner's rights and obligations as a member of the condominium community. The condominium association is the governing body that carries out the laws of the condominium.

The members of a condominium association comprise all the unit owners. When a person buys a condominium unit, he or she automatically becomes a mandatory member of the association and is bound by the declaration of condominium, the articles of incorporation, bylaws, and other legal instruments of the association.[993] The association works as a mini-government for the condominium, and operates through an elected board of directors.

To carry out their duties, condominium associations generally have a variety of quasi-governmental powers, including the power to tax unit owners

---

990   O.C.G.A. § 44-3-111(g).
991   O.C.G.A. § 44-3-111(g).
992   O.C.G.A. § 44-3-111(h).
993   O.C.G.A. § 44-3-100(a).

in the form of annual and special assessments, adopt reasonable rules and regulations regarding use of the units and common elements, fine owners for violation of the covenants or rules or regulations of the association, institute legal action to enforce the obligations set forth in the legal documents, and approve changes or alterations to the exterior of units or to the common elements. Therefore, it is not unusual for covenants contained in a set of condominium documents to regulate such things as parking, pets, use and leasing of units, and modifications to the exterior of units, buildings, and grounds.

The developer, during the period in which he or she is developing the condominium, may reserve the right to control the operation of the association by being able to appoint or remove the directors and officers of the association. The developer's right to control the association in this manner, however, cannot extend beyond any of the following dates:

(1) The date on which units to which eighty (80%) percent of the undivided ownership interest in the common elements pertain have been conveyed by the developer (unless the developer has an unexpired option to add additional property)[994]; or

(2) The expiration of seven years after the recording of the declaration in the case of an expandable or phased condominium or the expiration of three years after the recording of the declaration in the case of any other type of condominium.[995]

In an expandable condominium, the developer's right to appoint and remove board members and officers cannot extend beyond either of the following:

(1) Unless the developer still has the right to submit additional phases to the condominium, the date on which units to which eighty percent (80%) of the undivided interests in the common elements have been sold by the developer; or

(2) Seven years after the recording of the declaration in the county land records.

By appointing the board members and directors, the developer exerts substantial control over the affairs of the association, including decisions relating to assessment amounts, the physical appearance and maintenance of the property, and enforcement of the association's rules and regulations against owners and occupants. However, there are legal restrictions to limit developers from abusing this authority. In carrying out their duties, the developer appointed board members

---

994   O.C.G.A. § 44-3-101(2).
995   O.C.G.A. § 44-3-101(3).

and officers are held to the same standard of conduct and duty of care as board members elected by the unit owners. The developer appointed members and officers must discharge their duties in a manner they believe "in good faith to be in the best interest" of the association "[w]ith the care an ordinary prudent person in a like position would exercise under similar circumstances."[996] This means that the developer appointed board members and officers cannot act in a manner that unjustly favors the developer at the expense of the unit owners. For example, the developer appointed board members cannot purchase supplies from a company affiliated with the developer at prices substantially above market price for such supplies.

The Condominium Act does not require that the developer appoint a minimum number of directors. A developer will often appoint a single person to serve as the association's sole director and officer. One reason for limiting the number of director appointed board members and offers is to reduce the number of persons that may be subjected to claims by disgruntled owners against the individual developer appointed board members and officers.

§ 14.1.6   Remedies and Statutes of Limitations

A buyer who pays anything of value toward the purchase of a condominium unit that is the first bona fide sale of the unit in reasonable reliance upon any false or misleading material or any statement published by or under the authority of the seller in advertising and promotional materials, including brochures and newspaper advertising, or who has not been given the information required to be furnished by law, as listed above, is entitled to bring an action against the seller for damages.

This lawsuit must be brought prior to one year after the last of the following events: (1) closing of the transaction; (2) first issuance of a certificate of occupancy for the building containing the unit (or if no certificates of occupancy are issued, evidence of the date that lawful occupancy may first be allowed); (3) completion of the common elements and any recreational facilities, whether or not common elements, which the seller is obligated to complete or provide under the terms of the written contract for sale of the unit; (4) if the claim relates to the common elements and other portions of the condominium that are the responsibility of the association to maintain, the date upon which the declarant's right to control the association terminates under the GCA; or (5) if there is no written contract for the sale of the unit, the date of completion of the common elements and such recreational facilities the seller would be obligated to complete, whether or not the same are common elements. The outside limit for bringing a claim under this provision of state law is five years after the closing of the transaction.[997]

---

996   OCGA § 14-830(1) -842(1).
997   O.C.G.A. § 44-3-111(i).

The GCA also provides that a buyer who has a right of action for damages under the GCA also has the additional right to rescind any contract for the purchase of a unit at any time prior to the closing of the transaction.[998] This right to rescind exists regardless of whether the right is included in the contract.

§ 14.1.7   Resale Condominiums

The GAR Condominium Resale Purchase and Sale Agreement (GAR Condo Contract)[999] may be used for a transaction involving the purchase and sale of a resale condominium unit. This Contract should not be used for the initial sale of a condominium unit since certain required disclosures not included in the GAR Condo Contract must be included in the contract for the initial sale of a condominium unit.

A residential condominium unit is legally defined to include not only the space where the owner lives, but also an undivided ownership interest (along with the other unit owners) of the common elements of the condominium. To avoid disputes between buyers and sellers, a contract for the purchase of condominium unit must clearly specify whether the various provisions in the contract are applicable to just the residence being purchased or the residence plus the common elements of the condominium. The Condominium Resale Purchase and Sale Agreement is largely the same as the GAR Purchase and Sale Agreement except that some provisions are applicable to the unit including the common elements and other provisions are applicable to the unit excluding the owner's interest in the common elements.

§ 14.1.7.1   *Property condition*

The Condominium Resale Purchase and Sale Agreement provides that the unit (excluding the common elements of the condominium) shall be in the same condition on the date of closing as on the Binding Agreement Date. [1000]

This provision was limited to the unit excluding the common elements because it was felt that if the entire condominium complex had to be in the same condition on the date of closing as on the binding agreement date it would give too many buyers an opportunity to avoid their contractual obligations due to circumstances beyond the control of the individual condominium owner selling his or her unit. Otherwise, every time the condominium association altered or changed the common elements after the binding agreement date, the buyer could terminate the contract arguing that the common elements were no longer the same as on the binding agreement date.

---

998   O.C.G.A. § 44-3-111(i).
999   GAR Form F33
1000   GAR Form F33, paragraph 4A

§ 14.1.7.2   *Termite letter*

The Condominium Resale Purchase and Sale Agreement provides for two options with respect to a termite letter. First, the seller can provide the buyer with a termite clearance letter at closing confirming that the unit (excluding the common elements) is free of any visible evidence of termite infestation. The second option is for no termite letter at all to be provided by the seller to the buyer regarding termites.

The first option was limited to the unit excluding the common elements to prevent the unit owner from having to obtain a termite letter on the entire property (if the condominium association for some reason did not have a termite bond or policy on the entire property).

The second option was included because many condominiums, particularly mid-rise and high-rise residential complexes, are not constructed with wood and the buyer's mortgage lender may therefore not require a termite letter.

§ 14.1.7.3   *Inspection*

In the Condominium Resale Purchase and Sale Agreement, the common elements are sold "as is". This is because as stated in the contract, the seller cannot normally repair and/or replace defects in the common elements of the condominium. Instead, the common elements are normally maintained by the condominium association, which presumably will have some ongoing program for maintaining and repairing the common elements. If the condominium unit is being sold subject to a traditional right to request repairs, the buyer may only ask for the repair of defects in the unit itself rather than in the common elements.

§ 14.1.8   Conversion condominiums

A condominium may be created from existing apartments or from new construction. Typically, conversion condominiums are existing apartments or warehouses converted to the condominium form of ownership. The GCA defines a conversion condominium as a condominium, all or part of which may be used for residential purposes, which was occupied wholly or partially by persons other than persons who, at the time of the recording of the condominium documents, had contractual rights to acquire one or more units within the condominium.[1001] In conversion condominiums, existing tenants are required to receive a notice of conversion at least 120 days before the tenant is required to vacate the apartment.[1002]

1001   O.C.G.A. § 44-3-71(10).
1002   O.C.G.A. § 44-3-87(a).

The GCA also requires that a sale offer first be made to each existing tenant for the initial 60 days of sales[1003] which sale offer must be made at least 120 days before the tenant is required to vacate the unit.[1004] Additionally, if the tenants do not accept the sale offer presented to them during the first 60 days, they retain a right of first refusal to match any other contract accepted during the next 60 days.[1005]

The disclosure package for the first bona fide sale in a conversion condominium must include a statement describing the condition of certain components and systems, a statement regarding the expected useful life of certain components and systems, and certain information regarding any notices of violations of county or municipal regulations. Additionally, the covered contract must contain the following text in boldface type or capital letters:

THIS CONTRACT APPLIES TO A CONDOMINIUM UNIT THAT IS PART OF A CONVERSION CONDOMINIUM.[1006]

§ 14.1.9   Expandable condominiums

A developer has the right to develop a condominium in phases.[1007] In order to submit additional phases to the declaration of condominium, the initial declaration must explicitly reserve an option to expand the condominium and include a legal description by metes and bounds of the additional property which may be submitted.[1008] A developer's right to expand the condominium by adding additional phases cannot exceed seven years from the recording of the declaration except in very limited circumstances where unit owners other than the developer approve such expansion.[1009]

The disclosure package for the first bona fide sale in an expandable condominium must contain the following text in boldface type or capital letters:

THIS CONTRACT APPLIES TO A CONDOMINIUM UNIT THAT IS PART OF AN EXPANDABLE CONDOMINIUM.[1010]

1003   O.C.G.A. § 44-3-87(b).
1004   O.C.G.A. § 44-3-87(a).
1005   O.C.G.A. § 44-3-87(b).
1006   O.C.G.A. § 44-3-111(e)(6).
1007   O.C.G.A. § 44-3-77(b).
1008   O.C.G.A. § 44-3-77(b)(1).
1009   O.C.G.A. § 44-3-77(b)(2).
1010   O.C.G.A. § 44-3-111(e)(2).

§ 14.2. Homeowner Associations

§ 14.2.1　What is a Homeowner Association?

In a homeowner association (HOA), the owner owns his or her lot, which means that the owner owns the land beneath the building. All lot owners are normally automatic members of the homeowner association. There are common areas, such as recreational amenities and other properties such as greenbelts and entrance facilities. The common areas are typically owned by the HOA, which differs from a condominium where the common areas are owned by the unit owners jointly.

HOAs are commonly found in a townhouse development or a single-family detached development. A townhome development comprises of attached dwellings, commonly referred to as the "fee-simple townhome." However, the term is misleading as it is often interpreted to mean a townhome which is not part of a mandatory membership homeowner association. Legally, the term fee-simple refers to a freehold interest, as opposed to a leasehold interest.

Each lot owner normally has an easement to use and enjoy common areas for as long as she owns the property.

§ 14.2.2　Creating a Homeowner Association

A homeowner association is created by filing a declaration of covenants, which are often similar in length and scope to a declaration of condominium. A homeowner association is typically formed as a non-profit corporation and have traditionally been organized pursuant to the common law of covenants.[1011] The association is usually responsible for maintaining the common areas and operates through an elected board of directors.

As of July 1, 1994, a homeowner association may be created under or submit to a statutory scheme of development known as the Georgia Property Owners' Association Act ("POA").[1012] Homeowners associations created under or submitted to the POA have collection and enforcement powers similar to those in condominiums and have a statutory automatic lien for unpaid assessments.[1013] Under the POA, a developer may create a property owners development by recording a declaration of covenants, conditions, and restrictions expressly subjecting the property to the

---

1011　King v. Baker, 214 Ga. App. 229, 447 S.E.2d 129 (1994), reconsideration den. (July 29, 1994); County Greens Village One Owner's Ass'n v. Meyers, 158 Ga. App. 609, 281 S.E.2d 346 (1981).

1012　O.C.G.A. § 44-3-220, et seq.

1013　O.C.G.A. § 44-3-109 and O.C.G.A. § 44-3-232. Since the lien is automatic, it does not have to be recorded in the county land records. Title examiners in addition to doing their normal search of the land records must also check with the association to determine the existence of any automatic liens.

POA.[1014] If the property was not originally submitted to the POA, the owners in the community may subject the community to the terms of the POA by amending their declaration according to the amendment procedure set forth therein. Covenants in an instrument submitted to the POA continue for perpetual duration unless terminated by agreement of the lot owners.[1015]

A homeowner association which is not submitted to the POA is not regulated by statute and there are no disclosures or other consumer protections that are required by law to be included in the real estate contract. However, real estate brokers representing buyers should be aware of whether covenants exist and to ensure that the buyer receives a copy of the recorded covenants prior to entering into a sales contract or that it is conditioned upon receipt and/or approval of any such covenants. Some of the special stipulations mentioned in the sections below may be helpful in protecting buyers who may not be given the covenants.

§ 14.2.3   Contract Issues to Consider Regarding Homeowners Association

§ 14.2.3.1   Mandatory membership, voluntary association, or no association

Most new subdivisions are being developed with entry features, recreational facilities, and other amenities that require ongoing maintenance. Buyers should determine how those expenses will be paid. The buyer should review the covenants to see if there are provisions requiring membership in an owners association and the payment of assessments.[1016]   If the covenants do not require the payment of assessments or allow membership in the association to be voluntary, there is no assurance that sufficient owners will join the association to pay the operational expenses. To avoid confusion or surprise, the buyer should consider the following provision:

Special Stipulation #14-1: Seller's warranty on HOA membership type

Seller warrants:
____   membership in an owners association is mandatory
____   membership in an owners association is voluntary
____   the duty to pay assessments is mandatory
____   the common areas, including but not limited to the recreational facilities, are or will be owned by the owners association

---

1014   O.C.G.A. § 44-3-222.
1015   O.C.G.A. § 44-3-234.
1016   Owners of property in a condominium or subdivision subject to the Georgia Property Owners' Association Act are automatic members of the owners' association and obligated to pay assessments.

____ the common areas, including but not limited to the recreational facilities, will not be owned by the owners association

§ *14.2.3.2*   *Developer's obligations to build and turn over recreational facilities*

In many subdivisions, the recreational facilities are constructed prior to the sale of any lots. In others, the developer promises to build the facilities at a later time. If the declaration does not specify the size, type, number, quality, location, and construction time frame for the facilities to be constructed, this should be set out as specifically as possible in the purchase contract.

Special Stipulation #14-2: Seller's warranty on construction of recreational facilities

Seller warrants that the recreational facilities, including but not limited to the following: (i.e., a junior olympic size swimming pool, six lighted tennis courts, a clubhouse, a jogging trail, nature areas) as shown on the plans attached hereto as Exhibit "A" shall be completed in a good and workmanlike manner by _____ (date) and transferred to the____ Homeowners Association, free and clear of any liens and other title encumbrances.

Some developers build recreational facilities on the front end of the development but then attempt to either transfer them to the owners subject to a loan or attempt to sell the facilities to the owners at the end of the development process. Generally, the value of the recreational facilities is factored into the sales price of the homes; therefore, there should be no additional cost to the buyers for their recreational facilities. The declaration should require that specified recreational facilities and common areas be conveyed free and clear of all liens and encumbrances to the home-owners association by a specified time. If the declaration is silent on these issues, the buyer may want to specifically address them in the purchase contract.

Special Stipulation #14-3: Seller's warranty on transfer of recreational facilities to HOA

Seller warrants the recreational facilities of subdivision consisting of_____ shall be deeded to Homeowners Association, Inc., at no cost and free of any liens or other title encumbrances, no later than _____.

§ *14.2.3.3*   *Buyers' assurances that other homes in community will be of same standards and equal value*

Many homeowners become upset when a developer constructs homes in later phases of a development that are substantially smaller or less expensive than the homes which were initially developed. The concern is that values of the larger, more expensive homes in the community will drop. Most developers want to preserve as much flexibility on building as possible and therefore place few restrictions in the covenants on the type, price, or size of the homes in later phases of the subdivision. The absence of such restrictions can leave buyers vulnerable to changing market conditions, or the developer may sell out to another developer to complete the development, and the successor developer may have a different vision of what will be built in the community.

If the covenants contain limited restrictions on development and the community is just beginning to be developed, the buyer may propose a contract provision such as the following to protect her interests:

Special Stipulation #14-4: Seller's warranty on standard of construction of future property

Seller warrants on behalf of itself and successors and assigns in title that future residences constructed on lots subject to the Declaration of Covenants, Conditions, and Restrictions for_____ ("Declaration") will consist of at least _____ square feet of heated floor area and will be substantially similar in size, quality of construction including building materials used, architectural design, and cost to construct (calculated in present dollars) as the residences on the lots which are presently subject to the Declaration, and that the future lots submitted to the Declaration shall be of equal or larger size to the existing lots subject to the Declaration.

While this special stipulation may provide a remedy to a buyer against the seller for its breach, it will not provide the buyer with a remedy against builders or other third parties who purchase without notice of this restriction from the seller or who foreclose on the property. Such protections could be achieved only by amending the declaration to incorporate the obligation and having all construction lenders consent to its terms. Similarly, such a provision obligates the developer only if the property is, or may become, subject to the declaration for the association. Unless the developer is obligated to formally incorporate future phases of the subdivision into the association, she can also get around such an obligation by developing the future phases as a different subdivision.

§ 14.2.3.4   Changing declaration after buyer purchases property

Even if a buyer concludes that the covenants are acceptable, there is no guarantee that the covenants will not change. Most declarations include an amendment procedure which allows the members of the community to change the covenants in the future to address new issues and meet changing conditions. Both the Georgia Condominium Act[1017] and the Georgia Property Owners' Association Act[1018] permit

---

1017   O.C.G.A. § 44-3-93.
1018   O.C.G.A. § 44-3-226.

the covenants to be amended with the consent of owners holding at least two-thirds of the votes of the total association membership. Consequently, it is not possible to include a provision in the purchase agreement limiting amendments.

Buyers should be aware that amendments can affect fundamental property rights. Prior to the Fair Housing Amendments Act of 1988,[1019] which limited all-adult communities except in certain limited circumstances, the Georgia Supreme Court upheld the right of the members of a condominium association with a recorded declaration to amend the declaration to restrict the age of occupants.[1020] The result in that case was that a man who voted against the amendment and subsequently married a woman with a child under the age limitation was prohibited from having the child live in the community. In a recent case, condominium owners voted many years after the creation of the condominium to amend the declaration to restrict leasing.[1021] The owner leased her unit in violation of the amendment. The court upheld the amendment and upheld a $25.00 per day fine imposed by the association.[1022]

Buyers should also be wary of amendment procedures which require the consent of the developer for every amendment so long as the developer owns any property in the subdivision or which require the approval of a very high percentage of the owners. Such provisions can make it difficult to pass needed changes to the declaration in the future. Buyers should also confirm that the covenants contain an amendment procedure. Otherwise, the likelihood is that covenants can be amended only by a vote of all the owners.

§ 14.2.3.5   Approval of house plans by association

Most covenants require the written approval of the association before a home may be constructed or modified. The owner is required to submit plans and specifications to an architectural control committee for approval. In new construction, the developer typically retains control of the committee until all lots are sold or until a certain date, so that approval of the purchase agreement generally is an acceptance of the building plans. After that date, or if a purchaser wants to modify an existing structure, the purchaser must receive approval from the association board of directors or a committee of the board organized for this purpose. There is no guarantee that the board or the committee will approve the plans.

If architectural approval of new construction is not vested in the developer or if the buyer intends to modify the dwelling to be purchased and such modification

---

1019   42 U.S.C.A. 3601, et seq.

1020   Hill v. Fontaine Condominium Ass'n, Inc., 255 Ga. 24, 334 S.E.2d 690 (1985).

1021   Spratt a/k/a Sprain v. Henderson Mill Condominium Ass'n, Inc., 224 Ga.App. 761, 481 S.E.2d 879 (1997).

1022   Spratt a/k/a Sprain v. Henderson Mill Condominium Ass'n, Inc., 224 Ga.App. 761, 481 S.E.2d 879 (1997).

requires approval of the architectural control committee, the following provision in the contract will protect the buyer:

Special Stipulation #14-5: **Approval of house plans by association**

Notwithstanding anything in this Agreement to the contrary, this Agreement shall not become binding until the Board of Directors or Architectural Control Committee or Architectural Review Committee, as appropriate, of Association has approved Buyer's request for architectural approval of the following improvements [or changes and modifications], a copy of which is attached hereto as Exhibit "__" and incorporated herein, and written notice of such approval has been delivered to Buyer.

§ 14.3 Cooperatives

A housing cooperative is different from a homeowners association or condominium in that a cooperative corporation holds legal title to all of the property in the community, including the units. Members of the cooperative corporation receive membership certificates or shares which entitle them to lease a specific apartment, as long as they comply with certain provisions set forth in a lease agreement, typically called an occupancy agreement. Often, a blanket mortgage exists for the entire property. All of the rent payments made by the members of the cooperative, typically called carrying charges, are pooled by the cooperative association to pay the mortgage, taxes, and other operating expenses.

Most housing cooperatives in Atlanta were developed to provide affordable housing for low and moderate income people. However, the Atlanta area has recently witnessed cooperative developments as an upscale, higher priced housing alternative, as has been successful in New York and other major cities. As in the case of condominiums, cooperatives may be created from existing apartment properties or through new construction.

§ 14.3.1 Creating a Cooperative

Unlike condominiums, the creation of cooperatives is not regulated by state statute, but rather is governed by general principals of corporate and landlord and tenant law. The legal documents to organize a cooperative development are articles of incorporation, bylaws, subscription agreements, occupancy agreements, rules and regulations, and sometimes regulatory agreements with federal or other agencies providing financing or subsidies. Members execute the subscription agreements to purchase shares of stock or membership in the cooperative association. The members then execute a lease or occupancy agreement defining the terms of each member's occupancy of a unit and requiring compliance with the rules and regulations of the cooperative. In cooperatives where funding or loan guarantees are obtained from mandatory agencies such as the Department of Housing and Urban Development, a regulatory agreement is prepared and executed between the cooperative and the regulatory agency.

In cooperatives, unlike condominiums, the members generally are not responsible for maintenance and repair of the units. Cooperatives also differ from condominiums in that cooperative memberships may be terminated and members may be dispossessed for non-payment of carrying charges, but non-payment of condominium assessments does not automatically authorize termination of membership in the condominium association or eviction of a unit owner.

§ 14.4   Mixed Use Developments

The various forms of ownership discussed in this Chapter are increasingly being used in combination to create master planned communities. For example, a developer may take a large piece of property and subject it to the terms of a declaration of covenants which create a master association responsible for commonly used roadways, green belts and recreational amenities. The developer may then create a series of sub-associations within the community. The sub-associations may consist of homeowner associations, condominiums, office developments, country clubs and the like. Each sub-association may be subject to a declaration of condominium or a declaration of covenants which applies to just the sub-association. In addition, members of the sub-association are also bound by the declaration of covenants for the master association. The process of layering covenants in a community is being increasingly used as a means to regulate and control the large scale development of real property. The relationship between the sub-associations and the master association is often similar to that of city and county governments, with each performing defined tasks within the same or partially overlapping jurisdictions.

Such developments are often characterized by people living in close proximity to one another in housing designed to encourage social interaction. Cars are de-emphasized and commercial and office land uses are located in close proximity to residential uses. A legal framework has to be created that can preserve the aesthetic appearance of such communities, resolve land use conflicts, accommodate some degree of individuality and freedom of expression, and provide for the short- and long-term operation of the community. The legal structure must also be sensitive to the unique realities of many new mixed use communities.

OVERVIEW

This chapter discusses the contracts used by builders and developers, which are the GAR New Construction Purchase and Sale Agreement, Lot/Land Purchase and Sale Agreement, and Lease/Purchase Agreement. Since these contracts are all based on the GAR Purchase and Sale Agreement discussed throughout the book (and referenced as the GAR Contract), most topics have been discussed in the earlier chapters of this book. For example, discussions on purchase price and financing provisions can be found in chapter 2, earnest money in chapter 3 and so forth.

This chapter focuses on the unique provisions for builder contracts and issues of particular concern to builders and developers, such as liquidated damages, the handling of construction deposits, change orders and disclosures. The GAR New Construction Contract has several exhibits which should be incorporated in the contract. The New Construction Exhibit[1023] (GAR Exhibit) identifies a number of rights and obligations of both the seller and the buyer, and the Pre-Construction Specifications Exhibit[1024] (GAR Specs) allows the parties to identify specifications for each room in the home.

§ 15.1 Collecting deposits

§ 15.1.1   Earnest money

The earnest money provision of the New Construction Contract gives the parties two options with respect to the handling of earnest money. The first option is that a third party, generally the broker, will hold the earnest money. When the earnest money is held by the broker, it must always be deposited in an escrow/trust bank account.

The second option provides that the seller will hold the earnest money. Builders and developers frequently prefer this option. If the parties elect to have the seller hold the earnest money, the GAR exhibit modifying the earnest money provision should be used.[1025] The parties have to state on the form if the earnest money is to be paid into the seller's escrow account or general account.

§ 15.1.1.1 Earnest money as liquidated damages

The GAR Earnest Money Held by Seller Exhibit also provides that in the event the buyer defaults, the earnest money shall be retained by the seller and treated as full liquidated damages. This means that if the seller has performed seller's obligations, but the buyer refuses to close the purchase of the property by the closing date, then the seller is entitled to keep the earnest money. Georgia courts tend to

---

1023   GAR Form F24, New Construction Exhibit
1024   GAR Form F25, Pre-Construction Specifications.
1025   GAR Form F80, Earnest Money Held By Seller.

disfavor penalty clauses and will often strike them down as unenforceable. However, Georgia courts have created an exception to the this general rule by stating that a liquidated damages provision if properly written will not be deemed to be a penalty provision.

So, for example, in one case, the Georgia Court of Appeal held that such a provision, which allowed the builder to retain liquidated damages equal to about ten percent of purchase price was valid.[1026] The Court stated that the burden was on the defaulting party to show that liquidated damages provision was a penalty and therefore unenforceable.

The court will look closely at the wording of the liquidated damages clause to determine if the builder is entitled to retain the earnest money. In another case, the liquidated damages clause provided that the builder may retain the $250,000 earnest money deposit in the event of the buyer's breach, but only if the builder has performed all of its own obligations under the contract.[1027] The liquidated damages provision stated as follows:

> "Seller and Buyer acknowledge that it would be extremely impractical and difficult to ascertain the actual damages that would be suffered by Seller if Buyer fails or refuses to consummate the purchase of the Property for any reason *other than Seller's inability, failure or refusal to perform any of Seller's covenants herein* or because Buyer never had an unconditional obligation to close the purchase and sale on the closing date as the result of one or more contingencies in the Agreement not being fulfilled as of the closing date.... [I]f all the conditions precedent to Buyer's obligations to consummate the purchase of the Property have been waived by Buyer or have been satisfied, *and if Seller has performed Seller's covenants hereunder,* but Buyer has failed or refused to consummate the purchase of the Property by the closing date, then Seller shall be entitled to retain the earnest money as full and complete liquidated damages for such default....[1028]

The Court stated that the above provision clearly applies only if the seller was not in breach of the agreement. The seller had breached the contract by attempting to find a new buyer without first resorting to arbitration and by

---

1026   Liberty Life Ins. Co. v. Thomas B. Hartley Const. Co., Inc. 258 Ga. 808, 375 S.E.2d 222 (1989)

1027   Henderson v. Millner Developments LLC, 259 Ga.App. 709, 578 S.E.2d 289, (2003)

1028   The Greater Atlanta Home Builder's Association's (HBA) New Home Purchase and Sale Agreement has similarly provides, "If sale is not closed because of Seller's inability, failure or refusal to perform the Agreement...the earnest money shall be refunded to Buyer.

unilaterally extending the closing date for almost six months. Since the seller had not   performed all of its covenants, the liquidated damages clause was not applicable and the seller was not entitled to retain the earnest money.

Under the terms of the GAR Contract, the seller also reserves the right to bring an action for specific performance as a result of the buyer's breach in lieu of liquidated damages. [1029] The seller may, alternatively, wish to reserve the right to sue for specific performance and keep the earnest money as liquidated damages. In some cases, the seller may also want to retain the right to pursue actual damages instead of retaining the earnest money. The following stipulation may be used to provide the seller with such options:

Special Stipulation #15-1: Earnest money as liquidated damages

Seller and Buyer acknowledge that it would be extremely impractical and difficult to ascertain the actual damages that would be suffered by Seller if Buyer failed or refused to consummate the purchase of the Property for any reason other than Seller's inability, failure, or refusal to perform any of Seller's covenants herein. Seller and Buyer have considered carefully the loss to Seller as a consequence of the negotiation and execution of this Agreement; the personal expenses Seller has incurred in connection with the preparation of this Agreement; Seller's performance hereunder; and the other damages, general and special, which Seller and Buyer realize and recognize that Seller would sustain, but which Seller cannot calculate with absolute certainty. Based upon all these considerations, Seller and Buyer have agreed that the damage to Seller would reasonably be expected to be equal to the amount of $_____. If Seller has performed Seller's covenants hereunder, but Buyer has failed or refused to consummate the purchase of the Property by the closing date, then Seller shall be entitled to retain the earnest money toward payment of said amount of liquidated damages and to recover from Buyer the balance of said amount of liquidated damages for such default of Buyer. Said amount of liquidated damages is intended not as a penalty, but as full liquidated damages pursuant to O.C.G.A. § 13-6-7. In lieu of claiming said amount as full liquidated damages, Seller shall have the right to bring an action for specific performance of the terms of the Agreement or actual damages incurred by Seller as a result of Buyer's breach, including, but not limited to, all rents due, the cost of repairs and redecorating, continued insurance coverage, utility bills, maintenance costs, ad valorem taxes, loss of use of the proceeds of the sale and decrease in value.

If the buyer wants to limit his liability to the earnest money as liquidated damages and prohibit the seller from seeking specific performance or actual damages, he may incorporate the following special stipulation:

1029   The HBA New Home Purchase and Sale Agreement has similar provisions.

Special Stipulation #15-2: Seller's damages limited to earnest money as liquidated damages

Notwithstanding any provision to the contrary contained herein, Buyer and Seller hereby agree that in the event of Buyer's breach of this Agreement, Seller's sole remedy shall be to receive or retain the earnest money as liquidated damages, which is a reasonable estimate of the probable loss, and that Seller shall not be entitled to actual damages or specific performance.

§ 15.1.2   Construction deposit

Construction deposits are usually non-refundable and used to pay for the initial costs of construction. The main reason for a builder to collect a construction deposit is the assurance that the buyer intends to consummate the transaction. In other cases, the builder may wish to collect the initial overhead or base cost when building a custom home to reduce the out of pocket costs if the contract later falls through. However, collecting the construction deposit is only the first condition to be fulfilled before a builder will commence construction. In custom homes, most builders require a firm mortgage commitment and the release of all contractual contingencies.

Some contracts may provide for payment of earnest money as well as a construction deposit.[1030] The GAR New Construction Purchase and Sale Agreement does not provide for the payment of a construction deposit. If the builder wishes to collect a construction deposit, the builder may include the following stipulation:

Special Stipulation #15-3: Payment of construction deposit

Provided that Seller is not in default of this Agreement, Buyer shall pay to Seller the following sums:
$_____ *on __[date]_ ;*
$_____ *on __[date]_ ;, and*
$_____ *on __[date]*

as a construction deposit. Seller shall be authorized to immediately use said funds solely for the construction of the improvements on the Property. This construction deposit shall be non-refundable except where the Seller is in default of its obligations under this Agreement.

§ 15.1.2.1 Construction deposit as liquidated damages

Most contracts provide that the construction deposit is non-refundable and will be treated as liquidated damages upon the buyer's breach. The builder may additionally wish to reserve the right to bring an action for specific performance or the

---

1030   The HBA's New Home Purchase and Sale Agreement.

right to pursue actual damages. The builder may also wish to limit the amount of damages that the buyer can claim in the event of the builder's breach. The following stipulation may be used to provide for these options:

Special Stipulation #15-4: Construction deposit and other deposits as liquidated damages

If Seller elects to terminate due to the default of Buyer, Seller may elect to retain all construction deposits and other payments made by Buyer hereunder as agreed upon liquidated damages, it being acknowledged that it is impossible to more precisely estimate the specific damages to be suffered by Seller, but that the sum herein stipulated is a reasonable estimate of such damages and the parties hereto expressly acknowledge and intend that this provision shall be a provision for the retention of the construction deposit and other sums paid hereunder as liquidated damages and not as a penalty pursuant to the provisions of O.C.G.A. § 13-6-7, whereupon all rights, liabilities and obligations created under the terms and provisions of this Agreement shall be deemed null and void and of no further force and effect. Alternatively, Seller may elect to seek enforcement of this Agreement by specific performance. Upon default by Buyer prior to closing, Buyer shall, notwithstanding anything to the contrary herein, also immediately pay the full amount of the real estate commissions due hereunder. Listing Broker and Selling Broker may jointly or independently pursue Buyer for that portion of the commission which they would have otherwise received had this transaction closed. If prior to closing Seller defaults under this Agreement then Buyer as its sole and exclusive remedy shall be entitled to the following: (a) the return of Buyer's construction deposit and the other monies paid hereunder from Buyer to Seller, and (b) the sum of $250 as full and complete liquidated damages, it being agreed that it is impossible to precisely estimate the actual damages to be suffered by Buyer in the event of a default by Seller and that the same is a reasonable pre-estimate of Buyer's actual damages and is not intended as a penalty under O.C.G.A. § 13-6-7. Thereafter, all further rights, obligations, and liabilities created hereunder shall be deemed terminated and of no further force and effect.

§ 15.1.3 Protecting buyer's earnest money and/or deposit

In many new home sales contracts, builders often provide that the deposit money be paid into company accounts to pay construction costs or other expenses. There is a risk that the buyer will either have to wait a long time before receiving a refund in the event of a dispute or not get a refund at all if the builder has financial problems. To protect themselves, buyers should perform background checks on the builder, such as contacting the local homebuilder's association or Better Business Bureau to see if any complaints exist against the builder.

When substantial amounts of the buyer's money will be used for construction, some buyers may want to pay certain vendors directly for materials and supplies. Other buyers may want the money deposited with an escrow agent who disburses only in accordance with a specific construction draw schedule.

If the buyer is to provide substantial funds to the builder, the buyer may want to require the builder to execute a note and deed to secure debt on the property in favor of the buyer. Receipt of a promissory note and deed to secure debt will give the buyer a security interest in the property, thereby giving the buyer a right to accelerate and foreclose on the deed to secure debt if the seller defaults. Such a provision also includes a requirement that the buyer execute a quit-claim deed in favor of the builder to satisfy the deed to secure debt if the buyer defaults on the buyer's obligations. The quitclaim deed is generally held by the broker.

Although such a procedure may give the buyer some additional security, the security deed for the earnest money will generally be subordinate to the lender's construction loan or other loans and judgments against the property. So, for example, if there is a first priority construction loan of $200,000.00 on the property and the buyer has a security deed in an inferior position for $50,000.00, the buyer can still get wiped out if there is a foreclosure by the construction lender. To determine the priority of the security deed for earnest money or a construction deposit, it is recommended that a title search be performed before entering into such an agreement.

§ 15.2   Construction issues

The GAR New Construction Exhibit ("GAR Exhibit") addresses construction issues, such as the construction completion date, plans and specifications, selections, change orders, allowances, inspections, warranties and walk- throughs.[1031] These issues are discussed in the following paragraphs.

§ 15.2.1   Completion and closing

The GAR New Construction Purchase and Sale Agreement provides for closing to be on a stipulated date or on such other date as the parties may agree to in writing.[1032] Users of this GAR form contract should also attach the GAR Exhibit, which provides that the property is deemed ready to close upon the issuance of a certificate of occupancy, or final inspection certificate.[1033] The GAR Exhibit also states that it will prevail over the GAR form contract in the event of any inconsistency. This means that even if the parties agree on a closing date, the closing will not take place until the certificate of occupancy or final inspection certificate is issued.

1031   GAR Form F24
1032   GAR Form F23, paragraph 4c
1033   GAR Form F24, paragraph 1

In addition, the GAR Exhibit protects the builder in the event of unavoidable delays in construction due to strikes, acts of God or nature, or delays directly caused by the buyer's change orders and/or selection of materials. In such events, the builder may extend the closing for up to 30 calendar days in its sole discretion. The seller is obligated to notify all parties immediately of the cause of delay and the new closing date.[1034]

The GAR Exhibit does not cover other contingencies that may cause delays in construction. Examples of such contingencies are government moratoriums, inadequate or delay in the provision of utility services or shortage in construction materials. Builders may wish to include the following stipulation to take into account a broader range of contingencies and to provide that the builder has the right to extend the closing for the period of such delay:

Special Stipulation #15-5: Extension of closing date due to construction delays

Seller shall not be responsible for delays in construction caused by strikes, acts of God or nature, poor weather, failure or unavailability of adequate sewer, water, electricity, gas, fire protection or other utility service, material and labor shortages, theft, unanticipated soil conditions, sink holes, underground springs, sewer or other governmental moratoriums, delays in government approvals for land development and construction, and delays caused by buyer's change orders or selections. The Closing Date shall be extended for a period of time equal to such delays.

§ 15.2.2   Plans and specifications

Under the GAR Exhibit, the builder has to construct the property "substantially in conformance with the Plans and Specifications initialed and approved by the Buyer . . ."[1035] However, this provision still gives the seller the right to make "such changes in the Plans and Specifications as may be required by governmental authority or as may be required by job conditions as long as the size, overall quality and appearance of the house are substantially equal to or superior to that shown on the attached Plans and Specifications."

If the buyer is concerned about changes the builder/seller may make in the plans and specifications, the following special stipulation may be incorporated:

1034   GAR Form F24, paragraph 11.
1035   GAR Form F24, New Construction Exhibit, paragraph 2A.

Special Stipulation #15-6: Buyer approval for changes to plans and specifications

The home shall be constructed substantially in conformance with the Plans and Specifications initialed and approved by the Buyer attached hereto as an Exhibit to this Agreement and by reference incorporated herein. Buyer and Seller agree that if changes are required by governmental authority or required by job conditions, Seller shall submit proposed changes in writing to Buyer for Buyer's approval. Buyer shall approve or disapprove proposed changes within ___ days of the date received. Buyer shall not unreasonably withhold approval of changes. If Buyer fails to approve or disapprove a change within ___ days of receipt, Buyer shall be deemed to have waived his right to disapprove changes.

If the parties want to identify the manufacturer of certain items in the home, such as windows, ceiling fans, flooring, and other items, they may be identified on the GAR Pre-Construction Specifications exhibit ("GAR Specs").[1036] In addition, the GAR Exhibit allows the parties to identify allowances for floor coverings, fixtures, landscaping, and appliances and provides for identifying the make, model, and color of appliances.

§ 15.2.3 Inspection

The inspection provision of the New Construction Contract provides that the buyer and/or buyer's representatives shall have the right to enter the property at the buyer's expense and at reasonable times, including immediately prior to closing, to thoroughly inspect, examine, test, and survey the property. There is a blank in the New Construction Contract where the parties can indicate who will be responsible for ensuring that all utility services at any pool, spa, and similar items are operational so that the buyer can complete his or her inspections. The buyer agrees to hold the seller and all brokers harmless from all claims, injuries, and damages arising out of or related to the exercise of these rights. Under the New Construction Contract, the buyer has the right to provide the seller, within a reasonable time prior to closing, a list of defects to be corrected.

The term "defects" is defined as any portion of an item in the property which: (1) is not in good working order and repair, (2) constitutes any non-grandfathered violation of applicable laws or governmental codes and regulations; (3) has not been substantially completed or constructed in substantial accordance with the plans and specifications, if any, for the property; or (4) is a defect as that term is defined in any warranty provided by the seller. The seller agrees to correct the defects in a good and workmanlike manner prior to closing.

1036   GAR Form 25

§ 15.2.3.1 Inspection Standards

It should be noted that all contracts for new construction do not define defects in the same manner as defined in the GAR New Construction Contract. For example, some contracts provide that the only criteria and standards that will be used in connection with an inspection are those set forth in the warranty described and, if there is no warranty, then customary and generally accepted local area building industry criteria standards will be used. Although customary building standards may address the issues which would be commonly defined as "defects," they may not address work which has not been substantially completed in compliance with the plans and specifications for the property. Therefore, if the GAR New Construction Contract is not used, the buyer may want to modify the contract to more broadly define defects. The following stipulation may be used:

Special Stipulation #15-7: Standards for Inspection

Notwithstanding anything to the contrary contained herein, any inspection shall be limited and restricted to inspections of the Property for violations of applicable governmental codes and regulations. In the event of any dispute between a third party inspector and Seller regarding the existence of an alleged code violation, such dispute shall be resolved by the applicable governmental code enforcement officer and that individual's final determination shall be binding on Buyer and Seller. Notwithstanding the foregoing, the issuance of a certificate of occupancy, temporary certificate of occupancy, or final inspection certificate covering the Property by the applicable governing authority shall be conclusive and determinative of such approval and compliance with applicable governmental codes and regulations thereby indicating substantial completion of the home and obligating Buyer to close hereunder. Buyer acknowledges and agrees that at the time of any inspection certain utility services and similar items may not be fully operational and Seller shall have no liability for Buyer's inspector failing or being unable to inspect same. Upon the completion of any inspection, examination or test, Buyer shall restore the Property to its former condition. Buyer agrees to indemnify and hold Seller harmless from any and all loss and expense (including, without limitation, attorney's fees) resulting from claims and damages caused by, arising out of or incurred in connection with the exercise by Buyer of Buyer's rights under this Section.

§ 15.2.3.2 Inspector

The GAR New Construction Contract inspection provision does not require the inspector to be a member of ASHI or GAHI.[1037] This allows the buyer to perform

---

1037   American Society of Home Inspectors, Inc. or Georgia Association of Home Inspectors, Inc.

other specialized inspections in addition to conducting a building inspection. On the other hand, buyers may engage less credible inspectors who make partial or inaccurate findings. If the seller wishes to restrict building inspections to be conducted only by certified building inspectors, the following stipulation may be added:

Special Stipulation #15-8: Inspector to be ASHI or GAHI member

Any building inspection must be performed during normal business hours (Monday through Friday 9 a.m. – 5 p.m.) by an inspector (Inspector) with the following credentials:

1) *Inspector must be a current member of The American Society of Home Inspectors, Inc. or the Georgia Association of Home Inspectors, Inc. Prior to the inspection, the Inspector shall furnish to Seller a letter from the association of which it is a member identifying the Inspector as a member of such organization.*

2) *Inspector shall present to Seller evidence of general liability insurance insuring the Inspector in an amount of not less than One Million Dollars.*

3) *Inspector shall present a valid business license for the jurisdiction in which the Inspector is operating.*

4) *The Inspector shall be CABO 1 and 2 certified Family Dwelling Code (International Residential Code) (or state other certification) and shall present evidence to Seller of such certification.*

5) *Inspector shall sign an agreement prepared by Seller in which the Inspector agrees to indemnify and hold Seller harmless any loss, damage or injury to persons or property arising out of or related to the inspection of the Property.*

§ 15.2.4   Walk-through

In addition to the inspection, the GAR New Construction Contract provides that prior to closing, buyer and seller will inspect the property and execute a "walk-through list" or "punch list" specifying all items, including those noted in previous inspections, that remain to be completed.[1038] This paragraph also requires the buyer to acknowledge that the seller will make its best effort to complete all the items specified in the agreed-upon "walk-through list" on a timely basis as soon as reasonably possible after closing. However, the buyer may not fail or refuse to close because any repairs, touch-ups, or adjustments are incomplete.

The GAR Contract distinguishes between minor punch list items and "defects." Under the GAR New Construction Contract, defects would have to be remedied prior to closing; however, minor repairs, touch-ups, or adjustments may be completed subsequent to closing. Further, there is to be no withholding of any of

---

1038   GAR form F24, paragraph 9; GAR Form F26, Walk Through List.

seller's proceeds at closing for any walk-through items which may be completed after closing without the written approval of the seller.

Many builder contracts provide that "punch list" items do not have to be corrected until after closing. This gives the builder greater flexibility as to when repairs are to be made. However, it can sometimes be a problem for buyers if after closing, the builder loses interest in completing the repairs. Buyers can attempt to avoid this by asking the builder/seller to agree to the following special stipulations:

Special Stipulation #15-9: Completion of walk-through items

Notwithstanding anything contained herein to the contrary, Buyer and Seller agree that all items on the Walk Through List shall be completed by Seller within _____ days of the closing date.

Special Stipulation #15-10: Completion of walk-through items and escrow of funds

Notwithstanding anything contained herein to the contrary, in the event that items on the Walk Through List remain to be completed as of the closing date, then Seller shall deposit into a separate escrow account sufficient funds to cover the cost of completing the said items. In the event that Seller does not complete the said Walk Through List items within _____ days of the closing date, then the said funds (or so much of them as are necessary to complete the Walk Through List items) shall be immediately paid to Buyer.

§ 15.2.5   Change orders

Change orders are agreed upon deviations from the approved building plans or specifications. If buyers are careful in finalizing their construction plans, the need for change orders should be limited. However, even with careful planning, change orders often occur because buyers change their minds, mistakes are made by architects or draftsmen, previously unknown site conditions or building peculiarities are discovered, and shortages or price increases in particular materials necessitate a change in a chosen building product.

Under the GAR Exhibit, change orders are required to be in writing and delivered to the seller's office. [1039] All change orders must be signed by both the seller and buyer in order to be valid. Change orders must be submitted timely so that the seller has adequate lead time to schedule the change orders into the building sequence. The buyer must pay the seller in advance to carry out the change orders and also agrees that these payments are non-refundable.

1039   GAR Form F24, paragraph 10

Under the GAR Exhibit, the seller also has a right to refuse any change order delivered to seller within 30 days of closing. Lastly, the buyer acknowledges that any work done on the home pursuant to change orders or additions will not necessarily increase the appraised value of the property. This may be a significant issue for the buyer. If the price of the property increases, but the appraised value does not, the buyer may not be able to increase the amount of his loan to pay for the change order. This means that the buyer may need additional cash to close the transaction.

It is important for the parties to have any change orders signed off and paid for before the work is done. Change orders can easily inflate the construction budget and it is important that buyers are fully aware of the extent of the budget increase in order to avoid disputes later down the road. Often, disputes arise because buyers accuse builders of charging exorbitant amounts for change orders. With important change orders, some buyers feel that they have no choice but to pay the builders whatever price he or she demands for the change order to be completed. Disputes also arise when buyers refuse to pay for change orders necessitated by the mistake of the builder, architect or engineer. Therefore, builders may want to contract to state in the contract who will be responsible for contractor or subcontractor errors. One way of minimizing all disputes regarding construction costs is to set out the line items in detail, as set out in the GAR Exhibit and GAR Specs.[1040]

§ 15.2.6   Survey

As in the GAR Purchase and Sale Agreement, the GAR New Construction Agreement provides that any survey of the property shall be part of the contract and the buyer shall have the right to terminate the agreement upon written notice to the seller if a new survey performed by a surveyor licensed in Georgia is obtained which is materially different from the attached survey. Unlike the Purchase and Sale Agreement, the survey provision in the New Construction Contract incorporates language providing that the term "materially different" does not apply to any improvements constructed by the seller in their agreed-upon locations subsequent to the Binding Agreement Date.

In some cases, the precise location of the improvements will be critical to the buyer. In such cases, the buyer may want to incorporate a provision requiring the seller to obtain written consent from the buyer before changing the location of improvements as shown on the survey. The following provision may be used for this purpose:

Special Stipulation #15-11: Location of footprint for improvements

Seller and Buyer agree that the footprint of the improvements shall be constructed by Seller in the location shown on the survey attached hereto as

---

1040   GAR Form F24 & F25

Exhibit "___". No material changes in the location of the footprint of the improvements shall be permitted without the written consent of Buyer.

§ 15.2.7   Soil treatment bond

Unlike the GAR Purchase and Sale Contract which requires a termite letter, the GAR New Construction Contract has a check box system in which the builder can disclose the type of system used to control termites and other wood destroying mechanisms. These include treating the soil for termites prior to constructing the improvements on the property, installing a termite baiting system or using any other system meeting the standards of the Georgia Department of Agriculture to control termites. At closing, the builder is required to provide the buyer with a letter or report from a licensed Georgia Pest Control operator certifying that the property includes the agreed upon termite control system. Since the structures are new, the termites should not have had an opportunity to cause any damage.

§ 15.2.8   Topographical issues

Buyers will frequently be concerned with the grade of the property, particularly if the builder is planning on changing the grade, for example, to make it level with the street. In addition to aesthetic preferences, regrading will also be important if the adjacent property is affected. To address grading issues, the buyer may require a topographical survey of the property to be provided at closing, which showing that the grade of that portion of the lot upon which the improvements are to be made will have an elevation of not less than a specified number of feet above sea level. The buyer may use the following special stipulation for this purpose:

Special Stipulation #15-12: Specification on elevation

Seller and Buyer agree that the final grade of that portion of the Lot upon which improvements are to be made shall be at an elevation of not less than ____ feet above sea level. Seller agrees to provide to Buyer an as-built topographical survey of the Property at closing.

Georgia law prohibits an owner from altering his property so as to increase or alter the flow of water on adjacent property and thereby damaging that property.[1041] In one recent case, a neighbor brought a trespass and nuisance action against the homeowner, homebuilder, independent contractor, and subdivision alleging that construction on neighbors' property caused flooding.[1042]

The Court of Appeals ruled that a property owner may be held liable for trespass and nuisance when construction on the owner's property causes an increase

---

1041   Cox v. Martin, 207 Ga. 442, 62 S.E.2d 154 (1950).
1042   Greenwald v. Kersh, 265 Ga.App. 196, 593 S.E.2d 381, 4 FCDR 366 (2004)

421

in water runoff onto neighboring property. In this case, a husband and wife hired a builder to build a home on their property in a subdivision. The builder (who was an independent contractor of the owners) apparently brought in dirt to level the lot. The dirt altered the flow of surface water, resulting in increased water runoff onto the neighbor's property and subsequent flooding. The owners for whom the house was built argued that they should not be held responsible for this damage because their builder was an independent contractor. They also argued that they had very little to do with the construction and had no control over what the contractors did. However, the Court held that the owners were responsible because they moved into the property and therefore accepted the work of the contractor. The Court also held that the owners knew about the problem and refused to do anything about it.

Therefore, to limit potential liability when the buyer acquires title to the property, the buyer may want assurance from the seller that the grade will not been altered so as to increase or alter the flow of water on adjacent property. The buyer may incorporate the following language in the contract to accomplish this.

Special Stipulation #15-13: Grade change to channel water run-off prohibited

Seller warrants to Buyer that Seller shall not change the grade of the property so as to channel, direct, or increase the flow of surface water runoff onto adjacent properties.

§ 15.2.9   Construction debris

To ensure that construction debris is not buried on the property, the buyer may want to include the following special stipulation in the contract:

Special Stipulation #15-14: Disclosure of buried construction debris, stumps or other materials

Seller shall not bury any construction debris, trees, stumps, or other organic materials on the Property without the written consent of Buyer. Seller warrants that, to the best of Seller's knowledge and information, no construction debris, trees, stumps or other organic materials were buried on the Property during the development of the Property.

It is especially important to disclose construction debris in planned unit developments (PUD's) because many PUD covenants provide that fines will be levied against an owner if construction debris is left on the property. The buyer may want to incorporate a provision stipulating that all construction debris will be removed from the property prior to closing so that the buyer will not be subject to a fine when he takes title to the property. The following provision may be used for this purpose:

Special Stipulation #15-15: Seller to remove all construction debris before closing

Seller agrees that all construction debris shall be removed from the Property prior to the date of closing. Seller agrees that if all construction debris is not removed, Buyer may require that sufficient funds be placed in escrow at closing to cover the cost of removal.

§ 15.3   Special construction contract provisions

§ 15.3.1   Using builder disclosures

An effective way for a builder or developer to limit potential legal liability is to include disclaimers in their sales contracts. When a buyer is specifically told about a condition relating to the property, it will be difficult for the buyer to then argue that he or she did not know about the condition or that the builder concealed a problem.

§ 15.3.1.1   Sample property disclosures

Set forth below are general disclosures that builders and developers may include in their sales contract:

1. Buyer acknowledges and agrees to the following: (a) Property is located adjacent or near thoroughfares which may be improved or widened in the future and in an area where additional transportation improvements may be made; (b) the views from the Property may change over time due to, among other things, additional development and the removal or addition of landscaping; (c) No representations are made regarding the zoning or use of adjacent property, or which schools may now or in the future serve the Property; (d) Buyer acknowledges that the sizes, architectural styles and prices of any future homes constructed in the subdivision may be significantly different than what will be or has been constructed on the Property, and (e) Buyer shall be responsible to become fully acquainted with neighborhood and other off-site conditions affecting the Property by (1) diligently inspecting and (2) reviewing all reasonably available governmental records, maps and documents (examples of which are set forth in the Brokerage Relationships in Real Estate Transactions Act ("BRRETA") O.C.G.A. § 10-6A-1 et. seq.) relating to the surrounding neighborhood.

2. Since trees and landscaping existing on the Property prior to the commencement of construction thereon may be adversely affected or even killed by construction activities, Seller shall have no responsibility for the same. In particular, Buyer acknowledges that the underground root system of a tree often extends as much as its canopy and that the viability of the

tree can be affected when the root system, or a particular portion thereof, is damaged through construction activities.

3. Buyer hereby grants Seller the right to obtain and use photography of the Property for publication and advertising purposes.

4. This Agreement, together with all attachments, contains the entire agreement between Seller and Buyer with respect to the purchase of the Property and the construction of any home thereon. This Agreement replaces all prior agreements or understandings, if any. No representation, statement, promise or understanding not specifically set forth in this agreement shall be binding on seller. No real estate salesperson or construction personnel shall have any authority to make any verbal or written agreements on behalf of Seller.

5. Buyer consents to the Seller changing, in its sole discretion, the subdivision name and the street names and addresses in the subdivision including the street address of the Property before or after closing.

6. Seller has no control over installation and energizing of streetlights. Streetlights may not be in operation prior to Purchaser's move in.

7. Radon, Carbon Dioxide and Other Contaminates. The grading of the soil and other elements created by nature, as well as building materials developed by man, many times create unwanted and undesired gases and other contaminates in homes and residential buildings, both new and used. Also, since energy conservation has become a concern, there is a need to build homes and residential buildings that are more airtight. As a result, these homes and residential building trap unwanted gases in different degrees depending on how each person lives within their home or such residential building. To date, measurements of such unwanted gases (Such as the radon gas described below and carbon dioxide) are reported as parts of the air they occupy. Since the quality of air we breath can affect our health, Seller recommends frequent airing of Purchaser's home by simply opening windows to introduce fresh air uncontaminated with such gases.

8. Mold and/or mildew can grow in any portion of the Home that is exposed to elevated levels of moisture. Buyer acknowledges and agrees that it is necessary for Buyer to provide appropriate climate control in the Home, keep the Home clean, and take other measures to retard and prevent mold and mildew from accumulating in the Home. Buyer agrees to clean and dust the Home on a regular basis and to remove visible moisture accumulation, mold or mildew on windows, walls and other surfaces as soon as reasonably possible. Buyer agrees not to block or cover any of the heating, ventilation or air-conditioning ducts in the Home.

Buyer acknowledges that the Home may contain toxic mold. Molds are a type of fungus. More than 1,000 different species have been found in the United States. Most molds are not harmful; however, over 100 mold species are believed to potentially cause infection in humans. In addition, several types of molds are considered by some to be "toxic," which means that they can produce toxic agents (metabolites) called mycotoxins, which may cause serious health problems. Builder is not an expert with regard to mold or the health effects of mold exposure. Accordingly, it is the sole responsibility of Buyer to retain appropriate professionals to inspect any property that the Buyer may purchase to determine the presence of any toxic mold.

§ 15.3.1.2 Sample construction disclosures

Set forth below are construction disclosures that builders and developers may include in their sales contract, if applicable:

1. Any alarm systems installed in the home shall only be installed on all first floor operable windows (lower windows only) and doors, including basement level windows (lower windows only) and doors.

2. In constructing the home on the Property, Seller shall have the right to do the following:

   (a) Locate the heating, wiring and electrical system, hot water heater, all plumbing lines, and gas and electric meters at Seller's discretion;

   (b) Remove trees, plants, shrubbery and rocks from the Property;

   (c) Substitute construction materials, appliances, equipment and fixtures from those specified in the Home Plan and Construction Specifications in Seller's reasonable discretion, provided that the substitutions are of equal or better quality materials, appliances, equipment and fixtures than those originally specified and provided. Buyer agrees that industry standards, as determined in the reasonable exercise of Seller's discretion, shall govern the acceptability of any particular variance. The variations, substitutions and deviations referenced above shall not be the basis of any claim by Buyer against Seller nor shall it be a basis for Buyer not to accept the Property or otherwise not fulfill Buyer's obligations under this Agreement; and

   (d) Determine the ground elevation and location of the home on the lot and the siting of homes on neighboring home sites.

3. Buyer hereby acknowledges and agrees that any floor plans, advertising materials, brochures, renderings, drawings, and the like, furnished by Seller

to Buyer which purport to depict the home to be constructed or any portion thereof, are merely approximations and do not necessarily reflect the actual as-built conditions of the same. Due to the unique nature of the construction process and site conditions, room dimensions, size and elevations may vary from home to home. Seller makes no representation as to the location of mailboxes, utility boxes, street lights, fire hydrants or storm drain inlets or basins. Buyer further acknowledges and agrees that the decorations, furniture, furnishings, wallpaper, appliances, fixtures, floor coverings and window treatments, landscaping, displays and promotional materials, and the like, contained in any model home are for marketing and demonstrative purposes only, and are not included in the Property which is the subject of this Agreement.

4. Buyer acknowledges that the performance and methods and practices of operating heating and cooling systems can be directly affected by the orientation and location of a room or home in relation to the sun. Seller shall, therefore, have no obligation other than to install a heating and cooling system at the Property which has been sized and designed based on industry standards for the type and size of home to be constructed and which functions in accordance with industry standards.

5. Condensation may appear on the interior portions of windows and glass surfaces, and fogging of windows and glass surfaces may occur due to temperature disparities between the interior and exterior portions of the windows and glass.

6. While the drainage system for surface water runoff on the Property will be constructed in accordance with applicable governmental standards, the Property may still be subject to erosion and/or flooding during unusually intense or prolonged periods of rain.

7. Buyer acknowledges that small amounts of water may pond on sidewalks, driveways, patios and balconies.

8. The cost of upgrades may not necessarily result in a commensurate increase in the value of the Property.

9. No representations are made that any room, wall, ceiling or floor in any dwelling on the Property or any pipes located therein will be soundproof.

10. No representations are made that the systems in the Property including, by way of example only, heating and air conditioning and electrical systems will operate or perform at a level or standard greater than the minimum specifications of the manufacturer.

11. Since trees and landscaping existing on the Property prior to the commencement of construction thereon may be adversely affected or even killed by construction activities, Seller shall have no responsibility for the same.

12. Buyer acknowledges that the construction of other homes and improvements in the Development may create noise, odors, smoke and debris and agrees that none of these activities shall be considered to be a nuisance.

13. All power lines and electrical appliances that draw electric current have electromagnetic fields ("EMFs") around them. There are various types of studies currently being conducted by researchers to determine whether or not there are health risks associated with EMFs. The electric utility industry and local power companies monitor those research activities and work with their customers to explain what EMFs are and how people can find out more about them. Seller has no expertise regarding EMFs. As a result, Seller does not make representations or warranties of any kind, express or implied, or provide information about the presence or effect of EMFs on or in proximity to the Property. The local electric company servicing the property, the state or the local environmental, energy or health agencies, or the regional office of the EPA may provide such information about EMFs.

14. Lumber contains moisture when installed and will dry, shrink and settle after installation. As a result, nails pop from drywall locations, baseboards may move slightly and exposes wood may striate or crack. Doors made of wood may shrink, swell or warp. Swelling may affect the way a door fits in an opening and it may cause sticking. In some instances paint and/or drywall seams may slightly crack. These conditions are normal incidents of home ownership unless they occur in the extreme.

15. Purchaser is aware that certain materials used for fixtures in a new home (including, but not limited to, brass/chrome plumbing fixtures, brass/chrome bathroom accessories and brass/chrome light fixtures) are subject to discoloration and/or corrosion over time.

16. Natural wood has considerable color variation due to its organic nature. There may be shades of white, red, black or even green in areas. In addition, mineral streaks may also be visible. Grain pattern or texture will vary from consistent to completely irregular; wood from different areas of the same tree can also have variations in pattern or texture. It is because of these variations that wood is in such high demand of aesthetic products. These variations in grain will in turn accept stain in varying amounts, which will show throughout the wood products from one door to the next, one panel to the next or one piece of wood to the next. Also, cabinet finishes

427

(including gloss and/or matte finishes) will not be entirely consistent and some minor irregularities will be apparent. Additionally, wood and wood products may be subject to warping, splitting, swelling and/or delamination.

17. Marble and granite are natural pieces of stone. Marble and granite veins and colors may vary drastically from piece to piece and are all different. Marble and granite also have chips and shattering veins which look like scratches. The thickness of the joints between marble, granite or other materials against which they have been laid will vary and there will be irregularities in surface smoothness. Marble and other stone finishes may be dangerously slippery and Seller assumes no responsibility for injuries sustained as a result of exposure to or use of such materials. Periodic use of professionally approved and applied sealant is needed to ensure proper maintenance of the marble and granite, and it is the Purchaser's responsibility to properly maintain these materials. Marble, granite and other stone surfaces may scratch, chip or stain easily. Such substrates, as part of their desirable noise attenuating properties, may flex or move slightly in order to absorb impacts. Such movement may in turn cause grout to crack or loosen or cause some cracking in the stone flooring which may need to be repaired as part of normal home maintenance.

18. Purchaser is aware that it is impossible to avoid a certain amount of cracking in stucco and other cementitious materials. Cracks in Astucco≡, GFRC, GFRG and concrete, including, but not limited to, floors, foundations and building envelope, are to be expected due to normal curing, hot and cold weather, and general stress from movement. Stucco, GFRC and GFRG, like concrete, are cement-based products and are subject to cracking due to, among other reasons, settlement, lumber shrinkage and weather conditions. Cracking is customary at the corners of windows and doors. Concrete floors may not be perfectly flat when poured and some sloping and pooling are common.

§ 15.3.2   Arbitration

Unlike the GAR Purchase and Sale Agreement which does not address alternative dispute resolution options, the GAR New Construction Contract includes a provision to which the buyer and seller may stipulate, requiring the parties to settle any disputes they may have through arbitration. Builders will frequently insist on an agreement to arbitrate disputes because arbitration generally resolves disputes more quickly than court proceedings.

If the buyer and seller agree to this provision and initial it on the contract, all disputes between the parties must be submitted to arbitration, including disputes over construction as well as disputes regarding earnest money or other provisions of the contract. If the arbitration provision is not initialed by both parties, it will not be enforceable. The GAR New Construction Contract arbitration provision takes into account the new mediation procedure required by state law::

> "Buyer and Seller agree that any construction defect claim not resolved after following the procedure described in O.C.G.A. § 8-2-38 and all other claims between the parties shall be settled by arbitration through the services of an arbitrator mutually agreed upon by the parties. The decision of the arbitrator shall be final and may be enforced by any court having jurisdiction thereof. The arbitration shall be conducted in accordance with O.C.G.A. § 9-9-1 et seq. Notwithstanding the provisions of this subparagraph, if Buyer is claiming under a warranty provided by Seller, the terms and procedures of that warranty shall first apply to the resolution of the claim. In order for this paragraph to be a part of this Agreement it must be initialed by Buyer and Seller; if not initialed it shall be void and unenforceable."[1043]

§ 15.3.3   Warranty

The GAR New Construction Contract provides that except to the extent specifically identified, the seller agrees to warrant the property for a one-year period from the date of closing against all defects of labor and materials, normal wear and tear excepted.[1044] Many builders will also include either an insured limited warranty or a builder's limited warranty with the home. Under the New Construction Contract, any warranty in addition to the one-year warranty is to be attached to and incorporated in the contract.

Earlier versions of the GAR New Construction Contract required the seller to deliver to the buyer at closing a warranty as agreed to in the contract, either an insured limited warranty or a builder's limited warranty. However, if the seller failed to deliver to the purchaser at closing the required warranty, there was some question as to whether the merger doctrine precluded the seller from being obligated to provide the warranty to the purchaser. Incorporating the warranty into the agreement avoids this issue. Further, even if no warranty is attached to the contract, the buyer will have, at a minimum, a one-year workmanship warranty.

§ 15.4   New State Law for construction defect claims

On May 17, 2004, the "Right to Repair Act" ("Act"), became effective in Georgia. The Act applies to all dwelling-related construction defect claims against contractors from May 17, 2004 forward. It is one of the most significant new laws in decades for the building industry. Its principal goal is the resolution of residential

---

1043 GAR Form F23, paragraph 13.
1044 GAR Form F23,, paragraph 13.

construction disputes without costly and time-consuming legal proceedings. It is critical that persons covered by the Act understand its terms.

The Act sets out a new mediation procedure for resolving construction defect claims that must be followed before resorting to legal proceedings. The Act applies to both individual homeowners and property owners or condominium owners associations ("Associations") who intend to sue the developer for construction defects. Essentially, it requires the parties to communicate fully before going to court. The Act also requires an Association to follow a series of steps before it can sue for construction defects.

The new statute benefits developers in several ways. The Association is required to show evidence to support its claim at the outset, which gives the developer a chance to evaluate whether the claim is legitimate early in the process and therefore save time and cost. The fact that the Association has to obtain the consent of all the unit owners before making a claim avoids the possibility of the developer having to defend separate claims brought by unit owners who allege that they did not authorize the Association's action and is therefore not bound by any settlement agreement. In the event that the claimant decides to sue, the limitations on the amount of damages and costs that the claimant can recover gives the developer some control over the extent of its liability. A detailed discussion of the Act is set forth below.

§ 15.4.1   Meaning of "claimants"

Who is affected by the Act? It applies to construction defect claims by "claimants" against a remarkably broad range of building-industry players, who are collectively called "contractors." The term "contractor" includes any person or entity who is "engaged in the business" of:

(1) Designing, developing, constructing or selling dwellings;
(2) Designing or constructing alterations or additions to dwellings; or,
(3) Repairing dwellings.

In other words, the Act protects not only builders, but also developers, architects, real estate agents, renovation contractors and repair contractors. The term "contractor" also covers any owner, officer, director, shareholder, partner or employee of a contractor, any subcontractor or supplier of a contractor and any risk retention group (example, HBW) that insures any part of a contractor's liability for a construction defect.

The term "claimant" means anyone "who asserts a claim concerning a construction defect." That term plainly covers homeowners and purchasers. It also covers condominium and neighborhood associations. Whether it covers others is unclear.

§ 15.4.2   Meaning of "dwellings"

What kinds of claims are covered by the Act?   The Act covers only "dwellings."   It does not apply to commercial or industrial construction. However, the term "dwelling" is very broadly defined.   It includes single-family, duplex and condominium units as well as all systems and components of such units.   It also includes improvements, structures or recreational facilities that an owner of a dwelling had the right to use as of the initial sale.

§ 15.4.3   Meaning of "construction defects"

The alternative dispute resolution ("ADR") procedures of the Act apply only to "construction defect" claims relating to dwellings. That term can be defined in two ways: first, through an "express written warranty" and second, through the default definition provided in the Act.   Therefore, to a large extent, builders can generally control the meaning of "construction defects".

If the term "construction defect" is defined in an "express written warranty" provided by a contractor (example: builder limited warranty) or required by statute, that definition will apply.   Generally (HUD, VA and FHA statutory warranties being prominent exceptions), there will not be an express written warranty required by statute. Thus, in most cases, the starting point for understanding the term "construction defect" is the contractor's express written warranty. If "construction defect" is not defined in either an express written warranty given by a contractor or required by a statute, the following definition will apply by default:

> ...construction defect means a matter concerning the design, construction, or repair of a dwelling, or an alteration of or repair or addition to an existing dwelling, or of an appurtenance to a dwelling on which a person has a complaint against a contractor.

This default definition is very broad and includes all conceivable construction-related claims against a contractor relating to a dwelling, including claims for negligence, fraud, and breach of contract.

Since the default definition is likely to be broader than the term "construction defect" in an express written warranty and since, in almost all cases, the contractor will prefer the Act to apply, it is generally advisable to trigger the default definition in contracts and warranties. A specific statement in an express written warranty and sale or construction contract that, for the ADR purposes of the Act, the term "construction defect" will have the default meaning, should accomplish that goal.   Contractors should clarify in those documents, however, that the default definition is not intended to expand the contractor's warranty or contractual construction obligations beyond those set forth in those documents.

The Act states that the definition of "construction defect" "may" also include any physical damage to the dwelling or real property on which it is located that is caused by a construction defect. It is unclear whether the term "may" applies to the default definition as well as to the first definition of "construction defect" in the Act. As a practical matter, this confusion can be addressed by incorporating this permissive expansion of the term into the contractor's warranty and/or contract.

Notably, the provisions of the Act generally apply to any alleged construction defect, even if it is only one of several claims that the claimant has against the contractor. Moreover, the Act may apply to claims where an alleged construction defect is only tangentially or collaterally involved. For example, a claim for the return of earnest money or an adjustment in the contract price due to an alleged construction defect or to a delay in construction could be covered by the Act.

While some of the Act's provisions assume that a dwelling is already owned by the claimant, most of the provisions of the Act, including the definition of "construction defect," appear to apply to construction defect disputes arising before a closing as well as afterward. Application of the Act's ADR procedures to pre-closing disputes will often cause significant delays in closing.

Contractors should have future contracts and warranties reviewed and redrafted as appropriate by legal counsel to coordinate their terms with the Act. Since, however, the Act applies to prior and existing contracts and warranties, many questions arise about the interplay between those documents and the Act. With some exception, the Act does not attempt to coordinate its terms with those in contracts and warranties. To the extent that the Act conflicts with those terms, the Act will presumably prevail. However, as a general matter, the Act should be viewed as an addition or supplement to the procedural requirements of a contract or warranty, meaning those procedures should normally still govern.

§ 15.4.4   New ADR procedure

The Act sets forth a number of steps and a variety of alternatives aimed at resolving disputes without legal proceedings. Understanding these steps and alternatives is critical to effectively using the ADR procedures, which are the heart of the Act.

§ 15.4.4.1   *Notice of Claim must be provided to contractor*

The ADR procedures are initiated with a "notice of claim" ("NOC"). At least 90 days prior to a lawsuit or arbitration asserting a dwelling-related construction defect claim against a contractor, the claimant must "serve" a written NOC on the contractor. The term "serve" means "delivery" by certified mail or authorized next day delivery, return receipt requested, to the last known address of the addressee.

The NOC must contain substantial, specific information. First, it must affirmatively state that the claimant is asserting a construction defect claim and is providing the NOC under the Act. This distinguishes the NOC from other correspondence, such as a traditional warranty notice, which may still be sent to a contractor. Because the Act imposes obligations on contractors upon receipt of a NOC, it is important that contractors recognize when they have received a NOC.

The NOC must also describe the claims "in detail sufficient to explain the nature of the alleged construction defects and the results of the defects." Importantly, the NOC must also include "any evidence" depicting the nature and cause of the defects, including expert reports, photographs, and videotapes, if that evidence would be discoverable under evidentiary rules.

If a claimant plans to pursue a legal proceeding against multiple contractors, a NOC must be sent to each contractor. That can be accomplished with one or separate NOCs.

§ 15.4.4.2   Responding to NOC

Within 30 days after service of a NOC, the contractor must serve a written response on the claimant and on any other contractor that received the NOC. It is important to consider coordinating responses with other contractors, such as your subcontractors, to whom the NOC has been sent. It is also important to remember that a separate NOC, about which you have no knowledge, may have been sent to other contractors.

1.   Responding to NOC by offering to settle without inspection

A contractor receiving a notice of claim ("NOC") has various options. First, the contractor can make a settlement offer without verifying the claim by conducting an inspection of the property. Contractors can respond by offering to settle the claim by monetary payment, repairs, or a combination of the two. The offer should state a time for performance and any terms of importance to the contractor. If the claimant accepts the offer and it is performed, the ADR process ends.

If the claimant rejects the offer, he must serve a written rejection notice on the contractor and its attorney, if any. The claimant's rejection notice must include all known reasons for rejection. If a claimant believes the offer fails to address part of a claim, the notice must note that portion. If the claimant believes the offer is unreasonable "in any manner," the notice must "set forth in detail all known reasons" for that belief. Although not expressly contemplated by the Act, the claimant's notice may also contain a counteroffer.

If the claimant rejects the offer, the claimant can file a suit or demand for arbitration, unless, as discussed below, a supplemental offer is made by the contractor within 15 days after rejection. The ability of a claimant to ultimately pursue a legal action is an important limitation on the Act. The Act does not guarantee or force a settlement; it simply provides ADR procedures intended to promote settlement prior to suit or arbitration. The consequences of a claimant's rejection of a "reasonable offer" are discussed below.

Within 15 days after receiving a rejection notice, the contractor may make a supplemental settlement offer, which may include a monetary offer, a repair offer or a combination of the two. Although the Act does not specifically require the supplemental offer to be in writing, it should be. The Act does not expressly state that the claimant must delay filing a legal action during this 15-day period, however, a court or arbitrator will, upon request, probably stay the action if it is pursued during that period and a supplemental offer has, in fact, been made. It is important to note that the supplemental offer does not include the right to request for an inspection. Thus, if the contractor wants to insist upon an inspection, it must request one in its original response to the NOC. This does not mean that the contractor cannot ask permission to inspect, just that it is not entitled to such an inspection in the context of a supplemental offer.

If a supplemental offer is rejected by the claimant, the claimant must serve a supplemental rejection notice on the contractor setting forth "all known reasons" for rejection. Upon rejection of a supplemental offer, the claimant can file a suit or demand for arbitration.

Under the Act, an offer, whether original or supplemental, can be accepted in a traditional affirmative manner. Acceptance also occurs automatically if a claimant fails to reject an offer to "remedy a construction defect" within 30 days after receiving the offer. While the phrase "remedy a construction defect" plainly covers an offer of repair, it is not clear whether it applies to a monetary offer or a combination of money and repairs.

If a claimant accepts an offer that, in whole or in part, involves repairs, the claimant must provide the contractor and its subcontractors, agents, experts and consultants "unfettered access" to the dwelling for completion of the repairs.

If the claimant accepts an offer, whether original or supplemental, and it is performed, the claimant will thereafter be barred from bringing an action "for the claim described in the NOC." It is very important to appreciate that, after acceptance, the Act only bars a claimant from bringing a legal action for claims described in the NOC. If the contractor intends its settlement offer to fully resolve all potential claims by the claimant, it should condition that offer on a standard release of all claims.

2.   Responding to NOC by requesting inspection

The contractor can respond to a NOC by proposing an inspection of the dwelling. This proposal must be served on the claimant within 30 days after receiving the NOC. The claimant must then, within 30 days after receiving the proposal, provide the contractor and its subcontractors, agents, experts and consultants reasonable access to the dwelling. Reasonable access probably includes access during typical work hours.

In the inspection, the contractor is entitled to examine, document and test anything required to "fully and completely evaluate the nature, extent and cause of the claimed defects and the nature and extent of any repairs or replacements that may be necessary to remedy the alleged defects." The inspection may include destructive testing, although the contractor must give the claimant advance notice of such testing, presumably after the initial inspection, and the dwelling must be returned to its pre-testing condition. If the inspection reveals a condition that requires additional testing to fully evaluate a defect, the contractor must provide notice (written notice is not required, but preferable) to the claimant, after which the claimant must provide prompt and reasonable access to the dwelling.

Within 14 days after completion of the inspection and testing, the contractor must serve on the claimant either a written settlement offer or a statement that the contractor will not remedy the alleged defects. The settlement offer can propose monetary payment, repairs or a combination. If the offer includes repairs, it must include a description of the work and an anticipated timetable. Contractors should be realistic about timetables since claimants may only be required to provide access during that period and a legal action can be pursued if the contractor fails to complete the work during that period. If the contractor declines to remedy the alleged defects, it must state all reasons for declining to do so. In this scenario, contractors should exercise great care in preparing the list of reasons, since it may eventually be scrutinized by a judge, jury or arbitrator. The contractor should include all valid legal and factual reasons in the notice. If the contractor declines to address any defects, the claimant may pursue legal action.

If an offer is made, the claimant may accept it. If the claimant does so and it is performed, the ADR process ends. If a claimant accepts an offer following the inspection process and the contractor fails to make the monetary payment and/or repair the construction defect within the timetable, the claimant may bring an action against the contractor without further notice except as required by law. The claimant may also file the offer and acceptance in that action, which creates a rebuttable presumption that a binding and valid settlement occurred which should be enforced by the court or arbitrator.

If the claimant rejects the offer by the contractor, the claimant must serve a written rejection on the contractor. Presumably, the rejection notice must be served within 30 days after receipt of the settlement offer. The notice must state all known reasons for rejection. If the claimant rejects the offer, the claimant can file a suit or demand for arbitration, unless a supplemental offer is made by the contractor within 15 days thereafter.

Generally speaking, the rules and procedures governing acceptance, supplemental offers, responses to supplemental offers, unfettered access, barring of further claims and the ultimate right to pursue a legal action that were mentioned in the discussion above relating to offers of settlement without inspections apply in the context of offers of settlement following inspections. There are some differences, however, so the Act should be carefully reviewed if this alternative is selected.

3.   Responding to NOC by rejecting claim

The Act also contemplates that the contractor may wholly reject the claimant's NOC. It appears that such a rejection should include all known reasons for the rejection. Any rejection notice should be carefully considered and drafted since it may eventually become evidence at trial or arbitration. It should include all legal and factual reasons for rejection. Upon receipt of a written rejection, the claimant may bring an action against the contractor without further notice except as may otherwise be required by law.

4.   Not Responding to NOC

The Act also recognizes that a contractor may not respond at all to a NOC. If no response occurs within 30 days after service of the NOC, the claimant may bring an action against the contractor without further notice except as may otherwise be required by law.

§ 15.4.4.3   *Proposing an alternative procedure*

After the NOC is served, the Act allows a claimant and a contractor to alter the ADR procedures of the Act by written agreement. No guidance, restrictions or time limitations are provided for such procedures. The permission to alter these procedures only after the NOC is presumably intended to prevent contractors from sidestepping the terms of the Act by including superceding ADR procedures in contracts or warranty documents. The option of proposing alternative ADR procedures should be considered by a contractor in formulating a response to a NOC. If the contractor wishes to propose alternative procedures, it is preferable to do so well in advance of the end of the 30-day period for response to the NOC or include that proposal as an alternative in its response to a NOC. The contractor should also consider involving any other contractors in the written agreement for alternative procedures. Alternative procedures can be elaborate or as simple as extensions or limitations on the time for certain actions.

Regardless of the alternative response contemplated by a contractor, it is important that it immediately notify its insurer(s) of the receipt of a NOC. A contractor, who believes that insurance coverage may exist for a claim should not make a settlement offer without first notifying the insurer and requesting its involvement. Given the relatively short deadline for responding to a NOC, contractors should insist on prompt responses by their insurer(s). Because NOCs must contain more information than a suit or demand for arbitration, insurer(s) should theoretically be better equipped than otherwise to determine coverage and to participate in the ADR process.

§ 15.4.5   Consequences of rejecting a "reasonable offer"

Claimants that reject a "reasonable offer," including any reasonable supplemental offer, are not precluded from pursuing an action. However, they cannot recover an amount greater than:

(1)   the fair market value of the settlement offer;
(2)   the actual cost of the repairs made; or
(3)   the amount of a monetary settlement offer.

These limits could eliminate reduction in fair market value, loss of use, inconvenience, punitive and many other damages. The Act also precludes the claimant from recovering attorney's fees or costs otherwise recoverable that are incurred after the rejection of a reasonable offer. If the only real damages at issue are repair costs, the claimant may not suffer significant losses, other than self-inflicted attorney's fees, legal expenses, costs and lost time, from rejecting a reasonable offer.

The trier of fact (judge, jury or arbitrator) determines the reasonableness of the settlement offer. The trier of fact will presumably consider not only offers, but the reasons provided by the claimant in its rejection notice(s). The Act does not expressly state that in a subsequent legal proceeding the claimant will be limited to those reasons in defending its rejection, but that may be the legal or practical consequence. The admissibility of settlement offers and other communications relating to settlement is a major departure from the normal rule that settlement discussions are inadmissible in evidence. This change suggests that contractors exercise care to ensure that offers and other communications are, in fact, reasonable and are readily understood as such by a trier of fact.

The same damages limitations for rejections of reasonable offers apply when a claimant does not permit a contractor to make repairs per an accepted settlement offer. The Act does not expressly authorize enforcement of an agreement to repair, but a contractor might be able to enforce it by relying on legal principles not set forth in the Act.

Presumably, a contractor must assert that a claimant failed to accept a reasonable offer for that to be an issue in a suit or arbitration. If the contractor does not raise that issue, because it is concerned that its offer was not or may not be perceived by a trier of fact as reasonable or for any other reason, it is doubtful that the claimant will be able to raise the issue solely for the purpose of demonstrating the unreasonableness of the offer.

§ 15.4.6   Consequences of failing to comply with Act's procedures

If a claimant files a legal action, whether a suit or arbitration, "without first complying with the requirements" of the Act, the court or arbitrator is required, if requested by the contractor or other party to the action, to stay the action until the claimant has complied. This is the principal way for contractors to enforce compliance by claimants.

A failure by a claimant to comply with the "requirements of" the Act may mean almost any failure, including failing to: serve a NOC; include all information and documentation required in the NOC; serve a notice of rejection; include all reasons for rejection in the notice of rejection; or allow an inspection upon proper request by a contractor. A claimant's failure to allow access for repairs after accepting an offer involving repairs, even though required by the Act, does not appear to be grounds for a stay since the Act allows a claimant to pursue a legal action despite breaching that agreement.

In this context, it is important to understand the actions subject to a stay under the Act. The term "action" is defined very broadly to mean "any civil lawsuit, judicial action, or arbitration proceeding asserting a claim in whole or in part for damages or other relief in connection with a dwelling caused by an alleged construction defect." Thus, for a stay to apply, it is not necessary that all or even most of the claims in the case involve construction defects. It may be sufficient if a construction defect claim is only tangentially or collaterally involved. The stay probably does not apply to criminal code enforcement procedures against a contractor.

If a claimant has sent a NOC to more than one contractor, the claimant may have completed the Acts' prerequisites to a suit or arbitration as to some contractors, but not others. Thus, the claimant may be able to pursue a suit or arbitration against some contractors, but not others.

If a lawsuit or arbitration, as initially filed, does not assert a construction defect claim, but one is asserted by way of amendment, the action should be stayed upon request of any party. Whether a counterclaim by a claimant asserting a construction defect claim is covered by the Act is not clear. Since the overall intent of the Act is to promote resolution of construction defect claims, counterclaims are probably covered.

Although the Act does not provide a time within which a motion or request to stay must be filed, contractors should assume that it must be promptly filed. If it is not, the claimant may successfully argue that the contractor waived its right to a stay. If the grounds for a stay do not reasonably become apparent to a contractor until the discovery process or later, a contractor may be able to stay the action at that time.

If an action is filed without compliance by the claimant and the contractor is required to file a motion or request for stay, the contractor should consider a claim for attorney's fees and expenses incurred in obtaining the stay. Whether such a claim may be pursued in arbitration, as opposed to a lawsuit, is less clear under Georgia law.

The Act expressly authorizes an action to be filed before the ADR process is pursued or completed if a statute of limitation will expire during that process. However, that action must be immediately stayed. The stay does not apply to a claim for damages due to personal injury or death, although it does apply to construction defects claims asserted in the same action.

If, after serving the NOC, other construction defects are "discovered," a claimant cannot pursue a suit or arbitration against a contractor for those defects without first following the same ADR procedures outlined above for the original NOC.

§ 15.4.7   Mandatory notice required under the Act

The Act requires a contractor to provide written notice to a buyer or owner of a dwelling of the contractor's right to resolve construction defects before the buyer or owner commences an action against the contractor. That notice must be provided at the time the initial contract between the contractor and the buyer or owner is signed. It is not clear that the notice has to be provided before the contract is signed, but doing so is safer. The Act does expressly state that the notice may be included as a part of the contract and, as a matter of practice, that is probably the best approach.

In whatever manner the notice is provided, it must be conspicuous and must be in "substantially" the form set forth in the Act. The safest course is simply to include that exact language, which is as follows:

GEORGIA LAW CONTAINS IMPORTANT REQUIREMENTS YOU MUST FOLLOW BEFORE YOU MAY FILE A LAWSUIT OR OTHER ACTION FOR DEFECTIVE CONSTRUCTION AGAINST THE CONTRACTOR WHO CONSTRUCTED, IMPROVED, OR REPAIRED YOUR HOME. NINETY DAYS BEFORE YOU FILE YOUR LAWSUIT OR OTHER ACTION, YOU MUST SERVE ON THE CONTRACTOR A WRITTEN NOTICE OF ANY CONSTRUCTION CONDITIONS YOU ALLEGE ARE DEFECTIVE. UNDER THE LAW, A CONTRACTOR HAS THE OPPORTUNITY TO MAKE AN

OFFER TO REPAIR OR PAY FOR THE DEFECTS OR BOTH. YOU ARE NOT OBLIGATED TO ACCEPT ANY OFFER MADE BY A CONTRACTOR. THERE ARE STRICT DEADLINES AND PROCEDURES UNDER STATE LAW, AND FAILURE TO FOLLOW THEM MAY AFFECT YOUR ABILITY TO FILE A LAWSUIT OR OTHER ACTION.

This statutory language is an attempt to summarize the terms of the Act and should not be relied upon by the parties as sufficiently describing the terms of the Act.

One of the questions unanswered by the Act is the consequence to a contractor of failing to provide this notice. The Act does not expressly state that a contractor's failure to provide the notice excuses the claimant from providing the NOC and otherwise complying with the terms of the Act. That, however, is likely to be the interpretation by courts and arbitrators. Presumably, the notice requirement only applies to general contractors and others (real estate agents, buyer or owner-retained architects, etc.) who have a direct contract with the owner or buyer. Other persons and entities covered by the term "contractor," such as subcontractors, suppliers, contractor-retained engineers or architects, that do not have a contract with the owner or buyer appear to be excused from that obligation.

§ 15.4.8   Claims by associations

The statute makes it difficult for an association to sue a developer in a number of different ways. As of the date of publication of this book, there is some movement to modify these provisions as applied to associations.

Under the Act, the term "association" is defined as "a corporation formed for the purpose of exercising the powers of the members of any community interest community."[1045] This definition covers homeowners associations, property owners associations and condominium associations that have been incorporated. It does not cover unincorporated neighborhood associations, which, in some cases, can assert claims against developers.[1046] It also does not cover claims by individual unit owners, individually or collectively.

First, the new law only allows an association to sue a developer for claims involving the common elements and the limited common elements only. An association cannot sue for defects involving the individually owned condominium units.

The Act states that an association has to comply with a number of

---

1045   O.C.G.A. § 8-2-36 (2).
1046   O.C.G.A. § 9-2-24.

preconditions to a construction defect action for damages against a contractor.[1047] According to its wording, this subsection only applies to legal actions for "damages."[1048] Thus, legal actions for injunctive or declaratory relief are not covered by this subsection.

The statute then goes on to say that the association can only bring a claim after following a fairly cumbersome series of steps. The most significant is the requirement that the association obtain the written approval of each unit owner whose interest in the common elements or limited elements would be the subject of the lawsuit. Since all unit owners own an undivided interest in the common elements, this likely means that the association cannot commence a lawsuit involving a common element without first obtaining the written consent of all unit owners.

Third, the association will also have to hold a meeting to obtain the majority vote of the unit owners to commence the action. Before conducting such a meeting, the association must give each unit owner 21 days' notice of such meeting. The attorney representing the association will also have to send a written statement to each unit owner 3 days before the meeting. The statement must include in reasonable detail the following:

(1)   the defects and damages or injuries to the common elements or limited common elements;
(2)   the cause of the defects if known;
(3)   the nature and extent of the damage or injury caused by the defects;
(4)   the location of each defect;
(5)   a reasonable estimate of the cost to remedy, which should include attorney's fees and expert fees;
(6)   the disclosures that the unit owner must make upon the sale of the unit.

The next step is for the association's full board of directors and the developer to meet in person and make a good faith attempt to resolve the association's claim. If the parties cannot come to a solution, then they must proceed with the mediation procedure that is set out in the new statute.

1047   O.C.G.A. § 8-2-42 (e).
1048   O.C.G.A. § 8-2-42 (e). While the definition of "action" is broad enough to cover suits or demands for arbitration covering claims other than for damages, O.C.G.A. § 8-2-42 (e) covers only actions for damages for construction defects. Thus, an enforcement action by an association against a contractor for violation of architectural control standards will not be covered by the Act even though such a violation might fall within the Act's definition of "construction defect." If, however, that enforcement action seeks damages as allowed by the covenants or otherwise, the action may be covered by O.C.G.A. § 8-2-42 (e).

§ 15.5   Land/Lot Purchase and Sale Agreement

§ 15.5.1   Purchase price

The GAR Lot/Land Purchase and Sale Agreement ("GAR Lot/Land Contract") gives the parties two options for stating the purchase price.[1049] The first option is to provide a stipulated sum. The second option allows the parties to determine the purchase price on the basis of acreage. The parties designate one party to have a survey made of the property by a registered Georgia surveyor. The purchase price will be determined by multiplying the total number of acres, to the nearest one-hundredth of an acre, by a stipulated sum per acre. If the survey is not mutually acceptable, the parties agree to resolve that issue in accordance with the provisions of the GAR Survey Resolution Exhibit.[1050]

The GAR Survey Resolution Exhibit establishes a procedure to resolve differences between the buyer's survey and the seller's survey (if the seller elects to commission a survey after reviewing the buyer's survey.) If the seller and buyer are unable to agree upon a survey, then both the buyer and seller will cause their respective surveyors to name a third surveyor. If the two surveyors have not named a third surveyor within seven calendar days from the date they are requested to make an appointment, a superior court judge serving the county where the property is located may appoint a third surveyor. The third surveyor is employed by the buyer and seller to make a survey of the property, the cost of which is equally borne by the buyer and seller. The acreage on the survey by the third surveyor will be used in the formula to calculate the purchase price.

§ 15.5.2   Earnest money

The earnest money provision of the GAR Lot/Land Contract is identical to that set forth in the GAR Purchase and Sale Agreement. However, there are also a number of GAR Lot/Land special stipulations, including one providing that the earnest money will be held by the seller.[1051] If the parties elect to have the earnest money held by the seller, the parties should incorporate the GAR exhibit providing for earnest money held by seller.[1052] If the buyer wants to limit his liability to the amount of earnest money, the buyer may incorporate Special Stipulation #3-5 from this book.

§ 15.5.3   Disclosure

As in the GAR Purchase and Sale Agreement, the Lot/Land Contract provides that a Seller's Property Disclosure Statement[1053] is attached and incorporated in the

---

1049   GAR Form F27, Lot/Land Contract, paragraph 2.
1050   GAR Form F136, Survey Resolution Exhibit.
1051   GAR Form F28, Lot/Land Special Stipulations.
1052   GAR Form F80, Earnest Money Held by Seller.
1053   GAR Form F53, Seller's Lot/Land Disclosure Statement.

agreement.[1054] The buyer should carefully review this disclosure statement to determine if it addresses all issues which are of concern to the buyer. Unlike the GAR New Construction Contract, the Seller's Lot/Land Property Disclosure Statement addresses whether there is or will be any fill on the property. This disclosure should address the issue of whether the seller has buried trees or other construction debris on the property.

§ 15.5.4   Inspection

The inspection provision of the Lot/Land Contract provides that the buyer and/or the buyer's representatives has the right to enter the property at the buyer's expense at reasonable times to inspect, examine, test and survey the property. As in the GAR Contract, the seller is obligated to cause all utility services and any pools, spa, and similar items be operational so the buyer can complete all inspections under the agreement. The buyer agrees to hold the seller and all brokers harmless from all claims, injuries, and damages arising out of or related to the exercise of these rights. Under the Lot/Land Contract, the buyer has the right and responsibility to review and inspect all aspects of the property.

§ 15.5.5   GAR Land/Lot Special Stipulations

There are a number of optional special stipulations provided for in the GAR Land/Lot Special Stipulations.[1055] The special stipulations include allowing the parties to provide for a feasibility study, percolation tests, and well tests.

§ 15.5.5.1   Feasibility study

In many instances prior to committing to purchase undeveloped property, the buyer will want to review matters such as governmental ordinances, environmental issues, zoning issues, whether the property can support a septic system of the size needed for the contemplated improvements or the property (commonly referred to as a percolation test) and well and utility service matters. For example, if utilities are not available at the lot line, the buyer's expense in bringing such utilities can significantly increase the cost of the property to the buyer.

A significant issue for buyers purchasing larger tracts of land should be potential hazardous waste being discovered on the property. The federal Comprehensive Environmental Response, Compensation and Liability Act (CERCLA)[1056] addresses environmental contamination resulting from uncontrolled hazardous waste sites. CERCLA imposes liability on the current owner or operator of a facility as well as the owner or operator of the facility at the time of disposal. To address potential hazardous waste issues, as part of the feasibility study, buyers may

---

1054   See chapter 5 regarding the effect of making it part of the contract.
1055   GAR Form F28, Lot/Land Special Stipulations.
1056   42 U.S.C. §§ 9601-9675.

commission (and lenders will likely require) a Phase I Environmental Site Assessment to identify obvious or reasonably likely sources of hazardous or regulated materials that may be associated with the property.

The GAR Feasibility Study Contingency[1057] gives the buyer a specified number of days in which to notify the seller that the buyer is not satisfied with the results of the feasibility study, in which case the agreement will automatically terminate and the buyer's earnest money will be returned. If the buyer fails to provide this notice, then the contingency is deemed waived by the buyer.

§ 15.5.5.2   Well test

A buyer of property served by well water will likely want the well water tested to determine its suitability for drinking or any other use. Under the GAR Well Test Special Stipulation[1058], the buyer has the duty and responsibility of ordering, supervising, and paying for any well water sample tests he wants performed or that his lender requires to be performed prior to closing.

§ 15.5.5.3   Building permit

If the buyer intends to purchase the property for a particular purpose, the buyer may want to make the purchase contingent on the buyer obtaining authority to build on it. In such cases, the parties should incorporate the GAR Building Permit Stipulation,[1059] which provides that if the buyer is unable to acquire all required licenses and permits from the appropriate governmental authority to build on the property within a specified time frame, the agreement will automatically terminate and the buyer's earnest money will be refunded. If the buyer fails to provide notice under this provision, the contingency is deemed waived by the buyer.

§ 15.5.5.4   Rezoning

If the buyer must have the property rezoned in order to use it for its intended purpose, the parties should incorporate the GAR Rezoning Special Stipulation,[1060] which provides that the agreement is contingent on the property being rezoned to a specified category of zoning by the appropriate governmental authorities by a specified date. This special stipulation allows the parties to determine whether the buyer or seller will be responsible for pursuing the rezoning and the payment of all associated costs. The rezoning contingency provides that if the buyer notifies the seller and broker in writing within 48 hours after the specified date that the property cannot be rezoned, then the agreement will automatically terminate and the broker will refund the earnest money to the buyer.

1057   GAR Form F28, Lot/Land Special Stipulations.
1058   GAR Form F28, Lot/Land Special Stipulations.
1059   GAR Form F28, Lot/Land Special Stipulations.
1060   GAR Form F28, Lot/Land Special Stipulations.

There are two key issues to remember when property is contracted to be sold subject to being rezoned. First, the statute of limitations to challenge a rezoning approved by local government is 30 days from the date of the final governmental approval. As a result, most buyers will not want to close on a property, which has been rezoned until the appeal period has run. Therefore, the term "final zoning" in most real estate sales contracts is defined as 30 days from the date that the local government has approved the rezoning of the property.

Second, sellers need to carefully think through the wisdom of giving their buyers an open-ended ability to challenge a denial of rezoning request in court. Court challenges can often take several years, particularly if the case goes up on appeal. Therefore, many sellers will want to include an outside date for the closing of the property (even if a lawsuit has been filed), after which the seller may, but is not obligated, to terminate the contract.

§ 15.6 Lease/Purchase Agreement

A buyer may enter into a lease/purchase agreement when he does not have enough money to purchase the property, but anticipates that he will be able to purchase the property within some defined period of time. The GAR Lease/Purchase Agreement[1061] is not an option to purchase. Rather, the buyer and seller agree to close on a specified date or such earlier date as may be agreed to by the parties. Most of the provisions in the GAR Lease/Purchase Agreement are the same as in the GAR Purchase and Sale Contract; however, there are some differences.

§ 15.6.1   Earnest money

The earnest money provision of the GAR Lease/Purchase Agreement varies from the GAR Purchase and Sale Agreement. The GAR Lease/Purchase Agreement provides that the seller, rather than a third party, will hold the earnest money. The GAR Lease/Purchase Agreement also provides that the seller shall return the earnest money to the buyer only: (1) if the parties do not enter into a binding lease/purchase agreement; (2) upon failure of the seller to perform its obligations or warranties; (3) upon written agreement signed by the parties; (4) upon an order of a court or arbitrator having jurisdiction over the earnest money; or (5) upon failure of any of the conditions in the Lease/Purchase Agreement. The earnest money provision allows the seller to retain the earnest money as liquidated damages if buyer breaches buyer's obligations or warranties. If the seller fails to return the earnest money within seven days of a demand by the buyer for same, then the earnest money is deemed to have been claimed by the seller as liquidated damages and the seller will be precluded from pursuing the buyer for specific performance or actual damages.

§ 15.6.2   Lease compensation

1061   GAR Form F29, Lease/Purchase Agreement.

The GAR Lease/Purchase Agreement provides that the parties agree that lease payments made in accordance with the lease attached as an exhibit to the agreement are not to be applied to the purchase price of the property unless otherwise stipulated.[1062] If the parties desire that a portion of the lease payment is applied to the purchase price, the following special stipulation may be used:

Special Stipulation #15-16: Credit towards purchase price for rent

Buyer and Seller agree that at closing, Buyer shall receive a credit towards the purchase price in the amount of ___% of the rent payments, excluding any late charges.

§ 15.6.3   Credit report contingency

Since the seller is taking his property off the market for some period of time and assuming the role of landlord until the closing, the seller will want some assurance that the purchaser/lessee is credit worthy and will be able to meet the lease obligations. The credit report contingency[1063] provides that the agreement is contingent upon the seller's receipt of a satisfactory credit report on the buyer, which report must be provided by buyer at buyer's expense within seven days of the Binding Agreement Date. If the buyer does not provide the credit report, the seller may terminate the agreement by delivering a written notice to buyer within ten days of the Binding Agreement Date. If the buyer provides a credit report which is unsatisfactory to the seller, the seller may terminate the agreement by delivering written notice to the buyer within three days after seller receives the credit report, provided approval of the credit report is not unreasonably withheld.

§ 15.6.4   Lease agreement

When entering a lease/purchase agreement, it is important for the seller to ensure that the termination date of the lease is the same as the proposed closing date. The GAR Lease for Lease/Purchase exhibit provides that the term shall end at midnight on the closing date specified in the Lease/Purchase Agreement.[1064] The lease also provides that the earnest money cannot be applied against any rent payment due without the approval of the landlord.[1065]

The lessee has substantially more obligations under the GAR Lease for Lease/Purchase than under the standard GAR Lease[1066]. In part, the reason for increased tenant maintenance obligations is that the buyer/tenant performs the inspection under the Lease/Purchase Agreement within a specified number of days

---

1062   GAR Form F29, Lease/Purchase Agreement.
1063   GAR Form F29, Lease Purchase Agreement.
1064   GAR Form F30, Lease for Lease/Purchase Agreement.
1065   GAR Form F30, Lease for Lease/Purchase Agreement.
1066   GAR Form F40, Lease.

from the Binding Agreement Date and upon successful conclusion of the Repair Negotiation Period, the buyer accepts the property "as is." Therefore, the GAR Lease for Lease/Purchase provides that the tenant is responsible for maintaining the heating, sewer/septic, well, plumbing, air conditioning and electrical systems, and any built-in appliances and equipment in normal working order and keeping the roof watertight beginning on the commencement date of the lease; provided that any warranties commence on the date of the lease rather than the date of closing.[1067] Although a departure from the owner's responsibility under Georgia landlord-tenant law, as further consideration for entering the Lease/Purchase Agreement, the parties also agree that the tenant is solely responsible for all minor repairs and/or maintenance on the property from the date of occupancy to the date of closing or termination of the agreement.[1068]

If the parties structure a lease/purchase agreement in the form of a lease with an option to purchase instead of in the form set forth in the GAR Lease Purchase Agreement, the inspection would likely not be performed until the option was exercised. In such a case, the lease agreement could follow the standard GAR Lease format.[1069]

The GAR Lease for Lease/Purchase prohibits the tenant from making any alterations, repairs, or improvements to the property without first obtaining prior written consent of the landlord. If the landlord consents, the tenant is required to provide proof that labor, services, and materials have been paid for and the tenant agrees to indemnify the landlord from any liens which may be asserted relating the alterations, repairs, or improvements.[1070] If the tenant makes any such repairs, alterations, or improvements and the sale is not consummated, the alterations, repairs, or improvements are deemed to be the sole property of the landlord. The tenant is not entitled to be reimbursed or compensated for making the alterations, repairs, or improvements, and the tenant waives any right to assert or file a lien against the property.[1071]

The GAR Lease for Lease/Purchase also authorizes the tenant to cancel the lease at the election of tenant if the property is destroyed or substantially damaged by fire, storm, earthquake, or other casualty that is not the fault of the tenant, as of the date of destruction or damage.[1072] If the tenant elects to cancel the lease, the tenant must either cancel the lease/purchase agreement or consummate the lease/purchase agreement pursuant to its terms which are the same as set forth in the GAR Purchase and Sale Agreement for condition of property.[1073]

1067   GAR Form F30, Lease for Lease/Purchase Agreement.
1068   GAR Form F30, Lease for Lease/Purchase Agreement.
1069   GAR Form F40, Lease.
1070   GAR Form F30, Lease for Lease/Purchase Agreement.
1071   GAR Form F30, Lease for Lease/Purchase Agreement.
1072   GAR Form F30, Lease for Lease/Purchase Agreement.
1073   GAR Form F29, Lease/Purchase Agreement.

OVERVIEW

The Brokerage Relationships in Real Estate Transactions Act ("BRRETA") was enacted by the Georgia legislature in 1994 and was substantially revised effective July 1, 2000. The purpose of BRRETA is to define and to regulate the relationships between real estate brokers and the public through state statute rather than through the traditional common law rules of agency.

This chapter discusses BRRETA, the different types of brokerage relationships that are permitted in Georgia, the duties of brokers acting in each type of brokerage relationship, limitations on brokers' liability to customers and clients, brokers' disclosure obligations, handling the change from one type of brokerage relationship to another, and terminating the brokerage relationship. Also included are discussions of the GAR Brokerage Engagements and how they can be used by brokers to comply with BRRETA, and a section on choosing the appropriate form of agency for different situations.

§ 16.1 Types of brokerage relationships

BRRETA divides brokerage relationships into two different groups: (1) broker-client relationships, in which the broker is representing the party with whom the broker is working as a client and (2) broker-customer relationships, in which the broker is not representing the party with whom the broker is working. As discussed below, brokers are allowed to perform more services and owe greater duties to clients than to customers.

§ 16.1.1 The broker–client relationship

In a broker-client relationship the broker represents the client, and is permitted to perform a variety of services for her. BRRETA imposes a few requirements on establishing a broker-client relationship, but also substantially limits the duties owed from the broker to the client.

§ 16.1.1.1 Written agreement required for client relationship

BRRETA was revised effective July 1, 2000, to provide that a client relationship can only be formed by a written agreement between the broker and the party being represented as a client.[1074] The written agreement is referred to as the "brokerage engagement."[1075]

Prior to July 1, 2000, a client relationship could be formed through an express agreement of the parties. The express agreement could be either verbal or written. The

---

1074   O.C.G.A. § 10-6A-3(4), (6).
1075   O.C.G.A. § 10-6A-3(4).

new requirement for a written agreement protects consumers and real estate brokers because written agreements tend to minimize the likelihood of disputes between the parties[1076]. While the change in the law represents something of a departure from past practice, rules of the Georgia Real Estate Commission have long held that "exclusive brokerage agreements must be in writing."[1077]

§ 16.1.1.2   Contents of the brokerage engagement

Section 10-6A-10 of BRRETA requires that the brokerage engagement must do the following things:

(a)   <u>Advise the prospective client of the types of agency relationships available through the broker</u>.

To satisfy this requirement, the brokerage agreement must disclose to the prospective client which of the agency relationships permitted in Georgia (i.e., seller agency, buyer agency, designated agency and dual agency, landlord agency, and tenant agency) are practiced by the brokerage firm. BRRETA also specifically requires the brokerage engagement to state whether the broker practices or rejects dual agency.[1078] If the firm does not offer dual agency, it is not sufficient for the firm to list only those forms of representation that the firm offers without mentioning dual agency. Rather, the firm must affirmatively state that it does not practice dual agency. Since transaction brokerage (discussed in § 16.4.2.3.) is not an agency relationship,[1079] it does not need to be referenced in the broker's agency policy. Below are two sample agency policies:

(i)   <u>Single Agency Policy</u>:   It is the policy of _____ Realty Company to only represent buyers as clients in real estate transactions. Other than buyer brokerage, _____ Realty Company does not offer its clients other agency relationships and does not practice dual agency.

(ii)   <u>Multiple Agency Policy</u>:   It is the policy of _____ Realty Company to offer buyer agency, seller agency, dual agency, designated agency, landlord agency, and tenant agency.

(b)   <u>Advise the prospective client of any brokerage relationships held by the broker with other parties that would conflict with any interests of the prospective client actually known to the broker</u>.

1076   See, however, section * for a discussion of how the requirement of a written brokerage engagement could impact a broker's claim to a real estate commission.
1077   Substantive Regulations 520-1-.03.
1078   O.C.G.A. § 10-6A-12(f).
1079   O.C.G.A. § 10-6A-3(14).

This provision requires that brokers notify their prospective clients of other customer or client relationships they have that might conflict with the interests of the client entering into the brokerage engagement.

It is clear that the broker does not have to make a blanket disclosure that he may be representing other sellers, landlords and tenants in selling or leasing property or other buyers in purchasing property.[1080] BRRETA does not give any other guidance on the types of brokerage relationships held by the broker might be in conflict with the interests of the client and would therefore need to be disclosed to a prospective client. However, since the statute requires the broker to disclose conflicting agency relationships the broker has "with other parties", the provision does not appear to require disclosure of how one agency relationship might conflict generally with another agency relationship. Instead, this portion of the statute requires only the disclosure of specific conflicts between individuals both of whom are represented by the same broker. The problem below gives an example of such a conflict.

Problem: A large corporation plans to expand its corporate headquarters into a surrounding neighborhood of single-family homes. The corporation knows that when its plans become public, the prices of the homes will skyrocket. The corporation hires a local brokerage firm to quietly assemble as many homes in the neighborhood as possible at low prices. An owner of one of the homes in the neighborhood approaches the same brokerage firm. He says that he is thinking about hiring the firm to sell his home, but wants the firm's opinion as to whether holding onto the property would be a good investment. Would the firm have to disclose its agency relationship with the large corporation before listing the property?

Answer: The logical answer to this question would be "yes." This is a case where the broker holds a specific agency relationship with one client that conflicts with, or is substantially likely to conflict with, the interests of another client. Because the price of real estate in the neighborhood is about to rise dramatically because of confidential information known to the broker, the brokerage firm cannot answer the seller's question regarding the investment potential for his property without jeopardizing the interests of an existing client. Similarly, failing to disclose the plans of the large corporation could potentially harm the interests of the seller. The best solution to this potential conflict is to decline to represent the seller as a client and to allow the seller to be represented by another broker.

(c)   Advise the prospective client as to the broker's compensation.

To satisfy this statutory requirement, the brokerage engagement must state the terms under which the broker will receive a commission. The law also requires that the brokerage engagement state whether the broker will share the commission with other cooperating brokers. The law does not require that the amount of compensation to be paid to a cooperating broker be revealed, but only whether the commission will or will

---

1080   O.C.G.A. § 10-6A-10(2).

not be shared. However, the GAR Exclusive Seller Listing Agreement[1081] includes a place for the listing broker to fill in the amount of the commission to be offered to cooperating brokers. This change was made to insure that sellers were aware of the commission splits being offered by their listing brokers.[1082]

(d)   Advise the prospective client of the broker's obligations to keep information confidential under the law.

BRRETA requires that the broker's duty to keep information confidential also be explained in the brokerage engagement. All of the GAR Brokerage Engagement forms include an explanation of the broker's duties to keep confidences in dual agency transactions, and an explanation that brokers representing persons in a client capacity may not reveal any information they receive during the term of the brokerage agreement unless the client either allows the disclosure or the disclosure is required by law. The client may permit disclosure of confidential information by either words or conduct. BRRETA specifically states that a broker does not violate the duty of confidentiality by disclosing confidential information to any of the broker's affiliated licensees who are assisting the broker in the representation of the client,[1083] except in transactions where the brokerage firm is practicing designated agency. (Refer to § 16.2.5 of this Chapter for a complete discussion of the duty of confidentiality under BRRETA.)

§ 16.1.1.3   Broker can work with customer without written Brokerage Agreement

A written agreement is not needed to establish a broker-customer relationship in Georgia.[1084] For example, a broker can show a buyer property without establishing a client relationship. In such a relationship, the broker can perform only ministerial acts on behalf of the party being shown the property.[1085] Similarly, a broker can also have a verbal, non-client, non-exclusive agreement with a seller in which the seller agrees to pay the broker a commission if the broker procures a buyer to purchase the property (i.e., an "open listing"). Of course, the broker could not represent the seller as a client in such a transaction without a written agreement. BRRETA does not require that agency be explained or offered to customers.

1081   GAR Form *
1082   Cooperating brokers may be reluctant to show the property to prospective
          purchasers if the commission split is too low.
1083   O.C.G.A. § 10-6A-5(a)(5), 10-6A-6(a)(5), 10-6A-7(a)(5), 10-6A-8(a)(5).
1084   O.C.G.A. § 10-6A-3(8).
1085   O.C.G.A. § 10-6A-3(8).

§ 16.1.1.4 Sales contract is not a Brokerage Engagement

Buyer customers often get to a point in the transaction where they ask the broker with whom they are working to represent them as clients. Before undertaking such representation, the broker must be careful to enter into a written brokerage agreement meeting the requirements of BRRETA. The GAR Contract cannot serve as the written brokerage agreement because it does not contain all of the four items required by law to be included in a brokerage engagement. (See § 16.1.1.2 supra.) Therefore, the broker should use a GAR Buyer Brokerage Agreement[1086] as the written agreement to establish the client relationship.

§ 16.1.1.5 Different brokerage agreements needed to sell and buy property

It is not uncommon for buyers to also want their brokers to represent them in selling their existing homes or for sellers to ask their brokers to also represent them in buying new homes. Brokers representing the same client as both buyer and seller should enter into separate brokerage agreements for each type of representation. This is because the duties owed as a listing broker are different from the duties owed as a buyer broker.[1087]

§ 16.1.1.6 Representing a client without written agreement

What happens if a broker enters into an agreement to represent a party as a client without reducing the agreement to writing as required by BRRETA? While the answer is not clear, contracts made in violation of state law are subject to being challenged as unenforceable.[1088] Therefore, the broker's claim to a real estate commission on the basis of breach of contract could be jeopardized.[1089] This is in contrast to violations of the rules and regulations of the Georgia Real Estate Commission, which can subject the broker to being sanctioned but will not render the contract unenforceable.[1090]

§ 16.1.2 Types of Broker-Client Relationships

Prior to the enactment of BRRETA in 1994, brokers in Georgia almost exclusively practiced sub-agency, in which the broker working with the buyer in the transaction was the sub-agent of the listing agent (if the two brokers worked for

---

1086   GAR Form *

1087   Infra.

1088   Bowers v. Howell, 203 Ga. App. 636, 637; 417 S.E. 2d 392, 393 (1992); Harris v. Auto Finance Corporation, 135 Ga. App. 267, 268; 218 S.E. 2d 83, 84 (1975); O.C.G.A. § 13-8-2 (A contract which is against the policy of the law cannot be enforced.)

1089   See section 13.2 for a detailed discussion of the current state of the law regarding a broker's entitlement to a real estate commission when providing brokerage services to a client without a written brokerage agreement.

1090   Johnson Realty, Inc. v. Hand, 189 Ga. App. 706, 377 S.E. 2d 176 (1988).

different firms). Under this arrangement, all of the brokers represented the seller, and the buyer did not have representation. Brokers referred to the buyers with whom they worked (but did not represent) as "customers." Sellers were referred to by their brokers as "clients" because an agency relationship existed between the parties. Now, after BRRETA's adoption, there are multiple agency choices available to brokers, and sub-agency has almost completely disappeared in Georgia. The following sections discuss these newer forms of agency.

BRRETA permits a variety of broker-client relationships. One category of client relationship is single agency representation in which the broker represents only a single party as a client in the transaction. There are two kinds of single agency representation: seller agency and buyer agency. BRRETA also permits brokers to offer designated agency and dual agency to clients. When these two agency relationships are used, the broker represents two parties in the transaction (such as buyer and seller) as clients at the same time.

§ 16.1.2.1   Single agency representation

(a)   <u>Seller agency</u>.

With a seller agency, sometimes called listing agency, the broker represents only the seller in the transaction. Neither the broker nor the broker's affiliated licensees have a client relationship with the buyer. In the GAR Exclusive Seller Listing Agreement, [1091] the duties of the listing broker are to use his or her best efforts to find a buyer ready, willing and able to purchase the seller's property at a price agreed to by the seller, and to assist, to the extent requested by the seller, in filling out a pre-printed real estate sales contract.

(b)   <u>Buyer agency</u>.

Buyer agency, also known as buyer brokerage, is the other form of single agency representation. In buyer agency, the broker represents only the buyer as a client in the transaction. Since the enactment of BRRETA it has become common for buyers to have brokers representing them in real estate transactions. The broker working for the buyer is called the "selling broker" (not to be confused with the broker working for the seller, who is known as the "listing broker"). With a buyer agency the broker works for the buyer- client in locating property for the buyer and, to the extent requested by the client, assisting with negotiations for the purchase of the property. In most buyer brokerage agreements, including the GAR Buyer Brokerage Agreements, the broker representing the buyer receives a portion of the listing broker's commission under a cooperative brokerage arrangement even though the broker is not representing the seller as a client. Thus, except in a few situations, the seller ultimately pays the entire commission. In Georgia, the broker can be paid a commission by one party yet represent another party. BRRETA specifically provides that "[t]he payment or

---

1091   GAR Form *

promise of payment of compensation to a broker by a seller, landlord, buyer or tenant shall not determine whether a brokerage relationship has been created between any broker and a seller, landlord, buyer or tenant."[1092]

§ 16.1.2.2   Dual agency

Dual agency is the brokerage practice in which one real estate broker simultaneously represents both parties in the same transaction as clients [1093] (i.e., buyer and seller, or landlord and tenant) and where individual licensees affiliated with the broker have not been designated to exclusively represent each side of the transaction (i.e., designated agency). In other words, the buyer and seller or landlord and tenant are both clients of the same real estate broker and neither client has a designated agent exclusively representing their interests. While dual agency is permissible under Georgia law, it is inherently risky and is recommended only when 1) no other form of agency is practical and 2) both clients are sophisticated and can appreciate potential for the broker to find himself or herself in a conflict role.

Because of the risks associated with dual agency, BRRETA requires every broker to develop and to enforce a policy regarding whether the broker practices dual agency or rejects dual agency.[1094] This brokerage policy must be included in the brokerage engagement agreement used by the broker.[1095] As a practical matter, dual agency occurs most frequently when the listing agent representing the seller as a client sells his or her own listing to a buyer client.

(a)   What is considered the "Same Transaction"

BRRETA does not define what is meant by the term "same transaction" in determining whether a dual agency relationship has been created. The dictionary roughly translates these words to mean the "identical business deal." If, for example, a broker is representing both the buyer and seller as clients in the purchase and sale of a house, it is clearly the same transaction, and a dual agency exists. There are other situations, however, where it is not as clear whether the broker is dealing with the same or different transactions and whether a dual agency therefore exists. One such example is set forth below.

Example #1: A broker has a listing on property owned by Mrs. Jones. Mr. Smith, a buyer, visits the home during an open house and puts it under contract. Mr. Smith is not working with another real estate broker. The contract is conditioned upon a number of things, including the sale of Mr. Smith's present home. If the buyer now

---

1092   O.C.G.A. § 10-6A-11.
1093   O.C.G.A. § 10-6A-3(10).
1094   O.C.G.A. § 10-6A-12(f).
1095   O.C.G.A. § 10-6A-12(f).

asks the broker to list his home for sale, can the broker do so without being considered a dual agent with respect to the sale of Mrs. Jones' home?

Answer: There is no case law on this point. The correct answer, however, should be that this is not a dual agency situation. While the sale of Mrs. Jones' home and the sale of Mr. Smith's home are related transactions, they are not the same transaction. Certainly, if the purpose of the dual agency warning is to protect the buyer and seller in situations where the broker is representing them in negotiating the purchase and sale of a specific property, that situation does not exist here because the broker is representing the parties in the purchase and sale of different properties. It should be noted, however, that, a broker must disclose all adverse material facts to his or her client.

Until there is judicial clarification on this point, the broker should disclose to the seller client that he is now listing the buyer's house for sale and has a client relationship with the buyer for purposes of that transaction. Because the law in this area is unsettled, one approach to this situation would be to act as a dual agent in the transaction, to give the dual agency warnings, and to obtain the written consent of both parties based on those warnings. Since all parties will likely consent to the dual agency anyway, acting as a dual agent will eliminate the risk of a claim that the broker acted as a dual agent without the appropriate consent of both parties. Alternatively, and as discussed below the solution of choice, a designated agency relationship could be established.

(b)   Special written consent of all parties required for dual agency.

BRRETA only allows dual agency to be practiced by brokers with the written consent of both parties.[1096] There are no exceptions to this rule. Georgia real estate licensing law provides that a broker can be sanctioned (including the loss of the broker's license) by the Georgia Real Estate Commission if the broker represents more than one party in a transaction without the "express written consent of all parties to the transaction."[1097]

BRRETA mandates that the written consent to dual agency include the following:

(i)   A description of the transactions or types of transactions in which the broker will serve as a dual agent.

(ii)   A statement that, in serving as a dual agent, the broker represents two clients whose interests are or at times could be different or even adverse;

1096   O.C.G.A. § 10-6A-12(a).
1097   O.C.G.A. 43-40-25(a)(22).

(iii)   A statement that a dual agent will disclose all adverse material facts relevant to the transaction and actually known to the dual agent to all parties in the transaction except for information made confidential by request or instructions from another client which information is neither allowed to be disclosed nor required to be disclosed by BRRETA;

(iv)   A statement that the broker or the broker's affiliated licensees will timely disclose to each client in a real estate transaction the nature of any material relationship the broker and the broker's affiliated licensees have with the other clients in the transaction other than that incidental to the transaction. For the purposes of this Code section, a material relationship shall mean any actually known personal, familial, or business relationship between the broker or the broker's affiliated licensees and a client which would impair the ability of the broker or affiliated licensees to exercise fair and independent judgment relative to another client;

(v)   A statement that the client does not have to consent to the dual agency; and

(vi)   A statement that the consent of the client has been given voluntarily and that the engagement has been read and understood.[1098]

(c)   <u>Written consent which includes dual agency warnings is "conclusively deemed to have been given and informed."</u>

When the client signs a written consent that includes the dual agency disclosures discussed above, the consent of the client is conclusively deemed to have been given and informed."[1099] This means that after clients have signed a dual agency agreement they are barred statutorily from arguing that they did not give their consent or that their consent was not informed. Prior to this statutory protection a party could file a lawsuit against the broker and argue that he or she did not understand or give informed consent to the dual agency.[1100]

1098   O.C.G.A. § 10-6A-12(a).

1099   O.C.G.A. § 10-6A-12(b).

1100   Prior to the adoption of BRRETA, Georgia law did not preclude dual agency provided that there was meaningful disclosure and the consent of the seller and buyer. See Spratlin, Harrington & Thomas, Inc. v. Hawn, 116 Ga. App. 175, 156 S.E. 2d 402, 406 (1967). Unfortunately, Georgia case law did not clearly define the level of understanding and consent that was necessary to proceed safely in a dual agency relationship. In a New Jersey case, the Supreme Court of that state applying general principles of agency stated, "Full disclosure requires . . . an explanation of the pitfalls that may arise in the course of the transaction which

(d)   <u>Written consent must be obtained PRIOR to acting as a dual agent.</u>

The consent to dual agency discussed above must be obtained <u>before</u> the licensee acts as a dual agent(e.g., before the licensee performs anything more than ministerial services for a buyer-client with regard to a property in which the licensee will serve as a dual agent). Because the dual agency disclosure is contained in the GAR Contract, some real estate brokers have assumed that consent to dual agency is not necessary until the time the parties signed the purchase contract. This is not correct. BRRETTA provides that "a broker may act as a dual agent only with the written consent of all clients."[1101] This language mandates that the consent be obtained from all the clients <u>before</u> the real estate agent acts in a dual agency capacity.

To help licensees comply with the requirement of obtaining prior written consent, the dual agency disclosure is contained in the GAR Buyer Brokerage Engagement forms and the GAR Seller Listing forms, as well as in the various GAR Purchase and Sale Agreements. It is critical to include the dual agency consent in any brokerage agreement to avoid a later claim that the parties did not give informed consent to the dual agency. It should be noted that the disclosure in the brokerage engagement forms is not a statement that the broker will definitely be acting in a dual agency capacity. Rather, it is the client's consent to the <u>possibility</u> that the broker <u>may</u> act in a dual agency capacity. Then, at the point at which the broker actually shows a buyer client property in which the broker is also representing the seller as a client (and in which the broker is not acting in a designated agency capacity), the broker must disclose to the buyer that in showing this particular property the broker will be acting as a dual agent. This disclosure is necessary because BRRETA requires a broker with an existing brokerage relationship to disclose whenever the broker's agency relationship changes.[1102]

In the event that a broker finds herself in a potential dual agency situation in which one of the clients does not consent to dual agency, BRRETA allows the broker to withdraw from representing that client.[1103] In such a case, the broker is permitted to

---

would make it desirable that the buyer" be independently represented. The full significance of the representation of conflicting interests should be disclosed to the client so that he may make an intelligent decision before giving his consent. The Court went on to say that it would "not tolerate consents which are less than knowing, intelligent and voluntary. Consents must be obtained in such a way as to insure that the client has had adequate time . . . to reflect upon the choice, and must not be forced upon the client . . ." See Matter of Dolan, 384 A. 2d 1076 (N.J. 1978). Although the Dolan case was from another jurisdiction, the reasoning of the Court was consistent with the Spratlin case above. Therefore, prior to having a state statute creating a conclusive presumption of consent, parties could argue that their consent was not informed and should not bar them from asserting a claim arising from the broker acting in a dual agency capacity.

1101   O.C.G.A. § 10-6A-12(a).
1102   O.C.G.A. § 10-6A-(4)(b).
1103   O.C.G.A. § 10-6A-12(e).

continue to represent the client who gave his consent.[1104] When a broker withdraws from the representation of one client for this reason BRRETA permits the broker to refer that client to another broker in another real estate brokerage company. Although referral fees were not allowed in this situation under the 1994 version of BRRETA, the 2000 revisions allow brokers to receive a fee for such a referral.[1105] It is important to note that in such a situation the Georgia licensing law requires that the broker obtain the client's agreement to the referral and to inform the client whether or not the broker will receive a valuable consideration for the referral.[1106]

> (e)   Broker's duty to disclose adverse material facts to both clients in a dual agency transaction.

A broker acting in a dual agency capacity owes a duty to disclose adverse material facts known to the dual agent to both clients in the transaction. The only exception to this rule is if either party in the transaction instructs the dual agent to keep specific information confidential and the broker is permitted by law to keep the information confidential. The following examples illustrate this principle.

Example: Seller mentions to her listing broker that a neighbor's child is mentally disturbed and very aggressive towards other children in the neighborhood. Seller explains that this is one of the reasons she is moving. Seller instructs the listing broker to keep this information confidential. If the listing broker becomes a dual agent, is she obligated to disclose this information to her buyer - client?

Answer: The answer to this question should be "yes." By virtue of the dual agency the broker is obligated to disclose to her buyer-client all adverse material facts regarding the transaction. It is arguably reasonable to view this as a potentially adverse material fact. Accordingly, the broker is required to disregard the seller-client's wishes and make disclosure to the buyer-client.

The problem with dual agency, as reflected in the above example, is that regardless of whether the disclosure is or is not made, one of the broker's clients is benefited and another is potentially harmed by the broker disclosing or not disclosing the adverse material facts. If disclosure is made, the seller's ability to sell the house may be impaired. If disclosure is not made, the buyer's children may be put in harm's way. At the very least if disclosure is not made and the buyer later learns that the broker knew this sensitive information but chose not to disclose, the buyer will likely be extremely dissatisfied with the broker and may not speak well of him or her to friends and neighbors in the community. This creates something of a "no-win" situation for the broker and underscores the conflicts which can arise when the broker tries to represent two parties at the same time.

1104   O.C.G.A. § 10-6A-12(e).
1105   O.C.G.A. § 10-6A-12(e).
1106   O.C.G.A. § 43-40-25(a)(35)

In response to concerns about preserving client confidences, the GAR Contract and the various GAR Brokerage Engagements contain directives from both the buyer and seller to the dual agent to keep all information confidential which could affect the negotiating position of either party.

Example: A subdivision agent is aware that her builder client is experiencing serious financial problems and needs to sell a home quickly. If the subdivision agent becomes a dual agent, what are the agent's obligations to divulge this information to the buyer-client? What should the agent do or say if the builder asks to hold significant amounts of unrestricted earnest money?

Answer: If the parties have signed GAR Brokerage Agreements, the dual agent would be barred from revealing the builder's financial difficulties to a buyer. The seller's financial condition is arguably not an adverse material fact (it has no bearing upon the condition of the property or the neighborhood) and the GAR Listing Agreement directs the broker not to reveal any information which could harm the negotiating position of a client. However, this is another example where the dual agent is put in a "no-win" situation.

If the dual agent discloses the damaging information about the builder's situation, she may be further jeopardizing the builder's financial status. However, if the dual agent fails to disclose, the buyer may be at risk of losing his or her earnest money. While some real estate agents believe that being silent in these situations is a way of staying neutral, the reality is that silence hurts the buyer and helps the builder. Additionally, if the buyer loses his or her earnest money and then finds out that the dual agent knew of the builder's financial predicament, the buyer may feel that the agent has not adequately represented him in the transaction.

Example: Seller tells Listing Broker that he does not want it revealed that the exterior of his property is constructed with synthetic stucco. If Listing Broker becomes a dual agent, must this information be revealed to his buyer client?

Answer: BRRETA requires the disclosure of all adverse material facts to all parties in a dual agency transaction except those specific facts which either of the parties instructs be kept confidential and which are not otherwise required by law to be disclosed. In this case, the seller has specifically asked that the information about the synthetic stucco be kept confidential. However, BRRETA requires the disclosure of all material facts relating to the physical condition of the property which could not be observed upon a reasonably diligent inspection of the property. While it can be argued that the synthetic stucco could be discovered upon a reasonably diligent inspection of the property, the better answer is that the synthetic stucco is a material adverse fact regarding the physical condition of the property and that the duty to disclose is superior to the duty to keep the information confidential.

§ 16.1.2.3   Designated agency

Designated agency is a type of brokerage practice in which a broker appoints one or more licensees within the broker's firm to exclusively represent different clients (buyer and seller or landlord and tenant) in the same transaction.[1107] This situation most frequently arises when a real estate licensee has a client who desires to view a property that is listed by another licensee in the same brokerage firm.

(a)   How designated agency differs from dual agency.

Prior to the 2000 amendments to BRRETA the situation in which there were two different licensees affiliated with the same brokerage firm, each of whom was exclusively representing their own client in the same transaction, was defined to be a form of dual agency and. However, the 2000 BRRETA revisions changed the law by separating designated agency from dual agency and by establishing new regulations to control designated agency.[1108] Although designated agency is inconsistent with traditional common law principles of agency since the same broker is still representing both the buyer and seller as clients, the legislature has the power to enact statutes in derogation of the common law and has done so in this case. BRRETA explicitly states that in designated agency situations "neither the broker, the broker's licensees, nor the real estate brokerage firm" are to be considered dual agents.[1109]

One issue, which has not been completely settled, is whether a special written consent of the buyer, and the seller is needed to practice designated agency. BRRETA only requires that the buyer and the seller give a special written consent prior to practicing dual agency.[1110] However, Georgia license law still provides that a licensee can be sanctioned for "acting for more than one party in a transaction without the express written consent of all parties to the transaction."[1111] Since a broker is representing both the buyer and the seller in designated agency transactions, it would appear that license law requires the broker to obtain the express written consent of the parties prior to practicing designated agency. In light of this provision, the GAR brokerage engagements were modified to include not only a consent to dual agency but also to designated agency.

The most readily apparent consequence of carving designated agency out of dual agency is that a licensee can act in a designated agency capacity without having to provide the clients with a lengthy, written, dual agency consent.

1107   O.C.G.A. § 10-6A-3(9).
1108   O.C.G.A. § 10-6A-13.
1109   O.C.G.A. § 10-6A-13(b). However, two licensees from the same company, each of whom is working with their own client, can still be treated as a dual agency if each agent is not exclusively representing their respective client and if the broker has not assigned them as designated agents for their respective clients.
1110   O.C.G.A. § 10-6A-12.
1111   O.C.G.A. § 43-40-25(a)(22)

Designated agency is a much safer form of brokerage practice than dual agency because each client is exclusively represented by a licensee looking out for the client's interests. In essence, in a designated agency transaction, each licensee functions as if he or she was acting in a single agency capacity (or as if the licensee for the other client was affiliated with a different real estate brokerage firm). Thus, each agent owes his client the same duties as he would if it were single agency representation.

(b)   Designated agency and the duty to keep confidences.

In a designated agency transaction, each designated agent is prohibited from disclosing to anyone except his broker any information which the client has requested to be kept confidential, unless such disclosure is required by law. This prohibition means that designated agents cannot reveal any confidential information to any other agent in the firm, including the designated agent for the other party in the transaction. In addition, if the designated agent for one party had previously represented the other party in the transaction, the designated agent would be required to maintain previously learned confidences from the former client unless the confidences are waived through subsequent word or conduct, or the information is required by law to be disclosed.[1112] The problem below illustrates how this would work.

Problem: Agent A is representing Buyer as a client. During the course of the representation, Agent A learns many things about Buyer. Buyer becomes interested in a property on which Agent A is the listing agent. To avoid a dual agency, Agent A suggests that Agent B represent Buyer, to which Buyer agrees. What are Agent A's duties to keep confidential and not reveal to the seller the information Agent A has previously learned about Buyer?

Answer: Agent A would not be permitted to disclose any information made confidential by the Buyer unless the Buyer permits such disclosure by subsequent word of conduct, or the disclosure is required by law.

In a designated agency transaction, the broker still acts in a supervisory and managerial capacity with respect to each of the designated agents; however, the broker must act as a wall preventing the flow of information between the buyer's designated agent and the seller's designated agent. In a designated agency transaction BRRETA prohibits the broker from revealing any information made confidential by the client's request which he receives from a designated agent or that agent's client to the other designated agent or the other client unless the information is required by law to be disclosed. The statute defines confidential information for the purposes of designated agency to be any information that could harm the client's negotiating position which information the client has not consented to be disclosed.[1113]

1112   O.C.G.A. § 10-6A-13(d).
1113   O.C.G.A. § 10-6A-13(c).

BRRETA's limitations on the disclosure of confidential information by brokers and designated agents provides protection for licensees by eliminating the conflicting duties that are inherent in a dual agency setting. Thus, designated agency allows a brokerage firm to represent both sides of a transaction without as many risks as are associated with dual agency. Designated agency is also preferable from both the buyer and seller's standpoint because the licensee for each client does not represent the other client in the transaction.

(c)   Assigning designated agents.

In order to act as a designated agent, the broker must assign each licensee to act in that role.[1114] There are several ways in which brokers can accomplish this. A broker may directly assign designated agents on a case-by-case basis whenever a licensee in the firm representing the buyer as a client shows the buyer property which is listed by another licensee in the firm who is representing the seller. Such case by case assignments may be less practical in larger firms because licensees would constantly be calling their broker for permission to act in a designated agency capacity whenever they were showing their clients their own company's listings. BRRETA allows the broker to delegate to other management level personnel the responsibility for assigning designated agents through the adoption of company policy.[1115] In addition, the law also permits a brokerage firm to adopt firm-wide policies allowing for the automatic assignment of designated agents. However, the assignment of designated agents through the adoption of a company policy must be done in a way "reasonably calculated to ensure that each client is represented properly under that law."[1116] Adopting a policy which merely states that the firm's licensees will be designated agents in all situations where different licensees in the firm are representing the buyer and seller may create some risks for the brokerage firm. Specifically, brokerage firms should evaluate whether they are comfortable allowing for the automatic assignment of designated agents in following situations:

(1)   Where one spouse is representing the seller and the other spouse is representing the buyer or where a parent is representing the seller and a child is representing the buyer (or vice versa).
(2)   Where one member of a real estate team is representing the buyer and another team member is representing the seller.
(3)   Where a licensed real estate assistant is representing the seller and the licensee for whom she works is representing the buyer (or vice versa).

While the broker may not want to prohibit licensees from acting in a designated agency capacity in the above situations, it would probably be a good idea for the broker to insist that the licensee obtain permission from the broker on a case-by-case basis in such situations. An example of a sample policy is set forth below:

1114   O.C.G.A. § 10-6A-3(9).
1115   O.C.G.A. § 10-6A-13(a).
1116   O.C.G.A. § 10-6A-13(a).

<u>Sample brokerage policy on assigning designated agents</u>

It is the policy of ABC Brokers that whenever one licensee in our company is representing the buyer as a client and another licensee in our company is representing the seller as a client in the same real estate transaction, ABC Brokers does hereby automatically assign each of the licensees to act in a designated agency capacity in the transaction except in the following situations:

(1)   Where the licensees representing the parties are husband and wife, or parent and child, and

(2)   Where the licensees representing the parties are a licensee and the licensed assistant of said licensee.

In the above two situations, the licensees may not act as designated agents without the express permission of the managing broker of the office in which the licensees work.

(d)   <u>Broker acting as one of the designated agents.</u>

BRRETA defines a "designated agent" as "one or more licensees affiliated with broker who are assigned by the broker to represent solely one client to the exclusion of all other clients in the same transaction and to the exclusion of all other licensees affiliated with the broker."[1117] Since the definition of a designated agent is limited to "a licensee affiliated with the broker," rather than the broker himself, the broker cannot act as one of the designated agents in the transaction.

BRRETA was specifically written to limit brokers from acting as one of the designated agents out of a concern that both parties would not be fairly represented in a transaction where the broker was supervising one of the designated agents, and thus privy to the confidential information in possession of the agent, but was also acting as the designated agent in the transaction.

§ 16.2   Duties owed to clients by brokers

BRRETA sets forth the duties which a licensee owes to her client. Unless the parties expressly agree in a brokerage engagement to different or additional duties which the licensee owes to her client, the licensee owes no duties other than those set forth in BRRETA.[1118] Any agreement that alters the duties owed to the client must be in writing and signed by both parties.[1119]

BRRETA contains separate sections devoted to the duties owed by brokers in

---

1117   O.C.G.A. § 10-6A-3(9).
1118   O.C.G.A. § 10-6A-4(a).
1119   O.C.G.A. § 10-6A-4(a).

client relationships with sellers, landlords, buyers, and tenants.[1120] The duties owed by brokers to each of these types of clients is very similar. Consequently, the discussion that follows analyzes these duties together. Any difference in duties owed to different kinds of clients is noted. Also, since designated agents must function as if they were acting in a single agency capacity, the following discussion is applicable to designated agency as well. BRRETA mandates that a broker owes her client the following duties:

§ 16.2.1   Broker must perform terms of brokerage engagement agreement

Brokers must look to the written brokerage engagement, either the listing agreement or the buyer brokerage engagement, to determine precisely what services they must perform for their clients. As discussed previously, the duties imposed upon the broker under BRRETA can be altered, increased, or even eliminated by a written brokerage engagement.[1121]   While the GAR Brokerage Agreements all require compliance with BRRETA, the duties of the broker to the client are drafted very narrowly to limit the potential legal liability of the broker.

§ 16.2.2   Broker must promote interests of client

(a)   <u>The broker must seek a price and terms acceptable to the client.</u>

This requirement imposes a duty on the broker representing a seller/landlord to attempt to negotiate a sale or lease at the price established in the listing/leasing agreement or at a price that is acceptable to the seller/landlord. BRRETA specifically states that a listing agent is not obligated to continue to seek additional offers on the property for the seller or landlord client while the property is under a contract for sale or subject to a lease (or letter of intent to lease) unless the brokerage engagement agreement imposes this obligation.

A broker representing a buyer or tenant is required to attempt to find a property at the price and terms acceptable to the buyer or tenant. However, the broker is not required to search for other properties for the client while the buyer or tenant is a party to a contract to purchase or a party to a lease (or letter of intent to lease) unless the brokerage agreement imposes this duty of the agent.

(b)   <u>The broker must timely present all offers to and from the client.</u>

Brokers, regardless of whether they are representing seller, landlords, buyers, or tenants, must present in a timely fashion all offers to their clients. This requirement is consistent with the Georgia real estate licensing laws which also require licensees to "deliver within a reasonable time" all offers to buy or sell and completed purchase agreements.[1122]   Brokers must also present to the other party all offers which their

---

1120   O.C.G.A. § 10-6A-5, 10-6A-6, 10-6A-7, 10-6A-8.
1121   O.C.G.A. § 10-6A-4(a).
1122   O.C.G.A. § 43-40-25(19).

client desires to submit. This is the case even when the broker disagrees with some of the provisions in the offer. For example, if an offer is presented which includes a lower commission than the seller and listing agent have agreed to in their listing agreement, the listing broker <u>must</u> still present this offer to the seller. Of course, the listing broker is not obligated to accept the reduction in the commission. To protect his or her rights the broker can write in a note on the offer which states that the broker does not agree to the reduction in his or her commission.

When a seller or landlord's property is under a contract to sell or lease the broker must submit additional offers to the broker's client, even if the offer comes from a different buyer. Likewise, a broker representing a buyer or tenant must submit to the buyer any offers or counteroffers which the client wishes to make even if the buyer or tenant is a party to a sales contract or to a lease (or letter of intent to lease). Interestingly, the obligation to timely submit all offers likely extends to verbal offers, even though contracts for the purchase of real estate must generally be in writing to be enforceable.

(c)   <u>Brokers must disclose to the client adverse material facts of which the licensee has actual knowledge regarding the transaction.</u>

Whenever a broker learns of facts regarding the transaction that are unfavorable to his client he must disclose those facts if they are "material facts." BRRETA defines the term "material facts" to be those "facts that a party does not know, could not reasonably discover, and would reasonably want to know." [1123] Because the definition of the term "material fact" is limited to those facts which the client "could not reasonably discover," the broker's duty of disclosure has been greatly narrowed by the statute from the common law duty which brokers would otherwise owe to their clients. Whether a disclosure must be made under this provision requires a case-by-case determination as the examples below illustrate.

<u>Example #1</u>: A broker in a large city enters into a listing agreement with a seller whom he has just met. During the listing, another broker shows the house to a prospective buyer. As it turns out, the buyer is a close friend or relative of the listing broker. Should the listing broker disclose this fact to the seller?
<u>Answer</u>: Yes. The listing broker should disclose this fact to his seller client for two reasons: 1) this relationship is one about which the seller would reasonably want to know since it may affect the negotiations, and 2) this relationship is one which the seller could not reasonably discover in a large metropolitan area. However, in a very small, rural community this same relationship may not have to be disclosed to the seller if the facts are such that the prospective buyer lives in the same small community with the seller and the buyer is a person who is widely known throughout the community to be a friend or relative of the broker.

1123   O.C.G.A. § 10-6A-3(11).

Example #2: Two agents are working within a subdivision representing the builder/seller. A prospective buyer comes in and asks one of the agents to represent him as a buyer in the purchase of a home in the subdivision. Does the agent, who will now represent the buyer, have to make any disclosures to that buyer?

Answer: Yes. Under BRRETA the agent representing the buyer would have to disclose to the buyer that in other transactions within that subdivision he or she has represented the builder. Again, this is because the relationship between the agent and the builder might impact the negotiations between the buyer and the builder.

Example #3: A broker representing a buyer shows his client a home in which a murder took place several years before. The broker knows this fact. Does the murder have to be disclosed?

Answer: No. While this would normally be considered an adverse fact which the buyer-agent would have to disclose to his client, Georgia's "Stigmatized Property Statute" protects real estate agents from liability for not disclosing that the seller's property was the site of a homicide, felony or suicide.[1124] Of course, real estate agents are required to answer truthfully to the best of their knowledge any questions regarding homicides, felonies or suicides on the property and are not protected from liability if they lie about the same and are found to have defrauded their client.[1125]

(d)   The broker must advise the client to obtain expert advice regarding material matters which are beyond the expertise of the broker.

Whenever the broker feels that an issue is arising in a transaction which is outside of the scope of the broker's expertise, the broker should inform the client of this and advise the client to seek the advise of an expert in the area involved. The GAR Purchase Contracts contain a disclaimer, listing the areas in which the broker does not owe a special duty or have expertise. This paragraph is discussed in detail in Chapter 10. Nevertheless, verbal disclosures regarding a broker's lack of expertise are encouraged to insure that the client understands the broker's limitations.

(e)   The broker must timely account for all money and property received by the broker licensee in which the client has or may have an interest.

This section of BRRETA merely codifies long standing rules and regulations of the Georgia Real Estate Commission.[1126] Brokers must timely account for all money and property in their possession in which their client has an interest.

§ 16.2.3   Broker must exercise ordinary skill and care in performing duties under BRRETA and any other duties agreed between the parties in brokerage engagement

---

1124   O.C.G.A. § 44-1-16.
1125   O.C.G.A. § 44-1-16.
1126   See O.C.G.A. § 43-40-20

In addition to narrowing the scope of substantive duties owed to clients to only those duties set forth in BRRETA and in the written brokerage agreement, BRRETA has altered the legal standard of care with which brokers must perform when representing their clients. In common law agency situations, the agent is said to have a fiduciary relationship with the principal, i.e., the person who has appointed him as agent.[1127] In such a fiduciary relationship, the agent owes the highest degree of loyalty to the principal and must perform his duties for the principal with the utmost degree of care. BRRETA, by contrast, specifically states that unless the parties agree otherwise in a signed writing, a real estate broker is not in a fiduciary relationship with either a customer or a client.[1128]

In its original enactment, BRRETA lowered the standard of care from that of a fiduciary to a standard which required the broker to perform his duties with "reasonable" care. Under this standard, suits were still brought claiming that the broker did not carry out his duties in a manner consistent with the level of care that any broker, acting reasonably, would have performed. The broker's liability, therefore, often hinged on the testimony of experts. After the 2000 amendments to BRRETA, brokers must only exercise ordinary care in the performance of the duties listed in BRRETA and those duties to which they agree to in the written brokerage agreement.[1129] This means that in performing the duties listed in BRRETA and in the written brokerage agreement, brokers owe no greater duty of care to their clients than they would to any other person who is not a client. The example below explains these legal standards in greater detail.

Example: A buyer purchases an older home with the help of his selling broker. The buyer does not ask for an inspection and the seller does not provide a Seller's Property Disclosure Statement. After moving in, the buyer discovers defects in the roof which cause the roof to leak. The buyer sues the broker claiming that the broker was negligent and failed to perform his duties with reasonable care by not advising the buyer to have the property inspected. Will the broker be held liable for not recommending that an inspection be performed?

Answer: Prior to the 2000 revisions of BRRETA, if the buyer's expert witness testified that any reasonable, prudent selling broker would have recommended that the buyer have an inspection done on the house, the broker may be found to have not acted reasonably and may thus be liable to the buyer. However, the 2000 revisions to BRRETA afforded brokers additional protection by further lowering the standard of care with which brokers must perform to exercising ordinary care in the performance of those duties agreed to by the broker in her brokerage engagement. Since in the

---

1127   See Rayborn v. Long, 243 Ga.App. 128, 532 S.E.2d 433 (2000). It is interesting to note that the Court of Appeals appeared to reach its conclusions in this case without considering or citing BRRETA. The precedental value of this case would therefore appear to be extremely limited.

1128   O.C.G.A. § 10-6A-4(a).

1129   O.C.G.A. § 10-6A-5(a)(3), 10-6A-6(a)(3), 10-6A-7(a)(3), 10-6A-8(a)(3).

GAR Buyer Brokerage Agreement, the broker has no duty to advise the buyer to get an inspection, a good argument can be made that the broker should not have any liability to the buyer. See § 12-8-1 (Protections Against Liability in the GAR Brokerage Engagements) for a discussion of how GAR's Brokerage Agreements further reduce broker's liability by setting out the "sole duties of the broker."

§ 16.2.4   Broker must comply with all applicable laws and regulations including civil rights and fair housing statutes

This requirement means that the broker must comply with all applicable laws and regulations including the Federal Fair Housing Act[1130] and the Georgia Fair Housing Act[1131], as well as with all state and federal civil rights statutes and regulations.

§ 16.2.5   Broker must keep confidential all information received by broker during term of brokerage engagement made confidential by express request or instruction from client

If, while the broker is representing the client, the broker receives information from any source and the client expressly requests or instructs the broker to not reveal that information, BRRETA places a duty upon the broker to keep the information confidential. The statute provides that disclosing confidential information to other licensees within the same firm except in a designated agency situation, does not violate the duty of confidentiality.[1132] If the client requests that information not be disclosed the broker can only reveal the information if (1) the client subsequently permits the disclosure or (2) disclosure of the information is required by law. BRRETA provides that the client's permission can be given by "word or conduct."

Example: A seller asks his listing broker to not mention that the seller and his wife are getting divorced. Later the seller passes a prospective buyer and his agent in the doorway as the seller is leaving. The seller calls over his shoulder to his teenage son that he is hurrying to a meeting with his divorce lawyer. Must the listing agent now continue to treat this information as confidential?

Answer: The answer to this question should be "no" at least with respect to this buyer. The seller's conduct appears to indicate that his divorce is no longer confidential. However, in the event that the broker believes that the client has given his permission by conduct, the better approach is for the broker to verify with the client that the client's actions were meant to be interpreted as permission to disclose the information.

1130   42 USCA § 3602 et seq.
1131   O.C.G.A. § 8-3-206 et seq.
1132   O.C.G.A. § 10-6A-5(a)(5), 10-6A-6(a)(5), 10-6A-7(a)(5), 8(a)(5).

(a)   <u>Knowledge not imputed in designated agency or dual agency situation</u>.

In some relationships the law automatically deems that knowledge or responsibility is transferred from one party to another merely by virtue of the relationship, even though only one party has actual knowledge. This is known as implied knowledge. If that were the case in dual agency and designated agency situations it would not be possible for designated agents, dual agents, or their brokers to fulfill their duty of confidentiality to their clients. To prevent this automatic charging of knowledge held by one party to another, BRRETA defines both designated agency and dual agency such that there is no implied knowledge and information known to one party is not automatically considered to be in the possession of another party.[1133]

BRRETA specifically states that in a designated agency situation, the designated agents are considered to have only "actual knowledge" and that "there shall be no imputation of knowledge or information between and among the broker, designated agents, and the clients."[1134] This means that when an agent, broker or client is in possession of information, the other parties to the transaction, including the designated agent's client and broker, are not automatically deemed to have that information in their possession merely because they are also involved in the transaction. In other words, BRRETA mandates that until a piece of information is, in fact, known to a party in a designated agency situation, the party is not charged with knowledge of that information.

Similarly, in a dual agency situation, BRRETA states that "each client and broker and their respective licensees possess only actual knowledge and information" and that there is no "imputation of knowledge or information among or between the clients, brokers, or affiliated licensees.[1135]

§ 16.2.5.1   *Confidentiality after termination of brokerage engagement*

The duty of confidentiality also exists after the brokerage agreement has expired, has been terminated, or the broker withdraws from representing the client, unless the client permits the disclosure, the disclosure is required by law, or the information becomes public from "a source other than the broker."[1136]

<u>Example #1</u>: A buyer client asks to see a house on which his agent is the listing agent. To avoid a dual agency situation the agent refers the buyer to another

---

1133   <u>Wall v. Century 21 Winnersvile Realty, Inc.</u>, 244 Ga.App. 762, 536 S.E.2d 798 (2000).
1134   O.C.G.A. § 10-6A-13(c).
1135   O.C.G.A. § 10-6A-12(d)
1136   O.C.G.A. § 10-6A-9(b)(2)(C).

agent in the firm. Does the listing agent, who is now the designated agent of the seller, still have to keep the buyer's secrets confidential?

Answer: Yes. Even though the buyer is no longer a client, the agent must continue to preserve the buyer's confidences unless the disclosure is required by law, the information becomes public from a source other than the agent, or the buyer permits disclosure.

Example #2: A client has asked that his listing agent not reveal that he and his wife may be getting a divorce. After the listing agreement expires, the seller actually files suit for divorce. Does the agent still have to preserve the seller's secret?

Answer: What is meant by information becoming "public" through a source other than the broker is not defined in either BRRETA or in case law. Courts will likely apply a reasonableness test in making decisions in this area. The more widely the information has been disseminated, the more likely it is that the broker may treat the information as no longer confidential. In this case, the filing of divorce papers with the court may not be wide enough distribution of the information to allow the broker to treat the information as public. If, on the other hand, an article about the divorce is published in the local newspaper, the broker would be much safer in assuming that the information has been made public by a source other than himself.

§ 16.2.6   Conflicting duties

BRRETA imposes a duty on brokers to not give false information to customers. (See discussion in § 16.3.1.8, infra.) BRRETA provides that in the event of a conflict between the duty to keep client confidences and the duty not to give customers false information, the duty not to give customers false information shall control and that a broker shall not be liable for disclosing information in this situation.[1137] Assume, for example, that in the course of listing a property the seller tells his broker that he believes the kitchen and dining area of the house are much too small and are out of proportion with the rest of the house. He says he explored the possibility of adding on to the existing kitchen and eating area, but he discovered that even a small expansion would violate state regulations requiring a buffer and setback requirement for a river that flows by the back lot line. He asks the broker to not reveal this information to any prospective buyers or their agents.

If at a subsequent time a buyer's agent asks if it is possible to add on to the kitchen, a conflict has been created between the broker's duty to preserve the client's confidences and the broker's duty to not give a customer false information. Under BRRETA the duty to not give false information controls this situation. Thus, even though the broker is not required by law to disclose this information and the client has expressly asked that the information not be revealed, the broker must break the seller's

---

1137   O.C.G.A. § 10-6A-9(c).

confidence and tell the buyer's agent about the setback requirements to avoid telling a lie.

In other circumstances the broker may be able to avoid disclosing the confidential information without giving false information. Consider the situation in which a seller tells his listing agent that he and his wife are getting a divorce and asks the agent to not mention this to anyone. A prospective buyer later asks whether the sellers are getting divorced since they've only owned the house for a short period of time and neither the husband nor the wife are ever around. The listing broker can say that he has been asked by his clients not to discuss their personal situation. Taking this approach allows the broker to preserve this client's confidence without giving the buyer false information.

§ 16.3 Duty of care to customers

As discussed below, BRRETA imposes relatively minor duties upon brokers relative to customers (i.e., people with whom the broker does not have a client relationship).

§ 16.3.1 Duties owed by broker representing sellers and landlords to buyers or tenants

BRRETA imposes the following duties on brokers representing client sellers or landlords toward buyers and tenants whom the broker does not represent: (1) the duty to disclose adverse material facts regarding the physical condition of the property, (2) the duty to disclose materials facts relating to certain adverse off-site conditions, and (3) the duty to not knowingly give false information. Each of these conditions is discussed below.

§ 16.3.1.1 On-site and off-site disclosure obligations are exclusive

With regard to both adverse on-site conditions and adverse off-site conditions, BRRETA provides that brokers representing sellers or landlords shall not be liable for the failure to disclose to purchaser or tenant clients any matters other than those specified in the statute.[1138] This means that brokers are not responsible for disclosing to customer buyers or tenants anything except conditions described in the statute. The failure to disclose any other matter should therefore not be legitimate grounds for a claim against a broker.

§ 16.3.1.2 Duty to disclose adverse conditions on property

BRRETA requires brokers representing a seller or landlord to disclose to client buyers or tenants all "adverse material facts" regarding the physical condition of the property and improvements located on the property which are "actually known to the

---

1138   O.C.G.A. § 10-6A-5(b)(2), 10-6A-6(b)(2).

broker and which could not be discovered by a "reasonably diligent inspection" of the property by the buyer or tenant."[1139] As previously discussed, the term "material facts" is defined to include "those facts that a party does not know, could not reasonably discover, and would reasonably want to know."[1140] The statute lists two examples of such physical conditions: (1) material defects in the property, and (2) environmental contamination. The statute specifically says that the physical conditions required to be disclosed are not limited to these examples. The duties of brokers representing sellers and landlords to disclose adverse property conditions to customer buyers and tenants has been narrowed considerably by this provision from what these duties might otherwise be in the absence of BRRETA.

§ 16.3.1.3   Brokers representing sellers and landlords do not owe duty to discover adverse on-site conditions

As discussed above, brokers representing sellers and landlords are required to disclose to customers adverse on-site conditions which are <u>actually</u> <u>known</u> to the broker. The statute specifically provides that brokers are under no legal obligation to initiate an investigation or to seek to discover any adverse on-site conditions. This means that the broker does not have to conduct an inspection of the property searching for unknown adverse conditions. Nor does the broker have to order an inspection by a professional inspector. The law only requires the broker to disclose those adverse matters relating to the physical condition of the property which the broker is aware of or becomes aware of during the course of listing the property and which could not be discovered by the buyer upon a reasonably diligent inspection of the property.

It is important to note, however, that if the broker suspects or believes that there is a reasonable likelihood that an adverse condition exists on the property or its improvements, that suspicion or belief may be considered to be sufficient knowledge to trigger a duty on the part of the broker to investigate the suspicion and to determine if, in fact, an adverse material condition does exist on the property. For example, let's say that the roof on a property is in an obvious state of disrepair with water stains on the ceiling. Even if the seller indicates that the roof is not leaking, the listing agent would be well advised to point out these items to prospective buyers to avoid a claim that the listing broker had knowledge, but chose not to disclose. However, since these conditions should also be observable by the buyer upon a reasonably diligent inspection of the property, the broker should be able to successfully defend any claim which is asserted.

§ 16.3.1.4   Disclosure of on-site conditions only required if condition could not be discovered by buyer's reasonably diligent inspection

Many conditions may arguably be discoverable by a buyer upon a reasonably diligent inspection of the property. While such conditions are not legally required to

---

1139   O.C.G.A. § 10-6A-5(b)(1), 10-6A-6(b)(1).
1140   O.C.G.A. § 10-6A-3(11).

be disclosed, the safest approach is to always disclose the condition even if the broker believes that the buyer could discover the information for himself. Otherwise, the broker may find that he is defending a lawsuit about whether the buyer should have discovered the condition upon a reasonable inspection of the property.

(a) A reasonably diligent inspection may require the buyer to hire an inspector.

The question of whether a buyer has conducted a diligent inspection of a property is a question for the jury. What constitutes a diligent inspection varies with the facts of each case. Although a purchaser may be found to have exercised due diligence even though he did not hire a professional inspector,[1141] the failure of the buyer who has notice of a potential problem to either inspect a problem further themselves or to hire an inspector or other specialist may be sufficient grounds for a court to find that the buyer did not exercise due diligence.[1142] For example, a reasonably diligent inspection by a buyer should arguably include a survey of the property to determine, among other things, if the property is in a flood plain. Similarly, problems with synthetic stucco could probably be discovered by a diligent inspection by a home inspector employed by the buyer. However, in both these cases it is advisable to be cautious on such matters and disclose them. The GAR Seller's Property Disclosure Statement, supplied by the seller, should put prospective buyers on notice of conditions that need to be investigated further by the buyer.[1143] Additionally, under the 2005 GAR Contract and Seller's Property Disclosure Statement, the seller could be penalized for not disclosing the presence of the synthetic stucco if the buyer reserved the right to request repairs.

§ 16.3.1.5 *Disclosure of adverse on-site conditions shields broker from liability*

BRRETA provides that brokers cannot be held liable for complying with the statutory requirement to disclose adverse material facts relating to physical conditions on the property.[1144] Thus, even though BRRETA has narrowed brokers' liability, if there is any doubt about whether a condition on the property should be disclosed to a prospective buyer or tenant the broker should err on the side of disclosure on the theory that it is better to defend a lawsuit where the complaint is that the broker disclosed too much, rather than not enough.

1141 Aikens v. Couch, 271 Ga. App. 276, 278; 518 S.E. 2d 674, 676 (1999).
1142 Real Estate International v. Buggay, 220 Ga. App. 449, 451; 469 S.E. 2d 242, 245 (1996); Delk v. Tom Peterson Realtors, 220 Ga. App. 576, 577; 469 S.E. 2d 741, 742 (1996).
1143 See Chapter 6, supra, Property Disclosure Statement.
1144 O.C.G.A. § 10-6A-5(b)(2), 10-6A-6(b)(2).

If a seller is uncertain whether an adverse condition identified in an inspection report is a material fact or merely the incorrect opinion of the inspector, the broker would be well advised to treat the report as material and factual in nature, rather than merely the inspector's erroneous opinion. This is true because under the GAR Contract brokers disclaim any expertise with regard to the physical condition of the property. Therefore, choosing not to provide the report could be construed as an exercise of the very expertise that brokers have specifically disclaimed that they have. The safe answer is not to substitute your judgment for that of the buyer, and to treat all such reports as factual. The following example, based upon a case in North Georgia, illustrates this principal:

Two lots shared a common well. The owners of both lots used their property primarily as vacation homes. The owner of lot 1 put her property on the market with a broker. The owner of lot 2 paid a visit to the broker and told her that the shared well did not produce enough water to support both lots, and that they had to coordinate vacation schedules with the owner of lot 1 to avoid overtaxing the well. The owner of lot 1 denied this and explained that the owner of lot 2 was unhappy because he recently discovered that the well was actually located on lot 1, and not lot 2 as he previously believed. The broker already distrusted the owner of lot 2 because of some disparaging racial remarks he made several years earlier.

The broker took the position that her client, the owner of lot 1, was certainly in a position to know whether the well ran dry. She also assumed that the owner of lot 2 was just trying to chill any sale because he wanted to purchase lot 1 for a discount, and thereby obtain ownership of the shared well. Based upon this, the broker did not disclose the claims of the owner of lot 2 to the ultimate purchaser.

Of course, it turned out that the owner of lot 2 was not exaggerating his claims about the well. The purchaser of lot 1 moved into the property on a full-time basis and soon discovered that the well ran dry whenever the owner of lot 2 was also in town. When the purchaser spoke to the owner of lot 2 he was quick to tell her that he had disclosed the information about the well to the broker and warned the broker that she needed to let any prospective purchaser know about the well. Suit soon followed.

The broker argued that she had no liability to the purchaser based upon the GAR Contract's disclaimers and that she did not have actual knowledge regarding the well, just the word of a neighbor whom she thought had ulterior motives.

This point of this example is that the broker could have avoided the suit altogether (and thereby saved herself considerable time and money) by disclosing to prospective purchasers that there was some question about the capacity of the shared well. She could have then attempted to explain away the claims of the owner of lot 2 by also stating that the owner of lot 1 denied any problems. If the owner of lot 1 insisted that no such disclosure and explanation be given, the broker could have insisted that the owner of lot 1 have a well flow test performed and provide that information to prospective purchasers. Here, the broker made the subjective

476

determination that the owner of lot 2 was not telling the truth. This judgment call of whether to believe the owner of lot 2 is probably best left to the prospective purchaser.

§ 16.3.1.6 Sellers and landlords not relieved of disclosure duties for adverse on-site conditions

Sellers and landlords do not receive the benefit of the statutory protections that limit brokers' disclosure obligations. BRRETA does not in any way limit the obligation of a seller or landlord under any applicable law to disclose adverse material facts concerning the physical condition of the property.[1145] These obligations can include: the obligation of a landlord to disclose of whether the property has a propensity to flood[1146]; certain disclosure obligations regarding lead based paint[1147]; and the duty to disclose in situations where the seller has special knowledge not apparent to the buyer and is aware that the buyer is acting under a misapprehension as to facts which would be important to the buyer and would probably affect their decision to purchase (i.e., passive concealment).[1148]

§ 16.3.1.7 Duty to disclose adverse, off-site conditions prior to 2000 revisions to BRRETA

Prior to the 2000 revisions to BRRETA, the law in Georgia was unclear regarding a broker's duty to investigate and disclose adverse off-site neighborhood conditions to prospective buyer or tenant customers. Fraud claims had long been brought against brokers alleging that they had failed to disclose latent defects in property. (See §14.1.2, infra, for a discussion of these cases.) Fraud claims have also been asserted with regard to the broker's failure to disclose or correctly represent adverse off-site conditions. While there have been few appellate decisions regarding the scope of a broker's duty in this area, it is clear that such claims can be maintained.[1149] Brokers wanting to avoid claims in this area found it difficult to come up with clear rules on how to avoid trouble. Questions for which there were no clear answers included the following:

(a)   How far away from a property does a broker need to go in trying to identify adverse off-site conditions?

This question has been difficult to answer because some conditions such as a paper mill or chicken rendering plant might be 5-10 miles away, yet still impact the

---

1145   O.C.G.A. §§ 10-6A-5(b)(2), 10-6A-6(b)(2).
1146   O.C.G.A. § 44-7-20.
1147   42 U.S.C. § 4852, et seq.
1148   Deckert v. Foster, 230 Ga.App. 164, 495 S.E.2d 656 (1998).
1149   Hanlon v. Thornton, 218 Ga. App. 500; 462 S.E. 2d 154 (1995); Allen v. RE/MAX North Atlanta, Inc., 213 Ga. App. 644, 445 S.E. 2d 774 (1994).

property. Does this therefore mean that to be safe the broker should look for adverse conditions many miles away from the property?

(b)   What kinds of objectionable neighborhood conditions should the broker be looking for?

This question has also been hard to answer because things which are offensive or objectionable to some buyers or tenants might not bother other buyers or tenants at all. For example, a new grocery store at the entrance of a subdivision might be an objectionable condition to half of the neighborhood and a wonderful amenity to the other half of the neighborhood. In trying to define what is an adverse off-site condition, personal opinions can vary widely and there is much room for disagreement. To some extent the broker wishing to avoid a claim in this area had to either be a mind reader or ask extensive questions of buyers to learn of their concerns so that the broker could then evaluate whether the neighborhood contained the type of adverse conditions necessary to disclose.

(c)   Is there potential legal exposure in every transaction since if you go far enough away from any property, you will eventually run into some objectionable condition?

This question is rhetorical. However, it points out the difficulties in this area.

§ 16.3.1.8   Duty to disclose adverse, off-site conditions after adoption of 2000 revisions to BRRETA

The 2000 revisions to BRRETA statutorily limit the duty of brokers to disclose adverse off-site conditions. The law provides that brokers representing sellers and landlords have a duty to disclose the following to prospective buyers and tenants with whom the broker is working as customers:

> All material facts pertaining to existing adverse physical conditions in the immediate neighborhood within one mile of the property which are actually known to the broker and which could not be discovered by the buyer upon a diligent inspection of the neighborhood or thorough review of reasonably available governmental regulations, documents, records, maps, and statistics. Examples of reasonably available governmental regulations, documents, records, maps, and statistics shall include without limitation: land use maps and plans; zoning ordinances; recorded plats and surveys; transportation maps and plans; maps of flood plains; tax maps; school district boundary maps; and maps showing the boundary lines of governmental jurisdictions. . [1150] .

1150   O.C.G.A. § 10-6A-5(b)(2), 10-6A-6(b)(2).

The subsections below break down this statutory language into its component parts and explain how this part of the statute operates.

(a) <u>Disclosure required only if the condition is within one mile of the property</u>.

This requirement places a geographical boundary around the property in the transaction. Objectionable conditions within the one mile limit must be disclosed even if the property is separated from the condition by a physical barrier, such as a river or freeway, or by a political border such as a city-county boundary line. The statute does not describe how the one-mile boundary is to be measured. Presumably, the distance would be a one mile radius from any point in the property. However, some brokers may try to defend a failure to disclose by arguing that the standard should not be measured as the crow flies, but rather should be measured along major roads from the property. Such an argument would most likely not be successful. The one mile radius boundary should also be thought of in three dimensions to include one mile of air space above the property and one mile into the ground.

<u>Example</u>: A broker has a listing on a home in a suburb on the edge of a rapidly growing city. Three miles to the east there is a paper mill which has been there for many years. The prevailing winds at the home are from the west. However, periodically, the wind shifts and blows from the east, bringing a sulfurous odor from the paper mill to the home. A prospective buyer and his agent visit the property several times without smelling the odor before placing an offer on the property. Shortly after closing on the property, the buyers notice the odor. Can the buyer maintain a cause of action against the listing agent for failing to disclose the existence of the paper mill?

<u>Answer</u>: The broker representing the seller or landlord does not owe a duty to disclose to a customer buyer or tenant any material facts regarding adverse conditions that are more than one mile from the property, even if the broker is aware of the condition. While a disgruntled customer buyer might argue that the odor itself is within one mile of the property and that therefore a disclosure obligation exists, such an interpretation was certainly not intended and would render the statutory one-mile limitation on disclosing adverse conditions meaningless. This is because all adverse off-site conditions beyond one-mile from the property would obviously not be adverse unless they affected the property in some tangible way.

(b) <u>Disclosure required only if the condition is an existing condition</u>.

This limitation was included in BRRETA to try to minimize arguments that brokers were required to disclose potential, rather than existing, conditions. Arguments may arise regarding when a condition actually "exists" and is no longer a future or potential condition. For example, if a quarry operator purchases property and places heavy digging equipment on the land, does the quarry exist at that point in time, thus requiring disclosure? Although a case can be made that the quarry exists at that time, the better view is that the mere presence of machinery does not mean that the quarry is in existence. Moreover, even if it could be argued that the presence of the equipment signals the beginning of the quarry's existence, the better argument is that the equipment is not yet an adverse condition and thus does not have to be disclosed until the quarrying operation has actually begun.

Example: A broker has a listing in an in-town neighborhood which is within one mile of, but not adjoining, a two-lane thoroughfare. The broker is aware of the fact that the city transportation planning documents indicate that in the future the city will widen this road to four lanes to accommodate increasing traffic. However, the broker does not tell the prospective buyer or the selling agent about the city's plans. Shortly after the buyer moves into the home the city begins condemnation proceedings to widen the road. Has the broker violated BRRETA by not disclosing the city's plans?

Answer: The answer to this question should also be "no." Under BRRETA the broker is shielded from liability because the broker is only required to disclose existing adverse off-site conditions within one mile of the property. Potential or future conditions, such as road widenings or possible property rezonings should not be required to be disclosed even though the condition is within one mile of the property and even though the broker is aware of the future land use.

(c)   Disclosure required only if the condition is actually known to the broker.

This limitation is intended to protect brokers against claims that the broker "should have known" about an objectionable condition.

Example: A broker takes a listing on a friend's property in an area of town where the broker has never worked and with which he is unfamiliar. Within one mile of the property a telecommunications company has recently located a cellular phone tower on the rear of a commercial lot. After closing on the house the buyer discovers the presence of the tower in the neighborhood. Can the buyer win a claim against the broker for nondisclosure?

Answer: The answer to this question should be "no." The broker should not be liable to the buyer because the disclosure requirement only applies to those existing, adverse, physical conditions which are actually known to the broker. Furthermore, this section of BRRETA specifically provides that there is no duty on the part of a broker to discover or seek to discover either adverse material facts about the physical condition of the property or existing adverse neighborhood conditions.[1151]

1151   O.C.G.A. § 10-6A-5(b)(2), 10-6A-6(b)(2).

(d)   <u>Disclosure only required if the condition is a physical condition.</u>

BRRETA specifically limits the disclosure duty of brokers to those adverse off-site conditions that are physical in nature.

<u>Example</u>: While walking with the seller in the yard of a property being listed with his broker, a middle aged man walks up the street talking to himself and yelling obscenities. The seller mentions to the broker that the man lives several houses down from this property and that he has recently been released from a mental hospital. Does the broker have to disclose this fact to potential client purchasers?

<u>Answer</u>: The answer to this question should be "no." Under BRRETA, a seller's or landlord's broker only has a duty to disclose existing <u>physical</u> offsite conditions within one mile of the property. Non-physical conditions, such as the behavior or criminal record of the neighbors, should not be required to be disclosed to a customer buyer or tenant. For instance, in 1996, Georgia enacted a sex offender registration law which requires some convicted sex offenders to register, among other things, their name, address and place of employment with the Georgia Bureau of Investigation and the county sheriff's office.[1152] However, under BRRETA, brokers are not required to disclose such nonphysical conditions, nor are they required to investigate the neighborhood for the presence of such non-physical conditions. Although it may be possible to argue that people are physical conditions, the better view is that while people may exist physically, they are not "physical conditions" in relation to the property being purchased as contemplated by the statute.

(e)   <u>Disclosure required only if buyer could not discover the condition upon a diligent inspection of the neighborhood.</u>

This limitation on disclosure offers listing brokers fairly extensive protection from liability for nondisclosure of adverse neighborhood conditions. It effectively places on the buyer the responsibility to conduct his or her own investigation of the neighborhood. Furthermore, BRRETA states that the disclosure requirements placed on brokers under the Act do not limit the obligation of prospective buyers and tenants to familiarize themselves with potentially adverse conditions related to the physical condition of the property, any improvements located on the property, and the surrounding neighborhood.[1153]

It is also important to note that although buyers have a duty to conduct a diligent inspection of the neighborhood, brokers do not have any duty to discover or investigate the neighborhood for adverse off-site conditions. Therefore, unless it can be proven that the broker had <u>actual</u> knowledge of an adverse off-site condition, a

---

1152   O.C.G.A. § 42-9-44.1.
1153   O.C.G.A. § 10-6A-5(b)(2), 10-6A-6(b)(2).

buyer will have a difficult time maintaining a claim against the broker who has no duty to inspect, especially since the buyer has an affirmative duty under the law to conduct a diligent inspection.

Example: After moving into a new home during the summer, the buyers realize in the fall that they can hear athletic events from a nearby high school. Was the listing agent required to disclose this fact?

Answer: The answer to this question should be "no." The high school and its athletic fields should have been discovered by the buyers had they conducted a thorough investigation of the neighborhood. While the buyers may not have seen the athletic fields in use, it should be foreseeable to buyers that such fields will be used and generate noise during the school year.

(f)   Disclosure required only if buyer could not discover the condition through the review of reasonably available governmental regulations, documents, records, map and statistics.

This limitation on disclosure requires that a prospective buyer go beyond a physical inspection of the neighborhood. Rather, they are required to examine reasonably available governmental documents that may reveal the existence of an adverse off-site condition. BRRETA lists examples of documents that are considered to be reasonably available including: "land use maps and plans; zoning ordinances; recorded plat and surveys; transportation maps and plans; maps of flood plains; tax maps; school district boundary maps; and maps showing the boundary lines of existing governmental jurisdictions."[1154]   BRRETA states that this is not an exhaustive list of all documents that a buyer must consult in order to fulfill his duty of a diligent inspection. Thus, the buyer must interpret this provision as broadly as possible and must thoroughly investigate any relevant documents.[1155]

Example: After closing on a property near the edge of a subdivision, the buyer discovers that the property across the street is zoned for commercial uses. He believes that this will lower his resale value. Did the listing agent violate BRRETA by not disclosing this information?

Answer: The answer to this question should be "no." Even though this information is not apparent from a physical examination of the neighborhood, BRRETA protects the listing agent from liability in this case because the zoning ordinances are one of the specific examples of a governmental document readily available to the buyer. The buyer is obligated to conduct an investigation of such governmental records to discover adverse material facts in the neighborhood surrounding the property being bought.

1154   O.C.G.A. §§ 10-6A-5(b)(2); 10-6A-6(b)(2).
1155   O.C.G.A. §§ 10-6A-5(b)(2); 10-6A-6(b)(2).

§ 16.3.1.9   Duty not to knowingly give false information

BRRETA requires brokers representing sellers and landlords not to give information to prospective buyers or tenants which information they know to be false. Thus, a broker has a duty not to knowingly provide false information to a prospective buyer or tenant.

(a)   Brokers' liability for providing false information limited by BRRETA.

BRRETA protects brokers against liability in the event they unknowingly give a party false information. A broker has no liability for providing information that turns out to be incorrect if: (1) the broker does not have actual knowledge that the information is false; and (2) the broker discloses the source of the information to the party.[1156] The rational behind this portion of BRRETA is that the broker may be gathering information for the benefit of the buyer or seller, but he is only the messenger and not a guarantor.   If the buyer or seller knows the source of the information then he can, and should, use his own judgment to determine whether the source is reliable or whether he wants to investigate the matter further.

GAR has created an information disclosure form[1157] to help remind brokers doing research on behalf of a party to memorialize in writing the question being researched, the answer to the question and the source of the information. This form should be used by brokers and a copy of it kept in the broker's file to help prove that proper disclosures were made in the event that a party later claims that the broker gave him false information and did not disclose its source. The broker should also try to get the party for whom the research was done to acknowledge receipt of the disclosure form wherever possible. While this provision should help prevent "shoot-the-messenger" type claims against real estate brokers, the safest approach in this area is to try to encourage parties to do their own research when questions of importance arise.

Example: A prospective buyer asks the listing broker if the seller has ever had any problems with termites at the house. After reviewing the Seller's Property Disclosure Statement, the broker calls the seller to verify the information in the disclosure statement. The seller answers that he has had no such problems and has made no termite damage related repairs. The broker leaves a voice mail for the prospective buyer saying that she rechecked the Property Disclosure Statement and confirmed with the seller that there were no termite problems since the seller purchased the house. The termite clearance letter provided at the closing states that there are no visible signs of active termite infestation. After closing the transaction, when the buyer removes the carpet in the den to put down hardwood flooring, he discovers that a wooden patch has been put down in one corner of the floor concealing a soft spot and discovers that there are active termites in the sub-flooring

---

1156   O.C.G.A. § 10-6A-5(b)(2); 10-6A-6(b)(2); 10-6A-7(b); 10-6A-(8)(b).
1157   GAR Form F57.

underneath the patch. The buyer believes that the seller lied on the disclosure statement and that he tried to hide the termites with the patch and carpet. Is the broker liable under BRRETA for giving false information?

Answer: The answer to this question should be "no" provided that the broker identified the source of his information. If the broker did not actually know that the information provided by the seller was false, the broker should not be able to be held liable for misrepresentation or passive concealment since the broker disclosed the source of his or her information. Thus, even if the buyer can show that he could not have discovered the defect with a diligent inspection, the buyer should not be able to recover against the broker. Confirming the source of the broker's information in writing greatly reduces the likelihood of claims in this area.

§ 16.3.1.9   Elements of fraud must be proven

Since the initial passage of BRRETA in 1994, there has been some argument that the statute only required a showing that a broker had misrepresented a material fact in order for a client to maintain a claim against a broker for failure to disclose. The 2000 revisions to BRRETA make it clear that BRRETA does not create an independent, statutory cause of action against brokers. All the elements of fraud, including the requirement that the plaintiff prove that he or she exercised due diligence to discover and protect against the alleged fraud, must be shown in order to hold a broker liable for failing to disclose an adverse material property condition or an adverse neighborhood condition.[1158]   (Chapter 14.1.2.1, infra, discusses the elements which a plaintiff must prove to maintain a claim for fraud.)

Example: A prospective buyer asks if there have been any septic system problems on a particular property. The listing broker knows that there were past problems with the septic system but mistakenly answers "no" because the seller indicated that the problems had been corrected. Can the buyer maintain a claim against the listing broker for violating BRRETA without proving that the broker committed fraud?

Answer: No. BRRETA states that brokers are not liable for a failure to disclose an adverse material fact relating to the physical condition of the property or adverse material fact relating to the surrounding neighborhood unless there is a finding of fraud. The misrepresentation by the broker in and of itself does not give the buyer a claim against the broker absent a showing of fraud. Therefore, the buyer would have to show, among other things, that he or she could not have discovered the septic system problems upon a reasonably diligent inspection of the property.

1158   O.C.G.A. § 10-6A-5(b)(2); 10-6A-6(b)(2), 10-6A-7(b); 10-6A-8(b).

§ 16.3.2   Duties owed by buyer's or tenant's agent to seller or landlord

BRRETA imposes several duties on the part of brokers who are representing tenants and buyers as clients. These duties include: (1) disclosing certain adverse facts concerning the buyer/tenants financial status, and (2) not knowingly giving false information. Each of these duties is discussed below.

§ 16.3.2.1   *Financial status of buyer or tenant*

If a broker representing a buyer as a client is working with a seller in a transaction which will be financed either through partial or complete seller financing or through the assumption of a loan, BRRETA requires that the broker representing the buyer must disclose to the seller "all material adverse facts actually known by the broker" regarding the buyer's "financial ability to perform the terms of the sale."[1159]

Also, if it is a residential transaction and the seller is providing financing, the broker representing the buyer must inform the seller of the buyer's intent to occupy the property as his/her principal residence.[1160]   These disclosures serve to offer some protection to a seller when she will be acting as a lender in the transaction.

Similarly, brokers engaged by tenants are required to disclose to prospective landlords all adverse material facts "actually known" to the broker regarding the "tenant's financial ability to perform the terms of the lease or letter of intent to lease or intent to occupy the property."[1161]

Brokers representing buyers or tenants cannot be held liable for failure to disclose any matter other than those specifically listed in BRRETA. Furthermore, BRRETA prohibits causes of action against brokers representing buyers or tenants for complying with these disclosure requirements.[1162]

§ 16.3.2.2   *Buyer/tenant not relieved of duty to disclose to Seller/Landlord*

BRRETA specifically states that it does not in any way limit the obligation of prospective buyers "under any applicable law to disclose all adverse material facts actually known" to the buyer regarding the buyer's financial ability to perform the terms of the sale and in the case of a residential transaction, the buyer's intent to occupy the property as a principal residence.[1163]

Similarly, the statute does not limit the duty, under any applicable law, of prospective tenants to disclose to prospective landlords "all adverse material facts

---

1159   O.C.G.A. § 10-6A-7(b).
1160   O.C.G.A. § 10-6A-7(b).
1161   O.C.G.A. § 10-6A-8(b).
1162   O.C.G.A. §§ 10-6A-7(b), 10-6A-8(b).
1163   O.C.G.A. § 10-6A-7(b).

actually known by the tenant" regarding the tenant's financial ability to perform the terms of the lease or the letter of intent to lease or intent to occupy the property.[1164]

§ 16.3.2.3 Broker's duty to not knowingly give false information

As with brokers representing sellers and landlords as clients, BRRETA mandates that brokers representing buyers and tenants as clients not give information to prospective sellers and landlords which they know to be false.[1165]

(a)   Brokers' liability for providing false information limited by BRRETA

Brokers have no liability to providing information that turns out to be incorrect provided they did not know of its falsity and disclosed the source of the information. (See § 16.3.1.8 supra, for discussion.)

§ 16.4 Broker-customer relationships

A broker-customer relationship is one in which the broker does not represent the individual in an agency capacity but for whom the broker may perform ministerial acts pursuant to either a verbal or written agreement.[1166] In other words, the broker does not represent the individual in a legal sense, but may carry out a limited range of administrative tasks for the customer.

§ 16.4.1   Ministerial services may be performed for customers

Whenever a broker is in a broker-customer relationship, he may assist the customer in the transaction by performing limited brokerage services for the customer. These administrative services, known as "ministerial acts," are defined by BRRETA to be those acts which do not require the exercise of the broker's "professional judgment or skill."[1167] Prior to the 2000 revisions, BRRETA did not provide much guidance on what services would be considered ministerial acts that could be performed for customers. However, the 2000 revisions provided guidance in this area by listing the following examples of ministerial acts:

1.   identifying property;

2.   providing real estate statistics and information regarding property;

3.   providing preprinted real estate form contracts;

1164   O.C.G.A. § 10-6A-8(b).
1165   O.C.G.A. §§ 10-6A-7(b), 10-6A-8(b).
1166   O.C.G.A. § 10-6A-3(8).
1167   O.C.G.A. § 10-6A-3(12).

4. acting as a scribe in the preparation of form contracts;

5. assisting in the location and identification of relevant professionals, such as architects, engineers, surveyors, inspectors, lenders, insurance agents, and attorneys; and

6. identifying facilities and neighborhood amenities such as schools, shopping centers, and places of worship.[1168]

While this list is not exhaustive, it does give guidance to brokers on the broad range of services that can be performed for a customer. When in doubt, the rule of thumb should be that when working with a customer the broker can act as the customer's arms and legs but not as the customer's brains. In other words, the broker can perform administrative tasks for the customer at the customer's direction, such as those listed in the statute, but the broker cannot give advice to the customer requiring a high degree of professional judgment and skill.

§ 16.4.1.1   *Ministerial services must be performed with ordinary care*

BRRETA does not set out a standard of care with which a broker must perform ministerial acts for customers. However, Georgia case law holds that brokers must use reasonable and ordinary care when undertaking brokerage services for a customer.[1169] Although this is not a high threshold for performance, if a broker does choose to perform administrative tasks for a customer in a transaction the broker must carry through with ordinary care. It is interesting to note that the standard of care required of brokers in their performance toward clients (see discussion in § 16.2.3, supra) has been lowered by BRRETA to virtually the same level of care required when a broker performs administrative tasks for customers.

§ 16.4.2   Types of broker-customer relationships

A broker-customer relationship can arise in several situations: (1) Prior to entering a written brokerage agreement forming a broker-client relationship, the individual with whom the broker is working is a customer. (2) When a broker represents one party to a transaction as a client, the broker may, but is not required to, treat other parties to the transaction as customers. (3) When a broker does not enter into a broker-client relationship with any party to a transaction, the broker is acting as a transaction broker. Transaction brokers have a customer relationship with all of the parties to the transaction.

1168   O.C.G.A. § 10-6A-14(a).
1169   Shelts v. Epperson, 201 Ga. App. 405, 411 S.E. 2d 281 (1991).

§ 16.4.2.1 Customer relationship exists before entering into written brokerage agreement

Prior to forming a broker-client relationship by entering into a written brokerage agreement containing the specific items listed in § 16.1.1.2, supra, the individual with whom the broker is working is a customer.

§ 16.4.2.2 Broker representing client in a transaction may perform ministerial acts for other party to the transaction

When a broker represents one party to a transaction as a client, the broker may, but is not required to, treat other parties to the transaction as customers. § 16.3 above discusses the duties which a broker representing one party as a client in a transaction owes to the other parties whom they do not represent in the transaction. In addition to those duties, the broker is permitted to treat the other parties to the transaction as customers and thus the broker may perform ministerial acts for those other parties. BRRETA specifically states that the assisting of the other parties is not a violation of the broker's duty to his client.[1170] Furthermore, BRRETA states that the performance of such ministerial acts for the other parties to a transaction does not create a client relationship between the broker and the other parties.[1171]

§ 16.4.2.3 Transaction brokerage

Transaction brokerage is the practice in which a broker does not enter into a client relationship with any of the parties to a contract, performs only ministerial acts for one or more of the parties, and gets paid a valuable consideration for the performance of those services pursuant to a verbal or written agreement.[1172] In other words, a transaction broker does not represent any of the parties as clients, but may treat the parties as customers by assisting them in administrative tasks.

As originally enacted, BRRETA did not address transaction brokerage at all because this form of brokerage practice was essentially unheard of at that time in Georgia. Since 1994, however, transaction brokerage has become common practice in Georgia as more and more brokers are working with prospective buyers without entering into a client relationship.

§ 16.4.2.4 Duties of transaction brokers to all parties in transaction

As previously discussed, BRRETA allows a transaction broker to perform ministerial acts for the customers in a transaction. In addition to those forms of

---

1170   O.C.G.A. § 10-6A-5(c), 10-6A-6(c), 10-6A-7(c), 10-6A-8(c).
1171   O.C.G.A. § 10-6A-5(c), 10-6A-6(c), 10-6A-7(c), 10-6A-8(c).
1172   O.C.G.A. § 10-6A-4(14).

assistance that transaction brokers may provide, BRRETA specifically mandates that transaction brokers must fulfill the following duties:

1. timely presenting all offers to and from the parties;
2. timely accounting for all money and property received by the broker on behalf of any party to the transaction;
3. timely disclosing to buyers and tenants with whom the broker is working all adverse material facts about the physical condition of the property, improvements on the property, and all material facts pertaining to existing adverse physical conditions in the neighborhood within one mile of the property that are known to the broker.[1173]

BRRETA provides that transaction brokers cannot be held liable for disclosing information in compliance with this provision of the law.[1174] Additionally, transaction brokers can only be held liable for failing to disclose those matters specifically listed in the statute and cannot be held liable for failing to disclose any other matter.[1175] Finally, transaction brokers have no duty to familiarize themselves with the property or the surrounding neighborhood.

(a)   Disclosure of parties to the transaction not affected by disclosure duties of transaction broker

BRRETA provides that the disclosure duties of the transaction broker do not reduce or in any way affect any duty of sellers to disclose to prospective buyers all adverse material facts known to the seller relating to the physical condition of the property.[1176] Also, the duty of disclosure placed on transaction brokers does not affect the duty of buyers to familiarize him/herself with the surrounding neighborhood.[1177]

(b)   Transaction broker's duty not to knowingly give false information

In addition to the duties discussed above, BRRETA provides that transaction brokers must not knowingly give false information to any party. Transaction brokers must treat all of the parties to a transaction honestly. This is the same requirement discussed in § 16.3.1.8, supra, regarding a broker's duty not to give false information to the other party in a transaction when the broker is representing one side of the transaction as a client.

1173   O.C.G.A. § 10-6A-14(b). (See §§ 16.3.1.2 and 16.3.1.7 supra, for a complete discussion of a broker's duty to disclose adverse material conditions on the property adverse off-site conditions.)
1174   O.C.G.A. § 10-6A-14(c).
1175   O.C.G.A. § 10-6A-14(c).
1176   O.C.G.A. § 10-6A-14(c).
1177   O.C.G.A. § 10-6A-14(c).

(c)   Transaction brokers' liability for providing false information limited by BRRETA.

BRRETA protects transaction brokers in the event that they unknowingly give any party to a transaction false information by providing that the broker is not liable for giving a party false information if: (1) the broker does not have actual knowledge that the information is false and (2) the broker discloses the source of the information to the customer.[1178] GAR has designed a form[1179] that can be given to the parties for their signature when a broker provides answers to a party's questions. This form should be used by brokers and a copy of it kept in the broker's files.

§ 16.5   Changing the brokerage relationship

When a brokerage relationship changes, brokers must give notice of the change to all parties involved in the transaction. Specifically, BRRETA requires that whenever a broker with an existing brokerage relationship with a customer or client enters into a new brokerage relationship with the customer or client, the broker must "timely disclose that fact and the new brokerage relationship to all brokers, customers, or clients involved in the contemplated transaction.[1180] The purpose of this requirement is to notify all involved parties of changes in the broker's role and duties in the transaction. This disclosure requirement can come into play at various times during the course of a brokerage relationship including, for example, when the relationship changes from customer to client and vice versa, when a buyer agent or listing agent becomes a designated agent, and when a broker becomes a single-agent dual agent. The statute does not specify a time period within which this disclosure must be made, nor does it state whether the disclosure must be written. It would be advisable, however, for the broker to make the disclosure as soon as possible after the brokerage engagement has been signed, and when convenient for the disclosure to be in writing. If it is not possible to fax or mail the notice due to time constraints, a viable option would be to make the disclosure verbally and to then follow the conversation with a written confirmation sent to the parties. At the very least, the broker should put a written memo or note in her file stating that she made the required disclosure and giving the date of the disclosure to protect against claims that the broker did not comply with the statutory disclosure requirement. The following examples illustrate the application of this statutory requirement.

Example #1: A broker has shown a house listed with another real estate brokerage firm several times to a prospective buyer who has not signed a buyer brokerage engagement and who is thus a customer of the broker rather than a client.

1178   O.C.G.A. § 10-6A-14(c).
1179   GAR Form F57
1180   O.C.G.A. § 10-6A-4(b).

Upon deciding to make an offer on the property, the buyer asks the broker to represent him in the negotiations. The broker explains to the buyer that he cannot represent him as his legal agent unless the buyer becomes the broker's client by entering into a written brokerage engagement. When the buyer and broker sign the brokerage agreement, their brokerage relationship changes from a broker–customer relationship to a broker–client relationship. BRRETA requires that this change be disclosed in a timely fashion to the listing broker and the seller, as well as to any other customer, client or broker who might be involved in the transaction.

Example #2: A real estate licensee working with a prospective buyer-client under a buyer's brokerage engagement shows the client several houses listed by different real estate firms. The buyer then decides that he wants to see a listing in which the licensee is acting as the listing agent. Showing this property will involve a change of brokerage relationship to either designated agency or dual agency. This change must be disclosed to all other parties in the transaction.

Giving prompt notice of changed relationships is critically important if the relationship changes after a GAR Contract has been signed. This is because the notice requirements under the GAR Contract vary depending upon whether a client or customer relationship exits. Under the GAR Contract, notice to a broker is notice to that broker's client, but not notice to that broker's customer.

§ 16.6 Termination of brokerage relationship

The duties imposed on a broker by law begin at the time the client engages the broker. These duties are owed until either the engagement is completed or until the first one of the following events takes place: (a) the expiration date in the brokerage agreement passes, (b) the parties terminate the agreement in a manner agreed upon in the brokerage engagement, (c) if no expiration is provided for and no termination has occurred, then one year after the initiation of the engagement.[1181]

§ 16.6.1 When broker can terminate brokerage relationship

There are several instances in which a broker may desire to terminate her relationship with a client. If the broker and client have difficulty getting along with each other or difficulty communicating with each other to such extent that the broker feels she cannot adequately represent the client, it may be advisable for the broker to terminate the relationship.

Similarly, if a broker wants to avoid a dual agency situation that would arise by showing a buyer-client one of the broker's own listings, the broker can withdraw from representing the buyer, thus ending her client relationship with the buyer. The GAR Buyer Brokerage Engagement forms permit either party to terminate the client

---

1181   O.C.G.A. § 10-6A-9(a).

relationship without the consent of the other party upon giving written notice to that party.

§ 16.6.2   Duties of broker upon termination of brokerage relationship

After the brokerage relationship has terminated or expired, the broker owes no further duty to the client with two exceptions. First, the broker must account for all moneys and property relating to the engagement.[1182] Second, after the brokerage engagement has ended the broker must continue to keep confidential any information which the broker received during the term of the engagement and which the client requested to be kept confidential. Even though a brokerage relationship no longer exists, any such confidential information can only be revealed by the broker under the following circumstances: (a) the client permits the disclosure by subsequent word or conduct, (b) disclosure is required by law, or (c) the information becomes public from a source other than the broker.[1183] The same duties to account for money and property and to maintain confidences also arises when the brokerage relationship has changed such that the broker is no longer representing the individual as a client and broker-client relationship has technically ended..

§ 16.7   BRRETA and GAR's Brokerage Engagements

GAR's Listing Agreements and Buyer Brokerage Agreements have been designed to ensure that the broker-client relationship is formed in compliance with BRRETA. For example, all of the GAR form Brokerage Agreements include a bold face disclosure at the beginning of the form explaining that state law prohibits brokers from representing parties as clients without a written brokerage agreement. GAR's form Listing Agreements and Buyer Engagement Agreements include the four necessary elements of a brokerage engagement required under BRRETA discussed in § 16.1.1.2. These forms also set out specifically what other duties the broker has toward the client. The forms assume that the brokerage firm is offering the complete range of agency relationships: seller agency, buyer agency, dual agency, designated agency, landlord agency and tenant agency. Therefore, if a brokerage firm is not offering one or more of these agency relationships, the relationship or relationships not being offered would need to be specifically identified in the contract. The forms also include the disclosures that must be made if a firm practices dual agency.

§ 16.7.1   Protections against liability in the GAR Brokerage Engagements

The GAR form Brokerage Engagements limit the potential legal liability of brokers in two important ways.

1182   O.C.G.A. § 10-6A-9(b)(1).
1183   O.C.G.A. § 10-6A-9(b)(1).

First, the Brokerage Agreements provide that the maximum liability of the broker is the amount of the real estate commission paid to the broker. Excluded from this amount is that portion of the commission paid to any cooperating broker or retained by the listing broker. The case of Brainard v. McKinney, 220 Ga. App. 329, 469 S.E. 2d 441 (1996), established the legal precedent for enforcing such a limitation on liability. In the Brainard case, the Georgia Court of Appeals upheld a home inspection contract that included a clause limiting the inspector's liability to the cost of the inspection. A later companion case, Tanner v. Redding, 231 Ga. App. 250, 498 S.E. 2d 156 (1998), clarified the law further by holding that such a contractual limitation is enforceable only if the agreement is prepared and signed prior to the inspection. Thus, the GAR Brokerage Engagement forms not only ensure that the broker complies with BRRETA in the formation of the client relationship, but they also operate to cap the brokers liability and to substantially reduce the broker's legal exposure.

Second, the GAR Brokerage Agreements limit the duties owed by the real estate broker. BRRETA states that a broker only owes customers and clients the duties set forth in BRRETA unless the parties expressly agree in a signed writing to other duties.[1184] (§ 16.2, supra, discusses in detail the duties owed by brokers to their clients under BRRETA.) Each kind of GAR Brokerage Engagement form sets out the specific duties owed to the client. For example, the GAR Exclusive Buyer Brokerage Agreement (Form F-6) provides as follows:

> Broker's sole duties to Seller shall be to: (a) attempt to locate property suitable to Buyer for purchase; (b) assist to the extent requested by Buyer in negotiating the terms and filling out a pre-printed real estate purchase and sale agreement and (c) comply with all applicable laws in performing its duties hereunder including the Brokerage Relationships in Real Estate Transactions Act, O.C.G.A. § 10-6A-1 et seq.

BRRETA, in combination with the GAR Brokerage Engagement forms, significantly reduces the potential legal liability of a broker by narrowing the duties owed by a broker in his or her brokerage engagement and by limiting the potential damages in the event of an inadvertent breach of such duties.

§ 16.7.2   Getting buyer–clients to sign written brokerage agreement

Although it has never been difficult to get sellers to sign brokerage agreements (i.e., listing agreement), some buyers have been reluctant to sign written brokerage agreements. The reason for this reluctance seems to be two-fold: (1) fear of having to

---

1184 O.C.G.A. § 10-6A-4(a).

pay a real estate commission (even though the commission is normally paid by the seller), and (2) general anxiety with committing themselves contractually to one particular broker.

There are several possible actions which brokers can take to alleviate the fear on the part of some buyers to sign written brokerage agreements. First, brokers should explain to their buyer-clients that under the form GAR Brokerage Agreements, both the client as well as the broker can terminate the agreement with or without cause upon written notice to the other. Therefore, if the buyer no longer wants to work with the broker, all he or she has to do is send a letter of termination.

Second, there is nothing which requires a brokerage engagement to be of any particular duration. Therefore, the broker can offer to make the initial term of the brokerage engagement extremely short. For example, the brokerage agreement can be for one weekend or even one day. Of course, once the initial term of the agreement has ended the broker should seek to make the renewal term substantially longer.

Third, if the buyer is concerned about the possibility of having to pay a real estate commission, the broker can explain that if the following basic rules are followed, the buyer will not have to pay a real estate commission:

(a) The broker can agree to only show the buyer property listed in a multiple listing service where the seller is paying the commission. This can even be written into the GAR Buyer Brokerage Agreements as a special stipulation. In listing property in a multiple listing service ("MLS"), the seller is agreeing to pay a commission that may be shared with a cooperating broker who is the procuring cause of the sale. Therefore, if a broker explains to the buyer that if he or she only sees property with that broker, and if the broker agrees to only show the buyer property listed with the MLS in which the seller is paying the commission, the risk of the buyer having to pay a commission is significantly reduced.

(b) The broker can agree that he not show the buyer a property that is for sale by owner without first working out an arrangement with the seller to be paid a commission. In this way, the buyer will not have any unpleasant surprises.

(c) The buyer should be reminded to only see property with the broker if the buyer has signed an exclusive buyer brokerage agreement. This rule insures that the buyer broker will be the procuring cause of the sale in all transactions involving the buyer. This helps to avoid disputes regarding this issue with listing brokers. If the buyer is still uncomfortable, a special stipulation can be included in the Buyer Brokerage Agreement of the type similar to the following:

Special Stipulation #16-1: Broker to show property without written brokerage engagement

Broker agrees to show Buyer only property which is listed in a multiple listing service in which the seller is agreeing to pay a commission. Broker will not show Buyer a property offered For Sale By Owner without first working out a written commission agreement with the seller or notifying Buyer that in viewing the Property, the Buyer will be paying a commission of _____% of the purchase price.

§ 16.7.3   The commission and the GAR Brokerage Engagements

The GAR Contract no longer provides a space for the broker to fill in the amount of the commission or the split of the commission with any cooperating broker.[1185] The amount of the commission and any offer to split the commission is handled through separate agreements. This raises the question of how brokers can protect their right to a commission.

Historically, a selling broker would contact the listing broker and ask whether the listing broker was willing to split his commission. With the advent of the MLS and FMLS, the listing of a property in the systems indicates the amount of the split being offered. The rules of the FMLS or MLS require that brokers listing property with the services agree to cooperate with other members of the service. The GAR form Buyer and Seller Engagement Agreements discussed below help to further protect brokers' commissions.

§ 16.7.3.1   The Exclusive Buyer Brokerage Agreement

(a)   The commission obligation generally.

The GAR Exclusive Buyer Brokerage Agreement provides that the buyer's real estate broker will seek to be paid its commission from the seller or listing broker pursuant to a cooperative brokerage arrangement. In the event neither of these parties pays a commission to the selling broker, then the commission is paid by the buyer whether or not the property is one which the broker identified for the buyer.

The Exclusive Buyer Brokerage Agreement contains a blank to be filled in with the amount of the commission which the buyer will pay his broker in the event that the seller or listing broker does not pay the buyer's broker a commission. An issue may arise when the seller or listing broker agrees to pay a lesser commission than what has been designated by the buyer in the Exclusive Buyer Brokerage Agreement. In such situations, the broker cannot ask to be paid the difference from the buyer because

---

1185   GAR F20

the commission obligation only arises on the part of the buyer if the seller or listing broker pays no commission to the selling broker. Below is an example of this situation.

> Example: REALTOR® A enters into an exclusive buyer brokerage agreement using the GAR form in which the buyer agrees that in the event the seller or listing broker does not pay the selling broker a commission in accordance with a cooperative brokerage arrangement, the buyer will pay his broker a commission of 3 ½% of the purchase price of the property. The buyer purchases a property he viewed with his broker. The listing agreement and the MLS listing indicate that the commission to be paid to any cooperating real estate broker will be 2 ½%. Can the selling broker require the buyer to pay him any additional commission?

> Answer: No. The selling broker is entitled to only 2 ½% commission as set out in the listing agreement and the MLS listing. The selling broker would only be entitled to pursue the buyer for a commission under the exclusive buyer brokerage agreement if the listing broker or seller did not pay the selling broker any real estate commission. If the selling broker is paid a real estate commission in any amount by the seller or listing broker, the selling broker has no commission claims against the buyer.

The GAR Exclusive Buyer Brokerage Agreement specifically states that the commission is to be paid on all property which the buyer purchases during the term of this agreement whether or not it has been identified to the buyer by the real estate broker. This provision contractually modifies the general common law rule that the broker is only entitled to a commission if he or she is the procuring cause of the sale (i.e., the broker's efforts resulted in an uninterrupted series of events that resulted in the sale). However, under Georgia law, the parties to a contract are free to agree on whatever terms and about any subject matters in which they have an interest in the absence of a violation of public policy or law.[1186]

(b)   Entitlement to commission after expiration or termination of Buyer Brokerage Agreement.

The GAR Exclusive Buyer Brokerage Agreement provides that the broker is entitled to a commission if the buyer purchases or contracts to purchase, for a period of time after the termination or expiration of the brokerage agreement, a property "identified" to the buyer by the broker during the brokerage agreement. While the term "identified" is not defined, the term was intended to protect brokers in situations where the buyer learned of the property through the efforts of the

---

1186   Brainard v. McKinney, 220 Ga. App. 329, S.E. 2d 441, 442 (1996); First Capital Institutional Real Estate LTD v. Pennington, 1986 Ga. App. 617, 386 S.E. 2d 165, 166 (1988).

broker. As such, it should <u>not</u> require that the broker actually show the property to the buyer provided that the broker has taken other reasonable steps to make the buyer aware of the property. Let's look at the example below to see how this works.

Example #1: During the term of an exclusive brokerage agreement (entered into on the GAR form) the broker faxes MLS information sheets to the buyer on six (6) properties the broker believes the buyer would be interested in purchasing. The buyer thanks the broker for the information, but terminates the brokerage agreement a few days later without explanation and without seeing the property. Two months later, the broker learns that the buyer purchased one of the six properties identified to the buyer by the broker. Should the broker be protected for a commission?

Answer: The answer to this question should be "yes" assuming that the buyer entered into the purchase contract during the period of time after the termination of the contract in which the broker was protected for a commission. This is because while the broker did not actually show the buyer the property, the broker did identify the property to the buyer and cause the buyer to learn of its existence during the brokerage engagement. The broker's commission claim in this example would be against the buyer directly rather than the seller or listing broker of the property purchased by the buyer.

The amount of the commission and the number of days for which the broker is protected are shown in blanks on the GAR Exclusive Buyer Brokerage Engagement and must be filled in by the parties. Obviously, the greater the number of days specified, the greater the protection. If the parties fail to write into the agreement the amount of the commission or the number of days for which the broker's commission is protected, the broker would not be entitled to a commission if, after the termination of the agreement, the buyer purchases or contracts to purchase a property identified to the buyer by the broker. Below are several examples of how this process works.

Example #2: Broker shows buyer a property during the term of a buyer brokerage engagement. The agreement provides that the broker is protected for a commission for 120 days after the termination of the agreement. One hundred and ten days after the brokerage agreement terminates, the buyer enters into a contract to purchase the property shown to the buyer during the brokerage agreement. The closing is set for 45 days later, which is after the end of the broker's protected period. Can the broker recover a commission in this instance?

Answer: Yes. In order for the broker's commission protection provision to be effective, the buyer need only enter into a contract to purchase, during the protected time period, a property identified to the buyer during the brokerage agreement. The sale does not have to actually close within the protected time period. In this case, while the closing of the property takes place after the end of the protected time period, the buyer did enter into a contract to purchase the property during the protected time period thus entitling the broker to a commission. This entitles the broker to a commission in accordance with the brokerage agreement. The broker must carefully document the properties identified to the buyer to take advantage of this protection. Although this sounds difficult and tedious, it can be easily accomplished. Whenever the buyer brokerage agreement either expires or is terminated by one of the parties, the broker should send the buyer a letter specifically listing all the properties which the broker introduced to the buyer. This step lays the groundwork for the broker's claim to a commission in the event the buyer later contracts to buy a house identified by the broker.

Example #3: A buyer enters into an exclusive buyer brokerage agreement for a term of thirty (30) days with Broker No. 1. The agreement protects the broker's commission in the event the buyer within 90 days after the termination of the brokerage agreement, purchases or contracts to purchase a property identified to the buyer by the broker during the term of the buyer brokerage agreement. The broker shows the buyer numerous homes; however, the buyer does not submit an offer on any of the homes. After the term of the brokerage agreement expires, the buyer immediately enters into another exclusive buyer brokerage agreement with Broker No. 2. Within the 90 day protected period under the brokerage agreement with Broker No. 1, Broker No. 2 shows the buyer one of the same houses that Broker No. 1 had shown him earlier and the buyer enters a contract to buy this house. Is Broker No. 1 entitled to a commission?

Answer: The answer to this question should be "yes." This is because the buyer, within the protected time period, contracted to buy a house which Broker No. 1 had shown him during the term of their brokerage agreement. At closing the buyer would owe Broker No. 1 a commission on the sale. Interestingly, Broker No. 1's claim to a commission would be directly against the buyer. Broker No. 2 should also be entitled to a commission. Assuming that Broker No. 2 and the buyer entered into a GAR Exclusive Buyer Brokerage Engagement, Broker No.2 would be owed a commission either from the seller or listing broker, or, if no such commission was paid, from the buyer.

This is a different result from the parallel situation under an exclusive listing agreement. The GAR Exclusive Listing Agreement provides that if, after the termination of the listing agreement, the seller lists the property with a different broker and a buyer purchases the property who first saw the property during the initial listing, the first broker is not entitled to a commission.

(c)   Use of GAR Exclusive Buyer Brokerage Agreement can reduce disputes over procuring cause between competing brokers.

The growth in recent years of buyer brokerage in Georgia has created many disputes over whether the buyer broker is the procuring cause of the sale and thus entitled to share in the listing broker's commission. Although difficult to define, the term "procuring cause" refers to the principal that a broker who is unable to finalize a sale of property can still claim a commission if he or she can show that his or her efforts triggered a key series of events which, without significant interruption, resulted in the sale of the property. A variety of factors influence whether a broker is the procuring cause of a sale including: whether the broker initiated the series of events leading to the sale, whether there was a break in negotiations, and the reason for any break in the negotiations.[1187]

Non-exclusive buyer brokerage agreements and open listing agreements can create a situation in which a broker's right to a commission depends on whether he was the procuring cause of the sale.[1188] However, use of the GAR Exclusive Buyer Brokerage Agreement can eliminate the need for the broker to prove that he or she was the procuring cause and thus can eliminate many disputes between competing agents. First, this agreement clearly establishes an exclusive agency in which the buyer specifically agrees not to work with any other broker or real estate licensee for a specified period of time. This means that, during the term of the agreement, the buyer is contractually prohibited from establishing an agency relationship with another broker without terminating the buyer brokerage agreement with the first broker. If the buyer does purchase a property using another broker during the term of the agreement, the first broker is still entitled to his commission, even if the property purchased is one which the first broker never identified to the buyer. Furthermore, even if the buyer (or broker) terminates the brokerage agreement, the broker is still entitled to a commission if, within an agreed-upon time after termination, the buyer purchases or contracts to purchase any property identified to the buyer by the broker during the term of the brokerage agreement. For identified properties bought or contracted for during this protected time period, the broker can claim a commission without proving that he was the procuring cause of the sale.

§ 16.7.3.2   The Non-Exclusive Buyer Brokerage Agreement

The GAR Non-Exclusive Buyer Brokerage Agreement is similar to the GAR Exclusive Buyer Brokerage Agreement discussed in the previous section in that the broker agrees to look to the seller or listing broker for his commission. However, there is a critical difference between the two agreements. With the Non-Exclusive Buyer Brokerage Agreement the broker can only recover a commission from the buyer if the buyer purchases property identified to the buyer by the broker during the term of the agreement. This is in contrast to the Exclusive Brokerage Agreement under which the buyer's broker can claim a commission for sales made during the term of the agreement whether or not the property was identified to the buyer by the broker.

1187   See Chapter 13.
1188   Cartel Realty, Inc. v. Southern Bearings and Parts Co., Inc., 243 Ga.App. 653, 534 S.E.2d 119 (2000).

§ 16.7.3.3   The Exclusive Seller Listing Agreement

The GAR Exclusive Seller Listing Agreement sets the amount of commission which the seller will pay upon a sale of the property. The Agreement states that this commission will be due to the Broker if during the term of the Agreement, Broker either (1) procures a person "ready, willing and able" to purchase the property at a price agreeable to the seller, or (2) the seller enters into a contract to sell or exchange the property with any buyer. The agreement also contains blanks which the parties fill in to establish what commission split the broker will pay to any cooperating broker who procures a buyer. The Agreement specifically makes cooperating brokers third party beneficiaries to the agreement. This allows cooperating brokers, who are not directly in contract with the seller, to nonetheless pursue claims against defaulting sellers for their commission. It is critical that brokers fill in these blanks to protect their commission since the GAR Purchase and Sale Agreement no longer contains a place for the parties to write in the commission split for cooperating brokers.

Example: A seller enters into a GAR Exclusive Listing Agreement with a broker in which the seller agrees to pay the listing broker 7% of the purchase price. The listing broker fills in the blank in the listing agreement indicating that he will offer 50% of his commission to cooperating brokers. The listing broker enters the property into a multiple listing service at a commission of 7% with a 50/50 split on the commission. Later, the seller and listing broker verbally agree to reduce the commission to 6%, but they do not amend the listing agreement, modify the information contained in the multiple listing system, or tell the selling broker of the commission reduction. Is the selling broker's commission limited to 3% (half of 6%)?

Answer: The answer to the question should be "no." This is because when the listing broker offers to pay a selling broker a specific commission amount and the selling broker accepts the offer of the listing broker by producing a buyer ready, willing and able to purchase the property, a contract is created which should be capable of being enforced. Because the listing agreement specifically makes cooperating brokers third party beneficiaries to the listing agreement, the selling broker should be able to sue the seller for breaching the listing agreement, even though the selling broker is not a party to that contract.

§ 16.7.3.4   The GAR Commission Confirmation Agreement

In transactions where there is a cooperating broker, both brokers can further protect their right to their commission by entering into a GAR Commission Confirmation Agreement[1189]. Although there is no requirement that commission agreements between brokers be written, using this form protects brokers' commissions by serving as written evidence of their agreement. The form is an

---

1189   GAR Form F32.

agreement between the brokers only, and does not involve the buyer or seller. Therefore, the form should not be attached to the GAR Contract. This GAR Commission Confirmation Agreement contains blanks for the listing broker and the selling broker to write in their respective share of the commission for a specific transaction both as a percentage of the purchase price and a dollar amount. The form allows the selling broker to accept a split that differs from that set out in the listing agreement or to accept a different amount of commission from that set out in the listing agreement. The agreement also specifically supercedes any prior agreement the brokers may have entered into.

§ 16.7.3.5   *Commission Confirmation Agreement and Listing Agreement Should be Sent to the Closing Attorney*

If the real estate commission is not referenced in the purchase and sale agreement (as is the case with the GAR Contracts), the listing broker should send a copy of the listing agreement to the closing attorney so he or she knows the total amount of the commission to be paid at closing. In addition, the listing or selling broker should also send a copy of the commission confirmation agreement to the closing attorney so that he or she knows how to divide the commission between the listing and selling brokers.

§ 16.8   Making Smart Choices About Agency

Prior to the adoption of BRRETA in 1994, agency was relatively easy to understand. For the most part, all brokers represented sellers and practiced subagency when working with other brokerage firms. The introduction of buyer brokerage changed all of that. Suddenly, brokers were representing buyers, sellers, buyers and sellers at the same time in the same transaction and various other combinations. Most brokers have learned the different types of agency relationships which they can offer. If there has been confusion, it has tended to be in learning how to choose the right agency relationship for different situations. This section will discuss an approach on how to make smart choices when it comes to agency.

Rule No. 1. <u>Only offer agency to a party if you do not already have a client in the transaction</u>.

Many real estate brokers were incorrectly taught that they had to explain and offer agency at the first meaningful opportunity to all prospective clients and customers. In fact, the agency relationships offered by a real estate brokerage firm only have to be explained prior to entering into a client relationship. If agency is offered or explained to every party with whom the broker comes into contact, the effect is that the broker will needlessly end up acting in the high risk role of dual agent far more often than is wise. This is because most buyers, once they understand that being represented does not necessarily mean they have to pay a commission, will choose to be represented. Single agent dual agency is the agency relationship with the greatest risk and should be avoided wherever possible. Following the above rule will help avoid this problem.

Let's apply the above rule to several situations to see how it works. If a buyer walks into an open house on a Sunday afternoon, should the listing agent offer or explain agency to the buyer? The answer to this question is "no" because the broker already has a client in the transaction (i.e., the seller). The same would be the case if an unrepresented buyer approaches a subdivision agent to see a new home. However, if the buyer walks into the broker's office on a Saturday morning and asks for the broker's help in buying a new home it is fine to offer the buyer agency because the broker does not have a client relationship with the owner of any specifically identified real estate.

Not offering agency does not mean the broker cannot work with or help buyer as a customer and perform ministerial acts on his or her behalf. The listing broker does not have to let a good customer slip away. Let's say the broker meets an unrepresented buyer at an open house the broker is holding one afternoon. The broker does not offer agency to the buyer but instead treats the buyer as a customer. The buyer indicates that she is not interested in the listing. However, in speaking with her it is obvious to the broker that she is a ready, willing and able buyer. Should the broker let this hot prospect slip through the cracks because she is not your client?

The answer to this question is clearly "no." If the buyer is not interested in the listing, the listing agent should first determine if he or she has other listings which might meet the buyer's needs. If the listing agent has other suitable listings, the listing agent should offer to show the buyer those listings without offering or explaining agency to the customer. If the buyer rejects those listings, the broker should then offer to represent the buyer as a client in finding the buyer suitable property. By following this approach, the listing agent should be able to avoid acting in a high risk single-agent dual agent capacity. This is because when the broker shows the buyer the listings of other brokerage firms, the broker will be acting as a buyer agent. When the broker shows the buyer the listings of other agents in his or her own brokerage firm, the broker should be acting in a designated agency capacity.

> Rule No. 2.   Timely disclose who you represent but don't do it legalistically.

While real estate brokers are not required to offer or explain agency to everyone they meet, they are obligated to timely disclose to all parties in the transaction whom they are representing.[1190] This disclosure does not have to be made in an overly legalistic fashion. For example, if a buyer walks into a

---

1190   O.C.G.A. § 43-40-25(a)(31).

subdivision, the listing broker can merely say something to the effect of: "Hello. Welcome to Tall Pines Subdivision. My name is _____. As you probably know, I've been hired by AAA Developers to sell these lovely homes. May I show them to you?"

If the broker makes an overly legalistic disclosure, it may lead the buyer to view the transaction legalistically and heighten his or her concerns regarding the role of the listing broker.

Rule No. 3. Practice registration, not representation.

The reason that most listing agents offer to represent buyers is to ensure that they get paid the entire commission in the transaction. While this motivation is understandable, it is not necessarily smart business because of the high risks associated with practicing single agent dual agency. The better solution is to treat buyers as customers and register, rather than represent, them. In this way, the broker significantly increases the likelihood of being considered the procuring cause of the sale in the event a dispute arises over the commission at a later time.

Buyers are entitled to be represented by their own broker at any time they please. However, the listing broker is not obligated to share his or her commission with a selling broker unless the selling broker is the procuring cause of the sale. Listing brokers lose a significant portion of their real estate commissions by not preserving evidence that they, rather than another agent, were the procuring cause of the sale.

Questions of entitlement to a real estate commission are normally arbitrated at a Board of REALTORS® or litigated in court. Oftentimes, there is conflicting testimony by the listing broker, the selling broker and the buyer over when the selling broker first became involved with the buyer and the role of the selling broker in finding the buyer of the property. Such disputes are often quickly resolved if the listing broker has preserved the correct evidence regarding procuring cause.

Properly registering the buyer does not have to be done in an overly technical fashion. Getting the buyer to answer in writing two (2) basic questions is usually enough to protect the listing broker. They are as follows:

(1)   I am _____ or am not _____ working with another real estate agent or broker.

(2)   I found the property at _____ in the following way [check all of those which are applicable]:

_____ a. I saw the "For Sale" sign on the property.
_____ b. I saw an advertisement for the property in a newspaper or magazine.

_____ c. I found the property over the Internet.
_____ d. A friend told me about the property.
_____ e. Another real estate agent or broker found or told me about the property.

By having buyers provide this information, listing brokers can better ensure that they are entitled to the entire commission when a buyer is not working with his or her own agent at the time the buyer first identifies the property.

Rule #4. Avoid transaction brokerage.

A real estate broker can only perform ministerial acts on behalf of a party when acting in a transaction brokerage capacity. This essentially means that the broker can be the "arms and legs of the parties, but not the brains." The problem with transaction brokerage is that most brokers have an extremely difficult time limiting their role to performing only ministerial acts. Real estate brokers by their nature want to help the people with whom they work. Giving advise is second nature to most real estate brokers. As a result, some real estate brokers who call themselves transaction brokers end up crossing the line and start to represent one party or another in the real estate transaction as a client. This arguably is an undisclosed agency relationship and can subject the broker to being sanctioned by the Georgia Real Estate Commission.[1191] This can also lead to uncertainty as to whether the broker is entitled to pursue a breach of contract claim for his commission.[1192]

Rule #5. Avoid dual agency whenever possible.

Dual agency is the highest risk form of agency because of the potential for the dual agent to find himself or herself in the middle of conflicts between buyers and sellers. What are the alternatives to dual agency? First, the agent can treat the buyer as a customer and not offer to represent her. Second, the agent can get the buyer to sign an agreement that the agent will represent the buyer as a client except in situations where the agent is showing the buyer his or her own listing. Third, to avoid dual agency, the agent can refer one client to another agent in her brokerage firm. In doing so, each agent would be acting in a designated agency capacity.

Many real estate agents are reluctant to refer a client to another agent in their brokerage firm for fear that they will then be obligated to pay the other agent the entire selling side of the commission. However, the amount of commission shared between the designated agents is a matter between the agents and their real estate broker and can be any amount agreed to between the parties. So for example, to avoid acting as a dual agent, the agent could occasionally refer clients to another agent in his or her firm with the understanding that they would be paid only a nominal fee to represent the client and with the further understanding that the other

---

1191   O.C.G.A. § 43-40-25(a)(31).
1192   See Chapter 13.

agent would reciprocate and also occasionally refer clients to avoid being a dual agent. In this way, each agent should earn the same amount of commissions without having to act in a high risk, dual agency role.

TABLE OF SPECIAL STIPULATIONS

TABLE OF AUTHORITIES

517

TABLE OF STATUTES

525

INDEX